Brief Contents

Contents

Preface

THE REALITIES OF MANAGEMENT

We are deeply grateful for the feedback, encouragement, and support that we received on our first edition. When we set out to write a new management textbook, we sought to capture the realities of managing in an ever-changing and dynamic environment. The speed of change and the global interconnectedness of business necessitate that managers and their companies be flexible, quick, and nimble. Effective change and sustainable performance require that managers understand the impact of strategic choices, the optimal design of organizations, and the power of leadership. In our first edition of the textbook, we called these three core components (strategy, organizational design, and leadership) the pillars of management. These pillars stand together to form a solid foundation of support, yet they are not stationary or immobile. As the contextual environment changes so too must a firm's strategy. The adaptation of strategy often requires a reexamination and deployment of new organizational structures and leadership approaches.

Today's managers need to understand the subtleties of strategy and the nuances of organizational design to carve out a defensible and sustainable position in an increasingly competitive and volatile marketplace. And managers need to know the key leadership levers that enable them to build, inspire, and nurture high-performing teams to implement that strategy. To be effective and relevant for a long period of time, managers must understand the co-evolutionary nature of these three pillars—strategy, organizational design, and leadership. This understanding provides managers with a holistic view of the ways in which strategy informs organizational design, organizational design impacts external competitiveness and internal motivation, and leadership ultimately influences performance.

In this second edition, we have continued to explore how strategy influences organizational design, how leaders shape and defend strategic positions, how organizations impact performance and drive motivation, how leaders lead, and how global forces impact the competitive landscape. The second edition includes both core foundational components of strategic and organizational theory as well as contemporary research that are useful and relevant for aspiring and experienced managers. As with the first edition, we employ a performance edge—demonstrating the impact and result of decisions regarding strategic choices, organizational alignment, and individual leadership approaches. Our aim is to help students prepare for leadership roles by addressing the integrated facets of leading businesses in today's complex and ever-changing environment.

TEXT ORGANIZATION

Our management textbook is organized into four main parts including (1) setting the context for management; (2) the strategic perspective; (3) the organizational perspective; and (4) the individual perspective. The chapters in each of the sections have been expanded and updated to highlight new research and to showcase contemporary examples from the world of practice. Through this book, we have tried to bridge the divide between theory and practice by presenting examples that are relevant, illustrative, and compelling.

The initial section of the book includes three chapters that are focused on the contextual landscape of business. We discuss the historical context of business and introduce the three pillars. This section also includes an overview of the internal and external components of the business environment with a specific focus on the global nature of business. This global focus is interwoven throughout the book including discussions on effective cross-cultural teams, market-entry strategies, global communication, and cross-boundary negotiations. In addition, this first section includes an in-depth discussion of ethics and corporate social responsibility. Similar to the focus on globalization, these themes are referenced throughout the textbook. In this second edition, we have provided a broader overview of the volatility in the business environment, including a discussion of the global financial crisis and its impact on companies, individuals, and countries. Alongside this discussion, we have included a deeper dive into the various stakeholders of a firm. The new edition also includes more examples of personal and corporate moral dilemmas and how individuals can successfully navigate them.

The second part of the textbook showcases the strategic perspective and includes three chapters—an introduction to strategy as well as overviews of business-level and corporate-level strategy. The second edition contains more global cases, a new section on the implementation of strategy, and a streamlined focus on related and unrelated diversification.

The third part of the textbook is focused on the organizational perspective of management and includes five chapters. In this section, we focus on the organization as an instrument for achieving strategic objectives, and we examine the way leaders make important decisions regarding organizational design, culture, human capital, and measurement. The second edition includes a broader discussion on different organizational forms, new content on delegation and empowerment, and a richer overview of the ways in which culture impacts organizational performance. The chapter on performance management has been extensively revised; it includes a new section on financial management, a streamlined overview of the balanced scorecard, and a review of new models of benchmarking. Finally, this section includes a deeper discussion on organizational change models and the role of innovation in shaping organizational and strategic evolution.

The final section of the textbook delves into the role of the individual. It includes a focus on how to manage oneself as well as how to manage others. This section includes nine chapters that provide a comprehensive overview of the important leadership levers that are needed to drive organizational performance, including the ability to motivate and inspire others, to effectively wield power and influence, to successfully navigate conflict, to reach win-win negotiations, and to communicate with passion and purpose. The second edition includes additional information about the effectiveness of different leadership styles, an integrated discussion on the use of power and how to channel personal power, and a broader overview of various cognitive biases that impact decision making. In addition, this section includes a new discussion on collective intelligence, extrinsic and intrinsic motivation, and network characteristics.

"ENGAGE. CONNECT. PERFORM. LEAD." ADDRESSING MAJOR COURSE NEEDS THROUGH INTERACTIVE LEARNING

Management, 2e seeks to effectively engage the student to think and act like a manager. *Management, 2e* follows a path to obtain these results and other key course goals through various learning activities: *Engage* (pulling the student into the content and establishing relevance), *Connect* (mastering a body of knowledge, connecting terms and concepts), *Perform* (real-world applications pertaining to concepts and theories), and *Lead* (higher level critical thinking and application that puts the student in the shoes of a manager). These assignment types are fully utilized in the MindTap/Aplia product, as described below.

TEXT FEATURES

The focus on relevance and performance will be demonstrated in the text through the use of timely and relevant case examples, reflective exercises showcasing the diverse business landscape, and personal assessments to help students discover the key factors that drive organizational and individual results. Specifically:

- A *Self-Reflection* starts each chapter, giving students a quick way to assess their sense of the content of the chapter.

- *The Leadership Development Journey* is a comprehensive skills-based activity that allows students to develop who they are, or will be, as managers. From chapter to chapter, this activity translates theory into action—the "what" into "how."

- *A Different View* showcases unique applications of chapter content including strategic corporate philanthropy (Chapter 3), culture in crisis (Chapter 8), servant leadership (Chapter 12), difficult conversations (Chapter 16), and crisis communication (Chapter 19).

- *Case in Point* activities ask students to further explore case examples and provide research opportunities based on text content.

INSTRUCTOR SUPPORT

- **Instructor's Resource CD**

  Discover all of the key instructor resources at your fingertips with this all-in-one resource. The Instructor's Resource CD (IRCD) offers chapter-by-chapter tools for instructors who are new to the course as well as innovative materials ideal for experienced professors who are developing strong managers. The Instructor's Resource contains the Instructor's Manual, Test Bank, Examview Testing Software, and PowerPoint Presentation Slides for both the instructor and student. The Instructor's Manual consists of lecture outlines, answers to pedagogical features, sample syllabi, and recommended teaching notes and additional case studies.

- **MindTap**

  MindTap®

  MindTap for Management is a personalized, fully online, digital learning platform. It is composed of authoritative Cengage Learning content, assignments, and services that engage your students with interactivity. The platform allows you to choose the configuration of coursework and to enhance the curriculum via complimentary web-apps known as MindApps. MindApps range from ReadSpeaker (which reads the text aloud to students) to Kaltura (allowing you to insert inline video and audio into your curriculum) to ConnectYard (allowing you to create digital "yards" through social media—all without "friending" your students). The Gulati interactive ebook is a media rich reader complete with figure animations, multiple choice concept checks, and drag and drop figures—all aimed at raising student comprehension. *Management, 2e* is well beyond an eBook, a homework solution or digital supplement, a resource center website, a course delivery platform or a Learning Management System. It is the first in a new category—the Personal Learning Experience.

- **Aplia**

    Have your students "think like managers" with Aplia's premium student engagement tool for management. This tool allows you to easily manage the subtle dynamics of teaching Principles of Management, with problem sets that engage students, help them connect class concepts to the real world, facilitate their skill performance, and show them how to lead others. Assignable exercises are designed to get students to Engage, Connect, Perform, and Lead with the content. Engage exercises show students how management is relevant to their lives; Connect takes management theories and applies them to real-world applications; Perform scenarios provide students an opportunity to apply management concepts; and Lead illustrates higher-level problem types, such as video cases, giving students a chance to practice and improve leadership decisions. Engaging media is seamlessly integrated throughout including video cases, interactive diagrams, self-assessments, and vivid examples. Holding students accountable for their own engagement becomes easy with Aplia's dynamic and flexible grading system, including grade analytics and easy grade book export tools that allow Aplia to work with any learning management system. Aplia™ assignments match the language, style, and structure of *Management, 2e* allowing your students to apply what they learn directly to their work outside the classroom.

- **Write Experience**

    Cengage Learning's Write Experience helps students write effectively without adding to your workload! Write Experience utilizes artificial intelligence to score student writing instantly and accurately. It also provides students with detailed revision goals and feedback on their writing to help them improve written communication and critical thinking skills. Write Experience is the first product designed and created specifically for the higher education market through an exclusive agreement with McCann Associates, a Vantage Learning Affiliated operating company, and powered by e-Write IntelliMetric Within™.

Acknowledgments

First and foremost, we would like to thank the faculty who adopted the preliminary and first editions of our textbook. Adopting a new textbook is not an easy decision, and we greatly appreciate the trust and belief that was placed in us. We are also grateful for the feedback that we have received on the initial edition, and we have made a concerted effort to incorporate these invaluable suggestions. We would also like to acknowledge our partners at Cengage who have demonstrated a deep commitment and passion for this new approach to teaching the principles of management. In particular, we would like to thank Scott Person who has been a source of encouragement and support from the very beginning of this journey. In addition, we are indebted to the work of our colleagues at Cengage including Sara Ginn and Tara Singer for developmental editing support; Carol Moore, for her work on the digital side; and Joseph Malcolm for production support and oversight.

Over the last few years, we were fortunate to work with a team of dedicated individuals who provided thoughtful insights and relevant research support for various chapters including Sara Christopher, Stephanie Creary, Johnathan Cromwell, Alyssa Levy, Todd Maher, Lisa Riva, David Romney, William Russell, Franz Wohlgezogen, and Lara Zimmerman. We want to specifically acknowledge Samantha Cappelletti, Caroline de Lacvivier, Seah Lee, and Devlin McConnell who provided invaluable support for the second edition.

In launching this textbook on the principles of management, we sought the advice and counsel of several colleagues who provided thoughtful recommendations and input. In particular, we are extremely grateful for the thoughtful feedback and compelling insights of Bonita Austin (University of Utah), Francesca Gino (Harvard Business School), Geoffrey Love (University of Illinois), Svjetlana Madzar (University of Minnesota), and Lamar Pierce (Washington University, St. Louis). In addition, we are deeply indebted to Lynn Wooten (University of Michigan), who not only provided feedback on several chapters but also contributed key pedagogical elements to enhance the text.

We would like to thank our colleagues and the Division of Research at Harvard Business School for their support as well as our families who have provided unwavering encouragement.

Finally, we would like to thank the following individuals for their invaluable feedback and insights throughout the many stages of manuscript reviewing:

Darlene Andert, *Florida Gulf Coast University*
Corinne Asher, *Henry Ford Community College*
Karen Barr, *Pennsylvania State University – Beaver*
Richard Bartlett, *Columbus State Community College Delaware Campus*
Rebecca Bennett, *Louisiana Tech University*
Ellen Benowitz, *Mercer County Community College*
David Biemer, *Texas State University – San Marcos*
Charles Blalack, *Kilgore College*
Jeff W. Bruns, *Bacone College*
Deborah Butler, *Georgia State University*
Ken Butterfield, *Washington State University*
James Cashman, *The University of Alabama*
Wendy Casper, *University of Texas at Arlington*
Jim Cater, *Nicholls State University*
Joseph Chavez, *Nova Southeastern University*

John Cichy, *Davenport University*

Paul Coakley, *The Community College of Baltimore County*

Brad Cox, *Midlands Technical College*

Suzanne Crampton, *Grand Valley State University*

Aleta Crawford, *The University of Mississippi – Tupelo Campus*

Dan Creed, *Normandale Community College*

Margaret E. Deck, *Virginia Polytechnic Institute and State University*

Vinit Desai, *University of Colorado – Denver*

Joe Dipoli, *Bunkerhill Community College*

Robert Eliason, *James Madison University*

Ronald Emeigh, *Henry Ford Community College*

Bruce D. Fischer, *Elmhurst College*

Mary Ann Gaal, *Franklin Pierce University*

Patrick Geer, *Hawkeye Community College*

Tamara Giluk, *Xavier University*

David Glew, *University of North Carolina – Wilmington*

Mary E. Gorman, *University of Cincinnati*

George Griffin, *Spring Arbor University*

Carol Harvey, *Assumption College*

Ahmad Hassan, *Morehead State University*

Nathan Himelstein, *Essex County College*

Richard S. Hyland, *Westchester Community College*

Jonatan Jelen, *City College of New York*

Kathleen Jones, *University of North Dakota*

Rusty Juban, *Southeastern Louisiana University*

Jason Kanov, *Western Washington University*

Marv Karlin, *University of South Florida*

Rob Konopaske, *Texas State University*

Lee Lee, *Central Connecticut State University*

Jeffrey Lenn, *George Washington University*

Kristie Loescher, *University of Texas*

Jennifer Malfitano, *Delaware County Community College*

Doug McCabe, *Georgetown University*

Jeanne McNett, *Assumption College*

Lorianne Mitchell, *East Tennessee State University*

John Myers, *Jefferson College*

Daniel Nehring, *Morehead State University*

David Nemi, *Niagara County Community College*

John Nirenberg, *Walden University*

Rhonda S. Palladi, *Georgia State University*

Deana Ray, *Forsyth Technical Community College*

Sandra Robertson, *Thomas Nelson Community College*

Kim Rocha, *Barton College*

Stanley Ross, *Bridgewater State University*

Paul Sears, *The University of Findlay*

Amit Shah, *Frostburg State University*

Mansour Sharifzadeh, *California State Polytechnic University – Pomona*

Herbert Sherman, *Long Island University – Brooklyn*

Shane Spiller, *Western Kentucky University*

Gregory K. Stephens, *Texas Christian University*

John Striebich, *Monroe County Community College*

Charlotte D. Sutton, *Auburn University*

Kenneth R. Thompson, *DePaul University*

Mary Jean Thornton, *Capital Community College*

Mary Tucker, *Ohio University*

Valerie Ann Wallingford, *Bemidji State University*

Wendy Wysocki, *Monroe County Community College*

About the Authors

Ranjay Gulati

Ranjay Gulati is the Jaime and Josefina Chua Tiampo Professor of Business Administration and unit head of the Organizational Behavior Unit at the Harvard Business School. He is an expert on leadership, strategy, and organizational issues in firms. His recent work explores leadership and strategic challenges for building high-growth organizations in turbulent markets. Some of his prior work has focused on the enablers and implications of within-firm and inter-firm collaboration. He has looked at both when and how firms should leverage greater connectivity within and across their boundaries to enhance performance.

In his book, *Reorganize for Resilience: Putting Customers at the Center of Your Organization* (Harvard Business Press, 2009), he explores how "resilient" companies—those that prosper both in good times and bad—drive growth and increase profitability by immersing themselves in the lives of their customers. Based on more than a decade of research across a range of industries including manufacturing, retail, professional services, media, information technology, and healthcare, the book uncovers the path to resilience by showing companies how to break down internal barriers that impede action, build bridges across divisions, and create networks of collaborators. In another book, *Managing Network Resources: Alliances, Affiliations, and other Relational Assets* (Oxford University Press, 2007), he examines the implications of firms' growing portfolio of inter-firm connections. He demonstrates how firms are increasingly scaling back what they consider to be their core activities, and are at the same time expanding their array of offerings to customers by entering into a web of collaborations. He has also co-edited two books that focus on the dynamics of competition in emerging technology-intensive industries.

Professor Gulati is the past president of the Business Policy and Strategy Division at the Academy of Management and an elected fellow of the Strategic Management Society and the Academy of Management. He was ranked as one of the top 10 most cited scholars in Economics and Business over a decade by ISI-Incite. *The Economist, Financial Times,* and the *Economist Intelligence Unit* have listed him as among the top handful of business school scholars whose work is most relevant to management practice. He has been a Harvard MacArthur Fellow and a Sloan Foundation Fellow. His research has been published in leading journals such as *Administrative Science Quarterly, Harvard Business Review, American Journal of Sociology, Strategic Management Journal, Sloan Management Review, Academy of Management Journal,* and *Organization Science.* He has also written for the *Wall Street Journal, Forbes, strategy+business,* and the *Financial Times.* Professor Gulati sits on the editorial board of several leading journals. For the *Strategic Management Journal* he has been a co-editor of special issues including "Alliances and Strategic Networks" in 2000 and "Organizational Architecture" in 2011. He also co-edited a special issue of the *Academy of Management Journal* on "Multiplex Networks" that appeared in 2014.

Professor Gulati chairs the Harvard Business School's Advanced Management Program. He has directed several Executive Education programs on such topics as Building and Leading Customer Centric Organizations, Managing Customer Relationships, Managing Strategic Alliances, Mergers & Acquisitions, and Sustaining Competitive Advantage in Turbulent Markets. He is also active in custom executive education. He has received a number of awards for his teaching including the Best

Professor Award for his teaching in the MBA and executive MBA programs at the Kellogg School, where he was on the faculty prior to coming to Harvard.

Professor Gulati advises and speaks to corporations large and small around the globe. Some of his representative speaking and consulting clients include: GE, SAP, Novartis, Bank of China, Sanofi Aventis, Caterpillar, Allergan, Metlife, Target, Hitachi, Novartis, Honda, Qualcomm, Aetna, Future Brands, Ford, Seyfarth Shaw, LaFarge, McGraw-Hill, Rockwell Collins, Merck, General Mills, Abbott Laboratories, Baxter, Credit Suisse, and Microsoft. He has served on the advisory boards of several startup companies and has appeared as an expert witness in business litigations.

He has been a frequent guest on CNBC as well as a panelist on several of their series on topics that include: the *Business of Innovation, Collaboration*, and *Leadership Vision*. Professor Gulati holds a Ph.D. from Harvard University, a Master's Degree in Management from M.I.T.'s Sloan School of Management, and two Bachelor's Degrees, in Computer Science and Economics, from Washington State University and St. Stephens College, New Delhi, respectively. He lives in Newton, Massachusetts.

Anthony J. Mayo

Tony Mayo is the Thomas S. Murphy Senior Lecturer of Business Administration in the Organizational Behavior Unit of Harvard Business School (HBS) and the director of the HBS Leadership Initiative. He currently is the course head for FIELD, Field Immersion Experiences for Leadership Development, a required experiential, field-based course in the first year of the MBA Program which covers leadership, globalization, and entrepreneurship. Previously, he co-created and taught the course, "Great Business Leaders: The Importance of Contextual Intelligence." In addition, Tony teaches extensively in leadership-based executive education programs. He is the co-author of *In Their Time: The Greatest Business Leaders of the 20th Century*, which has been translated into 6 languages. He is also the co-author of *Paths to Power: How Insiders and Outsiders Shaped American Business Leadership* and *Entrepreneurs, Managers and Leaders: What the Airline Industry Can Teach Us About Leadership*. These books have been derived from the development of the Great American Business Leaders database that Dean Nitin Nohria and Tony created (see http://www.hbs.edu/ leadership/database/index.html).

As director of the Leadership Initiative, Tony oversees several comprehensive research projects on emerging, global, and legacy leadership and manages a number of executive education programs on leadership development. He was a co-creator of the High Potentials Leadership Development, Leadership for Senior Executives, Leading with Impact, Maximizing Your Leadership Potential, and Leadership Best Practices programs and has been a principal contributor to a number of custom leadership development initiatives. He launched the executive coaching component for the Program for Leadership Development and currently provides strategic support for a variety of executive coaching programs.

Prior to his current role, Tony pursued a career in database marketing where he held senior general management positions at advertising agency Hill Holliday, database management firm Epsilon, and full-service direct marketing company DIMAC Marketing Corporation. Most recently, Tony served as the General Manager of Hill Holliday's Customer Relationship Management Practice.

At Epsilon, he served as acting co-chief executive officer where he had full responsibility for the delivery and management of strategic and database marketing services for Fortune 1000 companies and national not-for-profit organizations. He also held senior management positions in Epsilon's sales and account management departments. At DIMAC Marketing Corporation, Tony served as vice president of strategic development and acting chief financial officer. In this capacity, Tony led the development of an integrated strategic plan for DIMAC's disparate business units and coordinated the ultimate sale of the company. Prior to his work in the database marketing industry, Tony served as the Director of MBA Program Administration at Harvard Business School.

Tony completed his MBA from Harvard Business School and received his Bachelor's Degree, *summa cum laude*, from Boston College. He lives in Needham, MA.

Nitin Nohria

Nitin Nohria became the 10th dean of Harvard Business School on July 1, 2010. He previously served as co-chair of the Leadership Initiative, senior associate dean of Faculty Development, and Head of the Organizational Behavior unit.

Dean Nohria's intellectual interests center on human motivation, leadership, corporate transformation and accountability, and sustainable economic and human performance. He is coauthor or coeditor of 16 books. The most recent, *Handbook of Leadership Theory and Practice*, is a compendium dedicated to advancing research on leadership based on a colloquium he organized during HBS's centennial celebrations. Dean Nohria is also the author of over 50 journal articles, book chapters, cases, working papers, and notes. He sits on the board of directors of Tata Sons and is on the board of trustees of Massachusetts General Hospital. He has served as an advisor and consultant to several large and small companies in different parts of the world. He has been interviewed by ABC, CNN, and NPR, and cited in *Business Week, Economist, Financial Times, Fortune, New York Times*, and *The Wall Street Journal*.

Prior to joining the Harvard Business School faculty in July 1988, Dean Nohria received his Ph.D. in management from the Sloan School of Management, Massachusetts Institute of Technology, and a B.Tech. in Chemical Engineering from the Indian Institute of Technology, Bombay (which honored him as a distinguished alumnus in 2007). He was a visiting faculty member at the London Business School in 1996.

P A R T **1**

SETTING THE CONTEXT FOR MANAGEMENT

CHAPTER

1

Introduction to Management

Learning Objectives

After reading this chapter, you should be able to:

LO1 Differentiate among the three pillars of managing organizations: strategic positioning, organizational design, and individual leadership.

LO2 Describe the complementary components of management and leadership and the relative importance of technical, interpersonal, and conceptual skills at various managerial levels in the organization.

LO3 Articulate how the practice of management has evolved.

LO4 Explain the changing perspectives on the purpose of business and how the relationship between the firm and its business environment has changed over time.

LO5 Describe the stakeholder theory of management and how various stakeholder relationships are managed to enhance overall firm performance.

SELF-REFLECTION

What Are Your Managerial and Leadership Strengths?

Please respond True or False to the following statements to assess your leadership and managerial strengths.

1. I excel at planning projects.

2. When working with a group, I think strategically by creating a vision and setting goals to make that vision a reality.

3. I am skilled at budgeting and financial planning.

4. I encourage change by challenging the status quo.

5. I can organize people to get a job done by establishing structures and delegating tasks.

6. I understand how to motivate people.

7. I enjoy creating solutions for complex problems.

8. I have the ability to work with a diverse group of people to accomplish a goal.

9. I am a take-charge type of person who brings order to a variety of situations.

10. I influence people through passion and emotional connections.

If you answered True to the majority of the odd-numbered statements, you have a solid foundation of managerial strengths. If you answered True to the majority of the even-numbered statements, you have a solid foundation of leadership strengths. If both are true, you are adept at balancing the roles of managers and leaders.

INTRODUCTION

Now, more than ever, the world needs leaders who are versatile and flexible. The increasing pace of globalization, rapid deployment of technology, and constantly changing competitive landscape require leaders who can nimbly adapt themselves and their organizations to new realities. The one constant in business is that it is not constant. Change is a reality, and businesses that stand the test of time are led by individuals who not only embrace change, but proactively prepare their organizations for its impact. Sustaining relevance in a dynamic business environment requires leaders to confront difficult decisions on a daily basis. Do they expand product offerings to anticipate consumer demand? Or do they eliminate waste and focus the company's efforts on fewer products? Should they compete directly with rivals? Or do they invest money to innovate an entirely new product or service? How do they motivate their employees? How do they gain trust and commitment in the organization? Should they focus on learning and development or bottom-line results?

Leaders need to understand how to harness technological advancements, manage and lead a dispersed and diverse workforce, anticipate and react to constant competitive and geopolitical change and uncertainty, compete on a global scale, and operate in a socially responsible and accountable manner.[1] One increasingly popular acronym that captures the context in which today's organizations compete is **VUCA**, which stands for volatile, uncertain, complex, and ambiguous. A volatile situation is characterized by unpredictability and requires managers to be agile and flexible. An uncertain situation calls for managers to gather and decipher large amounts of information, some of which will be conflicting. This uncertainty is sometimes accompanied by complexity, a situation that is based on the interconnection of various business elements. Separating these interconnections and structuring individual responses to them helps managers cope with complexity. Finally, managers often face very ambiguous situations where the cause-and-effect relationships are not always clear. Experimentation helps managers to achieve a greater sense of clarity about ambiguous situations (see Table 1.1).[2] Success for organizations in this VUCA environment requires a strong knowledge of (1) strategic positioning, (2) organizational design, and (3) individual leadership (see Figure 1.1).

The interaction between the formulation of strategy, the design of the organization, and the leadership of the firm is not a functional or linear process; it is a dynamic and interactive one. Throughout this textbook on the principles, purpose, and perspectives of management, we demonstrate the mutual interdependence and interconnectivity between strategy, organizational design, and individual leadership action. The strategy of an organization depends on the nature and context of the competitive and environmental landscape as well as the skills and capabilities of the management team. The understanding of this contextual landscape is, in turn, dependent on the ability of the firm's management to recognize opportunities and threats as well as lead and organize the company's resources to effectively compete in the marketplace.

A firm needs to adapt and change its strategic choices and leadership approaches to retain its relevance. Strategy often dictates the organizational design and leadership required for success. The type of leaders and the organizational design of a business can also influence the strategic choices in which a business can credibly compete. In essence, strategy, organizational design, and leadership must work together in an integrative and dynamic fashion.

The chapters of this textbook are organized according to the three pillars of managing organizations—strategy, organization, and individual leadership. The strategic level or perspective will encompass an understanding of the environmental landscape in which businesses compete and the elements of strategy that help organizations align their resources for success in a changing context. Key questions that will be addressed in the strategic perspective include the following: How should a business compete? How does the competitive landscape shape the potential for its

VUCA
An acronym for volatile, uncertain, complex, and ambiguous that captures the context in which today's organizations compete.

		Situation Characterized by...	Response
V	**Volatility**	Unstable and unpredictable change	Be agile and flexible
U	**Uncertainty**	Lack of knowledge about significance of change	Seek knowledge and information
C	**Complexity**	Many interconnected parts	Adjust operations to match the environment
A	**Ambiguity**	Lack of knowledge about cause and effect	Experiment

Table 1.1 ⟩ Context in Which Businesses Operate: VUCA—Volatility, Uncertainty, Complexity, and Ambiguity

Source: Adapted from Nathan Bennett and G. James Lemoine, "What a Difference a Word Makes: Understanding Threats to Performance in a VUCA World," *Business Horizons*, Vol. 57, 2014, pp. 311–317.

Global Business Context

Strategic Position

Organizational Design

Individual Leadership

Figure 1.1 The Pillars of Management

success or failure? What strategy will allow a firm to adapt as the context evolves? How has and will globalization impact the competitive positioning of a business?

Knowing what strategy to pursue is only the first part of the management puzzle. The next piece involves developing and aligning the organizational components (e.g., organizational design, culture, human resource practices, and performance management) to achieve these strategic objectives. Without this, no strategy will ever be properly implemented and all that thinking will come to nothing. To that end, the organizational perspective of the textbook will define the manner in which a business is structured to compete in its changing contextual landscape. Key questions include the following: What organizational structure will enable the firm to optimize its resources? How can the culture of the firm reinforce key values and lay the foundation for strong organizational performance? How will performance be measured? How does an organization remain relevant in a constantly changing competitive landscape?

Finally, an organization is nothing more than a collection of individuals who come together to achieve a common goal or objective. But how does one coordinate and motivate diverse individuals to work together? The answer is through effective leadership. The final section of the textbook addresses the key components and activities of leadership. This section is about you and how you can be a more effective leader in the global organizations of tomorrow. Leaders must first know who they are and what impels them to effectively motivate and influence others. Key questions addressed in the individual perspective section of the textbook include the following: How should managers wield power and influence? How do managers make critical decisions and navigate conflict? What motivates others, and how does one create and nurture effective teams? How do managers communicate with urgency and compassion?

The interplay of strategy, organizational design, and individual action operates within a broad contextual landscape. In fact, the context can directly impact the strategic opportunities open to a firm as well as the latitude of individual managerial action. That is why we have encircled the three perspectives of management in Figure 1.1 a contextual framing. While the context can shape the availability and viability of certain opportunities, managers can influence the context through a number of actions including their ability to commercialize technology, support or oppose government action, and capitalize on demographic movements.

In recent years, the growing importance of globalization and the expanding scope of corporate social responsibility have fundamentally impacted the business landscape. Chapters 2 and 3 of this opening section of the textbook will provide an overview of globalization and corporate responsibility, respectively, and how they have shaped the context for business.

In this first chapter, we will discuss how the perspective from which the firm is viewed has evolved over the years. As we'll see, the firm has shifted from owing a duty only to shareholders to owing a duty to various stakeholders. This view of a firm's purpose has changed as the complexity and turbulence in the marketplace have increased. We'll also discuss a firm's external and internal environments to demonstrate the various forces and stakeholders that a firm encounters in conducting its business. One thing that should become clear through the reading is that managing a firm's stakeholders and environments is a very difficult task, but doing so is critical to building a high-performing organization.[3] By responding to stakeholder concerns, the manager can drive the firm's performance and achieve a competitive advantage in the marketplace. Failing to understand the complexity of various stakeholders can have disastrous consequences, as evidenced by Walmart's attempt to enter the Inglewood, California, market.

Walmart's Business Environment

Walmart, the world's largest retailer, has followed a trajectory of growth and expansion since its inception in the 1960s. Started by the legendary Sam Walton, Walmart's historical strategy was to open stores in semirural markets to provide variety and competitive prices to customers who previously relied on a host of smaller stores for their shopping needs. Throughout the 1970s and 1980s, Walmart expanded aggressively across the United States, offering the lowest prices in many markets. As other retailing businesses such as K-Mart and Sears fell on hard times, Walmart continued to post ever-impressive results.[4]

In 2014, the company employed over 2.2 million people and earned net income of $16 billion on revenues of $476 billion.[5] Over the past two decades, Walmart has changed the mix of its retail stores, opening more Supercenters that offer groceries as well as traditional retail offerings (see Figure 1.2). Despite its growth, Walmart has struggled with expansion, especially in Vermont and California. Though rural Vermont would seem to be a natural fit for Walmart, the state has the fewest Walmarts per capita than any other state in the country. Several small Vermont communities have launched aggressive anti-Walmart campaigns in the state, concerned that the company's presence will erode the success of local retailers and irreparably damage the charm of the state's small towns.[6]

Andrew Nelles/Reuters

Walmart faced similar resistance in California. Following its first successful opening of a Supercenter in La Quinta, Walmart looked next to a market closer to Los Angeles. However, as the company drafted plans to open a Supercenter in Inglewood, it began to encounter serious opposition from the members of the city council, who had attempted to pass legislation in 2002 to prevent stores of Walmart's size from building new units in their town. Walmart executives were confused about why a town would not want a new commercial enterprise that could generate new jobs (estimated at 1,200) and additional tax revenue for the city (estimated at $5 million annually).

The company also faced typical competitive pressures as it sought to enter this new market. Like many markets in the United States, the grocery business in California was very competitive, with low gross margins prevalent across the industry. The California market was dominated by established grocers such as Safeway, Albertson's, and Kroger. Just as the Inglewood proposal hit the headlines, many of Walmart's grocery competitors in California responded to the chain's potential entry with a series of competitive actions. In many markets, a Walmart entry into the grocery business had resulted in prices dropping 3%–5% for certain products. As a result, many of the biggest grocery chains in California attempted to lower employees' wages and healthcare coverage in an effort to remain cost competitive with Walmart.[7] As rival grocery workers suffered from wage cuts, the United Food and Commercial Workers (UFCW) union continued to put pressure on the Inglewood city council

to block Walmart's Supercenter. Many argued that Walmart's arrival would continue to cause wage decreases across the city. This was a grim prospect for a city that already suffered high unemployment rates and lower income levels relative to those in other areas around Los Angeles.

As Walmart executives watched these events unfold, they debated what course of action to take. To many, it seemed pointless to take the proposal before a city council that had made its intentions clear. So the company moved forward with its efforts to put the proposal to a vote by citizen referendum. Critics responded that Walmart would hurt local citizens because its wage and healthcare programs kept employees below the poverty line. The city of Los Angeles commissioned a study showing that Walmart Supercenters destroyed jobs and forced competitors to pay lower wages.[8] In contrast, a report issued by the Los Angeles County Economic Development Corporation and funded by Walmart came to opposite conclusions, claiming that households shopping at Walmart saved on groceries, which allowed consumers to spend more on other items, in turn leading to job growth.[9] In the end, voters soundly rejected the initiative and Walmart was forced to abandon Inglewood.

Until recently, Walmart faced little if any opposition to new store openings. Today, it seems as though the company encounters resistance at every turn when opening new stores. If you were a manager at Walmart, how would you have dealt with the situation? What could they have done differently?

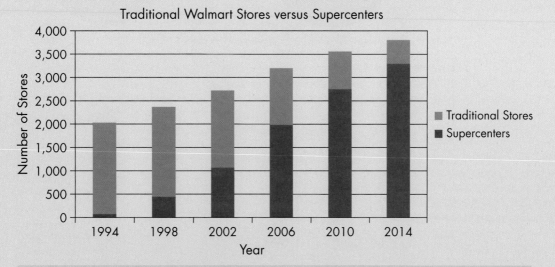

Figure 1.2 › Growth of Supercenters, 1994–2014

Source: Wal-Mart Stores, Inc. annual reports for 1999, 2004, 2010, and 2014.

The Walmart case highlights the complexity of managing and leading in today's business environment. Effective management is responsible for more than generating a profit; management's job often requires the ability to understand the needs of a variety of key constituents including its employees and the broader community. In essence, success in the global business environment requires effective management and skillful leadership.

MANAGEMENT AND LEADERSHIP

The distinction between **management** and **leadership** is often very subtle. In fact, most people use the terms interchangeably when they refer to the operation of a business. In a seminal analysis on the difference between managers and leaders, John Kotter noted that leaders set a direction for a firm, align people to focus on the organization's vision, and motivate and inspire people (see Figure 1.3).[10] Conversely, he noted that managers generally focus their efforts on planning and budgeting, organizing and staffing resources, and controlling and problem solving.

Management has generally been defined as the act of working with and through a group of people to accomplish a desired goal or objective in an efficient and effective manner. Leadership has been defined as the ability to drive change and innovation through inspiration and motivation. The development and execution of strategy requires the skills and expertise of leaders and managers, and both are equally important to an organization's success. A vision or direction without a sound plan for execution is often merely a dream. The execution of a plan without a vision often lacks strategic or competitive advantage.

For instance, at Southwest Airlines, a vision was born when former chief executive officer (CEO) Herb Kelleher learned of a short-haul commuter airline in

Management
The act of working with and through a group of people to accomplish a desired goal or objective in an efficient and effective manner.

Leadership
The ability to drive change and innovation through inspiration and motivation.

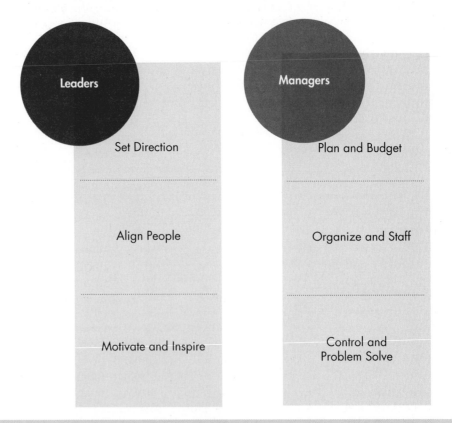

Figure 1.3 ⟩ The Roles of Leaders versus Managers

California that flew passengers over shorter distances than did major airlines. Kelleher surmised that many travelers were tired of driving long distances (between 500 and 1,000 miles) because the available flights were too expensive or not frequent enough. Kelleher's vision was to get passengers to trade their car trips for short flights. This vision of air travel competing with car travel differed greatly from the vision promoted by the major airlines that were more focused on long-distance flights. While Kelleher set forth the vision of the firm, his management team was able to execute it with precision and accuracy. They did so by organizing the resources of the company to focus on efficiency, consistency, speed, and cost-effectiveness.[11]

To be successful, organizations need to develop and nurture managers and leaders at all levels, not just at the top. In fact, organizations often evolve and innovate based on the suggestions and input of individuals who are several levels below the CEO.[12] The skills required for success in business are often different depending on a person's level and responsibilities in the organization.[13] While technical skills are very important early on, they tend to take a back seat to more strategic abilities as an individual advances in an organization. For instance, frontline supervisors must often focus on technical or process issues to ensure that operations are running smoothly, and new entry-level employees are often tasked with specific operational roles that require a certain level of proficiency and skills. While it is true that leadership skills become more critical as you move up in an organization, it is important to note that leadership is not just the monopoly of top management, and most organizations today expect even their lower-level managers to operate and think like leaders.

As individuals move up in an organization, they have to focus on managerial tasks such as financial reporting, planning, recruiting talent, and resource allocation. While technical skills are still important, middle-level managers sometimes have to spend more time applying their leadership skills such as motivating and developing teams while at the same time using managerial skills such as working with senior executives to provide analysis for the development or refinement of the organization's strategy.

And still higher up, senior executives are expected to set the vision and agenda for the organization as well as oversee strategic execution. They must balance short and long-term expectations while planning for certain expected and unexpected contingencies. To do so, they must leverage both leadership and management skills. If they lack one or the other they must ensure that someone with complementary skills is there to support them. To secure buy-in and support in the organization, senior leaders need to rely on strong communication and interpersonal skills.[14] The ability to think conceptually is vitally important at this level (see Figure 1.4).[15]

While an individual's abilities must transform as they go higher in an organization, it is important to note that each person can have a very unique style and still be successful. Some leaders are extroverted, while others make decisions by listening to their inner voice. Some are quick and impulsive, while others are cautious and take longer to make a decision. Some leaders are vain, some are humble. According to Peter Drucker, an effective leader is not someone who uses a specific leadership style; he or she is someone whose style enables him or her to obtain results.[16]

Technical, interpersonal, and conceptual skills are important and relevant for all individuals regardless of their place in the organization. The key difference is the level of intensity of each skill.[17] Conceptual skills consume more of a top executive's time, while technical skills are more important for new employees and frontline supervisors. This breakdown of skills is applicable to business and nonbusiness settings. Think about a soccer team. The players are focused on exercising their technical skills to the best of their abilities. They need to work as members of a team, and they need to know the team's plays (or strategies) but the players' primary concern is their own skills. The coaches are also focused on skills by providing instruction and training, but they must ensure that individual players work as a team. Coaches set strategy and create plays

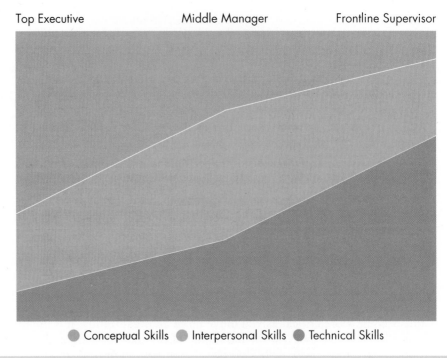

Figure 1.4 ⟩ Importance and Relevance of Skills by Managerial Level

Figure 1.5 ⟩ From Big Picture Strategy to Individual Action

to further develop the capacity of the team. Finally, the team's owners must be able to identify and support talent, but they spend the bulk of their time overseeing strategic issues such as revenue generation and long-term investment opportunities.

The primary skills of managers and leaders (conceptual, interpersonal, and technical) are aligned with the overall structure of this textbook (see Figure 1.5). In the strategic perspective, we will spend a considerable amount of time discussing ways in which business leaders develop strategies and positions to differentiate their operation in a competitive landscape. This ability to understand the landscape and one's position in it depends on the development of well-honed conceptual abilities.

The Leadership Development Journey

After you graduate from college and start your career, you will be expected to effectively incorporate fully developed technical, conceptual, and interpersonal skills needed for managing and leading. Identify your ideal career and consider the following questions:

- Can you identify the technical skills required for an entry-level job?
- What are the interpersonal skills needed to supervise a staff?
- How does a top executive use conceptual skills to set a vision and craft a strategy?

Based on your analysis of the skills needed for your ideal career, identify three goals that will enable you to succeed and to develop a career path.

Moving to the organizational perspective, our focus is on structural issues that involve conceptual as well as interpersonal and technical skills. For instance, how does one create an organizational structure that maximizes the talents of employees? In the final section of the textbook, we address the ways in which individuals can build the skills (technical, interpersonal, and conceptual) to develop as a leader and to prepare to make necessary organizational and strategic decisions.

We start with the big picture strategic perspective to define the company's position in the global business context. Once the strategy has been developed, it is important to move to execution and delivery. That's where organizational structure, design processes, and performance management come into play. What are the best structures and processes to support the desired strategic objectives? What resources are available? What resources must be acquired or developed? How can a business sustain its relevance in a changing contextual landscape? The answers to these questions define the organizational perspective.

Ultimately, managers must have the strategic abilities needed to understand a situation, the social skills to know what to do in that situation, and the behavioral skills to act.[18] Some leaders know what to do but can't do it, while others are less effective at recognizing the subtleties and complexities of nuanced situations. Still others treat all situations with the same managerial approach. Effective management requires the development of a broad set of skills and capabilities needed to act in a variety of situations. That's why it is so important to focus on the development of personal leadership skills.

HISTORICAL PERSPECTIVES ON BUSINESS

A formal theory of how large and complex organizations operate was first put forward in the early 1900s by German social scientist Max Weber. He was interested in explaining how organizations retain order and get things done as they get bigger. The underlying idea here was that as organizations get larger, they can become unwieldy as they tackle their internal division of labor. To maintain order, most organizations (in this case not just business but nonbusiness settings like the military and government) seek to implement systems and processes to create order. Weber's main contribution to the field was the conceptualization of the **bureaucratic organization structure**. According to Weber, the features of an ideal bureaucracy include the following: a clear differentiation of tasks and responsibilities among individuals; coordination through a strict hierarchy of authority and decision rights; standardized

Bureaucratic organization structure
A clear differentiation of tasks and responsibilities among individuals; coordination through a strict hierarchy of authority and decision rights; standardized rules and procedures; and the vertical separation of planning and execution so that plans are made in the upper ranks of an organization and executed in the lower ranks.

Scientific management
A focus on how jobs, work, and incentive schemes could be designed to improve productivity using industrial engineering methods.

Bettmann/CORBIS

Human relations movement
The belief that organizations must be understood as systems of interdependent human beings who share a common interest in the survival and effective functioning of the firm.

rules and procedures; the vertical separation of planning and execution so that plans are made in the upper ranks of an organization and executed in the lower; and the use of technical criteria for recruitment and promotion.[19] Most modern organizations have explicitly or implicitly based their structures on the basic principles of this bureaucratic form.[20] The classic example of the bureaucratic organization is the military. According to Weber, the bureaucratic form's greatest contribution was its ability to make organizations more rational and efficient.[21]

Following Weber's work, many social scientists began exploring how organizations could be set up around a set of scientific principles to make them orderly and efficient. Some of this work, pioneered by Frederick Taylor in the 1910s, came to be known as **scientific management**. Scientific management focused on how jobs, work, and incentive schemes could be designed to improve productivity using industrial engineering methods such as time and motion studies. The results of these studies formed the basis of Taylor's principles of effective supervision within the firm.[22] Through this approach, the organization was likened to a well-oiled machine and the manager was seen as a machine operator. The manager prescribed certain actions based on scientific study that were expected to produce definitive outcomes. Taylor believed that employees were economically driven and rational in their motives.

In the 1930s, theories of management shifted away from the view of the organization as a machine. During this period, the **human relations movement**[23] emerged, which emphasized the importance of informal social relations at work. As opposed to scientific management's view of the firm as a machine, human relations scientists believed that organizations must be understood as a system of interdependent human beings who share a common interest in the survival and effective functioning of the firm. Through the human relations movement, emphasis shifted from the output of the firm to the informal and social side of the firm. From this standpoint, organizations served as a means for people to interact and learn as well as turn a profit.

By the 1950s, theories of management had shifted yet again to examine the differences across organizations in the way they structured themselves. A debate raged on about how a firm should be organized. Some theorists believed that there was one optimal form of organizing all organizations. Others believed that the optimal form depended on the nature of the context in which the organization competed. This second group believed that organizational form depends on social, psychological, technical, and economic conditions.[24]

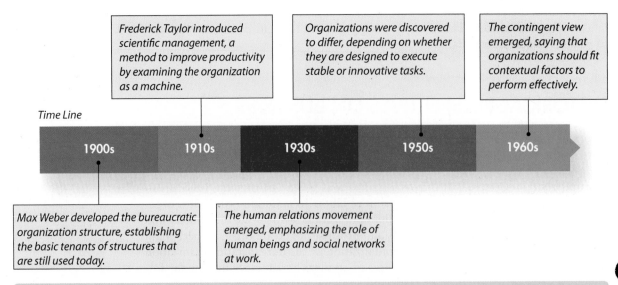

Frederick Taylor introduced scientific management, a method to improve productivity by examining the organization as a machine.

Organizations were discovered to differ, depending on whether they are designed to execute stable or innovative tasks.

The contingent view emerged, saying that organizations should fit contextual factors to perform effectively.

Time Line

1900s   1910s   1930s   1950s   1960s

Max Weber developed the bureaucratic organization structure, establishing the basic tenants of structures that are still used today.

The human relations movement emerged, emphasizing the role of human beings and social networks at work.

Figure 1.6 ⟩ Major Historical Events in the Study of Organizations

One of the most profound insights about organizational structure that came out of this period was the fact that organizations often differ based on whether they were designed to execute certain stable tasks or uncertain innovative tasks. Many researchers during the period believed that the nature of the environment and the tasks the firm had to accomplish should drive how organizations were structured and managed. According to this argument, firms that emphasized efficiency should maintain stable, mechanistic organizational structures. In contrast, firms that emphasized innovation should maintain flexible and organic organizational structures.[25]

In the 1960s, popular thought evolved and made a complete break from the notion that all firms should have a certain organizational structure. Ultimately a shared view emerged that there may not be one optimal form for all organizations and that the ideal form depends on its context. During this period, a **contingent view** of the firm emerged where effective organizational structure was based on fit or alignment between the organization and its environment.[26] This approach affirmed that the social, political, and business environments play a large role in shaping the way effective organizations are structured. According to this contingent view, the organization's structure should fit the firm's environment (see Figure 1.6).

Current research on the role of organizations has tended to be an extension of many of the previous theories. In general, there is no "one-size-fits-all" approach to organizational design. In making organizational design decisions, managers must evaluate their strategic objectives in relation to the contextual environment and their internal resource capabilities. That is why an understanding of the context is so important.

CHANGING PERSPECTIVES ON THE PURPOSE OF BUSINESS

Today's **business environment**, which includes all of the contextual forces and elements that shape or impact the internal and external environments of a firm, is infinitely more complex than it was just a few years ago. Over the years, the view of how to approach the business environment and drive performance has changed (see Figure 1.7).

Contingent view
A view of the firm where effective organizational structure is based on fit or alignment between the organization and various aspects in its environment.

Business environment
The combination of all contextual forces and elements in the external and internal environments of a firm.

Managerial View	• Up to 1960s • Key Focus: Production
Shareholder View	• 1960s–1980s • Key Focus: Financial Performance
Stakeholder View	• Since 1990s • Key Focus: Serving Multiple Constituencies

Figure 1.7 Changing Perceptions of the Business Environment

Library of Congress Prints and Photographs Division [LC-DIG-highsm-15747]

For a good part of the twentieth century, many managers subscribed to the **managerial view** of the firm, which saw the firm as a mechanism for converting raw materials into products to sell to customers. In this framework, managers focused on relationships between the firm and its suppliers, customers, owners, and employees. During this period, management often did not focus on the broader set of parties that Walmart was forced to contend with in Inglewood. In fact, many firms did not consider outside parties such as local governments or nongovernmental organizations (NGOs) as anything more than annoyances. In this context, managers were the boss, and in many cases, there were limited checks and balances on their power.

Up until the 1960s, shareholders did not have the power they do today. Mutual funds had not been developed, and corporate takeovers had yet to be popularized. As a result, managers did not face many threats from shareholders to improve performance or seek business in other industries.

However, in the late 1960s, many managers began to view the firm through a more shareholder-focused lens. During the 1970s, American corporations were under siege from two forces: (1) the combination of slow economic growth and high inflation and (2) increased penetration of foreign competition in the U.S. market.[27] Many firms stopped growing, and their profits began to stagnate.[28] The owners of the company who were technically the shareholders felt they had lost a voice in how the company was run and that their interests were no longer being served by managers. At the same time, shareholders were no longer individuals but rather institutions who had more collective clout and voice. As a result, managerial focus shifted to the interests of shareholders as the primary stakeholder for whom they worked.

According to the **shareholder view** of the firm, the job of top managers was to produce the highest possible stock market valuation of the firm's assets.[29] A series of factors during this period combined to promote this view. In the early 1980s, antitrust restrictions on mergers and acquisitions (M&A) were relaxed, prompting many firms to seek new growth opportunities by acquiring companies.[30] This period saw a huge increase in both M&A activity and corporate takeovers as managers attempted to seek growth in any way possible. Overall, no firm was immune to the pressures of the market and the threat of takeover.

Ford Motor Company took advantage of these relaxed rules. In an effort to provide more value to their shareholders and grow their business, Ford acquired British carmakers Jaguar and Aston Martin in the late 1980s. Both companies represented a market that Ford had failed to break into—Jaguar with luxury cars and Aston Martin with high-end sports cars.[31] By securing Jaguar, Ford also discovered a way to increase its presence in Western Europe.[32]

Managerial view
A business framework where the firm is seen as a mechanism for converting raw materials into products to sell to customers.

Shareholder view
A business framework where the job of top managers is to produce the highest possible stock market valuation of the firm's assets.

Rob Kinmonth/Getty Images

In a similar way, Frank Lorenzo capitalized on the new regulatory climate in the airline industry when he used his small Texas International Airline to undertake a hostile takeover of the much larger Continental Airlines in the early 1980s. Through some clever financial maneuvering, Lorenzo pushed his newly acquired firm into bankruptcy to break the power of the union and hence reduce the airline's cost structure. It worked. Profits soared. When the firm emerged from bankruptcy, Lorenzo went on a buying spree, acquiring Eastern Airlines, New York Air, and People Express in less than two years to make Continental one of the largest airlines in the United States. Lorenzo ran the airline as a financial model, focusing on profitability and shareholder value, and completely ignoring the impact of these financial decisions on employees and customers.[33]

Many managers, like Lorenzo, came to believe that the organization owed allegiance only to shareholders—that employees, communities, and customers were secondary. The results of an overemphasis on shareholder value emerged in the late 1980s as many U.S. companies started to lose ground to foreign competition. For some firms, this singular focus on shareholder value resulted in a short-term orientation, leading to a lack of investment in new products and erosion in quality standards. These firms were caught off guard as more nimble companies stole market share with new products, a greater focus on consumer needs, and a stronger commitment to quality. Lorenzo's success at Continental was short-lived. The lack of investment in the company, the inattention to customer needs, and the erosion of trust between management and employees resulted in Lorenzo's early departure from the company.

About the same time the shareholder view of the firm was reaching its zenith, both the internal and external environments of many firms began to increase in complexity. The external environment of the typical U.S. firm began experiencing turbulence through foreign competition. Many U.S. firms, such as the Big Three U.S. carmakers (General Motors, Ford, and Chrysler), had faced little foreign competition up until the 1980s because of protectionist measures that had insulated the industry. The Big Three also faced lower competitive pressures because of the infancy of many car firms in emerging economies. As Japanese carmakers made inroads into the U.S. market beginning in the 1970s, the Big Three had a new element of complexity to deal with in their environments.

But firms' environments were not increasing in complexity just because of foreign competition. Rather, firms during the 1980s began to face mounting pressure from a series of external groups, including environmental activists, animal rights groups, and local community governments. Many environmental groups emerged during this period (see Figure 1.8).

While it has become popular recently for corporations to focus on their environmental footprint or carbon emissions, this wasn't always the case. Many firms simply ignored environmental concerns for much of the twentieth century. High-impact industries such as mining, oil, and gas exploration as well as waste management rarely allocated any attention to environmental concerns. However, all of this changed in the 1980s as the public became aware of some of the by-products of these firms' activities. As acid rain and smog entered the average citizen's vocabulary, many firms were forced to address environmental concerns.

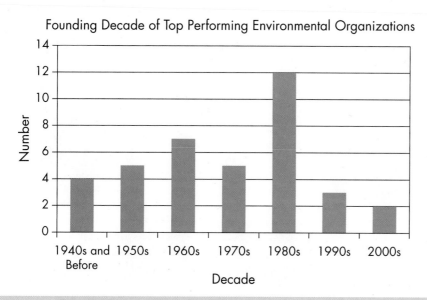

Figure 1.8) Founding Decade of Top Performing Environmental Organizations

Source: American Institute of Philanthropy, http://www.charitywatch.org/toprated.html#enviro, January 15, 2015.

At the same time, the firm's external environment was increasing in complexity; many firms had to deal with new pressures in their internal environments such as employee activism. As the shareholder view of the firm progressed, shareholders continued to push managers to achieve specific quarterly targets. The manager's focus was stretched between dealing with new sources of external and internal complexity and dealing with pressure from shareholders to produce results. The combination of these forces led to the development of a new paradigm from which to view the firm.

The **stakeholder view** of the firm emerged among this increasing complexity and turbulence in the economic environment. Made popular through E. Edward Freeman's 1984 book *Strategic Management: A Stakeholder Approach*, the stakeholder view of the firm identifies and analyzes multiple groups that interact with the firm and attempts to align organizational practices to satisfy the needs of these various groups (see Figure 1.9).[34] A typical firm may have relationships or duties to governments, local community organizations, owners, advocacy groups, customers, competitors, media, employees, environmentalists, and suppliers. While this list is not exhaustive, it demonstrates the various parties and groups with which a firm has relationships. The stakeholder view of the firm helps managers better understand the complex internal and external environment of the firm in today's marketplace. After Lorenzo's departure from Continental Airlines, the airline floundered with a series of unsuccessful CEOs until Gordon Bethune took the helm. Instead of running the airline as a financial entity focused exclusively on maximizing short-term performance, Bethune developed a comprehensive change plan to address the needs of customers, employees, investors, and suppliers. This holistic approach to running the airline fostered a sense of collaboration that had not previously

Stakeholder view
A business framework that identifies and analyzes multiple groups that interact with the firm and attempts to align organizational practices to satisfy the needs of these various groups.

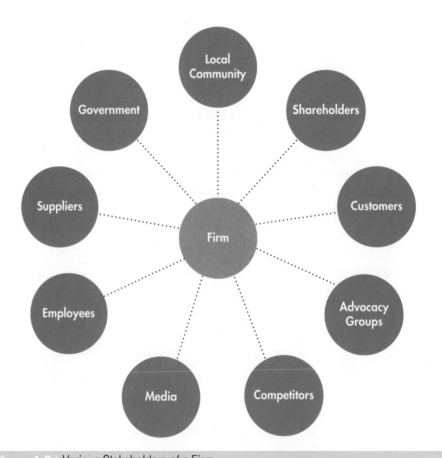

Figure 1.9 Various Stakeholders of a Firm

existed. In one year, the airline went from posting the worst reliability and performance metrics in the industry to the best. While Bethune employed a series of specific tactical actions to turnaround the airline, the key to the ultimate success was a broad stakeholder view.[35]

Each firm has a different set of stakeholders that affect its performance in the marketplace. The importance of various stakeholders also changes at different points in an organization's lifecycle.[36] For instance, the local community may be an influential stakeholder when a firm establishes a presence in a new location. After a period of successful operation in a local community, this stakeholder's level of influence may dissipate. In upcoming chapters, we'll define some of these stakeholders when we discuss the firm's external and internal environments in detail. For now, let's take a look at how managers can use the stakeholder approach to manage the firm more effectively and improve firm performance.

STAKEHOLDER APPROACH

According to the stakeholder theory, "a stakeholder is any group or individual who can affect or is affected by the achievement of an organization's purpose."[37] At its core, stakeholder theory is concerned with who can influence a firm's decisions and who benefits from those decisions.[38] The first step in organizing for stakeholder management is to identify all of the important stakeholders of the firm. While Figure 1.9 advances a certain group of stakeholders, this is by no means representative of every organization. The second component of stakeholder management involves designing formal processes and systems to deal with the firm's various stakeholders.

Stakeholder Mapping

The first step of stakeholder management is to map all of the stakeholder relationships relevant to the firm (see Figure 1.10). The manager must ultimately decide which groups or individuals can affect or are affected by the firm.[39] The manager can initiate this process by using the template from Figure 1.9 and adding or subtracting the firm's various stakeholders. As mentioned, each firm will have a specific group of relevant stakeholders. Some stakeholders will be more important than others. For instance, stakeholders that control vital resources are particularly important to consider.[40] Once the initial stakeholder map is constructed, the manager should identify specific subgroups within each stakeholder. For example, it is not sufficient to identify just the "government" as an important stakeholder on the map. Instead, the manager should seek to expand this group to a greater level of detail by mapping out the specific governmental agencies that affect or are affected by the firm.

The next step in the mapping process is to define the stakes that each group or subgroup seeks through its involvement with the firm. For example, one might have listed the government on his or her stakeholder map and the Environmental

A DIFFERENT View

Profit, planet, and people. First introduced in the mid-1990s, "the triple bottom line," or the three Ps, measures the financial (profit), environmental (planet), and social (people) performance of a corporation over a period of time. Sustainable corporations that emphasize social and environmental responsibility, regardless of their motives, are increasing their profits and often outperforming their more traditional competitors.

Timberland is one company that is focused on reducing its carbon footprint, boosting renewable energy use, and increasing the integration of recycled, organic, or renewable materials for its apparel lines while maintaining its profitability. Identify another sustainable corporation that focuses on the triple bottom line.

- How successful are they at each of the three Ps?
- How do they quantify "planet" and "people?"
- Is this practice always ethical and why?

Identify a more traditional corporation that focuses only on profit.

- Would a focus on the three Ps benefit them?
- What are ways that they could implement the three Ps?

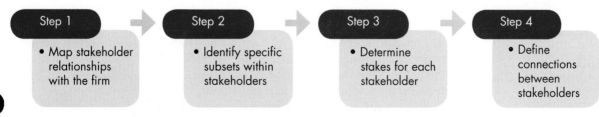

Step 1	Step 2	Step 3	Step 4
• Map stakeholder relationships with the firm	• Identify specific subsets within stakeholders	• Determine stakes for each stakeholder	• Define connections between stakeholders

Figure 1.10 ⟩ Stakeholder Mapping Process

Protection Agency (EPA) as a subgroup within this category. The EPA's relationship with the firm might be aimed at reducing the carbon emissions from production processes. By mapping out this relationship, one can start to better understand why the EPA has an interest in the organization and how one can start to address this interest.

In general, some important lessons may emerge from the mapping process. First, a firm's stakeholders and their interests are not static. Just because the EPA is concerned with carbon emissions does not mean it will not raise issues with waste disposal policies in the future. Second, many of the stakeholders on the map have the potential to become interconnected on a specific issue. As we saw in the Walmart case, the firm encountered powerful resistance because the city council and the local unions banded together. In this instance, two groups that typically did not work with each other joined forces to help block Walmart from entering the Inglewood market. As a manager, you must recognize the potential for these types of linkages to occur. In recent years, Walmart has tried to improve its reputation by investing more in employee health benefits (a key concern of unions) and by launching efforts to reduce the environmental impact of its operations (a key concern of environmentalists and community organizers).[41]

Stakeholder Management Processes

Once the stakeholder mapping process is completed, the manager should move on to develop mechanisms in the firm that can better identify and respond to new stakeholders and the complexity in the environment. This is by no means an easy task. Managers can develop these stakeholder mechanisms in several ways, including through strategic review processes and environmental scanning.

In a **strategic review process**, senior leaders of a corporation meet with business unit managers in a formal review session.[42] During these meetings, business unit managers review the performance of their unit or division and present their perspective on the future prospects of the unit. The strategic review process generally includes information on financial performance and targets, new business prospects, research and development updates, manufacturing capacity, talent management, and competitive threats. While the primary goal of the strategic review process is strategy formulation and target setting, the leader can use this forum to merge the firm's stakeholder map with new strategic projects. For example, when Walmart decided to expand the Supercenter format into California, managers might have initiated a strategic review process to discuss the operational, financial, and organizational strategies that would accompany this major initiative. At the same meetings, management also could have discussed the various stakeholders that would affect or be affected by this new strategic move. Based on these discussions, Walmart might have developed various strategies to deal with the possibility of resistance from the city council. In a sense, the merging of stakeholder analysis into the strategic review process is an attempt to ensure that new proposals are adequately understood and evaluated. Through this process, leaders can take preemptive action to address potential concerns of various stakeholders.

The second stakeholder process that can be used to identify and understand stakeholder response and activity is **environmental scanning**.[43] With environmental scanning, managers scour the business horizon for key events and trends that will affect the business in the future.[44] Managers who engage in environmental scanning tend to produce stronger financial results for their organization than those who refuse to pay attention to the contextual landscape. This is especially true for entrepreneurs who often capitalize on emerging trends.[45]

Managers can pursue environmental scanning through various avenues, including scenario building and trend analysis. In **scenario building**, a manager seeks to forecast the likely result that might occur when several events and stakeholders are

Strategic review process
The process by which senior leaders of a corporation meet with business unit managers to review progress toward specific goals.

Environmental scanning
A tool that managers use to scan the business horizon for key events and trends that will affect the business in the future.

linked together. For example, a Walmart manager may have used scenario building to determine that Supercenter expansion would push grocery prices lower, forcing other grocery chains to lower their cost structures to compete. This cost reduction effort could lead to other grocery chains lowering wages and health benefits, leading to protests from food worker's unions and ultimately to the unions pressuring the Inglewood city council to block Walmart from building in their town. This analysis is obviously variable, but it is extremely useful for identifying a potential scenario that might hurt or help a firm.

Having identified various potential scenarios, the manager can then turn his or her attention to **contingency planning** to prepare the firm for a reasonable range of alternative futures.[46] In contingency planning, the manager typically assigns probabilities to these alternative futures and begins to map out a series of preemptive action steps to prepare the firm.

Another technique used to predict stakeholder response and activity is **trend analysis**. In trend analysis, key variables are monitored and modeled to help predict a change that might occur in the environment. While trend analysis is an inexact science, it can be a useful tool for helping a manager better understand how certain environmental variables will affect the firm and its stakeholders. The success of environmental scanning and trend analysis is heavily dependent on the manager's ability to accurately assess the risks and opportunities that are confronting the firm.[47]

Knowing when and how to make strategic changes is not always easy. Managers must look beyond the boundaries of their internal operations to prepare for emerging competitive threats or capitalize on new potential opportunities.[48] In a sense, managers need to have peripheral vision—the ability to see beyond the boundaries of managing their day-to-day operations. Managers who excel at these boundary scanning activities possess **contextual intelligence**; they understand the impact of environmental factors on their business operations, and they understand how they can influence or react to those same factors.[49]

Managers can enhance their contextual intelligence by understanding historical precedents and how they have impacted an industry. An appreciation for historical trends and events in an industry can help managers be more attuned to the potential impact of similar occurrences in the future. Managers can enhance their environmental scanning skills by seizing opportunities to experience new situations that could impact their business (see Figure 1.11).[50] For instance, if a company is hoping to secure new suppliers in China or India, company executives need to visit these locations to better understand the opportunities that are available as well as the cultural implications of working in global locations.

Scenario building
Forecasting the likely result that might occur when several events and stakeholders are linked together.

Contingency planning
The systematic assessment of the external environment to prepare for a possible range of alternative futures for the organization.

Trend analysis
A tool where key variables are monitored and modeled to help predict a change that might occur in the environment.

Contextual intelligence
The ability to understand the impact of environmental factors on a firm and the ability to understand how to influence those same factors.

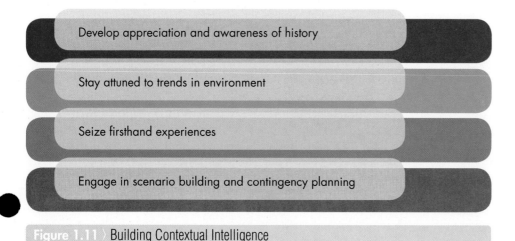

Develop appreciation and awareness of history

Stay attuned to trends in environment

Seize firsthand experiences

Engage in scenario building and contingency planning

Figure 1.11 〉 Building Contextual Intelligence

Managing Uncertainty

Many aspects of the business environment are difficult to interpret. It is especially difficult to predict the impact of contextual forces on how an industry will evolve or a business will operate in the future. Engaging in processes to build contextual intelligence like environmental scanning helps to mitigate some of this inherent uncertainty and risk.[51]

Despite a manager's best efforts, there will always be some level of uncertainty about the direction of the business environment.[52] It is important that managers appropriately estimate this level of uncertainty. If managers underestimate the nature of uncertainty in their industry, they will fail to prepare for competitive threats or to capitalize on potential opportunities. If managers overestimate the level of uncertainty, they may become paralyzed and fail to act, assuming that there is nothing that they can do to influence their business environment. Managers generally face greater uncertainty when many contextual forces impact an industry and when these same forces are constantly changing (see Figure 1.12).[53] The rate of change in the context will dictate the extent to which managers should engage in environmental scanning activities and the degree to which companies will need to adapt their operations.[54]

Now that we have discussed the stakeholder approach and how it can be applied, let's take a look at a firm that has a very diverse set of stakeholders to see how the firm dealt with their constituents in a very complex environment.

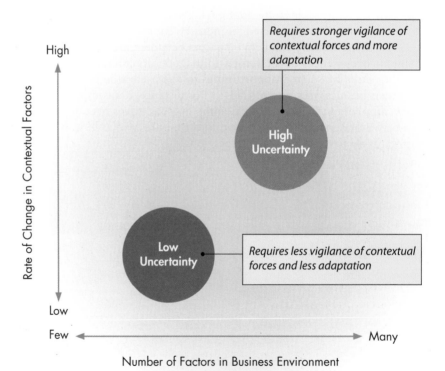

Figure 1.12 > How Contextual Forces Impact Uncertainty

BHP's Tintaya Copper Mine

While you may not have heard of BHP Billiton, you most likely own a product or live in a dwelling that uses its materials. In recent years, this metal mining company has grown in power and stature as the demand for base metals has increased in concert with the growth of economies in China and India. BHP is a global mining giant that maintains business in aluminum, iron ore, coal, lead, copper, and zinc extraction in 130 locations in 21 countries across the globe. In 2014, the company had revenues of $67 billion and net income of $14 billion.[55]

As part of its global expansion efforts, the company acquired the Tintaya Copper Mine, which was located in the Andean region of Peru known as Espinar province. While copper mining had contributed to greater prosperity for the Peruvian government, most of the local inhabitants of Espinar province did not see any benefits. In fact, the Tintaya mine had long been a source of contention between the locals and the mine's various operators. Established in 1985 as a state-owned enterprise, the mine originally stood on 2,368 hectares of land expropriated from 125 families in Tintaya Marquiri, an indigenous farming community.[56] In return for the land, the Peruvian government reportedly offered farmers as little as 10 soles per hectare (about $3 for 2.45 acres) and the promise of mining-related jobs.[57] The jobs, however, were few in number, and the loss of land pushed many local families into poverty.[58]

As metal prices continued to soar in the early twenty-first century, Peru's fortunes climbed in concert (see Figure 1.13). The rising profile of Peru's mining industry also attracted the attention of various NGOs and subsequently led to widespread unrest among some of the lower classes of society. Protests against large-scale mining and its environmental and social impacts became more frequent throughout the country.[59] BHP thought it had supported the local community by

Ric Francis/ZUMAPRESS.com/Newscom

creating jobs for over 600 locals and voluntarily contributing close to $2 million for a local development fund. However, many locals in the Espinar province had grown tired of the company because it continued to acquire land cheaply in the areas surrounding the Tintaya mine. As concerns about BHP's land purchases mounted, community members also began to speak up about the perceived environmental degradation the company had caused. Residents living near the company's operations claimed that wastewater from the company's processing plant had contaminated pasture lands and rendered the water unfit for consumption.[60]

In the spring of 2003, nearly 1,000 people stormed the Tintaya mine and took the general manager hostage. This group consisted of people from the Ccañipia river basin, who claimed that the company's tailings reservoir had polluted water sources used in the local dairy farming industry.[61] BHP negotiated with this group and agreed to set up a development fund that contributed a certain percentage of the mine's annual profits to the fund. At the same time, other groups in the mining community became angry that the company had negotiated a settlement with the Ccañipia group that had stormed the mine.[62] On May 23, 2005, 500 members of left-wing political parties and student groups from the provincial capital gathered outside the mine's gates to protest the terms of the agreement with the community. The decision was made to shut down the mine and evacuate all personnel.[63]

BHP failed to recognize the importance of its various stakeholders throughout the entire process. When the company obtained the mine from the Peruvian government in the 1990s, it was apparent that BHP did not have a stakeholder strategy in place. And despite subsequent attempts to develop one in the early 2000s, the company's inattention ultimately led to a crisis situation. Though the mine eventually reopened, BHP decided to sell it in 2006.

Figure 1.13 › Five-Year Copper Spot Price

Source: Kitco—Spot copper historical charts and graphs, kitcometals.com, www.kitcometals.com/charts/copper_historical_large.html, accessed October 7, 2009. Used by permission.

Case in Point   BHP's Tintaya Copper Mine

1. Often managers react to a crisis situation. An alternative strategy is to try to proactively prevent crises. What are some actions that BHP's managers could have done differently to prevent the crisis?

2. Contextual intelligence is an essential managerial skill. How could managers of BHP's Tintaya Copper Mine have analyzed the environment or its business operations to influence or react to the crisis?

3. For the executives of BHP's Tintaya Copper Mine, why was managing uncertainty a difficult task? How can scenario planning help you to manage uncertainty?

4. A stakeholder view of the firm takes into account how multiple groups interact with the firm. Who are the key stakeholders in the BHP's Tintaya Copper Mine case? Which stakeholders would you have collaborated with to prevent the crisis?

5. What are the important lessons learned from the BHP's Tintaya Copper Mine case? How can you apply these lessons to the management practices of other firms?

SUMMARY

LO1 There are three important pillars of managing organizations: strategic positioning, organizational design, and individual leadership. Success in business requires the ability to devise and nurture a defensible strategic position. The execution of this strategy, in turn, is dependent on a variety of organizational design decisions, including the allocation of resources, the structure of the organization, and the incorporation of key performance metrics. Ultimately, strategy and organizational design are the result of individual leadership actions. As such, it is critically important to understand how leaders identify and develop relevant skills.

LO2 Success in the global business environment requires effective management and leadership. Management is the act of working with and through others to accomplish a desired objective, and leadership is the ability to drive change and innovation through inspiration and motivation. Management and leadership skills are complementary.

Effective leaders develop and deploy technical, interpersonal, and conceptual skills. The relative importance of each of these skills is based on an individual's level in the firm. At the entry level, technical skills are vitally important. These technical skills often open the door for new employees. Interpersonal skills are also important for new employees as they join working teams, but new employees must rely on their technical skills to demonstrate competence in the organization.

At the managerial level, the technical skills are still important but are less relevant than interpersonal and cognitive skills. The work of managers involves many aspects of team management, which require strong interpersonal skills. Managers also provide support for innovative efforts and engage in scenario planning, both of which rely on conceptual abilities. At the senior level in a firm, leaders must focus on cognitive abilities to create the strategic positioning that will enable the firm to effectively compete in the marketplace. They do not do so in a vacuum. They must work with others and motivate the organization through effective communication, which is a central element of strong interpersonal skills.

LO3 The view of effective management has evolved over the last 100 years from a focus on the bureaucratic organization structure to scientific management to human relations to alignment or contingency theories. The contingent view of management states that there should be a fit or an alignment between an organization's structure, the business environment, and the leadership of the firm.

LO4 The business environment has grown more complex and the perspective on the purpose of business has changed in tandem. BHP and Walmart illustrate some of the immense challenges that managers may face. A manager can no longer evaluate his or her firm or its industry through a narrow managerial or shareholder viewpoint.

LO5 Rather, the manager must consider the numerous stakeholders with which the firm interacts and how those stakeholders impact or are impacted by the actions of the firm. In addition, the manager must be aware of all of the different dimensions in the company's external and internal environments.

Mapping out all of these stakeholders and environments is the first step in the stakeholder approach. Managers also use various stakeholder management processes such as strategic reviews, environmental scanning, and scenario planning to ensure that they are satisfying the important stakeholders of the firm. These processes help managers prepare for uncertainty and risk and help to ensure that the firm sustains its long-term relevance in the marketplace.

KEY TERMS

Bureaucratic organization structure
Business environment
Contextual intelligence
Contingency planning
Contingent view
Environmental scanning

Human relations movement
Leadership
Management
Managerial view
Scenario building
Scientific management

Shareholder view
Stakeholder view
Strategic review process
Trend analysis
VUCA

ASSIGNMENTS

Discussion Topics

1. Describe how the three pillars of management interact with each other. How can a firm's strategy influence the design of the organization? In what ways can a manager influence the strategy of an organization?

2. How do various contextual factors influence the business landscape? What levers can a manager use to influence the context?

3. What is the most important contextual factor impacting business today? How could a manager or firm influence this factor?

4. Combine the differences between managers and leaders with the various skills that are important to success in business (technical, interpersonal, and conceptual). What skills are more important to managers? Why? Do the same for leaders.

5. What are the advantages and disadvantages of the shareholder and stakeholder views of the firm? If you were a stockholder in a firm, what perspective would you want the management team to follow? Why? If you were an employee, would your perspective change?

6. What role do nonprofits and advocacy groups play in shaping the business context?

7. Review Figure 1.12. If you were starting a business, would you rather be in an industry with high or low uncertainty? What are the advantages and disadvantages of each environment? What skills would you need to be successful in each environment?

Management Research

1. Use resources in your library to identify examples of the different perspectives of management:

   • Bureaucratic Organization Structure
   • Scientific Management
   • Human Relations
   • Contingent View

2. How have management perspectives changed over time? How would you describe current management practices? What changes in management practices do you anticipate in the next five to ten years? How should individuals prepare for these changes?

3. Select a firm and draw a stakeholder map for it. What potential changes should the firm anticipate in its internal and external environments? How should the firm prepare for these changes?

In the Field

1. Spend some time with an experienced manager to learn how the individual "changed" while progressing through positions of greater career responsibility. Similar to Figure 1.4 in this chapter, create a map that identifies the importance of technical, interpersonal, and conceptual skills in that individual's career.

2. Visit a local business and collect the following information to enhance your contextual intelligence:

   • Identify historical events that have impacted its industry.
   • Scan its internal and external environments to identify current trends that affect the business.
   • Identify another industry or firm that the local business can learn from given its current environment.
   • Develop two future scenarios for the local business you visited. Given these scenarios, what type of contingency planning would you recommend?

ENDNOTES

1 Robert Hooijberg and James G. Hunt, "Leadership Complexity and Development of the Leaderplex Model," *Journal of Management*, Vol. 23, No. 3, 1997, pp. 375–408.

2 Nathan Bennett and G. James Lemoine, "What a Difference a Word Makes: Understanding Threats to Performance in a VUCA World," *Business Horizons*, Vol. 57 (2014), pp. 311–317.

3 Paul R. Lawrence and Jay W. Lorsch, *Organization and Environment* (Boston, MA: Graduate School of Business Administration, Harvard University, 1967).

4 Felix Oberholzer-Gee, "Walmart's Business Environment," Harvard Business School Case No. 9-706-453, rev. December 12, 2006 (Boston, MA: HBS Publishing, 2006), p. 3.

5 Walmart 2014 Annual Report.

6 Al Norman, "Vermont Governor Takes Heat for Warming Up to Wal-Mart," *Huffington Post*, March 28, 2013.

7 Steven Greenhouse, "Labor Raises Pressure on California Supermarkets," *The New York Times*, February 10, 2004.

8 Felix Oberholzer-Gee, "Walmart's Business Environment," Harvard Business School Case No. 9-706-453, rev. December 12, 2006 (Boston, MA: HBS Publishing, 2006), p. 7.

9 Ann Zimmerman, "Wal-Mart … [and the] Supercenter Vote," *The Wall Street Journal*, April 8, 2004, p. B7; and Tim Sullivan, "In a Bitter Strike, Grocery Workers Lost Ground," *High Country News*, June 7, 2004.

10 John P. Kotter, "What Leaders Really Do," *Harvard Business Review*, December 2001.

11 Anthony J. Mayo, Nitin Nohria, and Mark Rennella, *Entrepreneurs, Managers, and Leaders: What the Airline Industry Can Teach Us about Leadership* (New York: Palgrave-MacMillan, 2009), pp. 155–172.

12 Michael E. Porter and Nitin Nohria, "What Is Leadership? The CEO's Role in Large, Complex Organizations," *Handbook of Leadership Theory and Practice: A Harvard Business School Centennial Colloquium*, Nitin Nohria and Rakesh Khurana, eds. (Boston, MA: HBS Press, 2010).

13 Troy V. Mumford, Michael A. Campion, and Frederick P. Morgeson, "The Leadership Skills Strataplex: Leadership Skills Requirements across Organizational Levels," *The Leadership Quarterly* 18 (2007),

pp. 154–166; and Robert Hooijberg and James G. Hunt, "Leadership Complexity and Development of the Leaderplex Model," *Journal of Management*, Vol. 23, No. 3, 1997, pp. 375–408.

14 Michael E. Porter and Nitin Nohria, "What Is Leadership? The CEO's Role in Large, Complex Organizations," *Handbook of Leadership Theory and Practice: A Harvard Business School Centennial Colloquium*, Nitin Nohria and Rakesh Khurana, eds. (Boston, MA: HBS Press, 2010).

15 Robert L. Katz, "Skills of an Effective Administrator," *Harvard Business Review*, September–October 1974.

16 Peter F. Drucker, "Not Enough Generals Were Killed," *The Leader of the Future*, Frances Hesselbein, Marshall Goldsmith, and Richard Beckhard, eds. (San Francisco, CA: Jossey-Bass Publishers, 1996).

17 Robert L. Katz, "Skills of an Effective Administrator," *Harvard Business Review*, September–October 1974.

18 Robert Hooijberg and James G. Hunt, "Leadership Complexity and Development of the Leaderplex Model," *Journal*

of Management, Vol. 23, No. 3, 1997, pp. 375–408.

[19] Max Weber, *The Theory of Social and Economic Organization*, A. H. Henderson and Talcott Parsons, eds. (Glencoe, IL: Free Press, 1946 translation).

[20] Harold J. Leavitt, "Why Hierarchies Thrive?" *Harvard Business Review*, March 2003.

[21] Max Weber, *The Theory of Social and Economic Organization*, A. H. Henderson and Talcott Parsons, eds. (Glencoe, IL: Free Press, 1946 translation).

[22] Henri Fayol, *General and Industrial Management* (London: Pitman, 1949 translation); and Frederick W. Taylor, *The Principles of Scientific Management* (New York: Harper, 1911).

[23] Elton Mayo, *The Human Problems of an Industrial Civilization* (New York: Macmillan, 1933); and F. J. Roethlisberger and W. J. Dickson, *Management and the Worker* (Cambridge, MA: Harvard University Press, 1939).

[24] Eric L. Trist and K. W. Bamworth, "Social and Psychological Consequences of Longwall Method of Coal-Getting," *Human Relations*, Vol. 4, February 1951, pp. 3–28.

[25] Tom Burns and G. M. Stalker, *The Management of Innovation* (London: Tavistock, 1961).

[26] Paul R. Lawrence and Jay W. Lorsch, *Organization and Environment* (Boston, MA: Graduate School of Business Administration, Harvard University, 1967).

[27] Benjamin M. Friedman, *Corporate Capital Structures in the United States* (Chicago, IL: University of Chicago Press, 1985).

[28] Neil Fligstein, *The Architecture of Markets: An Economic Sociology of Twenty-First-Century Capitalist Societies* (Princeton, NJ: Princeton University Press, 2001).

[29] Neil Fligstein, *The Architecture of Markets: An Economic Sociology of Twenty-First-Century Capitalist Societies* (Princeton, NJ: Princeton University Press, 2001).

[30] Michael Useem, *Executive Defense: Shareholder Power and Corporate Reorganization* (Cambridge, MA: Harvard University Press, 1993).

[31] Steven Prokesch, "Ford to Buy Jaguar for $2.38 Billion," *The New York Times*, November 3, 1989; and The Guardian, "Ford Taking the Driver's Seat at Aston Martin," *Sydney Morning Herald*, September 9, 1987.

[32] Bradley A. Stertz, "Jaguar *PLC* Stock Soars on Rumor of Bid by Ford," *The Wall Street Journal*, May 30, 1989; and "Jaguar Agrees to £1.6bn Ford Takeover," *The Independent—London*, November 3, 1989.

[33] Nitin Nohria, Anthony J. Mayo, and Mark Benson, "Gordon Bethune at Continental Airlines," Harvard Business School Case No. 9-406-703, rev. November 29, 2010 (Boston, MA: HBS Publishing, 2006).

[34] R. Edward Freeman, *Strategic Management: A Stakeholder Approach* (Boston, MA: Pitman, 1984).

[35] Nitin Nohria, Anthony J. Mayo, and Mark Benson, "Gordon Bethune at Continental Airlines," Harvard Business School Case No. 9-406-703, rev. November 29, 2010 (Boston, MA: HBS Publishing, 2006).

[36] Waymond Rodgers and Susana Gago, "Stakeholder Influence on Corporate Strategies Over Time," *Journal of Business Ethics*, Vol. 52, No. 4, July 2004, p. 350.

[37] R. Edward Freeman, *Strategic Management: A Stakeholder Approach* (Boston, MA: Pitman, 1984), p. 53.

[38] Robert Phillips, R. Edward Freeman, and Andrew C. Wicks, "What Stakeholder Theory Is Not," *Business Ethics Quarterly*, Vol. 13, No. 4, October 2003, p. 487.

[39] R. Edward Freeman, *Strategic Management: A Stakeholder Approach* (Boston, MA: Pitman, 1984), p. 54.

[40] Waymond Rodgers and Susana Gago, "Stakeholder Influence on Corporate Strategies over Time," *Journal of Business Ethics*, Vol. 52, No. 4, July 2004, p. 351.

[41] Miguel Bustillo and Ann Zimmerman, "In Cities Fighting Wal-Mart, Target Welcomed," *The Wall Street Journal*, October 15, 2010.

[42] R. Edward Freeman, *Strategic Management: A Stakeholder Approach* (Boston, MA: Pitman, 1984), p. 66.

[43] Arnoldo C. Hax and Nicolas S. Majluf, "The Corporate Strategic Planning Process," *Interfaces*, Vol. 14, No. 1, January–February 1984, p. 52.

[44] R. Edward Freeman, *Strategic Management: A Stakeholder Approach* (Boston, MA: Pitman, 1984), p. 67.

[45] Marc J. Dollinger, "Environmental Boundary Scanning and Information Processing Effects on Organizational Performance," *Academy of Management Journal*, Vol. 27, No. 2, June 1984, pp. 351–368.

[46] Curtis W. Roney, "Planning for Strategic Contingencies," *Business Horizons*, March–April 2003, p. 36.

[47] L. J. Bourgeois, III, "Strategy and Environment: A Conceptual Integration," *Academy of Management Review*, Vol. 5, No. 1, January 1980, p. 31.

[48] Walter J. Ferrier, "Navigating the Competitive Landscape: The Divers and Consequences of Competitive Aggressiveness," *Academy of Management Journal*, Vol. 44, No. 4, August 2001, pp. 858–877.

[49] For more on contextual intelligence, see Anthony J. Mayo and Nitin Nohria, *In Their Time: The Greatest Business Leaders of the Twentieth Century* (Boston, MA: HBS Press, 2005).

[50] Anthony J. Mayo and Nitin Nohria, *In Their Time: The Greatest Business Leaders of the Twentieth Century* (Boston, MA: HBS Press, 2005), pp. 359–360.

[51] Robert B. Duncan, "Characteristics of Organizational Environments and Perceived Environmental Uncertainty," *Administrative Science Quarterly*, Vol. 17, No. 3, September 1972, pp. 313–327.

[52] Hugh Courtney, Jane Kirkland, and Patrick Viguerie, "Strategy Under Uncertainty," *Harvard Business Review*, November–December 1997.

[53] Robert B. Duncan, "Characteristics of Organizational Environments and Perceived Environmental Uncertainty," *Administrative Science Quarterly*, Vol. 17, No. 3, September 1972, p. 320.

[54] Moshe Farjoun, "Towards an Organic Perspective on Strategy," *Strategic Management Journal*, Vol. 23, No. 7, July 2002, p. 571.

[55] BHP Billiton 2014 Annual Report.

[56] Juan Aste, José de Echave, and Manuel Glave. "Procesos Multi-Actores para la Cogestión de Impactos Mineros en Perú: Informe Final" (Lima, Peru: La Iniciativa de Investigación Sobre Políticas Mineras, August 2003), p. 63.

[57] Oxfam America, " *Tintaya Copper Mine*," available at http://www.oxfamamerica.org /whatwedo/where_we_work/south_america /news_publications/tintaya/art6243.html, accessed November 2012.

[58] V. Kasturi Rangan, Brooke Barton, and Ezequiel Reficco, "Corporate Responsibility & Community Engagement at the Tintaya Copper Mine (A)," Harvard Business School Case No. 9-506-023, rev. May 20, 2008 (Boston, MA: HBS Publishing, 2006), p. 1.

[59] Ibid., p. 2.

[60] Ibid., p. 3.

[61] Ibid., p. 9.

[62] Ibid., p. 10.

[63] Ibid., p. 13.

CHAPTER

2

The Global Business Environment

Learning Objectives

After reading this chapter, you should be able to:

LO1 : Describe how changing contextual forces in the global business environment impact the competitive position of a firm.

LO2 : Understand the role that globalization, including trade agreements and trade associations, has played in shaping the business landscape.

LO3 : Define the primary dimensions of the external environment of a firm, including the components of the general and task environments.

LO4 : Differentiate between the four components of the internal environment of a firm, including owners, boards of directors, employees, and culture.

SELF-REFLECTION

You and Your Business Environment

The ability to scan, acquire, and learn from your business environment is an important management skill. Please respond True or False to the following statements to assess your competency in this area.

1. I read articles from the business press and surf the Web to stay up-to-date on current events.

2. I understand how the development and usage of technology influences the external environment.

3. I track economic data to assess the global business environment.

4. I can identify sociocultural trends that influence the competitive environment.

5. I comprehend how demographic data can be used to make business decisions.

6. I realize that companies operate in a global environment, and because of this pay attention to events that happen in different parts of the world.

7. When analyzing a firm, I identify its competitors and their impact on the firm's environment.

8. I understand the critical role that customers and suppliers play in shaping a firm's operations.

9. I understand the different ownership structures of a firm and the governance role of a firm's board of directors.

10. I realize that a company's employees and its culture are important components to its success.

If you answered True to the majority of these statements, you are aware of your business environment.

INTRODUCTION

Businesses and their leaders do not operate in isolation. They are part of a much larger ecosystem that is constantly evolving. As we discussed in Chapter 1, today's business context is often referred to as VUCA—volatile, uncertain, complex, and ambiguous. Successful business leaders not only respond to a VUCA context in the global business environment but also try to influence it. Some leaders focus their efforts on lobbying to influence the government's role in business. Other leaders identify growing market niches or target consumer segments and develop products or services to fill specific needs. Still other leaders invest in research and development to commercialize technological innovations. In these ways, business leaders take a proactive stance in managing their environment and adapting their strategies accordingly.[1]

The context of the last decade provides ample evidence of how the business landscape can change so quickly. These changes have required managers to be even more nimble in their adaptability. Managers in all types of businesses faced the aftereffects of a credit crunch, largely fueled by banks and other institutions lending money for homes to subprime customers. This practice went unnoticed as home prices in the United States experienced a meteoric rise through most of the first decade of the twenty-first century. The rise in home ownership fueled a host of other businesses, including automobiles, home improvement, appliances, and landscaping. However, by late 2007, many consumers could no longer afford the payments on their adjustable rate mortgages, and their inability to repay their loans contributed to an unprecedented financial collapse. By the end of 2008, financial giants Lehman Brothers, American International Group, and Merrill Lynch had imploded. In addition, venerable companies such as the 86-year-old KB Toys, 60-year-old Circuit City, and 34-year-old Linens 'n Things collapsed. Within a few short years, the entire business landscape had changed and managers had to scramble to define a new way of operating in an environment in which consumers were skeptical, financing was tight, and employees were on edge. Unemployment in the United States increased from 4.6% in 2007 to a peak of 9.6% in 2010.[2] While the unemployment rate has been steadily declining since its peak in 2010, many individuals, including recent college graduates, have struggled to find employment that is commensurate with their skills, education, and experience.

The aftereffects of the post-2008 recession have not been isolated to the United States. The financial crisis has been global with many countries in Europe, especially Greece and Spain, experiencing crippling debt and very high levels of unemployment. The struggles in Europe and other parts of the world, in turn, impact the success of many U.S. businesses demonstrating the interconnectedness of the global economy. As we will see throughout this chapter, managers can no longer only pay attention to the U.S. economy; they have to develop a better understanding of the global economy.

While many of the events of the last decade seem tumultuous, they represent the constant changing nature of global business. These events represent both challenges and opportunities for managers. A review of the companies that comprised the Dow Jones Industrial Average over the last 100 years provides a quick glimpse into how dramatic these changes can be and how they impact the rise and fall of businesses (see Table 2.1).

Only 7 of 30 companies that appeared on the Dow Jones Industrial Average (DJIA) in 1956 were still on the list in 2015, and two of them (Chevron and AT&T) were removed from the list at one or more points during the past 59 years. In 2013, Alcoa, which had been on the DJIA for 54 years, was replaced by Nike. The current list also includes several companies that represent the new titans of industry including Cisco, Home Depot, Microsoft, and Walmart. While these companies have ascended to the list in the last few decades, there is one company that has stood the test of time.

General Electric Company (GE) is the only firm that has been included on the Dow Jones Industrial Average since 1896. GE has sustained its relevance by constantly adapting and refining its strategy and business processes. For instance, if you reviewed GE's business portfolio in the early 1980s, you would discover that 75% of its business was based in manufacturing and 25% was based in services. At the turn of the twenty-first century, those numbers were reversed: 75% of GE's business was based in services, and only 25% was derived from manufacturing.[3]

Throughout its history, GE has been able to reinvent itself. For instance, its first Chief Executive Officer (CEO), Charles Coffin, created a centrally controlled function-based organizational structure, which was dismantled by a successor CEO Charles Wilson, who favored a decentralized structure. In the late 1950s and early 1960s, another CEO, Ralph Cordiner, invested in computers. His successor Frederick Borch bailed out of computers. In the late 1970s, CEO Reginald Jones established a layer of senior executives and invested in a coal mine. A few years later, CEO Jack Welch abandoned the sector approach and sold the mine.

May 26, 1896	July 3, 1956	January 31, 2015
American Cotton Oil	Allied Chemical	3M Company
American Sugar	American Can	American Express
American Tobacco	American Smelting	AT&T
Chicago Gas	AT&T	Boeing
Distilling & Cattle Feeding	American Tobacco	Caterpillar
General Electric	Bethlehem Steel	Chevron
Laclede Gas	Chrysler	Cisco Systems
National Lead	Corn Products Refining	Coca-Cola
North American	DuPont	DuPont
Tennessee Coal & Iron	Eastman Kodak	Exxon Mobil
U.S. Leather	*General Electric*	*General Electric*
U.S. Rubber	General Foods	Goldman Sachs
	General Motors	Home Depot
	Goodyear	Intel
	International Harvester	International Business Machines
	International Nickel	JPMorgan Chase
	International Paper	Johnson & Johnson
	Johns-Manville	McDonald's
	National Distillers	Merck
	National Steel	Microsoft
	Procter & Gamble	NIKE
	Sears Roebuck	Pfizer
	Standard Oil of CA (Chevron)	Procter & Gamble
	Standard Oil of NJ (Exxon Mobil)	Travelers
	Texas Company	United Technologies
	Union Carbide	UnitedHealth Group
	United Aircraft (United Technologies)	Verizon
	U.S. Steel	VISA
	Westinghouse Electric	Walmart Stores
	Woolworth	Walt Disney

Table 2.1 ⟩ Composition of Dow Jones Industrial Average, 1896, 1956, 2015

Source: "Dow Jones Industrial Average: Components," available at Dow Jones website at http://www.djaverages.com/, accessed January 31, 2015

This reinvention of the company has continued. While Welch invested in insurance and many financial businesses, his successor Jeffrey Immelt has offloaded many of these business lines (see Figure 2.1). The capacity of the company to sustain its relevance over such a long period of time is a testament to the ability of

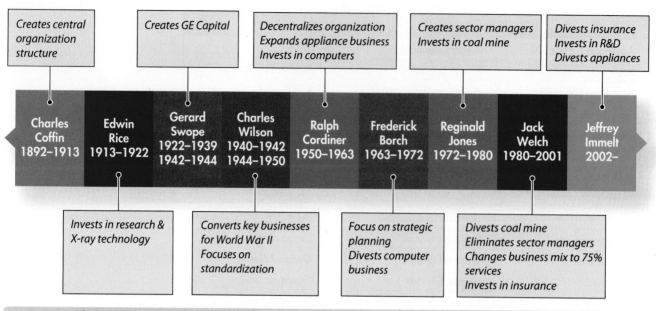

Figure 2.1 ⟩ General Electric's CEOs, 1892–Present

Source: Anthony J. Mayo

successive CEOs to accurately read and/or influence the global environment. This is one major way GE has been able to retain its place on the DJIA.

The increasing globalization of markets has hastened the pace and intensity of change. To remain competitive, companies can no longer sell exclusively in their domestic markets. Firms such as McDonald's, Starbucks, Apple, and Facebook have experienced slowing growth at home. In response to this trend, all of these firms (McDonald's in 1967, Apple in 1980, Starbucks in 1996, and Facebook in 2006) have ventured abroad for new sources of growth. By 2014, each of these firms obtained a significant portion of their revenues from international markets (McDonald's 67%, Apple 62%, Starbucks 31%, and Facebook 54%).[4] In emerging economies such as China and India, the opportunities are immense. In 2012, the Chinese middle class reached 300 million people, almost equivalent to the total population of the United States.[5] By 2020, China's middle class is expected to surge to over 500 million, and the Asia-Pacific region, as a whole, is expected to comprise 54% of the world's middle class (see Figure 2.2).[6] This growth provides many new opportunities for companies who can lead effectively across vastly different geographies.

Globalization has also presented challenges, including the emergence of new, powerful competitors in many industries. In computers, Dell and Apple must contend with the Chinese firm Lenovo, which purchased IBM's personal computer (PC) business. In automobiles, global producers such as GM must contend with Chery Automotive and Geely Automotive from China. The home appliance and electronics sector has also seen a number of formidable new competitors including Haier from China and Samsung and LG from South Korea.

Understanding the global business environment is vital to sustaining success. Many firms have failed in their attempts to expand globally. One company that has been able to build a consistently successful global presence in a constantly changing business environment is Coca-Cola.

In this chapter, we will explore the forces of globalization and the various internal and external entities that comprise a firm's business environment. Understanding the competitive landscape and knowing how and when to react to threats and opportunities are vitally important to a firm's long-term sustainability.

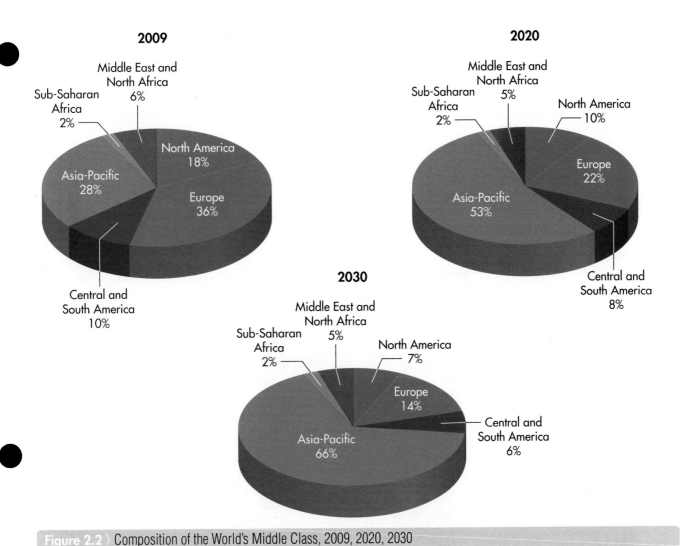

Figure 2.2 Composition of the World's Middle Class, 2009, 2020, 2030

Source: "Hitting the Sweet Spot: The Growth of the Middle Class in Emerging Markets," Ernst & Young, 2013, available at http://www.ey.com/GL/en/Issues /Driving-growth/Middle-class-growth-in-emerging-markets—China-and-India-tomorrow-s-middle-classes

Coca-Cola Company

In 2014, Coca-Cola celebrated its 128th anniversary and was ranked as the third best brand in the world, after having held the top spot from 2000 to 2012.[7] Like GE, Coca-Cola has been able to sustain its relevance and market viability for more than a century. Unlike GE, Coca-Cola has concentrated on the proliferation and expansion of a core product line for most of its history. The basis of that core product line is the secret cola formula that was stored in a vault at the SunTrust Bank in Atlanta from 1925 to 2011. As part of the brand's 125th anniversary, the secret formula was relocated to a special enclosure at the new interactive World of Coca-Cola Exhibit at company headquarters.

John S. Pemberton, a pharmacist in Atlanta, Georgia, founded the company in 1886 when he combined a unique syrup with carbonated water to sell at the soda fountain at Jacobs' Pharmacy. One of the customers at the soda fountain was Asa Candler, whose colleague recommended the drink as a treatment for Candler's persistent upset stomach and headaches. The combination of caffeine and carbonation seemed to relieve Candler's pains, and he soon became enamored with the product. Five years after that fateful first drink, Candler bought the concoction's recipe and formula from Pemberton and began an aggressive campaign to expand fountain sales of Coca-Cola. By 1895, Coca-Cola was sold and drunk in every state and territory of the United States.

Candler's first expansion outside the United States came in 1906 when bottling operations were opened in Canada, Cuba, and Panama. That was also the year that Candler signed D'Arcy Advertising Company as Coke's agency of record. This relationship would last 50 years and result in the creation of many memorable advertising and promotional campaigns including the indelible image of Santa Claus with a Coke. Tapping into the social consciousness of the country was vital to the sale of Coke and its ascendance into an iconic American and global brand. A quick survey of Coca-Cola's trademark slogans throughout its history highlights the way in which the company was able to build a connection with the American populace (see Table 2.2).

While Candler initiated the first globalization campaign for Coca-Cola, it was Robert Woodruff who was most responsible for making Coke a truly global brand. Woodruff became president of the company in 1923 and served in this capacity for more than six decades. He invested heavily in advertising and established the Coca-Cola Foreign Department in 1926 to service bottlers throughout the world. By this time, Coke had bottling operations in Belgium, China, Columbia, Germany, Mexico, and Spain, among others.

Coke's big push on the world stage came during World War II when Woodruff announced that Coke would be available to any soldier serving overseas for just five cents. Through this seemingly generous proposition, Woodruff was able to secure access to sugar, which was severely rationed during the war. The rationing could be lifted if a company demonstrated that their product fulfilled a vital military function. Though one would be hard-pressed to conceive of Coke

as a military necessity, the product did provide a morale boost for the troops, and Woodruff used this connection between the soldier and the slice of Americana to advance his cause. The strategy worked so well that the company received government subsidies to build 64 bottling plants throughout the world, which resulted in the consumption of over 5 billion bottles of Coca-Cola. American soldiers drinking Coke unwittingly became global marketing ambassadors for the firm.[8] When the war ended, the company had a ready-made global infrastructure and a giant head start on its global positioning. By the end of the 1950s, foreign sales accounted for approximately one-third of company revenues.

During the first half of its history, the company sold and marketed only one product—Coca-Cola. That began to change in 1955 when Fanta Orange was introduced by the company in Naples, Italy. Once the product was successful in Italy, it was brought to the United States. From this point, a series of new products were launched including Sprite in 1961, TAB in 1963, Fresca in 1966, Mr. PIBB in 1972, Mello Yello in 1979, and Diet Coke in 1982.

Coke's efforts to expand globally were not always smooth. For instance, though the company had established operations in China in the 1920s, they were forced to leave the country in 1949 when the Communist Party came to power. Over the next 30 years, Coke was only available on the black market in China. That changed in 1979 when Coke became the first U.S. company to return to China. By the end of the twentieth century, the company had 28 bottling plants in China, and by 2008, when China hosted the Summer Olympics, Coke had partnered with a number of local establishments to create and distribute products that were aligned with the Chinese consumer market, including Heaven & Earth (noncarbonated fruit juice, tea, and water) and Lanfeng (honey green tea).[9]

The company's biggest success on the global stage has been in Mexico where per capita consumption of soft drinks is one of the highest in the world. Though Coca-Cola operated in Mexico for a number of decades, its major growth came in the 1990s when the Mexican government lifted regulations on the sale, packaging, and distribution of soda. The new laws enabled Coke to expand and leverage its distribution network in the country. Distribution was essential in Mexico as most soda in the country was consumed not in the home but on the spot. Consumers then immediately returned the bottles for refunds. Having a strong distribution network was critical for Coca-Cola to regularly and systematically replenish supplies at small, local retail shops. The company also increased its presence in Mexico through the acquisition of a major juice producer.[10] The company's efforts have resulted in a significant increase in the per capita consumption of Coca-Cola products, rising from 290 eight fluid ounces per capita in 1991 to 745 by 2012.[11]

By 2014, Coca-Cola had expanded to over 600 brands, seven of which generate more than $1 billion in revenues each, with consumers in more than 200 countries.[12] Of the $46.9 billion in revenue that the company generated in 2013, approximately 45% was derived from sales outside North America. While per capita consumption of the company's beverages had stabilized in the United States at roughly 400 eight fluid ounces, there was tremendous opportunity in Russia, China, and India where the per capita consumption was 79, 39, and 14 eight fluid ounces, respectively. Though these consumption numbers were small in comparison to the United States and Mexico, they represented significant increases. In 1992, per capital consumption in Russia and China was 2 and 1 eight fluid ounces, respectively, and consumption in India was virtually zero.[13]

The company has also invested in a number of efforts to jump-start sales in the United States. One campaign that has shown promise is "share a Coke." During the summer of 2014, Coca-Cola put the 250 most popular names of teens and millennials on 20-ounce Coke bottles. The campaign also included personalized cans available at roving kiosks and "virtual" personalized Coke bottles that could be shared in personal media. The result was a 2% increase in domestic consumption, the first such rise in a number of years.[14] Moving forward, the company seeks to increase consumption across all its markets through a combination of promoting its core cola products as well as by adapting to local customs and tastes.

Year	Slogan	Historical Context
1900	For Headache and Exhaustion, Drink Coca-Cola	Positioned as a medicinal product; offered initially in pharmacies
1906	The Great National Temperance Beverage	Positioned as an alternative to alcohol as part of the Prohibition movement in the United States
1929	The Pause that Refreshes	Marketed as an opportunity to relax during the "go-go" 1920s
1937	So Easy to Serve, and So Inexpensive	During the height of the Great Depression, Coke is marketed as a value-priced, convenient product
1949	Along the Highway to Anywhere	Coke expands with the growing suburbanization of the country
1960	Relax with a Coke	Coke's marketing is attuned to the easygoing vibe of the 1960s
1971	I'd Like to Buy the World a Coke	Coke is aligned with the free spirit of the times to promote world peace during the Cold War
1990	Can't Beat the Real Thing	Part of an effort to stave off competition from Pepsi and other cola products
2005	Make it Real	Coke's continued effort to position its brand as the first, and original cola product

Table 2.2 > Selected Coca-Cola Slogans

Source: Coca-Cola Company, "Coke Lore: Slogans for Coca-Cola," available at http://www.thecoca-colacompany.com/heritage/cokelore.html, accessed July 18, 2012.

Case in Point

Coca-Cola Company

1. What factors contributed to making Coca-Cola such a strong global brand?
2. How was Coca-Cola able to stay relevant for over 128 years?
3. Why did Coca-Cola change its product strategy after 50 years?
4. How is the beverage market in Mexico different from the United States?
5. How will Coca-Cola be able to increase beverage consumption in emerging markets such as China, India, and Russia? Should they focus more on local brands or try to increase consumption of their core products?

GLOBALIZATION

Globalization refers to the integration and interdependence of economic, technological, sociocultural, and political systems across diverse geographic regions.[15] The idea of globalization can be traced back thousands of years. An early form of globalization existed during the Roman Empire when the nation-state had various far-flung territories it had conquered that absorbed the empire's culture and products and served as a source of raw materials and precious commodities. This path toward global integration continued sporadically throughout the next centuries, culminating in the sixteenth and seventeenth centuries with the emergence of the Portuguese and Spanish empires. Both empires expanded exploration and commercial activity.

At the same time, the Dutch East India Company of the Netherlands began trade relations between Europe and areas in Asia. Considered the first multinational company, the Dutch East India Company was created in 1602 as an association of merchants meant to reduce competition, achieve economies of scale, and increase trade throughout the world. It was also the first company to issue stock to shareholders. By 1670, the Dutch East India Company was the richest corporation in the world and employed more than 50,000 people. The Dutch East India Company was not only a financial asset to the Dutch, but also a political asset. Granted wide latitude from the Dutch government, the company had the right to build forts, maintain armed forces, and form treaties with native princes. Through the leadership of forceful commanders, the company defeated the British fleet and displaced the Portuguese in the East Indies, solidifying Dutch trade in the region. As a result, the company prospered for most of the seventeenth and eighteenth centuries and assisted the Dutch in their war of independence from Spain.[16]

International trade accelerated as European imperial powers traded with their colonies, but it broke down during and after World War I. The devastation of the war caused many countries to look inward and focus on self-reliance. Following World War II, many leading economists and politicians pushed more for globalization and less protectionism. This movement

Globalization
The integration and interdependence of economic, technological, sociocultural, and political systems across diverse geographic regions.

North Wind Picture Archives / Alamy

led to the creation of several international trade agreements and institutions, including the General Agreement on Tariffs and Trade (GATT), the World Trade Organization (WTO), the Association of South East Asian Nations (ASEAN), the European Union (EU), the North American Free Trade Agreement (NAFTA), and other alliances. All of these institutions have emerged to promote open trade among nations and better access to investment capital.

Global Trade Agreements

Following World War II, officials from the United States, Great Britain, and Canada met to design a set of international alliances and institutions that would strengthen the world's economies. From these meetings, several important international institutions emerged, including the World Bank and the International Monetary Fund (IMF). At the same time, the world powers attempted to create an international trade organization that would regulate tariffs. While this organization never came to be, GATT was formed as a temporary measure to lower tariffs. The agreement was based on three main principles: most favored nation status, national treatment, and consensus. The most favored nation principle meant that a tariff rate granted to one member of GATT would be extended to all members. The principle of national treatment meant that foreign firms would be subject to the same rules and regulations as a country's domestic firms. The consensus principle meant that trade disputes would be settled by the unanimous agreement of all parties to the dispute.[17]

Through GATT's numerous negotiation sessions, tariffs on traded goods were reduced from an average of 40% in 1940 to 50% in 1980.[18] From 1986–1994, GATT conducted the Uruguay Round, which cut tariffs and created agreements in areas as varied as services, capital, intellectual property, textiles, and agriculture. The Uruguay Round was also noteworthy because it launched the successor to GATT—the WTO, an organization created to supervise and liberalize international trade. The WTO was formed to deal with the rules of trade between nations and is responsible for negotiating and implementing new trade agreements as well as policing member countries' adherence to them.[19]

World Trade and Free-Trade Associations

World trade, defined by the value of the world's merchandise exports, stumbled after the global financial crisis of 2008, declining by about 12% in one year. Since then, global trade has improved, but it is still only growing less than 3% per year. For 2013, world trade was estimated to grow at 2.5%. The post–financial crisis slowdown in world trade has also been evident in the slow growth of global gross domestic product. The growth in global gross domestic product (GDP) was 2.2% in 2013, and the forecast for 2014 was projected to be 3.1%, well below the 20-year average of 5.3% (1983–2013).[20] In 2013, the pace of growth in GDP was not consistent across the globe; developed economies saw a 1.1% rise in GDP while emerging/developing economies posted a 4.4% increase led by China at 7.5% and India at 5.4% (see Table 2.3).

World trade is supported through a series of free trade agreements negotiated between various countries and overseen by the WTO. As of 2015, the WTO oversaw almost 400 regional trade agreements of which the EU, NAFTA, ASEAN, and MERCOSUR represented the largest ones (see Table 2.4). Trade within North America, Europe, and Asia is much higher than trade within Africa, the Middle East, and South and Central America. Europe has the highest concentration of trade (i.e., trade among countries within a particular region), and Africa has the lowest concentration. In 2013, 62% of EU merchandise exports went to EU member countries

Region	GDP	Exports	Imports
World	2.2	2.5	1.9
North America	1.8	2.6	1.2
South and Central America	3.0	1.4	3.1
Europe	0.3	1.5	−0.5
Commonwealth of Independent States	2.0	0.8	−1.3
Africa	3.8	−2.4	4.1
Middle East	3.0	1.9	6.2
Asia	4.2	4.7	4.5

Table 2.3 ⟩ GDP and Trade by Region (Annual Percentage Change, 2012–2013)

Source: World Trade Organization, "World Trade Report 2014," available at WTO Web site, http://www.wto.org /english/res_e/booksp_e/wtr14-1_e.pdf, accessed January 31, 2015.

Trade Agreement	Countries Represented
ASEAN (Association of South East Asian Nations)	Brunei Darussalam, Cambodia, Indonesia, Laos, Malaysia, Myanmar, Philippines, Singapore, Thailand, Vietnam
CACM (Central American Common Market)	Costa Rica, El Salvador, Guatemala, Honduras, Nicaragua
ECOWAS (Economic Community of West African States)	Benin, Burkina Faso, Cape Verde, Cote d'Ivoire, Gambia, Ghana, Guinea, Guinea-Bissau, Liberia, Mali, Niger, Nigeria, Senegal, Sierra Leone, Togo
EU (European Union)	Austria, Belgium, Bulgaria, Croatia, Cyprus, Czech Republic, Denmark, Estonia, Finland, France, Germany, Greece, Hungary, Ireland, Italy, Latvia, Lithuania, Luxembourg, Malta, Netherlands, Poland, Portugal, Romania, Slovak Republic, Slovenia, Spain, Sweden, United Kingdom
GCC (Gulf Cooperation Council)	Bahrain, Kuwait, Oman, Qatar, Saudi Arabia, United Arab Emirates
MERCOSUR (Southern Common Market)	Argentina, Brazil, Paraguay, Uruguay, Venezuela
NAFTA (North American Free Trade Agreement)	Canada, Mexico, United States
SADC (Southern African Development Council)	Angola, Botswana, Congo, Lesotho, Madagascar, Malawi, Mauritius, Mozambique, Namibia, Seychelles, South Africa, Swaziland, Tanzania, Zambia, Zimbabwe

Table 2.4 ⟩ Selected Regional Trade Agreements

while in Africa, only 16% of exports stayed within African borders. Africa's main export market was the EU (see Figure 2.3).[21]

European Union

The EU traces its roots back to the 1950s, when Europeans were searching for a way to promote political and economic stability in their region. The organization was originally known as the European Coal and Steel Community, which sought to reduce trade barriers in coal and steel trading. The organization eventually developed into its current form in 1993 with the signing of the Maastricht Treaty, which established the legal framework for the EU. The formation of the EU created a

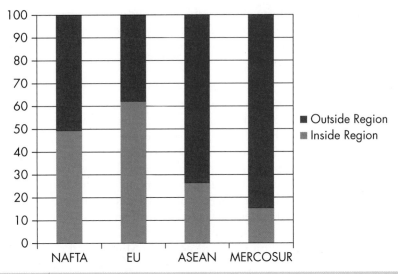

Figure 2.3 ⟩ Breakdown of Merchandise Exports of Selected Regional Trade Agreements, 2013

Source: World Trade Organization, "International Trade Statistics, 2014," http://www.wto.org/english/res_e/statis_e/its2014_e/its14_toc_e.htm, accessed January 31, 2015.

single market run by a system of laws that applies to all member states, guaranteeing the freedom of movement of people, goods, services, and capital.[22]

In 1999, the EU introduced a common currency, the euro, which has been adopted by 17 member states of the eurozone, an economic union of 28 of Europe's major economic states. The single European currency replaced numerous national currencies and unified a common marketplace, which created a competitive economy on par with the United States.[23] The euro was designed to help build a single market by, for example, easing travel of citizens and goods, eliminating exchange rate problems, providing price transparency, creating a single financial market, and supporting price stability and low interest rates.[24]

The global financial crisis in 2008 was particularly problematic for the EU. Several countries including Poland, Ireland, Italy, Greece, and Spain faced severe declines in their economies. Public debt and unemployment in many of these countries have hit unprecedentedly high levels. Various Eurozone leaders and the European Central Bank have been key players in helping to stabilize the crisis by encouraging more favorable loans and promoting fiscal reform policies throughout Europe. Despite these efforts, problems still persist. In 2013, overall unemployment in the EU was 10.5%, but it was more than 16% in Portugal and higher than

The European Union

Alex and Anna /Shutterstock.com

25% in Greece and Spain. Even more troubling, public debt as a percent of GDP was over 120% in Greece, Ireland, Italy and Portugal.[25] Given these conditions, encouraging trade inside and outside the EU is vital.

NAFTA

The NAFTA came into effect in 1994 when the United States, Canada, and Mexico signed the treaty to eliminate tariffs among each other. Today, this trading group forms the largest trading bloc in the world in terms of its members' combined GDP. Since its inception, tariffs on most goods traded between the partners have been reduced or eliminated, but the trading bloc still maintains restrictions on certain agricultural products. Through this agreement, the United States and Mexico have strengthened their ties economically and politically. The main export partners of the United States are Canada which receives 19% of U.S. exports followed by Mexico at 14%, and China at 7%.[26] In 2014, the United States exported more than $221 billion worth of goods to Mexico and over $280 billion to Canada.[27]

Many industries have benefited from the opening of borders and the reduction of tariffs, including automobile companies, construction equipment manufacturers, and agricultural firms. Trade has also increased dramatically among the three nations. Since NAFTA's inception, total trade between the United States and its NAFTA partners has increased by 208%.[28]

ASEAN

The ASEAN was originally established in 1967 to support three primary goals for the region, including: (1) accelerating economic growth; (2) promoting social and cultural development; and (3) ensuring peace and stability. The five original members of ASEAN included Indonesia, Malaysia, the Philippines, Singapore, and Thailand. Over the years, five other countries joined the Association including Brunei Darussalam, Cambodia, Laos, Myanmar, and Vietnam. Of all the major trade associations in the world, ASEAN has one of the most diverse populations as characterized by Singapore, whose economy is 80 times larger than that of the least developed country in the region, Myanmar. The differences are also evident in the population base, with Indonesia's population of 230 million being 50 times larger than Singapore's.[29]

This diversity in the makeup of the countries within ASEAN has created some challenges to enhancing integration within the region. As evident in Figure 2.3, trade within the region is far lower than trade within the EU and NAFTA. In an effort to facilitate greater integration, the ASEAN members have agreed to promote enhanced trade liberalization through the creation of the ASEAN Economic Community (AEC). AEC is designed to create a freer flow of goods, services, and investments within the region.

The fast pace of growth of many ASEAN countries as well as ASEAN's close proximity to the large developmental opportunities in China and India have provided a strong foundation for future expansion and economic growth. Since the 1990s, ASEAN trade with China has more than tripled while its trade with the United States has stagnated.[30]

MERCOSUR

The fourth largest regional trading group, MERCOSUR, comprises the countries of Argentina, Brazil, Paraguay, Uruguay, and Venezuela. Similar to other trading groups, MERCOSUR, established in 1991, was created to promote economic growth and integration through the reduction of tariffs and the free flow of goods within the region. MERCOSUR seeks to create an economic juggernaut in South America.

Like ASEAN, MERCOSUR has struggled to accelerate the rate of trade growth between member countries (see Figure 2.3). Fuel and mining products are increasingly important components of MERCOSUR's export base. Oil-rich Venezuela, which was admitted to MERCOSUR in 2012, will likely increase the importance of fuel trade both within and outside the region.[31]

Is Free Trade Good for the Global Economy?

In general, the proliferation of trading alliances has fueled international trade and provided economic opportunities for companies and countries around the globe. While many critics decry some of the by-products of these agreements, the overall economic effect has been mostly positive. However, these issues aren't always so black and white, and trade restrictions can have serious effects on the viability of a firm such as Chiquita.

Bananas are one of the most important and popular agricultural products in the world, with more than 70 million metric tons of production annually. For most of the twentieth century, Chiquita dominated the international banana industry, which was valued at $5.1 billion in 1994. In 1993, the EU adopted a new banana import regime that established a community-wide quota on bananas imported from the Latin American countries where Chiquita sourced its fruit.[32] Bananas produced in other countries, such as Dominica, St. Lucia, St. Vincent, and Grenada, received tariff-free access to the EU community. The new policy was instituted to provide an economic boost to these impoverished areas. As a result, Chiquita lost an estimated 20%–50% of its market share and its stock fell from $40 in 1991 to $13.63 in 1994.[33] In 1996, the WTO ordered the EU to stop imposing quotas because they were considered restrictive and protectionist.

As you can see, trade restrictions can have dramatic effects on a company's fortunes. In Chiquita's case, restrictive tariffs essentially shut the company off from its most important end markets. While arguments can be made in support of the EU's policy, the ultimate effect was to harm the most efficient producer in the marketplace.

Supporters of globalization and free trade claim that reducing trade barriers increases economic prosperity for all. These supporters point to the theory of **comparative advantage** as an argument for globalization. The theory of comparative advantage proclaims that countries should specialize in producing goods for which they have the lowest opportunity cost of production.[34] As a country continues to specialize in the production of a particular product or commodity, it generally becomes a much more efficient producer.[35] Economic theories of comparative advantage suggest that free trade leads to a more efficient allocation of resources, because free trade encourages countries to specialize in the production of products for which they are the lowest cost producers. As a result, all countries involved in trade benefit from access to cheaper products. In general, free trade between nations can lead to lower prices, more employment, higher output, and a higher standard of living for those in developing countries.[36]

EXTERNAL ENVIRONMENT

The forces of globalization have dramatically impacted all aspects of the business environment, but as we saw in the Walmart example in Chapter 1, the environment in which firms operate has become increasingly complex on a number of fronts. To be consistently successful, managers must understand all aspects of its business environment. The **external environment** of a firm represents all of the external forces that affect the firm's business.

Comparative advantage
An economic theory that proclaims countries should specialize in producing goods for which they have the lowest opportunity cost of production.

External environment
Represents all of the external forces that affect the firm's business.

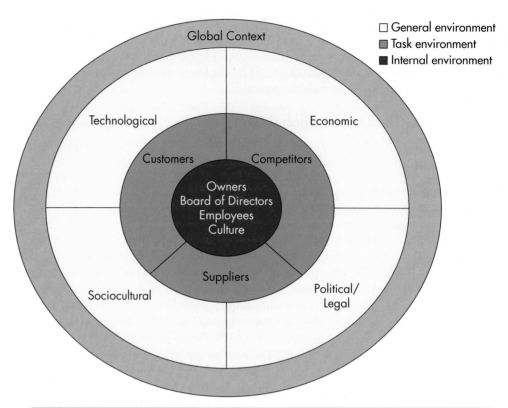

Figure 2.4 ⟩ A Firm's Business Environment

Source: Adapted from L. J. Bourgeois, III, "Strategy and Environment: A Conceptual Integration," *Academy of Management Review*, Vol. 5, No. 1, January 1980, p. 26.

For purposes of discussion, we will divide a firm's external environment into two separate components: the **general environment** and the **task environment** (see Figure 2.4). The global context can affect all of the elements of the firm's general and task environments, and as such, it forms the outer layer of the diagram in Figure 2.4. A firm's general environment represents the primary external forces that affect a firm. Some of these factors will have a stronger impact on the firm than others. For instance, the political/legal forces in the healthcare sector of the United States are potent; they have a significant impact on the manner in which health insurers and pharmaceutical firms operate. Sociocultural and technological forces have played a large role in the proliferation of social networking enterprises such as Facebook, Twitter, and LinkedIn. Political forces have impacted companies that rely on access to affordable raw materials such as oil, gas, and timber for their manufacturing processes.

The task environment forms the next layer. A firm's task environment includes entities that directly affect a firm on a continuous basis and include competitors, suppliers, and customers. When Apple introduced the iPad in 2010, it not only invented a new platform for computing, but it also put immense pressure on its competitors to release similar products. Companies such as Motorola, Dell, and Toshiba responded quickly. Just one year after the iPad's introduction, there were 11 tablets on the market.[37] In contrast to the dimensions of the general environment, these parties have the ability to exert a greater and more immediate influence over a firm.

General Environment

While the dimensions of the general environment seem broader and more diffuse than the dimensions of the task environment, they are important to understand because of the impact they can have on a firm and its industry. These dimensions form

General environment
Includes the technological, economic, political/legal, and sociocultural dimensions that affect a firm's external environment.

Task environment
Includes entities that directly affect a firm on a constant basis and include competitors, suppliers, and customers.

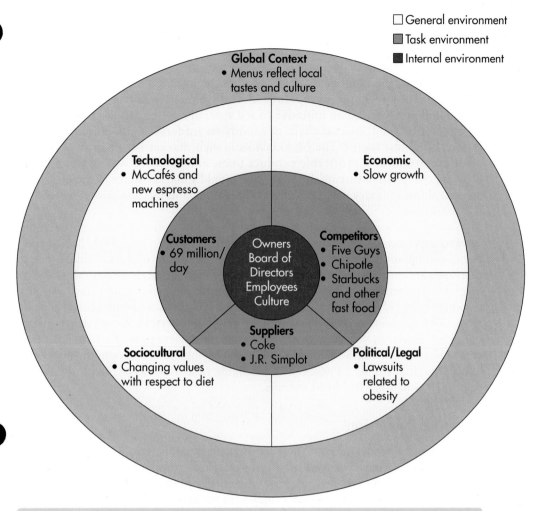

Figure 2.5 McDonald's Business Environment

the basis of the strategic context in which all businesses in a particular industry compete.[38]

The first step for a manager is to identify the external dimensions that are pertinent to the firm and to develop strategies to deal with them. In this section, we will look at how the external dimensions in the general environment affect McDonald's (see Figure 2.5).

Technological Dimension

The **technological dimension** of the general environment refers to the processes, technologies, or systems that a firm can use to produce outputs. The technological dimension often includes the technology behind a firm's manufacturing line or the hardware or software used to run its distribution system. This dimension has experienced accelerated changes in the last two decades.

While technology affects companies and industries in various ways, successful companies are able to capitalize on new innovations. Sometimes the most successful long-term companies are not necessarily the ones that first commercialized a technology or deployed a new innovation. For instance, Napster sparked the initial revolution in online digital music and was heralded by consumers, but its failure to

Technological dimension
The processes, technologies, or systems that a firm can use to produce outputs.

recognize the importance of other key stakeholders, including government regulators, artists, and record companies, paved the way for Apple to introduce a business model that was satisfactory to all constituents.

While McDonald's business is not driven as closely by technological forces as other firms, the company does depend on technology to drive new business opportunities and make its operations run efficiently. In the last few years, McDonald's introduced an initiative to sell specialty coffee drinks. The move was an attempt by the fast-food chain to solidify its leadership position in the quick service breakfast sector. The breakfast sandwich market is one of McDonald's most important and profitable product lines, and the firm was worried about growing competitive threats. In 2013, McDonald's market share in the quick service breakfast industry was 19%. Rivals Starbucks and Dunkin' Donuts each had 7% market share.[39]

To help McDonald's introduce a series of specialty coffee drinks such as espressos and cappuccinos, the firm relied on new technology. In late 2007, McDonald's began rolling out automated espresso machines to certain outlets. Unlike espresso machines at Starbucks, which require extensive manual intervention, McDonald's machines perform essentially all of the functions in the brewing and flavoring process automatically. These machines are aligned with McDonald's core focus on efficient production and help the company maintain its strict time and delivery standards for orders. In addition, the espresso machines were part of a larger effort to create McCafes within McDonald's that allow customers to linger in the restaurant while enjoying free Wi-Fi access and indulging in a wider assortment of pastries, smoothies, and other breakfast options.

Economic Dimension

The **economic dimension** of a firm's environment often includes GDP, inflation, unemployment, consumer sentiment, and interest rates of all the countries where it sells its products and services. Understanding the economic dimension of the global business environment is particularly important for any manager looking to conduct business abroad. To gain this knowledge, a manager should seek to understand economic components such as structure, resource position, currency, and labor issues in all the countries where it is doing business (see Table 2.5).

Developed countries such as Canada, Australia, Japan, and Germany are marked by high levels of free market principles that are similar to those in the United States. These countries have stable economic conditions, with lower variability than developing countries in terms of inflation and interest rates. In many less-developed countries, inflation and interest rates can fluctuate wildly because of the fragility and infancy of these economies. A manager must consider all of these factors prior to entering any new markets. These factors are also important to consider in the markets where a firm already operates as they can affect consumer demand in the region as well as a firm's day-to-day business operations.

Managers must also consider the resource position of global regions. Most global markets do not look like the United States in terms of resource development and availability. In the United States, most managers take infrastructure such as communication networks and highway systems for granted. Most developing countries, in contrast, do not have reliable highway systems, which can become an obstacle when conducting business in those countries. With less-developed resource positions and infrastructure, global managers need to remain flexible when running their businesses across different markets.

A manager also needs to investigate currency issues in operating their businesses across borders. In general, most developed countries have stable currencies that fluctuate along a fairly predictable spectrum. But in less-developed regions, local currencies can swing dramatically on a daily basis and change a consumer's buying

Economic dimension
The general economic environment (e.g., GDP, inflation, and unemployment) in the markets where the firm performs activities.

World Region	Economic Conditions
North America	Consisting of the United States, Canada, and Mexico, the United States led this region with a $16.7 trillion economy in 2013; Mexico's economy stood at $1.8 trillion, and Canada's was $1.5 trillion. With manufacturing jobs going overseas during the 1990s, the services-oriented industries in the United States account for more than 79% of GDP. With exports worth $1.58 trillion and imports worth $2.27 trillion, the United States had a $690 billion trade deficit in 2013.[40]
European Union (EU)	Consisting of 28 member states, the EU represented the world's second largest economy at $15.9 trillion in GDP in 2013. It holds an open internal market of exchange and a relatively open trade with the rest of the world, operating a mostly neutral trade deficit.[41] With higher levels of unionization, work rules, and government-run social systems, companies in the EU face higher costs than do most other regions.
China	Since the 1970s, China has slowly moved from a closed, centrally planned economy to a more market-oriented one by gradually introducing reforms. These reforms, along with increased efficiency, have led to massive economic growth as its GDP has increased more than tenfold since 1978. In 2013, its GDP stood as the world's third largest at $13.4 trillion and was increasing by 7.7% annually. Still, doing business in China is fraught with many complications including corruption and intellectual property theft. China's future challenges stem from a rapidly aging population, high domestic inflation, environmental degradation, and lack of consumer demand due to poor distribution of income.[42] One looming concern for business leaders today is the possible slowdown in China's economy. Many countries rely on China as a key trading partner and any slowdown in its economy could impact the ongoing fragile recovery from the global financial crisis.
India	India is the world's fourth largest GDP at $5 trillion. While more than half of the workforce is employed in agriculture, global knowledge-based services are a major source of economic growth, accounting for more than half of India's output. Beginning in the early 1990s, India has been developing into an open-market economy by deregulating industry, privatizing public companies, and reducing control on foreign trade. Major challenges include widespread poverty, inadequate infrastructure, and poor access to higher education.[43]
Japan	Japan was one of the fastest-growing economies during the second half of the twentieth century, with 10% annual growth during the 1960s, 5% during the 1970s, and 4% during the 1980s. Known for producing vehicles, electronics, machine tools, metals, ships, chemicals, and textiles, Japan currently ranks as the fifth-largest single-nation economy with $4.7 trillion in GDP in 2013. But with the government's debt currently at 226% of GDP and an aging population, Japan's economy faces considerable challenges.[44]

Table 2.5 ⟩ Characteristics of Major Economic Regions

power. This can pose problems for firms that use the global location to distribute to these local consumers. When the local currency devaluates significantly relative to the dollar, the firm can lose money if it does not make adjustments in its prices to account for this new disparity.

Finally, a manager needs to consider the labor situation in a global market. Global markets differ widely in terms of the skill and education of the labor force. For firms that engage in high-tech operations or other skilled manufacturing, a steady supply of skilled workers is crucial for success. In general, it is fairly expensive for a firm to relocate an employee from its domestic operations to a global site. While many firms relocate executives for high-level positions, relocating large numbers of lower-level workers is rarely a cost-effective solution. Many global firms rely on developing skills of the local workers to work at lower levels of their organization. A current debate in the United States is centered on the number of H1B visas (a visa that allows foreigners with specific skills to temporarily work in the United States) to grant for skilled workers. Many information technology companies are

Bloomberg/Getty Images

lobbying for the government to increase the number of visas to support the growing need for key technical skills.

The homebuilding industry is particularly prone to economic shifts. For instance, Toll Brothers, one of the largest builders of single family homes and planned communities in the United States, experienced 30% growth per year between 2003 and 2006.[45] Low interest rates and easily accessible financing fueled this spectacular growth. By 2007, however, the company had hit a major roadblock as housing construction dropped precipitously. Completed new home construction dropped from 1.98 million units in 2006 to 1.5 million in 2007 and continued to fall, reaching only 584,000 units by 2011.[46]

The slowdown was a result of many economic factors, including anemic GDP growth, increasing unemployment, a tightened credit market, and rising interest rates.[47] Housing construction often serves as a bellwether of the viability of the economic landscape. Since 2011, new housing construction has risen to 883,000 in 2014, still less than half the total from 8 years earlier.[48]

From its beginnings in 1948, McDonald's has grown to over 36,000 restaurants around the globe. In 2014, the firm had $27.4 billion in revenues and $4.8 billion in net income. While these numbers seem strong, McDonald's has actually struggled for the past few years, reporting flat or declining revenue and profitability since 2011. The lackluster performance has resulted in three CEO transitions in the past decade. McDonald's troubles are a result of a number of factors, including increased competition, shifting consumer tastes, and several other factors that we'll explore in the discussion of the remaining dimensions of a firm's general environment.

Political and Legal Dimension

The **political dimension** of the external environment refers to the political events and activities in a market that affect a firm. Firms that operate on a global scale experience significant political pressures in their business. For instance, local government policymakers can influence the opportunities available to businesses by restricting access to raw materials or charging exorbitant fees for permits. In essence, they have the power to change the competitive landscape.[49] For instance, in 2013, India revoked Pfizer's patent for the cancer drug, Sutent, to allow a local manufacturer to produce a cheaper version. Though the Indian Court System has required the Patent Office to reassess the case, it demonstrates some of the difficult challenges that businesses face when operating in markets with different regulatory regimes.[50]

Unrest and violence are an everyday occurrence in many countries. These factors can have a direct or indirect impact on a firm in a global market. Political unrest can directly impact a firm when civilian unrest leads to destruction of the firm's property. In the BHP copper mine example in Chapter 1, a politically sensitive situation morphed into a full-blown riot at the mine, forcing managers to evacuate and abandon the business. Political unrest can also indirectly impact a firm by destroying consumer confidence in the country. Finally, many firms need to be aware of the potential for asset expropriation in certain global markets. This has been, for instance, a recurring problem for international oil companies doing business in different parts of the world over the last several decades.

In November 2010, the government of Fiji revoked the visa of David Roth, the local manager of California-headquartered FIJI Water. FIJI Water, which accounts for 20% of the nation's exports, was accused of selling its water to its U.S. parent at

Political dimension
Refers to the political events and activities in a market that affect a firm.

artificially low prices in an effort to lower its tax obligation to Fiji. The government also threatened to revoke FIJI Water's access to the aquifer that supplies its product if the tax issue remained unresolved.[51] The company briefly decided to suspend operations in Fiji over the dispute but eventually reopened and agreed to comply with the new tax policies. This issue demonstrated the precarious nature of the company with so much dependence on a single product and a single source for that product. Since then, the company has expanded into a new product line: premium wines.

The **legal dimension** refers to the regulations and laws that a firm encounters in its markets. In some industries, laws and regulations dictate the way a firm must process its products (e.g., the food industry) or market to consumers (e.g., the pharmaceutical industry). For instance, Congress recently increased fuel-efficiency standards for all cars sold in the United States. Fuel-efficiency standards must increase from 27 mpg (miles per gallon) to 35.5 mpg by 2016. This legislation was enacted in response to concerns that the pace of global warming is quickening due to carbon dioxide emissions. All firms that sell cars in the United States are directly affected and many will be forced to overhaul their design of engines and fuel systems. In 2012, the Obama Administration announced even higher standards by requiring cars to achieve 54.5 mpg by 2025.[52]

In the last decade, McDonald's has come under intense scrutiny because of the food it sells. In general, the majority of McDonald's menu consists of high-calorie, high-fat items such as the Big Mac and Chicken McNuggets. In the late 1990s, many critics began to argue that firms such as McDonald's were directly responsible for the increasing incidence of obesity in both children and adults. In 2001, a lawyer filed a liability lawsuit against McDonald's, alleging that his client had become obese from eating at McDonald's.[53] While this suit was eventually dropped, the company has continued to come under increasing pressure to improve its menu. In 2012, McDonald's joined many other fast-food chains in agreeing to post the calorie counts of all its menu items. In doing so, the company sought to be more transparent and allow consumers to be better informed about their choices.[54] McDonald's decision to post calories was not completely altruistic. As part of the healthcare overhaul during President Barack Obama's first term, all restaurants with 20 or more locations will eventually have to post calorie counts for their menu items. For its part, McDonald's sought to act before the federal requirements forced them to do so.

Sociocultural Dimension

The **sociocultural dimension** of the external environment refers to demographic characteristics as well as to the values and customs of a society. Some of the more prominent demographic forces that can impact a firm are the aging and changing racial composition of a population. Managers must consider these forces in how they run their businesses and how they hire employees. By 2045, more than 21% of the U.S. population will be over 65, up from 15% in 2015.[55] The increase in the population over 65 is a result of the aging baby boom generation, the largest surge in the population of the United States. The baby boom refers to the over 78 million people who were born after World War II between 1946 and 1964. The first wave of these individuals began to turn 65 in 2011. Japan and Germany are facing an even sharper rise in the proportion of their population that is over 65, while India and Nigeria have a much younger population (see Figure 2.6). Concerned about the economic impact of an aging demography, Japan and Germany have even offered financial incentives to their citizens to encourage them to have more babies. The hope is that more babies will eventually result in a broader employment base to support the expected increase in costs for elder care.[56]

As the U.S. population ages (see Figure 2.7), large companies will be faced with replacing a sizeable portion of upper management with younger employees. Many firms will select this generation's replacements from a smaller pool of talent.

Legal dimension
The regulations and laws that a firm encounters in its markets.

Sociocultural dimension
Demographic characteristics as well as the values and customs of a society.

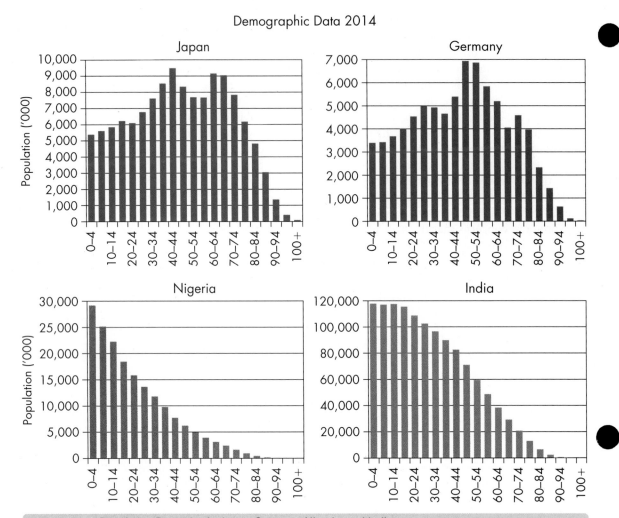

Figure 2.6 › Population Dynamics in Japan, Germany, Nigeria, and India

Source: U.S. Census Bureau, 2015.

To complete this task, firms will likely need to look outside the company to fill key positions. This practice contrasts from the previous experience of many large companies that traditionally hired and promoted from within the organization. Other companies might look at the experienced pool of aging employees as an opportunity to provide them with third or fourth careers. In doing so, these firms may create flexible work arrangements or job-sharing activities to extend the traditional retirement age for executives.

The aging demography has additional implications for firms, especially those that seek to develop products or services for this segment of the population. With greater disposable income and more leisure time, the older segment of the population is a particularly attractive target market for many industries. The Professional Golfers' Association (PGA) performed a study that labeled boomers' participation as the key to business growth because that group made up nearly 40% of golfers. As men and women became older, they entered their most active years of playing golf, and PGA officials claimed that cultivating participation from this segment was pivotal to the future of the sport.[57] Boomers are also more beauty conscious compared to previous generations, affecting industries such as plastic surgery. A study conducted in 2002 showed that from 1997 to 2001, the plastic surgery industry experienced a 352% increase in surgeries and a 300% increase in breast

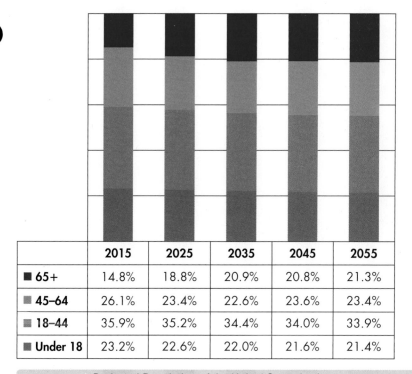

	2015	2025	2035	2045	2055
■ 65+	14.8%	18.8%	20.9%	20.8%	21.3%
■ 45–64	26.1%	23.4%	22.6%	23.6%	23.4%
■ 18–44	35.9%	35.2%	34.4%	34.0%	33.9%
■ Under 18	23.2%	22.6%	22.0%	21.6%	21.4%

Figure 2.7 ⟩ Projected Population of the United States by Age

Source: http://www.census.gov/population/projections/data/national/2012/summarytables.html

augmentation for individuals 65 years and older. Because of the boomers' emphasis on beauty, doctors are confident that their industry will continue to experience rapid growth.[58]

The aging demographic in China has also been a lucrative market for many companies. By 2030, the over-65 population in China is estimated to almost double to 210 million from 110 million in 2014. To serve this growing market, companies like Abbott Laboratories, makers of Ensure, is testing new flavors of nutritional drinks for Chinese senior citizens, and Kimberly-Clark has launched a new series of advertisements for its Depends adult diapers. Local Chinese companies are also targeting seniors. For instance, Alibaba, the eBay of China, has launched a new shopping section targeted to its 2 million online shoppers over 50, and Chinese electronics company, Hisense, has created a new smartphone, which includes an easy-to-use flashlight and easy access to medical assistance.[59]

In addition to aging, companies must adjust to or develop strategies for the population's changing racial composition (see Figure 2.8). Over the next few decades, the Hispanic population in the United States is expected to grow faster than any other group, reaching over 26% of the population by 2045.[60] Similar to companies targeting products to the aging population, some firms choose to develop products or services that are aimed specifically at diverse population subsegments. For instance, Home Depot launched a campaign in 2005 called Colores Origenes—the company's first paint palette featuring 70 vibrant colors to reflect Hispanic culture. Designed to create visuals of Latin America, Home Depot hoped to inspire consumers who were looking to capture Hispanic culture in their home décor.[61] The company used names such as *Azul Cielito Lindo* (Lovely Blue Sky) and *Chayote* (Chayote Squash) because it believed that Hispanics were more likely to purchase colors advertised in Spanish.[62]

A DIFFERENT View

More apple slices, less fries? Happy Meals across the country now offer a more nutritious kid's treat. In response to childhood obesity and healthier eating habits, McDonald's has imposed a healthier meal on their customers by automatically adding apple slices or yogurt to all Happy Meals while decreasing the number of fries. McDonald's recognized that evolving their business to meet the needs of their social environment is necessary to move forward successfully.

- Why is it important for businesses to be aware of their social environment?
- What is another example in which an organization's social environment influenced a product or business model?
- What is an example in which an organization's social environment should not influence a product or business model?

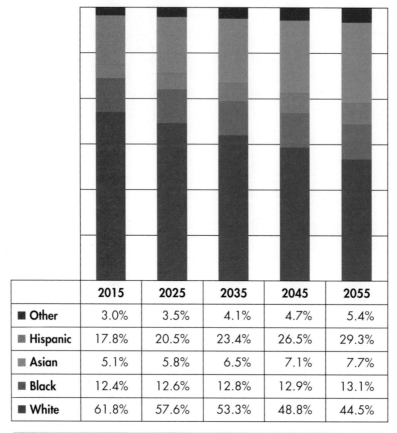

	2015	2025	2035	2045	2055
■ Other	3.0%	3.5%	4.1%	4.7%	5.4%
■ Hispanic	17.8%	20.5%	23.4%	26.5%	29.3%
■ Asian	5.1%	5.8%	6.5%	7.1%	7.7%
■ Black	12.4%	12.6%	12.8%	12.9%	13.1%
■ White	61.8%	57.6%	53.3%	48.8%	44.5%

Figure 2.8 ⟩ Projected Population of the United States by Race

Source: http://www.census.gov/population/projections/data/national/2012/summarytables.html

To capture some of the increase in Hispanic buying power, mall developer Macerich Co. has joined forces with real estate broker, Jose Legaspi, to convert vacant or underutilized malls in California and Arizona into destination shopping centers for Hispanics. For instance, a vacant Mervyns was transformed into a Mercado, housing several Hispanic-owned and themed retail stalls. The mall also hosts Latin-themed music and culinary events to serve the local community. The result was an almost immediate 30% boost in the bottom line performance of the mall.[63]

While the forces of globalization have caused many cultural tastes and practices to converge, most global markets still differ widely on important cultural dimensions. The first step for managers attempting to conduct business abroad is to gain an understanding or feel for the new culture. Most countries exhibit differences based on religious beliefs, race, social norms, and language. Language, for example, can have a huge impact on trade between firms from different countries. Trade between countries that share a common language is estimated to be three times greater than trade between countries that do not share a language.[64]

IKEA experienced the impact of language and social norms when it entered the Thailand market. Many of IKEA's furniture products use playful Scandinavian names, but sometimes these product names have very different connotations in other languages. For instance, IKEA's Redalen bed is named after a town in Norway and is a popular item in Scandinavia, but in Thailand, this name has a sexually explicit connotation.[65] As firms like IKEA expand globally, they need to be sensitive to language and local customs to ensure that they are not being offensive or

Social Dimensions	Description
Low versus High Power Distance	Individuals who gravitate toward low power distance prefer shared decision making and consensus while those who favor high power distance prefer deference to authority. Low power distance refers to more democratic societies such as Austria and Denmark. High power distance refers to autocratic societies such as China and parts of Latin America.
Individualism versus Collectivism	Individualism refers to a focus on individual goals and achievements while collectivism refers to a focus on group goals and relationships. The United States is mostly individualistic, while Latin America is strongly collectivistic.
Cooperative versus Competitive	Individuals who gravitate to cooperative relationships prefer collaboration and group participation while those who gravitate to competitive relationships prefer individual achievement, competition, and assertiveness. Previous research referred to these dimensions as feminine (cooperative) and masculine (competitive). The United States and Germany tend to be more competitive and Sweden tends to focus on more cooperative aspects of relationships.
Low versus High Uncertainty Avoidance	The extent to which members of a society cope with anxiety by minimizing uncertainty. Countries with high uncertainty avoidance, such as the majority of Latin American countries, prefer more rules, planning, and structure. Countries with low uncertainty avoidance are more comfortable with ambiguity and include Ireland, Sweden, Denmark, and Singapore.
Long- versus Short-Term Orientation	The importance attached to the future and the criteria that should be considered when making business decisions. Asian countries usually have a long-term orientation; Western nations, short-term.

Table 2.6 〉 Universal Social Dimensions

Source: Based on data from Geert Hofstede and Michael H. Bond, "The Confucius Connection: From Cultural Roots to Economic Growth," *Organizational Dynamics*, Vol. 16, Autumn 1988, pp. 4–21, and David Livermore, *Expand Your Borders* (East Lansing, MI: Cultural Intelligence Center, 2013).

misunderstood. It can be a tough balancing act since part of IKEA's global appeal is its quirky, fun Scandinavian terms for its products.

While language barriers may be easily overcome, **social values** often pose a much greater challenge for a company wanting to expand globally. Social values refer to the deeply rooted system of principles that guide individuals in their lives and interactions.[66] The social values of a society can affect a firm in two ways. First, a country's social values can affect the way a firm's local employees act and behave. Second, the social values of a country can affect the preferences of customers for certain product attributes. Some of the more important aspects of the social dimension of countries are discussed next (see Table 2.6).

The five broad dimensions outlined in Table 2.6 can help a manager better explain the social values of a particular country (see Figure 2.9). However, remember that these dimensions represent generalizations about certain societies and variations within a country. The particular people or companies that a firm works with may differ from these broad generalizations. To be effective, managers should understand the culture of the markets in which they hope to compete and should adapt their strategies accordingly. We will address issues of cross-cultural communication in Chapter 19 .

As was mentioned in the previous section, McDonald's has come under intense scrutiny in the last decade because of its menu offerings and the changing values of many customers. The rate of obesity and diabetes among children and adults has increased at an alarming rate. As these trends have emerged, many consumers have begun to change their beliefs and value systems with regard to diet and health. In addition, many people have begun to openly criticize fast-food chains such as McDonald's, implying a connection between increasing obesity and increasing sales.

In the popular documentary *Super-Size Me*, the director set out to eat McDonald's food at every meal for a month to see what the effects would be on his weight and health. Media such as this had a devastating effect on the company.

Social values
The deeply rooted system of principles that guide individuals in their everyday choices and interactions.

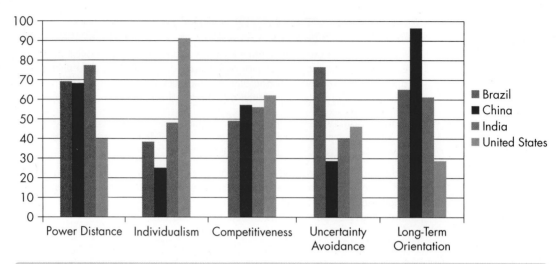

Figure 2.9 ⟩ Country Social Value Scores

Source: Adapted from Geert Hofstede and Michael H. Band, "The Confucius Connection: From Cultural Roots to Economic Growth." *Organizational Dynamics*, Vol. 16, Autumn 1988, pp. 4–21.

Since this movie and other critical books such as *Fast Food Nation*, McDonald's has begun to accept society's changing values with respect to diet and health. McDonald's has stopped offering its Super-Size variety of fries and drinks and has added new healthier items to its menu (e.g., salads, oatmeal, and fresh fruit).

More than most other firms, McDonald's has taken advantage of global opportunities in its environment. The firm operates restaurants in over 100 countries and serves 69 million people daily.[67] It maintains restaurants in far-flung places such as Moscow and Kuwait City. In 2014, McDonald's opened its first restaurant in Vietnam. To many, the restaurant offers the opportunity for a taste of America. However, others have criticized the company's expansion, claiming that the chain has reduced cultural identity in many places. Regardless, the global dimension of its environment has brought tremendous success to the firm by way of increased revenues and brand awareness.

Task Environment

A firm's task environment includes entities that directly affect the firm in a more immediate way, including competitors, suppliers, and customers. In contrast to the dimensions of the general environment, these parties have the ability to exert a greater and more constant influence over the firm. Once again, we'll discuss each component in the upcoming sections through the lens of the McDonald's Corporation.

Competitors

A **competitor** of a firm is any organization that creates goods or services targeted at a similar group of customers. The proliferation of technology, the rapid pace of globalization, and the speed of innovation have resulted in a vastly changed competitive landscape. Technological and global changes have fueled competition in industries such as electronics, automobiles, and computers.

The U.S. automotive industry has experienced two significant changes in the last decade. First, the biggest areas for growth are in emerging markets like India and China, requiring U.S. manufacturers to design new cars to fit these markets. At the same time, U.S. auto manufacturers are facing stiff competition from local car manufacturers in these emerging markets. Automobile production in China and India

Competitor
Any organization that creates goods or services targeted at a similar group of customers.

grew at double-digit rates annually over the last decade, giving these companies the financial power to expand beyond their borders. India's Tata Motors bought Jaguar and Land Rover from Ford in June 2008, and China's Geely Automobile Company was the first Chinese automaker to display a vehicle at the Detroit Auto Show in 2006. Geely went on to acquire Volvo from Ford in 2010. Other companies have merged with Western companies, expanded their exports to U.S. markets, and even announced new production in the United States.[68]

The U.S. semiconductor industry is also experiencing competitive pressure from Chinese companies. As the Chinese chip manufacturers SMIC, Actions, and Vimicro opened on the New York Stock Exchange in 2004, there were signs that China would soon dominate the industry.[69] From 2003 to 2013, China's semiconductor industry grew at a compound annual growth rate of 23%, and Chinese consumption of semiconductors grew at a 19% compound annual growth rate, compared to a worldwide consumption rate of 6%. By 2013, China accounted for over 55% of the global market for semiconductors, and the number of major Chinese semiconductor companies grew to 50.[70]

At McDonald's, the list of competitors is extensive. The firm essentially competes with every other restaurant in a local market. The local Chinese, Mexican, and Indian restaurants are all competitors of McDonald's. However, McDonald's considers other fast-food restaurants to be its direct competitors. Firms such as Wendy's, Burger King, Taco Bell, and Hardee's offer products similar to those of McDonald's. More recently, McDonald's has had to compete with a plethora of more focused, fast casual restaurants such as Chipotle Mexican Grille and Panera Bread. In its traditional burger space, Five Guys and Shake Shack have become formidable competitors.[71] In fact, if you drive down any major commercial road in the United States, you'll likely see many of these restaurants right next to each other. And while these firms are the company's traditional competitors, McDonald's also counts numerous other firms (e.g., Starbucks) as competitors. As we saw earlier, Starbucks introduced a line of breakfast sandwiches to its outlets in 2005. To McDonald's, this represented a major threat because consumers could now go to Starbucks for a complete breakfast, rather than grab a coffee at Starbucks and then head to McDonald's for a breakfast sandwich.

Suppliers

A **supplier** provides resources or services for a firm to help in its creation of products and services. In many cases, it is not economical for firms to produce everything in-house. As a result, firms rely on various suppliers to produce inputs for their products. For instance, Apple only physically makes about 10% of the iPhone; the other 90% is made by its network of suppliers. In addition to having a wide variety of discrete suppliers, firms generally maintain several sources of supplies for specific components to reduce their reliance on one particular company.

Like many firms, McDonald's has a long list of suppliers. The company relies on certain firms (e.g., J.R. Simplot) to provide potatoes for its french fries, ground beef for its hamburgers, and soda (Coca-Cola) for its beverages. In 2010, McDonald's purchased 800 million pounds of beef (3% of all beef consumed in the United States), 231 million pounds of cheese, 750 million pounds of chicken, and 60 million pounds of apples.[72] Over the years, McDonald's has gained the reputation of being a good customer to work with from a supplier standpoint. The firm tends to develop deep, long-term relationships with a few suppliers. In its negotiations, the company focuses on quality and exact specification of products. For example, the meat in McDonald's hamburgers must be 83% lean chuck (shoulder) from grass-fed cattle and 17% choice plates (lower rib cage) from grain-fed cattle.[73] This level of detail has allowed the company to maintain consistent operations and products throughout its global franchises.

Supplier
A company that provides resources or services for a firm to help in its creation of products and services.

Customers

The **customers** of a firm are the people or organizations that buy the firm's products and services. To many managers, the customer represents the most important aspect of the firm's environment. Without customers and sales, the firm would not exist. At many firms, you'll hear slogans such as "The customer is king" and "The customer is always right." These statements reflect the importance attributed to this component of the task environment. Many firms have different sets of customers. For example, a company such as Staples has both retail and commercial customers. In fact, you might be considered one of the firm's retail customers if you purchase your school supplies there. However, the firm also has a long list of commercial customers (e.g., local businesses) that use Staples for their office supply needs. And while both sets of customers are important to the company, the relationships and sales processes involved in the two are vastly different.

While McDonald's has been a forerunner in offering convenience and consistency to customers, it has also tried to attract a broader audience through the introduction of Happy Meals and indoor playgrounds. Through these efforts, McDonald's is trying to serve customers who value speed and convenience as well as customers who seek a destination dining experience. Although McDonald's has based a majority of its success on a consistent dining experience, the company has experimented with localized menu modifications as it has expanded on a global scale. Firms, like McDonalds, often have to grapple with how much to standardize their products and services across geographies and how much to customize them for local markets.

In 2003, McDonald's introduced the McArabia across the Middle East to grab a foothold in consumer branding in the region. These sandwiches, which featured significantly more spice than American menu items, were dressed with a garlic-based tahini sauce. But this item was modified even further in Moroccan franchises to cater to their consumers' unique palette. Rather than tahini sauce, McDonald's used cumin, coriander, a piquant tomato sauce, bell peppers, and a pita. McDonald's has also sold Shrimp Burgers in Hong Kong, lemon pepper Shaka Shaka Chicken patties in Japan, and chili-spiced SingaPorridge breakfast dishes in Singapore. These are only a few examples of modifications McDonald's has made worldwide to adapt to local customers' tastes.[74]

INTERNAL ENVIRONMENT

A firm's **internal environment** consists of several dimensions that affect the firm from within its boundaries. The typical components of a firm's internal environment include owners, the board of directors, employees, and culture. Each of these dimensions can directly impact a firm's performance and competitive position.

Owners

The **owners** of a firm are the people or institutions that maintain legal control of the organization. In many instances, firms are owned by one person or a small group of people (see Figure 2.10). In fact, sole proprietorships make up the majority of businesses in the United States; more than 79% of U.S. firms employ fewer than 10 individuals (e.g., the local dry cleaner or pizza shop).[75] Other firms may be larger in size, yet still remain under private ownership. These firms do not trade their securities over an exchange such as the New York Stock Exchange. Instead, they have a set amount of stock that represents the owners' equity in the business. Some firms avoid public ownership to escape the pressures and scrutiny that come from Wall Street's expectations of achieving quarterly earnings estimates.

At the other end of the spectrum, many large firms are publicly owned by shareholders and are actively traded on the stock market. Companies that are publicly

Customers
The people or organizations that buy a firm's products and services.

Internal environment
A group of parties or factors that directly impact a firm, including owners, the board of directors, employees, and culture.

Owners
The people or institutions that maintain legal control of an organization.

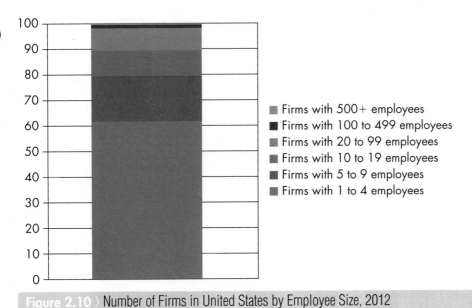

Figure 2.10 ⟩ Number of Firms in United States by Employee Size, 2012

Source: U.S. Census Bureau, "Number of Firms, Number of Establishments, Employment, and Annual Payroll by Enterprise Employment Size for the United States and States, Totals: 2012," released January 23, 2015.

owned and traded on the stock market must comply with several federal and state policies including the reporting of their earnings on a regular basis.

For a firm such as McDonald's, both individual and institutional shareholders own the company. You could go online right now and purchase shares in McDonald's. And while your share of ownership would be very small, you would still be considered a fractional owner in the business and be given the opportunity to vote on proxy matters. A company such as McDonald's also has institutional shareholders (e.g., Fidelity Investments or CalPERS). Typically, institutional shareholders hold thousands—even millions—of shares in a company. As a result, institutional shareholders wield greater influence over companies, often pressuring firms to change strategies or management when performance does not meet expectations.

Board of Directors

The **board of directors** is a group of individuals elected by shareholders and charged with overseeing the general direction of the firm. Though shareholders are part owners of the company, it is difficult for them to oversee what managers actually do to serve their interests. As such, the board of directors serves as an intermediate group, and they oversee managers to ensure that they serve the interests of a diverse group of shareholders. Boards come in different shapes and sizes. Some boards are made up mostly of company executives, while others have substantial representation from nonexecutives. More recently, firms have begun to diversify the structure of their boards in response to some of the corporate scandals of the early 2000s. The main criticism of boards at companies such as Enron and WorldCom was a lack of adequate oversight. One of the board's main functions is to provide oversight of the firm's strategies and management practices. Many critics wondered what Enron's board was doing while its executives engineered several financial frauds. Because of these events, many firms have moved to make their boards more independent, with less representation from their executive ranks.

When Enron filed for bankruptcy and WorldCom grossly misreported annual earnings, massive corruption was exposed and government officials enacted new legislation to protect a variety of constituents.[76] By July 2002, the Sarbanes-Oxley Act was passed, fundamentally changing the role that board members played in companies. Rather than being responsible for the general oversight of operations,

Board of directors
A group of individuals elected by shareholders and charged with overseeing the general direction of the firm.

board members were now mandated to prepare financial statements and ensure sound reporting. The act codified new responsibilities for corporate executives, corporate directors, lawyers, and accountants, putting everything under the supervision of a new regulatory board.[77] While this established more stringent rules for public companies, it also increased costs for items such as audit fees, legal fees, board compensation, and insurance premiums. Still, the act has been deemed effective because companies and auditors have since developed a rigorous new accounting discipline.[78] If fraud is detected today, directors can be held accountable by shareholders.

At McDonald's, the board consists of executives, nonexecutive members, and various individuals from other companies who have an understanding of McDonald's business and its customers. In 2015, McDonald's board of directors included its CEO, Steve Easterbrook, and 12 other nonexecutives such as the former CEO of Mattel, Robert Eckert, the President of the Art Institute of Chicago, Walter Massey, and the President of Products and Merchandising for Nike, Jeanne Jackson.

Employees

A firm's **employees** are an extremely important component of its internal environment. Employees are the people who make the products and provide the services that allow the firm to exist. Without a capable and motivated employee base, a firm cannot expect to generate a competitive advantage in the marketplace. Most firms have a mix of permanent and temporary employees. Permanent employees are employees whose work contract does not expire on a given date. On the other hand, a temporary employee may be brought in to help during the busy Christmas season. Amazon, for instance, has partnered with recreational vehicle (RV) parks in towns close to their massive distribution warehouses to house temporary workers for the preholiday sales rush. Retirees looking for a little extra money and a new experience have flocked to these "Amazon towns" and set up camp for a few months. Amazon recruits these new employees at RV shows and agrees to pay the local parking fees. In this way, Amazon has found a unique way to solve a temporary staffing issue.[79]

Just as a firm's external environment has grown more complicated recently, the firm's internal environment has increased in complexity as well because of a new mix of employees. Today, more than ever, the workplace is populated by people of different genders, races, ages, religions, and nationalities.

McDonald's 1.9 million employees can be categorized in two distinct groups. At its corporate offices in Illinois, the company has thousands of employees who work in key functions that support the entire company around the world. These include corporate functions such as sales and marketing, finance, and operations. These employees perform some of the company's traditional activities that are coordinated from the corporate center. Like many firms, McDonald's provides its employees with training opportunities through its Hamburger University programs. At the individual store level, the company has some staff who are restaurant managers and others who are hourly employees who work behind the counter in food preparation and delivery. And while McDonald's has received criticism over the years for its treatment of this group, the company does provide direct opportunities for its staff to be promoted to restaurant managers and to positions in the corporate office. In fact, 40% of executive officers began as crew members working in local McDonald's restaurants.[80]

Culture

Culture is a word that likely means something to you. People are often talking about the culture of a particular company, school, classroom, or sports team. At one time, you might have said that the culture of your college class is lighthearted and collegial. In fact, your school's culture may have been one of the reasons you

Employees
The people who make the products and provide the services that allow a firm to exist.

decided to attend the school. Despite being an almost ubiquitous term to describe an organization, culture is difficult to define. At its core, culture embodies who and what an organization is or represents.

Some people define a firm's culture based on certain tangible factors such as the firm's physical environment. These observable characteristics can include physical space, the way people dress, the hours and patterns of work schedules, or the overall behavior of its members.[81] Based on these observations, many people label a particular culture as formal or informal. However, these visible signposts do not represent the full culture of an organization.

At its core, culture is a pattern of basic assumptions about the way an organization should work and the manner in which individuals in an organization should interact with each other. As members join an organization, they are taught both implicitly and explicitly about what is accepted behavior.[82]

Cultures at firms develop over a long period of time. For many firms, the culture is a by-product of the founder's personality. In these cases, the company is based on the values, beliefs, and assumptions of an individual or a small group of individuals. Steve Jobs's impact on Apple's culture, Herb Kelleher's impact on Southwest Airlines culture, and Richard Branson's influence on Virgin's culture have transcended decades. At other firms, the culture is a product of the community in which the firm resides.

Like many firms, McDonald's culture can be traced back to its founder, Ray Kroc. In the 1950s, Kroc bought the rights to franchise the business from the original McDonald's brothers in California. Kroc saw the awesome potential of franchising the restaurant throughout the country. He also saw tremendous profit opportunities in bringing strict assembly-line discipline to the food preparation and delivery processes. This attention to detail defines the culture at corporate headquarters and can be seen in many outlets around the world. Despite the high employee turnover associated with fast-food establishments such as McDonald's, the company has been able to diffuse this culture to its thousands of outlets so that consumers receive the same experience whether they are eating a Big Mac in Madison, Wisconsin, or Moscow, Russia.

A firm's culture is very important for attracting, developing, and retaining a competent workforce and for creating a competitive advantage in the marketplace. Chapter 8, Organizational Culture, will discuss this topic in greater detail and explain how a manager can affect positive change in an organization through the development and growth of the culture.

The Leadership Development Journey

Astute leaders are attuned to their business environment. If a government official in your hometown asked you to prepare a memo that assesses the business environment, what environmental factors would you discuss? For example, in the memo would you include:

- Economic indicators such as GDP, inflation, and employment?
- Current political activities?
- Regulations and laws?
- Demographic projections and census data?
- Sociocultural trends?

What are the leadership implications of each environmental factor you would discuss in the memo? Based on your analysis of the environmental factors, what recommendations would you make to the government official?

SUMMARY

LO1 Several environmental forces have combined to create a more global marketplace than that which existed just 10 years ago. Globalization has resulted from an overall reduction in trade barriers and tariffs around the world. And, while globalization has led to jobs being shipped from higher-cost regions to lower-cost regions, its effects have been mostly positive. As markets around the world open up, citizens and consumers gain better access to employment, commercial, and product opportunities.

LO2 While globalization has made life better for many, it has also made life more challenging and complex for managers. Managers must realize that the global business environment affects their firms and industries even if they don't conduct business in the global arena. With lower trade barriers, firms can expect to see more competition in the marketplace. Trade agreements such as GATT, NAFTA, ASEAN, and MERCOSUR and trade organizations such as the WTO have changed the way managers think about competition.

LO3 A firm's external environment includes two primary components—the general environment and the task environment. The general environment represents the primary external forces that impact a firm including technology, economic conditions, political and legal structures, and sociocultural factors. The task environment consists of the dimensions that have the most immediate impact on a firm, including its competitors, suppliers, and customers.

LO4 In addition to reacting to and influencing the external environment, managers also need to pay close attention to their internal task environment. The internal environment consists of several dimensions that affect the way in which a firm operates, including owners, boards of directors, employees, and organizational culture. Each of these dimensions requires a particular level of attention to create and sustain a competitive advantage.

KEY TERMS

Board of directors
Comparative advantage
Competitor
Customers
Economic dimension
Employees

External environment
General environment
Globalization
Internal environment
Legal dimension
Owners

Political dimension
Social values
Sociocultural dimension
Supplier
Task environment
Technological dimension

ASSIGNMENTS

Discussion Topics

1. Why are some companies more successful in their global expansion than others? What factors should a manager consider when expanding globally?

2. Do you think that it is easier for a U.S.-based company to expand in an emerging market like China or India or for a Chinese or Indian firm to expand in the United States? If you were an advisor to a company in each of these scenarios, what advice would you provide? How would the advice be similar? How would it be different?

3. Where do you believe the greatest opportunity for global expansion exists: Asia, South America, or Africa? Why?

4. What are the advantages and disadvantages of trade associations and regional trade agreements? Have these been good for business and society? Who benefits the most from regional trade alliances? Why?

5. How has social media impacted the way companies do business locally and globally? What other technological forces do you think will impact the global business landscape in the next five years?

6. Of the major dimensions of the general environment—technology, economy, political/legal, and sociocultural—which one do you believe is the most complicated? How can managers influence each one?

7. What opportunities does the aging population of the United States present to business? What challenges do they present?

8. How should companies think about the changing racial composition of the population in the United States? What challenges and opportunities does the change present? What firm appears to be doing a good job leveraging this greater diversity?

9. In what ways can a manager influence the internal environment of the firm?

10. How well positioned do you think McDonald's is for the next 10 years? What are the company's key advantages and potential challenges?

Management Research

1. GE and Coca-Cola have retained their relevance for more than 100 years. Why? Find another company that has been able to remain relevant for at least 50 years. What is the secret to its success?

2. Select a company on which you can conduct an environmental analysis. Consider the following in your analysis.

   - Name and describe the various forces that affect its external environment.
   - Name the various components of the firm's internal environment and how they affect the firm.
   - Predict what contextual forces will have the greatest impact on the business in the next five years. Evaluate if these forces will present opportunities or challenges.

3. Identify a company that recently had to manage a crisis.

   - What environmental factors led to the crisis?
   - Create a timeline for how management reacted to the crisis.
   - Were management actions effective?
   - Did management behave ethically?

In the Field

1. Work with a leader of a nonprofit organization to assess both its external and internal environments. Be prepared to share the assessments with your classmates.

   - How did your assessment differ for a nonprofit organization in comparison to a for-profit organization?
   - What can corporations learn from the environment of nonprofit organizations?

2. Create a video that documents the business environment of a retail firm in your college town. The following segments should be included in the video.

   - An analysis of the firm's stakeholders.
   - A discussion of the different dimensions of the external environment.
   - A discussion on how the firm manages its competitors and suppliers.
   - An analysis of its customer segments.
   - A discussion on the firm's organizational culture and how it affects performance.

3. Identify two managers who were born in different countries. Using Hofstede's model of National Values in Table 2.6, ask each manager to describe the values of their birth country on the following dimensions:

   - Low versus high power distance
   - Individualism versus collectivism
   - Cooperative versus competitive
   - Uncertainty avoidance
   - Long- versus short-term orientation

After each manager describes his or her country's national values, ask how these values influence his or her leadership style.

ENDNOTES

[1] Justin Tan and David Tan, "Environment—Strategy Co-Evolution and Co-Alignment: A Staged Model of Chinese SOEs under Transition," *Strategic Management Journal*, Vol. 26, 2004, p. 143.

[2] United States Department of Labor, "Labor Force Statistics from the Current Population," available at http://www.bls.gov/cps/cpsaat01.htm, accessed February 3, 2015.

[3] Nitin Nohria, Anthony J. Mayo, and Mark Benson, "General Electric's 20th Century CEOs," Harvard Business School Case No. 9-406-048, rev. July 25, 2007 (Boston, MA: HBS Publishing, 2006).

[4] McDonald's Corporation, "Geographic Segments," via the OneSource® Business BrowserSM, accessed January 29, 2015; Starbucks Corp, "Geographic Segments," via the OneSource® Business BrowserSM, accessed January 29, 2015; Apple Inc., "Geographic Segments," via the OneSource® Business BrowserSM, accessed January 29, 2015; and Facebook Inc., "Geographic Segments," via the OneSource® Business BrowserSM, accessed January 29, 2015.

[5] Helen H. Wang, "The Chinese Middle Class View of the Leadership Transition," *Forbes*, November 9, 2012.

[6] "Hitting the Sweet Spot: The Growth of the Middle Class in Emerging Markets," Ernst & Young, 2013, available at http://www.ey.com/GL/en/Issues/Driving-growth/Middle-class-growth-in-emerging-markets–China-and-India-tomorrow-s-middle-classes.

[7] Interbrand, "Best Global Brands 2014," http://www.bestglobalbrands.com/2014/ranking/, accessed January 31, 2015.

[8] Anthony J. Mayo and Nitin Nohria , *In Their Time: The Greatest Business Leaders of the Twentieth Century* (Boston, MA: HBS Press, 2005), p. 76; and Coca-Cola, "125 Years of Sharing Happiness: A Short History of the Coca-Cola Company," http://www.thecoca-colacompany.com/heritage/ourheritage.html, accessed July 18, 2012.

[9] Frank Cespedes, "Cola Wars: Going Global," Harvard Business School Case No. 9-709-451, rev. September 30, 2009 (Boston, MA: HBS Publishing, 2008), p. 3.

[10] Ibid., p. 2.

[11] Coca-Cola, "Coca-Cola: Per Capita Consumption of Company Beverage Products," http://www.thecoca-colacompany.com/ourcompany/ar/pdf/2011-per-capita-consumption.pdf, accessed July 18, 2012.

[12] Anne Vandermey, "Keeping a Sparkle, as Sodas Fizzles," *Fortune*, May 19, 2014.

[13] Coca-Cola, "Coca-Cola: Per Capita Consumption of Company Beverage Products," http://www.coca-colacompany.com/annual-review/2012/pdf/2012-per-capita-consumption.pdf, accessed January 31, 2015.

[14] Mike Esterl, "'Share a Coke' Creates Pop in Sales," *Wall Street Journal*, September 26, 2014.

[15] Theodore Levitt, "The Globalization of Markets," *Harvard Business Review*, May–June 1983; and Vijay Govindarajan and Anil K. Gupta, *The Quest for Global Dominance* (San Francisco: Jossey-Bass, 2001).

[16] "A Taste of Adventure," *The Economist*, December 19, 1998, via LexisNexis, accessed March, 2011; and Britannica Online Encyclopedia, "Dutch East India Company," www.britannica.com/EBchecked/topic/174523/Dutch-East-India-Company, accessed March 2011.

[17] Jack High and George C. Lodge, "The World Trade Organization: Toward Freer Trade or World Bureaucracy," Harvard Business School Case No. 9-795-149, rev. August 16, 1995 (Boston, MA: HBS Publishing, 1995), p. 2.

[18] Ibid., p. 2.

[19] World Trade Organization, "About WTO: What We Do," http://www.wto.org/english/thewto_e/whatis_e/what_we_do_e.htm, accessed July 17, 2012.

[20] World Trade Organization, "WTO Lowers Forecast after Sub-par Trade Growth in First Half of 2014," September 23, 2014, http://www.wto.org/english/news_e/pres14_e/pr722_e.htm, accessed January 29, 2015.

[21] World Trade Organization, "International Trade Statistics, 2014," http://www.wto.org/english/res_e/statis_e/its2014_e/its14_toc_e.htm, accessed January 31, 2015.

[22] "The EU Single Market: Fewer Barriers, More Opportunities," European Commission, http://ec.europa.eu/internal_market/index_en.htm, accessed September 27, 2007; and "Activities of the European Union: Internal Market," European Commission, http://ec.europa.eu/internal_market/index_en.htm, accessed September 27, 2009.

[23] "Outs and Ins; the European Union and the Euro Zone," *The Economist*, March 12, 2011, via LexisNexis, accessed March 2011.

[24] "The Euro: Our Currency" European Commission, available at http://ec.europa.eu/internal_market/index_en.htm, accessed September 27, 2009.

[25] Central Intelligence Agency World Fact Book, "Europe: European Union," https://www.cia.gov/library/publications/the-world-factbook/index.html, accessed January 31, 2015.

[26] Central Intelligence Agency World Fact Book, "North America: United States," https://www.cia.gov/library/publications/the-world-factbook/index.html, accessed January 31, 2015.

[27] "Trade in Goods with Mexico," United States Census Bureau, https://www.census.gov/foreign-trade/balance/c2010.html, accessed January 29, 2015; and "Trade in Goods with Canada," United States Census Bureau, https://www.census.gov/foreign-trade/balance/c1220.html, accessed January 29, 2015.

[28] "Trade in Goods with Mexico," United States Census Bureau, https://www.census.gov/foreign-trade/balance/c2010.html, accessed January 29, 2015; and "Trade in Goods with Canada," United States Census Bureau, https://www.census.gov/foreign-trade/balance/c1220, accessed January 29, 2015.

[29] Margareta Drzeniek Hanouz and Thierry Geiger, "Enabling Trade in the Greater ASEAN Region," World Economic Forum, 2010.

[30] Ibid.

[31] World Trade Organization, "International Trade Statistics, 2011," http://www.wto.org/english/res_e/statis_e/its2011_e/its11_toc_e.htm, accessed July 24, 2012; and Joanna Klonsky, Stephanie Hanson, and Brianna Lee, "Mercosur: South America's Fractious Trade Bloc," Council on Foreign Relations, July 31, 2012, http://www.cfr.org/trade/mercosur-south-americas-fractious-trade-bloc/p12762, accessed August 7, 2012.

[32] Debora Spar and Terrence Mulligan, "Chiquita Brands International (A)," Harvard Business School Case No. 9-797-015, rev. September 12, 2007 (Boston, MA: HBS Publishing, 1996), p. 7.

[33] Ibid.

[34] Theodore H. Cohn, *Global Political Economy: Theory and Practice*, 5th edition (New York, NY: Pearson Education, 2010).

[35] Peter Debaere, "Why Countries Trade: The Theory of Comparative Advantage," University of Virginia Darden Business Publishing Note No. UV2702, rev. July 24, 2009 (Charlottesville, VA: University of Virginia Darden School Foundation, 2007).

[36] Jeffrey Sachs, *The End of Poverty* (New York, NY: The Penguin Press, 2005).

[37] "Tablet PC Reviews," http://tabletpc-comparisons.com/, accessed September 2011.

[38] L. J. Bourgeois, III, "Strategy and Environment: A Conceptual Integration," *Academy of Management Review*, Vol. 5, No. 1, January 1980, p. 26.

[39] Lisa Baertlien, "McDonald's Looking to Heat Up U.S. Sales with Breakfast, Coffee," Reuters, February 11, 2014.

[40] Central Intelligence Agency World Fact Book, "North America: Mexico," and "North America: Canada," https://www.cia.gov/library/publications/the-world-factbook/index.html, accessed January 31, 2015.

[41] Central Intelligence Agency World Fact Book, "Europe: European Union," https://www.cia.gov/library/publications/the-world-factbook/index.html, accessed January 31, 2015.

[42] Central Intelligence Agency World Fact Book, "East and Southeast Asia: China," https://www.cia.gov/library/publications

/the-world-factbook/index.html, accessed January 31, 2015.

[43] Central Intelligence Agency World Fact Book, "South Asia: India," https://www.cia.gov/library/publications/the-world-factbook/index.html, accessed January 31, 2015.

[44] Central Intelligence Agency World Fact Book, "East and Southeast Asia: Japan," https://www.cia.gov/library/publications/the-world-factbook/index.html, accessed January 31, 2015.

[45] Calculated from annual revenue and sales figures. Toll Brothers Inc., *Toll Brothers 2007 Annual Report*, Global Reports LLC, 2007.

[46] United States Census Bureau, "New Residential Construction," available at http://www.census.gov/construction/nrc/pdf/compann.pdf, accessed February 4, 2015.

[47] Patrice Hall, "Blame Abounds for Housing Bust; Easy Money, Greed a Toxic Mix," *The Washington Post*, December 26, 2007; and J. W. Elphinstone, "Mortgage Volume Drops to 4-Year Low, Latest Sign of Slowing Real Estate Market," *The Associated Press*, August 2, 2006.

[48] United States Census Bureau, "New Residential Construction," available at http://www.census.gov/construction/nrc/pdf/compann.pdf, accessed February 4, 2015.

[49] Gerald D. Keim and Amy J. Hillman, "Political Environments and Business Strategy: Implications for Managers," *Business Horizons*, 2008, p. 48.

[50] Ian Bremmer, "The New Rules of Globalization," *Harvard Business Review*, January-February 2014.

[51] Caroline Winter, "FIJI Water: Shutting Off the Tap?" *Bloomberg Businessweek*, November 25–December 5, 2010.

[52] The White House, Office of the Press Secretary, "Obama Administration Finalizes Historic 54.5 MPG Fuel Efficiency Standards," August 28, 2012.

[53] David P. Baron, "Obesity and McLawsuits," Stanford Graduate School of Business Case No. P-49, (Stanford, CA: Stanford Graduate School of Business, 2005), p. 1.

[54] Stephanie Strom, "McDonald's Menu to Post Calorie Data," *New York Times*, September 12, 2012.

[55] U.S. Census Bureau, 2015, available at http://www.census.gov/population/projections/data/national/2012/summary-tables.html.

[56] Daisuke Wakabayashi and Miho Inada, "Baby Bundle: Japan's Cash Incentive for Parenthood," *The Wall Street Journal*, October 8, 2009.

[57] Tim Triplett, "Golf Industry Links Future to Aging Boomers," *Marketing News*, Vol. 30, Issue 12, 1996, p. 2.

[58] David Frabotta, "Riding the Wave of the Future," *Cosmetic Surgery Times*, Vol. 5, Issue 8, 2002, p. 22.

[59] Laurie Burkitt, "China's Aging Boomers Are Lucrative Market," *Wall Street Journal*, January 20, 2015.

[60] U.S. Census Bureau, 2015 available at http://www.census.gov/population/projections/data/national/2012/summarytables.html.

[61] "Homing In on Hispanics," *Home Channel News*, Special Reports, December 12, 2005.

[62] "The Home Depot's New Splash," *Chain Store Age*, Vol. 81, Issue 10, 2005, p. 17.

[63] Miriam Jordan, "Mall Owners Woo Hispanic Shoppers," *Wall Street Journal*, August 14, 2013.

[64] Pankaj Ghemawat, "Distance Still Matters: The Hard Reality of Global Expansion," *Harvard Business Review*, September 2001.

[65] James Hookway, "IKEA Products Makes Shoppers Blush in Thailand," *The Wall Street Journal*, June 5, 2012.

[66] Pankaj Ghemawat, "Distance Still Matters: The Hard Reality of Global Expansion," *Harvard Business Review*, September 2001.

[67] McDonald's Corporation, "Our Company," http://www.aboutmcdonalds.com/mcd/our_company.html, accessed January 31, 2015.

[68] Efraim Levy, "Industry Surveys Autos & Auto Parts: Global," *Standard & Poor's Industry Surveys*, August 2008, www.netadvantage.com, accessed October 15, 2009.

[69] Vivek Wadhwa, "Why China's Chip Industry Won't Catch America's," *Business Week*, September 3, 2009, www.BusinessWeek.com, accessed October 15, 2009.

[70] Raman Chitkara and Jianbin Gao, PWC, "A Decade of Unprecedented Growth: China's Impact on the Semiconductor Industry—2014 Update," available at http://www.pwc.com/gx/en/technology/chinas-impact-on-semiconductor-industry/index.jhtml, accessed February 4, 2015.

[71] Jason Dean, Ilan Brat, and Annie Gasparro, "McDonald's CEO Is Out Amid Decline in Sales," *Wall Street Journal*, January 29, 2015.

[72] Beth Kowitt, "Why McDonald's Wins in Any Economy," *Fortune*, September 5, 2011.

[73] David Upton and Joshua D. Margolis, "McDonald's Corporation," Harvard Business School Case No. 9-693-028, rev. September 23, 1996 (Boston, MA: HBS Publishing, 1992), p. 3.

[74] Erik German, "Morocco Loving the McArabia," *GlobalPost*, August 26, 2009, www.globalpost.com/dispatch/morocco/090825/morocco-loving-the-mcarabia, accessed October 13, 2009.

[75] U.S. Census Bureau, "Number of Firms, Number of Establishments, Employment, and Annual Payroll by Enterprise Employment Size for the United States and States, Totals: 2012," accessed January 23, 2015.

[76] Lynn Sharp Paine and James Weber, "The Sarbanes-Oxley Act," Harvard Business School Case No. 9-304-079, rev. July 12, 2004 (Boston, MA: HBS Publishing, 2004).

[77] Deloitte & Touche, Ernst & Young, KPMG, and PricewaterhouseCoopers, "Perspectives on Internal Control Reporting: A Resource for Financial Market Participation," p. 5.

[78] Diya Gullapalli, "Living with Sarbanes-Oxley: How Companies Are Coping in the New Era of Corporate Governance," *The Wall Street Journal*, October 17, 2005.

[79] Stu Woo, "Welcome to Amazon Town," *The Wall Street Journal*, December 20, 2011.

[80] Regina Wolfe, Laura Hartman, Justin Sheehan, and Jenny Mead, "Started as Crew (C): McDonald's Strategy for Corporate Success and Poverty Reduction," University of Virginia Case Study No. UV1156 (Charlottesville, VA: Darden Business Publishing, 2008), p. 10.

[81] Clayton M. Christensen and Kirstin Shu "What Is an Organization's Culture?" Harvard Business School Case No. 9-399-104, rev. August 2, 2006 (Boston, MA: HBS Publishing, 1999).

[82] Ibid.

CHAPTER

3

Ethics and Corporate Social Responsibility

Learning Objectives

After reading this chapter, you should be able to:

LO1 : Differentiate between various ethical frameworks and describe how they influence the way managers navigate complex ethical decisions.

LO2 : Describe the different types of moral dilemmas that managers face both inside and outside their organizations.

LO3 : Explain the ethical, legal, and financial obligations of a business and how these influence a firm's approach to corporate social responsibility.

LO4 : Outline the link between corporate social responsibility and the overall performance of a firm.

SELF-REFLECTION

What Are Your Ethical Beliefs?

Ethics is the study of morality, and morality is defined as the standards used to judge what is right or wrong, good or evil. Our ethical beliefs are influenced by life experiences, cultural heritage, and personal values. Reflect upon your ethical beliefs by responding True or False to the following statements.

1. Behaviors are considered moral if they produce the greatest good for the greatest number of people.

2. Right or wrong actions should be judged solely by their consequences, not by their intent.

3. People should seek to maximize the total good of their actions even when this means ethical rules are violated.

4. Rules are designed to produce good consequences.

5. Motives are important when judging ethical behavior.

6. People should use a standardized process when making ethical decisions.

7. When people confront a difficult decision, their values or morals should guide their actions.

8. Ethical behaviors are the result of conforming to societal expectations.

9. An evaluation of ethical practices should consider differences in the values, opinions, and beliefs of others.

10. Managers should consider the social impact of their decisions.

Based on your responses, what are your views on ethics? How do you think your ethical beliefs will influence your managerial behaviors?

INTRODUCTION

Mark Yang was excited about his summer internship for a technology security firm. He felt his previous internships and business education would allow him to contribute to the market research and product development efforts for one of the company's core products. Yang's initial excitement turned to concern after a conversation with his direct supervisor. His supervisor asked Yang to represent himself as a student working on a school research project when he conducted the market research. The supervisor believed that existing and potential customers would be more open to talk about their core concerns and issues if they were not speaking with a company representative. Yang felt deeply conflicted about the request. He really liked the company and wanted to do well so that he could secure a permanent position after graduation. As he thought about the situation, he believed that a case could be made to justify the company's request. He technically was a student, after all. As Yang continued to contemplate the issue, though, he grew increasingly uncomfortable about having to misrepresent himself. He did not know what to do.[1]

What, on the surface, may seem like a simple choice between right and wrong is not always so simple, especially when there are personal costs that one must pay. For instance, Yang believes that if he does not do what is asked, he will not get a permanent offer. Does this seemingly small misrepresentation warrant a loss of a career opportunity? From an outside perspective, it may seem very clear, but when you are in the midst of the situation, it can seem quite murky.

As a manager, you will face many ambiguous situations. Decisions will have no clear or correct answer; carefully laid plans will face unforeseen obstacles; and key relationships may come under severe pressure, causing conflict and division. You will undoubtedly have to rely on your personal values, beliefs, and **ethics** to navigate these difficult decisions. Although this may seem like a simple concept, the study of ethics is one of the most complex topics in business.[2] At its core, ethics is the study of moral standards and their effect on conduct and behavior. **Morality** is defined as the standards that people use to judge what is right or wrong, good or evil.

As a manager, you will face pressures from your boss, shareholders, customers, and subordinates to satisfy economic, legal, and ethical obligations. Rarely do these interests align. Competing priorities and performance pressures often cause managers to ignore their inner voice, especially when they fear retribution, embarrassment, or the loss of a promotion. For his part, Yang decided that he could not in good conscience misrepresent himself in the market research project. After raising his concerns to his manager, he was relieved by the response. The manager apologized for placing him in an uncomfortable position, and they worked together to define a mutually agreeable summer project.[3]

Ethical dilemmas can become even more complicated as managers operate on a global scale. The morals developed in one society often clash with those of another. For example, while bribery is forbidden in many countries, it is commonly accepted in other parts of the world. As a result, managers may sometimes have a point of view that is only relevant in one region of the world. Further, still many people know how to do the right thing but do not always do it. Why? In this chapter, we provide multiple perspectives about ethical decision making designed to help you better navigate morally gray or unclear situations.

When making ethical decisions, it is important to weigh the interests of all of the stakeholders of your organization.[4] Shareholders expect businesses to maximize profits. Employees expect businesses to provide a safe work environment and fair compensation. Customers expect businesses to be truthful and transparent about the quality of their products and services. And the public expects businesses to serve as "good citizens." Recall from Chapter 1 the discussion of how the purpose of business has transformed from a shareholder's perspective to a multiple stakeholders' perspective. Many organizations today are evaluated both domestically and globally on whether they are responsible corporate citizens. In 2013, 72% of S&P 500 companies published a corporate social responsibility (CSR) report, up from less than 20% in 2011.[5] Through CSR efforts, companies seek to pursue activities that benefit society in some meaningful way.

CSR can improve a company's brand, enabling them to charge more for their products, attract better employees, and ultimately improve their stock price.[6] As competition among businesses raises the standard of living and provides more opportunities to more people, two key components of many CSR initiatives—sustainability and energy efficiency—have become more important. It's not surprising that the words *energy efficiency* and *sustainability* have dominated political and corporate discussion in recent years. But CSR is not right for every organization. A company needs to carefully consider whether CSR is appropriate, cost-effective, and aligned with its overall strategy. Without this alignment, CSR efforts can be ineffective and costly.

In this chapter, we explore multiple theories of ethics and CSR that help companies and managers balance the demands of stakeholders and achieve economic

Ethics
The study of moral standards and their effect on behavior and conduct.

Morality
The standards that people use to judge what is right or wrong, good or evil.

results while maintaining high ethical and legal standards.[7] Learning to recognize ethical issues in a corporate setting is difficult, and implementing ethical decisions is even more difficult. But it's a skill that comes with experience and training.[8] Let's look at how Merck managed one of its ethical decisions under incredible stress and uncertainty.

Merck and River Blindness[9]

River blindness is a disease that afflicts nearly 25 million people in remote villages along the banks of rivers in tropical regions of Africa and Latin America.[10] The disease is caused by a tiny parasitic worm, which is passed from person to person through the bite of a black fly that breeds in river waters. The worms burrow under a person's skin and grow up to 2 ft. long, producing nodules that are half an inch to an inch in diameter. Within the nodules, the worms reproduce by releasing millions of offspring that wriggle their way throughout the body beneath the skin, discoloring it as they migrate. Victims experience such intense itching that some commit suicide. Eventually, the offspring invade the eyes and gradually blind the victims. Because other plots of land are not fertile enough to sustain the villages, most villagers must live along the rivers and accept the disease as an inescapable part of life.

The only drugs to treat the parasite in humans were very expensive, had severe side effects, and required lengthy hospital stays, all of which made treatment impractical for most victims. But in 1979, Dr. William Campbell, a research scientist at Merck, discovered that one of the company's best-selling animal drugs, ivermectin, might kill the parasite. Further analysis showed that ivermectin might provide a low-cost, safe, and simple cure for river blindness. Upon discovering the possibility, Campbell petitioned Merck's chairman, Dr. P. Roy Vagelos, to develop a human version of the drug. The decision was not easy. The cost of developing the drug would top $100 million, and even if it was successful, the victims were too poor to afford the drug and there was no way to easily distribute it in

these rural areas. In addition, there was a possibility that people would misuse the drugs, which would cause side effects and stimulate bad press for Merck.

Merck's managers were undecided about what to do. Healthcare costs were on the rise, Medicare and Medicaid reimbursements were limited, and Congress was getting ready to pass an act that made it easier for competitors to copy and market generic drugs.[11] While Merck faced worsening economic conditions and industry pressures, managers were reluctant to undertake an expensive product that showed little economic promise. Vagelos conducted several meetings with his management team, trying to make a decision about developing a human version of ivermectin. They eventually came to the conclusion that the human benefits of a drug for river blindness were too significant to ignore. Many managers believed, in fact, that the company was morally obligated to develop the drug despite the costs and slim chance of economic reward. Ultimately, Vagelos approved a budget that provided the funding needed to develop human ivermectin.

After 7 years of clinical testing and research, Merck succeeded in developing a human version of ivermectin—a single pill taken once a year would completely eradicate the parasite and prevent new infections. Unfortunately, Merck's initial fears came true. Nobody stepped forward to buy the drug, including the governments of affected regions, the U.S. government, or the World Health Organization (WHO). As a result, Merck decided to give the drug away for free to potential victims.[12] Merck then faced another roadblock: There were no effective distribution channels to get the drug to the people who needed it most. Working with the WHO, Merck also financed an international committee to provide the infrastructure to distribute the drug safely and prevent the drug from being sold on the black market. By 1996, millions of people received the drug, transforming their lives and relieving the intense suffering and potential blindness caused by the disease.

Asked why the company invested so much money in developing, manufacturing, and distributing a drug that made no money, Vagelos replied in an interview that once the company thought that one of its animal drugs might cure a severe human disease, the only ethical choice was to develop it. Moreover, he said that people would remember how Merck helped them.[13] He claimed that the company had learned how these actions have strategically important long-term advantages.

Case in Point   Merck and River Blindness

1. Why was Merck hesitant about developing a human version of ivermectin?
2. What were the benefits and cost of developing a human version of ivermectin?
3. Why did Dr. P. Roy Vagelos and his team ultimately decide to develop a human version of ivermectin?
4. How do you think Merck's investments in the human version of ivermectin create value for its stakeholders and corporate goodwill?

ETHICAL FRAMEWORKS

Should managers only consider the law, and not ethics, when making business decisions?[14] Many people share this attitude. Because the law is a set of enforceable rules that applies to everyone, many believe that the law should be applied to public life while ethics should be applied to private life. Some even believe that the law already embodies the ethics of business; therefore, there is no need to take extra steps to be ethical.[15]

The law, however, does not always result in the right approach. Consider the use of asbestos in the construction industry. Asbestos, during the 1950s, was used in building materials because of its strength, durability, and fire resistance. Although producers knew it could lead to devastating diseases, including cancer, they continued to use it. As a result, more than 100 million Americans were exposed to asbestos through construction or by living in buildings constructed with it.[16] While it was legal to use asbestos, it was clearly not ethical. In addition, ideas that are considered lawful may not necessarily be ethical.[17] For example, racial segregation was legal for nearly a century after the Civil War. While many claim that laws provide the moral backbone to businesses, in reality, they often simply reflect society's minimum standards.[18]

Investors expect businesses to maximize profits, while many customers expect businesses to demonstrate leadership in socially responsible initiatives such as reducing pollution and waste and promoting civil and human rights. To effectively manage these complex decisions, leaders must not only meet competing interests and responsibilities but also behave in ways that are aligned with their own values. Therefore, they need to have a strong moral compass.[19] A moral compass is a set of guiding principles that help an individual navigate complex ethical challenges. The compass is generally derived from a deep understanding of one's personal values. This understanding enables an individual to better find their "true north," when confronted with morally ambiguous situations. Yang most likely relied on his moral compass when he decided to confront the company on the summer internship. This section provides some insights on ethical principles and concepts, which should help managers develop their own moral compass so that they can more clearly see their way through ethical uncertainties.[20]

Utilitarianism

Thomas Jefferson wrote in the Declaration of Independence "that all men are created equal, that they are endowed by their Creator with certain unalienable Rights, that among these are Life, Liberty and the pursuit of Happiness." Here, Jefferson proclaims what he believes to be the proper ethical foundation of a nation. Life and liberty seem obvious, but of all possible things to define his ethical foundation, he also chose happiness. **Utilitarianism** undoubtedly had its influence on the founding fathers as well as numerous other nation builders. One of the most popular and widely used ethical frameworks, utilitarianism operates under the "greatest happiness principle" as the foundation to its ethical theory.

Utilitarianism is defined as the ethical philosophy claiming that behaviors are considered moral if they produce the greatest good, or utility, for the greatest number of people.[21] With this approach, people should use a cost–benefit analysis of all possible decisions and select the alternative that results in the greatest utility.[22] In business, managers should seek good outcomes for affected parties, be objective in identifying others' interests and the likely consequences of their actions, and be impartial when balancing others' interests with their own.[23] "Good" things are considered to be happiness, utility, and pleasure, while "bad" things are considered to be pain and displeasure. Actions are right if they promote happiness or the absence of pain and wrongdoing.[24]

Despite utilitarianism's strengths and widespread influence, it can fall short in some instances. For example, obeying the principle of the greatest good for the greatest number can lead to a tyranny of the majority and a failure to respect individuals such as minorities.[25] Can a company produce the greatest good for its shareholders *and* also the greatest good for its employees and the community? If not, which stakeholder represents the greatest good? In a multistakeholder world, it is often very difficult to make the right choice. Decisions often mean making trade-offs. Other frameworks can balance these shortcomings.

Kantianism

Kantianism is another dominant ethical model, but it differs from utilitarianism in a fundamental way. Rather than focusing purely on the positive and negative consequences of actions, Immanuel Kant believed that motives are critically important when judging moral action. In other words, people must make the right decisions for the right reasons.[26] For example, some corporations do the right thing only when it is profitable or when they expect to receive good publicity. By Kantian standards, these decisions are prudent, not moral.[27] But why does it matter whether intentions are good as long as the end result is moral? Kant argued that these actions do not build trust. If someone with bad or even neutral intentions produces a good outcome, can we trust that he or she will produce good outcomes in the future?[28] One leader who adopted this approach is Kazuo Inamori, founder of Kyocera, who explained his performance management process as follows:

> I graded the performance of the employees on four levels. The first level is the individual who achieved performance results with a challenging spirit and positive attitude. If someone does not achieve the performance results but tries with a positive attitude, they are considered the second level. If someone happens to enjoy a successful result without making a sincere or hard effort, just because of luck or something else, that is the third level. No positive effort and no results is the fourth level. We don't just look at results. We regard the process as a very important factor.[29]

Utilitarianism
The ethical philosophy claiming that behaviors are considered moral if they produce the greatest good, or utility, for the greatest number of people.

Kantianism
An ethical philosophy claiming that motives and universal rules are important aspects in judging what is right or wrong.

At Kyocera, employees were rewarded for their intent as well as their actions and results.

Think about the business leaders that you admire. What about them do you admire—the outcomes that they produced or the way they produced them? Many individuals admire Steve Jobs for his creativity, consumer insight, and design expertise. His ability to develop products that were elegant and functional has been well documented. He is often cited as the reason for Apple's phenomenal performance in satisfying consumer needs and shareholder interests. But, the way Jobs led the company has also been well documented. He was considered a temperamental and inflexible leader and some accounts suggest that he didn't always treat employees with respect and dignity. Is he a great business leader? Many would say yes—for them, the ends justify the means. For others, though, they harbor deep concerns about the way in which those results were produced. One framework that can be helpful in evaluating leaders assesses three components (1) the intent or objectives of the leader; (2) the means by which the leader sought to realize his or her intent to achieve his or her objectives; and (3) the outcomes that were actually produced from this effort (see Figure 3.1). For Kant, motives are extremely important.

Kant argued that people should be treated as ends and never purely as a means to an end. Doing so would be like treating humans as machines, denying them the respect they deserve.[30] According to Kant, respect for the human is not just necessary, but an obligation.[31] Organizations can benefit from having this attitude. At Southwest Airlines, for example, a key aspect of the company's mission is "respect for the individual." As a result, employees felt free to express themselves and became extremely loyal to the company. Following the 9/11 attacks, employees worked overtime without pay to save the company money, which enabled the airline to continue operations under severe economic uncertainty.[32]

Good motives are not the only criterion that makes a behavior moral from the Kantian perspective. Kant believed that universal laws or rules should also govern the way rational human beings behave. According to Kant, one fundamental law that should influence individual action is: "I ought never to act except in such a way that my maxim should become a universal law." In other words, people should envision their actions as if they became a universal rule. Only those actions that remain logical and good under universal conditions are considered moral.

Virtues and Character

While the previous ethical theories focus on being obligated to people and honoring fundamental rights, virtue ethicists do not believe this goes far enough. Many argue that a person who follows the rules of obligation is not as trustworthy as a person who exhibits strong moral character and integrity.[33] Scholars have defined character by (1) a person's ability to recognize the moral elements of a situation, (2) how well a person makes moral judgments, (3) how consistent a person's actions are with those judgments, and (4) how well a person can teach others to exhibit character.[34]

In business, some believe that people should rely on decisions made by virtuous individuals, those with good character, rather than focusing on rights and obligations.[35] An individual cannot solve a moral situation if he or she does not first recognize it as such.[36] For most of the twentieth century, many believed that the only good business virtues were profit and competitiveness. If managers let these virtues guide their decisions and behavior, organizations would be profitable and competition would be healthy. But these virtues often lead to managers such as Al Dunlap, chief executive officer (CEO) of Sunbeam, who earned the nickname "Chainsaw Al" for his propensity to fire people and shut down plants, even when they were marginally profitable. To him, stock price and profitability were the only worthy goals of business; as a result, many lost their jobs and livelihoods when it was unnecessary.[37]

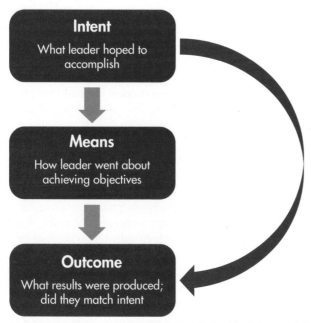

Intentions	Means	Outcomes
• *Purpose*: Financial Gain or Personal Advancement or Advancement of Society • *Vision*: Defined or Emergent • *Innovation*: Incremental or Breakthrough • *Goal*: Growth or Stability	• Clear Values or Flexible Pragmatism • Empowering or Exploiting People and Processes • Inclusive or Exclusive	• Transforming Society or Financial Success or Personal Wealth Accumulation (or some combination) • Unlikely or Inevitable (What is the starting position of the individual? What was his/her access to power and opportunity?) • Positive or Negative Unintended Consequences • Long-term or Short-term Horizon • Tangible vs. Intangible

Figure 3.1 ⟩ Intent, Means, and Outcome

Source: Anthony J. Mayo.

Descending from Aristotle and Plato, **virtue ethics** claims that morality's primary function is to develop virtuous character, similar to the way people develop skills such as creativity and conflict management.[38] The most seminal research on moral development was done by Lawrence Kohlberg who outlined six stages spread across three levels of moral development (see Table 3.1). Preconventional morality usually occurs earlier in life during childhood, but adults can also exhibit this moral reasoning. Conventional morality develops as people transition from highly dependent children to more independent adolescents, but this level of reasoning is also exhibited by many adults. The final level, postconventional morality, is exhibited by those with a higher awareness of moral values, who can understand where values

Virtue ethics
An ethical philosophy claiming that morality's primary function is to develop virtuous character.

Level	Stage	Description
Preconventional Morality	Obedience and Punishment	Usually common in children, who see rules as fixed or absolute. Obeying rules means avoiding punishment.
	Individualism and Exchange	Children account for individual points of view and judge actions based on how they serve individual needs.
Conventional Morality	Interpersonal Relationships	Focused on living up to social expectations and roles; there is an emphasis on conforming, being "nice," and considering how choices influence relationships.
	Maintaining Social Order	People begin to consider society as a whole as they focus on maintaining order by following the rules, doing their duty, and respecting authority.
Postconventional Morality	Social Contracts and Individual Rights	People begin to account for differing values, opinions, and beliefs of others. While laws are important for maintaining a society, members of society should agree on these standards.
	Universal Principles	Based on universal principles and abstract reasoning, people follow these internalized principles of justice even when they conflict with laws and rules.

Table 3.1 › Moral Development

Source: Adapted from Lawrence Kohlberg and Richard H. Hersh, "Moral Development: A Review of the Theory," *Theory Into Practice,* Vol. 16, No. 2, 1977.

come from and compare the values of different cultures. Some people never achieve this level of reasoning.

Utilitarianism, Kantianism, and virtue ethics can provide useful insight into ways in which an individual may think about and act upon moral issues. As we have seen, these philosophies can also inform the ways in which a business leader cultivates a certain culture in a firm. In addition to individual actions, leaders must also consider the overall moral obligations of their firm and the legal environment in which the firm operates.

Justice

Justice provides the framework for society to judge what is morally right or wrong, fair or unfair, and establishes ways to evaluate or punish those who behave immorally.[39] Justice is the notion that moral behaviors must be based on standards of equity, fairness, and impartiality to preserve order in society.[40]

Distributive justice deals with the distribution of wealth among members of a society. People who follow this line of thought are egalitarians, and they believe that individual differences are morally insignificant. For example, they support heavily progressive taxes for an equal distribution of wealth.[41] But what if more capable people could provide better services for others if they had more money? Wouldn't society benefit from this inequality? Think about the Gates Foundation, founded by billionaire Bill Gates, which contributes millions of dollars to education and social good. Is society better off because of Gates's accumulated wealth? Philosophers, politicians, and other leaders have continuously wrestled with questions about what is best for society.

According to the philosopher John Rawls, each person should be permitted the maximum amount of basic liberties (moral rights), but once this basic equality

Justice
An ethical philosophy that provides the framework for society to judge what is morally right or wrong, fair or unfair, and establishes ways to evaluate or punish those who behave in immoral ways.

Distributive justice
A subset of justice that deals with the distribution of wealth among members of a society.

The Leadership Development Journey

Leaders are responsible for creating an ethical climate in their organizations. This begins with the leader modeling ethical behavior, making fair decisions, and building a culture of trust. Also, leaders must take responsibility for disciplining employees who violate ethical standards and ensuring that employees not only focus on results but also focus on "doing the right thing" when making decisions. Leaders incorporate ethical practices and behaviors in the following areas.

- Recruiting and selecting employees
- Onboarding and training employees
- Instituting policies and codes
- Rewarding and punishing behavior
- Maintaining managerial accounting systems
- Supervising performance management systems
- Managing decision-making processes[45]

Think of a time when you observed a leader creating an ethical climate. How did this leader inspire and motivate ethical behavior? What were the support systems that reinforced this leader's ethical standard? What have you learned from this leader's ethical behavior? How will you apply these lessons learned to your leadership development journey?

is achieved, inequalities may exist between members if it will benefit everyone in society.[42] Because the inequalities of birth, family history, and natural endowment are undeserved, society should make these inequalities more equal and provide support for naturally disadvantaged people.[43] This balance of basic rights and wealth inequality is important for government and business. For example, in business, if two people have the same position in a company but one has more years of experience, that person should receive a bigger salary because he or she is conceivably more capable of performing the job well. In turn, that employee has more ability to improve the company's financial standing and consequently everyone else's financial standing. While this example may be simple, managers' decisions get more difficult when they weigh the pressures from multiple stakeholders.

Procedural justice is the notion that rules should be clearly stated, consistently obeyed, and impartially enforced. It provides the framework for societies to develop laws and procedures that result in fair or just outcomes.[44]

CONFRONTING MORAL DILEMMAS

Being a good person and having sound personal ethics may not be enough to deal with the ethical issues in business.[46] Ethical dilemmas are rarely as simple as knowing what is right or wrong. Many times managers must decide between two wrongs, such as which employee to fire during a restructuring process. Because managers must interpret company policy, enforce rules, hire, fire, discipline, and supervise employees, they perform a crucial role in organizations and serve as role models.[47]

It is also important to understand that, while most people are inherently good and have good intentions, there are situations where an individual may make immoral decisions. For example, as accountants develop an attachment to their clients, they can become less likely to report faulty information or even notice suspicious

Procedural justice
A subset of justice claiming that rules should be clearly stated, consistently obeyed, and impartially enforced.

behavior, making them more susceptible to the influence of bias.[48] Even more striking is the behavior of some doctors. Before 2002, liver transplants were prioritized to patients depending on how sick they were. Accordingly, anyone in an intensive care unit (ICU) was usually close to the top of the list. In an effort to help patients who needed a liver transplant but were not sick enough to be in an ICU, some doctors created fake ICU admissions. How do you evaluate the morality of the doctors who fabricated the ICU patients, especially when considering the Hippocratic Oath, which requires doctors to promise to fully serve their patients' health needs and to neither mistreat nor over treat their patients? Their intentions were well meaning, but their actions are questionable. Under this system, the patients with the most honest doctors, who didn't create fake ICU admissions, were less likely to get transplants.[49]

Fiduciary Responsibilities

One of the most important moral obligations in business is characterized by the fiduciary relationship. A fiduciary relationship exists when a party—an individual or a business—is entrusted with property, information, or power to make decisions on behalf of another party. In business, an investment adviser is a **fiduciary** for his or her client; members of a partnership are fiduciaries for one another; and corporate officers, directors, and executives are fiduciaries for the corporation and its shareholders.[50]

Fiduciary relationships carry a set of legal responsibilities that go beyond those of ordinary professional relationships. Those responsibilities include candor and disclosure, diligence and care, and loyalty and self-restraint. In regular relationships, each party is allowed to disclose as much or as little information as he or she likes. But in a fiduciary relationship, the fiduciary is obligated to be candid with his or her beneficiary and disclose all relevant information. Fiduciaries also have a duty of undivided loyalty, which means that they must not only protect and promote their beneficiary's interests but also avoid putting their own interests ahead of the beneficiary's.[51] Overall, the law requires fiduciaries to exert their best efforts on behalf of their beneficiaries and never personally benefit at their beneficiaries' expense.[52]

Common Moral Dilemmas Faced by Organizations

Fiduciary
A person who is entrusted with property, information, or power to act on behalf of a beneficiary.

Organizations and the managers who lead them face many moral dilemmas in their relationship with the environment, consumers, and employees. As the United States industrialized during the twentieth century, businesses made sweeping progress in all three categories. They not only became more environmentally responsible but also upheld a more honest relationship with their consumers and employees. Some of this progress was driven by companies themselves, but external advocacy groups such as Consumers Union also contributed. In addition, legislative actions such as consumer protection laws, food and drug testing, equal opportunity employment laws, and environmental protection legislation have forced companies to comply with new standards of performance.

As the economy transitions from the manufacturing age to the information age, management ethics must evolve. Moral reasoning now deals with the transmission of information. Information can be empowering, but it also can be used for control, power, and manipulation. For

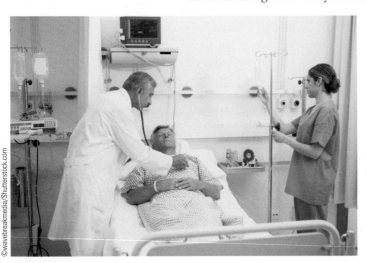
©wavebreakmedia/Shutterstock.com

example, companies now engage in personalized marketing to seek information about consumers and tailor the advertisements they view. While this can improve a consumer's experience, the information shared between companies can be very personal and may fall into the wrong hands. Identity theft is a major problem in the United States. In 2012, over 16 million Americans experienced some form of identity theft, and that number was projected to be close to 20 million in 2014.[53] When someone steals an identity, he or she uses personal information such as Social Security numbers, names, and credit card information to commit fraud or other crimes. Consequences for the victims can become serious as they spend thousands of dollars and several days to restore their good name and credit.[54] One organization that has been a recent target of identity theft is the Internal Revenue Service (IRS). Criminals have been able to break into the IRS computers to hijack the identities of taxpayers, and use these identities to receive fraudulent tax returns. For instance, Rashia Wilson secured enough false refunds to purchase a $92,000 Audi. She was so excited about her success in securing false refunds that she posted pictures of herself with stacks of money on her Facebook account and declared that she was the "queen of IRS tax fraud." While that picture was used in a successful trial against Wilson, there are so many other criminals who are not prosecuted. During the first half of 2013, over 1.6 million taxpayers were affected by identity theft.[55]

Environmental Dilemmas

As one of the most discussed topics in business ethics, pollution has been at the heart of public debate for many years. With increasing focus on long-term sustainability and global warming on the national stage, pollution will likely remain there for years to come. The overarching question for managers is this: What obligations do businesses have to future generations to preserve the environment?[56] As industrialization expanded throughout the nineteenth and twentieth centuries, the social costs of air pollution increased exponentially. As a result, many industries have been negatively affected, including agriculture and timber. In areas with high concentrations of sulfur oxides in the air, acid rain can have devastating effects on the local ecology. More significant and lasting consequences include long-term health concerns for the general public and the greenhouse gas effect on the world's climate and weather.[57]

Water pollution is another problem that has challenged business and society. Pollutants such as salts, metals, and biological material can impair aquatic life and threaten humans' well-being.[58] For example, the British Petroleum (BP) oil spill in 2010 leaked millions of gallons of oil into the Gulf of Mexico, threatening much of the wildlife and ultimately endangering the entire coast's economy. When designing the oil rig and its safety systems, BP engineers knew that an explosion was possible if they drilled an oil reserve with abnormal pressure. Hours before the crisis, unusually high-pressure readings warned managers that they should alter their drilling. But a decision was made to continue working. Later, a report on the incident revealed several concerns with BP's safety mechanisms and maintenance history leading up to the disaster.[59] Managers must determine the balance between their ethical obligations to the environment and the costs incurred by their business.

Beyond pollution, environmental dilemmas are apparent in the increasing depletion of natural resources. While the depletion may not impact the current generation, there will be consequences for future generations. As companies make decisions about the utilization of natural resources, they often have to weigh short-term efficiency and profitability against long-term environmental sustainability. In many cases, companies and managers make choices that favor the short term.[60] This short-term thinking can result in disastrous consequences for future generations.

Privacy Dilemmas

Privacy is one of the trickier ethical issues; it impacts consumers and employees. While it is not protected in the Bill of Rights, people feel passionately about their right to privacy, defined as a person's right to determine the type and extent of information that is disclosed about him or her.[61] In recent years, companies such as Google and Facebook have pushed the limits on what people are comfortable with sharing, and these companies have come under criticism for their loose policies. The Consumer Reports organization recently conducted a review of Facebook's privacy policies and uncovered some disturbing information. For instance, Facebook receives a report every time an individual visits a Web site with a Facebook "Like" button regardless of whether or not the individual clicked the button or is even a Facebook member. In addition, even if a Facebook user restricts his or her information to friends only, those same friends, who use certain Facebook apps, can inadvertently transfer information about their friends and contacts to third parties without anyone knowing.[62]

In a business environment, it is nearly impossible for managers to avoid such intrusion, especially because they are responsible for monitoring their subordinates' work. Although it is acceptable to learn about a subordinate's skills and career aspirations to improve group performance, some overly intrusive practices include listening to phone conversations, installing hidden cameras, or using monitoring systems that can track time spent on the phone or the number of strokes keyed on a computer.[63]

The key for managers is to strike the right balance between respecting privacy and learning about their subordinates. To do this, managers should follow three simple rules about the information they seek from subordinates: information should be directly relevant to the issue at hand; employees must have the opportunity to give consent; and the methods of learning information should be ordinary and reasonable. For example, investigating an employee's political beliefs and using devices such as hidden cameras, hidden microphones, and lie detector tests are invasions of privacy. However, as employees move higher in the organization, they are required to represent their company more publicly. As a result, more private activities may become relevant. For example, a vice president's drinking problem may affect his or her ability to represent the firm professionally.[64]

The Role of the Individual in Confronting Moral Dilemmas

While companies can develop policies and make statements about how they address (or should address) difficult environmental, consumer, and employee dilemmas, the actual decisions are made by individuals. Most people make the right decisions when confronted with common ethical challenges, though there are certain cases when a few individuals can go astray. These can be gray areas where there is limited information and lots of ambiguity, but these can also be clear-cut situations when an individual decides to follow a more precarious and potentially illegal path. Individuals often rationalize the decisions that they make using one of three common arguments including the following:

1. *Everyone is already doing it. What difference does it make if I go along as well?* In essence, this argument tries to make the case that the questionable action is already standard practice in the organization, and in some cases, it might be what is expected of individuals.
2. *The impact of this action is not that big of a deal. It is so small that it is immaterial and won't really hurt anyone.* This argument can be a slippery slope. If one makes decisions based on this argument for small items, it can easily lead to larger and more complex issues.
3. *I am just doing what I have been told.* This argument deflects the accountability and blame to other parties, thus absolving the individual from any responsibility.[65]

Privacy
A person's right to determine the type and extent of information that is disclosed about him or her.

While these arguments may make the individual feel better about his or her decision in the moment, they are quite dangerous and can easily lead one to make poor judgment calls with more severe issues. Some of these more severe ethical dilemmas involve conflicts of interest, insider trading, trade secrets, and bribery. Misguided incentives often play a role in leading individuals astray.

Conflicts of Interest

When employees or managers engage in activities on behalf of the company and have a personal interest in the outcome of those activities, they are engaging in a **conflict of interest**. It is a particular problem when their own interests oppose the company's interests or their judgment is biased against their duty to the company.[66] For example, if a manager's daughter-in-law is a salesperson for a firm that manufactures tools that the company needs, the manager may be motivated to give her company business instead of a more trusted and/or less-expensive source.[67] Other examples include situations where people exercise biased judgment, engage in direct competition with their employer, misuse their power, and violate confidentiality.[68]

Insider Trading

Leaders often have access to proprietary information such as earnings forecasts, research experiments, or potential lawsuits. It can be very tempting to use this inside information for personal gain. If a manager uses inside information to bet for or against a company's stock before that information is publicly available, he or she is engaging in the illegal practice of **insider trading**. Unfortunately, the allure of a quick financial win can cloud one's judgment. In 2002, Steve Madden, founder of the women's shoe line, admitted to helping penny stock firms manipulate more than 20 initial public offerings, resulting in losses to investors that approached $100 million. As a result, Madden was sentenced to 41 months in prison and had to pay more than $4 million in fines and restitution.[69]

Recently, SAC Capital agreed to a $1.2 billion fine to settle insider trading charges brought against them by the U.S. government. Though the firm's principal, Steve Cohen, has avoided prosecution, eight of his former employees have been charged, and the firm has become a mere shadow of its former self. The most significant charges against the former employees involved the trading of stock from Dell and two drug companies, Elan and Wyeth. One trader gained access to information about Dell's third quarter financial performance in 2008 before it was publicly available. The trader used this information to sell SAC's holdings in Dell and to bet against the stock before the earnings announcement was made public. This inside information allowed SAC to reap an enormous profit while avoiding a loss in holding onto Dell stock. The trader who used this inside information was sentenced to a 3-year prison term. Similarly, another trader used inside information he had learned about the potential underperformance of two Alzheimer drugs produced by Elan and Wyeth before it was publicly available to bet against the companies. By doing so, SAC avoided losses and yielded profits of $275 million, and the trader received a $9 million bonus. The trader who orchestrated this deal was eventually sentenced to 9 years in prison and was forced to repay his bonus.[70]

Trade Secrets

Some of the most important assets of a company are its trade secrets. A **trade secret** is any type of information used in conducting business that is not commonly known by others. Trade secrets are especially valuable in research and development (R&D), as they often provide strategic advantage for a company over its competitors.[71] For example, Google's search algorithm is a heavily guarded trade secret. Trade secrets, along with patents, copyrights, and trademarks, are considered intellectual property

Conflict of interest
Conflicts that occur when employees or managers engage in activities on behalf of the company and have a personal interest in the outcome of those activities.

Insider trading
Insider trading occurs when a manager uses inside information to bet for or against a company's stock before that information is publicly available.

Trade secret
Any type of information used in conducting business that is not commonly known by others. It often provides a strategic advantage for a company over its competitors.

Owen Hoffmann/PatrickMcMullan.com/Sipa USA/Newscom

(IP) by law, which means that they are treated the same as tangible property. The owner has a right to sell, license, or assign ownership of a trade secret to others.[72] The owner of the IP is generally the company itself, not an individual employee. As such, individual employees should not reveal trade secrets without the express consent of the company. Doing so could result in legal action as well as undermine the competitive strength of the company.

The pharmaceutical industry, in particular, relies heavily on IP law to protect its intellectual assets and to secure financial longevity. Due to years of R&D, regulation by the Food and Drug Administration, and clinical trials, pharmaceutical companies incur costs that are higher than those of almost any other industry. As a result, they go to extra lengths to ensure that laws protect IP. They not only lobby for longer patent protection domestically but also ask the U.S. government to protect their IP abroad by reducing pharmaceutical fraud in countries that have more lax IP laws.[73]

Bribery

Bribery is defined as offering something valuable to a party as an incentive to act on his or her behalf, often to an unfair advantage. Bribery is fundamentally about creating a breach of trust. While the oldest forms of bribery involved public officials, today it also manifests itself in private organizations.[74] The problems caused by bribery are numerous. Organizations can suffer negative economic consequences such as the diversion of resources to inefficient uses, higher costs of doing business, and loss of investor confidence.[75] In 2011, U.S. regulators accused IBM of a decade-long campaign of bribery in Asia, claiming that more than 100 employees handed over shopping bags of money to government officials in exchange for millions of dollars in contracts. To avoid litigation, IBM agreed to pay a $10 million settlement.[76] At the governmental level, bribery undermines economic development because it decreases efficiency, breeds cynicism, and distorts international competition.[77]

Because the negative consequences of bribery are so high, most countries condemn bribery and have adopted laws to prohibit it among public officials.[78] There are even international laws against it. Despite the domestic and international efforts, bribery remains a pervasive problem worldwide. In many cases, the financial penalties are not very severe. Consider IBM's case. The $10 million the company paid to avoid litigation represented only 0.06% of the company's net income in 2011. How does that compare to the additional business that IBM may have secured from the alleged bribery? In some cases, firms even conduct a cost–benefit analysis to determine the potential upsides and downsides of engaging in bribery.

PixelPro / Alamy

Transparency International, a nongovernmental agency that combats corruption, publishes a "Corruption Perceptions Index." According to the 2014 report, nearly 70% of 175 countries worldwide scored below a 50 (out of a best possible clean 100), signaling a high problem with corruption (see Table 3.2).[79] Many of these countries host multinational corporations, and many U.S. managers must deal with local organizations to secure resources and sell goods. If you were a manager faced with intense pressure to meet financial goals, would you offer a bribe to secure a distribution channel? What if you were competing for a promotion and knew your colleagues would offer a bribe to get ahead of you?

Whistle-Blowing

While employees have a moral obligation to stakeholders, they also have a duty to the business. In fact, their main duty is to work toward the goals of the firm and avoid activities that might harm those goals.[80] But employees may at times egregiously violate moral standards, and

Top 10 Country (score)	Bottom 10 Country (score)
Denmark (92)	Somalia (8)
New Zealand (91)	North Korea (8)
Finland (89)	Sudan (11)
Sweden (87)	Afghanistan (12)
Norway (86)	South Sudan (15)
Switzerland (86)	Iraq (16)
Singapore (84)	Turkmenistan (17)
Netherlands (83)	Uzbekistan (18)
Luxembourg (82)	Libya (18)
Canada (81)	Eritrea (18)
No. 17 - United States (74)	

Table 3.2 2014 Transparency International Corruption Index Top 10 and Bottom 10 Country Rankings

Source: Transparency International 2014 Index available at http://www.transparency.org/cpi2014/results, accessed February 14, 2015.

others may need to step in and blow the whistle. **Whistle-blowing** is the release of evidence by a member of an organization that proves illegal or immoral conduct to executives in a company or regulating agencies outside a company.[81]

In 2002, *Time* magazine named three women, Sherron Watkins, Coleen Rowley, and Cynthia Cooper, as their persons of the year for blowing the whistle on their respective organizations. A vice president at Enron, Watkins, warned the Chairman of Enron, Ken Lay, that the company was using improper accounting methods to inflate the value of its assets and earnings. Rowley, a staff attorney at the FBI, wrote a memo to the Director, Robert Mueller, about how the bureau failed to act on information from the Minneapolis field office about Zacarias Moussaoui, who was later indicted as a co-conspirator in the September 11, 2001 terrorist attacks. Finally, Cooper informed the board of WorldCom that the company had covered up $3.8 billion in losses through phony bookkeeping. All three were reluctant whistle blowers, and their names only became public through leaked memos at their organizations.[82]

More recently, Sherry Hunt, a vice president and chief underwriter at CitiMortgage, spoke up about the bank's mortgage fraud. Like many banks, Citi-Mortgage got caught up in the freewheeling mortgage lending that contributed to the global financial crisis. To sustain growth, some members of the bank's underwriting department approved mortgages based on fabricated information including inflating an applicant's annual income. After being unsuccessful in getting the attention of senior executives in the firm, Hunt reached out to the U.S. Department of Justice.[83]

Although whistle-blowers are acting ethically, they usually pay a high price for their acts of dissent. They can be blacklisted, fired, threatened, and treated unfairly, and they often endure financial hardship. For instance, Hunt was threatened by two senior executives who demanded that she retract her memo about the fraud and that she change the results of her quality control reports.[84] In addition, those who have blown the whistle have difficulty finding other jobs because they are seen as disloyal.[85] What is interesting to note is that regardless of the consequences, many whistle-blowers said that they couldn't live with themselves if they did nothing and would do the same if given the choice.[86]

Whistle-blowing
The release of evidence by a member of an organization that proves illegal or immoral conduct to executives in a company or regulating agencies outside a company.

CORPORATE SOCIAL RESPONSIBILITY

Today there is increasing pressure on business organizations to fulfill broader goals, those that go beyond financial performance.[87] While some managers face pressure from external organizations such as Human Rights Watch, the Animal Defense League, and the Environmental Protection Agency, they also feel pressure from their own employees to engage in CSR activities.[88] Over the years, corporations have responded. Between 2011 and 2013, the *Fortune* Global 500 spent almost $20 billion on CSR. Three companies, Oracle, AstraZeneca, and Halliburton, contributed over $1 billion each to CSR activities.[89]

CSR was first described in 1953 as business's obligation to pursue the policies, decisions, and actions that align with the objectives and values of society.[90] The basic assumption behind CSR is that business and society are intimately interwoven: Businesses rely on consumers to buy their products, and consumers rely on businesses to provide goods that will sustain their well-being.[91] Like the government, business has a social contract with the public—an implied set of rights and obligations. While the specifics of the contract may change as society changes, the contract remains as a source of legitimacy for business.[92] In other words, if a company does not hold up its end of the bargain, society can take action against the firm. For example, consumers can choose not to purchase goods from a company they dislike, and talented employees can leave a company they do not respect.

Economic, Legal, and Ethical Responsibilities

Theorists have identified three core domains in which businesses have a responsibility: economic, legal, and ethical. Many believe that if businesses promote each of these domains, they will achieve a fair distribution of wealth to their stakeholders. While these three seem separate and unique, overlap is possible and business activities can support one, two, or all three domains (see Figure 3.2).[93]

Economic responsibilities refer to a business's duty to make a profit and increase shareholder value. Business institutions are the basic economic units in society; therefore, they have a duty to produce goods and services that people want and to sell them at a profit. Most aspects of business are built on this fundamental assumption.[94] Companies engage in a variety of activities to increase profits, both directly and indirectly. Direct activities can include decreasing production costs

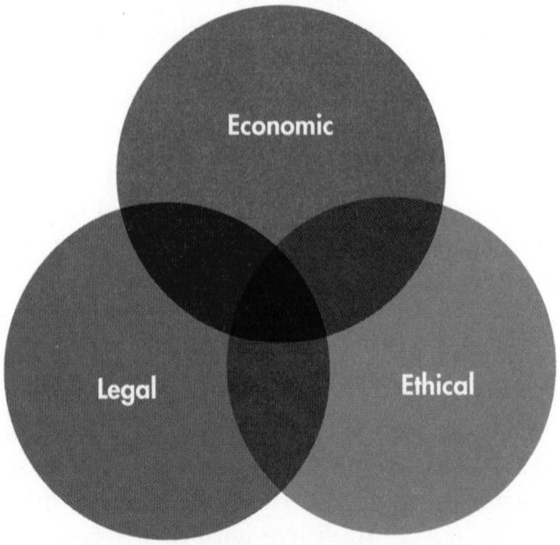

CSR
A business's obligation to pursue policies, decisions, and actions that align with the objectives and values of society.

Economic responsibilities
A business's duty to make a profit and increase shareholder value.

Figure 3.2 ⟩ Core Responsibilities of Business in Society

and improving efficiency. Indirect actions refer to the intangible things that, over time, improve economic performance (for instance, improving employee morale, increasing brand awareness among consumers, and fostering strong leadership throughout an organization).[95]

The **legal responsibilities** to society are to obey the state and federal laws pertaining to business activity. Just as society allows business to assume the role of producer, it also lays down the boundaries in which a business must operate. There are several ways in which a company can maintain this responsibility. The most common are complying with laws, anticipating future laws, and avoiding civil litigation.[96] For example, Toyota avoided heavy lawsuit costs by voluntarily recalling more than five million cars worldwide when it was reported that accelerators would stick to the floor of the car.[97] Generally, laws serve as the minimum standard that businesses should hold (see Figure 3.3). Recent scandals have forced lawmakers to raise the bar on business standards, evidenced by the Sarbanes-Oxley Act of 2002. In response to Enron's accounting fraud, Congress passed this law to prohibit officers, directors, and others from influencing their financial auditors or altering financial statements. It also illegalized the destruction of any documents used to obstruct a federal investigation.[98] Again, in the aftermath of the global crisis of 2008, Congress passed a law in 2009 to increase the government's ability to regulate financial markets, reflecting a renewed distrust in the American corporation. The law created a new council to detect risks in the financial system, created a new powerful regulator to protect consumers of financial products, and called for regulation of complex trading instruments called derivatives.[99]

Beyond the economic and legal responsibilities, businesses have **ethical responsibilities** to society. These can be defined as the expected behaviors of the general population. Although ethical responsibilities are difficult to define, managers can use the ethical frameworks discussed earlier in this chapter to understand how to make ethical decisions based on their stakeholders' expectations. For example, it is no longer good enough just to practice fair hiring and provide a safe work environment. Today's ethical climate calls for businesses to address issues of sustainability and pollution. Ritz Camera, a leading retail camera and photo company, recently launched its "Call2Recycle" campaign. As part of this initiative, Ritz offers its customers a free and easy way to properly dispose of their used rechargeable batteries. This program is based on the idea that recycling improves sustainability and reduces waste.[100]

Legal responsibilities
A business's duty to pursue its economic responsibilities within the boundaries of the law.

Ethical responsibilities
A business's duty to meet the expectations of society beyond its economic and legal responsibilities.

Figure 3.3 ⟩ Duties of Corporate Social Responsibility

Source: Adapted from Archie B. Carroll, "The Pyramid of Corporate Social Responsibility: Toward the Moral Management of Organizational Stakeholders," *Business Horizons*, 1991, pp. 39–48.

Corporate social responsiveness
The practice of businesses responding to pressure from society to engage in socially responsible ways.

Corporate Social Responsiveness

Many researchers have looked beyond the scope of the economic, legal, and ethical framework for ways that companies can practice CSR. One of the main questions these researchers explore deals with accountability. How do businesses create programs and policies to produce good outcomes for society? **Corporate social responsiveness** refers to how businesses should respond when society pressures them to do more.[102] When BP caused the 2010 oil crisis in the Gulf of Mexico, it responded to public criticism by setting up a relief fund worth $20 billion to compensate those affected by the spill.[103] When responding to these pressures, managers have numerous tools at their disposal. They can react, accommodate, defend, lead, use public relations, use law, bargain, or problem-solve. Responsive firms are characterized by three behaviors: (1) they monitor and assess environmental conditions on a constant basis, (2) they seek to identify the needs of their stakeholders, and (3) they design plans and policies to respond to the changing conditions.[104] In the next section, we show how these responsive CSR behaviors can be incorporated into a firm's strategy and become a potential source for competitive advantage.

IS CORPORATE SOCIAL RESPONSIBILITY GOOD FOR BUSINESS?

Some observers believe that CSR not only detracts from financial performance but also undermines the purpose of business in a capitalistic society. None were more vocal about this perspective than Milton Friedman, who in 1970 claimed that "the only social responsibility of business is to increase its profits." He believed that, while social welfare is important, it should be left to the government. The best thing businesses can do is maximize their profit within the limits of the law. Anything else would undermine society, moving it from capitalism to socialism.[105]

Dozens of research studies have supported Friedman's view, showing that CSR activity negatively affects economic performance. Using numerous financial indicators such as profit, return on investment, or stock price and CSR indices to reflect CSR activity, these researchers argue that higher CSR activity causes lower financial performance in the future.[106] They reason that CSR involves definite costs that fall on the bottom line, but only uncertain gains that may never reach the bottom line.[107] More recently, other studies have refuted these claims, finding a positive or neutral effect on financial performance with similar criteria.[108] These researchers argue that CSR should be viewed as an investment that will lead to improved efficiency, innovation, and long-term financial success.[109]

One individual who has tried to reconcile corporate philanthropy and financial performance is Tony Hsieh, founder of the online shoe retailer, Zappos. In 2011, Hsieh committed to investing $350 million to revitalize the neglected and abandoned downtown area of Las Vegas. He moved Zappos' offices from the suburbs of Las Vegas into the old City Hall, and bought 60 acres and 100 buildings in the downtown area. Over the next few years, he invested in new local businesses and built new apartment complexes. He personally relocated to one of the new apartments and convinced many other employees to leave their gated communities for the downtown Las Vegas district. In addition, Hsieh has funded a number of start-up tech firms that are also located in the downtown area. These firms' employees, in turn, need local restaurants, grocery stores, and entertainment venues all of which contribute to the creation of a vibrant, renewed city center. Hsieh believes that these investments will result in a significant financial return as well as what he calls a "return on the community."[110]

Though not universally accepted, a positive link between CSR and profit has become more commonly acknowledged, which has significantly strengthened its business case.[111] Consumers are a major source for this phenomenon: they not only have a favorable attitude toward companies engaging in CSR but also make purchasing decisions based on CSR activity.[112] For instance, a recent Nielsen survey found that 55% of global online consumers are willing to pay more for products and services from companies that are socially and environmentally responsible.[113] Other benefits for companies come in the form of making tax deductions, attracting talented employees, avoiding litigation, and saving costs.[114] For example, firms such as Arco and Procter & Gamble generally credit part of their profits and reputation to proenvironment corporate behavior.[115]

CSR as a Competitive Advantage

While a healthy society needs successful businesses, successful businesses need a healthy society to sustain increasing demand.[116] Practicing CSR can be a source of opportunity, innovation, and competitive advantage. It can be an investment in the company's future.[117] As a result, companies must treat CSR the same way they treat their strategy—they must plan, implement, and evaluate CSR goals.[118] In 2010, Ron Shaich, founder of Panera Bread, reevaluated his firm's philanthropic activities. Even though the company was giving more than $100 million a year in cash and products to various communities, Shaich felt that the efforts were too diffused and disconnected. After learning about a "pay-what-you-can" café in Denver, Shaich decided to start Panera Cares, a full-scale Panera bakery-café. Panera Cares is essentially identical to the traditional Panera establishment except that they are based in communities that are economically troubled where individuals who need a meal can gain access to one. With no listed prices and no cash registers, Panera Cares operates on a donation basis, asking patrons to pay what they can. To be self-sustaining, the company has been careful to choose locations that offer access to a diversity of customers, some who can make larger donations than others.[119] As of 2014, the company served over 1 million people each year at their Panera Cares locations, and the company brought in about 75% of what they would have earned with a traditional outlet.[120]

Supporting Core Business Activities

CSR is strategic when it supports core business activities that contribute to a firm's mission, vision, and strategy.[121] One of the most important areas is the labor force. Attracting and retaining employees who are skilled, creative, and driven is essential for satisfying customers and differentiating a company from its competitors.[122] Previously, firms succeeded by emphasizing process technology, access to financial markets, patents, and industry attractiveness. While these sources of competitive advantage are still important, recruitment of top candidates is becoming even more important.[123] In an effort to be the "nation's first zero-landfill car factory," Subaru of Indiana Automotive launched an employee incentive program whereby workers, who make suggestions for reducing packaging and identifying process reductions in the assembly line, are eligible for bonuses including a new Subaru Legacy. The program has resulted in significant cost savings that are reinvested in the business while also increasing the profile of the company as an attractive and sought-after employer.[124]

Marc Benioff, founder of Salesforce.com, a technology that enables companies to keep track of their

ZUMA Press, Inc. / Alamy

customers, has embraced CSR as a strategic initiative since he founded the company in 1999. At the time, he introduced the 1-1-1 model of corporate philanthropy whereby the company would send 1% of its stock, products, and employees' work hours to the company foundation. The company foundation supports a number of civic initiatives, including healthcare, education, and affordable housing around San Francisco where Salesforce is headquartered. Benioff believes that his company is a much more attractive place of employment based on their CSR approach, which is a distinct competitive advantage in an environment (Silicon Valley) that needs lots of technological talent. The influx of technological talent and the growth of the tech sector in San Francisco have resulted in a decline in affordable housing and the gentrification of many parts of the city. Benioff realizes that his company has contributed to this situation, and he wants to be a part of the solution. To that end, he has been active in convincing other technology companies in the area to increase their civic mindedness and to make investments in new affordable housing as well as other programs.[125]

Research shows that companies with higher CSR activity, like Salesforce.com, are seen as more attractive places to work, which means that talented employees are more willing to pursue these employers and are more willing to stay with them over time.[126] By attracting a higher-quality workforce, firms can develop a competitive advantage. Employees participating in CSR activities tend to have a better self-image, which in turn improves their morale and increases company profitability.[127] For example, Home Depot allows its employees to take company time to participate in volunteer organizations around the community. By doing so, employees are happier and often acquire new skills that help them in their jobs.[128]

Beyond human relations, companies can use CSR to improve the quality of the business environment in which they operate. By investing in education, pollution reduction, and economic development in emerging markets, for instance, companies can improve their productivity and generate new business opportunities while promoting social welfare. For example, Cisco created an educational program called the Cisco Networking Academy to train computer network administrators. This program not only provided attractive job opportunities for high school graduates but also secured long-term growth opportunities by educating net administrators who would later need Cisco's products to perform their job. In another case, Exxon-Mobil has devoted substantial resources to improving basic infrastructure such as roads and the rule of law in the developing countries where they operate. By doing so, the company is improving both its business operations and consumer demand in developing regions of the world.[129]

Creating a Strategic CSR Platform

CSR can be difficult to implement, especially when a company is engaging in CSR activities for the first time. Companies should strive to engage in **strategic CSR**, where they identify CSR initiatives that are directly related to their business activities so that they can combine social welfare with financial welfare. The following four-step process is a useful tool for managers engaged in this effort (see Figure 3.4).

First, companies should identify the inside-out linkages as well as the outside-in linkages. The inside-out linkages consist of all of the activities in a firm's value chain that impact society, including the firm's hiring and layoff policies, greenhouse gas emissions, and supply chain practices.[130] Outside-in linkages consist of social dimensions that can affect a firm's ability to improve productivity and execute strategy. Examples include industry regulations, access to natural resources, availability of human resources, and competitive rivalry.

When a company is choosing what social issues to address, the essential guideline for CSR is not whether a cause is worthy, but whether there is an opportunity to generate a benefit for society while also benefiting the business. Companies should refrain from supporting generic issues, which have no connection to a business's

Strategic CSR
Corporate social responsibility activities that are directly related to business activities so that they can combine social welfare with financial welfare.

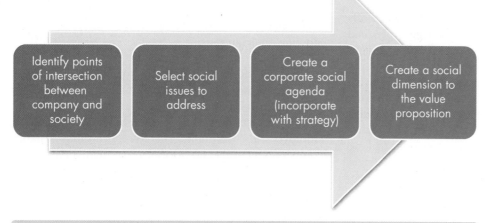

Figure 3.4 Four-Step Process to Implementing CSR

activity. Instead, they should support issues that are directly related to their value chain or they should support issues that can change the competitive context of their business. For example, supporting a local dance company is a generic issue for a utilities company such as Southern California Edison, but that same dance company may influence the competitive context for a company such as American Express, which depends on high-end entertainment and tourism for business.[131]

After choosing specific issues, companies should create a corporate social agenda that supports both inside-out and outside-in dimensions. Whole Foods' business model is built around the notion that people will pay a premium for food that is healthy, tasty, and environmentally friendly. Whole Foods uses its buying power to change modern factory farming so that animals are treated humanely before slaughter. The company also owns and operates its own seafood processing plants to ensure that its sourcing tactics do not affect other marine life. In January 2006, the company also made the largest-ever purchase of renewable energy credits from wind farms, which was enough to cover all of the company's electric energy consumption.[132]

Finally, companies should use their social agenda to add a social dimension to their value proposition, which is the unique set of needs a firm can meet for its customers. By adding a social dimension to this value proposition, a firm can show that making a social impact is integral to the overall strategy. For example, Whole Foods's value proposition is to sell organic, natural, and healthy food to customers who are passionate about food and care about the environment. This emphasis has enabled the company to command premium prices for its products.[133] Not all companies can benefit in the same way as Whole Foods, where customers are willing to pay extra for the firm's CSR activity. As a company considers its various strategic alternatives, one potential avenue can be CSR, but it should be evaluated in light of the industry context and competitive landscape.

SUMMARY

Ethics is the study of what is right or wrong, moral or immoral. However, many business decisions are not simple choices between right and wrong. Conflicting interests, ambiguous data, and differing personal and cultural perspectives contribute to the complexity of managerial decision making. Managers often need to navigate these unclear situations. An ethical framework can help a manager in many of these cases.

....
LO1 These ethical frameworks can provide guidance when the interests of a company conflict with the interests of society. How does a manager decide what trade-offs are most important and relevant? A manager's personal moral philosophy and understanding of what is right and wrong often play an important role in confronting ethical dilemmas. Some individuals, who take a utilitarian approach, believe that morality is derived from making decisions that produce the greatest good for the greatest number of people. Other individuals believe that morality is derived by motives and moral obligations; they believe that individuals must make the right decisions for the right reasons. Still others base moral decisions on their conception of justice.

....
LO2 Organizations have long been confronted by common moral dilemmas in their relationship to the environment, consumers, and employees. As the business landscape evolves, organizations will need to constantly reassess their relationship to these constituents to ensure that they are properly addressing them. Ultimately, individuals make decisions, and some of the difficult dilemmas faced by individuals involve conflicts of interests, insider trading, trade secrets, and bribery. When businesses or individuals fail to navigate these dilemmas in an appropriate and ethical way, they can be susceptible to whistle-blowing, then lawsuits.

....
LO3 CSR is an application of ethics in business whereby businesses are expected to engage in socially responsible behavior. A firm has economic, legal, and ethical responsibilities to shareholders, customers, employees, and the public. Therefore, firms must balance competing interests and priorities to remain competitive. This is part of the stakeholder view of management.

....
LO4 The link between CSR and financial performance of a firm is not always clear. What is clear is that CSR should not be pursued in a vacuum. CSR can be a competitive advantage if it is linked with the firm's strategy and business activities. Being socially responsible in a strategic sense allows firms to apply considerable resources, expertise, and insight to activities that benefit society and that have economic impact.

KEY TERMS

Conflict of interest
Corporate social responsibility (CSR)
Corporate social responsiveness
Distributive justice
Economic responsibilities
Ethical responsibilities
Ethics

Fiduciary
Insider trading
Justice
Kantianism
Legal responsibilities
Morality
Privacy

Procedural justice
Strategic CSR
Trade secret
Utilitarianism
Virtue ethics
Whistle-blowing

ASSIGNMENTS

Discussion Topics

1. Think about your personal values and beliefs. Where did your values come from? What or who shaped your perspectives on business and leadership?

2. Compare and contrast utilitarianism and Kantianism. How are these ethical frameworks similar and different? Which one is more aligned with your personal values? Why?

3. Do businesses have a moral obligation to the development of society? Is the moral obligation the same or different in emerging markets?

4. Review the stages of moral development in Table 3.1. How might each stage influence the way an individual leads?

5. What incentives or situations might cause someone to struggle with conflicts of interests or trade secrets? How can a company ensure that its employees do the right thing?

6. What motivates a student to cheat in class or to plagiarize a paper?

7. Why do whistle-blowers pay a high personal price for their actions?

8. How should a business evaluate its obligations to the environment?

9. Why should a firm pursue CSR? What are the right and wrong reasons for pursuing CSR?

10. Consider the economic, legal, and ethical responsibilities of a business. Which one is most important? Least important?

Management Research

1. Think of a film that portrays business managers and focuses on an ethical dilemma. What was the ethical issue in this film? What was management's role in creating the ethical issue? Did stakeholders pressure management to resolve the ethical issue?

2. The Ethisphere Institute composes an annual list of the World's Most Ethical Companies. In some years, more than 3,000 companies were nominated or self-nominated. The Ethisphere Institute uses a rating system called the Ethics Quotient. This rating system evaluates each nominee's codes of ethics, litigation and regulatory infraction histories, investment in sustainable business practices, and corporate citizenship practices. The evaluation system also takes into account feedback from the nominee's industry peers, suppliers, and customers. Research a company that has been included in the list of the World's Most Ethical Companies. What are its ethical management practices? How do you think organizational culture and leadership action influence these ethical practices? How do you think this company's investment in ethical practices creates value for its stakeholders? Does

this company create synergies between its values and CSR?

3. Identify a company that has benefited from CSR. What did they do? How did they benefit? In what ways were their actions strategic?

In the Field

Select an organization in your community to conduct an ethics and CSR audit. Use the checklist below to evaluate the organization's ethical management practices and approach to CSR.

- If the organization has a code of conduct that defines appropriate behavior for its members, review it.
- If the organization has a training program for ethics, what is the curriculum?
- If the organization has a system of checks and balances for managing its financial resources, review it.
- How do the leaders of the organization model ethical behavior?
- How does the organization incorporate ethics and CSR into its strategic planning process?
- Are employees evaluated and rewarded for ethical behavior?
- How does the organization punish inappropriate ethical behavior?
- Does the organization have performance metrics for its CSR initiatives?
- Does the organization publicly report its CSR initiatives?

ENDNOTES

[1] Sandra J. Sucher and Matthew Preble, "An Intern's Dilemma," Harvard Business School Case No. 9-611-401, rev. August 6, 2013 (Boston, MA: HBS Publishing, 2011).

[2] Manuel G. Velasquez, *Business Ethics: Concepts and Cases*, 4th edition (Upper Saddle River, NJ: Prentice Hall, 1998), p. 8.

[3] Sandra J. Sucher and Matthew Preble, "An Intern's Dilemma," Harvard Business School Case No. 9-611-401, rev. August 6, 2013 (Boston, MA: HBS Publishing, 2011).

[4] Rebecca Henderson, Ranjay Gulati, and Michael Tushman, eds. *Leading Sustainable Change: An Organizational Perspective* (Oxford: Oxford University Press, 2015).

[5] Laurie Havelock, "U.S. Companies Rally toward Sustainability Reporting," *IR Magazine*, June 13, 2014.

[6] Charles Fombrun and Mark Shanley, "What's in a Name? Reputation Building and Corporate Strategy," *The Academy of Management Journal*, Vol. 33, No. 2, 1990, pp. 233–258.

[7] John R. Boatright, *Ethics and the Conduct of Business*, 3rd edition (Upper Saddle River, NJ: Prentice Hall, 2000), pp. 9–10.

[8] Ibid., p. 19.

[9] Manuel G. Velasquez, *Business Ethics: Concepts and Cases*, 4th edition (Upper Saddle River, NJ: Prentice Hall, 1998), pp. 2–5.

[10] Centers for Disease Control and Prevention, "Onchocerciasis FAQs," available at http://www.cdc.gov/parasites/onchocerciasis/gen_info/faqs.html, accessed February 21, 2015.

[11] Standard & Poor's Corporation, *Standard & Poor's Industry Surveys*, Vol. 1, 1979, pp. H13–H16.

[12] "Merck to Donate Drug for River Blindness," *The Wall Street Journal*, 1987, p. 42.

13 David Bollier, *Merck & Company* (Stanford, CA: The Business Enterprise Trust, 1991), p. 5.

14 John R. Boatright, *Ethics and the Conduct of Business*, 3rd edition (Upper Saddle River, NJ: Prentice-Hall, 2000), p. 16; and Tom L. Beauchamp and Norman E. Bowie, *Ethical Theory and Business*, 7th edition (Upper Saddle River, NJ: Prentice-Hall, 2004), p. 4.

15 John R. Boatright, *Ethics and the Conduct of Business*, 3rd edition (Upper Saddle River, NJ: Prentice-Hall, 2000), p. 16.

16 Tom L. Beauchamp and Norman E. Bowie, *Ethical Theory and Business*, 7th edition (Upper Saddle River, NJ: Prentice Hall, 2004), p. 5.

17 Ibid.

18 Linda K. Treviño and Katherine A. Nelson, *Managing Business Ethics: Straight Talk About How to Do It Right*, 3rd edition (Hoboken, NJ: Wiley, 2004), p. 16.

19 Augusto Blasi, "Moral Cognition and Moral Action: A Theoretical Perspective," *Development Review*, Vol. 3, 1983, pp. 178–210.

20 Manuel G. Velasquez, *Business Ethics: Concepts and Cases*, 4th edition (Upper Saddle River, NJ: Prentice Hall, 1998), p. 6.

21 Tom L. Beauchamp and Norman E. Bowie, *Ethical Theory and Business*, 7th edition (Upper Saddle River, NJ: Prentice Hall, 2004), p. 17.

22 O. C. Ferrell, John Fraedrich, and Linda Ferrell, *Business Ethics: Ethical Decision Making and Cases*, 5th edition (Boston, MA: Houghton Mifflin, 2002), p. 59.

23 Thomas L. Beauchamp and James F. Childress, *Principles of Biomedical Ethics* (New York, NY: Oxford University Press, 2011), pp. 337–377.

24 Tom L. Beauchamp and Norman E. Bowie, *Ethical Theory and Business*, 7th edition (Upper Saddle River, NJ: Prentice Hall, 2004), p. 17.

25 Tom L. Beauchamp and James F. Childress, *Principles of Biomedical Ethics* (New York: Oxford University Press, 2001), p. 347; and Michael Sandel, *Justice: What's the Right Thing to Do?* (New York: Farrar Strauss and Giroux, 2009), p. 37.

26 Tom L. Beauchamp and Norman E. Bowie, *Ethical Theory and Business*, 7th edition (Upper Saddle River, NJ: Prentice Hall, 2004), p. 23.

27 Ibid.

28 Ibid., p. 24.

29 Anthony J. Mayo, Masako Egawa, and Mayuka Yamazaki, "Kazuo Inamori, A Japanese Entrepreneur," Harvard Business School Case No. 9-408-039, rev. April 7, 2009 (Boston, MA: HBS Publishing, 2008), p. 15.

30 Tom L. Beauchamp and Norman E. Bowie, *Ethical Theory and Business*, 7th edition (Upper Saddle River, NJ: Prentice Hall, 2004), p. 22.

31 Ibid., p. 23.

32 Mary Schlangenstein, "Workers Chip In to Help Southwest Employees Offer Free Labor," *The Seattle Times*, September 26, 2001, p. E1.

33 Tom L. Beauchamp and Norman E. Bowie, *Ethical Theory and Business*, 7th edition (Upper Saddle River, NJ: Prentice Hall, 2004), p. 32.

34 Nitin Nohria, Sandra J. Sucher, and Bridget Gurtler, "Note on Human Behavior: Character and Situation," Harvard Business School Note No. 9-404-091, rev. February 1, 2011 (Boston, MA: HBS Publishing, 2004), p. 2.

35 Tom L. Beauchamp and Norman E. Bowie, *Ethical Theory and Business*, 7th edition (Upper Saddle River, NJ: Prentice Hall, 2004), p. 31.

36 Nitin Nohria, Sandra J. Sucher, and Bridget Gurtler, "Note on Human Behavior: Character and Situation," Harvard Business School Note No. 9-404-091, rev. February 1, 2011 (Boston, MA: HBS Publishing, 2004), p. 2.

37 Tom L. Beauchamp and Norman E. Bowie, *Ethical Theory and Business*, 7th edition (Upper Saddle River, NJ: Prentice Hall, 2004), p. 32.

38 Ibid., p. 31.

39 Tom L. Beauchamp and Norman E. Bowie, *Ethical Theory and Business*, 7th edition (Upper Saddle River, NJ: Prentice Hall, 2004), p. 631; and Carolyn Wiley, "The ABC's of Business Ethics: Definitions, Philosophies and Implementation," *IM*, 1995, pp. 22–27.

40 Gerald F. Cavanaugh, Dennis J. Moberg, and Manuel Velasquez, "The Ethics of Organizational Politics," *Academy of Management Review*, Vol. 6, No. 3, 1981, pp. 363–374.

41 Tom L. Beauchamp and Norman E. Bowie, *Ethical Theory and Business*, 7th edition (Upper Saddle River, NJ: Prentice Hall, 2004), p. 632.

42 Ibid., p. 633.

43 Ibid.

44 Carolyn Wiley, "The ABC's of Business Ethics: Definitions, Philosophies and Implementation," *IM*, 1995, pp. 22–27.

45 David M. Mayer, "How Can We Create Ethical Organizations?," July 22, 2011, http://www.centerforpos.org/2011/07/how-can-we-create-ethical-organizations/

46 O. C. Ferrell, John Fraedrich, and Linda Ferrell, *Business Ethics: Ethical Decision Making and Cases*, 5th edition (Boston, MA: Houghton Mifflin, 2002), p. 16.

47 Linda K. Treviño and Katherine A. Nelson, *Managing Business Ethics: Straight Talk about How to Do It Right*, 3rd edition (Hoboken, NJ: Wiley, 2004), p. 138.

48 Max H. Bazerman, George Loewenstein, and Don A. Moore, "Why Good Accountants Do Bad Audits," *Harvard Business Review*, November 2002.

49 Jason Snyder, "Gaming the Liver Transplant Market," *Journal of Law, Economics, & Organization*, Vol. 26, No. 3, December 2010.

50 Lynn Sharp Paine, "The Fiduciary Relationship: A Legal Perspective," Harvard Business School Note No. 9-304-064, rev. April 10, 2009 (Boston, MA: HBS Publishing, 2004), pp. 1–2.

51 Robert C. Clark, "Agency Costs versus Fiduciary Duties," *Principles and Agents: The Structure of Business*, eds. John W. Pratt and Richard J. Zeckhauser (Boston, MA: HBS Press, 1985), pp. 55–79.

52 Lynn Sharp Paine, "The Fiduciary Relationship: A Legal Perspective," Harvard Business School Note No. 9-304-064, rev. April 10, 2009 (Boston, MA: HBS Publishing, 2004), p. 4.

53 Alexander Trowbridge, "Identity Theft Rises, Consumers Rage," CBS News, July 1, 2014 accessed at http://www.cbsnews.com/news/identity-theft-rises-consumers-rage/.

54 Federal Trade Commission, "About Identity Theft-Deter, Detect, Defend, Avoid ID Theft," Federal Trade Commission, www.ftc.gov/bcp/edu/microsites/idtheft/consumers/about-identity-theft.html#Howdothievessteal anidentity, accessed March 2011.

55 Michael Kranish, "IRS Is Overwhelmed by Identity Theft Fraud," *Boston Globe*, February 16, 2014.

56 Manuel G. Velasquez, *Business Ethics: Concepts and Cases*, 4th edition (Upper Saddle River, NJ: Prentice Hall, 1998), p. 252.

57 Ibid., pp. 253–255.

58 Ibid., p. 258.

59 "BP Oil Spill Investigation Reveals 'Fundamental Mistake,' Highlights Potential Cost Implications," *BMI Industry Insights—Oil & Gas, Americas*, May 26, 2010, available via Factiva, accessed March 2011.

60 Manuel G. Velasquez, *Business Ethics: Concepts and Cases*, 4th edition (Upper Saddle River, NJ: Prentice Hall, 1998), p. 290.

61 Ibid., p. 449.

62 "Facebook and Your Privacy," *Consumer Reports*, June 2012.

63 John R. Boatright, *Ethics and the Conduct of Business*, 3rd edition (Upper Saddle River, NJ: Prentice Hall, 2000), pp. 162–165.

64 Ibid.

65 Mary C. Gentile, *Giving Voice to Values* (New Haven, CT: Yale University Press, 2010), p. 179.

66 Manuel G. Velasquez, *Business Ethics: Concepts and Cases*, 4th edition (Upper Saddle River, NJ: Prentice Hall, 1998), pp. 430–432.

67 Ibid.

68 John R. Boatright, *Ethics and the Conduct of Business*, 3rd edition (Upper Saddle River, NJ: Prentice Hall, 2000), pp. 143–145.

69 Robert F. Worth, "Shoe Designer Jailed 41 Months, Fined $3.1M: IPO Manipulation," *The New York Times*, April 5, 2002, p. FP3, available via LexisNexis, accessed March 2011.

70 Sheelah Kolhatkar, "Why SAC Capital's Steven Cohen Isn't in Jail," Bloomberg.com, January 2, 2014; Matthew Goldstein, "Ex-Trader at SAC Fund Is Sentenced to 3 Years," *New York Times*, May 16, 2014; and Nathan Vardi, "Matthew Martoma Sentenced to Nine Years for Insider Trading," *Forbes*, September 8, 2014.

71 John R. Boatright, *Ethics and the Conduct of Business*, 3rd edition (Upper Saddle River, NJ: Prentice Hall, 2000), p. 130.

72 Ibid., p. 132.

73 "Pharma Chief Says He Supports the US Administration's Moves on IP Priorities," *Pharma Marketletter*, May 5, 2006, available via LexisNexis, accessed March 2011.

74 John T. Noonan, Jr., *Bribes* (New York, NY: Macmillan, 1984), pp. 578–579.

75 Lynn Sharp Paine and Christopher M. Bruner, "Bribery in Business: A Legal Perspective," Harvard Business School Note No. 9-306-012, rev. August 18, 2006 (Boston, MA: HBS Publishing, 2006), p. 2.

76 Jessica Holzer and Shayndi Raice, "IBM Settles Bribery Charges," *The Wall Street Journal*, March 19, 2011, p. B1.

77 Lynn Sharp Paine and Christopher M. Bruner, "Bribery in Business: A Legal Perspective," Harvard Business School Note No. 9-306-012, rev. August 18, 2006 (Boston, MA: HBS Publishing, 2006), p. 2; and Rajib Sanyal and Subarna Samata, "Correlates of Bribe Giving in International Business," *International Journal of Commerce & Management*, Vol. 14, No. 2, 2004, pp. 1–2.

78 O. Thomas Johnson, Jr., "International Law & Practice: Foreign Corrupt Bribery: A Comparison of National and Supranational Legal Structures," www.abanet.org/genpractice/lawyer/spring97/johnson.html, accessed March 2011.

79 Transparency International, 2014 Index available at http://www.transparency.org/cpi2014/results, accessed February 14, 2015.

80 Manuel G. Velasquez, *Business Ethics: Concepts and Cases*, 4th edition (Upper Saddle River, NJ: Prentice Hall, 1998), p. 429.

81 John R. Boatright, *Ethics and the Conduct of Business*, 3rd edition (Upper Saddle River, NJ: Prentice Hall, 2000), p. 107.

82 Richard Lacayo and Amanda Ripley, "Persons of the Year," *Time*, December 30, 2002.

83 Adam Waytz and Vasilia Kilibarda, "Through the Eyes of a Whistle-Blower: How Sherry Hunt Spoke Up About Citibank's Mortgage Fraud," Northwestern University Kellogg School of Management Case No. KEL862 (Chicago, IL: Kellogg School of Management, 2014).

84 Ibid.

85 John R. Boatright, *Ethics and the Conduct of Business*, 3rd edition (Upper Saddle River, NJ: Prentice Hall, 2000), p. 106.

86 Ibid., pp. 122–123.

87 Ruth V. Aguilera, Debora E. Rupp, Cynthia A. Williams, and Jyoti Ganapathi, "Putting the S Back in Corporate Social Responsibility: A Multilevel Theory of Social Change in Organizations," *Academy of Management Review*, Vol. 32, No. 3, 2007, pp. 836–863.

88 Abagail McWilliams, Donald S. Siegel, and Patrick M. Wright, "Corporate Social Responsibility: Strategic Implications," *Rensselaer Working Papers in Economics*, No. 0506, May 2005; Ruth V. Aguilera, Debora E. Rupp, Cynthia A. Williams, and Jyoti Ganapathi, "Putting the S Back in Corporate Social Responsibility: A Multilevel Theory of Social Change in Organizations," *Academy of Management Review*, Vol. 32, No. 3, July 2007, pp. 836–863; and Roger L. Martin, "The Virtue Matrix: Calculating the Return on Corporate Responsibility," *Harvard Business Review*, March 2002.

89 Varkey Foundation, "Business Backs Education, 2014," available at https://www.varkeyfoundation.org/sites/default/files/BBE%20EPG%20Report%20online.pdf.

90 H. R. Bowen, *Social Responsibilities of the Businessman* (New York: Harper & Row, 1953), p. 6.

91 Donna J. Wood, "Corporate Social Performance Revisited," *The Academy of Management Review*, Vol. 16, No. 4, 1991, pp. 691–718.

92 Steven L. Wartick and Philip L. Cochran, "The Evolution of the Corporate Social Performance Model," *The Academy of Management Review*, Vol. 10, No. 4, 1985, pp. 758–769.

93 Mark S. Schwartz and Archie B. Carroll, "Corporate Social Responsibility: A Three-Domain Approach," *Business Ethics Quarterly*, Vol. 13, No. 4, 2003, pp. 503–530.

94 Archie B. Carroll, "A Three-Dimensional Conceptual Model of Corporate Performance," *The Academy of Management Review*, Vol. 4, No. 4, 1979, pp. 497–505.

95 Mark S. Schwartz and Archie B. Carroll, "Corporate Social Responsibility: A Three-Domain Approach," *Business Ethics Quarterly*, Vol. 13, No. 4, 2003, pp. 503–530.

96 Ibid.

97 Kate Linebaugh, "The Toyota Recall: Toyota Is Unable to Hit the Brakes on Crisis," *The Wall Street Journal*, 2010.

98 Sarbanes-Oxley Act of 2002, Pub. L. No. 107-204, 116 Stat. 745(2002), summarized in Lynn Sharp Paine and Christopher M. Bruner, "Deception in Business: A Legal Perspective," Harvard Business School Note No. 9-306-019, rev. August 10, 2009 (Boston, MA: HBS Publishing, 2006), p. 2.

99 "Financial Regulatory Reform," *The New York Times*, November 4, 2010, http://topics.nytimes.com/topics/reference/timestopics/subjects/c/credit_crisis/financial_regulatory_reform/index.html, accessed March 2011.

100 "Rechargeable Battery Recycling Corporation; Ritz Camera Western Stores Join the Rechargeable Battery Recycling Corporation's Call2Recycle Program," *Entertainment & Travel*, August 11, 2008, p. 230.

[101] Rosabeth M. Kanter, *Supercorp: How Vanguard Companies Create Innovation, Profits, Growth, and Social Good* (New York: Crown Business, 2009).

[102] Archie B. Carroll, "A Three-Dimensional Conceptual Model of Corporate Performance," *The Academy of Management Review*, Vol. 4, No. 4, 1979, pp. 497–505.

[103] John Schwartz, "Comments by Overseer of BP Fund Irk Lawyers," *The New York Times*, December 22, 2010, p. A18.

[104] R. W. Ackerman, *The Social Challenge to Business* (Cambridge, MA: Harvard University Press, 1975).

[105] Milton Friedman, "The Social Responsibility of Business Is to Increase Its Profits," *The New York Times Magazine*, September 13, 1970, p. 32.

[106] Kenneth E. Aupperle, Archie B. Carroll, and John D. Hatfield, "An Empirical Examination of the Relationship between Corporate Social Responsibility and Profitability, *The Academy of Management Journal*, Vol. 28, No. 2, 1985, pp. 446–463; and Moses L. Pava and Joshua Krausz, "The Association between Corporate Social Responsibility and Financial Performance: The Paradox of Social Cost," *Journal of Business Ethics*, Vol. 15, No. 3, 1996, pp. 321–357.

[107] Sandra A. Waddock and Samuel B. Graves, "The Corporate Social Performance-Financial Performance Link," *Strategic Management Journal*, Vol. 14, No. 4, 1997, pp. 303–319.

[108] Jennifer J. Griffin and John F. Mahon, "The Corporate Social Performance and Corporate Financial Performance Debate: Twenty-Five Years of Incomparable Research," *Business and Society*, Vol. 36, No. 1, 1997, pp. 5–31; and Marc Orlitzky, Frank L. Schmidt, and Sara L. Rynes, "Corporate Social and Financial Performance: A Meta-Analysis," *Organization Studies*, Vol. 24, 2003, pp. 403–441.

[109] Lee Burke and Jeanne M. Logsdon, "How Corporate Social Responsibility Pays Off," *Long Range Planning*, Vol. 29, No. 4, 1996, pp. 495–502; Michael V. Russo and Paul A. Fouts, "A Resource-Based Perspective on Corporate Environmental Performance and Profitability," *The Academy of Management Journal*, Vol. 40, No. 3, 1997, pp. 534–559; and Sandra

A. Waddock and Samuel B. Graves, "The Corporate Social Performance-Financial Performance Link," *Strategic Management Journal*, Vol. 14, No. 4, 1997, pp. 303–319.

[110] Susan Berfield, "Hard Times in Happy Town," *Bloomberg Businessweek*, December 29, 2014-January 11, 2015.

[111] C. B. Bhattacharya and Sankar Sen, "Doing Better at Doing Good: When, Why, and How Consumers Respond to Corporate Social Initiatives," *California Management Review*, Vol. 47, No. 1, Fall 2004, pp. 9–24.

[112] Lois A. Mohr, Debora J. Webb, and Katherine E. Harris, "Do Consumers Expect Companies to Be Socially Responsible? The Impact of Corporate Social Responsibility on Buying Behavior," *Journal of Consumer Affairs*, Vol. 35, No. 1, Summer 2001, pp. 45–72; and C. B. Bhattacharya and Sankar Sen, "Doing Better at Doing Good: When, Why, and How Consumers Respond to Corporate Social Initiatives," *California Management Review*, Vol. 47, No. 1, Fall 2004, pp. 9–24.

[113] Patrick Sullivan, "Consumers Will Pay More for Corporate Social Responsibility," *The NonProfit Times*, June 17, 2014

[114] Geoffrey B. Sprinkle and Laureen A. Maines, "The Benefits and Costs of Corporate Social Responsibility," *Business Horizons*, Vol. 53, 2010, pp. 445–453.

[115] Michael V. Russo and Paul A. Fouts, "A Resource-Based Perspective on Corporate Environmental Performance and Profitability," *The Academy of Management Journal*, Vol. 40, No. 3, 1997, pp. 534–559.

[116] Michael E. Porter and Mark R. Kramer, "Strategy & Society: The Link between Competitive Advantage and Corporate Social Responsibility," *Harvard Business Review*, December 2006.

[117] Ibid.

[118] Oliver Falck and Stephan Heblich, "Corporate Social Responsibility: Doing Well by Doing Good," *Business Horizons*, Vol. 50, 2007, pp. 247–254.

[119] Beth Kowitt, "A Founder's Bold Gamble on Panera," *Fortune*, August 13, 2012; and Panera Cares, "Our Mission," available at http://paneracares.org/our-mission/, accessed October 1, 2012.

[120] Panera Cares, "FAQs," available at http:// paneracares.org.

[121] Lee Burke and Jeanne M. Logsdon, "How Corporate Social Responsibility Pays Off," *Long Range Planning*, Vol. 29, No. 4, 1996, pp. 495–502.

[122] C. B. Bhattacharya, Sankar Sen, and Daniel Korschun, "Using Corporate Social Responsibility to Win the War for Talent," *MIT Sloan Management Review*, Vol. 49, No. 2, Winter 2008, pp. 37–44.

[123] Jeffrey Pfeffer, "Competitive Advantage through People," *California Management Review*, Vol. 36, No. 2, 1994, pp. 9–28.

[124] Roben Farzad, "The Scrappiest Car Manufacturer in America," *Bloomberg Businessweek*, June 6–12, 2011.

[125] Brad Stone, "Pay Up, You Stingy Nerds," *Bloomberg Businessweek*, December 29, 2014-January 11, 2015.

[126] Daniel B. Turban and Daniel W. Greening, "Corporate Social Performance and Organizational Attractiveness to Prospective Employees," *The Academy of Management Journal*, Vol. 40, No. 3, 1997, pp. 658–672; and Ruth V. Aguilera, Debora E. Rupp, Cynthia A. Williams, and Jyoti Ganapathi, "Putting the S Back in Corporate Social Responsibility: A Multilevel Theory of Social Change in Organizations," *Academy of Management Review*, Vol. 32, No. 3, 2007, pp. 836–863.

[127] Daniel W. Greening and Daniel B. Turban, "Corporate Social Performance as a Competitive Advantage in Attracting a Quality Workforce," *Business and Society*, Vol. 39, No. 3, 2000, pp. 254–280.

[128] C. B. Bhattacharya, Sankar Sen, and Daniel Korschun, "Using Corporate Social Responsibility to Win the War for Talent," *MIT Sloan Management Review*, Vol. 49, No. 2, Winter 2008, pp. 37–44.

[129] Michael E. Porter and Mark R. Kramer, "The Competitive Advantage of Corporate Philanthropy," *Harvard Business Review*, December 2002.

[130] Michael E. Porter and Mark R. Kramer, "Strategy & Society: The Link between Competitive Advantage and Corporate Social Responsibility," *Harvard Business Review*, December 2006.

[131] Ibid.

[132] Ibid.

[133] Ibid.

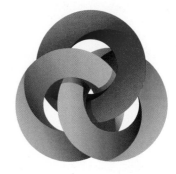

P A R T **2**

STRATEGIC PERSPECTIVE

CHAPTER

4

Introduction to Strategy

Learning Objectives

After reading this chapter, you should be able to:

LO1 Describe the historical roots of strategy.

LO2 Create a strategic framework for a firm by outlining its purpose, analyzing its internal and external environments, defining its vision, mission, and objectives, and describing its strategic formulation process.

LO3 Describe how a firm can achieve competitive advantage by defining specific activities, making trade-offs among activities, and creating fit among the activities.

LO4 Explain the differences between business-level strategy and corporate-level strategy.

LO5 Explain the advantages and disadvantages of different global strategies.

LO6 Describe the ways in which companies enter global markets.

SELF-REFLECTION

Are You a Strategic Thinker?

Strategic thinking is a process that enables leaders to analyze information and make decisions so that an organization can build a sustainable competitive advantage. Evaluate your strategic thinking skills by responding True or False to the following statements.

1. When working with a group, I can craft a vision that will direct our strategy.

2. When reflecting upon a situation, I can comprehend the big picture to see things in a new and different way.

3. When analyzing a company, I think about its competitors and how they would respond to strategic actions.

4. I excel at using data to make sense of patterns and relationships.

5. I understand the relationship between environmental trends and an organization's strategy.

6. I understand how a customer orientation is an important aspect of a firm's strategy.

7. When studying a company, I think about its strategic positioning within its industry.

8. I am able to cognitively map how a firm's internal environment supports its strategy.

9. I am familiar with business models that help evaluate a firm's strategy.

10. I am good at asking the right questions to make sense of information.

If you answered True to the majority of statements, you are thinking like a strategic leader.

Source: Richard L. Hughes and Katherine M. Beatty, *Becoming a Strategic Leader: Your Role in Your Organization's Enduring Success* (San Francisco, CA: John Wiley & Sons, 2005).

INTRODUCTION

In the first section of the textbook, we saw how the business environment is constantly changing and becoming more complex. To succeed in a constantly changing contextual landscape, a firm must develop and execute a defensible strategy. At its core, **strategy** includes pursuing a set of unique activities that provide value to customers; making trade-offs about which businesses to pursue, what products to produce, and which customers to serve; and aligning resources to achieve organizational objectives.[1] In other words, strategy is the manager's "game plan" for the organization—specifying how the firm intends to achieve its goals. Adopting a specific strategy requires a set of choices and trade-offs that revolve around what a firm intends to do and how it intends to do it.[2] In essence, strategy involves "placing bets and making hard choices."[3]

A firm achieves a **competitive advantage** when it creates more economic value than competitors by engaging in a strategy that is difficult or impossible for others to duplicate. For this competitive advantage to be sustainable, a firm's strategy must adapt and continue to be appropriate for its changing external environment. At the same time, the firm's strategy must be aligned with its internal capabilities.[4]

Strategy
Pursuing a set of unique activities that provide value to customers; making trade-offs about which businesses to pursue, what products to produce, and which customers to serve; and aligning resources to achieve organizational objectives.

Competitive advantage
A firm achieves a competitive advantage when it creates more economic value than competitors by engaging in a strategy that is difficult or impossible for others to duplicate.

In this chapter, we'll discuss a framework that will help you understand the components of strategy. Strategy is not simply the domain of business. Strategy is a critical component of not-for-profit organizations, athletic teams, nations, and other organizations that seek to carve out a defensible and competitive position within their respective environments. The manner in which two baseball teams, the Oakland Athletics and the Baltimore Orioles, competed during the last decade illustrates the importance of applying smart, strategic choices in a hypercompetitive sports environment.

Arms Race in the Major Leagues

During the late 1990s, the payrolls of Major League Baseball (MLB) began to rise to unprecedented levels. Teams such as the New York Yankees and Boston Red Sox started competing with each other for a limited number of highly prized players. Bidding wars for talented players such as Alex Rodriguez sent annual payrolls into the $150 million to $200 million range. Major market cities could afford to pay large salaries because of the revenues they made from ticket sales and lucrative cable contracts. But midmarket cities such as Baltimore and Oakland could not generate enough annual revenue to match the salaries of large market teams.

As teams such as the Yankees and Red Sox dominated the standings and the market for players, many critics began to complain that the structure of the system prevented midmarket to lower-market teams from competing with major market teams. While the critics were, for the most part, correct about MLB not being a level playing field, one team seemed to suggest that smaller-market teams could compete with the big boys.

The Oakland Athletics were once a big market team of sorts. In the 1980s, the team was owned by a group that spent freely on top players such as Mark McGwire and Jose Canseco. The owners didn't see the team as a money-making enterprise, but as an instrument to boost community pride. When the team changed hands in the early 1990s, the new owners did not have the resources to run the team in the same manner. With an old, decaying stadium and smaller fan base, the owners needed a new way to compete.

John G. Mabanglo/epa/Corbis

In 1997, they hired the former major leaguer, Billy Beane, as general manager (GM). At one time, Beane was one of the brightest prospects in the New York Mets system. He was referred to as a "can't miss type of player" because scouts believed that he would become a superstar. Despite his immense physical skills, Beane never achieved success in the majors. Following his mediocre baseball career, he began working in Oakland's front office before eventually becoming the GM. Beane knew that he could not employ the same tactics used by other GMs; he needed a new strategy to locate high-quality, low-priced talent to fit the constraints the owners placed on him.

At the core of Beane's strategy was the idea that most MLB teams evaluated talent improperly. From his own experience, Beane knew that most scouts evaluated prospects by simply watching games. They tended to favor young, physically impressive high school players. Most scouts didn't use a computer or statistics to evaluate players. Instead, they wanted to see how fast a player could run, how fast he could throw, and how far he could hit a ball.

Through research and statistical analysis, Beane discovered that what scouts had traditionally evaluated did not always predict success in baseball. While the three things they looked at were important, so too was a player's on-base percentage (OBP), a measure of how often a player reaches base through hits, walks, or errors (hit by pitcher). OBP differs from the more commonly used batting average statistic by taking into consideration the ability of the batter to reach base with walks and hits by pitches as well as hits. Walks were previously just attributed to poor pitching, but Beane considered a batter's ability to manage the pitch count and lay off bad pitches as an important skill. Some players who had the traditional attributes that scouts wanted also had favorable OBPs, but many unknown players had comparable OBPs.

In 1997, Beane began to deploy the drafting strategy of picking players with high OBPs. Most of these players went unnoticed by other teams and thus were relatively cheap compared to superstars. Beane's main strategy was to draft players who had the ability of a fourth or fifth round pick and pay them less money.

In this way, he could minimize his risk by drafting 10 reasonably strong players while still staying under the salary cap. Other teams in large markets often overpaid for their first draft choice and then their next nine selections were players with lower talent levels. At 21 and 23 years old, respectively, Ben Grieve and Miguel Tejada signed with the Athletics in 1997 and went on to greater success in the Major League. Grieve was the American League Rookie of the year in 1998; Miguel Tejada was a six-time All-Star and the American League's Most Valuable Player (MVP) in 2002.[5] When word of Beane's strategy spread to

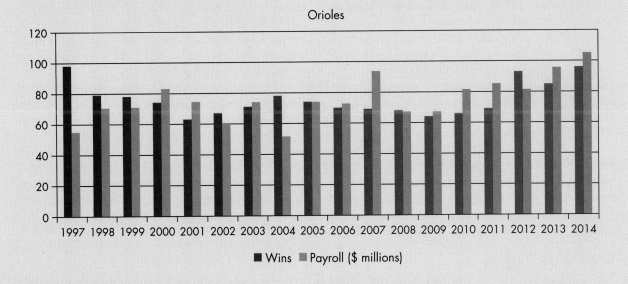

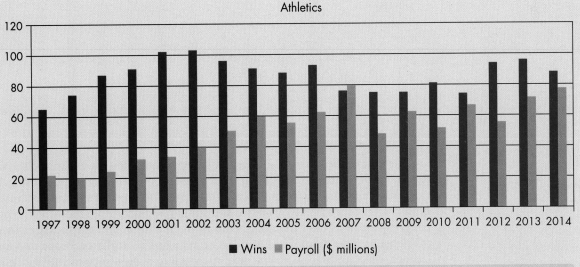

Figure 4.1 Wins and Payroll of Baltimore Orioles and Oakland Athletics, 1997–2014

Sources: Baltimore Orioles, "Year by Year Results," at http://baltimore.orioles.mlb.com/bal/history/year_by_year_results.jsp, accessed February 20, 2015; Oakland Athletics, "Year by Year Results," available at http://oakland.athletics.mlb.com/oak/history/year_by_year_results.jsp, accessed February 20, 2015; and USA Today, "MLB Salaries," available at http://www.usatoday.com/sports/mlb/athletics/salaries/2014/team/all/ and http://www.usatoday.com/sports/mlb/orioles/salaries/2014/team/all/, accessed February 20, 2015.

other GMs, the initial response was one of derision. However, the results speak for themselves. Since Billy Beane's second year as GM in 1999, the Athletics have averaged a winning percentage of 58 while maintaining a team salary in the bottom third quartile of MLB teams.[6] While the Athletics have not won a World Series during Beane's tenure, they have made the playoffs 8 out of 17 years.

In contrast, the Baltimore Orioles have been one of the most successful franchises in MLB, making six appearances in the World Series and winning three of them over the last five decades. In fact, the organization was one of the most dominant in MLB during the 1960s and 1970s when they went to the postseason nearly every year. However, the team entered a decade-long slump after winning the World Series in 1983, never reaching the postseason. Many attributed the decline to the team selling its young assets in the early 1980s to obtain veteran players. Under new ownership and with few prospects, the team floundered for most of the decade, even losing their first 21 games to start the 1988 season (an MLB record).

About the same time Billy Beane came to the Athletics, the Baltimore Orioles began to pursue a new strategy. A new owner bought the team in 1993, and he was willing to open his wallet to get high-priced free agents. Rather than finding a different way to compete through strategy, Baltimore followed the lead of the Yankees and Red Sox, expanding its payroll to unsustainable levels. However, Baltimore didn't have the resources to compete head-to-head with these teams, ultimately missing out on some of the best players and spending too much on one or two prime players. While this strategy led the Orioles to the postseason for the first time in a decade in 1996 and 1997, the team lost both times to big market teams. Following the 1997 season, the team continued to acquire high-priced free agents, although to a smaller degree because of falling attendance and revenue levels. With fewer resources and an undifferentiated strategy, the team spiraled into perpetual decline. From 1998 to 2006, the team averaged a winning percentage of 44, never achieving a winning season once, while maintaining an average team salary 59% higher than the Oakland Athletics (see Figure 4.1).

The success of the Oakland Athletics led to Beane's approach being chronicled in the 2003 bestselling book *Moneyball: The Art of Winning an Unfair Game*, which was later developed into a major motion picture starring Brad Pitt. With this exposure, more teams decided to engage in sophisticated statistical analysis in choosing players. As a result, the competitive advantage the Athletics had achieved with Beane's approach began to be diffused.

Case in Point

Arms Race in the Major League

1. What environmental and competitive factors explain the rise of the payroll for MLB players?

2. What is the role of a baseball team's GM in formulating and implementing a team's strategy?

3. Compare and contrast the strategies of the Oakland A's and the Baltimore Orioles.

4. What can corporations learn from the strategies of MLB teams?

As you can see, forming a coherent strategy that allows a leader to take advantage of his or her resources is often the difference between winning and losing. These examples demonstrate the importance of strategy and performance in competition. Both the Orioles and the Athletics had similar resources, yet the Athletics consistently performed better than Baltimore through a differentiated strategy. Now that other teams have employed a similar strategy as the Athletics, Beane and his colleagues will have to look for the next approach to achieve a competitive advantage.

Like successful sports teams, all successful companies have a well-designed strategy, and the formulation of this strategy does not come from chance. Rather, it is formed after a careful assessment of a firm's internal and external environments and the resources and capabilities available to the firm. By carefully considering these factors, the manager places the firm in a position to achieve its goals and obtain a competitive advantage in the marketplace. In the past, a firm's most dangerous competitors were often similar businesses, but in today's environment, competition can sometimes come out of a totally different industry or geography. As such, the real challenge is to maintain competitive differentiation from current and future competitors.[7] When there is no differentiation among competitors in an industry, there is a growing commoditization of the products or services offered and then firms tend to compete mostly on price, which can erode profitability for the entire industry.

A BRIEF HISTORY OF STRATEGY

The concept of strategy is not a new one. Its roots are deeply imbedded in ancient military terminology. The word *strategy* comes from the Greek word *strate-gos*, which, in turn, derives from the two words *stratos* (army) and *e-gos* (to lead). The Greeks used the term *strategy* to refer to the leader or general of an army. In a broad sense, the term described a leader's ability to marshal a large set of resources.

Many believe that the notion of strategy in the context of war was first described in detail in *The Art of War*, a Chinese military treatise said to have been written sometime between 480 and 221 BC by Sun Tzu.[8] In this work, Tzu noted: "Those who win one hundred triumphs in one hundred conflicts do not have supreme skill. Those who have supreme skill, use strategy to bend others without coming to conflict." He continued: "Those who are skilled at executing a strategy, bend the strategy of others without conflict, uproot the fortifications of others without attacking, [and] absorb the organizations of others without prolonged operations." In essence, Tzu believed that success over an opponent could be achieved using a well-honed strategy instead of force. He believed it was more important to outthink an opponent than to outmaneuver the opponent on the battlefield. To him, the avoidance of conflict through strategy was the essence of success.[9] This notion is similar to the ongoing debate in geopolitics between using diplomacy and using force to resolve conflicts. Most nations pursue both courses of action simultaneously.

For thousands of years, the development and use of strategy in the military has often mirrored the success of nation-states. In fact, nation-states such as the Roman Empire successfully used military strategy to devise an overall plan to defeat rival states. In this setting, Roman military strategists constructed battle plans based on an assessment of their own forces (internal environment) and the enemy forces and conditions (external environment). For the Romans, military strategy often changed from battle to battle depending on the enemy. In this context, strategy was considered a plan of action designed to achieve a specific goal. Military strategists such as Sun Tzu made a clear distinction between strategy and tactics. To military leaders, tactics represented the specific moves or actions their armies would perform on the battlefield (charging or flanking, for instance). The strategy represented the grand plan for the war, and it was usually aimed at creating a military advantage.

It is from these military foundations that the study and application of business strategy emerged. In applying the concept of strategy to business, it should not be surprising that many people have referred to business as war. At its basest level, war and business have much in common—the desire to beat the opponent and succeed in competition. Regardless of whether you are waging a war on the battlefield or on Main Street, the rules of engagement have not changed in the manner in which an organization attempts to gain a competitive stronghold. They do so by the following methods:

- Generating better information than their rivals.
- Analyzing that information to make strong, informed choices.
- Selecting among different choices.
- Converting strategic choices into decisive action.[10]

charistoone-images / Alamy

According to Tzu, the process of gathering information was an integral component of developing strategy. In *The Art of War*, he noted: "Those who triumph, compute at their headquarters a great number of factors prior to a challenge. Those who are defeated compute at their headquarters a small number of factors prior to a challenge. Much computation brings triumph. Little computation brings defeat."[11] The data gathering and analysis that is so important in the theater of war is also relevant to understanding the landscape of business. In war, it is important to understand the enemy and, similarly in business, leaders must understand their competitors and the overall competitive landscape.

This need to understand the competitive landscape led early business leaders to focus on corporate planning and analysis as the basis of strategy. The corporate planning function became popular in the post–World War II era as many businesses grew in size, scope, and complexity. This was particularly evident in the age of **conglomeration** when businesses grew through unrelated diversification, essentially by acquiring companies in different industries. Managers turned to corporate planning to make sense of their various business lines. The planning process involved the development of detailed forecasts and business-level goals and objectives. These goals were then institutionalized through a specific action plan whose steps were to be implemented over a defined period. Companies often developed 3- or 5-year business plans that were periodically updated.

While the planning process provided general managers and other executives with a potential road map for their businesses, the plan was often quickly out of sync with the shifting competitive landscape. Instead of modifying the plan based on the changes in the competitive marketplace, many businesses slavishly continued to implement it. Not surprisingly, the results were not very effective, and the usefulness and importance of planning began to wane.[12] This was particularly evident in the 1970s and 1980s as markets became more dynamic and competitive, leading many large firms to lose their competitive edge to more nimble and flexible competitors. Many people blamed this stringent attachment to corporate planning as one of the culprits in the loss of competitiveness for many U.S. firms. Some researchers believed that planning actually decreased a firm's innovative capabilities because of management's adherence to rigid formulas.[13]

While planning does have a downside, especially when it is performed in a vacuum and is not updated with changing market conditions, firms would be equally naive to make critical investment and resource allocation decisions without understanding the potential consequences. Without some form of strategic planning, key decisions will likely lack a sound rationale. The key to planning is to not only ensure that the plan is robust and well thought out, but also is fluid and adaptable. Robust business plans should not sit in the drawers of executives, and they should not be followed with zombielike mindlessness. Plans should be dynamic. They should be a living document that helps managers prepare for potential opportunities and threats. To retain their usefulness, plans should be constantly monitored and updated. This fluid process of updating plans is a critical component to the development of strategy in an increasingly competitive environment. When Alan Mulally was the CEO of Ford Motor Company, he held two-and-a-half hour weekly business plan reviews with the heads of key departments to ensure that the company's plans were on track and in sync with the changing market conditions. Mulally used a color-coded system to review plans; red meant there was a problem while green signified progress. When Ford picked a new CEO in 2014, they tapped Mark Fields, who was responsible for managing these weekly business reviews. His experience in the review process enabled him to clearly understand Ford's challenges and opportunities. By holding these sessions on a frequent basis, Ford ensures that its business plans are both relevant and timely.[14]

Conglomeration
The act of growing through unrelated diversification, essentially by acquiring companies in different industries.

STRATEGY AND THE ORGANIZATION: A FRAMEWORK

As we discussed in Chapter 1, managers need to understand their internal and external environments to ensure that they are able to effectively satisfy a broad group of stakeholders. Understanding who the vital stakeholders are and what the firm hopes to achieve are prerequisites for developing the firm's strategy. When developing a firm's strategy, managers must make a series of decisions, including the following:

- What is our purpose?
- How will environmental forces impact our business?
- What stakeholders are important?
- In what business or areas will we compete?
- Who will we serve?
- How will we distinguish our firm from competitors?

While all of these questions are important to the development of strategy, the first question is critical because it speaks to the reason the firm exists.

The Purpose of Business

What is the business for? Who does it serve and to what purpose? These questions have been widely debated for decades and speak to the **goal** of a firm. In a general sense, the goal of a firm can be defined as an organizationally desired result, product, or end state. According to the Nobel prize–winning economist Milton Friedman, the goal of a business is to make profits.[15] In other words, a business should strive to produce revenues that exceed costs by the widest margin possible. Friedman argued that a firm should focus exclusively on this task and concern itself only with creating value for shareholders or owners of the business within the limits of the law.

More recently, academics and managers alike have debated whether a firm's sole focus should be on profits, claiming that a firm owes a duty to many other stakeholders. As we saw in Chapter 3, many firms are embracing CSR as a competitive advantage to serve a broader array of stakeholders. Despite the increasing attention given to the stakeholder theory of the firm, many still believe that the primary purpose of a firm is to make profits for shareholders, but to do so in an ethical and responsible manner.

Analyzing the Internal and External Environments of a Firm

As we discussed, strategy formulation begins with an analysis of a firm's internal and external environments (see Figure 4.2). Without a strategy that assesses those environments, a great idea may lose out to a competitor who has carefully evaluated the factors and formed a strategy based on this assessment. Chapter 2 noted that every firm is influenced by numerous forces within their internal and external environments. A manager must identify all of the components of his or her firm's internal environment, including its goals, resources, and competencies, to assess the firm's capabilities and potential. In addition, a manager must explore the components of the external environment with a special emphasis on the contextual forces, which can influence the potential success or failure of the firm. In analyzing the internal and external environments, managers must build a comprehensive understanding of the power and needs of the firm's various stakeholders. Depending on the business or industry, certain stakeholders have more influence than others. As such, a manager must identify which stakeholders possess the greatest leverage and develop specific approaches to address their needs.

Goal
An organizationally desired result, product, or end state.

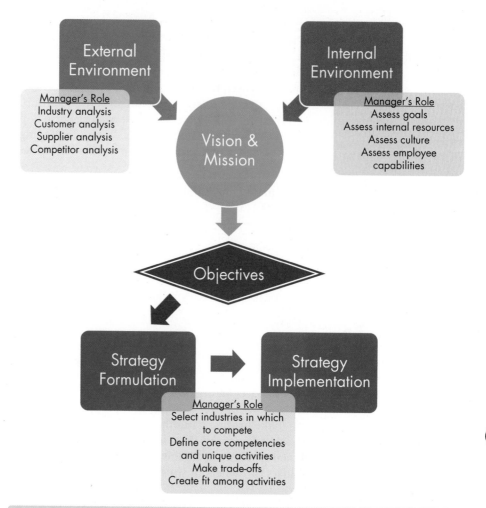

Figure 4.2 ⟩ Strategic Framework

Once a manager has examined these factors, he or she can better articulate the firm's reason for existence and begin to make a series of decisions and construct a system of activities that will enable the firm to reach its potential. The ultimate goal of this process is to create a network of activities that strategically fit together and are difficult to replicate. This network of activities forms a firm's **core competencies**, which, in turn, helps to establish the firm's competitive advantage. Netflix, the online streaming DVD rental company, explicitly states its core competencies as follows:

- Easy to use and intuitive Web site
- Personalized movie recommendations based on more than two billion ratings from subscribers
- Relentless focus on continuously improving the customer experience
- Proven competence in making unlimited subscription a profitable business model[16]

Netflix hopes to distinguish itself from its competitors by reinforcing these core competencies.

Vision, Mission, and Objectives

For a firm to be successful, it must have a clear **vision** of how it wants to bring value to customers and satisfy its various stakeholders. Warren Bennis and Burt Nanus noted that "a vision articulates a view of a realistic, credible, attractive future for an organization,

---

Core competencies
A network of unique activities that strategically fit together and are difficult to replicate.

Vision
A concept or picture of what a firm wants to achieve.

a condition that is better in some important ways than what now exists."[17] A vision is a concept or picture of what a firm wants to achieve. The development of a vision for a company is one of the critical roles for leaders of an organization because it is often what motivates people to join a firm and perform beyond expectations.

While a firm's vision promotes a lofty idea of where the firm wants to go, the **mission** of the firm is a definition of what it stands for and what its purpose is.[18] Many firms codify this idea through a **mission statement**. A mission statement defines a firm's reason for existence. It often states what activities the firm performs or what markets it is trying to serve and how it distinguishes itself from competitors.[19] Most firms spend a lot of time developing and honing their mission statements to communicate to customers and to motivate employees. Mission statements provide employees with a sense of the firm's priorities and, in so doing, they serve as a guide to direct a firm's activities.[20] The result is often more productive employees. Some researchers have even shown that firms with comprehensive mission statements tend to perform better than those with loosely defined ones.[21] Effective mission statements can provide the following benefits:

- Define the purpose of the company
- Build motivation and commitment among employees
- Provide direction and inspiration
- Serve as a focal point
- Assist in making strategic trade-offs[22]

Look at the different mission statements presented in Table 4.1. As you can see from these high-tech companies, most mission statements define the purpose of the firm. Interestingly, many of these mission statements seem to be interchangeable, making them sometimes less effective, as employees perceive them as generic. Without the company names next to them, would you be able to tell which one belonged to Intel or Microsoft? Mission statements are often inspirational and potentially motivating, but they lack specific details on how the missions will be accomplished. The specifics become clearer when the firm's strategy is defined.[23]

While the vision and mission set forth an overarching direction for the firm, **objectives** provide a series of quantifiable milestones or benchmarks by which the firm can track its progress. Objectives outline what the firm hopes to achieve within a specific time frame in a number of areas, including financial performance, market

Mission
The activities a firm performs for its customers.

Mission statement
A statement that defines a firm's reason for existence.

Objectives
Series of quantifiable milestones or benchmarks by which a firm can assess its progress.

Company	Mission Statement
facebook	To give people the power to share and make the world more open and connected.
(intel)	Delight our customers, employees, and shareholders by relentlessly delivering the platform and technology advancements that become essential to the way we work and live.
Microsoft	To enable people and businesses throughout the world to realize their full potential.
SAP	Our mission is to help every customer become a best-run business.

Table 4.1 Sample Mission Statements

Sources: Intel, "General Company Information," Intel Web site available at http://www.intel.com/intel/company/corp1.htm, accessed February 20, 2015; Microsoft, "Our Mission," Microsoft website available at http://www.microsoft.com/enable/microsoft/mission.aspx, accessed February 20, 2015; SAP, "About SAP AG," SAP website available at http://global.sap.com/corporate-en/investors/pdf/sap-fact-sheet-en.pdf accessed February 20, 2015; and Facebook, "About," Facebook website available at https://www.facebook.com/facebook/info?tab=page_info, accessed February 20, 2015.

share, and new product introduction. These objectives are usually woven into the annual planning process at most companies.

Once a manager has established a vision, a mission, and objectives for the firm, he or she must also define the strategy of the business. The process of analyzing a firm's external and internal environments as well as the firm's vision and mission is an input for **strategy formulation**.[24] It is important to note that strategy is distinct from a firm's vision and mission. It is also different from objectives and tactics. **Tactics**, such as launching new products, entering new markets, and redesigning the organizational structure, are the actions that a firm takes to enact its strategy. In formulating a firm's strategy, a manager seeks to identify the manner in which a firm can best align its resources to carve out a defensible position in the marketplace. Objectives define what the firm seeks to achieve. Tactics describe how the firm seeks to achieve its objectives, and strategy is the way in which a firm positions itself in the marketplace and aligns its resources around that positioning.[25]

Strategy Formulation

The development of strategy should be both a planned and emergent process that develops and is adapted over time. The planned component of strategy development involves the systematic assessment of the external and internal environments and is generally derived from a subset of individuals in the firm. They are typically strategic planning resources and line managers who have a solid understanding of the day-to-day operations of the company and the competitive landscape.[26] It is often a top-down process with the CEO and his or her team, outlining the firm's core vision and mission along with the planned strategy.

Even with the best-developed plans, a firm will not anticipate all aspects of a competitive marketplace. It is often difficult to predict the manner in which competitors will respond to another firm's actions or to changing environmental factors. As such, a leader may need to rethink the firm's strategy, objectives, and tactics. Are they still relevant in an evolving business environment? This process of reassessing strategy, objectives, and tactics on an ongoing basis is part of the emergent aspect of the strategy formulation process.[27] Frontline managers are often at the forefront of change in an industry and, as such, they are in a position to understand potential new opportunities or serious threats. Including frontline managers in the reassessment of strategy tends to increase organizational consensus on new tactical moves and boosts the likelihood of successful implementation.[28] While the planned aspects of strategy development are often top-down, the inputs to the emergent aspects of strategy development are more bottom-up. That is, they bubble up from individuals throughout the organization.

The strategy development process does not always flow in a linear fashion as shown in Figure 4.2; rather, it evolves over time. The constantly changing nature of the external environment requires managers to engage in environmental scanning on an ongoing basis to determine its impact, if any, on the firm. Some aspects of a firm's strategy will remain constant for a long period, while other aspects may be more susceptible to frequent changes.[29] Some changes start as a simple tactical maneuver (e.g., offer a discount to clear inventory) but may quickly turn into a major strategic shift (e.g., the organization discovers there is a huge market at a lower price point).

Some firms have very stable strategies. This is especially true for businesses in mature industries and in industries that are heavily regulated. In these situations, many aspects of a firm's strategy tend to be relatively consistent and sometimes predetermined. It is unlikely that the actions of one firm will dramatically impact the business environment.

In a dynamic, fast-changing industry, strategies and choices that follow from it may be subject to constant change. Managers must develop the ability to identify what aspects of the external environment will impact their firm and what the extent of that

Strategy formulation
The process of identifying how a firm can best align its resources to carve out a defensible position in the marketplace.

Tactics
The actions that a firm takes to enact its strategy.

impact will be. In these settings the only constant is change and it may be hard to pin down a definitive strategy.

Groupon, a company that offers discounted prices for local entertainment such as museums, restaurants, and tourist attractions, illustrates the balance between a planned and emergent strategy and how unforeseen market forces can have a hand in changing a company's trajectory. Founder Andrew Mason launched a Web site, www.ThePoint.com, while pursuing a master's degree at the University of Chicago. Determined to expose the truth behind political issues, he wanted to provide a platform to anyone who wanted to raise support for a cause. The Web site soon drew national press, not for its influence in public life, but for its controversial and at times silly campaigns. For example, one initiative drew

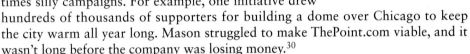

hundreds of thousands of supporters for building a dome over Chicago to keep the city warm all year long. Mason struggled to make ThePoint.com viable, and it wasn't long before the company was losing money.[30]

In reviewing his business model, Mason discovered one important trend: the most successful campaigns were those that banded consumers together to generate massive buying power. With this knowledge, he changed his strategy and, with seven employees, began contacting local vendors to strike deals for products and services. These local establishments, often with low marketing budgets, had an opportunity to gain thousands of new customers who would otherwise not look at their business. In exchange for this exposure, they would sacrifice profit by splitting sales 50/50 with Groupon. For example, in early 2010, Groupon sold nearly 20,000 tickets for a $25-Chicago-boat tour for only $12; the two companies split the $238,000 generated through Groupon's website. By modifying his original strategy, Mason became very successful; by 2010, Groupon expanded into more than 85 cities and was on its way to becoming the fastest company ever to generate $1 billion in revenue (beating Apple, Google, and Amazon).[31]

In 2010, Google offered Mason over $6 billion to acquire Groupon. Unfortunately, Mason passed on the deal. The subsequent few years were very difficult. Groupon's success emboldened a number of competitors who have since eroded the company's market share and stock position. Groupon shares have fallen over 70% from 2011 to 2015. As a result, Mason ultimately lost his job. Groupon will, once again, need to reassess their strategy to find a defensible position in the market. To that end, the company formed a new Groupon Goods business that uses the company's 200 million e-mail addresses to sell reduced-priced electronics and other home goods. The new venture has grown rapidly. By 2013, Groupon Goods accounted for over 70% of the company's $2.6 billion in revenues.[32]

In considering a strategy for a firm, its leaders must make a series of choices, including the following:

- The range and variety of products and services to offer
- How the firm seeks to position itself within the marketplace
- The scale and scope of its operations
- The firm's organizational structure
- How success will be measured

As we will see throughout the rest of this chapter, these choices are often mutually dependent and reinforcing.[33] That is, the way a firm is organized depends on what it plans to produce and how it plans to produce it. The combination of the choices that a firm makes should form an integrated whole that is greater than the sum of the individual parts.[34] While the choices of where the firm will compete (industry) are very important, so too are the choices of how the firm will compete—the manner in which the firm will implement its strategic choices.

DEFINING STRATEGY

As a manager develops a strategy, he or she needs to consider three elements (see Figure 4.3).[35] First, the manager must realize that competitive strategy is primarily about being different. Strategy involves consciously picking a different set of activi-ties to deliver value for the customer.[36] If the product or service offered does not include activities that help to deliver value to the customer, the business will not remain profitable in the long term.

Second, while it is imperative to choose a set of unique activities, the manager must also decide what not to do. In other words, the manager must make trade-offs in the formulation of strategy. Without trade-offs, the company will end up trying to compete in too many markets where it does not have a competitive advantage.

Finally, the manager must create a solid fit among the activities so that the prod-uct or service being offered cannot be easily copied by competitors. The activities

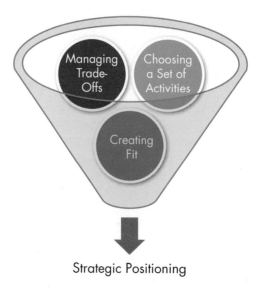

Strategic Positioning

Figure 4.3 ⟩ Three Components of Strategy

must be sustainable and interlocking in order to produce a product or service the customer wants.

The whole system of activities must be based around a performance theme. Otherwise, the firm will lose out to competitors. By themselves, activities and fit are not enough. Performance and execution must complement the system. While this definition sounds simple in theory, many managers fail to grasp the importance of each step and end up creating an incomplete strategy that ultimately fails. To help us better understand the strategy definition process, let's consider the three steps in greater detail and also look at some relevant examples.

Choosing a Set of Activities

A strategy should outline what the firm hopes to achieve (i.e., the markets it will serve, the products it will produce, and so on) as well as the manner in which it seeks to achieve those objectives.[37] For example, Southwest Airlines maintains a unique set of activities that differentiates it from competitors and allows it to maintain a low-cost model. The company concentrates on flying to airports that are both underutilized and near a metropolitan area; flying only one type of aircraft (Boeing 737s); and making short-haul trips, in contrast to the traditional hub-and-spoke system. In addition, the airline does not serve meals and does not offer seat assignments. When Southwest enters a new market, it often stipulates that fares be 70% below the average cost of flights already existing in the market. All of Southwest's activities are directed at bringing low-cost services to customers who might otherwise consider another form of transportation (for instance, a car or train).[38]

From its inception, Southwest has encouraged its employees to focus on the customer and have fun while doing it.[39] According to Southwest's former CEO, Herb Kelleher, "Fun is a stimulant to people. They enjoy their work more and work more productively."[40] This culture of fun at Southwest is promoted by every executive at the firm. With this culture, Southwest has been able to keep its employee turnover rate extremely low, averaging about 5% during the last decade. The culture has also allowed Southwest to pay lower average salaries relative to other airlines because employees want to work for the company.

In contrast, major airlines offer all of the things Southwest doesn't. For example, Delta uses a traditional hub-and-spoke system, serves meals, offers seat assignments, flies almost anywhere, and utilizes different types of aircraft. The different approaches of Delta and Southwest have resulted in dramatically different levels of profitability. While Delta has struggled, Southwest has created a unique set of activities that forms a clear strategy, resulting in 41 straight years of profitability.

In the consumer products industry, Gillette seeks to differentiate its products from those of its competitors by performing certain activities. Some of these activities include massive research and development (R&D) that has led to the continuous introduction of innovative products such as the Mach 3, Fusion, ProGlide, and FlexBall. Gillette performs these activities so that its products will have a higher perceived value in the marketplace. With Gillette's heavy expenditures on R&D and advertising, the company makes an active decision not to pursue a low-cost model. Compare this with their competitor, Bic that focuses heavily on a cost leadership strategy. They spend less than Gillette on R&D and advertising and can therefore charge significantly lower prices for their product.[41] On the flip side, Gillette's strategy enables them to charge premium prices for Mach 3 and Fusion blades because of the perceived value of the product in the marketplace. In 2015, Gillette

iStockphoto.com/Sjoerd van der Wal/Sjo

Fusion razors were priced at $12 with $5 replacement blades, while Bic disposable razors were as low as 40 cents each.

Southwest Airlines and Gillette have created a set of unique activities that delivers value to their customers. These unique activities allow companies to occupy a **strategic position** within their industry. A strategic position refers to a place in an industry that a firm occupies relative to its competitors by way of the products or services it offers and the method in which it delivers them.[42] When a company chooses its set of activities, they are, in effect, choosing to occupy a strategic position in a certain industry. The most common strategic positions are based on cost leadership, differentiation, and focus.[43] Southwest Airlines competes based on a cost leadership position. Gillette competes based on a differentiation strategy.

Another common strategy, a focus strategy, narrows the scope to focus on a niche market within an industry. In a focus strategy, cost leadership and differentiation are still the most common strategic positions, but companies use them to cater to market segments that are overlooked by larger companies. As a result, these companies are generally smaller.[44] Edward Jones is an example of one of these companies and is detailed in the next section.

Making Trade-Offs

Companies cannot effectively be all things to all people. If they try to do so, they often lack focus. This lack of focus is confusing to potential consumers as well as employees who are trying to deliver services for the firm.[45] The concept of a trade-off is often misunderstood and misapplied at companies and in life. Trade-offs are pervasive in all parts of people's lives. In fact, people make trade-offs every day without noticing what they are doing. For example, you may decide to grab a quick lunch between classes so that you can review your notes for the next class. The review provides a quick refresher of the material that will be covered and prepares you to engage in class discussion. In this instance, you are making an explicit trade-off between being prepared for class and enjoying a more leisurely sit-down meal with friends.

Edward Jones is one of the largest and most profitable retail investment brokers in the country, with over 11,000 offices in the United States. Like Southwest Airlines, the Midwestern-based investment firm has chosen a distinct set of activities to perform for its customers. Edward Jones defines its strategy as "offering trusted and convenient face-to-face financial advice to conservative individual investors who delegate their financial decisions through a national network of one-financial-adviser offices."[46] Edward Jones is explicit about the numerous trade-offs it has made. One key trade-off is the type of customer the firm endeavors to serve. The firm seeks to bring financial services to rural customers, who typically have fewer financial assets than people who live in metropolitan markets. The company has adopted a set of activities aimed at keeping costs low while simultaneously catering to the more conservative needs of its rural customers.

The firm also limits the activities its brokers perform. Compared to other brokerage houses, Edward Jones does not offer as many financial products and services (e.g., commodities, options, and full-scale investment banking). This set of activities contrasts sharply with the set of activities that many large brokerage houses maintain. However, Edward Jones believes that it is better able to serve its rural customer base by making these explicit trade-offs. The firm studied the marketplace to understand what its customers valued and were willing to pay for, then it structured its organization to deliver for them.

Creating Fit among Activities

For a strategy to be effective and defensible, a manager must create fit and alignment among its chosen activities. Companies that have superior strategies and profitability often employ a set of activities that reinforce each other and make the whole system difficult to duplicate. The goal of creating this "fit" among activities is to reduce cost

Strategic position
A place in an industry that a firm occupies by way of the products or services it offers and the methods it uses to deliver them.

or increase differentiation at a firm relative to that of its competitors. Strategic fit among many activities is fundamental not only to competitive advantage, but also to the sustainability of that advantage. In fact, it is often harder for a rival to match an array of interlocked activities than it is to imitate a particular advertising campaign or a set of product features.[47]

For example, the Toyota Motor Corporation employs an interlocked system of activities that have led to its overall success and profitability. This system, known as the Toyota Production System, involves a set of interlocked activities that promotes learning and constant improvement on the manufacturing line. Like strands of DNA, these rules govern how people carry out their jobs, how they interact with each other, how products and services flow, and how people identify and address process problems. The rules rigidly specify how every activity—from the shop floor to the executive suite, from installing seat belts to reconfiguring a manufacturing plant—should be performed. Deviations from the specifications become instantly visible, prompting people to respond immediately with real-time experiments to eradicate problems in their work.[48]

To many outside observers, the most important features of the Toyota Production System are structural, such as the andon cords that workers can pull when problems occur at their station. In fact, many of Toyota's competitors have tried to model their manufacturing systems after the company, in hopes of attaining Toyota's level of profitability.[49] But while many of Toyota's activities are widely known by competitors, very few firms have been able to replicate the entire system because of the unique fit that Toyota has created.

While the steps in defining and forming a strategy may seem simple, they are often very difficult to create and even harder to implement. The process is ultimately about creating fit among a company's activities. As we saw in many of the previous examples, firms that create a system of unique activities often maintain a performance edge over competitors in their industry. Managers should evaluate their strategy based on a number of key criteria (see Table 4.2).

PHILIPPE HUGUEN/AFP/Getty Images

Criteria	Evaluation
External Fit	Does the strategy fit with the environmental landscape?
Internal Fit	Does the strategy leverage the firm's key resources?
Differentiation	Does the strategy provide a distinct, differentiated, and sustainable position in the marketplace?
Implementable	Can the firm effectively execute the strategy?

Table 4.2 Criteria for Evaluating the Quality of a Firm's Strategy

Source: Adapted from Donald C. Hambrick and James W. Fredrickson, "Are You Sure You Have a Strategy?" *Academy of Management Executive,* Vol. 15, No. 4, November 2001.

BUSINESS-LEVEL VERSUS CORPORATE-LEVEL STRATEGY

Throughout most of this chapter, we have discussed a firm's strategy at a very broad level—what it hopes to achieve and how it hopes to achieve it. The manner in which an organization creates and sustains competitive advantage in an industry or a

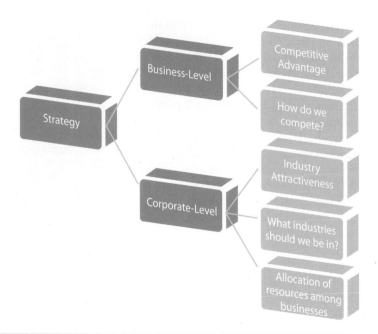

Figure 4.4 Business-Level and Corporate-Level Strategy

Source: Adapted from Robert M. Grant, *Contemporary Strategy Analysis: Concepts, Techniques, Applications* (Cambridge, MA: Blackwell Publishers, 1991), p. 20.

group of industries is driven by two types of strategy: **business-level strategy** and **corporate-level strategy** (see Figure 4.4). We'll briefly describe these two aspects of strategy next. Chapters 5 and 6 will provide greater detail.

Business-Level Strategy

Business-level strategy entails "how a company will compete in a given business and position itself among its competitors."[50] In setting business-level strategy, a manager evaluates both the attractiveness of the industry structure and the firm's resources to determine how the firm should compete. Based on these evaluations, the manager typically chooses among three generic strategic approaches: low cost, differentiation, and focus. As was discussed earlier in the chapter, Southwest Airlines has adopted a low-cost business strategy in the airline industry, Gillette has chosen a differentiation strategy in the male-targeted consumer products industry, and Edward Jones has pursued a focus strategy in the investment industry. As we will see in Chapter 5, business strategy is tightly intertwined with industry dynamics and evolution.

Corporate-Level Strategy

Corporate-level strategy decisions are made at a higher level than business-level strategic decisions and typically apply to companies that operate in multiple businesses. They typically include how many industries to compete across, whether to vertically integrate, whether to buy or sell companies, and how to share resources across divisions. In addition, corporate-level strategy often entails identifying and developing strategic alliances with other firms. In summary, corporate-level strategy is the way a company seeks to create value "through the configuration and coordination of multimarket activities."[51] Corporate-level strategy essentially defines the portfolio of businesses and approaches of the organization.

Different industries have different profitability profiles, and these differences greatly influence the way in which a manager should define his or her firm's

Business-level strategy
The determination of how a company will compete in a given business and position itself among its competitors.

Corporate-level strategy
The way a company seeks to create value through the configuration and coordination of multimarket activities.

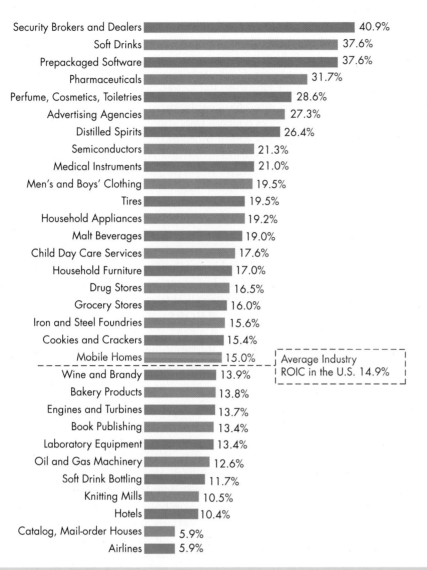

Security Brokers and Dealers	40.9%
Soft Drinks	37.6%
Prepackaged Software	37.6%
Pharmaceuticals	31.7%
Perfume, Cosmetics, Toiletries	28.6%
Advertising Agencies	27.3%
Distilled Spirits	26.4%
Semiconductors	21.3%
Medical Instruments	21.0%
Men's and Boys' Clothing	19.5%
Tires	19.5%
Household Appliances	19.2%
Malt Beverages	19.0%
Child Day Care Services	17.6%
Household Furniture	17.0%
Drug Stores	16.5%
Grocery Stores	16.0%
Iron and Steel Foundries	15.6%
Cookies and Crackers	15.4%
Mobile Homes	15.0%
Wine and Brandy	13.9%
Bakery Products	13.8%
Engines and Turbines	13.7%
Book Publishing	13.4%
Laboratory Equipment	13.4%
Oil and Gas Machinery	12.6%
Soft Drink Bottling	11.7%
Knitting Mills	10.5%
Hotels	10.4%
Catalog, Mail-order Houses	5.9%
Airlines	5.9%

Average Industry ROIC in the U.S. 14.9%

Figure 4.5 ⟩ Average Return on Invested Capital for U.S. Industries, 1992–2006

business-level and corporate-level strategies (see Figure 4.5). In the next chapter, we'll introduce a tool called the 5-Forces Framework that will help you better understand what dynamics occur in an industry and how different interactions determine profitability in industries. Regardless of their industry, every firm faces the challenge of how and when to expand globally.

STRATEGIES FOR GOING GLOBAL

As the world becomes more integrated, we see firms operating across multiple geographies. Sometimes it is hard to even pin down the country of origin of some companies as they operate at a very large scale in many geographies. Operating in multiple markets simultaneously can be very complicated. One of the central challenges such companies face is to balance the opposing forces of scale and local responsiveness. At one level, they need to leverage their global scale to take advantage of being big and operating in many markets at once. At the same time, each market requires them to behave and adapt to local market conditions so they can effectively compete with other local competitors.

While the names of the various global strategies seem to connote similar approaches and are often used interchangeably, there are significant differences between them. The main differences concern operational efficiency and customization. Some firms seek global strategies to sell more of the same products to a larger potential customer base. These firms are centrally managed and focused on production efficiency and cost effectiveness. Other firms pursue customization to ensure that its products are aligned with local customs and tastes. In this situation, local operations are granted considerable autonomy. Still other firms pursue a hybrid form of these two approaches by balancing local customization and operational efficiency.

Firms use **multinational strategies** when it is important to be responsive and sensitive to local needs and tastes; this approach usually involves significant customization of a firm's products. **Global strategies** focus on developing overall scale economies and global efficiency instead of catering to local tastes; as such, a primary goal is cost management. **International strategies** are a cross between global and multinational strategies. Like a global strategy, it maintains control over subsidiaries, but like a multinational strategy, it allows subsidiaries to develop new products and ideas to match local tastes. The **transnational strategy** focuses on efficiency, local responsiveness, and organizational learning.

Multinational Strategy

In the multinational model, the parent company organizes local subsidiaries and gives them autonomy to develop products tailored to local tastes. The local subsidiary may perform all corporate functions at the local level. For example, multinational subsidiaries often perform sales and marketing functions at the local level to account for strong local preferences. Creating several sales and marketing organizations in subsidiaries can be costly. Depending on how the multinational organizes, a firm could have dozens of marketing organizations attempting to localize products according to specific preferences. This practice not only creates additional costs in the system, but also makes coordination among units difficult.

Global Strategy

In contrast to a multinational strategy, a global strategy attempts to provide a standardized product to all markets. One of the main goals of a global strategy is to take advantage of scale economies in production. By manufacturing products in one centralized location on a large scale, a firm can take advantage of the efficiencies and cost savings that come with massive production. The electronics industry has come to be dominated by firms using the global strategy. In the 1950s and 1960s, introduction of the transistor and integrated circuit reduced the cost of manufacturing and increased the minimum efficient scale of production. As a result, the efficient scale for production of color TVs rose from 50,000 sets per year in the early 1960s to 500,000 sets in the early 1980s.[52] At the same time, R&D and marketing costs increased to a level that prevented more local players from competing in the business. Consumer electronics retailers such as Best Buy also emerged, placing even more pressure on manufacturers to lower their cost structures.

Constant technical changes and the homogenization of tastes have continued to fuel the consumer electronics industry's pursuit of world scale economies.[53] Many Japanese competitors such as Matsushita used this form of global strategy to dominate consumer electronics markets in the 1970s. Under its Panasonic name brand, the Japanese company achieved high profits and market share by producing fairly

Multinational strategies Strategies in which the parent company organizes local subsidiaries and gives them autonomy to develop products tailored to local tastes.

Global strategies Strategies that focus on developing overall scale economies and global efficiency instead of catering to local tastes.

International strategies Strategies that combine elements of multinational and global strategies by using foreign subsidiaries to produce and distribute products.

Transnational strategy Strategies that balance a firm's international activities among efficiency, local responsiveness, and organizational learning.

standardized consumer electronic products in its centrally located plants. More recently, Apple has adopted this strategy in the dissemination of its iPhone, iPod, and iPad products. But while this strategy has worked for products that are conducive to standardization, it does not work for all products. Local markets often differ in their tastes and preferences. When considering a global strategy, a manager must consider if the company's products can be standardized for all geographic markets or if they need to be customized to fit local tastes and preferences.

International Strategy

An international strategy combines elements of multinational and global strategies. Like a multinational strategy, international strategies focus on using foreign subsidiaries to produce and distribute products. Like a global strategy, critical processes such as R&D are performed by the parent company in its home market. In a sense, firms that pursue an international strategy compete in markets that do not require high levels of local customization or low-cost production through economies of scale. With international strategies, local subsidiaries rely on the parent firm for core processes and for the diffusion of technology and other innovations. This model allows the parent firm to tightly control the development of products and innovation. However, this model is not particularly useful for adapting products to local preferences or achieving economies of scale.

Transnational Strategy

The key attribute of the transnational firm is the ability to balance strategy among three factors: efficiency, local responsiveness, and organizational learning. Because some markets may require more local responsiveness than others, this flexibility enables a firm to respond to dynamic environmental factors. Firms using the transnational strategy develop flexibility by balancing scales of efficiency while responding to local needs. For example, some production may be centralized to a few locations in order to take advantage of low costs and scale economies, and other production activities may be conducted at the local level in order to adapt to local preferences. As part of this strategy, the transnational centralizes some resources at home and distributes other resources among global units, which can result in a complex configuration of assets and capabilities.[54]

A transnational firm must also have the ability to share and diffuse information across the entire firm. For example, Intel relies on foreign subsidiaries to help the company spot innovation trends in markets around the world. For much of its history, Intel focused on processor chips to achieve growth, and it fueled 20% annual growth throughout the 1980s and 1990s. But in the late 1990s, with growth slowing down, Intel decided to broaden its business focus to include networking devices, wireless phones, information appliances, and anything related to e-commerce. To help with this transition, Intel spent $6 billion acquiring 12 companies in 1999 alone.[55] Many of the firm's important technologies, such as flash memory, were discovered or developed in foreign markets and later diffused throughout the company.[56]

Managers have numerous options to consider when forming a global strategy, and they must match their firm's strategy to the global business environments in which it competes. When Weber, maker of the iconic cooking barrel grill, decided to ship their products to India, they created the Weber Experience Center in Bangalore to teach Indians about the practice of grilling. The Indian market had some inherent challenges, not the least of which was that most Indians are vegetarian. Indians also do not tend to have large backyards where grills are commonly placed in the United States. Despite these challenges, the Indian market had some strong opportunities such as the common practice of grilling vegetables, fish, and pizza. In addition to teaching the advantages of grilling in India through the Weber Experience Center, Weber heavily marketed their smallest grill, a 145 in. grill called the Smokey Joe. This portable grill has also been a key to Weber's success in China.[57]

MARKET ENTRY STRATEGIES

Determining which country to enter depends on its market and learning potential.[58] Market potential refers to the overall market size of a particular region and its growth prospects. For many companies like Weber, emerging markets such as China are attractive because of the growth of the middle-class population. As consumers in emerging markets start earning higher incomes, they will demand more commodities.

Following market selection, a manager needs to decide on a mode of entry. First, a manager must decide the extent to which a firm will export its goods or produce them locally.[59] Second, a manager must decide whether the firm will own all of the production assets or share ownership with another party. Within this dimension, a manager can choose low ownership structures, such as franchising or licensing, or higher ownership structures, such as alliances or joint ventures. In other cases, firms can choose total ownership through a wholly owned subsidiary. Let's look at the four major forms of market entry to help us discern which mode is appropriate for different situations.

Exporting

The practice of **exporting** involves shipping a firm's products from its domestic home base to global markets. For example, toys made in China are shipped to the United States. To accomplish this task, a firm usually contracts with international officials to transport and distribute its products in global markets. The practice of exporting has positive and negative outcomes. On the positive side, exporting provides many firms an opportunity to begin the global expansion process in an inexpensive and low-risk way.

On the negative side, one of the biggest challenges of an exporting strategy is the loss of control over sales and marketing in the international market. This occurs when a firm cedes control to a foreign group that may not understand the product and sales process as well as the firm does. A firm can avoid this challenge by managing the sales process itself. Exporting is also susceptible to political or economic instability and can be dramatically impacted by tariff legislation.

Licensing and Franchising

Two other low-cost methods that firms entering foreign markets can use are licensing and franchising agreements. **Licensing** is a contractual arrangement "whereby the licensor (selling firm) allows its technology, patents, trademarks, designs, processes, know-how, intellectual property, or other proprietary advantages to be used for a fee by the licensee (buying firm)."[60] The majority of international licensing involves technology transfer among industrialized nations. Licensing agreements also occur in other industries—consumer products, food, and entertainment. In 2005, MTV Networks and Warner Music Group announced a licensing agreement that would allow MTV to include Warner's music video catalog in programming it sells over mobile phone networks worldwide.[61]

Licensing allows many firms to test a foreign market before seeking a higher-impact entry strategy. However, licensing can involve many risks, the most important being the potential loss of proprietary advantage.[62] When Angela Ahrendts took the helm of Burberry in 2006, she was concerned by the way in which the firm had licensed its products.

Exporting
Shipping a firm's products from its domestic home base to global markets.

Licensing
A contractual arrangement whereby the licensor (selling firm) allows its technology, patents, trademarks, designs, processes, know-how, intellectual property, or other proprietary advantages to be used for a fee by the licensee (buying firm).

Franchising
Common arrangements in many retail businesses where a firm contracts with individual owners to operate its retail units. This arrangement typically involves a corporation sharing management and marketing techniques with the owner in exchange for a fee and some percentage of the unit's revenues.

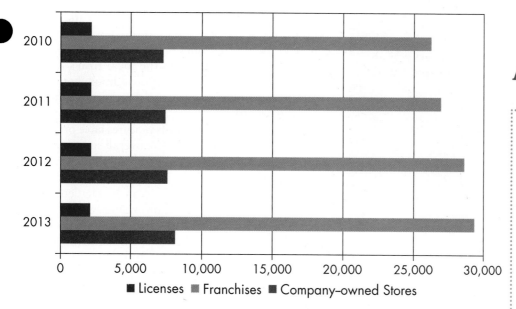

Figure 4.6 〉 Composition of YUM! Brands Restaurants, 2010–2013

Source: YUM! Brands, "YUM! Financial Data," at www.yum.com/investors/restcounts.asp, accessed March 5, 2015.

In her view, the company had too aggressively licensed the Burberry name, creating a global presence that lacked cohesion and consistency. One of her first acts was to buy back the licensing rights and redirect them to products that were aligned with the company's positioning as a high-end, hip brand for young, wealthy consumers.[63]

As a market entry mode, **franchising** shares many similarities with licensing. Franchising is an organizational form "where the franchisor (parent company/owner) of a service, trademarked product, or brand name allows the franchisee to use the name in return for a lump sum payment or royalty, while conforming to required standards of quality and service."[64] While licensing most often occurs between manufacturing firms, franchising is used by service firms such as hotels and fast-food chains. YUM! Brands, which runs the Kentucky Fried Chicken, Pizza Hut, and Taco Bell chains, has embraced franchising for their expansion efforts (see Figure 4.6). By 2013, almost 75% of Yum's outlets were franchises, and many of them were in international markets. For example, more than 65% of Kentucky Fried Chicken's (KFC) 14,000 outlets are located outside the United States.[65] Yum has made a concerted effort to target Africa for its most recent expansion plans. Trying to tap into the growing urbanization and consumerism of major African cities, Yum has almost 1,000 KFC locations in 17 African countries with plans to add more in the near future.[66]

Like licensing, franchising is a low-cost means of market entry. Typically, the franchisor provides the brand name and other managerial processes while the franchisee assumes most or all of the capital risk. The firm does not control much of the operations or quality of service in franchised locations. For example, a hotel franchisee in an overseas market might delay upgrading the décor of rooms, despite a contract stating that it must update room furnishings every 5 years. In practice, the corporate parent may have a difficult time enforcing this guideline because revoking a franchise agreement is often a long and arduous process.

Joint Ventures and Alliances

In a **joint venture**, two firms come together to form a new company in a market. Joint ventures were popular with many firms looking to expand in the Chinese market in the 1980s when the country was not as open to international expansion as

A DIFFERENT View

Is the World Flat?

Do we live in a globalized world? Technology and trade certainly support the notion that the world is flat. Brands like McDonald's and Coca-Cola permeate even remote areas of Asia and Africa. Author Tom Friedman first presented the notion that the world has been flattened by influences such as outsourcing and smartphones. But economics professor Pankaj Ghemawat studied the notion of a globalized economy and found surprising data. He looked at a variety of metrics such as cross-border trade and Internet traffic and found that the extent of globalization is only about 10%. Ninety percent of business activity is still within national borders.

1. What data can you find to support the notion that the world is flat? What data supports the notion that the world is not flat or only partly flat?
2. What organizations are truly global? What percentage of their business is global?
3. What conclusions about the global economy can you draw from the findings of both Friedman and Ghemawat?

Joint venture
A structure where two firms come together to form a new company in a market.

Aly Song/Reuters

it is today. For firms such as General Motors, a joint venture may be the only vehicle through which the firm can enter an international market. In a joint venture, the foreign firm learns from the local firm's knowledge of the market and country. In addition, both firms typically contribute resources to the venture, allowing both to share risks.

Despite these benefits, joint ventures have produced varied results over the years. The overall success rate of joint ventures globally is about 50%.[67] This low success rate exemplifies the numerous risks inherent in joint ventures. They tend to encounter challenges involving strategy, governance, or organizational issues. Regarding strategy, members of the joint venture may have different strategic interests, consequently affecting their ability to collaborate. For governance, most joint ventures are designed to allow both partners to share control, a construct that often leads to disagreement. Finally, many partners in joint ventures find it difficult to overcome the vast cultural differences that exist between the partners.

Walmart launched its international strategy in 1991 by forming a joint venture with Cifra, a leading retailer in Mexico. This joint venture lasted for 6 years. In 1997, Walmart acquired the majority shares of Cifra and formally changed the name of its operations to Walmart de Mexico. Walmart has been very successful in Mexico despite some early missteps. When they initially built new stores in the country, they replicated the U.S. model including large parking lots, but in Mexico, most consumers arrived at Walmart by bus. There was no need for large parking lots. The company quickly changed its approach to accommodate the shopping requirements of bus travelers. By 2013, the company operated over 2,000 stores and had a 55% market share of the Mexican retail market.[68]

In contrast to joint ventures, contractual alliances do not create a new entity. In an **alliance**, partners come together by contract to engage jointly in activities in a market. An alliance involves a firm sharing resources or capabilities with a counterparty for the mutual benefit of both. Alliances can be used to obtain a competitive advantage in a market or to achieve a competitive balance. In general, a firm pursues a strategic alliance when the cost of creating an internal entity or developing a capability is higher than the cost associated with forming the alliance. Alliances are low cost but take time and effort to establish and cultivate.

In general, a firm should pursue alliances or joint ventures based on the environmental conditions in the market—for example, when the local market is substantially different from the firm's home market or when language and cultural habits differ dramatically.[69] While this knowledge of the local market can also be obtained through an acquisition, many firms struggle to integrate foreign acquisitions because of cultural differences. When Ford entered the Indian market, it considered numerous entry options but ultimately settled on a joint venture with the local firm Mahindra & Mahindra to help navigate the local business environment. Three years after the establishment of the joint venture, Ford increased its stake from 50% to 92%.[70]

A firm should also pursue a joint venture or alliance when the potential for integration of global operations is low.[71] One of the benefits of having global operations is the learning that can take place. But for learning to occur, different units must be well integrated with the corporate center. If global integration is unlikely or not possible, firms should enter the market with a partner. Finally, firms are forced to engage in local alliances or joint ventures in countries that require local equity

Alliances
A structure where partners come together by contract to engage jointly in activities in a market.

participation. Countries such as China and Brazil have required foreign firms to work with a local company when entering their markets.

When Disney began construction on its 963-acre Shanghai Disneyland in 2011, it partnered with three state-owned enterprises that collectively hold a 57% stake in the operation. While Disney was required to partner with a local Chinese operation to open in China, they have been able to gain invaluable insights from their partners. For instance, their partners have provided advice about the types of food to serve at the park (more dim sum and noodle dishes), and the types of rides to build (a combination of Disney movie-themed rides as well as rides based on Chinese culture). A visitor to Shanghai Disneyland will likely encounter Mickey Mouse, but instead of being clad in his signature U.S. attire, he will be wearing a traditional, red Chinese outfit to symbolize good fortune. By paying attention to cultural differences and norms, Disney hopes to attract the 300 million people who live within a three-hour drive of the park.[72]

Wholly Owned Subsidiaries

Finally, a firm can enter a foreign market through a **wholly owned subsidiary**. In this case, a firm sets up a fully operational, independent entity in a foreign country to conduct business in that market. Many firms use this mode of market entry exclusively because of the sensitive nature of their technology or processes. For technology and pharmaceutical companies, intangible assets represent the bulk of the value of their firms. As a result, many firms feel uncomfortable with licensing or alliance structures. In addition, the wholly owned subsidiary allows the parent company to maintain tight control over the new enterprise. This control becomes important when the firm's products or services involve tightly fitting activities that may be difficult for an alliance or joint venture partner to understand.

Establishing a wholly owned subsidiary is an expensive and risky proposition. A firm must establish production facilities and train employees in the new market. For managers who have grown accustomed to the sophisticated infrastructure and technology environments of the United States, foreign markets can be a marked contrast. In this sense, the manager of a wholly owned subsidiary needs to maintain creativity and flexibility when adapting a firm's processes to the local infrastructure and overall environment.

The tale of Walmart and Target Stores in Canada offers an interesting perspective on international expansion through local market acquisitions. Walmart has been very successful in Canada since its entry in 1994. In that year, the company acquired 120 of 142 Woolco discount stores in Canada and rebranded them as Walmart but retained the employees and the top leadership team. When Walmart acquired the Woolco stores, they were largely unprofitable. In a few short years, Walmart was able to reverse this situation by leveraging its successful technology and supply management practices from the United States. Walmart even tailored some of its product offerings to Canadians who sought a larger variety of furniture, pet supplies, and consumer electronics.[73]

For its part, Target did not enter Canada until 2011 when it acquired 220 stores from Zellers. This purchase marked Target's first effort to expand beyond the United States. While Walmart was able to apply its business practices with success in Canada, Target struggled. The company spent $4 billion dollars to set up the Canadian operation but has not been able to make it profitable. After just a few years, Target decided to close all its stores and exit the market. Though the company used a similar strategy as Walmart to enter the market, the stores that Target purchased were in poor locations, were hard to access, and were smaller, requiring significant costs to transform them. In addition, Target made some poor decisions

Wholly owned subsidiary
A fully operational, independent entity that a firm sets up in a foreign country to conduct business in that market.

regarding its inventory. Though Target was aware that Canadians came to the United States to shop for interesting, trendy, and unique items at Target stores along the border, when they opened their operations in Canada, they did not stock similar items. They opted to carry mostly basic merchandise. Canadian shoppers who expected a unique experience similar to the United States were disappointed. Even with these basic products, Target was not able to keep shelves stocked due to its poor supply management processes. Target senior executives estimated that the company would not be profitable in Canada until 2021. This sobering statistic was a key reason behind the company's decision to exit Canada.[74]

SUMMARY

For companies, the development and implementation of strategy is often the difference between winning and losing in an industry. Without a consistent, unique set of activities and resources, a firm will not be able to create a competitive advantage in the marketplace.

LO1 The concept of strategy has been around for thousands of years, and its roots are deeply imbedded in the military. Military strategists must identify the landscape of battle, understand the strengths and weaknesses of their opponents, and determine appropriate tactical maneuvers. Business leaders must do the same. They need to be aware of the competitive landscape, understand the strengths and capabilities of their rivals, and develop a plan of attack for the market.

LO2 The framework for understanding a firm's strategy involves multiple components, starting with defining the firm's purpose. The next step is to analyze the internal and external environments to determine what resources, challenges, and opportunities are available to achieve a firm's vision, mission, and objectives. A firm's mission statement outlines the firm's reason for existence and states what activities the firm will perform, what customers it will serve, and how it will distinguish itself. Having analyzed the internal and external environments and defined its mission, a firm can then formulate its strategy. The formulation of strategy is often a planned and emergent process. The planned component is derived from the assessment of the environment and the capabilities of the firm. Strategic planning is used for this purpose. The emergent process is developed through an ongoing reevaluation of the competitive landscape usually performed by frontline managers.

LO3 In defining its strategy, a firm must choose a unique set of activities, make trade-offs, and create fit among these activities to develop core competencies that will distinguish the firm from competitors. At the same time, the manager must focus on the performance of these activities to create value for customers and other stakeholders.

LO4 The manner in which a firm builds and sustains a competitive advantage in an industry is driven by business-level and corporate-level strategies. A firm's business-level strategy outlines the manner in which it will compete in a specific industry. The three most common strategic approaches to competition are being the low-cost provider, providing a differentiated product or service, and being focused on a specific customer or market segment. A firm's corporate-level strategy outlines the number of industries that a firm will compete across and the manner in which it will share resources and produce outputs across various divisions.

LO5 When expanding globally, managers need to choose a strategy—multinational, global, international, or transnational—that fits with their firm's goals. As firms progress in their global development, managers should consider transitioning from a focus on local responsiveness or global efficiencies to a transnational form, a blend of both factors. A transnational firm views its global subsidiaries not only as sources of revenue, but also as sources of innovation and learning.

LO6 As managers evaluate their global strategies, they must weigh the advantages and disadvantages of various market entry strategies—from exporting to licensing to alliances to wholly owned subsidiaries. The right market entry approach depends on a number of factors, including the size of the market, the availability of raw materials, access to key resources, capital requirements, the presence of local partners, and the country's social and economic policies.

KEY TERMS

Alliances
Business-level strategy
Competitive advantage
Conglomeration
Core competencies
Corporate-level strategy
Exporting
Franchising

Global strategies
Goal
International strategies
Joint venture
Licensing
Mission
Mission statement
Multinational strategies

Objectives
Strategic position
Strategy
Strategy formulation
Tactics
Transnational strategies
Vision
Wholly owned subsidiary

ASSIGNMENTS

Discussion Topics

1. Certain companies like Apple, Southwest Airlines, and Amazon seem to be able to maintain a strong competitive advantage within their respective industries. How are they able to do so? What do they need to do to sustain their competitive advantage?

2. What are the advantages and disadvantages of strategic planning?

3. What is the purpose of business? Complete the following statement with the first word that comes to your mind: "Medicine is to health, as Law is to justice, as Business is to _____." What did you say/write? Why? What does that mean?

4. Consider a company such as McDonald's or Walmart. How would they define their purpose? What is their mission?

5. In what ways is the development of strategy a planned process? An emergent process? Which process do you believe provides greater value?

6. What is the difference between strategy and tactics?

7. Southwest Airlines has begun to modify its strategy by serving more major market areas. Do you think they will continue to be successful? What challenges will they face and how should they address those challenges?

8. Toyota often lets other companies view their production lines. Why aren't other companies as successful in implementing the well-proven Toyota production system? Why can't you just "plug and play" best practice processes from one company to another?

9. What are the advantages and disadvantages of each of the global strategies? Why would a company choose one approach over another?

10. What are the advantages and disadvantages of each of the global market entry modes? Rank the market entry modes in order of difficulty. When should a firm adopt a particular approach?

Management Research

1. Select a firm and describe its vision, mission, and mission statement. How is the vision and mission aligned with the firm's strategy? Does the firm's mission or vision emphasize its values? In what ways is the mission motivating to employees?

2. Pick a firm and analyze its business strategy. Is there an aspect of the firm's strategy that incorporates its ethical practices?

3. Examine the list of industry profitability in this chapter (Figure 4.5). Can you hypothesize why some industries on the list have higher profits than others? Which industry do you find more attractive? Why?

4. Find one example for each of the foreign entry modes discussed in the chapter.

In the Field

1. Earlier in this chapter, you learned that strategy is not simply the domain of business and can be a critical component of athletic teams.

With a few of your classmates, attend a local athletic team event.

- How would you describe the team's strategy?
- What are some examples of the team aligning its talent management practices with its strategy?
- How does the coach empower the team to execute its strategy?

- Does the team have an observable competitive advantage?

2. Visit a local franchise in your community and interview the manager to learn how the corporate office works with the local franchisee to craft a strategy. Are there differences between the corporate-level strategy and the strategy of the local franchisee?

ENDNOTES

1 Michael E. Porter, "What Is Strategy?," *Harvard Business Review*, November–December 1996.

2 Kenneth R. Andrews, *The Concept of Corporate Strategy* (Homewood, IL: Dow-Jones-Irwin, 1971), p. 28.

3 Roger L. Martin, "The Big Lie of Strategic Planning," *Harvard Business Review*, January–February 2014.

4 David Collis and Jan W. Rivkin, "Strategic Renewal," Harvard Business School Module Note No. 9-708-503, rev. April 6, 2009 (Boston, MA: HBS Publishing, 2008), p. 1.

5 Online database of players and statistics, www.baseball-reference.com, accessed November 18, 2009.

6 Michael Lewis, *Moneyball: The Art of Winning an Unfair Game* (New York: W.W. Norton, 2003).

7 Bruce D. Henderson, "The Origin of Strategy," *Harvard Business Review*, November–December 1989, p. 141.

8 R. L. Wing, *The Art of Strategy: A New Translation of Sun Tzu's Classic "The Art of War,"* (New York: Doubleday, 1988), p. 13.

9 Ibid.

10 Mark B. Fuller, "Business as War," *Fast Company*, December 19, 2007, www.fastcompany.com/magazine/00/war.html.

11 R. L. Wing, *The Art of Strategy: A New Translation of Sun Tzu's Classic "The Art of War,"* (New York: Doubleday, 1988).

12 Henry Mintzberg, *The Rise and Fall of Strategic Planning* (New York: Free Press, 1994), pp. 239–245.

13 C. Chet Miller and Laura B. Cardinal, "Strategic Planning and Firm Performance: A Synthesis of More Than Two Decades of Research," *Academy of Management Journal*, Vol. 37, No. 6, 1994, p. 1649.

14 Keith Naughton, "The Happiest Man in Detroit," *Bloomberg Businessweek*, February 7–13, 2011; and Jena McGregor, "Ford Appoints Mark Fields New CEO," *Washington Post*, July 5. 2014.

15 Milton Friedman, "The Social Responsibility of Business Is to Increase Its Profits," *The New York Times Magazine*, September 13, 1970, pp. 122–126.

16 Netflix, "Corporate Fact Sheet," http://ir.netflix.com, accessed October 1, 2009.

17 Warren Bennis and Burt Nanus, *Leaders: The Strategies for Taking Charge* (New York: Harper & Row, 1985), p. 89.

18 Chris Groscurth, "Why Your Company Must Be Mission-Driven," *Gallup Business Journal*, March 6, 2014 at http://www.gallup.com/businessjournal/167633/why-company-mission-driven.aspx, accessed February 28, 2015.

19 John A. Pearce II and Fred Davis, "Corporate Mission Statements: The Bottom Line," *Academy of Management Executive*, Vol. 1, No. 2, 1987, p. 109.

20 Chip Jarnagin and John W. Slocum, Jr., "Creating Corporate Cultures Through Mythopoetic Leadership," *Organizational Dynamics*, Vol. 36, No. 3, 2007, p. 292.

21 Forest R. David and Fred R. David, "It's Time to Redraft Your Mission Statement," *Journal of Business Strategy*, Vol. 24, No. 1, 2003, p. 11; and John A. Pearce II and Fred Davis, "Corporate Mission Statements: The Bottom Line," *Academy of Management Executive*, Vol. 1, No. 2, 1987, p. 112.

22 Forest R. David and Fred R. David, "It's Time to Redraft Your Mission Statement," *Journal of Business Strategy*, Vol. 24, No. 1, 2003, p. 11; and Jerome H. Want, "Corporate Mission: The Intangible Contributor to Performance," *Management Review*, 1986, p. 47.

23 David J. Collis and Michael G. Rukstad, "Can You Say What Your Strategy Is?," *Harvard Business Review*, April 2008, p. 3.

24 Henry Mintzberg, "The Design School: Reconsidering the Basic Premises of Strategic Management," *Strategic Management Journal*, 1990, pp. 171–195.

25 Arthur A. Thompson, Jr. and A. J. Strickland III, *Strategy Formulation and Implementation: Task of the General Manager*, 5th edition (Boston, MA: Irwin, 1992), pp. 5, 7.

26 Arnoldo C. Hax and Nicolas S. Majluf, "The Corporate Strategic Planning Process," *Interfaces*, Vol. 14, No. 1, 1984, p. 49.

27 Henry Mintzberg, "Crafting Strategy," *Harvard Business Review*, July–August 1987.

28 Adelaide Wilcox King, Sally W. Fowler, and Carl P. Zeithaml, "Managing Organizational Competencies for Competitive Advantage: The Middle-Management Edge," *Academy of Management Executive*, Vol. 15, No. 2, 2001, p. 98.

29 Kenneth R. Andrews, *The Concept of Corporate Strategy* (Homewood, IL: Dow-Jones-Irwin, 1971), p. 29.

30 Christopher Steiner, "Meet the Fastest Growing Company Ever," *Forbes*, August 30, 2010, http://www.forbes.com/forbes/2010/0830/entrepreneurs-groupon-facebook-twitter-next-web-phenom.html.

31 Ibid.

32 Ingrid Lunden, "Groupon Goes after Costco and Sam's Club with Groupon Basics, A Portal for Home Goods," Techcrunch.com, May 1, 2014, and Douglas MacMillan, "Groupon CEO Andrew Mason Fights to Keep His Job," *Bloomberg Businessweek*, January 10, 2013.

33 Richard P. Rumelt, Dan E. Schendel, and David J. Teece, "Fundamental Issues in Strategy," *Fundamental Issues in Strategy: A Research Agenda*, Richard P. Rumelt, Dan E. Schendel, and David J. Teece, eds. (Boston, MA: HBS Press, 1994), p. 9.

34 Donald C. Hambrick and James W. Fredrickson, "Are You Sure You Have a Strategy?," *Academy of Management Executive*, Vol. 15, No. 4, November 2001, p. 54.

[35] Michael E. Porter, "What Is Strategy?," *Harvard Business Review*, November–December 1996, pp. 3–18.

[36] Ibid., p. 8.

[37] Donald C. Hambrick and James W. Fredrickson, "Are You Sure You Have a Strategy?," *Academy of Management Executive*, Vol. 15, No. 4, November 2001, p. 52.

[38] Charles O'Reilly and Jeffrey Pfeffer, "Southwest Airlines (A)," Stanford Graduate School of Business Case No. HR-1A, rev. April 5, 2006 (Stanford, CA: Stanford Graduate School of Business, 1995), p. 3.

[39] Ibid.

[40] Ibid., p. 7.

[41] Paul Betts, "Bic Struggles to Shave into Gillette's Market Leadership," *Financial Times*, October 31, 2007, available via LexisNexis, accessed September 2011.

[42] Michael E. Porter, "What Is Strategy?," *Harvard Business Review*, November–December 1996, p. 3.

[43] Michael E. Porter, *Competitive Strategy: Techniques for Analyzing Industries and Competitors* (New York: The Free Press, 1980), pp. 34–46.

[44] Richard S. Allen, Marilyn M. Helms, Margaret B. Takeda, and Charles S. White, "Porter's Generic Strategies: An Explanatory Study of Their Use in Japan," *Journal of Business Strategies*, Vol. 24, No. 1, Spring 2007, p. 74.

[45] Michael E. Porter, "What Is Strategy?," *Harvard Business Review*, November–December 1996, p. 10.

[46] David J. Collis and Michael G. Rukstad, "Can You Say What Your Strategy Is?," *Harvard Business Review*, April 2008, p. 1.

[47] Michael E. Porter, "What Is Strategy?," *Harvard Business Review*, November–December 1996, pp. 10–14.

[48] Steven Spear and H. Kent Bowen, "Decoding the DNA of the Toyota Production System," *Harvard Business Review*, September–October 1999, p. 1.

[49] Ibid., p. 2

[50] Kenneth R. Andrews, *The Concept of Corporate Strategy* (Homewood, IL: Richard D. Irwin, Inc., 1980), p. 13.

[51] David Collis and Cynthia Montgomery, "Corporate Strategy: A Conceptual Framework," Harvard Business School Note No. 9-391-284, rev. April 17, 1995 (Boston, MA: HBS Publishing, 1991), p. 6.

[52] Christopher A. Bartlett and Sumantra Ghoshal, *Managing across Borders: The Transnational Solution*, 2nd edition (Boston, MA: HBS Press, 1998), p. 26.

[53] Ibid.

[54] Ibid., p. 69.

[55] "The New Intel: Craig Barrett Is Leading the Chip Giant into Riskier Terrain," *Bloomberg BusinessWeek*, March 13, 2000, http://www.businessweek.com/2000/00_11/b3672001.htm, accessed September, 2011.

[56] Ashlee Vance, "Stretching Intel Flash Memory," *International Herald Tribune*, December 3, 2008, available via Factiva, accessed September, 2011.

[57] Ryan Bradley, "Where Grills Are Born," *Fortune*, August 13, 2012.

[58] Anil K. Gupta and Vijay Govindarajan, "Managing Global Expansion: A Conceptual Framework," *Business Horizons*, March–April 2000, p. 47.

[59] Ibid., p. 48.

[60] Paul Beamish, "Note on International Licensing," *Ivey Management Services*, 2005, p. 1.

[61] Ibid., p. 10.

[62] Ibid., p. 3.

[63] Beth Kowitt, "High Tech's Fashion Model," *Fortune*, June 11, 2012.

[64] Paul Beamish, "Note on International Licensing," *Ivey Management Services*, 2005, p. 1.

[65] Yum!, "YUM! Financial Data," at http://www.yum.com/investors/restcounts.asp, accessed February 20, 2015.

[66] Bradley Seth McNew, "Following China, This Is Where Yum! Brands' Growth Could Come From Next," *The Motley Fool*, January 20, 2015.

[67] Joe Bleeke and David Ernst, "The Way to Win in Cross-Border Alliances," *The McKinsey Quarterly*, Vol. 28, No. 1, 1992, pp. 113–133.

[68] Juan Alcacer, Abjishel Agrawal, and Harshit Vaish, "Walmart around the World," Harvard Business School Case No. 9-714, 431, rev. December 6, 2013 (Boston, MA: HBS Publishing, 2013).

[69] Anil K. Gupta and Vijay Govindarajan, "Managing Global Expansion: A Conceptual Framework," *Business Horizons*, March–April 2000, p. 49.

[70] Ibid.

[71] Ibid.

[72] "Disney Gets a Second Chance in China," *Bloomberg Businessweek*, April 18–24, 2011.

[73] Juan Alcacer, Abjishel Agrawal, and Harshit Vaish, "Walmart around the World," Harvard Business School Case No. 9-714, 431, rev. December 6, 2013 (Boston, MA: HBS Publishing, 2013).

[74] Paul Ziobro and Rita Trichur, "Target Bails Out of Canada," *Wall Street Journal*, January 16, 2015; and Matt Townsend, "Why Target is Raking Up Its Maple Leaves," *Bloomberg Businessweek*, January 26, 2015-February 1, 2015.

CHAPTER

5

Business-Level Strategy

Learning Objectives

After reading this chapter, you should be able to:

LO1 Describe the way a firm competes within its industry.

LO2 Outline how various forces in the external environment impact the attractiveness of an industry.

LO3 Describe how a firm's internal environment impacts its strategic approach.

LO4 Describe a firm's value chain.

LO5 Perform a SWOT analysis of a firm by describing its internal strengths and weaknesses and defining the opportunities and threats that it faces in the marketplace.

LO6 Describe how a firm can generate competitive advantage through one of the three generic strategies: cost leadership, differentiation, or focus.

SELF-REFLECTION

Framing for Competitive Advantage

The ability to frame a situation is an essential managerial skill. Framing entails observing, interpreting, and acting to make sense of a situation. When managers create a frame of reference for a firm's business-level strategy, they are focusing on the key actions that will result in a competitive advantage. On a scale of 1 to 5, evaluate your strategic framing skills as you read the following statements:

1 = never 2 = rarely 3 = sometimes 4 = usually 5 = always

1. I can map out how a firm creates value for its customers. _____

2. When evaluating a product, I consider its quality. _____

3. When studying a company, I try to identify ways that expenses can be reduced. _____

4. I know how a firm positions itself to differentiate its products and services. _____

5. I realize that some firms are at a competitive disadvantage because they lack a clear strategy. _____

6. I understand how an industry structure influences a firm's strategy. _____

7. I understand the rationale for why some firms target a smaller segment of an industry. _____

8. I recognize that a firm's tangible and intangible resources are an important determinant of competitive advantage. _____

9. When studying a firm's strategy, I am aware of the primary and support activities needed for implementation. _____

10. When thinking about a firm's strategy, I consider how the contributions of employees create value. _____

Based on this assessment, what are your strategic-framing strengths? What can you improve?

INTRODUCTION

This chapter focuses on how a firm competes in its industry and builds competitive advantage through a clearly articulated strategy. As a manager, it is helpful to think of two questions regarding the choice of competitive strategy. The first question a manager must ask is, "How attractive is the industry?" Industries have unique structures and characteristics that shape the manner and level of competition among firms and the potential for profit.[1] Some industries are characterized by high growth and constant change, while others are relatively stable. In the airline industry, for instance, profits have traditionally been low for various reasons: high fuel costs, legacy cost structures, and intense competition. Poor structural industry conditions, however, do not preclude smart players from earning outsized profits. As we saw in Chapter 4, Southwest Airlines is the perfect example of a company that succeeds despite difficult

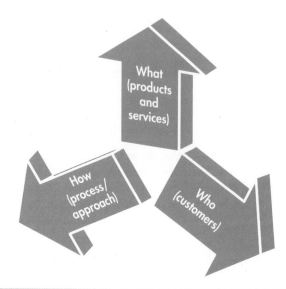

Figure 5.1 〉 Three Components of Strategy

Source: Adapted from Constantinos Markides, "Strategic Innovation," *Sloan Management Review*, Spring 1997, p. 12.

industry conditions. Having evaluated the characteristics of the industry, a manager must then ask a second question, "How will the firm compete in the industry?" This positioning of a firm within its industry is the essence of business-level strategy.

In setting business-level strategy, a manager evaluates the attractiveness of the industry structure, the opportunities and threats in the external environment, and the firm's internal resources to determine how to compete. In developing a business-level strategy, a manager must answer three fundamental questions: (1) Who do we serve (a broad or narrow market segment)? (2) What do we provide (a small or large range of products or services)? and (3) How do we provide it (our unique production approach or delivery processes)? Those three questions are illustrated in Figure 5.1. The answers to these questions often determine which generic strategic approach a firm will follow: a low-cost strategy, a differentiation strategy, a focused strategy, or some combination thereof.

To outline the concepts of business-level strategy, we'll discuss two firms that have experienced different levels of success. One firm has been able to sustain strong growth in an extremely competitive marketplace while the other has struggled to develop a consistent growth strategy.

Starbucks vs. Krispy Kreme

Many professionals, parents, and students begin their mornings with a cup of coffee, and increasingly, that cup is from Starbucks. The company's products can be found almost anywhere—on street corners, in bookstores, in office buildings, in shopping malls, and in cafeterias. Starbucks has become so popular in America today that it is not unusual for busy urban streets to have two or three Starbucks outlets within

sight of each other. However, while the well-known coffee maker is ubiquitous today, the specialty coffee market barely existed just two decades ago.

Howard Schultz, the individual most responsible for the growth of Starbucks, began his career as a salesperson for a housewares company. He was first introduced to specialty coffee when he visited an account named Starbucks in Seattle that was buying many of his company's plastic cone filters. Upon seeing and tasting the local company's products, Schultz became convinced that this type of coffee could be sold nationwide in stand-alone restaurant facilities. Following his trip, Schultz left his job in New York and signed on with the fledgling company. Unable to convince senior management to open additional retail outlets, Schultz eventually left Starbucks.

After leaving Starbucks, Schultz and his colleagues opened several specialty coffeehouses in the Seattle area. When the original owners of Starbucks looked to exit their business, Schultz gathered capital to buy it. Following the acquisition in 1987, Schultz planned to open 125 stores in 5 years using the Starbucks name.

Despite the fact that the market for specialty coffee was still fragmented and most consumers had little concept of the product or its benefits, Schultz believed that premium coffee engulfed in a certain retail ambience had broad appeal.[2] The retail ambience that he sought to recreate was a European coffee house where patrons linger for hours. He hoped to build a brand and a customer experience, which linked Starbucks with fine coffee.[3]

Starbucks quickly gained a cult following in major metropolitan areas and later spread across the country. Through a unique strategy and well-defined activities, Schultz brought value to both consumers and shareholders. The results of his strategy were nothing less than breathtaking. By 2014, the company boasted $16.4 billion in annual revenues with over 21,000 outlets in the United States and abroad (see Figure 5.2).[4]

As you can see from the example of Howard Schultz at Starbucks, performance and strategy make a difference in terms of profitability. Prior to the late 1980s, the coffee industry appeared to be a low-growth, low-profit segment of the global beverage industry. Market leaders such as Folgers and Maxwell House competed based on price and concentrated on selling coffee for consumption in the home. Schultz's strategy was predicated on creating an environment where individuals would pay a premium to enjoy coffee outside their home. Though other coffee shops are direct competitors of Starbucks, the company also competes against Folgers and Maxwell House for overall coffee consumption.

Schultz developed a competitive advantage relative to large coffee

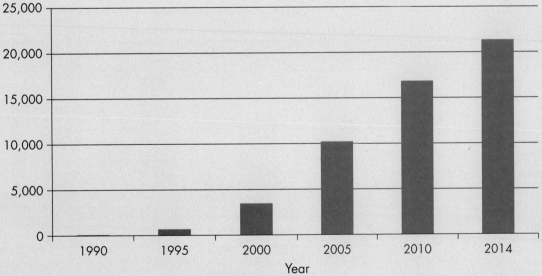

Figure 5.2 Growth of Starbucks Stores, 1990–2014

Source: Starbucks Corporation, 10-K (Seattle, WA: Starbucks Corporation, 2000–2014); and Nancy F. Koehn, "Howard Schultz and Starbucks Coffee Company," Harvard Business School Case No. 9-801-361, rev. September 30, 2005 (Boston, MA: HBS Publishing, 2001), p. 29.

producers and other coffee shops by differentiating his product and constructing a system of internal and external firm activities that shielded the company from many threats. In hindsight, Schultz gambled on the assumption that consumers would pay premium prices for this added quality and experience. He mitigated these risks through a defensible strategy and the development of core competencies (human resources, for instance) that further differentiated his offering relative to competitors. However, the experience has been very different for many other food and beverage companies that have attempted to expand rapidly into structurally challenging segments of the market.

The story of Krispy Kreme doughnuts is marked by extreme highs and lows. Despite launching the most successful initial public offering (IPO) of the year in 2000, the company became the subject of a Securities and Exchange Commission (SEC) investigation just 3 years later. While the SEC investigation centered on accounting irregularities, many of the company's core problems stemmed from overexpansion and lack of attention to changing eating habits.

Krispy Kreme was started by Vernon Rudolf in 1937 when he purchased a recipe for doughnuts from a French chef in New Orleans. As the doughnut chain gained recognition in its home market, the company began to expand to other regions of the country. During this period, Krispy Kreme pursued expansion through company-owned outlets and franchised operations. In 2000, when Krispy Kreme went public, the company's stock was pushed to new highs as investors watched consumers line up for hours at a new outlet to get hot glazed Krispy Kreme doughnuts.[5] Flush with IPO funds and a mandate from investors, the company began an aggressive push across the United States and Canada. In 5 years, the company expanded from fewer than 200 stores to 433, mainly through its franchising model (see Figure 5.3).

At the same time Krispy Kreme began ramping up its expansion strategy, many Americans began new dieting fads such as the Atkins and South Beach diets. Both promoted the lower intake of carbohydrates (i.e., breads and cereals). Despite such widespread media attention focused on new weight loss strategies, Krispy Kreme failed to recognize the potential negative effect that such a shift in consumer preferences might have on demand for its products. The company also failed to expand into new products that might insulate it from a drop in demand for doughnuts. As the company continued to open new stores in 2004, profitability began to free fall, declining from $50 million in 2004 to a loss of $157 million in 2005.[6] As Krispy Kreme's sales began to slip in 2003, senior managers started to engage in suspect accounting practices in an effort to maintain and sometimes boost profitability. When these

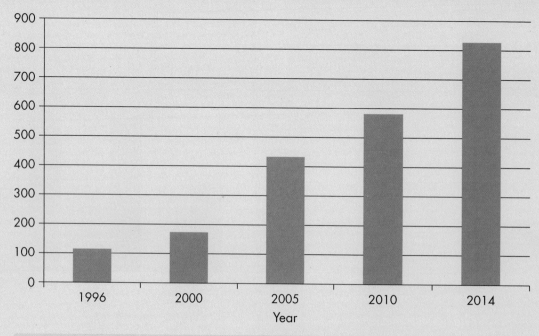

Figure 5.3 › Growth of Krispy Kreme Stores, 1996–2014

Source: Krispy Kreme Doughnuts Inc., 10-K (Winston-Salem, NC: Krispy Kreme Doughnuts Inc., 2001–2014).

accounting misdeeds came to light, the stock price fell from $44 in 2003 to $6 in 2005,[7] and the senior management team was replaced.

If you look back at some of the press clippings or analyst reports from 2000 when it became a public company, you will see a very different view of Krispy Kreme. Many analysts initially hailed the company as a great brand with superior growth prospects, but the company lost sight of changes in the external marketplace and lost control of internal operating procedures. One key to a firm's long-term survival is its ability to understand and adapt to expected and unexpected changes in the marketplace. Krispy Kreme failed to adjust to changes in Americans' eating habits. In an effort to regain its former prominence, Krispy Kreme has closed poor performing stores, cut operational costs, and streamlined less profitable businesses. These cost containment measures have enabled the company to begin to pursue an expansion plan. In doing do, the company has to be careful not to make the same mistakes again. To that end, it is being more careful about store formats and locations. With weaker domestic demand for its products, Krispy Kreme is heavily investing in international expansion.[8]

In contrast, the phenomenal growth of Starbucks is partially attributed to the company's ability to ride the wave of free spending and indulgence during the last two decades of the twentieth century when Americans were willing to pay over $3 for a cup of specialty coffee. In the aftermath of the global financial crisis of 2008, Starbucks had to reevaluate its business proposition—streamlining some of its offerings and slowing down its expansion plans. To achieve growth in the past, Starbucks relied on rapid expansion of stores both domestically and internationally. Since then, they have shifted their strategy to operate in a leaner economy. For example, in 2011, Starbucks announced that it would pursue expansion into items like juices and teas that would be sold in grocery stores.[9] To enhance its product offerings in grocery stores as well as its own retail outlets, Starbucks acquired juice company Evolution Fresh and bakery La Boulange and formed an alliance with Danone for yogurt. These acquisitions and alliances have enabled the company to control more of its operations. Previously, the company sold Pepsi's Naked Juice in its Starbucks cafes. These have now been replaced with its own Evolution products. In early 2012, Starbucks unveiled a new service whereby customers could pay for purchases with their smartphones. Within a few short weeks, Starbucks became the largest and most popular retailer to offer this level of convenience.[10] By 2014, Starbucks was processing 5 million mobile payments per week.[11] Through this effort, Starbucks sought to further differentiate its business in a marketplace that was increasingly competitive.

Throughout this chapter, we'll discuss many examples of companies like Starbucks that have been able to achieve market success based on a superior strategy. Some companies have achieved this advantage through differentiation while others have focused on cost efficiency. Still others have found success by narrowing their scope to focus on a small segment of the market. We will explore all three approaches in the chapter.

The Leadership Development Journey

Translating strategy into action is the work of strategy implementation. Many managers will work hard at formulating a strategy, but struggle with the work of implementation. Yet, strategy implementation is a vital aspect of a firm's business-level strategy. Think about a time when you were a member of a student club, participated on an athletic team, worked at a job, or volunteered at a nonprofit organization.

1. How were the strategic goals translated into action steps?
2. How did leadership engage others to work toward its goals?
3. What did you contribute to the implementation of the strategy?
4. Was the implementation of strategy a success? Why or why not?

HOW THE EXTERNAL ENVIRONMENT IMPACTS INDUSTRY ATTRACTIVENESS

As we saw in Chapter 1, every firm is affected by its external environment. Most firms are affected by a common set of forces, including technological forces, economic forces, political and legal forces, sociocultural forces, and global forces. An effective strategy aligns a company's resources and strengths with the opportunities presented in the external environment.[12] In the examples of Chapter 1, we saw how turbulence in a firm's external environment may create challenges. In the Walmart case, the firm faced extreme challenges as it attempted to expand its Supercenter format into California. The lesson from this example and the others in Chapter 1 was the importance of recognizing and developing strategies for a firm's various stakeholders. While the stakeholder tools help a manager recognize influential factors, they do not necessarily provide an understanding of a firm's industry environment. To comprehend Walmart's context, we would need to understand their relationship with their suppliers, customers, and also the nature of the competitive environment they are facing. One such tool to comprehend the industry context within which firms operate is the 5-Forces Model developed by Professor Michael Porter.

Porter's 5-Forces Model

The model's original intent was to provide a comprehensive framework to assess an industry's long-run profit potential. It suggests that any industry's attractiveness can be assessed by exploring five basic forces.[13] The 5-Forces Model, as shown in Figure 5.4, includes the threat of new entrants, bargaining power of customers, threat of substitutes, bargaining power of suppliers, and rivalry among existing competitors. By examining

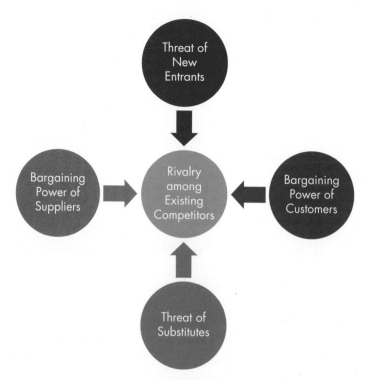

Figure 5.4 ⟩ Porter's 5-Forces Model

Source: Michael E. Porter, "The Five Competitive Forces That Shape Strategy," *Harvard Business Review*, January 2008.

these five factors, a manager can obtain a sense of the long-term prospects of the industry and the strategic forces that guide it. Any good strategist uses this tool as a starting point for identifying the strengths and weaknesses of an industry. This tool can also be used to assess which forces a firm might try to modify to make the industry more attractive for them.

Threat of New Entrants

A common threat to any industry is the threat of entrants. While some industries have barriers that reduce this threat, others are easy to enter. When a new competitor enters an industry, it often means that more of the same products are supplied to the same customer base, which ultimately decreases profits for all players. While all industries have some threat of entry from competition (except regulated or nationalized industries), the level of threat can differ from industry to industry. According to the 5-Forces Model, the threat of entry into an industry depends on the **barriers to entry** that are present and on the reaction from existing competitors that entrants can expect.[14] Barriers to entry tend to vary by industry, and they are the obstacles that a new entrant may face while trying to enter a market or an industry. Some of the most common entry barriers include high capital investments needed to enter the industry and the high costs associated with customers switching from one company to another. There are other forms of entry barriers, which we'll explore in a moment. The personal computer (PC) industry provides an interesting example of entry barriers in action.

The PC has become so ubiquitous today that it's easy to forget what the industry looked like just a few years ago. Prior to PCs, the computer market was dominated by firms such as IBM that produced large mainframe and minicomputers for industrial and governmental use. Not only was it very costly to develop a new mainframe at the time, but convincing customers to switch was very hard as their costs of switching were very high. In the early 1980s, several start-up firms began developing computers for use by individuals including Apple, which achieved success among certain groups.[15] When IBM launched its version of the PC, it quickly gained 42% of the market in only two years.[16] However, unlike its mainframe computers, IBM outsourced its PC processor to Intel and its operating system to Microsoft. In addition, IBM opened up its product architecture to encourage software developers to write programs for its PCs.[17]

At the outset of the PC market, IBM maintained a huge competitive advantage over other firms because of its brand name, sales force, and relationship with lucrative corporate accounts. However, when IBM opened up its architecture to software and peripheral manufacturers, it also opened the door for competitors. In the past, IBM had kept system architectures in-house, developing proprietary systems for its mainframe computers. This made it hard for any new entrants to enter this market. But with the PC, IBM was late to the market and thus sought to make up time by outsourcing certain components and allowing those suppliers to sell those same components to any other company that might want to enter the PC market. Through this singular move, IBM tore down a huge entry barrier to the PC industry, allowing others to procure the same inputs from those suppliers.

As demand for IBM PCs exploded, other firms started making "IBM clones."[18] In fact, Compaq made over $100 million in revenue in its first year of offering IBM clones.[19] Other clone manufacturers followed suit, including Dell, Gateway, and Hewlett-Packard. By 1986, IBM realized that it had set an open standard but, in doing so, it had spawned a set of imitators.[20]

Barriers to entry
Obstacles a firm may face while trying to enter a market or an industry.

Tomasz Bidermann/Shutterstock.com

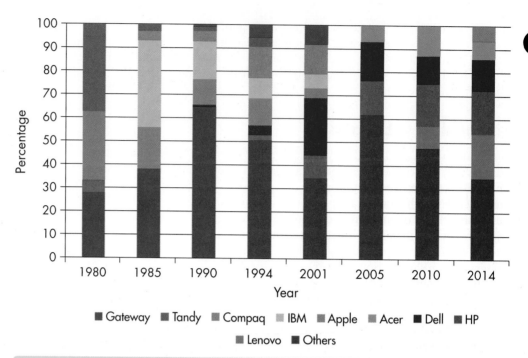

Figure 5.5 PC Market Share Trends, 1980–2014

Sources: V. Kasturi Rangan and Marie Bell, "Dell—New Horizons," Harvard Business School Case No. 9-502-022, rev. October 10, 2002 (Boston, MA: HBS Publishing, 2002) John Steffens, Computer Industry Forecasts and New Games: Strategic Competition in the PC Revolution (New York: Pergamon Press, 1994) "Home Personal Computers—US—December 2008," December 2008, Mintel www.mintel.com, accessed December 14, 2009 Gartner, "Garner Says Worldwide PC Shipments in Fourth Quarter 2010 Grew 3.1 Percent; Year-End Shipments Increased 13.8 Percent," January 12, 2011 at http://www.gartner.com/newsroom/id/1519417, accessed March 9, 2015; Garner, "Gartner Says EMEA Region Became Largest PC Market in the World Based on Unit Shipments in 2005," January 18, 2006, at http://www.gartner.com/newsroom/id/492237, accessed March 9, 2015; and IDC, "PC Leaders Continue Growth and Share Gains as Market Remains Slow," January 12, 2015, at http://www.idc.com/getdoc.jsp?containerId=prUS25372415, accessed March 9, 2015

By 1989, IBM's share of the PC market had fallen to 17% as customers began purchasing cheaper cloned PCs (see Figure 5.5). Over the past 20 years, there has been a tremendous shake up in the personal computer industry. Compaq was purchased by HP in 2002, and in 2004, IBM sold its PC business to Lenovo, a Chinese multinational firm for $1.25 billion.[21] Ten years later, Lenovo became the top worldwide seller of personal computers.

As you can see from IBM's foray into the PC industry, the lowering of barriers to entry encourages competition and, in turn, creates a less profitable industry for everyone. When these barriers are high, as was the case with IBM's mainframe business, prospective competitors found it difficult to enter the industry, so the industry was more profitable for IBM and others who were already in it.

Now that we've seen what can happen to an industry when entry barriers drop, let's discuss some of the major sources of barriers to entry, including supply-side economies of scale, demand-side benefits of scale, customer switching costs, capital requirements, incumbency advantages independent of size, unequal access to distribution channels, and restrictive government policy. As you'll see, many of these barriers are interrelated, which can increase the challenges for new entrants. Barriers to entry are also related to the lifecycle stage of an industry. When an industry or a market is new and emerging, barriers are generally low and many firms scramble to enter and build a dominant position.[22] When an industry becomes more established and mature, it is often difficult for a new entrant to enter on a similar scale or level as an incumbent.

Supply-Side Economies of Scale

Supply-side economies of scale arise when a firm manufactures products or services in high volumes. The ability to produce and sell large volumes results in a much lower production cost.[23] These lower costs in turn can deter entry by new firms since they cannot generate the same production scale at the time of entry.[24] Scale-based forms of entry barriers are present in many industries, including microprocessors, steel, and automobiles. In each of these industries, there are fixed costs of entry, such as the cost of building a plant and purchasing equipment, which are extremely high. These large fixed costs, in turn, often warrant even larger scale production to generate profits, which can be a major obstacle for new entrants.

Demand-Side Benefits of Scale

These benefits for a product arise in situations where any buyer's willingness to pay for that product increases as the number of other buyers for that product increases.[25] In essence, buyers benefit by buying something that others are also buying. Some classic examples of this are the telephone and fax machines where individual buyers benefited greatly when others also bought those products. The effect usually kicks in when there is a critical mass of people who have bought the product. These benefits of scale often discourage entry by reducing consumers' preference to purchase from a newcomer to the industry.[26] The traditional example of demand-side benefits of scale is the Microsoft operating system, Windows. As Windows continues to dominate the operating system market (with more than a 90% market share in 2014), potential entrants are essentially locked out because of consumers' preference to buy systems that are compatible with the existing universe of software.[27] Interestingly, Microsoft is confronting this very challenge as it tries to make inroads in the smartphone market with its Windows Phone operating system. Consumers are already loyal to operating systems using the Apple or Android platform. As of 2014, Windows Phones only had 2.7% market share.[28]

Customer Switching Costs

Switching costs are fixed costs that buyers encounter if they change the supplier of a particular product or service.[29] A switching cost often arises because the buyer has to make changes to their product or operating procedure when using a new supply source.[30] A classic example was faced by computer companies like Apple whose customers early on had to incur significant costs to switch over to them. Apple software was not compatible with other PC providers and customers wanting to transfer their files from a PC product to an Apple product faced considerable challenges. The investment brokerage industry is another example where customers face high switching costs. Many consumers conduct all of their investment activities through a single brokerage entity such as Fidelity Investments. The typical consumer may have stocks, mutual funds, and retirement accounts with the broker. Many consumers encounter roadblocks when attempting to transfer assets to another broker. In this case, the high costs that consumers face include the time and patience needed to complete the transfer. These high switching costs are also seen in online banking. Once a

customer sets up his or her accounts, payment schedules, and billing information, the process of switching to another bank, regardless of potentially better interest rates, is not very appealing.

Capital Requirements

In many industries, large amounts of capital are required by any new entrant just to begin operating. Capital may be necessary not only for fixed facilities but also for customer credit, inventories, and possibly start-up losses.[31] Many industries require new entrants to make huge capital expenditures for entry, including copper mining, pharmaceuticals, and steel production. The research and development costs in the pharmaceutical industry are tremendous, with average drug development costs exceeding $2 billion prior to approval.[32] With this requirement, many potential entrants are restricted from entering the industry.

Incumbency Advantages Independent of Size

In many industries, incumbent companies maintain cost or quality advantages that are not easily available to a potential rival.[33] These advantages may include superior technology, preferential access to raw materials, government subsidies, or even a strong brand.[34] As we saw in the case of IBM, proprietary technology can act as a significant barrier to entry. When IBM outsourced several components of its PC to other firms, it effectively destroyed an important barrier to entry.

Unequal Access to Distribution Channels

Every company must distribute its product or service to customers through what are known as distribution channels. These include wholesalers and even local retailers where the ultimate customer purchases the product or service. However, many industries (e.g., beverages) are marked by limited distribution channels. If you've ever walked into a convenience store, you've probably noticed the proliferation of soft drinks, bottled waters, and juices. Many of these products are not only manufactured but also distributed by firms such as Coke and Pepsi through some wholly owned bottlers or others who have an exclusive agreement with them. For new entrants such as VitaminWater, the barriers to entry were significant because they needed to find distribution channels for their product. Ultimately, they needed someone to deliver their product to the retailer. At the same time, they needed to convince retailers to offer them valuable shelf space for their new and untested product. To combat this problem, VitaminWater courted independent distributors through extensive promotion and marketing. VitaminWater's founder, Darius Bikoff, aggressively marketed his product to distributors and retailers, often going door to door in Manhattan to gain shelf space in stores. Through this effort, VitaminWater slowly gained a toehold in what is traditionally a difficult market to enter.[35]

Restrictive Government Policy

Governments can limit or even foreclose entry to industries via controls such as license requirements, patent protection, foreign investment barriers, and limits on access to local raw materials markets.[36] The New York City cab industry represents an industry marked by restrictive government policy. In New York, the number of cabs is capped at approximately 14,000 licenses. These licenses, known as medallions in New York City, are valuable commodities controlled by a few private firms. Since the number of taxi medallions is fixed, those sold on the open market can fetch up to $1 million.[37] This system has historically prevented an aspiring entrepreneur from buying a car and running his or her own taxi service. The emergence of ride service companies such as Uber and Lyft has diminished the traditional power of these restrictions in the taxi industry. It is not surprising then that taxi companies in major metropolitan cities have worked vigorously to restrict the entrant of these new companies.

Bargaining Power of Suppliers

The second of five forces that shapes industry profitability is the relative bargaining power of suppliers to that industry. If the suppliers are strong compared to the buyers in that industry, they can dictate their terms and, in turn, reduce the profitability of that industry. Suppliers provide firms in an industry with essential inputs in the manufacturing or production process. For most firms, the term "supplier" connotes a broad group, including entities such as the utility company, raw material producers (e.g., steel producers), employees (supplying

Stuart Monk/Shutterstock.com

labor inputs), manufacturers of preassembled components, and services ranging from security to consulting. Every industry and the firms within it have a long list of suppliers that exert different degrees of power over them. Some of the most common aspects of supplier power occur when there are no substitutes for the supplier's product, when the supplier limits production, or when the supplier does not consider the industry as one of its major customers.[38] There are several other forms of supplier power that we'll explore in a moment. For now, let's look at an example that demonstrates supplier power in action.

For the last two decades, Microsoft has exerted tremendous supplier power over PC makers. As the dominant producer of operating system software, Microsoft has maintained a market share in the 90% range for the last two decades. The company has maintained this share because of the barriers to entry in the operating system software industry. As mentioned previously, Microsoft enjoys demand-side benefits of scale. When IBM outsourced the production of its operating system to Microsoft in 1981, it provided the firm with a **first-mover advantage** that has proved difficult to overcome. First-mover advantage occurs when a firm is the first to offer desirable products or services that secure customer loyalty. One study has shown that first movers can sometimes enjoy a decade long advantage over second movers in an industry.[39]

As the standard for IBM and PC clones, Microsoft Windows became an essential component of every PC. As the years passed and the number of Windows users increased, Microsoft's supplier power grew stronger, making it difficult for competitors to enter the industry. While the company sells Windows directly to consumers, the majority of its sales go through original equipment manufacturers (OEMs) that build the PCs. With the network of Windows in the hundreds of millions, most OEMs have little choice but to include the Windows system in its offerings and pay whatever price Microsoft dictates.

As you can see, every industry has a long list of suppliers that manifest different sources of power relative to the firms in that industry. While Microsoft exhibits extreme supplier power over OEMs in the PC industry, other suppliers that sell to OEMs in that same industry may exhibit low bargaining power (for instance, disk drive manufacturers). The important thing to remember is that every industry and market is different in terms of who has the power in the buyer–supplier relationship.

First-mover advantage
A competitive advantage that occurs when a firm is first to offer desirable products or services that secure customer loyalty.

Characteristics of a Powerful Supplier Group

Among an industry's list of suppliers, several characteristics determine whether a group is powerful relative to the firms in that industry. A supplier industry will tend to be powerful when the following happens:

- **The supplier industry is more concentrated than the industry it sells to.** We saw this form of supplier power in the Microsoft example, where a single firm clearly dominates the operating system industry while a dozen firms compete in the PC industry.
- **Industry participants in the buyer industry face switching costs in changing suppliers.** Many utilities are forced to purchase certain varieties of coal because their boilers are commissioned to accept coal with specific chemical properties. To switch to another variety of coal, utilities must decommission the plant for a time to retrofit it with equipment to handle the new coal. In this case, utilities face extreme switching costs in terms of coal use.
- **No substitutes exist for what the supplier group provides.** In the pharmaceutical industry, individual drug and medical device makers produce extremely differentiated products that are protected by patents, making it impossible for anyone to copy their product for the duration of the patent. Through the duration of patent protection, consumers and hospitals that need the product have low bargaining power relative to the drug maker. In many cases, the drugs or devices are unique and no one has produced anything close to it, which concentrates power with the supplier. As we will see later in this chapter, individuals suffering from certain diseases have no alternative treatments. A company such as Genzyme and other pharmaceutical companies that make unique offerings by developing treatment for rare diseases can price their products with almost total discretion.
- **The supplier group can threaten to integrate forward into the buyer industry.** This tends to happen when an industry earns significant profits, the barriers to entry in the industry are low, and the supplier to that industry has the resources and capabilities to move downstream into it. Diesel, a luxury clothing producer, forward integrated into the retail industry when it opened its own mono-brand stores to sell its jeans.
- **The supplier group does not depend heavily on the industry.** If the supplier group does not count the industry as a major customer, it may seek to extract maximum profits from the industry through aggressive

pricing.[40] By virtue of the fact that the industry is not a major customer of the supplier industry, the supplier has greater power. It can threaten to walk away at very little cost to itself if the buyer industry doesn't accept its terms. If it's a critical input for the buyers, they may have no choice.

A DIFFERENT View

Threat of Substitutes

The possible threat of substitutes or the appearance of real substitutes can also limit the profitability of an industry. Take the example of the local taxi industry in many markets around the world where it was quite profitable with few threats of substitutes and high entry barriers due to government restrictions and licensing requirements. Companies like Uber that provide links between passengers and drivers have upended the traditional taxi service in many major cities around the world. Uber has been able to circumvent the traditional restrictions on taxi regulations and licenses in the cities in which it operates by claiming that it is a technology platform for matching people with specific transportation needs. It asserts that it is not an actual transportation company and therefore should not be subject to the typical regulations that apply to taxis and limos thereby bypassing an important entry barrier.

Launched in 2009, Uber began as a private limo service and quickly evolved into a broader ride matching service. Uber has a proprietary technology platform that enables it to connect local drivers with passengers. By 2014, the company had rapidly expanded to over eighty-five cities in thirty-two countries and had become a significant competitive threat to local taxi and limousine service companies.[41]

Many passengers were happy to substitute the traditional taxi service for an Uber ride. Some customers found taxis to be poorly maintained and uncomfortable. Other customers were frustrated that taxis refused to service certain areas in the city.[42] With Uber, passengers generally pay about the same as a traditional cab, but the application provides other conveniences including a wider coverage area. Passengers who have downloaded the app on their phones can track cars in their area, which allows them to better manage their time. Payment is also much easier. All charges are made through a credit card that passengers register with Uber. The company takes care of the payment process so no money changes hand in the car. Uber keeps 20% of the fare and pays 80% to the driver.[43] This direct payment to drivers eliminates the traditional middleman or dispatcher at a taxi company. In addition, passengers are able to rate drivers, and drivers are also able to rate passengers. These ratings allow passengers and drivers to make quick decisions on whether or not to "work together."

Despite its success in creating a viable substitute for taxis and limos, Uber has been criticized by taxi and limo services for inadequate driver screening and training and by customers for its practice of surge pricing. With surge pricing, the company moderates the fares that passengers pay based on the level of demand. For instance, Uber pricing tends to increase during peak holidays, snow storms, and at 2 a.m. on weekends when many bars close. These criticisms have led to concerns about passenger safety and renewed calls for local municipalities to regulate the company. As the company expands it will undoubtedly have to contend with potential regulation from local municipalities and increased competition from local taxi and limo companies. Potentially more concerning to Uber is that Google may soon enter the market and offer its own substitute for local transportation. Though Google invested over $250 million in Uber in 2013, the company announced its plans to sever its relationship in 2015. Google is exploring an Uber-like service of its own using its Google maps as a precursor to a future transportation system that includes self-driving cars.[44]

Many industries today face the threat of substitutes. A substitute could be a competitor's product or some other product that satisfies the same consumer needs.

According to the 5-Forces Model, the very threat of substitute products or services can limit an industry's profit potential by placing a ceiling on the prices the companies in an industry can charge.[47] If they exceed that limit, it can make the industry sufficiently attractive for substitutes to quickly enter the market.

Some substitutes are not immediately obvious. For instance, when Southwest Airlines introduced its low point-to-point airfares, the goal was not to compete with traditional airlines. The company sought to offer an alternative to individuals who typically used their cars or the Greyhound bus company to travel relatively short distances. Southwest offers a substitute for car and bus travel as well as an alternative to other airlines.

Bargaining Power of Customers

Depending on the industry, a firm's customers may look and act very differently. In some industries, their customers/buyers may have a lot of power over them. You can look at this dynamic between two industries where one buys from the other or between two firms where one buys from the other or between a firm and its individual customers. Let's look at the industry level. Take the case of consumer packaged goods companies that sell their products to large retailers like Walmart and Costco. Because their customers are large and powerful, they are under a lot of pressure to offer their products at the lowest possible cost leading to very low margins and profits. The only way to mitigate this issue is by being large and powerful such as a Proctor and Gamble (P&G). In P&G's case, they can exert a countervailing power, which can lead to a more balanced relationship.

Another example can be seen with steel manufacturers. Their customers are typically large corporations—automakers or personal appliance manufacturers, for instance. Large customers such as automobile manufacturers are likely to have a lot of power over this industry by virtue of how much they buy from them.

The point is that different types of customers can exert different levels of pressure on a company based on their **bargaining power**. A buyer industry will tend to have high power relative to the supplier industry when the buyer purchases in very large volumes or when the supplier's products are largely undifferentiated. In these cases, the buyer or customer has the power to force down prices in an industry.[48] Let's look at an example that demonstrates customer power in action.

The steel industry was dominated by a few integrated producers for much of the twentieth century. In 1950, the Big Three steel producers—U.S. Steel, Bethlehem Steel, and Republic Steel—produced approximately 60% of the total steel produced in the United States. During this period, successful steel producers were well-capitalized firms that exercised tremendous supplier power over buyers.[49] Most buyers often had little choice but to purchase steel from the producer located closest to their plant, as transporting steel was a significant cost. However, bargaining power began to shift during the late 1950s and early 1960s when foreign competitors entered the market. During this period, large, integrated Japanese producers became the dominant exporters into the U.S. market.[50] Through manufacturing enhancements, Japanese companies steadily increased their productivity and were able to overcome the additional transportation costs they incurred to ship their products to the United States. The Japanese could achieve this price leadership because their entire steel industry was essentially rebuilt with newer technology following World War II. This more efficient technology, coupled with government aid and lower labor costs, allowed Japanese producers to beat their U.S. competitors on price, even with the added transportation costs.[51]

As imported steel flooded the U.S. market, steel buyers began to exercise more power over steel companies that produced largely undifferentiated products. As the power shifted from supplier to buyer in the steel industry, many steel

Bargaining power
The pressure that a supplier or buyer can exert on a company.

firms experienced a decline in both market share and profitability.[52] The shift in bargaining power, coupled with extremely high legacy cost structures, led to a permanent decline in the fortunes of U.S. steel producers. By 2002, the second, third, and fifth-largest U.S. steel producers had all declared bankruptcy.[53] Ten years later, the U.S. steel industry was still struggling with cheaper imports, but this time they were dealing with a new type of competitor, government subsidized steel producers in China and South Korea. The government subsidies in these countries allowed steel producers to export steel at very low prices, increasing the bargaining power of customers and further eroding the U.S. steel industry. Almost 1,000 U.S. steelworkers lost their jobs in 2014 due to the impact of these cheaper imports.[54]

Characteristics of a Powerful Customer Group

As we saw in the case of the steel industry, powerful customer groups can harm a company by exacting both price and quality pressures on their sellers. A customer group can come in the form of large individual customers or a group of customers that comes together to coordinate a form of collective buying. In general, a customer group will tend to have power in the following circumstances:

- **The group is concentrated or purchases in large volumes relative to the supplier.** Walmart exerts extreme buyer power over a number of firms because of its size. As the largest retailer in the world, Walmart is often the largest customer of many firms. Because of its size and scope, Walmart is able to exert downward price pressure on its suppliers. Walmart and Amazon have had a similar impact on the book publishing industry; both have forced publishers to reduce prices, even on their best sellers.
- **The sellers' products are undifferentiated.** We saw this type of bargaining power in the example of the steel industry. Most steel companies produced a largely undifferentiated product that was ultimately vulnerable to lower priced competitors.
- **Buyers face few switching costs in changing vendors.** Switching costs tend to be low in several industries, including the paper and office supply industry. Paper and office supplies are generally cheap commodities, which can be purchased from numerous suppliers. This means the sellers of office supplies face very powerful customers. As such, most businesses do not maintain exclusive contracts with a particular office supplies firm, often switching suppliers based on price.
- **Buyers could potentially integrate backward to produce the industry's product.** Automobile manufacturers, General Motors (GM) and Ford, produce some car components themselves, but they also rely on a large group of suppliers for the hundreds of parts that are needed to assemble a completed car. Given GM and Ford's vast manufacturing capabilities, they could easily produce more parts in-house. It is this threat of backward integration that enables the large automobile manufacturers to exert pressure on their suppliers to cost-effectively deliver parts.

Rivalry among Existing Competitors

The intensity of rivalry among firms in an industry also shapes its long-term profitability. Some industries are marked by intense rivalry, with firms competing on a whole range of factors including price, service, variety, and product introduction. In certain intense rivalries, the potential for profit is reduced as each competitor seeks to outdo the other rather than focus on a specific niche or a set of activities.

Conditions That Promote Intense Rivalry and Price Competition

In general, industry rivalry will be most intense and lead to depressed industry profitability when competition focuses mainly on price. Under the following circumstances, competition and rivalry will be greatest:

- **The product or service offered by the industry lacks differentiation and has low switching costs for its buyers.** Most commodity markets (e.g., sugar, cocoa, and wheat) exhibit this type of rivalry because their products are usually indistinguishable from each other and, at the same time, it's easy for buyers to switch from one seller to the other at no additional cost.

- **Fixed costs for firms in the industry are high, and marginal costs are low.** Fixed costs are the costs you must incur up front regardless of how much or how little you produce. Marginal costs are the costs incurred to produce every additional unit output. The airline industry has relatively high fixed costs and, at the same time, quite low marginal costs. The fixed costs are in the form of purchasing airplanes, gates, a ticketing system, and so on. Once a plane is scheduled to go from one place to another, the marginal cost of adding one additional passenger is low. This combination of high fixed costs and low marginal costs is a recipe for intense competition because, once you have incurred the fixed costs, you are inclined to use the investment you have made. Otherwise, it will be wasted. An airline would be loath to have its planes inactive while they have to make lease payments and also cover the payroll of its entire staff. From their vantage point, all they can see are the marginal costs of adding more passengers to their flights and this, in turn, leads many to lower their prices right up to their marginal costs, which can often result in low or no profits. As such, in the airline industry, firms are often encouraged to price close to their marginal costs when the plane has capacity to cover at least a portion of the fixed costs. This is true for other travel-based businesses that often offer attractive "last-minute" deals to entice customers. The movie theater business is another example of a low marginal cost operation but with relatively high fixed costs.

- **Capacity must be expanded in large increments.** In industries where there are economies of scale and it is not cost effective for a firm to manufacture low volumes of products, another dynamic can arise that leads to greater competition. In such contexts, not only are the set up costs to initiate production very large, which warrants a correspondingly large output, but, in addition, production capacity is only augmented in large batch increments. This means that when any firm wants to increase its capacity, they cannot do it in small increments. Instead, the technology requires them to increase it in large chunks. Sometimes the market is not ready for such a large increase in output, causing the industry to go from a shortage to a surplus. This, in turn, leads to a price decline. This dynamic is quite common in several large-scale industries such as chemicals.

- **The product is perishable.** In industries where the product is perishable, the seller may be pressured to sell at any price before their product is of no use. This happens not only in obvious cases like food and meats, but in other contexts as well. Many technology-focused products such as microprocessors are subject to this type of rivalry where the components sold can become obsolete within months. The same is true for the personal electronics industry. As the speed of innovation quickens, firms stuck with last-generation models will be tempted to cut prices significantly to unload outdated products.

- **Competitors are numerous or are roughly equal in size and power.** This type of rivalry often occurs in local service industries (e.g., dry cleaning) in which numerous undifferentiated competitors compete in a low-growth market and with all rivals of similar size, they jockey to outdo each other.

- **Industry growth is slow.** In the breakfast cereal market, consumption growth has been slow for the last decade. When the pie stops growing, then the players involved work harder to capture a larger share of it. As a result, competitors such as General Mills and Kellogg have competed intensely on price.
- **Exit barriers are high.** Sometimes the costs of exiting a business can be prohibitive, which can force a business to operate much longer than it should. In the steel industry, exit barriers were historically high, as producers faced numerous legacy and environmental costs regardless of whether they were operating. As a result, many U.S. steel producers remained in business despite annual operating losses to the detriment of the entire industry.[55]

Limits of the 5-Forces Model

Over the years, many have questioned the usefulness of the 5-Forces Model because it typically looks at an industry at one point in time. However, competition is driven by constantly changing competitive dynamics, and these changes must be monitored since they can impact the overall attractiveness of the industry. At the same time, these forces are not a given but rather can be shaped by the actors in those industries over time. For IBM, the PC industry became a structurally difficult industry overnight when IBM decided to outsource the major components of its system to competitors.

Despite these criticisms, the 5-Forces Model remains one of the most important tools for evaluating the attractiveness of industries and developing business-level strategy. While industries vary in their exposure to specific forces, it seems clear that the five forces generally work to increase or decrease profit potential (see Figure 5.6).

Managers should use this tool before, during, and after they enter a market or an industry to better understand its structural components. This tool is particularly useful in helping managers decide where to focus their attention. The forces provide

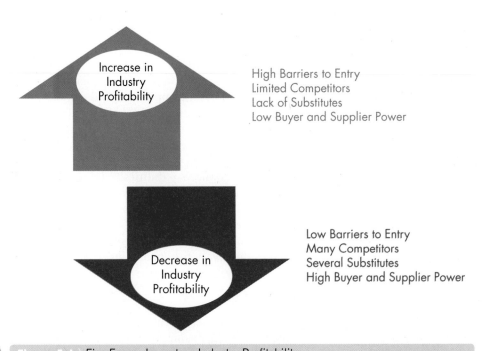

Figure 5.6 〉 Five Forces Impact on Industry Profitability

Source: Adapted from Michael E. Porter, "Understanding Industry Structure," Harvard Business School Note No. 9-707-493, rev. August 13, 2007 (Boston, MA: HBS Publishing, 2006), pp. 3–4.

a guide for making strategic choices such as how and where to compete. Not all forces are equally relevant in an industry. The analysis of the five forces in an industry should help managers identify which are most important for them.[56]

HOW A FIRM'S INTERNAL ENVIRONMENT IMPACTS STRATEGY

Up to this point, we've focused our discussion on the evaluation of a firm's external environment or industry structure. We've discussed the different profit potentials of industries and introduced a tool, the 5-Forces Model, to evaluate the attractiveness of a particular industry. We haven't fully discussed how the internal environment of a firm affects the development of strategy and the performance of the firm. A firm's internal resources can be just as important as the industry context. To create a lasting competitive advantage, managers must rely on both superior internal resources and favorable industry dynamics.

The focus on internal resources as a source of competitive advantage was derived from an analysis of why certain firms in attractive industries perform poorly and why certain firms in unattractive industries perform well. The difference seemed to be related to factors within the firm itself.[57] This led researchers to examine a series of firm-level activities, processes, or resources that distinguished winners from losers.

Resource-Based View of the Firm

The idea that a firm is a collection of resources is often referred to as the **resource-based view of the firm**. This theory, originally developed in the 1990s, states that resources are "strengths that firms can use to conceive of and implement their strategies."[58] Based on this theory, a firm can develop a competitive advantage through the collection and harvesting of resources.[59] The theory also assumes that not all firms have the same resources and capabilities within the same industry and that these advantages can be long lasting.[60]

The other insight that can be gained from the resource-based view of a firm involves the firm's relationship with the external environment.[61] External forces such as government regulatory bodies, consumer tastes, competitors, and demographics are constantly evolving. A company with a useful and profitable product may one day discover that the market for its product is no longer relevant. As the environment changes, a firm needs to reassess its internal resources to ensure that they are still relevant for the market in which it is trying to compete. If not, the firm needs to create or develop new internal resources and capabilities.[62] In general, long-term success depends on management's willingness and ability to adopt a learning mind-set.[63] This learning mind-set, in turn, will help managers to become more attuned to the impact of changes in the environment.[64]

Now that we've established the importance of a firm's resources, let's look at examples of specific resource categories that every firm maintains.

Company Resources

All firms have a long list of resources. To many, a firm's resources are the most recognizable aspect of their business. Certain resources (for instance, plant and equipment) can be valued and sold readily. Other resources (e.g., employees or patents) are less easily valued and rarely sold. For a company such as Toyota, all of these resources are important. As we saw in Chapter 4, this system, or fit among its

Resource-based view of the firm
A theory that a firm can develop a competitive advantage through the collection and harvesting of resources.

Ian Shipley IND / Alamy

resources and activities, enables Toyota to maintain a competitive advantage in its industry. For Toyota and other companies, resources can be classified under three categories: tangible resources, intangible resources, and human resources.

Tangible Resources

A firm's tangible resources tend to be most recognizable. They often include a firm's plant and equipment, or what it uses to manufacture products. Other types of tangible resources include real estate, inventory, raw materials, and computing systems. At Toyota, the tangible resources are important and numerous. For example, Toyota has 68 manufacturing companies around the world, including 11 in North America.[65] These automobile manufacturing facilities represent one of the largest assets on Toyota's balance sheet. The company also has significant tangible resources in the form of real estate around the world.

Toyota has used a strategy of situating its tangible resources (auto plants) in lower-income rural areas in the United States. This strategy evolved in the 1980s when the U.S. government placed restrictions on the number of foreign-imported cars coming into the country. Toyota maneuvered around these restrictions by locating plants inside the United States. To overcome the higher labor costs inherent in the U.S. market, Toyota placed its plants in rural areas, away from traditional car manufacturing areas such as Detroit. With this strategic decision, Toyota has been able to reduce the labor component of its cars and extract concessions from state governments trying to attract industry to rural areas.

Intangible Resources

While a firm's tangible resources are easy to visualize, its intangible resources may not be as familiar. They often include a firm's internal processes or systems, brand names, technology, culture, and intellectual property.

At Toyota, the intangible resources are a little harder to describe, but they are just as important. As we saw in Chapter 4, Toyota has become legendary through its Toyota Production System. This system is a combination of the manufacturing line and processes the company uses to assemble cars. While the line may look like one in any other automobile plant, it is vastly different in its philosophy and the processes that govern it. For example, above each worker's head is a device called an andon cord. A worker can pull the cord when he or she encounters a problem at his or her work station. A supervisor then comes to the station, and both of them try to troubleshoot the problem. If the problem is not correctable in a certain amount of time, the worker or the supervisor pulls the cord again and the line stops until the problem is fixed. The philosophy behind this mechanism is to prevent errors in manufacturing from accumulating, which can require costly rework. Toyota encourages every line worker to look for ways to make its processes more efficient. While this system may sound simple, competitors have found it nearly impossible to replicate. It is intimately intertwined in the Toyota manufacturing environment and is, by all accounts, an intangible resource.

Human Resources

Finally, a firm's human resources include employees of all levels, from entry-level workers to the CEO. For some firms, their human resources are their primary resource. Consider consulting or accounting firms, for example. While each of these firms may have proprietary processes, models, or frameworks that they use to solve clients' problems, their most important assets are their employees, who put these ideas and models to use. When a star performer or a client manager leaves a firm, the company loses a big source of value.

Toyota's human resources are just as important as its tangible and intangible resources. As noted, Toyota's Production System has been the envy of the automobile industry for decades. The model is studied and scrutinized by managers and academics around the world, with the hope of finding other industrial applications for it. And while some of the structural components of the system, such as the andon cord, are important, Toyota's line employees are just as important. Toyota recruits workers who possess not only certain technical skills but also certain key attributes (e.g., the ability to troubleshoot, to think creatively, and to work as part of a team).

As we've seen from these examples, Toyota has created its famous production system through the use of its many resources. With all of this success, customers and competitors have taken notice. In fact, Toyota recently surpassed General Motors as the largest carmaker in the world and has been the most profitable carmaker for the last decade. Many firms have attempted to replicate the Toyota Production System in their factories. To this end, many firms have asked and been granted permission to tour Toyota's facilities to see how it operates.

You may be asking, "Why would Toyota allow its competitors to get a glimpse of its vaunted production system? Wouldn't this allow its competitors to copy the activities, obtain similar resources, and thus erode Toyota's competitive advantage?" Well, the reason Toyota allows competitors to tour its facility is based on something we talked about in Chapter 4.

The idea is that, while a firm's activities and resources are important, they are only a part of the picture. A firm must create a system in which all of these activities fit together, allowing the firm to develop specific core competencies to create a sustainable competitive advantage.[66] Toyota knows that other firms will be able to replicate certain activities from its production system. But Toyota also knows that no company will be able to replicate the entire system.

THE FIRM AS A VALUE CHAIN

Value chain analysis
A systematic way of examining all of the activities a firm performs and determining how they interact to form a source of competitive advantage.

Firms that are successful for a long time possess unique resources that help them pursue a defensible strategy. One way to better understand how a firm's resources can support the firm's strategy is to conduct a **value chain analysis**. This analysis is a systematic way of examining all of the activities a firm performs and determining how they interact to gain competitive advantage. Value chain analysis separates a firm into its various activities to better understand total costs in the system and potential sources of firm differentiation.[67] As many of the examples in this chapter have shown, all firms possess a unique set of activities that they perform to bring their product or service to market.

Primary and Support Activities

The firm's value chain can be divided into two major activities: **primary activities** and **support activities** (see Figure 5.7). Primary activities refer to the activities involved in the physical creation of the product and its sale and transfer to the buyers.[68] The primary activities of a firm can be divided into five categories: inbound logistics, operations, outbound logistics, marketing and sales, and service. Support activities provide the support necessary for the primary activities to occur. The support activities of a firm can be divided into four categories: firm infrastructure, human resource management, technology development, and procurement. The firm's primary and secondary activities are defined in greater detail in Tables 5.1 and Tables 5.2.

Value Systems

Through value chain analysis, a manager should attempt to analyze three aspects of the firm's overall value system. First, the manager can study how the firm uses its resources and capabilities to develop core competencies. To be a source of competitive advantage, a capability must allow a firm to perform a primary or support activity better than its competitors do.[69] For example, the manager may discover through this process that the firm's main value-adding activity resides in the marketing and sales function of the organization. The manager may also discover that outbound logistics has presented a major challenge for the company. Through these realizations, the manager can then seek to emphasize the value-creating activities and improve those that do not add value.

Primary activities
The activities involved in the physical creation of the product and its sale and transfer to the buyer.

Support activities
Activities that provide the support necessary for the primary activities to occur.

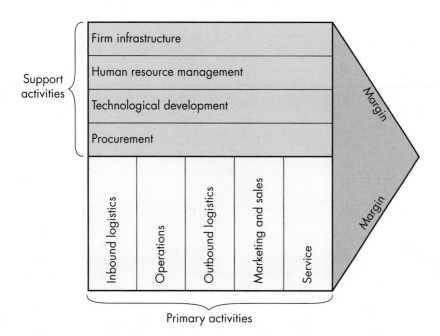

Figure 5.7 ⟩ The Basic Value Chain

Source: Adapted from Adelaide Wilcox King, Sally W. Fowler, and Carl P. Zeithaml, "Managing Organizational Competencies for Competitive Advantage: The Middle-Management Edge," *Academy of Management Executive*, Vol. 15, No. 2, 2001, pp. 96–97.

Inbound Logistics	Activities such as materials handling, warehousing, and inventory control that are used to receive, store, and disseminate inputs to a product.
Operations	Activities necessary to convert the inputs provided by inbound logistics into final product form. Machining, packaging, assembly, and equipment maintenance are examples of operations activities.
Outbound Logistics	Activities involved with collecting, storing, and physically distributing the final product to customers. Examples of these activities include warehousing, material handling, and order processing.
Marketing and Sales	Activities completed to provide the means through which customers can purchase products. To effectively market and sell products, firms develop advertising and promotional campaigns; select appropriate distribution channels; and hire, develop, and support their sales force.
Service	Activities designed to enhance or maintain a product's value. Firms engage in a range of service-related activities, including installation, repair, training, and adjustment.

Table 5.1 ⟩ Primary Activities

Source: Adapted from Michael E. Porter, *Competitive Advantage: Creating and Sustaining Superior Performance* (New York, NY: The Free Press, 1985).

Procurement	Activities completed to purchase the inputs needed to produce a firm's products. Purchased inputs include items fully consumed during the manufacture of products (e.g., raw materials and supplies) as well as fixed assets—machinery, lab equipment, office equipment, and buildings.
Technological Development	Activities completed to improve a firm's product and the processes used to manufacture it. Technology development takes many forms, such as process equipment design, basic research and product design, and servicing procedures.
Human Resource Management	Activities involved with recruiting, hiring, training, developing, and compensating all personnel.
Firm Infrastructure	Activities such as general management, planning, finance, accounting, legal support, and governmental relations that are required to support the work of the entire value chain.

Table 5.2 ⟩ Support Activities

Source: Adapted from Michael E. Porter, *Competitive Advantage: Creating and Sustaining Superior Performance* (New York, NY: The Free Press, 1985).

Second, the manager must compare the firm's value chain with competitors' value chains to better understand the competitive forces in the market and to determine how to improve the firm's value-creating activities and gain advantage over its competitors. Finally, managers must view the firm's value chain in the context of a larger value system that includes the value chains of suppliers and distribution channels. By studying these other value chains, the manager can better understand the connections among the different systems involved in bringing a product to market. Understanding these connections can enhance a firm's competitive advantage.[70] Toyota has regularly accomplished this by creating tight links with its suppliers through sharing data and processes.

SWOT ANALYSIS

One tool that has been useful in helping managers better understand their internal and external environments along with the linkage between them is called **SWOT analysis**.[71] This simple tool allows managers to take a snapshot of their firm's internal strengths and weaknesses as well as the opportunities and threats that are evident in the external environment (see Figure 5.8). Internal strengths might include specific human resources skills, proprietary technology, or lean manufacturing techniques. These items generally enable the organization to function more efficiently than its competitors do and are key aspects in the company's value chain. Weaknesses are potential vulnerable aspects in a firm's operations. These may include an older plant and equipment, an aging workforce, or a dependence on a certain supplier for core materials. The opportunities and threats aspect of the analysis encompasses many of the techniques discussed in Chapter 1, including environmental scanning and contingency planning. These activities are core components of gaining a better understanding of the contextual landscape. Key questions of this analysis typically include the following:

- What core internal resources set us apart from the competition?
- What is our unique selling proposition or core competitive advantage?
- In what internal areas are we vulnerable?
- What capabilities do we need to develop?
- In what ways is the external context changing?
- What is our position relative to the 5-Forces within the industry?
- What opportunities or threats do these changes present?

SWOT analysis is one way to combine a manager's understanding of the external environment in relation to his or her firm's capabilities and competitive advantage.[72] Like the 5-Forces Model, the SWOT analysis presents a snapshot of the firm at one point in time but requires managers to think about current and future opportunities and threats.[73] To be effective, the analysis should be revisited on a regular basis and should be the basis of strategic action, not just an isolated academic exercise. Firms that adapt their strategic approaches to the realities of the context in which they operate tend to perform better than those that stick to a rigid strategy.[74] By doing so, a firm can maintain a higher level of **strategic flexibility**—the capability to identify and react to changes in the external environment and to mobilize internal resources to deal with those changes.[75]

SWOT analysis
A tool that allows managers to take a snapshot of their firm's internal strengths and weaknesses as well as the opportunities and threats that are evident in the external environment.

Strategic flexibility
The capability to identify and react to changes in the external environment and to mobilize internal resources to deal with those changes.

Figure 5.8 › SWOT Analysis

COMPETITIVE ADVANTAGE

By understanding the forces in the external environment and the resources within the firm's internal environment, a manager is better equipped to assess how the firm can develop a strategy to achieve a competitive advantage in the marketplace.

Competitive advantage derives from a firm's ability to create value for its customers that exceeds the cost of producing the product or service.[76] **Value** refers to the amount consumers are willing to pay for a product or service, and it comes from offering a lower price than that of competitors or providing a unique product whose benefits outweigh a higher potential cost to consumers.[77] A competitive advantage in an industry is the result of creating a strategy that will allow a firm to outperform its competitors.

Southwest Airlines was able to build a competitive advantage over rival airlines by creating a system of low-cost activities that brought affordable air travel to customers. It did so in an industry that is considered structurally weak, by neutralizing the unattractive features and exploiting the attractive elements of the industry.[78] We also saw how Billy Beane of the Oakland Athletics developed a competitive advantage by discovering new techniques for evaluating baseball players. These organizations were able to maintain a competitive advantage by creating value through their development of core competencies that rivals could not match.[79]

Competitive advantage can come from three generic strategies that a manager can choose for the firm: cost leadership, differentiation, and focus. The focus strategy is just a variant of the first two, where the manager chooses to target a smaller segment than usual through cost leadership or differentiation (see Figure 5.9).

Cost Leadership

A company that pursues a **cost leadership** strategy aims to provide a product or service at as low a price as possible to a broad audience. For firms competing on cost leadership, several important trade-offs are necessary in designing the activities they will perform. These trade-offs are often centered on price and product features or price and product quality. The goal of such firms is to offer a basic set of features

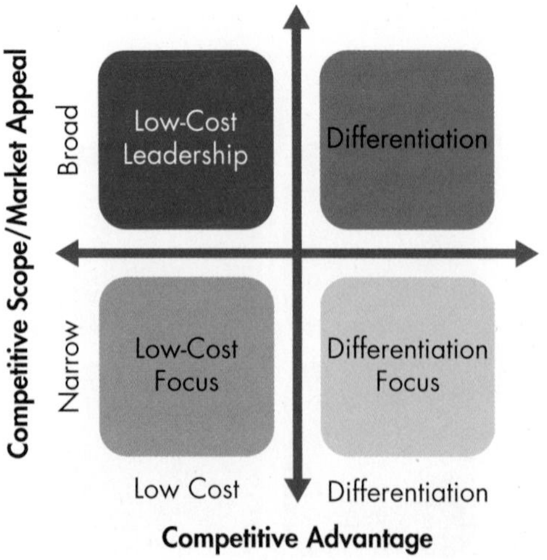

Value
The amount consumers are willing to pay for a product or service. It comes from offering a lower price than that of competitors or providing a unique product whose benefits outweigh a higher potential cost.

Cost leadership
A strategy that aims to provide a product or service at as low a price as possible to a broad audience.

Figure 5.9 Three Generic Strategies

Source: Adapted from Michael E. Porter, "The Five Competitive Forces That Shape Strategy," *Harvard Business Review,* January 2008.

with acceptable quality at the lowest possible price to the largest possible group of customers. If possible, it strives to be able to price its product or service below the cost of all competitors. The ideal goal here is to have a cost advantage over competition that is greater than the price disadvantage, allowing the firm to have greater margins than its competition.

The sources of cost advantage that help to reduce a firm's cost may include **economies of scale**, proprietary technology, or unique access to raw materials.[80] Economies of scale are achieved when the large volume of a product produced by a firm enables it to reduce the per unit cost. In this way, a firm's fixed costs are spread across more units. Walmart is a classic example of a firm that has such an advantage.

In a cost leadership strategy, the manager must continuously pursue multiple sources of low-cost advantage to compete effectively. While it is important to seek multiple sources of low-cost advantage, a manager must also consider its position in comparison to its competitors in the market. For example, a firm's product cannot be so different or inferior from that of its competitors in the industry that the customer no longer recognizes the product as a viable alternative. If buyers don't see the product as being comparable, a firm might be forced to discount its offerings.[81]

In industries where several firms compete to be the cost leader, competition is usually fierce, with some players sometimes selling items below cost to gain or retain market share. By establishing itself as the dominant lowest cost producer in an industry, a firm can often dissuade others from pursuing low-cost strategies, and in so doing, it can gain a competitive advantage.[82] Walmart, on their way to becoming the world's largest company, has translated an extremely efficient distribution system into low operating costs. These low costs help them offer prices that are impossible for other retailers to match. As a result, most others have shied away from going head-to-head with Walmart on price. Now that we've established some of the key components of cost leadership, let's look at another firm that successfully employs this strategy.

Economies of scale
Cost savings achieved when the volume of a product produced by a firm enables it to reduce per unit costs.

The Vanguard Group

The Vanguard Group is one of the largest asset managers in the United States, with over $2.5 trillion in assets under management and 12,000 employees at the end of 2014.[83] Vanguard provides individual and institutional investors with mutual funds, exchange-traded funds, bonds, certificates of deposits, annuities, 529 college savings plans, brokerage services, and investment advisory services.[84] The majority of Vanguard's assets are housed in instruments called mutual funds. Vanguard's mutual fund business is among the largest in the United States, competing with players such as Fidelity Investments and T. Rowe Price. Unlike many other mutual fund companies, Vanguard primarily distributes its funds directly to consumers rather than through outside brokerage houses.

From inception, Vanguard has focused all of its activities on bringing low-cost and high-quality service to customers. The company's average expense ratio is among the lowest in the business,[85] and all of its mutual funds are no-load funds, which have no transaction costs because they are sold without commission or sales charges.

Another component of Vanguard's low-cost approach involves promoting index funds. Index funds typically mirror a major market index such as the S&P 500 and allow the investor to own a broad array of stocks. This model offers the investor diversification and low trading costs as the fund manager constructs the portfolio and does not make changes unless a company falls out of the mirrored index. In contrast, managers of nonindexed mutual funds may buy or sell different stocks for a fund on a weekly or even daily basis, increasing overall costs for the investor. While Vanguard focuses primarily on index funds, it also offers actively managed mutual funds similar to those at Fidelity. Through this activity, Vanguard is able to meet some of the differentiation measures that other firms have established, yet still maintains its overall cost leadership focus.

Vanguard also performs other activities that lead to its cost leadership position in the industry. The firm rarely advertises in traditional media, preferring word-of-mouth publicity instead. Most of the firm's transactions occur on the Web, in contrast to many firms that conduct trades by phone. This Web approach creates a much lower cost per transaction than that of many of its competitors.

As you can see by Vanguard's activities, every aspect of the business revolves around bringing low costs to the consumer (see Figure 5.10). While many competitors have attempted to copy some of Vanguard's activities by offering their own index funds, Vanguard has been able to maintain its strategic position because of the fit among its activities created by promoting low cost in every aspect of the business.

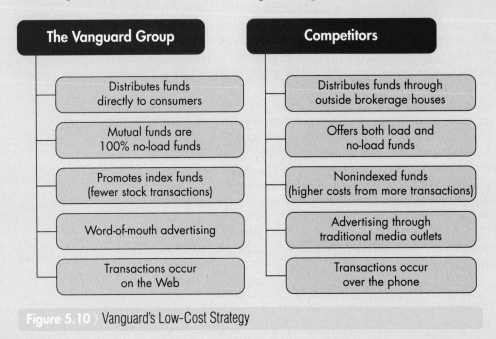

Figure 5.10 Vanguard's Low-Cost Strategy

Case in Point   The Vanguard Group

1. How has The Vanguard Group positioned itself as an asset management firm?
2. Map out the activities that support the core components of The Vanguard Group's low-cost strategy.
3. How does a low-cost strategy create value for The Vanguard Group's customers?
4. Elaborate on why you think competitors have not succeeded at imitating The Vanguard Group's strategy.

Differentiation

Differentiation
A strategy in which a firm seeks to be unique in its industry along a dimension or a group of dimensions that are valued by consumers.

When pursuing a **differentiation** strategy, a firm seeks to be unique in its industry along a dimension or a group of dimensions that are valued by consumers and can command a premium price.[86] To accomplish this, a firm must position itself to offer certain product attributes or services that customers value and competitors cannot easily replicate. In contrast to cost leadership, consumers should be willing to pay a premium price for that firm's product.[87] Differentiation can be based on a broad range of factors, including product features, service offerings, distribution systems, and marketing approaches.[88]

A firm that can achieve and sustain differentiation has the ability to create long-term profitability as long as its price premium exceeds the extra costs incurred by being unique.[89] While a firm seeks a price premium in a differentiated strategy, that premium cannot be so great that it prices itself out of the market or becomes a narrow niche player. To accomplish this task, a firm needs to focus on those facets of its value proposition that are most valued by its target customers and, as a result, increase differentiation and garner a premium price from customers.[90] Such companies should, at the same time, seek to reduce their investment in other activities that do not add much value to their customers. For example, if a firm sells bike locks to customers who care about durability, it may consider lowering costs related to the lock's styling to increase investment in antitheft materials.

The basic premise of a differentiation strategy is that a firm must choose dimensions in which to differentiate relative to those of its rivals, and those dimensions must in turn be relevant to consumers.[91] Multiple firms can simultaneously compete based on differentiation in an industry. Now that we've established some of the key components of a differentiation strategy, let's look at a firm that successfully employs this approach.

Patagonia: Adding Value to Customers and the Environment

Patagonia was formed in 1973 by legendary mountain climber Yvon Chouinard to sell performance apparel and equipment for customers who participated in outdoor sports such as mountain climbing and skiing. The company is one of the most successful and well-recognized firms in the U.S. outdoor apparel industry, which consists of high-end competitors such as North Face, Marmot Mountain Inc., and Mountain Hardwear. The industry also includes middle-market players such as Columbia Sportswear and other sports-related players (for instance, Nike and Reebok). Manufacturers often sell their products through several different channels—in general and outdoor sports stores such as Dick's, Eastern Mountain Sports, and REI; on the Internet; in catalogues; and in company-owned retail-branded stores.

Chief among the firm's sources of differentiation is product quality. To produce higher quality products, Patagonia works closely with suppliers. Rather than buying commodity fabrics, the firm collaborates with suppliers to create innovative materials for Patagonia garments.[92] In contrast, many competitors use commodity fabrics and lower cost methods to assemble seemingly similar products. While focusing on high-quality and innovative fabrics, Patagonia also attempts to lower costs in its manufacturing processes to remain competitive with other lower priced competitors.

Patagonia also derives its competitive advantage through its differentiated approach to environmental awareness. In fact, the firm is considered by many to be one of the most environmentally conscious companies in the world. From its use of organic fabrics to its donation of 1% of annual sales to environmental organizations, Patagonia seeks to consider the environment in every

Ed Endicott/WYSIWYG Foto, LLC/Alamy

decision it makes. In an effort to promote recycling and reduce excess waste, the company encourages customers to have their ripped Patagonia ski jackets repaired instead of buying a new one. Patagonia will even do the mending.[93] In addition, the company has set the goal of making 100% recyclable, landfill free products in the near future. By 2014, they were at 70% and climbing.[94]

Through this differentiated strategy, Patagonia can sell its products at higher prices.[95] This premium often translates into prices typically 15–20% higher than other specialty producers and 50% higher than mass market producers (see Figure 5.11).

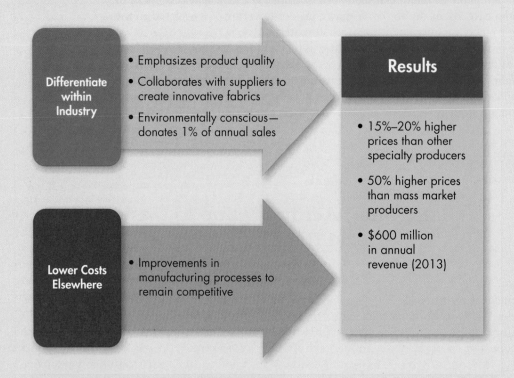

Figure 5.11 〉 Patagonia's Differentiation Strategy

Sources: Adapted from Forest Reinhardt, Ramon Casadesus-Masanell, and Hyun Jin Kim, "Patagonia," Harvard Business School Case No. 9-711-020, rev. October 19, 2010 (Boston, MA: HBS Publishing, 2010); Patagonia, Inc. Company Profile," 2009, www.onesource.com, accessed December 10, 2009, and Christopher Steiner, "A Fight for the Mountaintop: Yvon Choinard's Disciple Challenges Patagonia," *Forbes*, September 10, 2014.

Case in Point   Patagonia

1. Why do you think Patagonia's differentiation strategy has resulted in a high profit margin for the firm?

2. Can you identify another clothing manufacturer that has formulated and implemented a differentiation strategy?

3. Visit Patagonia's website and read about its corporate social responsibility practices. How does this firm integrate its corporate social responsibility practices into its strategy? How are corporate social responsibility practices a component of a differentiation strategy?

Focus

In a **focus** strategy, a company "focuses" its sales efforts on a specific geographical region, a specific group of purchasers, or a specific product type. While pursuing a focused strategy, a firm may do so by either being low-cost or differentiated. For instance, a firm can decide to be low-cost and focused, where it offers low-cost products to a small geographical region or group of customers, or it can offer a differentiated focused approach, where it offers a differentiated product to a specific region or audience.

The two types of focus strategies aim to exploit a unique opportunity that may exist in certain market segments. In a low-cost focus strategy, a firm attempts to target cost-conscious customers who may have been underserved historically. In a differentiation focused approach, a firm attempts to target customers with special needs who also have been underserved historically. In these instances, certain segments may have been overlooked or discarded by traditional competitors and the focuser can often achieve competitive advantage by concentrating exclusively on these segments.[96]

Firms that achieve sustainable cost leadership (cost focus) or differentiation (differentiation focus) in a segment, can expect to have a competitive advantage in those market segments.[97] Now that we've established some of the key components of a focus strategy, let's look at a firm that successfully employs this approach.

Focus
A strategy in which a company "focuses" its sales efforts on a specific geographical region, a specific group of purchasers, or a specific product type.

Genzyme and the Orphan Drug Market

Genzyme is one of the most recognized and profitable companies in the high-growth biotechnology industry. Unlike traditional drug development, biotechnology uses tools to create synthetic or artificial proteins that look similar to human proteins.[98] This approach has yielded drugs that successfully treat diseases such as anemia, diabetes, and rheumatoid arthritis.

Because of the cost constraints and incredible odds involved in the FDA approval process, most companies focus their drug discovery efforts on diseases that contain large patient populations. Thus, a rare disease that affects only a few thousand people is often too small to ultimately recover the substantial investment required to develop, manufacture, and sell a new drug therapy.[99] As a result, most manufacturers seek to develop "blockbuster drugs" that have the potential to generate above $1 billion in annual revenues. Based on this data, it is easy to understand why big pharmaceutical companies leave many market segments untouched. Instead of evaluating the total market size of patients, Genzyme decided to focus on particularly severe disease states where no

remedies existed. Genzyme managers believed that particularly severe diseases that lacked any effective treatment might allow the company to charge a high price per patient for an effective therapy, particularly if the cost was less than the medical and social costs of caring for untreated patients.

Genzyme ultimately decided to pursue the orphan drug segment, typically defined by those diseases occurring in fewer than 200,000 patients worldwide (see Table 5.3). Producers of orphan drugs are provided protection under The Orphan Drug Act of 1983. According to the act, public funds are used to subsidize orphan drug development through a variety of benefits such as a 7-year period of market exclusivity, the ability to apply for federal grant funding to defray costs of qualified clinical testing expenses, and a 50% tax credit for certain clinical research expenses incurred in connection with product development.[100] Through the Orphan Drug Act, Genzyme recoups some of its development costs while simultaneously enjoying market exclusivity on developed drugs. This

Year	Drug Name	Disease	Company	U.S. Patients
2005	Retisert	Chronic noninfectious uveitis	Bausch & Lomb	175,000
2004	Acetadote	Acetaminophen overdose	Cumberland Pharmaceuticals	100,000[a]
2003	Serostim	AIDS wasting syndrome	Serono Laboratories, Inc.	100,000
2002	Xyrem	Cataplexy, a form of narcolepsy	Orphan Medical, Inc.	100,000
2002	Zevalin	Non-Hodgkin's B-cell lymphoma	IDEC Pharmaceuticals	90,000
2007	Doxil	Multiple myeloma	Johnson & Johnson Pharmaceuticals	80,000
2006	Revlimid	Multiple myeloma	Celgene Corporation	80,000
2007	Nutropin Depot	Low growth hormone secretion	Genentech, Inc.	80,000
2007	Saizen	Low growth hormone secretion	Serono Laboratories, Inc.	80,000
2004	Apokyn	Parkinson's disease	Mylan Bertek Pharmaceuticals	50,000[a]
2008	Banzel	Severe epilepsy	Novartis Pharmaceuticals Corporation	45,000
2004	Vidaza	Myelodysplastic syndrome (MDS)	Pharmion Corporation	40,000
2007	Norditropin	Noonan syndrome	Novo Nordisk Pharmaceuticals	40,000
2006	Prograf	Preventing organ rejection during organ transplants	Astellas Pharma, Inc.	35,000
2007	ReFacto	Hemophelia A	Wyeth Pharmaceuticals, Inc.	23,000
2006	Remicade	Crohn's disease	Centocor, Inc.	21,000
2006	Sprycel	Myelogenous leukemia	Bristol-Myers Squibb Company	20,000
2008	Xenazine	Huntington's disease	Cambridge Laboratories Group	16,000
2005	Arranon	T-cell acute lymphoblastic leukemia	GlaxoSmithKline US	10,000
2006	Myozyme	Pompe disease	Genzyme Corporation	10,000[b]
2002	Gleevec	Gastrointestinal stromal tumors (GIST)	Novartis	6,000[a]
2003	Fabrazyme	Fabry disease	Genzyme Corporation	5,000
2004	Clolar	Acute lymphoblastic leukemia (ALL)	Genzyme Oncology	4,000[a]
2004	Alimta	Mesothelioma	Eli Lilly and Company	3,000[a]
2006	Elaprase	Mucopolysaccharidosis II (MPS II)	Shire Plc	2,300

Table 5.3 ⟩ Orphan Drugs Released in the United States

[a] Number of new patients each year in United States.
[b] Number of patients worldwide.

exclusivity has allowed the firm to generate tremendous profitability.

Genzyme maintains a competitive advantage through a differentiated focus strategy that takes advantage of favorable dynamics in the orphan drug segment (see Figure 5.12). Genzyme saw an opportunity to develop treatments for a group that had been neglected, while simultaneously devising ways for insurance companies and governments to pay for the treatment. This strategy has led to several successful biologic products aimed at orphan diseases and historically strong profitability.

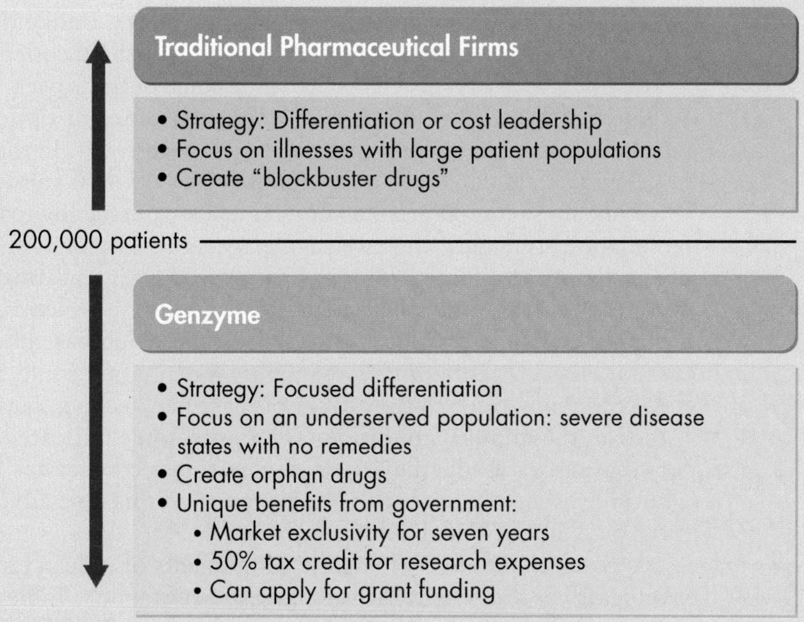

Traditional Pharmaceutical Firms

- Strategy: Differentiation or cost leadership
- Focus on illnesses with large patient populations
- Create "blockbuster drugs"

200,000 patients ─────────────────────────────

Genzyme

- Strategy: Focused differentiation
- Focus on an underserved population: severe disease states with no remedies
- Create orphan drugs
- Unique benefits from government:
  - Market exclusivity for seven years
  - 50% tax credit for research expenses
  - Can apply for grant funding

Figure 5.12 > Genzyme's Focused Differentiation Strategy

Case in Point   Genzyme and the Orphan Drug Market

1. Describe how Genzyme was able to create a niche in the biotechnology industry.
2. How did the external environment support a focused differentiation strategy?
3. Why is a firm's ability to innovate important when implementing a focused strategy?

Stuck in the Middle

In the previous sections, we saw examples of firms that competed based on each of the three generic strategies. Each firm clearly defined its activities to develop a competitive advantage based on one of the strategies. However, some firms are not as consistent or clear in their activities and strategy. In fact, many firms do not clearly stake out a competitive position using any one of the generic strategies. A firm that engages in numerous strategies simultaneously and in the process fails to master any one is referred to as being "stuck in the middle."[101] These firms are usually at a disadvantage because other players are better positioned to pursue a singular approach and achieve competitive advantage.[102] While the firm that is stuck in the middle may produce profits in the short run, more disciplined competitors will be more successful in the long run.[103] In many industries, firms are seduced into this middle ground by the prospect of being all things to all customers. It is very difficult to say no to a potential revenue opportunity even if it does not fit your chosen strategy. When firms pursue revenue for revenue's sake, they often lose focus and become less efficient.[104]

Delta Air Lines attempted to respond to the low-cost threat of Southwest by creating the low-cost subsidiary Delta Express. While the subsidiary was profitable at first, other low-cost airlines eventually eroded Delta's profits by stealing its market share. In Delta's Florida market, both Southwest and JetBlue were better positioned to bring low-cost air travel to customers. Unlike these low-cost carriers, Delta's overall cost structure prevented it from pushing costs to a comparable level. In addition, Delta had problems matching some of the aspects of differentiation that JetBlue maintained, including elaborate entertainment options and leather seats, which the airline was able to provide in a low-cost way. In the end, Delta's position in the middle ultimately led to the failure of its low-cost subsidiary.

While most companies that simultaneously pursue low-cost leadership and differentiation strategies tend to struggle, recent research has shown that some firms, especially in the digital economy, can succeed by integrating the two approaches. Web technologies and social media formats have enabled firms to target specific groups of people at very low costs.[105] In essence, Web-based firms can pursue a low-cost focused differentiation strategy. Target marketing could be very expensive and time consuming prior to the advent of these new technologies, thereby creating the "stuck-in-the-middle" condition. The Internet has mitigated many of these issues for e-businesses. While the low cost of customer contact has been a cornerstone of e-business, successful companies have married this cost advantage with a specific focus on a differentiated market segment.[106]

A manager should evaluate the components of industry structure to determine whether it has the potential for long-term profitability. Table 5.4 combines the different generic strategies that firms can pursue with the 5-Forces Model. The generic strategies can reduce, but cannot eliminate the impact of the five forces.

Employees in Generic Strategies

As we saw in many of the previous examples, the three generic strategies require firms to operate in very different ways. These strategies also differ from the perspective of the employee.

A cost leadership strategy generally involves tight control systems and cost minimization.[107] These activities are typically shaped by a culture at a firm that is focused on frugality, discipline, efficiency, and attention to detail, as seen at

	Threat of New Entrants	Bargaining Power of Suppliers	Bargaining Power of Customers	Threat of Substitutes	Rivalry Among Competitors
Low Cost	Provides cost advantage, harder for new entrants to have same cost advantage	Usually immune as cost leader typically buys in bulk	Already operating at low cost, less impacted by powerful buyers	Less susceptible to cost-based substitutes, but could miss new product opportunities	Strong cost advantage, but susceptible to new innovations
Differentiation	Distinctive competence, but need to maintain price/value balance	Able to pass through price increases to buyers	Target markets, buyers are less price sensitive, they want the differentiated product	Often requires big investment to build customer loyalty	Harder to overcome brand loyalty
Focus	Customer loyalty, focused on a specific niche but could grow in size attracting more competitors	Could pass through price increases, but often not a large buyer	Exclusivity—only a few options, but need to continue to offer price/value balance	Brand loyalty, limited market to service a specific niche	Exclusivity of offering, generally limits competition

Table 5.4 › Combining Generic Strategies with the 5-Forces Model

Source: Based on data from Arthur A. Thompson, Jr. and A. J. Strickland III, *Strategy Formulation and Implementation: Tasks of the General Manager,* 5th edition (Homewood, IL: Irwin, 1992), pp. 106–112.

Southwest Airlines. At Southwest, the firm's culture is tightly integrated with its low cost strategy. The firm pays its employees similar to other airlines, but does not lavish employees with luxurious perks. At the same time, the firm promotes a positive and fun environment for its employees. If above-industry compensation or lavish perks are important factors for you, Southwest Airlines or other firms pursuing cost leadership may not be a good fit.

For firms competing on differentiation, culture can also be an important factor in enacting the strategy. Many firms pursuing differentiation have a culture that encourages innovation and risk-taking.[108] The culture of Patagonia exemplifies many of these characteristics. At Patagonia, the employees are encouraged to experiment with products and fabrics to produce better designs. In addition, Patagonia encourages employees to leave work early to surf or rock-climb. To Patagonia's managers, these activities help employees gain inspiration for their products while simultaneously promoting a work–life balance. If creativity, innovation, and individuality are characteristics that appeal to you, a firm that competes based on differentiation may be a good fit.

SUMMARY

LO1 A firm's business strategy is defined by the manner in which it answers three primary questions: (1) Who do we serve?; (2) What products and services do we provide?; and (3) How do we provide those products and services? Different firms answer these primary questions in fundamentally different ways, and it is these responses that lay the foundation for the competitive landscape of an industry.

LO2 In defining a firm's business strategy, a manager must conduct a thorough assessment of the external environment. This assessment will generally reveal the attractiveness of an industry. Certain industries are inherently more attractive than others. The 5-Forces Model, which includes an assessment of entry barriers, buyer power, supplier power, competitive rivalry, and available substitutes, is one way to assess the relative attractiveness of an industry.

However, strategy development based on an evaluation of the external environment is incomplete.

LO3 A manager must also evaluate a firm's internal resources to determine how its capabilities and access to resources can provide a competitive advantage. Internal resources that can provide these advantages include tangible items such as real estate, inventory, and equipment, as well as intangible assets such as production processes, brand name, and culture. A firm's employees can also be a strong internal resource that can create a core competency within an industry.

LO4 Having outlined a firm's strategy and analyzed its internal resources and the external environment, a manager can use the value chain tool to break the firm into various activities to discover where it is adding value. The manager can then explore the connections between the firm and the other value chains in its value system to better create fit among its primary and support activities. In so doing, the manager will have a better sense of the firm's competitive advantage and how to sustain it.

LO5 A SWOT analysis, which outlines a firm's internal strengths and weaknesses as well as the opportunities and threats in the marketplace, can be an effective way to gauge a firm's current and future position within an industry. This analysis is also useful in determining a firm's competitive advantage.

LO6 Competitive advantage is derived from a firm's ability to create value for its customers. The way in which a firm creates this value is often through cost or differentiation. From these positions emerge three generic business-level strategies: cost leadership, differentiation, and focus. Firms that compete based on cost leadership provide a product or service at the lowest possible cost. Firms that compete on differentiation provide a product or service that is unique and that competitors cannot easily replicate. Finally, firms that compete with a focused strategy apply either cost leadership or differentiation to a specific target market, geography, or some other defined entity.

KEY TERMS

Bargaining power	First-mover advantage	Support activities
Barriers to entry	Focus	SWOT analysis
Cost leadership	Primary activities	Value
Differentiation	Resource-based view of the firm	Value chain analysis
Economies of scale	Strategic flexibility	

ASSIGNMENTS

Discussion Topics

1. Consider the three fundamental questions that must be answered to define a firm's strategy: (1) who do we serve?; (2) what do we provide?; and (3) how do we provide it? Which question is most difficult to answer for a firm? Why? When answered, which question best addresses a firm's competitive advantage in a marketplace?

2. If you were an executive at Coca-Cola, which of the five forces would you pay the most attention to? Why? If you were an executive at Red Bull, would your answer change?

3. What industries have low barriers to entry? How would a new entrant in this industry best exploit this low barrier?

4. Why do first movers in an industry enjoy special competitive advantages for long periods of time? What could prevent a first mover from capitalizing on these advantages?

5. Most individuals consider Southwest Airlines to be a substitute for other airline carriers such as Delta or United, but they are also a substitute for car travel between cities that are a few hundred miles apart. What other businesses act as a unique substitute?

6. Compare and contrast the bargaining power of suppliers and buyers. In which ways do powerful suppliers and buyers have an impact on an industry? How are these impacts similar and different?

7. Why does overall industry profitability decrease in industries that are characterized by intense rivalries?

8. In reviewing the three primary aspects of a firm's internal environment—tangible resources, intangible resources, and human resources—which one is most important in a mature industry? What about a new, emerging industry?

9. In Chapter 2, we discussed how General Electric has been able to sustain its relevance for over 100 years. In many ways, the company was characterized by strong strategic flexibility. What other companies have demonstrated a similar strategic flexibility? Do you think Facebook will still be a viable business in 20 years? What will they have to do to sustain relevance?

10. Would you rather work for a firm that is pursuing a cost leadership or differentiation strategy? How would your job be different?

Management Research

Identify three firms that use a different generic strategy to compete: low cost, differentiation, and focus.

1. For each of the three firms you identified, list the activities that support its generic strategy.

2. Take each of the three firms and apply Porter's 5-Forces Model to them. Decide whether each of the three firms is in a structurally attractive industry based on your analysis.

3. Take each of the three firms and list each one's tangible, intangible, and human resources.

4. Construct a value chain for each of the three firms.

5. Which firm would you invest in and why?

In the Field

1. For this assignment, interview a manager at a company that does not have a clearly defined business strategy. Use the interview to understand why this company is "stuck in the middle." Based on your interview, identify which generic strategy would position the firm for a competitive advantage. Develop a set of recommendations for how the firm could implement this strategy.

2. Which of the five forces can be applied to an assessment of the not-for-profit sector? Would you add any forces?

ENDNOTES

[1] Michael E. Porter, "Understanding Industry Structure," Harvard Business School Note No. 9-707-493, rev. August 13, 2007 (Boston, MA: HBS Publishing, 2006), p. 1.

[2] Nancy F. Koehn, "Howard Schultz and Starbucks Coffee Company," Harvard Business School Case No. 9-801-361, rev. September 30, 2005 (Boston, MA: HBS Publishing, 2001), p. 11.

[3] Ibid.

[4] *Starbucks Corporation, 10K* (Seattle, WA: Starbucks Corporation, 2014).

[5] Madhav V. Rajan and Brian Tayan, "Financial Restatements: Methods Companies Use to Distort Financial Performance," Stanford Graduate School of Business Case No. A-198 (Stanford, CA: Stanford Graduate School of Business, 2008), pp. 6–7.

[6] Krispy Kreme Doughnuts Inc., April 28, 2006 10-K (Winston-Salem: Krispy Kreme Doughnuts Inc., 2006), p. 44, http://investor.krispykreme.com/secfiling.cfm?filingID=950123-06-5450, accessed December 10, 2009.

[7] Datastream, "Interactive Price Chart, Krispy Kreme Donuts," http://banker.thomsonib.com, accessed December 9, 2009.

[8] Erika Fry, "Gorging on Krispy Kreme," *Fortune*, December 9, 2013.

[9] Bob Horovits, "Starbucks' Growth Strategy Thinks Outside the Cup," *USA Today,* March 24, 2011.

[10] Rachel Z. Arndt, "Adam Brotman: How Not to Reinvent the Wheel and Still Merrily Roll along," *Fast Company*, 2012.

[11] Julie Jargon, "Starbucks CEO to Focus on Digital," *Wall Street Journal*, January 30, 2014.

[12] R. Duane Ireland, Michael A. Hitt, S. Michael Camp, and Donald L. Sexton, "Integrating Entrepreneurship and Strategic Management Actions to Create Firm Wealth," *Academy of Management Executive,* Vol. 15, No. 1, 2001, p. 53.

[13] Michael E. Porter, "Understanding Industry Structure," Harvard Business School Note No. 9-707-493, rev. August 13, 2007 (Boston, MA: HBS Publishing, 2006), pp. 2–7.

[14] Ibid.

[15] Jan W. Rivkin and Michael E. Porter, "Matching Dell," Harvard Business School Case No. 9-799-158 (Boston, MA: HBS Publishing, 1999), p. 2.

[16] Ibid.

[17] Ibid.

[18] Ibid.

[19] Ibid.

[20] Ibid.

[21] Martyn Williams and Paul Kallender, "IBM Sells Its PC Business," *IDG News Service*, December 8, 2004.

[22] David Lei and John W. Slocum, Jr., "Strategic and Organizational Requirements for Competitive Advantage," *Academy of Management Executive,* Vol. 19, No. 1, 2005, p. 32.

[23] Michael E. Porter, "Understanding Industry Structure," Harvard Business School Note No. 9-707-493, rev. August 13, 2007 (Boston, MA: HBS Publishing, 2006), p. 3.

[24] Ibid.

[25] Ibid.

[26] Ibid.

[27] Jon Brodkin, "Windows on Verge of Dropping below 90% Market Share," *Network World*, January 13, 2011, http://www.networkworld.com/news/2011/011311-windows-on-verge-of-dropping.html, accessed August 15, 2012.

[28] Gladys Rama, "Microsoft's Windows Phone Market Share Declined in 2014," *Redmond Magazine*, December 2, 2014.

[29] Michael E. Porter, "Understanding Industry Structure," Harvard Business School Note No. 9-707-493, rev. August 13, 2007 (Boston, MA: HBS Publishing, 2006), p. 3.

[30] Ibid.

[31] Ibid.

[32] Jason Millman, "Does It Really Cost $2.6 Billion to Develop a New Drug?" *Washington Post*, November 18, 2014.

[33] Michael E. Porter, "Understanding Industry Structure," Harvard Business School Note No. 9-707-493, rev. August 13, 2007 (Boston, MA: HBS Publishing, 2006), p. 3.

[34] Ibid., p. 4.

[35] Gwendolyn Bounds, "Move Over Coke: How a Small Beverage Maker Managed to Win Shelf Space in One of the Most Brutally Competitive Industries," *Wall Street Journal*, January 30, 2006.

[36] Michael E. Porter, "Understanding Industry Structure," Harvard Business School Note No. 9-707-493, rev. August 13, 2007 (Boston, MA: HBS Publishing, 2006), p. 4.

[37] Virginia Weiler, Paul Farris, Gerry Yemen, and Kusum Ailawadi, "Uber Pricing Strategies and Marketing Communication," University of Virginia Darden School Foundation Case No. UV6878, rev. July 30, 2014 (Charlottesville, VA: University of Virginia Darden School Foundation, 2014).

[38] Michael E. Porter, "The Five Competitive Forces That Shape Strategy," *Harvard Business Review,* January 2008.

[39] David J. Ketchen, Jr., Charles C. Snow, and Vera L. Street, "Improving Firm Performance by Matching Strategic Decision-Making Processes to Competitive Dynamics," *Academy of Management Executive,* Vol. 18, No. 4, 2004, p. 31.

[40] Michael E. Porter, "Understanding Industry Structure," Harvard Business School Note No. 9-707-493, rev. August 13, 2007 (Boston, MA: HBS Publishing, 2006), pp. 4–5.

[41] Virginia Weiler, Paul Farris, Gerry Yemen, and Kusum Ailawadi, "Uber Pricing Strategies and Marketing Communication," University of Virginia Darden School Foundation Case No. UV6878, rev. July 30, 2014 (Charlottesville, VA: University of Virginia Darden School Foundation, 2014).

[42] David Hoyt and Steven Callander, "Uber: 21st Century Technology Confronts 20th Century Regulation," Stanford Graduate School of Business Case No. P-81 (Stanford, CA: Stanford Graduate School of Business, 2012).

[43] Virginia Weiler, Paul Farris, Gerry Yemen, and Kusum Ailawadi, "Uber Pricing Strategies and Marketing Communication," University of Virginia Darden School Foundation Case No. UV6878, rev. July 30, 2014 (Charlottesville, VA: University of Virginia Darden School Foundation, 2014).

[44] Brad Stone, "Uber and Google Move toward a Breakup," *Bloomberg Businessweek*, February 9–15, 2015.

[45] USPS, "A Decade of Facts and Figures," available at https://about.usps.com/who-we-e/postal-facts/decade-of-facts-and-figures.htm, accessed at February 21, 2015.

[46] Juliette Garside, "OMG, Number of UK Text Messages Falls for First Time," *The Guardian*, January 12, 2014.

[47] Michael E. Porter, "Understanding Industry Structure," Harvard Business School Note No. 9-707-493, rev. August 13, 2007 (Boston, MA: HBS Publishing, 2006), p. 7.

[48] Michael E. Porter, "The Five Competitive Forces That Shape Strategy," *Harvard Business Review,* January 2008.

[49] Timothy A. Luehrman, "Kaiser Steel Corporation, 1950," Harvard Business School

Case No. 9-291-005, rev. August 1, 1990 (Boston, MA: HBS Publishing, 1990), p. 4.

50 Timothy A. Luehrman, "Kaiser Steel Corporation, 1972," Harvard Business School Case No. 9-291-012, rev. December 21, 1990 (Boston, MA: HBS Publishing, 1990), p. 5.

51 Ibid.

52 Ibid., p. 6.

53 William E. Fruhan, Jr., "Restructuring the U.S. Steel Industry," Harvard Business School Case No. 9-203-042, rev. June 19, 2003 (Boston, MA: HBS Publishing, 2002), p. 8.

54 Terrence P. Stewart, Elizabeth J. Drake, Stephanie M. Bell, Jessica Wang, and Robert E. Scott, "Surging Steel Imports Put Up to Half a Million U.S. Jobs at Risk," *Economic Policy Institute*, May 13, 2014 at http://www.epi.org/publication /surging-steel-imports/

55 Michael E. Porter, "Understanding Industry Structure," Harvard Business School Note No. 9-707-493, rev. August 13, 2007 (Boston, MA: HBS Publishing, 2006), pp. 7–8.

56 Ibid., p. 2.

57 Richard P. Rumelt, Dan E. Schendel, and David J. Teece, "Fundamental Issues in Strategy," *Fundamental Issues in Strategy: A Research Agenda,* Richard P. Rumelt, Dan E. Schendel, and David J. Teece, eds. (Boston, MA: HBS Press, 1994).

58 Jay Barney, "Firm Resources and Sustained Competitive Advantage," *Journal of Management,* 1991, Vol. 17, No. 1, pp. 101–102.

59 David G. Sirmon, Michael A. Hitt, and R. Duane Ireland, "Managing Firm Resources in Dynamic Environments to Create Value: Looking Inside the Black Box," *Academy of Management Review,* Vol. 32, No. 1, 2007, p. 273.

60 Margaret A. Peteraf, "The Cornerstones of Competitive Advantage: A Resource-Based View," *Strategic Management Journal,* Vol. 14, No. 3, 1993, pp. 179–191.

61 David J. Collis and Cynthia A. Montgomery, "Competing on Resources," *Harvard Business Review,* July–August 2008; and Moshe Farjoun, "Towards an Organic Perspective on Strategy," *Strategic Management Journal,* Vol. 23, No. 7, 2002, p. 564.

62 David G. Sirmon, Michael A. Hitt, and R. Duane Ireland, "Managing Firm Resources in Dynamic Environments to Create Value: Looking Inside the Black Box," *Academy of Management Review,*

Vol. 32, No. 1, p. 280; and Nils Stieglitz and Klaus Heine, "Innovations and the Role of Complementarities in a Strategic Theory of the Firm," *Strategic Management Journal,* Vol. 28, 2007, p. 2.

63 R. Duane Ireland, Michael A. Hitt, S. Michael Camp, and Donald L. Sexton, "Integrating Entrepreneurship and Strategic Management Actions to Create Firm Wealth," *Academy of Management Executive,* Vol. 15, No. 1, 2001, p. 58.

64 David Lei and John W. Slocum, Jr., "Strategic and Organizational Requirements for Competitive Advantage," *Academy of Management Executive,* Vol. 19, No. 1, 2005, p. 35.

65 Toyota Motor Corporation, "Worldwide Operations," at http://www.toyota-global. com/company/profile/facilities/worldwide_ operations.html, accessed February 22, 2015.

66 Adelaide Wilcox King, Sally W. Fowler, and Carl P. Zeithaml, "Managing Organizational Competencies for Competitive Advantage: The Middle-Management Edge," *Academy of Management Executive,* Vol. 15, No. 2, 2001, p. 96.

67 Michael E. Porter, *Competitive Advantage: Creating and Sustaining Superior Performance* (New York: The Free Press, 1985), p. 33.

68 Ibid., p. 38.

69 David J. Ketchen, Jr. and G. Tomas M. Hult, "Bridging Organization Theory and Supply Chain Management: The Case of Best Value Supply Chains," *Journal of Operations Management*, Vol. 25, No. 2, 2007, pp. 573–580; and Michael E. Porter, *Competitive Advantage: Creating and Sustaining Superior Performance* (New York: The Free Press, 1985).

70 Michael E. Porter, *Competitive Advantage: Creating and Sustaining Superior Performance* (New York: The Free Press, 1985), p. 51.

71 Richard P. Rumelt, Dan E. Schendel, and David J. Teece, "Fundamental Issues in Strategy," *Fundamental Issues in Strategy: A Research Agenda,* Richard P. Rumelt, Dan E. Schendel, and David J. Teece, eds. (Boston, MA: HBS Press, 1994), p. 17.

72 Arnoldo C. Hax and Nicolas S. Majluf, "The Corporate Strategic Planning Process," *Interfaces,* Vol. 14, No. 1, 1984, p. 55.

73 Moshe Farjoun, "Towards an Organic Perspective on Strategy," *Strategic Management Journal,* Vol. 23, No. 7, 2002, pp. 562, 565.

74 C. Brooke Dobni and George Luffman, "Determining the Scope and Impact of Market Orientation Profiles on Strategy Implementation and Performance," *Strategic Management Journal,* Vol. 24, 2003, p. 583; and R. Duane Ireland, Michael A. Hitt, S. Michael Camp, and Donald L. Sexton, "Integrating Entrepreneurship and Strategic Management Actions to Create Firm Wealth," *Academy of Management Executive,* Vol. 15, No. 1, 2001, p. 53.

75 Katsuhiko Shimizu and Michael A. Hitt, "Strategic Flexibility: Organizational Preparedness to Reverse Ineffective Strategic Decisions," *Academy of Management Executive,* Vol. 18, No. 4, 2004, p. 44.

76 Michael E. Porter, *Competitive Advantage: Creating and Sustaining Superior Performance* (New York: The Free Press, 1985), p. 3.

77 Ibid., and Pankaj Ghemawat and Jan W. Rivkin, "Creating Competitive Advantage," Harvard Business School Note No. 9-798-062, rev. February 25, 2006 (Boston, MA: HBS Publishing, 1998), p. 3.

78 Pankaj Ghemawat and Jan W. Rivkin, "Creating Competitive Advantage," Harvard Business School Note No. 9-798-062, rev. February 25, 2006 (Boston, MA: HBS Publishing, 1998), p. 4.

79 Marvin B. Lieberman and Shigeru Asaba, "Why Do Firms Imitate Each Other?," *Academy of Management Review,* Vol. 31, No. 2, 2006, p. 367.

80 Michael E. Porter, *Competitive Advantage: Creating and Sustaining Superior Performance* (New York: The Free Press, 1985), p. 12.

81 Ibid., p. 13.

82 Ibid.

83 "The Vanguard Group, Inc. Company Report," 2014, http://www.premium. hoovers.com, accessed February 16, 2015.

84 Luis M. Viceira and Helen H. Tung, "The Vanguard Group, Inc. in 2006 and Target Retirement Funds," Harvard Business School Case No. 9-207-129, rev. January 28, 2008 (Boston, MA: HBS Publishing, 2007), p. 2.

85 Ibid., p. 3.

86 Michael E. Porter, *Competitive Advantage: Creating and Sustaining Superior Performance* (New York: The Free Press, 1985), p. 14.

87 Pankaj Ghemawat and Jan W. Rivkin, "Creating Competitive Advantage," Harvard Business School Note No. 9-798-062, rev. February 25, 2006 (Boston, MA: HBS Publishing, 1998), pp. 7–8.

88 Michael E. Porter, *Competitive Advantage: Creating and Sustaining Superior Performance* (New York: The Free Press, 1985), p. 14.

89 Ibid.

90 Marvin B. Lieberman and Shigeru Asaba, "Why Do Firms Imitate Each Other?," *Academy of Management Review,* Vol. 31, No. 2, 2006, p. 374.

91 Michael E. Porter, *Competitive Advantage: Creating and Sustaining Superior Performance* (New York: The Free Press, 1985), p. 14.

92 Forest Reinhardt, Ramon Casadesus-Masanell, and Hyun Jin Kim, "Patagonia," Harvard Business School Case No. 9-711-020, rev. October 19, 2010 (Boston, MA: HBS Publishing, 2010), p. 4.

93 Brian Dumaine, "Built to Last," *Fortune,* August 13, 2012.

94 "Patagonia, Inc. Company Report," 2015, http://www.hoovers.com, accessed February 17, 2015.

95 Forest Reinhardt, Ramon Casadesus-Masanell, and Hyun Jin Kim, "Patagonia,"

Harvard Business School Case No. 9-711-020, rev. October 19, 2010 (Boston, MA: HBS Publishing, 2010), p. 5.

96 Michael E. Porter, *Competitive Advantage: Creating and Sustaining Superior Performance* (New York: The Free Press, 1985), p. 15.

97 Ibid.

98 Barbara Martinez and Jacob Goldstein, "Industry Fails to Find New Drugs to Replace Wonders Like Lipitor," *Wall Street Journal,* December 6, 2007.

99 Henry Chesbrough and Clarissa Ceruti, "Genzyme: Engineering the Market for Orphan Drugs," Harvard Business School Case No. 9-602-147, rev. May 13, 2002 (Boston, MA: HBS Publishing, 2002), p. 3.

100 Ibid., p. 7.

101 Michael E. Porter, *Competitive Advantage: Creating and Sustaining Superior Performance* (New York: The Free Press, 1985), p. 16.

102 Ibid., and Gregory G. Dess and Peter S. Davis, "Porter's (1980) Generic Strategies

as Determinants of Strategic Group Membership and Organizational Performance," *Academy of Management Journal,* Vol. 27, No. 3, 1984, pp. 480, 484.

103 Stewart Thornhill and Roderick E. White, "Strategic Purity: A Multi-Industry Evaluation of Pure vs. Hybrid Business Strategies," *Strategic Management Journal,* Vol. 28, 2007, p. 559.

104 Nitin Nohria, William Joyce, and Bruce Roberson, "What Really Works," *Harvard Business Review,* July 2003.

105 Eonsoo Kim, Dae-il Nam, and J. L. Stimpert, "The Applicability of Porter's Generic Strategies in the Digital Age: Assumptions, Conjectures, and Suggestions," *Journal of Management,* Vol. 30, No. 5, 2004, p. 571.

106 Ibid., p. 577.

107 Michael E. Porter, *Competitive Advantage: Creating and Sustaining Superior Performance* (New York: The Free Press, 1985), p. 23.

108 Ibid., p. 24.

CHAPTER

6

······································

Chapter Outline

Corporate-Level Strategy

Learning Objectives

After reading this chapter, you should be able to:

LO1 Understand that corporate-level strategies include decisions regarding diversification and vertical integration.

LO2 Describe the strategy of and rationale for diversification.

LO3 Explain the difference between related and unrelated diversification and outline the advantages and disadvantages of each approach.

LO4 Describe the results that diversification strategies have produced.

LO5 Define the process of vertical integration and explain the reasons why a firm would choose to pursue this path.

SELF-REFLECTION

Strategizing for Growth

Corporate-level strategy entails developing a plan for the management of multiple businesses and deciding how to expand the boundaries of the firm. It also involves organizational design and ownership choices so that the firm can maximize its resources across multiple businesses. Please respond True or False to the following statements to assess your ability to understand strategies for growing a corporation through the management of multiple businesses.

1. I can explain the difference between business-level and corporate-level strategies.

2. I understand why firm diversification is a growth strategy.

3. I can explain the difference between related and unrelated diversification.

4. I take the cost of entering a new business into consideration when analyzing growth plans.

5. I am aware of the leadership skills that are needed to pursue an effective corporate-level strategy.

6. I recognize that the attractiveness of an industry should be incorporated into the decision-making process when a firm is diversifying.

7. I know how firms create synergy between various businesses.

8. I can explain the rationale for pursuing an international approach to diversification.

9. I understand the rationale for vertical integration.

10. I am familiar with the different forms of vertical integration.

If you answered True to most statements, you have a solid grasp of corporate-level strategies.

INTRODUCTION

As we learned in Chapter 4, a firm's strategy involves two major components: business-level strategy and corporate-level strategy. Through business-level strategy, a manager determines how the company will compete in a specific industry and position itself among competitors within that industry. However, a large number of firms do not compete in just one industry. Rather, many companies—General Electric (GE), Procter & Gamble (P&G), Kyocera, Tata Group, and Westinghouse, for instance—compete across numerous industries, each with different profit potentials and competitive threats.

To be successful in leading multiple businesses, a manager must develop a corporate-level strategy. Corporate-level strategy is defined as the way a company seeks to create value "through the configuration and coordination of multimarket activities."[1] Corporate-level strategy includes decisions on how many industries to compete across, whether to vertically integrate, whether to buy or sell companies, and how to share resources across divisions.[2] In essence, these choices can be summarized into three categories: (1) scope, the markets, and businesses that the firm

The Leadership Development Journey

Working across organizational boundaries and partnering with other organizations enable managers to formulate and implement corporate-level strategies. Once partnerships are formed, effective leaders have the ability to envision the "big picture" while focusing on common goals. Reflect upon a time when you partnered with another person to achieve a common goal.

1. What was your strategic rationale for partnering with the other person?
2. What were the advantages and disadvantages of partnering with the other person?
3. Did the partnership result in personal growth and pooling of resources?
4. How did the partnership benefit others?
5. What did you learn from the partnering relationship that can be applied to the management of a corporate-level strategy?

will compete in; (2) organizational design, the manner in which resources of the firm will be coordinated; and (3) ownership, the relationship between business units; that is, whether businesses should be acquired (owned) or aligned through other means (partnerships, alliances, or joint ventures).[3] The ultimate goal of developing a corporate-level strategy is to build a **corporate advantage**, which occurs when a firm maximizes its resources to build a competitive advantage across its various business units.[4] In other words, a company derives a corporate advantage when it is able to secure collective benefits from its businesses that would not exist if the businesses were owned independently.[5]

In this chapter, we will review the major decisions that a manager must make regarding the firm's corporate-level strategy. First, we discuss the reasons why diversification strategies may make sense for certain firms. Second, we discuss different approaches to diversification. Third, we will review the results of diversification. Finally, we discuss whether the firm should vertically integrate. These major strategic and organizational decisions are often called "big bets" because they fundamentally define the manner in which a firm will compete.[6] Let's look at how Disney has successfully developed and deployed its corporate-level strategy.

Corporate advantage
Occurs when a firm maximizes its resources to build a competitive advantage across its various business units.

The Walt Disney Company

Over the last half-century, The Walt Disney Company has been one of the most recognizable and successful entertainment companies in the world. While the company has experienced its share of ups and downs, it remains a case study in how a firm can achieve competitive advantage and long-term profitability through the successful implementation of corporate-level strategies.

Walt Disney and his brother Roy formed Walt Disney Studios in 1923 in Hollywood, California. While the business struggled at first, they found success when Walt developed the Mickey Mouse character.[7] In the late 1930s, Walt shifted his business from cartoon shorts to full-length feature films, including the 1937 release of *Snow White and the Seven Dwarfs*, the first full-length animation film.

During the World War II era, the company struggled financially as the demand for animated films slowed. However, Disney survived this period by producing educational cartoons for the government and by diversifying into other businesses. This initial diversification included the creation of the Walt Disney Music Company to control Disney's music copyrights and recruit top artists. In the beginning of the 1950s, Disney began producing live-action movies such as *Treasure Island* and *Old Yeller*. The company also created Buena Vista Distribution to distribute its films and ultimately save one-third of each film's gross revenues. In addition, during the 1950s, Disney diversified into TV shows with the production of the TV series *Disneyland*, which was used to promote the company's new theme park in California.

Disney followed up the success of Disneyland with another theme park in Orlando, Florida, called Disney World. The new park was an instant success, grossing $139 million from 11 million visitors in its first year. To generate traffic in the park, Disney opened an in-house travel company to work with travel agencies, airlines, and tour companies. However, following Walt Disney's death in 1966, the company began to languish as the corporate focus shifted from film-making to theme park construction. The company was almost lost to corporate raiders in 1984 but was ultimately saved by a cash infusion from a private investor who reinstated Roy Disney to the company's board. At this low point in the company's history, the reins were handed to Michael Eisner.

Eisner's first order of business was to breathe new life into the company's TV and movie units. In the early 1980s, Disney had stopped producing network TV shows for fear it would cannibalize its Disney Network offerings on cable. Eisner took the opposite approach, producing several shows on network TV to bolster the company's brand image. Eisner next turned his attention to the ailing movie division, which maintained a paltry 4% share of the box office in 1984. The new management team completely changed both the type and way in which movies were made at Disney. During this period, Disney produced more films on average (16 per year versus 4 per year), began producing comedies and live-action films for older audiences,

GABRIEL BOUYS/AFP/Getty Images

cast lower-priced actors, and held all film budgets to strict financial controls. Of Eisner's first 33 movies, 27 were profitable versus an average hit rate of only 40% for the industry.[8]

Over the next 10 years, Disney expanded its corporate reach into new businesses and reemphasized its core through significant investment. With its launch of Disney Stores in 1987, the firm pioneered the "retail-as-entertainment" concept, generating sales per square foot at twice the average rate for typical retail stores.[9] Disney also expanded the theme park division, building Euro Disney, Typhoon Lagoon, and Disney-MGM Studios. Through its Buena Vista Home Video unit, Disney achieved tremendous success by selling videos directly to consumers. Further diversification occurred through Broadway theater productions; the purchase of an NHL hockey team, The Mighty Ducks; and the development of new production studios under the Miramax and Touchstone names for films aimed at adults.

While all these initiatives broadened Disney's scope, the company cemented itself as one of the most diversified and vertically integrated firms in 1995 with the acquisition of ABC. This acquisition made Disney the largest entertainment company in the world, with worldwide distribution outlets for its creative content. Through the $19 billion acquisition, Disney controlled TV stations, cable networks, radio stations, newspapers, and periodicals. Eisner believed that Disney's ability to leverage its brand and create value depended on corporate synergy. For instance, in the year before a movie's release, creators from Disney's animation group would make presentations to the heads of the consumer products, home video, and theme parks units. The participants would then discuss product options and reconvene monthly to update one another.[10] In short, Eisner believed that Disney's structure created value through horizontal, vertical, and geographical synergies that allowed different business units to share resources and transfer skills (see Figure 6.1).

Eisner's successor as CEO, Robert Iger, has continued this approach. In 2006, Disney acquired

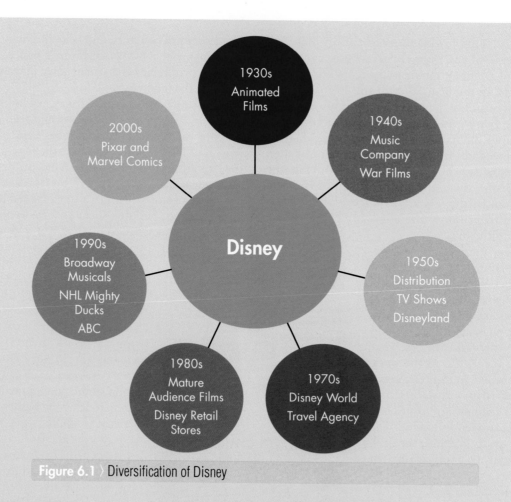

Figure 6.1 ⟩ Diversification of Disney

Pixar Studios from Apple for over $7 billion. Through this acquisition, the company gained access to a treasure trove of new characters from *Toy Story*, *Cars*, *Brave*, and other Pixar movies. With this access, Disney has been able to continue its strategic process of leveraging key assets across its theme parks, retail stores, and movie franchises. Disney hopes to do the same with the Star Wars franchise that was acquired for $4 billion from Lucasfilms in 2012.

Case in Point   Walt Disney

1. What is Disney's core competency? How did Disney align its core competency into its different businesses?

2. In recent years, what key investments did Disney make to expand its corporate advantage?

3. What future investments do you recommend to strengthen Disney's portfolio of businesses over the next 5 years?

Success with diversification can be difficult to achieve. Many scholars believe that firms should leverage their core competencies in one or two defined industries instead of trying to be successful across a broad array of industries. However, success, as evidenced by Disney, can be achieved with corporate strategy by developing organizational processes and sharing best practices among various business units.

DIVERSIFICATION STRATEGY

One of the cornerstones of corporate-level strategy is the concept of **diversification**. Through diversification, a firm engages in several different businesses that may or may not be related in an attempt to create more value than if the businesses existed as stand-alone entities (see Figure 6.2). The ultimate goal of a diversification strategy is for the whole (the combined companies) to be greater than the sum of the parts (the individual business units). Before we get into the details of diversification, let's review a brief history of the subject so that you'll better understand how the practice of this strategy evolved over time.

History of Diversification

The practice and popularity of diversification strategies in the United States has experienced cycles of boom and bust. In the 1950s, the majority of Fortune 500 companies derived revenues from a single core business. However, this singular focus began to shift during the 1960s as a result of regulatory changes that inadvertently promoted corporate diversification. In an effort to expand their revenue base, many firms attempted to acquire competitors and/or build internal capabilities that were previously provided by suppliers. With the passing of the Celler-Kefauver Act, the Federal Trade Commission (FTC) discouraged both activities. Since firms could not acquire "like businesses," they could either try to grow their existing business through a focus on core sales or try to acquire businesses in other industries. In most cases, businesses did both. They focused on growing their core business and sought to expand into new arenas. This expansion into new industries was a major factor in the adoption of diversification strategies by many firms during the 1960s and 1970s.[11]

A common approach to this form of diversification was the "firm as a portfolio" model, where the company functioned as an internal bank for all of its various acquired businesses. The diversity of businesses within the overall firm was seen as a means to mitigate risk since the firm's investments were spread across multiple businesses. Management consultants promoted this structure by comparing it to a diverse stock portfolio.[12] When most individuals and institutions invest in the stock

Diversification
A strategy in which a firm engages in several different businesses that may or may not be related in an attempt to create more value than if the businesses existed as stand-alone entities.

| Energy Infrastructure
Aviation
Healthcare
Transportation
Home & Business Solutions
Financial Services | Industrial & Transportation
Healthcare
Consumer & Office
Safety & Security
Displays & Graphics
Communications | Test & Measurement
Environmental
Life Sciences
Dental
Industrial Technologies | Insurance
Railroad
Utilities & Energy
Manufacturing
Retail
Financial Services |

Figure 6.2 Examples of Diversified Companies

Source: "Business Description," *Reuters,* via the OneSource® Business Browser, an online business information product of OneSource Information Services, Inc. ("OneSource"), accessed March 2015.

market, they maintain a diverse portfolio of stocks. By having a diverse portfolio, an individual is not overly dependent on the performance of just one or two companies. The diversity helps to balance high-performing and low-performing stocks and lowers overall risk. In a similar way, many firms during this time period sought to maintain a portfolio of businesses to minimize their risk of being overly dependent on the performance of one business. In fact, by 1979, 45% of the Fortune 500 companies had adopted portfolio planning techniques for diversification.[13]

The growth-share matrix (also called the BCG matrix), which was introduced in the 1970s by the Boston Consulting Group, was a popular and relatively easy way for companies to assess their portfolio of businesses (see Figure 6.3). The matrix classified businesses or product lines along two dimensions—rate of growth and market share. Market share was used as a proxy for a company's competitive advantage within an industry. Businesses or products that were deemed to have a large market share and a high growth rate were classified as stars. The rapid growth associated with stars generally required a significant cash infusion from the company to sustain that rate of growth. The goal of this investment was to allow the star to become the market leader as the growth rate slowed. At the other end of the spectrum, businesses that had low growth potential and low market share were named dogs. Businesses in the "dog" category were candidates for divesture.

The other two classifications are question marks and cash cows. Businesses that were named question marks were determined to have significant growth potential but low market share. These businesses often needed significant investments to enable them to build market share. If they could build market share, they could have the potential to first become a star and then, as the growth rated slowed, they could evolve into a cash cow. Alternatively, they could become dogs if they were unable to secure sufficient market share when the growth rate declined. Cash cows were mature businesses that had significant market share and relatively low growth potential. Since these businesses had low growth potential and high market share, they did not need significant cash infusions from the corporate entity. Instead, the profits generated by cash cows could be "milked" for reinvestment in stars or question marks.[14]

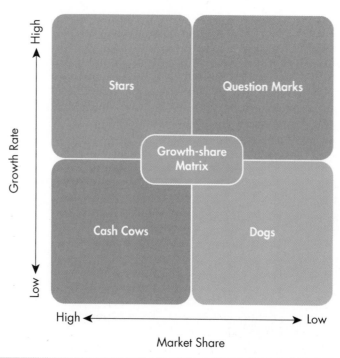

Figure 6.3 BCG's Growth-Share Matrix

Source: Adapted from Bruce D. Henderson, *On Corporate Strategy* (Cambridge, MA: Abt Books, 1979).

The growth-share matrix was used extensively in the 1970s and 1980s to enable corporate leaders to quickly assess their portfolio of businesses and determine a course of action. The prevailing wisdom of the time encouraged corporate leaders to sustain cash cows, divest dogs, invest in question marks to make them stars, and increase market share of stars to enable them to become cash cows.[15] While the matrix is still used today, it is often only one piece of a much larger portfolio evaluation process, and like the SWOT analysis that we discussed in Chapter 5, it represents a depiction of the company at one point in time. The increased complexity in the global landscape and the rapid pace of change has forced corporate leaders to evaluate their business portfolios on a number of dimensions beyond market share and growth including (1) the value that is created across businesses; (2) the ability of the business to quickly adapt and change to new market conditions; and (3) the ability of the business to innovate.[16]

The regulatory environment began to change during Ronald Reagan's presidency in the early 1980s. The FTC began to evaluate mergers based on factors that were different from those of previous decades, making it easier for firms to expand by acquiring similar businesses, essentially reversing the impact of the Celler-Kefauver Act. Firms were now able to expand by buying businesses that were similar and, as such, a firm's portfolio could include both similar and dissimilar businesses.

At the same time, as legal barriers to takeovers fell and easy financing became available, investment firms pursuing hostile takeovers emerged. These investment firms, also known as corporate raiders, at the time, sought to purchase a firm with various divisions and break it up into its components to sell to other buyers, leaving the core business to function as a stand-alone entity.[17] They believed that by breaking apart the firm, they could generate more value. In essence, they were convinced that the value of the parts (the individual business units) were greater than the sum of the whole.

During the late 1980s, the diversification trend among firms largely reversed itself as managers lost faith in the portfolio model and corporate raiders divided up companies. Some firms began to preemptively divest divisions during this period to focus on their core business. Others divested poor-performing companies and reorganized around a smaller group of more focused units. Though the level of diversification among firms has ebbed and flowed over the years, it is still a very important part of many companies' strategies.

Why Firms Pursue Diversification Strategies

Managers seek to diversify their organizations for several reasons: (1) the opportunity to leverage core assets or skills between different businesses, (2) the opportunity for growth, (3) the potential to manage or minimize risk, (4) the opportunity to expand internationally, and (5) the potential for personal gain. By combining either related or unrelated businesses, managers believe they can create **synergy**. Synergy is created when a firm generates sustainable cost savings by combining duplicate activities or deploying underutilized assets across multiple businesses.[18] Expected synergies are generally the primary reason firms acquire businesses in the same industry. By combining entities, a firm seeks to capture a benefit that could not be achieved if the entities were independent.

As we noted earlier, many managers have pursued diversification strategies in the interest of corporate expansion, especially as the business matures and opportunities for internal organic growth diminishes.[19] For instance, Google's entry into the mobile phone industry is an effort to expand beyond its maturing Internet search

A DIFFERENT *View*

Small Giants and Their Business Mojo

"Business mojo" is that unique charm and passion that defines a small giant. In the book *Small Giants: Companies That Choose to Be Great Instead of Big*, Bo Burlingham describes small giants as companies that place a greater emphasis on vision and culture than on the bottom line and growth. Small giants measure their success by achieving their goals for workplace culture, customer service, and community contributions. Typically privately held, these organizations are not required to make their goals or financial status public, so readily available information is more difficult to find. ECCO, operating out of Boise, Idaho, is an example of a small giant.

1. Based on research, explain why ECCO is considered a small giant?
2. What goals are more important to ECCO than financial performance?
3. How does ECCO differ from a larger corporation that is driven by the bottom line and pressures for growth?
4. Choose another company that is an example of a small giant. Why did this company choose to be great instead of big?

Synergy
Created when a firm generates sustainable cost savings by combining duplicate activities or deploying underutilized assets across multiple businesses.

CAMERA PRESS/Rob Welham/Redux

capabilities. In many cases, growth through diversification is pursued as an alternative means to profitability, especially in response to changes in internal and external environmental factors.[20]

Another main argument for diversification strategies is the reduction of risk.[21] This argument is based on portfolio management and states that by holding several different businesses, a manager will be able to spread the risks of one business across an entire spectrum of businesses. In this situation, it is argued that diversified business units will smoothen overall firm performance when one or a few units perform poorly.[22]

Firms may seek to diversify internationally to find new markets for their products and services. For many mature products, growth opportunities are often constrained in a firm's domestic market. As such, these companies sometimes seek growth in international locations. Firms also diversify internationally to achieve economies of scale. As we discussed in Chapter 5, a firm may achieve economies of scale when it produces a larger volume of products. In this case, a firm can spread the fixed costs associated with producing a product over a larger number of units, which ultimately increases the firm's profits. Additionally, many firms diversify internationally to take advantage of local factors. These factors may include lower cost sources of labor and access to natural resources.

A final reason for diversification is based on the self-interests and preferences of senior managers. Senior-level compensation is often tied to the size and complexity of a firm. Growth through diversification is one strategy that some managers use to attempt to minimize risk while simultaneously building their domain of control. This incentive-based justification for diversification has often resulted in suboptimal performance unless managers focus as much attention on integration as they do on acquisition.[23] We will discuss issues of implementation in "Results of Diversification" later in this chapter, but first, let's explore various approaches to diversification.

APPROACHES TO DIVERSIFICATION

There are three main approaches that companies utilize as they enact their corporate strategies. Some firms pursue a **single-product strategy** while others focus on either **related diversification** or **unrelated diversification** (see Figure 6.4).

Single–Product Strategy	• Focuses on one specific product, typically in one market. • Develops greater core competency, but suffers from more cyclicality.
Related Diversification	• Utilizes a similar set of tangible and intangible resources for multiple businesses. • Takes advantage of resources to achieve economies of scope.
Unrelated Diversification	• Involves managing several businesses with no connection. • Creates value through financial economies, distributing capital over many business units.

Figure 6.4 Types of Diversification Strategies and Definitions

A single-product strategy is fairly self-explanatory. In this strategy, a firm focuses on one specific product, typically in one market. Through this strategy, a firm attempts to develop core competencies in a specific market, using its resources and capabilities. While focusing on a single product often allows a firm to develop superior core competencies, it can also expose the firm to greater vulnerability if demand for the product or service wanes.

Firms that pursue related and unrelated diversification strategies often avoid the vulnerability that comes with a single-product focus. Most large companies diversify their operations in some manner to avoid the risks inherent in offering a single product. In fact, in 2005, "the average U.S.-based Fortune 500 company operated in four distinct industries, with some operating in more than ten."[24]

Related Diversification

Firms that have excess capacity or potential in their physical assets (e.g., production capability) or their intangible assets (e.g., strong brand name or research and development capabilities) tend to pursue related diversification. This approach enables a firm to leverage its assets across related industries.[25] Through related diversification strategies, managers attempt to achieve **economies of scope**, which exist when the costs of operating two or more businesses or producing two or more products with the same corporate structure are less than the costs of operating the businesses independently or producing each product separately.[26] Economies of scope that emerge from the sharing of resources and capabilities often become a way to achieve competitive advantage.

A prime example of a company that has successfully transferred skills across different business units to generate a competitive advantage is 3M. 3M is a diversified technology company that sells into very different markets, including the healthcare and highway safety industries. Over the years, 3M has developed a stable of world-famous products that have grown out of the company's technology and research capabilities. These products include Post-It Super Sticky Notes, Scotch Transparent Duct Tape, optical films for LCD televisions, and a family of Scotch-Brite Cleaning Products. Through its sharing of knowledge, 3M's research community has created a robust development program.[27] In fact, 3M's company

Single-product strategy
A strategy in which a firm focuses on one specific product, typically in one market.

Related diversification
A firm that owns more than one business that uses a similar set of tangible and intangible resources.

Unrelated diversification
A firm that manages several businesses with no reasonable connection.

Economies of scope
Exists when the costs of operating two or more businesses or producing two or more products with the same corporate structure is less than the costs of operating the businesses independently or producing each product separately.

norm is "While products belong to the businesses, technology belongs to the company."[28] This culture was instilled during the early days at 3M and has persisted over the years to help the company create a sustainable competitive advantage in the marketplace. With 50,000 products and counting, 3M's CEO in 2013 commented that "research and development is the heartbeat of this company and it's a competitive advantage."[29]

The challenge for a manager is finding these types of linkages to drive that competitive advantage. In most related diversification strategies, managers attempt to create value through the sharing and transferring of resources and skills among units, including the following:

- Sharing sales forces, advertising expenses, and distribution channels for similar products
- Exploiting closely related technologies or research and development activities like 3M
- Transferring operational knowledge or processes
- Leveraging a firm's strong brand name and reputation across multiple product lines[30]

P&G has pursued a related diversification strategy over the years by buying consumer products companies such as Gillette. While P&G has developed many well-known consumer brands in-house (e.g., Tide laundry detergent), the firm also relies on the acquisition of other consumer products companies to bring value to its many customers. P&G believes that it can create greater value through this related diversification because of the significant marketing and branding capabilities it has developed over the years. Company managers at P&G have successfully transferred these core competencies across new acquisitions for the past half-century. Since 1979, P&G has acquired more than 120 companies from multiple industries in several countries (see Table 6.1).

The pursuit of economies of scope can occur through the leveraging of tangible resources, administrative and support functions, internal practices, and intangible resources. In the case of tangible resources, firms often spread many fixed costs across several business units. When a firm acquires a new unit, the core of the firm may be able to eliminate duplicated functions such as distribution and sales, resulting in cost savings for the combined entity. The new firm can share the

existing sales and distribution infrastructure among the different business units. This is a strategy that many consumer goods companies, P&G, for example, have followed. When P&G acquired The Gillette Company in 2005, P&G's managers surmised that the firm could achieve economies of scope through the combination of several internal functions (e.g., distribution). These same managers posited that buyers such as Walmart would be comfortable buying diverse products such as laundry detergent and shaving cream from the same company. P&G also believed that its distribution network could effectively and cost-efficiently distribute both sets of products to buyers.

Firms can also achieve economies of scope by sharing administrative or support functions (e.g., human resource

Year	Industry Sector	Company Name	Deal Value ($ million)	Target Nation
1982	Food and Kindred Products	Coca-Cola Bottling Midwest Inc.	Undisclosed	United States
1985	Drugs	Richardson-Vicks Inc.	1,674	United States
1987	Personal Care Products	Blendax Group	400	Germany
1989	Food and Kindred Products	Sundor Group Inc.	300	United States
1989	Personal Care Products	Noxell Corp	1,340	United States
1990	Food and Kindred Products	Del Monte Corp—Hawaiian Punch	150	United States
1990	Personal Care Products	Shulton—Toiletries, Fragrances	370	United States
1991	Paper and Allied Products	Canadian Pac Forest—Facelle	161	Canada
1991	Personal Care Products	Revlon Inc.—Max Factor, Betrix	1,060	United States
1993	Paper and Allied Products	VP-Schickedanz AG	580	Germany
1994	Personal Care Products	Giorgio Beverly Hills (Avon)	150	United States
1996	Paper and Allied Products	Kimberly-Clark (four businesses)	220	United States
1997	Paper and Allied Products	Tambrands Inc.	2,003	United States
1997	Paper and Allied Products	Loreto y Pena Pobre	170	Mexico
1999	Food and Kindred Products	IAMs Co.	2,300	United States
1999	Machinery	Recovery Engineering Inc.	276	United States
1999	Paper and Allied Products	Prosan	375	Argentina
2001	Personal Care Products	Bristol-Myers Squibb—Clairol	4,950	United States
2003	Personal Care Products	Wella AG	6,121	Germany
2004	Drugs	Laboratorios Vita—Commercial	207	Spain
2004	Personal Care Products	Procter & Gamble—Hutchison Ltd	2,000	China
2005	Metal and Metal Products	Gillette Co.	54,906	United States
2005	Personal Care Products	Colgate-Palmolive Co—Southeast	Undisclosed	Malaysia
2009	Personal Care Products	Sara Lee Corp.	467	United Kingdom
2012	Personal Care Products	Arbora & Ausonia, S.L.U.	973	Spain

Table 6.1 P&G Acquisitions, 1982–2012

Source: SDC Platinum, a Thomson Financial product, accessed February 2015. © Reuters. Used with permission. http://thomsonreuters.com

management and research and development) across a broader array of business units. By adding another business unit, a firm may be able to increase revenues while maintaining the same level of costs, because it can share these resources among units.

In addition to sharing resources, firms can generate synergies by sharing internal practices and processes. When Kyocera, a large fine ceramics and integrated technology producer, acquires firms, it introduces its unique financial reporting and operating philosophy to the acquired companies. Kyocera has developed a tightly integrated business reporting process that enables it to understand the profitability of various departments and work groups in an overall business. This level of detail helps the firm better understand what products and services are most profitable, which enables the company to make quick changes. This reporting capability has become one of Kyocera's core competencies in its internal value chain.

Finally, firms can achieve economies of scope through the sharing of intangible resources. When a parent firm acquires other related businesses, the parent can lend many intangible factors to the acquired firm, such as its brand name or reputation. Through this activity, the parent transfers a major source of internal value to the new unit. This unit can, in turn, take advantage of the parent's brand name to achieve greater awareness in the market.

Beyond economies of scope, some firms may also pursue related diversification strategies to gain **market power**. Firms pursuing related diversification to increase market power are attempting to increase the price at which they sell their products to levels above the normal prices found in the market. To gain market power, some firms use their size to push a competitor out of the market.

An example of a firm that used its market power to push other firms out of an industry is Microsoft. In the mid-1990s, Netscape, the creator of the Internet browser Navigator, went public and had one of the most successful initial public offerings of the decade. As a first mover, Netscape quickly gained a leading share of the newly formed Internet browser software business. In response to this success, Microsoft began offering an Internet browser of its own, Internet Explorer, as a bundled product with its Windows operating system. Through this product bundling strategy, Microsoft essentially gave away its Internet browser software for free. Although Microsoft did not explicitly state it, the company's ultimate goal was to drive Netscape out of the browser business. Microsoft's market power originated from its dominant position in operating systems software.[31] With this market power in operating systems, Microsoft ensured that Netscape's early lead in browser software would evaporate. Microsoft's aggressive practices of trying to secure market dominance in many product areas led to a series of lawsuits from smaller competitors as well as an antitrust suit from the federal government. Though Microsoft was able to withstand most of these lawsuits, the company's expansion plans were vigilantly scrutinized for a number of years.

Unrelated Diversification

A firm that pursues an unrelated diversification strategy maintains several businesses that are not related in any way. A prime example is Vivendi. Vivendi traces its roots back to the mid-nineteenth century. The original company, known as Compagnie Generale des Eaux, operated as a water utility in France. During the twentieth century, the company used the cash flows from its core utility business to diversify into a range of industries including real estate, healthcare, and telecommunications. While the strategy worked well for years, the company encountered financial difficulties in the 1990s. The company focused on restructuring and divesting certain units and reducing the overall corporate debt that it had assumed to fund its diversification. By the beginning of the new millennium, Vivendi embarked on an aggressive diversification strategy, buying companies in industries such as music content and publishing (Universal Music) and video game development (Activision Games) and selling off its core water utility business. While the firm has successfully restructured itself several times in the last two decades, it has struggled to achieve consistently strong performance. Recently, Vivendi has decided to shed almost all of its nonmedia-related businesses as the company seeks to be a more focused and smaller media company.

The ultimate goal of an unrelated diversification strategy is usually to create some form of **financial economies**. Financial economies involve cost savings that a firm achieves through the distribution of capital among business units. In general, a firm can achieve financial economies in one of two ways: (1) by efficiently allocating capital among units and (2) by purchasing a new business and restructuring its assets with the goal of selling it back into the marketplace at a higher price. The downside of unrelated diversification is that it can open a firm to higher levels of risk

Market power
Achieved when a firm attempts to increase the price at which it sells products to levels above the normal price seen in the market.

Financial economies
Cost savings that a firm achieves through the distribution of capital among business units.

and uncertainty. Trying to extract the financial value from unrelated diversification is often quite complex and requires significant managerial expertise, especially since the business entities are so different.

The underlying rationale for unrelated diversification is that the efficient distribution of capital between business units will reduce the overall risk of the business. As we discussed earlier, the reduction of risk through unrelated diversification is difficult to achieve. However, in a few situations, unrelated diversification strategies can achieve financial economies. One advantage of using unrelated diversification is that it can allow a sick or dying company to use capital generated in a profitable division to prop it up for a short period of time. Without these internally generated funds, the company may be forced to enter bankruptcy prematurely.

Unrelated diversification strategies can also achieve financial economies through restructuring. Under this scenario, managers often acquire poorly performing businesses and try to restructure or streamline them to achieve greater profitability. Restructuring could include firing employees, shutting down certain product or service lines, or selling specific assets. To extract value in a meaningful way, managers must accurately assess the core strengths and weaknesses of the businesses that are being restructured.

The Diversification Test

Diversification can both add and destroy value at the corporate level. So when should a manager pursue a diversification strategy? The decision about whether to pursue related or unrelated diversification is often not an either/or choice. Many companies pursue both paths simultaneously. In all cases, a manager should seek to identify conditions under which diversification (related or unrelated) will create shareholder value.[32] These conditions can be described in a three-pronged test (see Figure 6.5).

How Attractive Is the Industry?

In the long run, the rate of return available from competing in an industry is a function of its underlying structure. As we discussed in the previous chapter, attractive industries have certain structural components that allow them to earn greater profitability compared to other industries. Attractive industries are often marked by high barriers to entry, lack of substitutes, low intensity of competition, and low supplier and buyer power. However, because these industries often have high entry barriers, many firms find it difficult to diversify into the most attractive industries.[33]

A prime example of a company diversifying into a structurally unattractive industry occurred when Time Warner purchased AOL in 2001 for $106 billion.[34] This transaction provided the old media giant Time Warner with greater diversification and more control over the delivery of its content. However, at the time of acquisition, the Internet provider industry had started to become structurally unattractive for several reasons. While AOL dominated the early Internet service business, cable and telephone companies entered the industry in the late 1990s with significant distribution and technological advantages. As consumers shifted from dial-up to high-speed digital subscriber line (DSL) and cable service, AOL's market share began to decline rapidly. When Time Warner acquired AOL, the industry was already threatened by intense rivalry among well-capitalized firms.

Stephen Hilger/Bloomberg/Getty Images

What Is the Cost of Entry?

Many managers also fall into the trap of diversifying into unattractive industries because the cost of entry is low. The cost of entering an

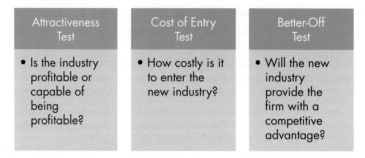

Attractiveness Test	Cost of Entry Test	Better-Off Test
• Is the industry profitable or capable of being profitable?	• How costly is it to enter the new industry?	• Will the new industry provide the firm with a competitive advantage?

Figure 6.5 ⟩ The Diversification Test

Source: Adapted from Michael E. Porter, "From Competitive Advantage to Corporate Strategy," *Harvard Business Review*, May–June 1987.

industry cannot exceed the benefits that management expects to derive from competing in the industry. Many acquisitions fail the cost of entry test because management teams do not accurately assess either the cost of getting in or the benefits that are likely to accrue to the company from being in the industry. While low-cost acquisition opportunities do exist in the market, their presence typically involves industries with low entry barriers that managers should avoid altogether.

Conversely, high entry costs in diversification strategies can be just as harmful for corporate value because the higher initial price impacts the potential for an effective return on investment. Typically, many forces converge to prevent a firm from buying into a new industry on the cheap. Private equity firms, investment banks, and other investors work tirelessly to find undervalued assets in the market. The result of this process is that undervalued companies are more difficult to find, because the sale process often attracts multiple bidders, driving up the price of the target.

Will the Business Be Better Off?

According to Michael Porter, when a firm undertakes an acquisition, the new unit (or new ownership of the business unit) must gain a competitive advantage from its link with the corporation or vice versa.[35] He asks whether the presence of the corporation improves the total competitive advantage of business units above and beyond what they could achieve on their own. A negative answer suggests the corporation should either avoid entering the market or should exit the market. If the answer is affirmative, managers should ask an additional question. Namely, "Does ownership of the business unit produce a greater competitive advantage than an alternative arrangement would produce?" In other words, if the two businesses cannot add value above the value they create on their own as independently owned operations, the firm should not diversify.

A positive answer to the better-off test and a negative answer to the ownership test implies managers should enter the industry, but through some alternative arrangement to full ownership such as a strategic alliance.[36] As you can see from this set of tests, the decision to diversify into other businesses should be made after rigorous analysis. These strict guidelines ensure that a manager will only add businesses to the firm when there is the possibility of creating real value to the overall enterprise.

RESULTS OF DIVERSIFICATION

The evidence that diversification strategies are better than more focused strategies is mixed.[37] According to one key study, a firm's performance increases as it shifts from single-business strategies to related diversification, but performance decreases

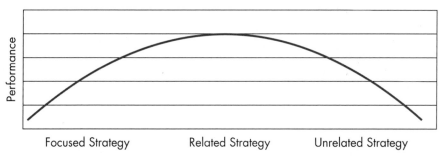

Figure 6.6 ⟩ Impact of Diversification on Firms' Performance

as firms change from related diversification to unrelated diversification.[38] This research shows that firms' performance often resembles an inverted U, with performance increasing up to a point of optimal related diversification and then decreasing as the firms diversify too far into unrelated industries (see Figure 6.6).

Firms that have been successful with related or unrelated diversification have spent a considerable amount of time on implementation strategies and processes. Managers are key players in the success or failure of diversification. The extent to which these managers work together to ensure the successful implementation of shared resources or leveraged assets often separates the winners from the losers. Unfortunately, many firms spend too much time on the "potential benefits" of synergy but not enough time on the hard work necessary to make that potential a reality.[39]

While the results of unrelated diversification are mixed in the United States, there is ample evidence that this strategy works well in emerging economies such as India, China, South Korea, and Chile. Large family business groups with many unrelated companies or highly diversified conglomerate groups have been successful in emerging economies for a number of years. These economies are often characterized by limited financial markets, political instability, restrictive flows of information, and variable human resource skills. In these environments, diversified business groups often mitigate many of these challenges by generating their own internal markets for funds and resources. Select family-owned firms have preferential access to financial resources and talent. Family-owned firms leverage these advantages by investing in a series of unrelated businesses. In spite of the complexity of running unrelated businesses, they gain advantage by providing preferential access to resources for their businesses.[40]

A strong overall corporate brand, such as Tata, can also play an important role in the success of unrelated diversification. Tata Group, an Indian business founded in 1868, used an unrelated diversification strategy to become the largest and most successful company in India. Using strong ethics and values to lead the company, the Tata Group owns 95 companies (e.g., steel, tea, and hospitality) that compete in seven business sectors. In 2014, Tata recorded $103 billion in revenue, with $69 billion coming from international sources.[41]

The manner in which corporate headquarters interact with the separate businesses in a diversified firm is another key factor in generating sustainable results.[42] Successful diversified organizations can balance centralized control levers (e.g., centralized purchasing and information technology) that provide leverage and cost savings throughout the firm with decentralized autonomy that allows business units that are closer to the customer to define real-time operational and market strategies.[43] This balance is especially important in firms pursuing unrelated diversification, where the corporate office generally has limited understanding of each operational business.

Canadapanda/Shutterstock.com

VERTICAL INTEGRATION

Firms that are successful with their corporate strategies know when it is right to diversify and what form of diversification to pursue—related or unrelated. In many ways, related and unrelated diversification are examples of a horizontal expansion plan. Another key lever in many corporate strategies revolves around vertical expansion. A vertical expansion strategy is often pursued in an effort to more effectively share resources and manage costs up and down the firm's value chain. One avenue that some firms pursue to manage costs is vertical integration. In general, **vertical integration** occurs when one corporation owns business units that make inputs for other business units in the same corporation.[44] There are essentially two different types of vertical integration: **backward integration** and **forward integration** (see Figure 6.7). Backward integration occurs when a firm owns or controls the inputs it uses. Forward integration occurs when a firm owns or controls the customers or distribution channels for its main products. Let's take a closer look at examples of each type.

An example of backward integration is The Hershey Company's strategy in the early twentieth century. The familiar candy company backward integrated into sugar production following World War I to guarantee its own supply of sugar. However, the company bought so much sugar capacity in Cuba that it essentially became a sugar exporter to other companies. Hershey's lack of knowledge of the sugar market and a collapse in the price of the commodity almost led to the company's demise in the 1920s. More recently, many large oil companies have also pursued a backward integration strategy by purchasing oil site exploration services.

An example of forward integration can be seen in the example of Walt Disney's acquisition of the ABC television network. Through this move, Disney acquired one of its former customers to control a distribution channel for its content. Other examples of successful forward integration include car manufacturers who own dealer networks and Apple Computer's entry into the retailing sector. Through the introduction of its own retail stores, Apple Computer has been able to better manage its relationship with customers. With this strategy, the company does not need to rely on less savvy retail clerks at large electronic stores; it can rely on its own knowledgeable employees.

Vertical integration
Occurs when one corporation owns business units that make inputs for other business units in the same corporation.

Backward integration
Occurs when a firm owns or controls the inputs it uses.

Forward integration
Occurs when a firm owns or controls the customers or distribution channels for its main products.

Costs Associated with Vertical Integration

To understand why a firm should vertically integrate, we must understand the total cost of conducting a set of activities. When a firm looks to forward or backward integrate into something, it must not only consider how its ownership of those activities

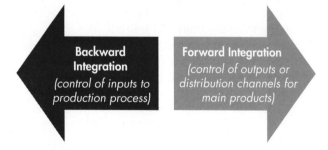

Backward Integration (control of inputs to production process)

Forward Integration (control of outputs or distribution channels for main products)

Figure 6.7 ⟩ Backward and Forward Integration

will affect the production costs, but also the costs of overseeing those activities. Similarly, if a firm chooses not to enter those activities and contract for them from a partner, it has to consider not only the production costs incurred by its partner, but also additional costs it must incur to oversee that relationship. In this context, we must consider the difference between transaction and administrative costs. **Administrative costs** refer to the costs a firm incurs to coordinate activities between its business units. **Transaction costs** are costs to obtain products or services from a contractor or supplier as well as the costs associated with writing and administering the contracts for these products and services.[45]

Over the years, the prevailing wisdom regarding the benefits of vertical integration has changed. During the 1960s and 1970s, many managers believed that vertical integration provided a source of competitive advantage by offering a firm a steady and more cost-effective supply of inputs for its main business. In this period, companies expanded their vertical scope due to a growing belief that the administrative costs of performing functions in-house were lower than the transaction costs of procuring those from an outside entity. However, more recently, managers have placed less emphasis on controlling a firm's entire value chain through vertical integration.[46] They have increasingly found that suppliers can produce those inputs cheaper and better than they can themselves and leverage much greater economies of scale. At the same time, firms have become better at managing the associated transaction costs that result from external procurement.

In some situations, the benefits of vertical integration are greater than the costs (see Figure 6.8). For example, the transaction costs may be so great between stages in a firm's supply chain that the only reasonable action is vertical integration. In general, the more specific or technical the linkage between steps in a value chain, the greater the transaction costs and the more reason to vertically integrate. As we will see in an upcoming example, the clothes maker Zara has chosen to vertically integrate along certain portions of its value chain because of the complexity and time-sensitive nature of a select group of its activities.

While vertical integration may allow firms to avoid some types of transaction costs, it often creates additional administrative costs that must be weighed against

Administrative costs
The costs of coordinating activities between a firm's business units.

Transaction costs
Costs to obtain products or services from a contractor or supplier as well as the costs associated with writing and administering the contracts for these products and services.

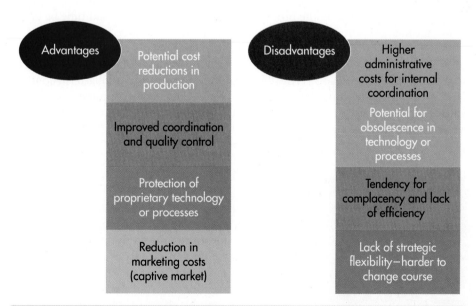

Figure 6.8 Advantages and Disadvantages of Vertical Integration

Sources: Charles W. L. Hill and Gareth R. Jones, *Strategic Management: An Integrated Approach*, 2nd edition (Boston, MA: Houghton Mifflin Company, 1992), pp. 208–212; and Kathryn Rudie Harrigan, "Formulating Vertical Integration Strategies," *Academy of Management Review*, Vol. 9, No. 4, 1984, pp. 638–652.

the benefits. One administrative cost that vertically integrated firms encounter is a reduced ability to develop core competencies in activities along the value chain. Because a firm's activities are spread across the entire value chain, it is often more difficult for management to develop specific core competencies in key areas. In many cases, it is difficult for a vertically integrated firm to develop a true source of differentiation in its activities because it is spread across so many different parts of the value chain.

Finally, incentives are often misaligned in vertically integrated firms. At vertically integrated firms, managers may not exert maximum effort to produce inputs for the larger production process because their internal profitability is guaranteed by "selling" their products to a sister company. In these situations, internal units do not face the same market pressures that firms outside the control of the corporation do.

As you can see, firms encounter numerous costs when they decide to vertically integrate. These costs can outweigh the benefits received from vertical integration. In these cases, a firm should seek alternative approaches to vertical integration.

Alternatives to Vertical Integration

For just about every input that a firm uses to generate its outputs, a manager is confronted with the "make versus buy" decision. That is, should the firm make that specific product or service or should the firm buy it from an outside provider. The extreme form of a buying arrangement is one where the buyer puts out a bid and simply gives the contract to the lowest bidder. Such short-term contracts, sometimes referred to as **spot contracts**, involve a firm's commitment to buy a commodity product at a specific price. When a food processing company needs a bushel of wheat, a manager can purchase it through a spot contract arranged on a commodity exchange. At the other extreme is vertical integration (or "make") where the firm chooses to produce that input in-house.

Firms must consider the relative costs of each choice. In addition to comparing the relative costs for the production of the product or service across the make or buy spectrum, the manager must also consider the administrative and transaction costs associated with that input. Finally, managers must consider the time and attention that is expended on the process. Could these costs, effort, and time be better spent on other areas that have the potential to create more value for the firm?

A number of novel hybrid choices to the stark alternatives of vertical integration (or "make") and buying it from an outside vendor are now available to firms. The most common alternative to vertical integration is to engage in a long-term contract with a supplier for certain products or services. A manager can pursue long-term contracts to stipulate certain services or inputs to be provided to the company. An even stronger form of commitment with an external partner may be an alliance or joint venture where both firms create a new entity that both of them own. Such intermediate arrangements are ones that are neither "make" nor "buy" and provide firms the benefits of both forms.

In **outsourcing**, a firm contracts with an entity outside the corporation to perform certain tasks or functions that the corporation used to do on its own. For example, many companies outsource their customer service operations to outside vendors rather than vertically integrating this function. Firms that specialize in call centers may be able to provide better quality service to the firm at a lower price. When a company outsources this function, it often signs a long-term contract that stipulates activities performed over a certain period of time.

Spot contracts
Contracts that allow a buyer to purchase a commodity at a specific price.

Outsourcing
Contracting with a firm outside the corporation to perform certain tasks or functions that the corporation used to do on its own.

Bloomberg/Getty Images

Companies such as San Antonio–based Rackspace have concentrated on outsourcing as their primary business function. Founded in 1998, Rackspace supplies Web-hosting services to small and medium-sized businesses that do not have the internal capabilities to perform these functions. With dedicated technology teams, Rackspace often operates as the firm's de facto technology department.[47]

Many argue that outsourcing noncore activities brings Rackspace's customers cost savings while simultaneously allowing them to focus on more core functions.[48] The long-term contracting in some ways mitigates the likely transaction costs associated with their working with an external partner like Rackspace. A manager must consider the balance of transaction costs at the firm when making an outsourcing decision. As with all vertical relationships at a firm, certain transaction costs are incurred when the firm decides to outsource an activity. If these costs are lower than the administrative costs the firm would incur by keeping this function in-house, the firm should seriously consider outsourcing it. However, a manager must weigh this cost-benefit analysis against what constitutes a "core" function at the firm. While information technology may not seem like a core function today, the firm's industry may be moving toward competition based on information systems. A manager must realize that outsourcing too many activities may damage the firm's core competencies. Finding the right balance between vertical integration and strategic outsourcing is tricky, but it can result in a stronger and more defensible competitive position.[49] Too much focus on vertical integration can result in isolating a firm from the external market. Conversely, a heavy outsourcing approach can lessen a firm's internal capabilities.[50]

Zara: A Vertically Integrated Apparel Maker

The apparel industry is one of the most visible industries from a retail and marketing standpoint. As a consumer, you can find apparel choices in many different venues—from department stores to upscale shops to Target. Some of the most successful firms in the industry are those that have mastered the art of the apparel value chain through an effective corporate-level strategy.

While many of the major apparel makers choose to focus their activities on specific parts of the value chain, the Spanish apparel maker Inditex has chosen to vertically integrate along many parts of the value chain to differentiate its products and drive performance. Inditex operates six chains: Zara, Massimo Dutti, Pull & Bear, Bershka, Stradivarius, and Oysho. Zara is the largest, operating over 2,000 stores worldwide and generating the majority of the company's sales. Zara produces fashionable apparel for men and women in major markets across the globe.

Zara manufactures most of its fashion-sensitive products internally and aims to draw repeat shoppers into its highly visible stores by rolling out new designs twice a week. With a constantly changing store inventory, Zara relies heavily on its store managers to provide updated sales data on a daily basis. With these data, "Zara's designers continuously track customer preferences and place orders with internal and external suppliers for nearly 11,000 distinct items that are produced during the year—several hundred thousand products given variations in color, fabric, and sizes—compared with 2,000–4,000 items for key competitors."[51] To achieve this customization, production is conducted in small batches, with production of the most time-sensitive items vertically integrated.[52] From production centers, clothing batches are sent twice a week to stores, eliminating the need for warehouses while simultaneously keeping inventories low. In 2014, the company invested over $200 million in a new logistics hub to expand its ability to quickly deliver hundreds of thousands of garments to retail stores in 87 countries.[53]

From this tightly interlocked system of activities, Zara has developed an advantage in the highly competitive global apparel industry. Traditional fashion retailers often outsource large aspects of their fashion lines to reduce production costs. While outsourcing can reduce costs, it often does not provide as much flexibility in the design and delivery process. Traditional retailers tend to produce large quantities of various fashion items that they store in warehouses until the products are needed in the individual retail stores.

This process requires a considerable amount of lead time. Alternatively, Zara has focused on delivering highly fashionable products on a timely and continuous basis. Without its vertically integrated structure for certain products, the company would not be able to bring garments to fashion-conscious customers as rapidly as it does.

Case in Point   Zara

1. How does Zara's strategy differ from a traditional retailer?
2. What key activities are aligned to support Zara's vertical integration strategy?
3. For Zara, how has vertical integration resulted in a competitive advantage?
4. Can Zara's strategy be easily imitated by its competitors?

SUMMARY

LO1 Corporate-level strategy entails developing a plan for the management of multiple businesses and deciding how to expand the boundaries of the firm. It also involves organizational design and ownership choices so that the firm can maximize its resources across multiple businesses. A manager has numerous corporate-level tools to choose from, including related diversification, unrelated diversification, and vertical integration.

LO2 Through diversification, a firm engages in several different businesses that may or may not be related in an attempt to create more value than if the businesses existed as stand-alone entities. Transferring skills and resources between different units can create synergies for a firm and is one reason that a firm decides to diversify. Firms also diversify to achieve financial objectives including the generation of new revenues or the reduction of operational costs.

LO3 There are two primary approaches to diversification: (1) related diversification, and (2) unrelated diversification. With related diversification, a firm owns more than one business that uses a similar set of tangible or intangible resources. The goal of related diversification is to achieve economies of scope that enable a firm to leverage their skills, resources, or other assets across similar businesses. Firms that pursue unrelated diversification strategies maintain a portfolio of companies that are not related in any way. The goal of unrelated diversification is not necessarily focused on leveraging the firm's capabilities across businesses, since it is harder

to create these synergies between inherently different units. The goal of unrelated diversification is to create financial economies. In general terms, firms that pursue related diversification are relying on a strategic approach to growth and profitability. Alternatively, firms that pursue unrelated diversification attempt to drive profitability through more financial means.

LO4 Given the complexity associated with diversification strategies, the overall results have been mixed. Firms that have been successful with related or unrelated diversification have spent a considerable amount of time on implementation strategies and processes. Managers are key players in the success or failure of diversification. The extent to which these managers work together to ensure the successful implementation of shared resources or leveraged assets often separates the winners from the losers.

LO5 Vertical integration can be another component of a firm's corporate strategy. Vertical integration occurs when a firm owns business units that make inputs for other business units in the same firm. In deciding whether or not to vertically integrate, a firm must consider if integration will provide a greater competitive advantage than purchasing from outside suppliers. The key to success with vertical integration is finding the right balance between what to do in-house and what to buy from others. This ultimately means that the firm must evaluate the costs of internal coordination (administrative costs) against the costs of buying from external suppliers (transaction costs).

KEY TERMS

Administrative costs	Forward integration	Synergy
Backward integration	Market power	Transaction costs
Corporate advantage	Outsourcing	Unrelated diversification
Diversification	Related diversification	Vertical integration
Economies of scope	Single-product strategy	
Financial economies	Spot contracts	

ASSIGNMENTS

Discussion Topics

1. Compare and contrast business-level and corporate-level strategies. How do these strategies complement each other? What leadership skills are most needed to execute each approach?

2. At what point in its lifecycle should a firm consider the development and execution of a corporate-level strategy?

3. What role should the government have in regulating or overseeing the way in which firms pursue diversification strategies? In today's business environment, do you believe that the level of regulation of corporate-level strategies is too much, too little, or about right?

4. What are the advantages and disadvantages of related and unrelated diversification strategies? How should a firm consider which diversification path to follow?

5. Why have firms found it so hard to reap the potential benefits of diversification? What could a firm do to increase its chances of reaping the benefits of diversification?

6. Why have large family-based firms like the Tata Group in India been successful with unrelated diversification? What aspects of the context in emerging markets are conducive to the pursuit of unrelated diversification?

7. What risks do firms face when they diversify on an international level? How can these risks be mitigated?

8. When does vertical integration make sense for an organization?

9. How do companies derive the most value from pursuing vertical integration?

10. Outsourcing has become an increasingly popular alternative to vertical integration. What are the costs and benefits of outsourcing?

Management Research

1. Find a firm that employs a diversification strategy and list the different industries in which it competes. Use the diversification test (see Figure 6.5) to decide if this company should be in these different industries. Use the Internet and public filings such as Annual Reports or 10-Ks to gather this information.

2. P&G has made a practice of acquiring related firms to build their market power with certain retail chains such as Walmart and Target. What other firms have been able to pursue a similar path?

3. Find a firm that employs a vertical integration strategy and list the stages of production that make it vertically integrated. Use the Internet and public filings such as Annual Reports or 10-Ks to gather this information.

In the Field

Facilitate a brainstorming session with a local business that historically has not pursued a corporate-level strategy. Work with managers to explore the firm's options for a corporate-level strategy. You may discuss the following questions:

- What are the firm's options for a diversification strategy?

- For each diversification strategy proposed, what are the pros and cons?

- Are there opportunities for the firm to vertically integrate?

- Does the firm have any alliances? If so, what are the benefits of those alliances?

ENDNOTES

[1] David Collis and Cynthia Montgomery, "Corporate Strategy: A Conceptual Framework," Harvard Business School Note No. 9-391-284, rev. April 17, 1995 (Boston, MA: HBS Publishing, 1991), p. 6.

[2] Michael E. Porter, "From Competitive Advantage to Corporate Strategy," *Harvard Business Review*, May–June 1987.

[3] Bharat N. Anand, "Corporate Strategy: Course Introduction," Harvard Business School Note No. 9-705-482, rev. April 11, 2005 (Boston, MA: HBS Publishing, 2005), pp. 2–3.

[4] David Collis and Cynthia Montgomery, "Corporate Strategy: A Conceptual Framework," Harvard Business School Note No. 9-391-284, rev. April 17, 1995 (Boston, MA: HBS Publishing, 1991), p. 6.

[5] Bharat N. Anand, "Corporate Strategy: Course Introduction," Harvard Business School Note No. 9-705-482, rev. April 11, 2005 (Boston, MA: HBS Publishing, 2005), p. 1.

[6] R. Duane Ireland and C. Chet Miller, "Decision-Making and Firm Success," *Academy of Management Executive*, Vol. 18, No. 4, 2004, p. 9.

[7] Michael G. Rukstad, David Collis, and Tyrrell Levine, "The Walt Disney Company: The Entertainment King," Harvard Business School Case No. 9-701-035, rev. January 5, 2009 (Boston, MA: HBS Publishing, 2001), p. 2.

[8] Ibid., p. 5.

[9] Ibid., p. 7.

[10] Ibid., pp. 11–12.

[11] Gerald F. Davis, Kristina Diekmann, and Catherine Tinsley, "The Decline and Fall of the Conglomerate Firm in the 1980s: The Deinstitutionalization of an Organization Form," *American Sociological Review*, Vol. 59, 1994, p. 552.

[12] Ibid., p. 553.

[13] Ibid.

[14] Bruce D. Henderson, *On Corporate Strategy* (Cambridge, MA: Abt Books, 1979), pp. 164–166.

[15] David J. Collis and Cynthia A. Montgomery, "Competing on Resources: Strategy in the 1990s," *Harvard Business Review*, July-August 1995.

[16] Martin Reeves, Sandy Moose, and Thijs Venema, "BCG Classics Revisited: The Growth Share Matrix," *BCG Perspectives*, June 4, 2014 available at https://www.bcgperspectives.com/content /articles/corporate_strategy_portfolio_management_strategic_planning_growth_share_matrix_bcg_classics_revisited/, accessed June 9, 2015.

[17] David Collis and Cynthia Montgomery, "Corporate Strategy: A Conceptual Framework," Harvard Business School Note No. 9-391-284, rev. April 17, 1995 (Boston, MA: HBS Publishing, 1991), p. 1.

[18] David Collis, "Managing the Multibusiness Corporation," Harvard Business School Note No. 9-391-286, rev. April 24, 1997 (Boston, MA: HBS Publishing, 1991), p. 5.

[19] Cynthia A. Montgomery, "Corporate Diversification," *Journal of Economic Perspectives*, Vol. 8, No. 3, 1994, p. 166.

[20] Carolin Decker and Thomas Mellewigt, "Thirty Years After Michael E. Porter: What Do We Know About Business Exit?," *Academy of Management Perspectives*, Vol. 21, No. 2, 2007, p. 42.

[21] Michael Lubatkin and Sayan Chatterjee, "Extending Modern Portfolio Theory into the Domain of Corporate Diversification: Does It Apply," *Academy of Management Journal*, Vol. 37, No. 1, 1994, p. 109.

[22] Carolin Decker and Thomas Mellewigt, "Thirty Years After Michael E. Porter: What Do We Know About Business Exit?," *Academy of Management Perspectives*, Vol. 21, No. 2, 2007, p. 47.

[23] Rajesh K. Aggarwal and Andrew A. Samwick, "Why Do Managers Diversify Their Firms?: Agency Reconsidered," *Journal of Finance*, Vol. 58, No. 1, 2003, pp. 71–118.

[24] Mikolaj Jan Piskorski, "Choosing Corporate and Global Scope," Harvard Business School Note No. 9-707-496, (Boston, MA: HBS Publishing, 2007), p. 1.

[25] Mary Kwak, "Maximizing Value through Diversification," *MIT Sloan Management Review*, Winter 2002, p. 10.

[26] Mikolaj Jan Piskorski, "Choosing Corporate and Global Scope," Harvard Business School Note No. 9-707-496 (Boston, MA: HBS Publishing, 2007), p. 3.

[27] Christopher A. Bartlett and Afroze Mohammed, "3M: Profile of an Innovating Company," Harvard Business School Case No. 9-395-016 (Boston, MA: HBS Publishing, 1995), p. 3.

[28] Ibid., p. 3.

[29] James R. Hagerty, "50,000 Products Aren't Enough," *Wall Street Journal*, November 19, 2013.

[30] Arthur A. Thompson, Jr., and A. J., Strickland, III, *Strategy Formulation and Implementation: Tasks of the General Manager*, 5th edition (Homewood, IL: Irwin, 1992), p. 170.

[31] David B. Yoffie, Dharmesh M. Mehta, and Rudina I. Seseri, "Microsoft in 2005," Harvard Business School Case No. 9-705-505, rev. January 9, 2006 (Boston, MA: HBS Publishing, 2006), p. 4.

[32] Michael E. Porter, "From Competitive Advantage to Corporate Strategy," *Harvard Business Review*, May–June 1987.

[33] Ibid.

[34] Julie Chen, Anchor, "CBS News: Morning News," January 12, 2001, www.factiva.com, accessed January 2010.

[35] Michael E. Porter, "From Competitive Advantage to Corporate Strategy," *Harvard Business Review*, May–June 1987.

[36] Mikolaj Jan Piskorski, "Choosing Corporate and Global Scope," Harvard Business School Module Note No. 9-707-496 (Boston, MA: HBS Publishing, 2007).

[37] Cynthia A. Montgomery, "Corporate Diversification," *Journal of Economic Perspectives*, Vol. 8, No. 3, 1994, p. 172; and Peter Taylor and Julian Lowe, "A Note on Corporate Strategy and Capital Structure," *Strategic Management Journal*, Vol. 16, No. 5, 1995, pp. 411–414.

[38] Douglas J. Miller, "Technological Diversity, Related Diversification, and Firm Performance," *Strategic Management Journal*, Vol. 27, 2006, pp. 601–619; Leslie E. Palich, Laura B. Cardinal, and C. Chet Miller, "Curvilinearity in the Diversification Performance Linkage: An Examination of Over Three Decades of Research," *Strategic Management Journal*, Vol. 22, 2000, pp. 155–174; and Michael Lubatkin and Sayan Chatterjee, "Extending Modern Portfolio Theory into the Domain of Corporate Diversification: Does It Apply," *Academy of Management Journal*, Vol. 37, No. 1, 1994, pp. 130–133.

[39] Michael Shayne Gary, "Implementation Strategy and Performance Outcomes in Related Diversification," *Strategic Management Journal*, Vol. 26, 2005, pp. 643–664.

[40] Tarun Khanna and Krishna Palepu, "The Future of Business Groups in Emerging Markets: Long-Run Evidence from Chile," *Academy of Management Journal*, Vol. 43, No. 3, 2000, pp. 368–285; Tarun Khanna, Krishna G. Palepu, and Jayant Sinha, "Strategies That Fit Emerging Markets," *Harvard Business Review*, June 2005; and Michael E. Porter,

"From Competitive Advantage to Corporate Strategy," *Harvard Business Review*, May–June 1987.

[41] Tata at http://www.tata.com/company/index/Tata-companies, accessed February 7, 2015.

[42] David Collis, David Young, and Michael Goold, "The Size, Structure, and Performance of Corporate Headquarters," *Strategic Management Journal*, Vol. 28, 2007, pp. 383–405.

[43] Michael E. Raynor and Joseph L. Bower, "Lead from the Center: How to Manage Divisions Dynamically," *Harvard Business Review*, May 2001.

[44] Mikolaj Jan Piskorski, "Choosing Corporate and Global Scope," Harvard Business School Note No. 9-707-496, (Boston, MA: HBS Publishing, 2007), p. 5.

[45] R. H. Coase, "The Nature of the Firm," *Economica* Vol. 4, 1937, pp. 386–405.

[46] John Stuckey and David White, "When and When Not to Vertically Integrate," *Sloan Management Review*, Spring 1993, pp. 71–83.

[47] James L. Heskett and W. Earl Sasser, "Rackspace Hosting in Late 2000," Harvard Business School Case No. 9-808-166 (Boston, MA: HBS Publishing, 2008).

[48] Gregory G. Dees, Abdul M.A. Rasheed, Kevin J. McLaughlin, and Richard L. Priem, "The New Corporate Architecture," *Academy of Management Executive*, Vol. 9, No. 3, 1995, pp. 7–18.

[49] Frank T. Rothaermel, Michael A. Hitt, and Lloyd A. Jobe, "Balancing Vertical Integration and Strategic Outsourcing: Effects on Product Portfolio, Product Success, and Firm Performance," *Strategic Management Journal*, Vol. 27, 2006, p. 1051.

[50] Ibid.

[51] Pankaj Ghemawat and Jose Luis Nueno, "Zara: Fast Fashion," Harvard Business School Case No. 9-703-497, rev. December 21, 2006 (Boston, MA: HBS Publishing, 2003), p. 9.

[52] Ibid.

[53] Christopher Bjork, "Zara Owner Prepares for Expansion," *Wall Street Journal*, March 20, 2014.

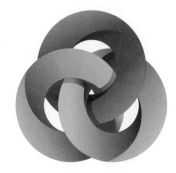

P A R T **3**

ORGANIZATIONAL PERSPECTIVE

CHAPTER 7

Organizational Design

Learning Objectives

After reading this chapter, you should be able to:

LO1 : Understand the role that organizations play in helping a firm achieve its strategic objectives.

LO2 : Define the various organizational design decisions that are central to creating an organization that is aligned with a firm's strategic objectives.

LO3 : Explain the different forms of organizational structure including functional, divisional, matrix, network, and hybrid and outline the advantages and disadvantages of each form.

LO4 : Determine what organizational choices and leadership approaches correspond to specific life-cycle stages of a business.

LO5 : Describe how firms are redefining their organizations to better meet the demands of customers and improve their operational efficiency.

SELF-REFLECTION

Organizational Acumen

Acumen is defined as the ability to make good judgments and quick decisions because of keenness in perception or discernment. Often when managers discuss business acumen, they are referring to an understanding of a firm's financial, accounting, or marketing status. However, managers also need acumen in understanding how organizations are designed to achieve strategic objectives. Please respond True or False to the following statements to assess your acumen in understanding the design of an organization.

1. I can identify the three functions of an organization.

2. I understand how organizations employ different mechanisms to control behavior.

3. I can differentiate between a decentralized organization and a centralized organization.

4. I understand why organizations are designed for the division of labor.

5. I know why job specialization is an organizational design consideration.

6. I can give examples of coordinating mechanisms that organizations use.

7. I acknowledge that organizations have informal structures for getting work done that may not be documented.

8. I recognize that there are advantages and disadvantages associated with different types of organizational structures.

9. I am familiar with how the design of an organization may change over its life cycle.

10. I understand how some organizations are designed for flexibility to better serve customers.

If you answered True to the majority of these statements, you have begun to develop acumen for understanding how organizations are designed to achieve their strategic objectives.

INTRODUCTION

In the previous section of this book, we focused on the strategic perspective of a company. We analyzed how managers evaluate the industry in which they compete and pursue a particular strategy that will best position their firm against competitors to achieve dominant market share and/or to maximize profits. Managers need to analyze the environmental context, decide how best to compete (cost leadership, differentiation, or focus), determine success criteria, and assess the overall competitive landscape. Having decided on a strategic direction, the next challenge is implementation. How is strategy translated into everyday action? How does a firm achieve its objectives?

Organizations are the primary mechanisms by which individuals (and their firms) come together to create desired outcomes.[1] While strategy is vitally important, execution is critical to a firm's long-term success. In fact, while a competitor can often "steal" or adopt another company's strategic perspective, it is more difficult to implement it. One element in particular that makes imitation hard is the unique organizational configuration that drives excellent implementation and performance.[2] Recall the discussion of Southwest Airlines. Many airlines have tried to copy Southwest's fun, low frills, low-cost approach to point-to-point air travel. For the most part, however, the results of these efforts have been disastrous. While other airlines can observe and read about Southwest's strategy in great detail, they still cannot copy the unique organizational design and culture that forms the foundation of Southwest's success. Companies have had similar trouble replicating Toyota's production system even though Toyota allows many visitors to tour its operations.

In this section of the book, we will focus on the organization as an instrument for achieving strategic objectives. We will unpack this black box of the organization and examine the way leaders make important decisions regarding its key elements, which include organizational design, culture, human capital, and measurement. We will explore various organizational design choices and associated organizational structures in this chapter. The formal structure of an organization is a key design choice that leaders must make and regularly revisit as they evolve their strategy. The formal structure of an organization is like the architecture of a building. It shapes how people experience and work in the organization. Who do they report to, how is work divided up, how are the different pieces brought back together and by whom? In some instances, you can get a glimpse into this structure by looking at a company's formal organization chart that shows the reporting structure in the firm, but in most cases, the structure is too complicated to be truly captured in a single graph. There are many design choices that leaders must make, and these, in turn, can have a significant impact on the organization and the employees within it.

The way employees feel about a company and the values they hold are part of the organization's culture. Those values provide a roadmap for the way in which work is accomplished and the manner in which individuals relate to one another in the organization. The development and nurturing of an organization's culture will be explored in Chapter 8. Ultimately, an organization is a collection of individuals working together to advance the strategic objectives of the firm. In Chapter 9, we will explore the manner in which firms hire, retain, and develop employees.

The results of the choices a firm makes to achieve its strategy need to be monitored and measured regularly. Performance management, which is discussed in Chapter 10, is a key component of the organizational perspective as it provides the means by which executives can evaluate the processes and procedures they have adopted to achieve specific objectives.

Preparing for and implementing change is the final component of the organizational perspective (Chapter 11). A firm's organizational design choices can result in a competitive advantage, especially when it helps to align the firm's resources in the pursuit of a common purpose and set of goals.[3] Successful firms modify and adjust their organizations and culture to fit changing contextual situations.

This opening chapter on organizational design will present an overview of the purpose of organizations and the various design elements that managers must consider as they define their approach to strategic implementation. The transformation of the Federal Bureau of Investigation (FBI) over the past decade is an interesting example of the importance of having an organizational perspective while implementing a new strategy.

Federal Bureau of Investigation

The FBI was established under the umbrella organization of the Department of Justice (DOJ). In 1908, the DOJ identified 34 special agents to focus on criminal investigations, and by 1930, under the leadership of J. Edgar Hoover, 30 field offices were established throughout the country. Hoover continued his role as the director of the FBI until 1972, working to bring the FBI to the national stage. With the help of cinema and widely publicized cases, the FBI gained national recognition for being the primary crime fighter against America's most serious criminals. Originally, the FBI was divided into two areas: criminal investigation and intelligence. While the former determined what happened in the past, the latter tried to predict the future. In the 1970s, the FBI's major priorities included counterintelligence, organized crime, and white-collar crime. Drug offenses were added in the 1980s, and counterterrorism was added in the 1990s. During this time, each category did not receive the same level of attention in the organization.[4]

The FBI's culture was heavily shaped by its field agents. Field agents were committed to justice and gained great satisfaction from prosecuting criminals. One agent was heard saying, "I'm here to fill jail cells, not file cabinets."[5] FBI agents also valued autonomy—as one agent said, "Real men don't type. The only thing a real agent needs is a notebook, a pen, and a gun, and with those three things, you can conquer the world."[6] As a result, field agents sought to work in criminal investigations because their work put criminals in jail. Intelligence jobs, on the other hand, were seen as less powerful positions. Because these jobs focused solely on predicting events that had not yet happened, intelligence agents had to request permission from higher authorities to pursue their work. With more definite guidelines, deadlines, and significantly more autonomy, criminal investigation jobs were far more popular.[7]

The September 11, 2001, attacks on the World Trade Center and Pentagon sent shockwaves throughout the organization. Follow-up investigations revealed that the FBI and Central Intelligence Agency (CIA) had enough information to prevent the attacks but failed to share the information. As a result, new priorities were set immediately from the attorney general and the director of the FBI, Robert Mueller.[8] The FBI's traditional priorities were flipped: they were ordered to prevent attacks first and prosecute criminals second. To do so, the FBI had to reorganize its structure, reallocate its resources, and revise its purpose.

The first changes occurred shortly after 2001 as Mueller worked to restructure the FBI to focus more on counterintelligence and counterterrorism. These two areas were combined under the same leadership and were centralized at FBI headquarters. Rather than field offices working independently on case leads, all information was submitted to an executive assistant director (EAD) of the FBI.[9] To improve the communication and facilitation of information, field intelligence groups, which reported to headquarters, were established in all field offices. With an increased emphasis on intelligence, the FBI heavily recruited new intelligence analysts, invested in new technology, and increased the amount of intelligence training for all agents. But like any organization, these changes were met with resistance.

Mueller understood that restructuring the FBI was not enough; he also had to change the FBI's overall mission and purpose. The old system relied on field agents to scan the environment for case leads, work autonomously on the cases, and prosecute criminals. This system proved unreliable because threats were becoming more nationally and internationally connected. Beginning in 2007, Mueller envisioned an "intelligence-led, threat-based" FBI that "served as a national security organization."[10] In the new system, all efforts would be led by intelligence. Agents would learn about new threats, assess the information gap, and conduct field work to fill in those gaps. Based on the data that were obtained, field agents would proactively fight criminals and terrorists. Essentially, it was an effort to use intelligence tactics to lead law enforcement activities.[11]

To implement this strategic and organizational change, Mueller introduced three initiatives: strategy management systems (SMS), a strategic execution team (SET), and strategy performance sessions (SPSs). These were meant to more clearly define the FBI strategy, clarify priorities, establish objectives, and monitor progress toward those objectives.[12]

The SMS was responsible for identifying the key metrics and objectives that would help the FBI morph into its new organization. The FBI adopted a modified balanced scorecard, a system that helps businesses translate strategy into action, to fit the needs of a government crime agency. The balanced scorecard is discussed more thoroughly in Chapter 10. The SMS identified key areas to monitor and review, improving the FBI's ability to perform long-term analysis on threats to the nation.[13] The SET was used to implement a long-term, sustainable change. Needing to overcome the change paralysis experienced at the FBI, SET helped bring the law enforcement and intelligence "sides of the house" under one mission: to promote national security. The SET promoted a unified culture by emphasizing the need to understand threats through a national and international lens, not through single field offices.[14] Finally, the SPSs communicated the overall strategy throughout the FBI and assessed progress. Functioning as performance reviews for field offices, SPSs were conducted by members from headquarters asking local agents to assess how they gathered and analyzed information, set priorities, allocated resources, and tracked progress toward their objectives.[15]

The three initiatives were responsible for producing a fundamental change in the FBI's organizational structure and culture. One of the goals of the changes was to enhance the coordination and integration of work across the organization. Like many companies, the FBI faced challenges during implementation, primarily through organizational resistance. Still, the efforts exposed areas for improvement and helped Mueller understand the challenges and identify the triumphs. By 2009, he discovered that agents needed fewer administrative obligations and better information technology (IT) support. He also saw that newly hired intelligence analysts needed to be integrated with field officers. While the change effort showed promise, he still needed to overcome many challenges to deliver a permanent change to the FBI.[16]

As the FBI story demonstrates, organizations are often a work in progress. As environmental conditions or internal priorities change, an organization must adapt to ensure that it is efficient and relevant.

Case in Point   Federal Bureau of Investigation

1. Why did the organizational design of the FBI change over time?

2. During the change process, how did the FBI employees so that it was aligned with the organization's strategy?

3. What key organizational design components did Robert Mueller, the director of the FBI, identify as essential for focusing on counterintelligence and counterterrorism?

4. What were the goals of Mueller's three initiatives? How did the three initiatives achieve these goals?

FROM STRATEGY TO ORGANIZATIONAL DESIGN

The growing complexity of the competitive landscape, the rapid pace of change and globalization, and the need to properly align and motivate employees have contributed to the importance of linking a firm's **organizational design** with its espoused strategy.[17] Organizational design refers to the formal systems, levers, and decisions an organization adopts or employs in pursuit of its strategy.[18] While some have argued that there is a hierarchical relationship between strategy and organizational design whereby design follows strategy, considerable evidence shows that strategy and organizational design are co-evolutionary and reciprocal in nature.[19] For instance, a firm that hopes to pursue a cost leadership strategy will most likely make a series of organizational design decisions that emphasize operational efficiency, cost reduction, and internal integration or alignment. Companies that seek to pursue a differentiation strategy will make different organizational

Organizational design
The formal systems, levers, and decisions an organization adopts or employs in pursuit of its strategy.

design decisions, including ones that emphasize innovation, creativity, flexibility, and speed.

From our discussion thus far, it should be clear that without a well-defined organizational design, many firms will struggle to develop and maintain a competitive advantage in the marketplace. Organizational design encompasses several important decisions. For instance, how will jobs be divided and how much autonomy will be allowed throughout the organization? Should jobs be formalized, structured, and standardized? Should the company focus on customers, geographic regions, product categories, or functions? The choices made in each of these areas will influence the overall context of the organization.[20]

Division of Labor

The concept of **division of labor** dates back to the seminal work of Adam Smith and refers to how work in a firm is divided among employees. At an elementary level, firms exist to accomplish more than individuals can do alone. At the same time, when you bring employees together, you need to clearly delineate who will do what. A manager must make several important decisions about the division of labor, including the scope of each individual's position. For example, an engineer responsible only for designing the circuits for a new cell phone has a focused role, which is characterized by a narrow scope of responsibility. However, an engineer involved with a more complete set of activities within circuit design from project budgeting to managing the transition from research to mass manufacturing has a greater degree of responsibility and a broader job scope. In this case, the engineer is overseeing many aspects of the delivery process from the product design to construction.

As a manager contemplates designating the division of labor across all its employees, he or she needs to be aware of the trade-offs inherent in this decision. On the one hand, the creation of highly specialized jobs can help a firm develop deep expertise or competency in a certain skill or function. On the other hand, extreme specialization can lead to low job satisfaction for a worker, especially if that specialization results in tedious, repetitive work. With high levels of job specialization, firms are often unable to prevent turnover. Interestingly, though, the repetitive and specialized nature of these types of jobs lends itself to quick and efficient training of new resources.

Coordinating Mechanisms

The first part of setting up the division of labor in an organization is dividing up the work among individuals and groups. The other side of this division of labor is to coordinate these disparate efforts to bring it all together in a coherent manner. To do so, a manager must decide which specific activities need to be coordinated with which others, and how to coordinate those activities.

As we consider how work should be divided and coordinated, two opposing schools of thought have emerged on how tightly this division and coordination should be controlled. On one side, **organizers** believe that more control is warranted in organizational design to ensure that jobs are performed satisfactorily and efficiently. More control generally includes greater job standardization, clear and specific definitions of roles and responsibilities, and more hierarchical leadership. Many fast-food retail chains are based on a system of tight controls to ensure quality, consistency, and speed in preparing and serving their primary products. Efficiency is often the overriding concern in these locations, and every job facet, including how long to toast a bun or deep fry a chicken patty or wrap a sandwich is defined and timed in seconds.

Division of labor
The manner in which work in a firm is divided among employees.

Organizers
Those who believe that more control is warranted in organizational design to ensure that jobs are performed satisfactorily and efficiently.

www.sunhydraulics.com

The extreme form of control is best exemplified by Weber's delineation of the **bureaucratic approach** to management that was discussed in Chapter 1. Bureaucratic systems are highly formalized and are characterized by extensive rules, procedures, policies, and instructions. Positions are arranged hierarchically with top management dictating the direction and activity of the organization while lower-level managers and employees follow orders.[21] The fundamental mechanism of monitoring involves close personal surveillance of superiors over subordinates.[22] To be successful in a bureaucracy, individuals must accept the formal authority and learn the expected rules and regulations.[23]

As firms grow in size and complexity, bureaucracies can be an efficient way to cope by structuring activities and creating more formal mechanisms of communication and control.[24] In addition, bureaucracies can withstand a diverse workforce and high turnover.[25] While a bureaucracy is often considered the most fair and efficient method of control, the formalized rules and surveillance can be troublesome. The hierarchy and constraints that are advantageous in some environments are, for the same reasons, disadvantageous in others. Bureaucracies are not useful in creative and innovative environments, ones that need to respond to changing, dynamic markets.[26]

Behaviorists, on the contrary, believe that too much control leads to lower job satisfaction, inertia, and lack of creativity. Behaviorists support a more open organizational design where roles and responsibilities are more loosely defined.[27] One company that has adopted an extreme form of the behaviorist approach is Sun Hydraulics, a manufacturer of hydraulic cartridge valves and manifolds used by companies that produce industrial fluid power applications. When Bob Koski founded the company in Florida, he sought to create a new model for an industrial manufacturer. The company does not have job titles, organizational charts, departments, close supervision, or defined work rules. Koski commented that "our one rule is that there are no rules." He went on to state that "we expect that people can decide for themselves, based on widely shared information on operations, how best to contribute to the company's objectives." New employees enter the company in a job rotation format where they move from one area to another to see where their skills are best utilized.[28] Of course, this type of organization is not for everyone. Many people thrive with structure; thus, they would feel lost or uncomfortable at Sun Hydraulics.

In many ways, Sun Hydraulics has adopted what Weber called a **clan approach** to organizational control. The key characteristics of clans include self-supervising teams that are responsible for a set of tasks. In the clan, each member is cross-trained to be able to perform multiple tasks, and individual goals and values completely overlap with the organization's values.[29] One of the core advantages to the clan is the self-regulating characteristics of its employees. Workers collaborate on projects and must negotiate proper team behavior, often using the organization's mission and values as a guide.[30]

While bureaucracies are more efficient for large organizations operating in steady environments, clans are preferred when conditions are uncertain and work activities are difficult to measure.[31] When a company is subjected to uncertainty in the environment, employees need to adapt and change along with the context, which happens most easily in a clan because it tolerates diverse working styles and performance. Because low turnover and guaranteed employment are important to sustain a clan system, companies that operate in price-competitive and cost-sensitive industries find clan systems to be challenging (see Figure 7.1).[32] Having made some broad organizational design choices regarding division of labor and coordinating mechanisms, a leader should then consider specific organizational structures that, in turn, shape how the firm will implement its strategy.

Bureaucratic approach
An extreme form of organizational control in which systems are highly formalized and are characterized by extensive rules, procedures, policies, and instructions.

Behaviorists
Those who support a more open organizational structure where roles and responsibilities are loosely defined.

Clan approach
A type of organizational control that includes self-supervising teams that are responsible for a set of tasks.

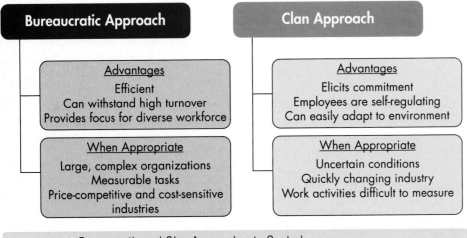

Figure 7.1 ⟩ Bureaucratic and Clan Approaches to Control

Source: Adapted from B. R. Baliga and Alfred M. Jaeger, "Multinational Corporations: Control Systems and Delegation Issues," *Journal of International Business Studies*, Vol. 15, Fall 1984, pp. 25–40.

ORGANIZATIONAL DESIGN: FORMAL AND INFORMAL STRUCTURES

Organizational design decisions about how work should be divided and coordinated impact the **organizational structure** that is adopted to fulfill the firm's strategy. While the degree of control is one high level way of thinking of design choices, there are a lot more specific choices to be made as well that, in turn, can have a dramatic impact on the likelihood of organizational success. Organizational structure is defined as the pattern of organizational roles, relationships, and procedures that enable coordinated action among employees. Most people assume that organizational structure simply involves making a chart. But there are various nuanced choices to be made such as whether to divide up work into units by function, product, or geographic region. Coming to a decision about such choices involves a detailed analysis about a firm's capabilities, the competitive environment, and the overall context. A well-defined and utilized organizational structure enables a firm to maximize the internal resources at its disposal to be competitive in the marketplace while at the same time prepare for changes on the horizon.

In general, the organizational structure serves three primary functions within a firm (see Figure 7.2). First, an organizational structure allows a firm to perform a variety of activities by dividing the firm's labor force. Second, an organizational structure allows the members of a firm to coordinate their activities through mechanisms such as supervision, formal rules and procedures, plans and budgets, training, and socialization. Coordination is important because of the interdependencies

Organizational structure
The pattern of organizational roles, relationships, and procedures that enable coordinated action among employees.

Figure 7.2 ⟩ Three Functions of an Organization

within organizations. In other words, the actions and decisions of one group often impact the way another group works.[33] Finally, an organizational structure defines the borders of a firm and its relationships with both the business environment and other firms.

The three basic types of organizational structures that a firm may adopt are functional, divisional, and matrix. Most firms follow an evolutionary pattern with respect to organizational structure, modifying it to account for business complexity and strategic changes. In general, many firms begin with a **functional structure**. As firms expand and grow in complexity, they may reorganize into a **divisional structure**. Some firms may ultimately move to a **matrix structure**.

Functional Form

When people envision a firm's organizational structure, they tend to think of the traditional functional form (see Figure 7.3). In a functional structure, a firm divides people into units in terms of the main activities that need to be performed, such as production, marketing, sales, and accounting.[34] For example, a sales manager resides in the sales portion of an organization and is managed by the vice president (VP) of sales. This person manages all of the firm's sales managers in a hierarchical manner. Employees such as the sales manager are committed to achieving functional goals (e.g., sales targets) and firm-wide goals (e.g., total revenue growth). While employees strive for numerous goals in the functional structure, their career progression is often determined by a department's success. Each functional department typically conducts its own budgeting and planning processes separate from those of the larger organization.[35]

The functional structure works very well for small businesses as well as businesses with a limited number of products or services. This form tends to support an easy flow of communication in the firm, a straightforward approach to supervision, and a reduced level of redundancy. One of the most important benefits of the functional structure is the functional expertise and efficiency it creates. By grouping employees according to a functional group, many firms develop competencies and competitive advantages based on functional expertise. Sometimes, functional groups even develop their own unique culture and value system.

While the functional cohesion that ensues in this kind of structure can lead to the development of competencies, it can also create coordination problems in the firm if each of the functional groups becomes isolated from the others. For a firm to compete effectively, all of the functional groups must act in a coordinated fashion. For example, production and sales must communicate constantly so that the sales group can better understand the product and the production team can receive feedback based on sales' interactions with customers. The general manager, within a functional organizational form, helps to support this communication and coordination through numerous formal mechanisms, such as planning and budgeting

Functional structure
A structure that organizes a firm in terms of the main activities that need to be performed, such as production, marketing, sales, and accounting.

Divisional structure
A structure that groups diverse functions into separate divisions.

Matrix structure
A structure where both divisional and functional managers have equal authority in the organization.

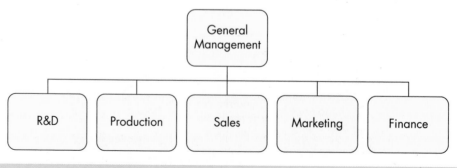

Figure 7.3 Functional Organizational Structure

systems, which we will discuss in greater detail in Chapter 10. Such formal systems are, in turn, supported by the informal connections between the individuals working across different functions as well.

Functional organizational structures are best suited for competitive situations where the most important aspect of competition is efficiency of production or functional expertise. In these situations, the development of economies of scale in production is a key aspect in the creation of competitive advantage. The functional structure is optimal for creating economies of scale. At the same time, such organizations are also suited for more stable and less complex environments.

An important weakness typical of organizations with a functional form is their inability to deal with changes in the business environment.[36] When a firm's business environment undergoes rapid change, those organized by function find it difficult to coordinate the various functions to create a rapid response to the change. Many functional groups in such organizations find it difficult to collaborate with other functional groups, which, in turn, makes it hard for the organization to adapt quickly to changes around it. Another weakness of the functional structure is that many employees have a narrow view of the firm's overall goals as they focus solely on their function; they may be unable to take a step back and see the bigger picture. This focus on the function as opposed to the overall organization can sometimes lead to suboptimal business decisions. It also makes it hard to hold functions accountable for their overall contribution to the business as it is hard to measure their contributions. The only measure for each function is what it costs the firm, and it can be difficult to connect each function (except the sales function) to the sales of the business.

Divisional Form

In contrast to a functional structure, a divisional structure groups diverse functions into separate divisions (see Figure 7.4). In this structure, firms can be organized around products, geographies, or even clients with each division run as a

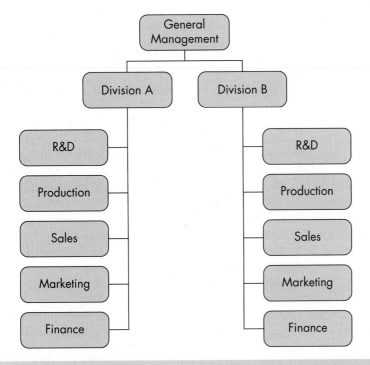

Figure 7.4 Divisional Organizational Structure

self-contained business with its own profit and loss measurements that are monitored by the headquarters. In this structure, each division gets credit for its own sales and monitors its own costs. In a product-divisional organization, each unit is focused on developing and selling specific products. In a geographic-divisional organization, each unit is focused on a specific geography. In a client-based divisional organization, each unit focuses only on selected clients to which they are assigned. Each division has its own resident functional capabilities, such as human resources, sales and marketing, and finance. In a sense, the divisional form is organized around the outputs the firm produces (products or services) or the way it goes to market instead of the functions that are needed to produce those goods (e.g., sales and production).

The divisional form is different from the functional form in many important ways. First, each division is like a self-contained unit and as a result, employees tend to feel more loyal toward their division than their function. Second, the divisional form allows for greater accountability. In many ways, the division is a business within a business. It has its own revenues and its own costs, allowing leaders to clearly assess the contributions of each business unit to the organization. As such, employees in the divisional form often see the larger outcomes of their actions for their specific business and have a better sense of the opportunities and threats that are facing the firm as a whole. Third, promotion in a divisional form is not only based on functional expertise but also can be based on management capabilities that cut across divisions. This allows for the development of talent that includes both functional specialists and also unit generalists. Finally, coordination among functions in the divisional structure is more fluid and easier to manage because the different functions are all represented within the division. Their loyalty and focus is first and foremost to their division, enabling greater teamwork and focus on the objectives of the division.

The divisional structure relies on senior leaders to coordinate actions among the various divisions should there be a need to do so. The general managers of a divisional form have different tasks than the general managers in the functional form. General managers who lead each division must coordinate action and communication among various functions within their division and ensure that the division achieves its targets. Above them are likely to be senior leaders whose job is to develop and guide strategy for the overall firm while also facilitating coordination among the divisions. These individuals are often considered to be the corporate headquarters staff.

The divisional structure is best suited to business environments marked by high degrees of uncertainty, requiring a quick response to market shifts. The divisional structure is also suited for competitive situations where coordinated action is needed for innovation or customer requirements.[37] Divisional structures tend to work in these types of environments because each division has its own slate of functional capabilities and a management team with clear deliverables and focus on a specific market. In this way, the company can quickly adjust to customer demands or a changing business environment.[38]

Divisional structures also have several weaknesses relative to the functional form. First, in divisional structures, several core functions are duplicated in each division, preventing the development of economies of scale for those functions. For example, a firm with high R&D needs may lose the capability to develop economies of scale if each division has its own R&D units. This may, of course, be necessary if each divisions' needs are drastically different.

Another common problem in the divisional structure is the potential for competitive behavior between divisions. It is not uncommon for two divisions of a company to share certain customers. In these cases, divisions may act in their own self-interest as opposed to the firm's overall best interests. In certain cases, one division may even refuse to share information about a particular customer with another division who also services that same customer. They may believe that by doing so they would jeopardize their own relationship with the customer.

Finally, divisional structures often do not develop the same level of functional expertise that a pure functional structure can. In general, divisional structures are best suited for firms that operate in a diverse business environment and produce multiple lines of products, serving different geographical regions, or serving a diverse set of customers.[39]

Matrix Form

Organizations that face multiple pressures can lead them to organize themselves as a matrix structure. Instead of the organization being simply organized by function or division, management elects to simultaneously have multiple overlapping units. As a result, most employees work for two or more units at once. The units themselves each have their own leadership with objectives that can sometimes be in conflict with each other. The units themselves can be one or more of the divisional types we discussed above (product, geography, or client) and/or may also include functional units as well.

Through the matrix structure, an effort is made to create an organization that simultaneously focuses on multiple dimensions. For instance, many global companies have regional units so that local management can focus on tailoring their products to each local market. At the same time, they may have global products units to allow them to have a globally coherent approach to bringing those products to market. They may also have global functions like human resources to reap the benefits of efficiency and standardization. The goal of matrix structures is to combine the positive elements of different organizational configurations at the same time.

The organizational structure in Figure 7.5 illustrates one common format of the matrix structure whereby functional teams (R&D, manufacturing, and sales) provide services for multiple product groups. In this type of organization, many employees have two bosses who have equal authority; they work for a product or division boss and also a functional boss. The product boss is focused on the success of the products while the functional boss is focused on the efficiency of the function (for example, marketing, accounting, or manufacturing). This is an instance of what is called a two-dimensional matrix. Some organizations may add another dimension like geography to allow them to have distinct geographical units to serve each geography.

This matrix reporting structure is appropriate under certain conditions. First, when environmental pressures derive from multiple sources, an organization should adopt a matrix structure to have distinct units that are focused on addressing each of those pressures in a dedicated manner. Second, an organization should consider a matrix structure when there is a high degree of interdependence between distinct units.[40] Overlaying a matrix forces interaction across the units by virtue of individuals working for multiple units. The FBI is an example we discussed earlier that essentially transitioned from a divisional structure to a matrix structure as they sought to better coordinate activities between the criminal investigation and intelligence divisions.

The main weakness of the matrix structure is its complexity. It often creates confusion for its managers who are simultaneously accountable to distinct units that don't always share the same objectives.[41] In many situations, a manager will have competing pressures from each of their multiple bosses. Because the manager has more than one reporting relationship, it is difficult to reconcile which group has priority or how the manager should allocate his or her time among the groups. For this reason, matrix structures require tremendous amounts of coordination among the different units so that resources are allocated appropriately and conflicts are resolved. To achieve this level of coordination, the matrix structure requires leaders

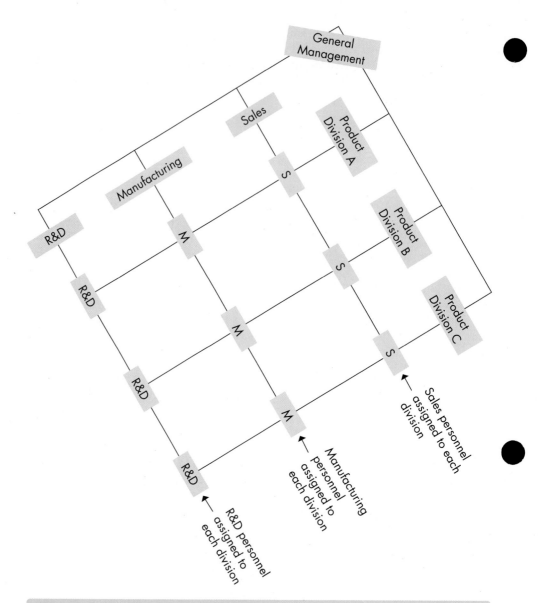

Figure 7.5 ⟩ Matrix Organizational Structure

of the different units to align their goals and objectives as best as they can.[42] Some amount of stress in the system is inevitable and some argue that this may be a good thing. It forces the members of the organization to come up with creative solutions that allow it to simultaneously tackle different constraints. This can, however, be time-consuming and can create inefficiency in the organization. Such organizations have to be attentive to the types of leaders they recruit and promote in the organization. In a matrix structure, managers can no longer rely on vertical authority. Instead, they must be good at influencing others in different parts of their organization. They must also be good at resolving conflicts and tackling ambiguity in their jobs and career paths.

Network Form

The pace of change and complexity in today's business environment forces many organizations to look for alternative ways to organize in order to meet the demands of innovation in a particular industry.[43] In many sectors where the main

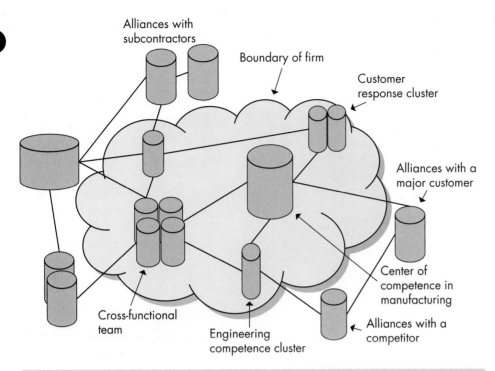

Figure 7.6 ⟩ Network Organizational Structure

organizational asset is people and the output differs dramatically from one client to the next, the organization may choose a more flexible modular structure than any we have discussed before. One approach has been to use a **network structure** as an organizing framework. The network structure is marked by a very different division of labor. In the network structure, "knowledge workers" are organized to work as individual contributors or to be a part of a work cluster that provides a certain expertise for the organization.[44] The various clusters of the organization form the building blocks of the network organization (see Figure 7.6). For each new project, the organization assembles a new unit that includes different clusters based on the requisite knowledge required for that project. And once the project is completed, each cluster is then redeployed to another project.

A typical example of a network structure is a professional service organization such as a consulting firm or an advertising agency. For each client engagement they may assemble a team of disparate groups of individuals who work closely for the duration of the engagement. Once completed, they will be reassigned to another client engagement. In some instances where they have long-term engagements, those groups may become a division of sorts. Many of these types of organizations also create functional groups (e.g., human resources, technology, and so on) to support the network structure.

In some instances, a network structure may span across individual organizations and encompass an entire industry in what some researchers refer to as an "ecosystem." The organizational system in Hollywood to produce movies is an example of such an ecosystem where the network structure spans across multiple individuals and organizations. Once the plan for a movie is hatched, a team, including producers, directors, actors, and so forth are quickly assembled for the task at hand. Once the task is completed, they disburse and reassemble in different teams again for another movie.

Network structures can also emerge in more traditional organizations in the form of project teams. The goal of project teams is to bring together different combinations of workers and help coordinate their actions. For example, a cross-functional team might be established to help develop a new product. The team

Network structure
A structure where "knowledge workers" are organized to work as individual contributors or to be a part of a work cluster that provides a certain expertise for the organization.

2003 David McIntyre/Black Star/Newscom

would be composed of workers from engineering, sales, marketing, and production. It is not uncommon for networked teams to be disbursed among many different locations, creating a virtual team. Flextronics, a contract manufacturing firm, deployed a virtual team to oversee the assembly and delivery of Microsoft's Xbox for the 2001 holiday season. Microsoft contracted with California-based Flextronics to simultaneously launch the Xbox in North America and Europe. To complete the simultaneous launch, Flextronics created a virtual team with members from its corporate offices in San Jose, California, and its manufacturing operations in Mexico and Hungary. The virtual team met on a regular basis to share best practices that would facilitate the simultaneous delivery of Xbox across two continents. Flextronics also included Microsoft in many of these meetings in an effort to ensure transparency about the delivery process.[45]

In the network structure, cross-unit teams can be both permanent and temporary.[46] While management provides broad oversight to these cross-unit teams, the decision rights in a network organization tend to reside at the lower levels. Network organizations tend to be flat, with few or no middle managers to coordinate communication and resources between upper and lower management. To support this flat organizational structure, information and communication technology are important means to ensure that resources and information can be shifted quickly between clusters.

A unique feature of a network organization is the emphasis on the informal structure of the firm. While most organizational structures place more emphasis on formal structure, network organizations are designed so that informal relationships between clusters of workers and cross-functional teams dominate the operation of the firm. In addition, because of the informal nature of network organizations, a person's formal position is not as important as it is in traditional organizational structures.[47]

With a network structure, a firm can move quickly to adapt to a change in the marketplace or respond to a competitor's action.[48] This capability can be a source of competitive advantage in industries that are marked by high degrees of change or innovation.[49] This level of adaptability, however, often results in the duplication of resources and low levels of accountability in an organization. For example, a cross-functional team in a network structure can be unwieldy, making it difficult to hold

The Leadership Development Journey

Leaders wear many hats to produce results for their organizations. Mastering the different roles of leadership requires organizational decisions that enable stability, efficiency, and control, while simultaneously encouraging collective action, adaptation, and innovation. Think about an organization that you are affiliated with through work, membership, or volunteer activities. Respond to the following questions as you reflect upon your observations.

1. Was the organizational structure aligned with leadership goals?
2. Did the leader ever change the organizational structure in response to external pressures?
3. Did the leader design the organization to encourage collective actions and shared responsibilities?
4. How did the leader use the organizational structure as a control system?
5. Was there a clear link between the organizational structure and performance metrics?
6. Based on your observations of that organization, what did you learn about the synergies between leadership and organizational structure? How can you apply these lessons to your leadership practices?

people accountable for discrete tasks and goals. In addition, virtual teams often require a considerable amount of coordination and communication to ensure that all team members are aligned. Technology can play an important role in facilitating such coordination and communication activities, but the investment in these tools can be costly.

Each of the organizational structures discussed thus far has certain advantages and disadvantages (see Table 7.1). A manager must weigh the benefits with the downsides of any organizational structure decision. When designing the organizational structure, a manager should consider a number of dimensions including efficiency, responsiveness, adaptability, and accountability. Firms that are focused on operational efficiency and are located in stable industries are best served by the functional form. On the other hand, organizations that emphasize managerial accountability and adaptability are better served by the divisional structure. When facing multiple strategic pressures, a matrix structure may be most appropriate. It is important that the appropriate design should be aligned with the firm's strategy and

	Functional	Divisional	Matrix	Network
Resource Efficiency	Excellent	Poor	Moderate	Good
Responsiveness	Poor	Moderate	Good	Excellent
Adaptability	Poor	Good	Moderate	Excellent
Accountability	Good	Excellent	Poor	Moderate
Best in Which Environment	Stable	Heterogeneous	Complex	Volatile

Table 7.1 Advantages and Disadvantages of Different Organizational Structures

Source: Adapted from Exhibit 7 in Nitin Nohria, "Note on Organization Structure," Harvard Business School Note No. 9-491-083, rev. June 30, 1995 (Boston, MA: HBS Publishing, 1991), p. 19.

objectives. Regardless of which approach is used, an organization needs to be able to adapt to changes in the competitive environment.

Informal Structure

Our discussion thus far has been about the formal structure of the organization. This refers to the formal architecture that an organization has in place within which individuals' roles and job descriptions are provided. While a lot of interaction happens within the formal structure of the organization, some would argue that the majority of interactions among individuals are shaped by the informal structures.[50] This refers to the relationships that individuals form with each other as a result of their prior interactions. Such interactions can come from prior work together or through social interaction at work or outside of work. Most employees build social relationships at work and those, in turn, can be important in shaping who they interact with afterward.

DECISION RIGHTS

When the leaders choose a formal structure for their organization, it has profound implications for the flow of information through the organization since the unit structure shapes the conduits through which communications are likely to flow.[51] Along with the flow of information, another key aspect of organizing is the specification of decision rights within the organization. This means, who makes which decisions in the organization. Each type of formal organization discussed may have a different way of going about this. **Decision rights** include the right to initiate, approve, implement, and control various types of strategic or tactical decisions.

In general, decision rights for specific decisions should be given to individuals at a firm who have the best information with regard to making those decisions. In instances where the best information resides lower in the organization, it would be optimal to push the decision rights down lower in the organization. The process by which managers transfer decision rights to individual employees is called **delegation**. In many manufacturing businesses, workers on the factory line know a great deal more about the firm's production capacity and how the operation works; as such, they are in the best position to make production-level decisions.

Despite the advantages of delegation, many managers are often reluctant to "let go" of decisions. This apprehension can be driven by a number of factors including a lack of confidence in the subordinate to make the right decisions or an intense need to personally control every decision. A manager may also be concerned that he or she would ultimately be blamed for the actions of subordinates. Though the drawbacks of delegation are clear, so too are the potential benefits. Delegation enables managers to better leverage their time and has the potential to increase employee motivation and satisfaction (see Figure 7.7).[52] If delegation is not feasible, and senior leaders prefer to make certain decisions themselves, then it becomes important for them to look for ways to move all the relevant information up the organization to their level so they can make a more informed decision.

While centralized hierarchical organizations remain common because of their efficient decision making, decentralized companies are becoming more popular as they offer a better environment for delegation and participation. As we will see in Chapter 10, decisions regarding centralization and decentralization are important because they have implications on the monitoring systems and measurement methods that are most effective.

Decision rights
Rights that include initiating, approving, implementing, and controlling various types of strategic or tactical decisions.

Delegation
The process by which managers transfer decision rights to individual employees.

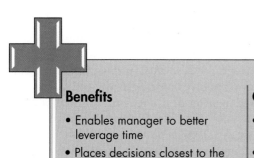

Benefits	Concerns
• Enables manager to better leverage time	• Lack of confidence in subordinates' abilities
• Places decisions closest to the actual action	• Fear of blame for subordinates' actions
• Drives quicker responses	• Personal desire to maintain absolute control over decisions
• Creates opportunity for employee development	• Potential problems with coordination and standardization of activities
• Increases employee engagement and motivation	

Figure 7.7 Benefits and Concerns about Delegation

Source: Adapted from Gary A. Yukl, *Leadership in Organizations* (Englewood Cliffs, NJ: Prentice-Hall, 1981).

A **centralized organization** is characterized by formal structures that control employee behavior by concentrating decisions in a top-down, hierarchical fashion. This is often seen in a functional organizational structure. Centralized organizations tend to be larger and older, and they exist in more mature industries.[53] Concentration of authority shortens the time it takes to make strategic changes and facilitates tight coordination of activities between divisions.[54] At the same time, the burden remains on senior leadership to collate all the information they need in order to make the right decisions in a timely manner. Otherwise, they run the risk of either making costly mistakes or becoming a decision-making bottleneck as they painstakingly collect all the information they need to make each decision in the best possible way.

In a **decentralized organization**, key decisions are made at all levels of the firm, not only at the top. Many network organizations as well as divisional organizations have elements of such decentralization. As uncertainty increases, companies must be more agile, and it becomes more efficient to delegate responsibility and decision-making to local units.[55] In general, decentralized companies provide more flexibility to react to environmental threats and opportunities because they attract highly skilled employees, coordinate efforts through standardization, and allow more individual-level decision-making.[56]

Well-defined roles and responsibilities tend to lessen the need for close supervision, which enhances an organization's ability to adjust to environmental changes and uncertainty.[57] In allocating decision rights, it is tempting to delegate and move decisions lower down in the organization. However, managers also need to be aware of potential conflicts of interest.[58] For example, in some organizations, manufacturing employees may be compensated based on how much they produce. If a manufacturing worker has the decision right to change the speed of the line, that worker may increase the speed of operations to an unsafe level to increase his or her total compensation. In addition, decision rights may also need to be balanced between lower and upper levels because many lower-level workers do not have access to the breadth of information that senior leaders do. For example, a salesperson may want to change pricing to close a sale. However, this salesperson may not have complete information with regard to the product's cost or the margin needed for the firm to

Centralized organization
An organizational structure characterized by formal structures that control employee behavior by concentrating decisions in a top-down, hierarchical fashion.

Decentralized organization
An organizational structure where key decisions are made at all levels of the firm, not mandated from the top.

be profitable. They may not realize the cascading implications of discounting a sale for one customer when other customers may want similar discounts once they hear about it.

Despite the distinct organizational structures described in this chapter, in reality, most organizations are rarely pure forms of any one model. We seldom observe a highly centralized or decentralized organization or a pure bureaucracy or clan. Instead we see hybrids that blend elements of these ideal forms. An organization may have a divisional structure but within each division they may have a matrix structure or a network structure. Or, you may see a functional organization that sits alongside a divisional structure.

ORGANIZATIONAL DESIGN AND THE LIFE CYCLE OF A FIRM

Mutual adaptation
The process by which firms impact the nature of their overarching industrial environment and adapt their organization in response to evolving contextual factors.

Silos
A functional or divisional unit that operates by its own rules and guidelines and does not openly share information with other units.

The choices that managers make regarding organizational design options should be aligned with the life cycle stage of the firm—start-up, growth, maturity, and decline. For instance, start-up firms are generally characterized by less job specialization, heightened coordination, broad decision rights, and open boundaries. When such firms evolve from an informally run organization to greater formalization, they typically embrace a functional structure. As a firm matures and grows in size, it tends to emphasize division of labor and specify distinct coordinating mechanisms to ensure greater efficiency and control, leading to a divisional structure.[59] Once a firm reaches maturity, it may face more complex markets necessitating it to operate an organization that simultaneously tackles multiple constraints, leading it to embrace a matrix structure.[60]

When a firm evolves, the nature of leadership should also fit its life cycle stage (see Figure 7.8). The leadership activities and priorities that are important in the early stage of a business often need to change in the growth or maturity phase. Managers, for their part, have to learn to change their styles and priorities to meet

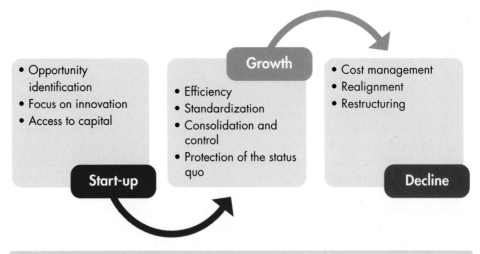

Figure 7.8 ⟩ Role of Leadership across Life Cycle Stages

Source: Adapted from Anthony J. Mayo, Nitin Nohria, and Mark Rennella, *Entrepreneurs, Managers, and Leaders: What the Airline Industry Can Teach Us About Leadership* (New York: Palgrave MacMillan, 2009), pp. 1–20.

the changing demands of the business as well as the fundamental changes in the contextual environment.[61]

Organizational Flexibility

To sustain long-term competitiveness, firms need to implement organizational design decisions that support current strategic imperatives yet are flexible enough to adapt to changing market conditions.[62] Firms need to evolve and change to respond to shifts in external forces (context shifts in regulation) but may also have to change in response to internal forces (loss or addition of key resources or capabilities). In addition, firms do not just respond to environmental conditions; firms can impact those conditions as well. The process by which firms impact the nature of their overarching environment and adapt their organization in response to evolving contextual factors is called **mutual adaptation**.[63] The process of mutual adaption is critically important in industries where change is a constant, such as technology and fashion.

As we will discuss in Chapter 11, firms that make an effort to be efficient in running their current strategic operations while, at the same time, embarking on ambitious exploration into future opportunities are often referred to as ambidextrous.[64] The most common approach to becoming ambidextrous is creating a separate organization or team to work on future opportunities, while the rest of the firm focuses on the primary business. Away from the structure and bureaucracy of the larger organization, these small units are allowed to pursue a more free-flowing development process and explore new opportunities.[65] While there are many advantages to this approach, especially in terms of creating a forum for innovation and creativity, managers need to make sure the separate team is not too isolated. If it is, managers will have more difficulty integrating the team's activities or recommendations with the mainstream business.[66]

More recently, firms have tried to build ambidexterity in individual job roles, not as part of a separate organization. In certain cases, employees are expected to spend a portion of their time on forward-looking activities and are encouraged to develop recommendations that will enable the organization to adapt to new contextual realities.[67] These organizations support employee initiative and innovation.

RECENT TRENDS IN ORGANIZATIONAL DESIGN

In the past, many firms had come to view their customers' wants and needs through their existing products rather than seeing them from the customer's perspective. Their organization was designed to optimize how they produced and distributed their products instead of starting with a focus on what their customers may want. This model worked in contexts where customer preferences were stable and there was limited competition. Such business environments are increasingly rare. Most businesses today have to confront a more transparent marketplace where customers have more choices and more information to make those choices. With greater competition in many markets, firms are being forced to adopt what has been described as a more customer-centric or outside-in model of organizing themselves.

Adapting the firm's perspective to start with the customer and not with themselves is harder than it sounds. The biggest impediments to making such a fundamental shift emanate from the way those firms are organized. In particular, most organizations whether functional, divisional or matrixed, have units that become

A DIFFERENT View

A Democratic Workplace

Are employees at a democratic workplace happier and healthier? Yes, says World-Blu, a nonprofit organization championing transparency, accountability, and decentralization at organizations worldwide. Democratic companies boast lower turnover and absenteeism, more top talent, higher levels of productivity and efficiency, and more innovation. Generation X and Y, the current economic crisis, savvy customers, and advanced technology are all factors influencing the democratic workplace trend. Brainpark, a small democratic company based in San Francisco, California, allows their employees to regularly review senior management, including the option to vote out an inadequate CEO. Zappos.com is an example of a large organization that believes that happy employees and happy customers are good for business.

1. How does Zappos.com treat their employees? How do they treat their customers? What other aspects of their business make it a democratic workplace?
2. What is another example of an organization with a democratic workplace? Why?
3. What is an example of an organization that could increase their revenue by implementing a democratic workplace? Why?

"**siloed**," meaning their focus remains on themselves and less on the organization or the customers they may serve. Not only are such silos not always collaborative with other silos in the organization, but they also develop an inward focus that detaches them from their customers and the marketplace. At the same time, silos that are closest to the customers may not always have the ability to shape key strategic decisions like product design. Shifting such organizations toward greater customer-centricity may thus entail fundamental changes in the organization that transcend simple structural adjustments.

In recent years, many leading companies have successfully shifted their focus to a more customer-centric organizational design by incorporating five specific activities: coordination, cooperation, capability development, clout, and connection.[68] Coordination involves creating structural mechanisms and processes at a firm that allow employees across silos to coordinate their activities to focus on creating value for the customer. Since organizational silos don't naturally coordinate very well, management is forced to identify those areas that need coordination and then put in place formal mechanisms to ensure greater coordination. This could be in the form of interim steps like setting up shared task forces, working groups, or, in the extreme, reshaping the silos and placing those tasks that need the greatest coordination within a single silo.

The journey of Cisco Systems and its reorganizations over the past 15 years is an example of an organization that has adjusted its organizational structure and processes to ensure coordination where it was necessary while, at the same time, trying to take advantage of economies of scale wherever possible. The company reorganized its divisional structure from customer groups to technology groups after the "tech meltdown" in 2001. The move was initiated to deal with redundancies that had emerged at the firm. For example, different internal groups had developed nearly identical products for different customers, resulting in wasted resources. The reorganization centralized marketing and research and development. At first, many at the company were worried that the move would distance Cisco from its customers. To assuage these fears, management created various coordinating mechanisms at the firm to maintain customer-centricity. The centralized marketing group included a cross-functional engineering team that brought technologies together from different parts of the company. Ultimately, even this became too cumbersome and complex, and the firm then overhauled the organization again to remain agile and customer-centric.

While coordination involves aligning the actions of disparate silos through explicit direction, cooperation is more about aligning behavior. Here, the focus is

not only directing who should collaborate with whom, but, rather, developing a more collaborative mind-set across silos with a common goal of serving customers more effectively. Building greater cooperation involves shaping an organization's culture and aligning incentives to encourage employees across silos in the organization to come together in the spirit of serving customers.

Fostering such a cooperative environment can require both formal and informal elements. On the formal side, a firm adopts incentives and measurement systems that focus on customer-centric activities. On the informal side, managers work to create an environment and culture that puts the customer first. At Cisco, such a cooperative environment that focused on customers dated back to its founder's commitment to customers. While the company focuses on developing innovative technology, employees are taught that technology that doesn't fit a customer's needs is wasteful. It's been a long time since the days of its founders and the company is much larger than before, making it much harder for its leaders to continue to foster and maintain these founding principles. Cisco must reinforce this customer-centric culture through a host of formal and informal structures.

A third ingredient for firms seeking to become more customer-centric is capability development. When a firm creates coordinating mechanisms to transcend organizational silos, its employees need a new skillset to deal with the new activities required by the organization. In customer-centric organizations, employees must be able to work across multiple products and services while creating connections across the boundaries of the firm.[69] As companies increase customer-centricity, they must remember to help employees build these skills by rewarding this behavior and creating career paths that these new generalists can follow.

The fourth element of customer-centricity ties back to our earlier discussion about allocating decision rights. Most large organizations don't always allocate comprehensive decision rights to its customer-facing silos like sales and marketing. At the same time, the rich customer information that resides with them doesn't always trickle to the silos that have the decision rights to create, develop, manufacture, and distribute its products and services. The end result can be a disconnect between the location of information and the assigned decision rights, which can lead to suboptimal decisions. In this context, organizations can either relocate information to those who have the decision rights or choose to reallocate decision rights—what some have called "clout"—to those who have the requisite information. Clout encompasses providing greater power to customer-facing units in the organization such that they can influence decisions that directly impact customers.

The final ingredient for customer-centricity is developing a connection with external partners. Firms can fight the commoditization of their products and become more customer-centric by redefining the boundaries of their firm.[70] This redefinition can occur in many ways, including outsourcing noncore functions or aligning with another firm to offer a product or service that delivers greater value for the customer. For example, Starbucks has pursued customer-centricity by joining forces with other players to increase its breadth of offerings. The company realized that many of its customers wanted their products in times and places where Starbucks could not serve them. To address this need, Starbucks joined forces with Pepsi to distribute its cold Frappuccino product (because Pepsi had greater expertise in bottling and distributing beverages) to bring customers more value.

In short, many firms have maneuvered their organizational design to become more customer-centric. These moves were prompted by a changing business environment and increased competition from global markets. A key aspect of such organizational designs is their fluid nature. These adjustments are continuous and require diligent attention by a firm's leadership.

SUMMARY

LO1 A well-defined strategy is important, but, by itself, it is often meaningless. Execution is vital to fulfilling the goals and objectives of a firm's strategy, and one of the primary mechanisms by which these objectives are achieved is through the way those firms are organized. Organizational design includes decisions regarding organizational structure, culture, human resources, and performance criteria and measurement. All those elements come together in aiding an organization to implement a strategy.

LO2 Strategy and organizational design are co-evolutionary. One does not necessarily follow the other, but they must be aligned. Organizational design elements often require a manager to balance a series of tensions that will best position a firm to compete effectively as the business environment evolves. The resolution of these tensions involves decisions about how to divide labor, define roles and responsibilities, and coordinate activity. The culmination of these decisions results in the development of the roadmap for execution.

LO3 Depending on a firm's strategy, a functional, divisional, matrix, network, or other hybrid structure may be appropriate. Each structure has specific advantages and disadvantages. The functional structure supports efficiency and economies of scale. The divisional form is best suited to business environments with high levels of uncertainty. The matrix form combines elements of multiple divisions and functions and is a useful way of leveraging certain core capabilities across business units. Finally, the network structure is appropriate for leveraging diversity and creating a forum for innovation. No one structure is perfect and each comes with a set of trade-offs.

LO4 Following the selection of an organizational structure, a manager must design the subtler elements of a firm such as decision rights. While these decisions are vitally important, they must be evaluated and re-assessed in light of changes in the contextual environment and internal resources. Organizations that are successful over the long term are able to change and adapt to sustain their relevance. As such, leaders must adapt their approaches to fit the contextual realities of their firm and its life cycle stage.

LO5 In recent years, many firms have attempted to realign their organizations to either perform services more efficiently or to better service customers. A move toward customer-centricity has often required firms to break down organizational silos and reexamine their operational procedures. Managers must constantly monitor whether or not their organizational design decisions are providing the foundation to enable the firm to succeed.

KEY TERMS

Behaviorists
Bureaucratic approach
Centralized organization
Clan approach
Decentralized organization
Decision rights

Delegation
Division of labor
Divisional structure
Functional structure
Matrix structure
Mutual adaptation

Network structure
Organizational design
Organizational structure
Organizers
Silos

ASSIGNMENTS

Discussion Topics

1. In what ways are decisions about strategy and organizational design co-evolutionary? Under what situations should one precede the other?

2. What are the advantages and disadvantages of the functional, divisional, and matrix forms of organizational structure? Why do firms progress from the functional to the matrix structure as they grow?

3. What leadership challenges are important to consider when embarking on a network organizational structure? How can a manager mitigate some of the challenges in a network structure?

4. Which organizational structure is most conducive to unleashing creativity and innovation in employees?

5. In what type of organizational structure do you think you would thrive? Which organizational structure would be most difficult for you? Do you want to pursue a functional career path or a generalist career path?

6. Today, many organizations do not use formal organizational charts to outline their structure. Why would a firm not want to use formal organizational charts?

7. Make the case for why you support the view of organizers or behaviorists. Would you thrive in a bureaucratic organization or in a clan? Why?

8. Why do certain managers have trouble delegating responsibility within an organization?

9. What challenges must a leader confront in overseeing a decentralized organizational structure?

10. How do informal structures influence the design of an organization?

Management Research

1. Evaluate two companies in the same industry that seem to be pursuing a similar strategy. How has each firm decided to implement its strategy? What decisions did each firm make about organizational design?

2. Compare and contrast a start-up company with a mature company. How do their organizations differ? What is more important and less important at each life-cycle stage?

3. Create a fictional firm. This fictional firm should be basic (e.g., an airline that competes based on low price). Write a paragraph describing its strategy, and then design an organization to fit your fictional firm's strategy.

In the Field

1. Visit a local company that is customer-centric and sells a product or service. During your visit, spend time as an anthropologist observing its organizational practices. Take pictures of customer interactions and write down your observations to capture the organizational practices. Based on the pictures and your observations, write a brief article about the company's practices. Discuss how the processes are designed to cater to customers.

2. With a group of classmates, attend a performing arts event such as a music concert, a dance production, or a play. As you are watching the show, create a mental image of the organizational structure. Think about how the organizational structure enables the performers to do their job. Analyze if the organizational structure is designed for improvising or if it is static. Can a corporation learn from the structure of a performing arts organization?

ENDNOTES

[1] W. Richard Scott, *Organizations: Rational, Natural, and Open Systems*, 5th edition (Upper Saddle River, NJ: Prentice Hall, 2003), p. 11; and R. H. Coase, "The Nature of the Firm," *Economica*, Vol. 4, No. 16, 1937, pp. 386–405.

[2] Danny Miller and John O. Whitney, "Beyond Strategy: Configuration as a Pillar of Competitive Advantage," *Business Horizons*, May–June 1999, pp. 5–17.

[3] Edgar H. Schein, "Three Cultures of Management: The Key to Organizational Learning," *Sloan Management Review*, Fall 1996, p. 9.

[4] Jan W. Rivkin and Michael Roberto, "Federal Bureau of Investigation, 2001 (Abridged)," Harvard Business School Case No. 9-710-450, rev. May 24, 2010 (Boston, MA: HBS Publishing, 2010), pp. 1–2.

[5] Ibid., p. 4.

[6] Ibid., p. 6.

[7] Ibid., pp. 4–5.

[8] Ibid., p. 10.

[9] Jan W. Rivkin, Michael Roberto, and Ranjay Gulati, "Federal Bureau of Investigation, 2007," Harvard Business School Case No. 9-710-451 (Boston, MA: HBS Publishing, 2010), p. 2.

[10] Ibid., p. 5.

[11] Ibid.

[12] Jan W. Rivkin, Michael Roberto, and Ranjay Gulati, "Federal Bureau of Investigation, 2009," Harvard Business School Case No. 9-710-452, rev. May 18, 2010 (Boston, MA: HBS Publishing, 2010), p. 1.

[13] Ibid., pp. 1–2.

[14] Ibid., pp. 2–4.

[15] Ibid., pp. 4–5.

[16] Ibid., pp. 5–8.

[17] Alfred D. Chandler, Jr., *Strategy and Structure: Chapters in the History of American Industrial Enterprise* (Cambridge, MA: MIT Press, 1962).

[18] Robert Simons, *Levers of Organization Design: How Managers Use Accountability Systems for Greater Performance and Commitment* (Boston, MA: HBS Press, 2005), p. 17.

[19] Terry L. Amburgey and Tina Dacin, "As the Left Foot Follows the Right? The Dynamics of Strategic and Structural Change," *Academy of Management Journal*, Vol. 37, No. 6, 1994, pp. 1427–1452.

[20] This section on Organizational Design Decisions is extensively drawn from Nitin Nohria, "Note on Organization Structure," Harvard Business School Note No. 9-491-083, rev. June 30, 1995 (Boston, MA: HBS Publishing, 1991).

[21] Gregory A. Bigley and Karlene H. Roberts, "The Incident Command System: High-Reliability Organizing for Complex and Volatile Task Environments," *Academy of Management Journal*, Vol. 44, No. 6, 2001, pp. 1281–1299.

22 William G. Ouchi, "A Conceptual Framework for the Design of Organizational Control Mechanisms," *Management Science*, Vol. 25, No. 9, 1979, pp. 833–848.

23 Ibid.

24 Peter H. Grinyer and Masoud Yasai-Ardekani, "Dimensions of Organizational Structure: A Critical Replication," *Academy of Management Journal*, Vol. 23, No. 3, 1980, pp. 405–421.

25 William G. Ouchi, "Markets, Bureaucracies, and Clans," *Administrative Science Quarterly*, Vol. 25, 1980, pp. 129–141.

26 James R. Barker, "Tightening the Iron Cage: Concertive Control in Self-Managing Teams," *Administrative Science Quarterly*, Vol. 38, 1993, pp. 408–437.

27 *Organization Theory: Selected Readings*, 2nd edition, D. S. Pugh, ed. (Middlesex, England: Penguin, 1984), p. 10.

28 Linda A. Hill and Jennifer M. Suesse, "Sun Hydraulics: Leading in Tough Times (A), Abridged," Harvard Business School Case No. 9-403-139, rev. May 6, 2003, (Boston, MA: HBS Publishing, 2003).

29 Richard E. Walton, "From Control to Commitment in the Workplace," *Harvard Business Review*, March–April 1985, pp. 77–84.

30 James R. Barker, "Tightening the Iron Cage: Concertive Control in Self-Managing Teams," *Administrative Science Quarterly*, Vol. 38, 1993, pp. 408–437.

31 Richard L. Daft and Norman B. Macintosh, "The Nature and Use of Formal Control Systems for Management Control and Strategy Implementation," *Journal of Management*, Vol. 10, No. 1, 1984, pp. 43–66.

32 B. R. Baliga and Alfred M. Jaeger, "Multinational Corporations: Control Systems and Delegation Issues," *Journal of International Business Studies*, Vol. 15, Fall 1984, pp. 25–40.

33 Jan W. Rivkin and Nicolaj Siggelkow, "Balancing Search and Stability: Interdependencies among Elements of Organizational Design," *Management Science*, Vol. 49, No. 3, 2003, pp. 290–311.

34 Nitin Nohria, "Note on Organization Structure," Harvard Business School Note No. 9-491-083, rev. June 30, 1995 (Boston, MA: HBS Publishing, 1991), p. 4.

35 Ibid.

36 Ibid.

37 R. Duane Ireland and Justin W. Webb, "Strategic Entrepreneurship: Creating Competitive Advantage Through Streams of Innovation," *Business Horizons*, 2007, p. 55.

38 Nitin Nohria, "Note on Organization Structure," Harvard Business School Note No. 9-491-083, rev. June 30, 1995 (Boston, MA: HBS Publishing, 1991), p. 4.

39 David Collis, "Managing the Multibusiness Corporation," Harvard Business School Note No. 9-391-286, rev. April 24, 1997 (Boston, MA: HBS Publishing, 1991), p. 1.

40 Nitin Nohria, "Note on Organization Structure," Harvard Business School Note No. 9-491-083, rev. June 30, 1995 (Boston, MA: HBS Publishing, 1991), p. 6.

41 Michael Goold and Andrew Campbell, "Making Matrix Structures Work: Creating Clarity on Unit Roles and Responsibility," *European Management Journal*, Vol. 21, No. 3, 2003, pp. 361–363.

42 Ibid.

43 Alan Hurwitz, "Organizational Structures for the 'New World Order,'" *Business Horizons*, May–June 1996, pp. 5–14.

44 Nitin Nohria, "Note on Organization Structure," Harvard Business School Note No. 9-491-083, rev. June 30, 1995 (Boston, MA: HBS Publishing, 1991), p. 6.

45 Jeffrey T. Polzer and Alison Berkley Wagonfeld, "Flextronics: Deciding on a Shop-Floor System for Producing the Microsoft Xbox," Harvard Business School Case No. 9-403-090, rev. August 23, 2004 (Boston, MA: HBS Publishing, 2003).

46 Gregory G. Dees, Abdul M.A. Rasheed, Kevin J. McLaughlin, and Richard L. Priem, "The New Corporate Architecture," *Academy of Management Executive*, Vol. 9, No. 3, 1995, pp. 7–18.

47 Nitin Nohria, "Note on Organization Structure," Harvard Business School Note No. 9-491-083, rev. June 30, 1995 (Boston, MA: HBS Publishing, 1991), p. 8.

48 Melissa A. Schilling and H. Kevin Steensma, "The Use of Modular Organizational Forms: An Industry-Level Analysis," *Academy of Management Journal*, Vol. 44, No. 6, 2001, pp. 1149–1168.

49 Nitin Nohria, "Note on Organization Structure," Harvard Business School Note No. 9-491-083, rev. June 30, 1995 (Boston, MA: HBS Publishing, 1991), p. 8.

50 David Collis, "Managing the Multibusiness Corporation," Harvard Business School Note No. 9-391-286, rev. April 24, 1997 (Boston, MA: HBS Publishing, 1991), p. 2.

51 Herbert A. Simon, *Administrative Behavior: A Study of Decision-Making Processes in Administrative Organizations*, 3rd edition (New York: The Free Press, 1976).

52 Gary A. Yukl, *Leadership in Organizations* (Englewood Cliffs, NJ: Prentice-Hall, 1981), pp. 226–230.

53 Khandwalla (1977), Stinchcombe (1959), Kimberly (1976), Blau et al. (1976), Reimann (1973), and Pugh et al. (1968) quoted in B. R. Baliga and Alfred M. Jaeger, "Multinational Corporations: Control Systems and Delegation Issues," *Journal of International Business Studies*, Vol. 15, Fall 1984, pp. 25–40.

54 Jeffrey A. Alexander, "Adaptive Change in Corporate Control Processes," *Academy of Management Journal*, Vol. 34, No. 1, 1991, pp. 162–193.

55 Ibid.

56 Jeffrey A. Alexander, "Adaptive Change in Corporate Control Processes," *Academy of Management Journal*, Vol. 34, No. 1, 1991, pp. 162–193, and B. R. Baliga and Alfred M. Jaeger, "Multinational Corporations: Control Systems and Delegation Issues," *Journal of International Business Studies*, Vol. 15, Fall 1984, pp. 25–40.

57 D. S. Pugh, "The Measurement of Organization Structures: Does Context Determine Form?," *Organization Theory: Selected Readings*, 2nd edition, D. S. Pugh, ed. (Middlesex, England: Penguin, 1984), p. 75; and William G. Ouchi, "A Conceptual Framework for the Design of Organizational Control Mechanisms," *Management Science*, Vol. 25, No. 9, 1979, pp. 833–848.

58 David Collis, "Managing the Multibusiness Corporation," Harvard Business School Note No. 9-391-286, rev. April 24, 1997 (Boston, MA: HBS Publishing, 1991), p. 5.

59 Allen C. Bluedorn, "Pilgrim's Progress: Trends and Convergence in Research on Organizational Size and Environments," *Journal of Management*, Vol. 19, No. 2, 1993, pp. 163–191.

60 Ken G. Smith, Terrence R. Mitchell, and Charles E. Summer, "Top Level Management Priorities in Different Stages of the Organizational Life Cycle," *Academy of Management Journal*, Vol. 28, No. 4, 1985, pp. 815–816.

61 Ibid., pp. 817–818.

62 Jan W. Rivkin and Nicolaj Siggelkow, "Balancing Search and Stability: Interdependencies among Elements of

Organizational Design," *Management Science*, Vol. 49, No. 3, 2003, pp. 290–311.

[63] Paul R. Lawrence and Davis Dyer, *Renewing American Industry* (New York: The Free Press, 1983), p. 4.

[64] Charles A. O'Reilly III and Michael L. Tushman, "The Ambidextrous Organization," *Harvard Business Review*, April 2004.

[65] David Lei and John W. Slocum, Jr., "Organization Designs to Renew Competitive Advantage," *Organizational Dynamics*, Vol. 31, No. 1, 2002, pp. 1–18.

[66] Julian Birkinshaw and Cristina Gibson, "Building Ambidexterity Into an Organization," *Sloan Management Review*, Vol. 45, No. 4, Summer 2004, pp. 47–55.

[67] Ibid.

[68] Ranjay Gulati, "Silo Busting: How to Execute on the Promise of Customer Focus," *Harvard Business Review*, May 2007.

[69] Ibid.

[70] Ibid.

CHAPTER

8

Organizational Culture

Learning Objectives

After reading this chapter, you should be able to:

LO1 Explain the ways in which culture provides the framework and foundation for how work is accomplished and what activities and practices are valued in a firm.

LO2 Explain how a firm's culture can impact organizational performance.

LO3 Differentiate between the three levels of culture: (1) artifacts, (2) beliefs and values, and (3) assumptions.

LO4 Discuss the ways in which culture is developed, influenced, and socialized in a firm.

LO5 Explain the role that culture plays when a firm is acquired.

SELF-REFLECTION

Are You a Corporate-Culture Anthropologist?

Corporate-culture anthropologists are not digging in dirt to retrieve artifacts of ancient civilizations. Instead, they study organizational behavior by systematically observing how an organization's members collectively think, act, and feel as they work to accomplish goals. Consider yourself a corporate-culture anthropologist and respond True or False to the following statements.

1. I recognize that the shared assumptions of appropriate behavior guide the actions of an organization's members.

2. I understand how values and beliefs help organizational members make sense of their roles.

3. I understand how stories and myths convey an organization's values.

4. I realize that an organization has heroes and heroines who are iconic representatives of its culture.

5. I have observed how rituals reinforce an organization's culture.

6. I am familiar with how ceremonies help to socialize organizational members.

7. When analyzing an organization, I look for physical artifacts to understand its culture.

8. I understand how an organization's founder influences its culture.

9. I know that leaders are role models for exemplifying an organization's culture.

10. I can make a mental connection between an organization's culture and its performance.

If you answered True to the majority of these questions, you are well on your way to becoming a corporate-culture anthropologist.

INTRODUCTION

It is a place where everyone from the president to the janitors calls themselves "Ladies and Gentleman," where every employee says to a guest, "The answer is yes. Now, what is the question?"[1] It is a company whose reputation for excellence not only has lasted longer than many companies have been around, but also has continued to grow year after year. When other companies were eliminating many expenses related to customers and employees, this company invested in more training, raising the effectiveness of its people and processes while delivering services of even better quality. The company is Ritz-Carlton. How has Ritz-Carlton shown such growth and sustainable quality for so long? There is, of course, not just one answer to that question. But if there was a foundation to its success, a fountain from which all other reasons fortify its roots, it is the company's organizational culture. Within its culture, employees know what is expected of them. They embody a generous spirit of service and a dedication to high quality. Service and quality are the hallmarks of the Ritz-Carlton brand and the essence of the organization's culture. In fact, each employee is authorized to spend up to $2,000 to solve a customer issue—no questions asked.[2]

Jb Reed/Bloomberg/Getty Images

One such Ritz-Carlton employee even helped with a marriage proposal for one of the hotel's guests. The guest had asked a hotel employee to leave two chairs on the beach because he was planning to return later that evening to propose to his girlfriend. When the guest arrived, he found the chairs situated under a beautiful flower-filled canopy. The hotel employee, who had changed into a tuxedo, escorted him and his girlfriend. He brought them to the table, lit a candle, and later presented the newly engaged couple with a bottle of champagne—all without the consent or approval of hotel management.[3] This Ritz-Carlton employee did not just do what he was asked; he went above and beyond to create an unforgettable experience for the two hotel guests. Creating these experiences is a core part of Ritz-Carlton's culture, which, in turn, serves as a blueprint for all its employees. While formal rules and guidelines in an organization can be a powerful way to shape employee behavior, what seems to matter even more are the informal rules that are embodied in its culture.

Like Ritz-Carlton, most organizations want to reach new levels of growth and performance. They seek to implement cutting-edge technology, new strategies, and other change initiatives to increase profits, lower costs, improve productivity, and build value. Yet initiatives fail, mergers falter, and improved performance does not always last. Such failures often result from inadequately addressing organizational culture.

An organization's culture provides the foundation and framework for how work is accomplished and what activities and practices are valued by its employees. The previous chapter examined how organizations are designed to enable employees to pursue specific strategic objectives. By itself, however, organizational design cannot enable employees to achieve strategic objectives. It is the culture of the organization that shapes how employees actually behave and, by extension, drives performance. These are the unwritten rules that can be the central drivers of employee behavior and can even override any formal rules or even organizational units that may be pushing employees in a different direction.

Many companies offer lip service to culture while allowing daily demands to pull them away from allocating the correct or the necessary resources to shape the culture. Yet consistently, the highest performing organizations point to their culture as one of the key reasons for their success. Consider 3M. Famous for Post-it Notes, 3M has continually led its industry and has done so by shaping a culture that fosters creativity and innovation. At 3M, "employees believe in developing new and improved products and processes by working in teams, challenging ideas, and taking risks."[4]

At its core, an organization's culture represents the invisible rules that guide employees' behaviors and hence defines how people think, feel, and act and it functions at an almost subconscious level.[5] Building a culture doesn't happen overnight and can sometimes take years. At the same time, organizations that have strong cultures can find it hard to change when certain learned behaviors persist over long periods of time. As organizations evolve and the contextual landscape changes, they often need to adjust their cultures, which can involve reinforcing what works, eliminating what does not work, and shaping new rituals or activities.[6] In this sense, culture is dynamic.[7] Organizations that succeed over the long term have been successful in adapting their cultures.

In this chapter, we will explore the essence of culture—how it develops and how it can drive competitive advantage. In addition, we will examine the role that leaders play in shaping the culture of an organization. Finally, we will discuss specific situations in which understanding culture is particularly important, including when one organization merges with another and when there's a change in the external environment in which a firm competes. To investigate culture further, let's look at a case study of Ben & Jerry's Ice Cream.

Ben & Jerry's Ice Cream

Ben Cohen and Jerry Greenfield of Ben & Jerry's ice cream present anything but the picture of typical business executives. Both owners are chubby and sport scruffy beards and wild hair; both wear T-shirts and flannel rather than a shirt and tie. The two friends enrolled in a correspondence course in ice cream making. The result was an ice cream store and then a company that rapidly overtook the market share of the superpremium corner of the ice cream industry.

When their company was young, Ben and Jerry were successful at shaping their company's culture. Besides the company being characterized by its funkiness—a trait also seen in the crazy flavors and combinations of mix-ins the company produced—it was also considered family by its employees. The company was based in a small Vermont town to attract people who valued local color and close relationships. Initially, their production was a small operation. When big orders came in, employees pulled together to complete the job the way a close-knit family works together in a crisis. Employees did whatever they could to help out, whether it was in their job descriptions or not. When successes came, employees celebrated together. They also conferred together about key company decisions.

The two founders played a specific role in shaping other aspects of the company's culture. Neither of them began marketing ice cream to get rich; rather, the business was an adventure. In spite of the company's size, Jerry was determined to keep the same spirit of fun. He made himself a joy manager of sorts, evangelizing joy at company meetings. Ben, on the other hand, was concerned with the company's moral soul.

© Sami Serf/istockphoto.com

Under Ben's direction, the company's marketing—including product packaging—became a way to educate the public about social causes. As such, they partnered with ingredient vendors, with social activism in mind. For instance, they bought their brownies from a bakery run by homeless people. In 1985, Ben oversaw the creation of Ben & Jerry's Foundation, an organization that funds community-oriented projects. Later, the company organized 1% for Peace, a group designed to help redirect 1% of the national defense budget to peace-promoting endeavors. The firm championed many other causes—from the protection of family farms to global warming.

They also managed the company internally with an eye to social change. Among other things, Ben instituted the 5-to-1 compensation rule that mandated that top executives couldn't make more than five times what the company's lowest-earning employee made. As the company grew in revenues and numbers of people, it became more corporate and less familial. Not everyone was involved in every decision. Job descriptions held firm. A lot more planning took place.

To aid in the firm's development, Ben and Jerry brought on other senior-level executives who were skilled at growing companies. Their tutelage brought the company even more success. But these new employees valued economic gain, and their basic assumptions about the company often conflicted with the idea of corporate responsibility. A mission statement, drafted at this point in the company's development, clarified the values of the organization. This document described the company's focus as three interrelated parts: a product mission, a social mission, and an economic mission.[8] Ben had to concede to give equal weight to each of the three missions. It was also a concession for the new senior executives who believed profit and growth were the lifeblood of any company.

As the company expanded, the 5-to-1 policy came under fire. Initially, the owners and executives believed this policy helped them find professionals who were socially motivated. Because of this rule, many of the senior executives had taken an economic step down to work for the company. Most of them were willing to do it because they agreed with the company's culture. As time passed, however, senior executives believed the policy made it impossible to hire other qualified business executives.

Ultimately, Ben & Jerry's 5-to-1 policy was sacrificed. By 1990, the policy had been modified to 7-to-1. When Unilever acquired Ben & Jerry's in 2000, it discontinued the practice of reporting on the ratio altogether, a response to the increased complexities involved in compensation and salaries across the company. The death of the 5-to-1 policy didn't diminish the organization's social activist constituency, however. The company's social mission is alive and well. The company donates at least $1.1 million annually to worthy causes, and this corporate philanthropy is largely prompted by employees.

While the assumptions underlying the 5-to-1 policy proved dysfunctional, the assumptions underlying the larger social mission weren't. For one, the corporate responsibility bottom line really did affect the economic bottom line for the better. The social causes touted in the product packaging and in marketing pieces, on the website and in publicity events became a unique voice in the food industry. The company's social activism resonated enough with the larger world culture to give it a competitive edge. In fact, studies showed that ice cream consumers are willing to pay a little more for products that encourage social responsibility.[9] Although the company had to rethink how and where it acted on its social mission, it successfully maintained its two-part bottom line.

Ben & Jerry's is an example of a company that has had to modify certain aspects of its corporate culture to fit changes in the competitive marketplace. The key to success is to ensure that the aspects of culture that provide a competitive edge are reinforced while those that hamper an organization's adaptability are modified.

Case in Point

Ben & Jerry's Ice Cream

1. How did the founders of Ben & Jerry's influence its culture?
2. How would you describe the culture of Ben & Jerry's in the early years?
3. In what ways did the culture of Ben & Jerry's change after it was acquired by Unilever?

WHAT IS CULTURE?

Culture is often defined as "a pattern of shared basic assumptions that was learned by a group as it solved its problems … that has worked well enough to be considered valid, and, therefore, to be taught to new members as the correct way to perceive, think, and feel in relation to those problems."[10] In other words, **culture** provides employees with a road map and a set of rules for how work gets done and how people interact in a company.[11] Culture responds to humans' basic need for stability, consistency, and meaning. If you are trying to assess an organizations culture, several elements can be helpful in deciphering it:

Culture
Culture provides employees with a road map and a set of rules for how work gets done and how people interact in a company.

- *An appreciation for the company's values and philosophy or purpose.* Broad policies and ideological principles guide a group's actions toward stockholders, employees, customers, and other stakeholders. What are the articulated, publicly announced principles and values that the group claims to be trying to achieve? What is the purpose of the company? With Ritz-Carlton, the key value is customer service.

- *An understanding of the group's boundaries.* Understanding a group's rules for inclusion helps a new member determine what the group assumes to be valuable and what is expected of employees. This will help focus attention on the most important aspects of the company.
- *An understanding of the power structure in a company.* Identifying the rules for achieving, keeping, and losing power also helps lay bare the group's assumptions about what is and is not appropriate. It can also help to observe who has power in the organization and who doesn't. This observation can provide some insights into the sources from which people obtain power.
- *An understanding of the work rules and norms.* How do people in the organization interact? The implicit standards and values that evolve in working groups, such as the particular norm of "a fair day's work for a fair day's pay" that are transmitted from one generation of employees to another through stories and through sanctions for inappropriate behavior help decipher what is valued.[12] Strong norms clarify the priorities and expectations of the organization which, in turn, lead to a better understanding of performance and, ultimately, greater efficiency.[13]
- *An evaluation of the company's reward and punishment system.* This can be evaluated by looking at the ways in which a group celebrates key events that reflect important values or important "passages" by members, such as promotions, completion of important projects, and milestones.[14] Conversely, looking at behavior that is punished or ignored provides further clues about the culture of the organization.

Think about your college search process. A key piece of advice that you may have received was to find a college that "fits" who you are. Some counselors might have told you that when you step on the "right campus," you will know it. It will feel right, and you will be able to picture yourself there. In essence, the college search process is about finding a culture that fits your values, who you are, and who you want to become. The campus climate, its learning model and philosophy of education, its extracurricular activities, and its overall spirit are all elements of its culture. Some of these elements are readily apparent, such as the campus infrastructure, while others are more subtle and require you to obtain a deeper understanding of what you value and what is important to you. At the heart of the search process, you are trying to find a match between you and the culture of your intended college. The same lessons apply when looking for a job—finding a culture that fits who you are and what you value.

IMPACT OF CULTURE ON PERFORMANCE

Quality products and services (such as Ben & Jerry's ice cream), innovative strategy (like that employed by Google), and impeccable customer service (such as Ritz-Carlton's) are a few of the by-products of companies with strong cultures. So are the scandals, such as the cellphone hacking in Rupert Murdoch's News Corporation and huge trading losses incurred at JP Morgan Chase.

A strong positive culture can significantly contribute to the achievement of an organization's strategic goals and has been linked to better levels of performance, higher financial metrics, and, ultimately, distinctive competitive advantage.[15] In fact, in one survey of 1,200 global senior executives, 91% believed that culture was as important as strategy to a firm's success.[16] At some point, the size of the company will no longer allow a general manager to guide every decision to ensure they align with company objectives. In a strong culture, those goals are clear and serve as instinctive guidelines that allow an organization to scale up more easily and operate with fewer overt control systems to regulate employee behavior.[17] Strong cultures often have greater role clarity because they're explicit about what is expected in an organization.[18] This clarity of expectation, in turn, enables employees to operate more autonomously and with greater consistency.[19]

Several benefits ensue for organizations with a strong culture. If an organization has a strong culture, there is a greater chance that decisions made throughout the company will be in line with company goals and thus require less coordination and monitoring.[20] In essence, a strong culture allows a company to run more smoothly and quickly and in a cost-effective manner because the company's personnel doesn't have to debate every course of action.[21]

An organization's culture can also serve as a moral compass for the organization as it defines acceptable and unacceptable behavior. In fact, culture has been shown to be the most influential factor in defining the right types of behaviors in organizations, even more so than ethical compliance programs.[22] One study found that if employees "have a personal commitment to the organization and if they believe the rules are morally right, they are motivated to obey the rules even in the absence of monitoring." In essence, compliance becomes ingrained.

Employees in organizations with strong cultures tend to experience lower levels of turnover, especially because the culture plays a large role in identifying who is likely to "fit" and succeed in the organization.[23] In this manner, hiring practices are tightly intertwined with the culture of an organization.

While there are many benefits of a strong culture, there is also a potential dark side. Strong cultures are likely to discourage disagreement and can, in turn, result in a rush to decisions that are not properly vetted.[24] Organizations with strong cultures may also encourage unethical behavior by rewarding the wrong actions or emphasizing only one goal at the expense of others.[25] Strong culture organizations can also be difficult to change. In fact, one study shows that strong cultures lead to increased performance in stable environments, but decreased performance in more turbulent environments.[26] A strong culture can make adapting to change more difficult, especially if adaptability is not a core part of the company's culture.[27] Company leaders must pay close attention to the company's environment, goals, and actions to determine when to change a strong culture that has become dysfunctional.

In strong cultures, there are high levels of agreement among employees about what is valued and a correspondingly high level of intensity about these values (see Figure 8.1). When there is no agreement on what is valued in a firm, and little

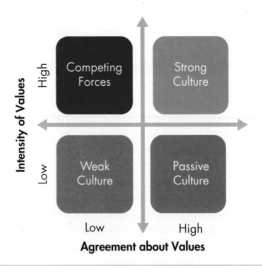

Figure 8.1 > The Impact of Values on Culture

Sources: Jennifer A. Chatman and Sandra Eunyoung Cha, "Leading by Leveraging Culture," *California Management Review*, Vol. 45, No. 4, Summer 2003, pp. 24–25; and Yoash Wiener, "Forms of Value Systems: A Focus on Organizational Effectiveness and Cultural Change and Maintenance," *Academy of Management Review*, Vol. 13, No. 4, 1988, pp. 534–545.

passion or intensity for these values, firms experience weak cultures. When there is high agreement about values, but little intensity or passion for these values, a firm's culture is considered passive. Employees recognize what is important but are not necessarily willing to make the appropriate effort. In the opposite situation, when there is a lot of intensity surrounding values but little agreement about which ones are important, firms are typically undermined by competing forces and rivalries. The number of values a firm holds is not as important as how strongly held they are and how much organizational buy-in they generate.[28]

In many cases, a company will develop **subcultures** that form around subunits within the organization, such as those that may occur around geography, product, or function. Groups often find their identity by comparing themselves to other groups—and this is true of groups within an organization. But while this identity formation can pull groups together and empower them to accomplish more than could be done on an individual level, their strong local culture can make those groups rigid and less open to different ideas. This can cause problems when members of different groups try to work together or communicate. Managers should recognize that conflict between divisions of a company is often due to differences in thinking, feeling, and acting that come from members of different groups operating within their own local cultures. If managers accurately identify these conflicts as cultural differences, they can point out the different assumptions and better confront the problems.

LEVELS OF ORGANIZATIONAL CULTURE

Culture can be inferred from a number of aspects about an organization—some are visible while others are hidden. To understand culture, you must comprehend the different levels of culture and its manifestations. When walking into a Nordstrom store, a customer will begin to get a feel for its culture. Nordstrom typically uses higher-quality lighting and floor materials than do most other department stores. The stores are clean and orderly. Beyond their impeccable appearance, you'll notice the friendliness and helpfulness of the sales staff. And if you shop at Nordstrom frequently enough, you will notice how far the salesclerks will go to serve you. As an example, a foreign national who bought a pair of pants halfway around the world brought them to a Nordstrom near his office in the United States and asked if they could be returned. To his disbelief, the young clerk (not a manager) asked him how much he had paid for them and then reached into the till and gave him that amount.[29]

How and why did this employee feel empowered to service the customer in this manner? The answer to this question lies in the culture that is embedded in Nordstrom. Much like Ritz-Carlton, Nordstrom has built a culture that allows employees to do whatever it takes to serve its customers. These employees do not need to be told what to do. They know what is expected within the culture of their organization.

An organization's culture can be understood on a number of levels, each of which provides a more nuanced understanding of it. At the most basic level, there are artifacts (day-to-day behaviors that can be observed), below which are beliefs and values (what is deemed important by members of an organization), and, finally, there are assumptions (the underlying essence of why members of an organization act as they do).[30] For managers to understand and assess the potential of an organization's culture, they must start with the visible artifacts and move backward through the process by which they were created. This means uncovering the assumptions behind the artifacts as well as identifying the problems and the setting that formed the assumptions.

Subcultures
Cultures that form around geographic or organizational units in a company.

AP Photo/Elaine Thompson

Artifacts

Artifacts are visible organizational structures, processes, and languages. The most visible level of culture is a company's artifacts which include "all the phenomena that one sees, hears, and feels when one encounters a new group with an unfamiliar culture. Artifacts include the visible products of the group … its language; its technology; its artistic creations; its style … its published lists of values; its observable rituals and ceremonies."[31] As in the above example, this visible level of an organization's culture is deceptively easy to identify. It is fairly simple to note what artifacts are present in a company and how they are put into practice. It is another thing altogether to understand the reasons why those artifacts exist. When you enter an organization's headquarters for example, you may notice the layout of the offices, how people are dressed, and other physical symbols like the logo or a poster outlining the company values. These are all visible artifacts that communicate some sense of an organization's culture.

Beliefs and Values

Beyond artifacts, culture is created in a group setting from the **beliefs and values** that members bring to the table or that a group learns together.[32] Generally, these beliefs and values are the meanings that members of an organization attach to artifacts. An organization's beliefs and values drive what is considered important in the organization. As we will see, organizational values sometimes originate from the founder and are passed along as others join the company. In some instances, they take the form of a formal statement and in other cases they are communicated formally or informally from one generation of employees to the next.

Assumptions

Artifacts
Visible organizational structures, processes, and languages.

Beliefs and values
The meanings that members of an organization attach to artifacts.

Assumption
A behavior that stemmed from a belief held by a group that is no longer visible, but has become deeply embedded in the organization.

Lurking beneath a company's articulated beliefs and values are a group's underlying assumptions. An **assumption** was once a behavior that stemmed from a belief held by a group. When that behavior successfully solved the problem it was addressing, it set a precedent for all future iterations of that problem.[33] Once a behavior has become an assumption, unlike beliefs or values, it is no longer visible. Rather, it is intrinsic, instinctive, and unconscious.[34] In essence, it becomes deeply embedded in the organization.

When joining a new company, the greatest temptation of managers and employees is to note the artifacts of a culture—the physical layout and quality of an office space, for instance—and jump immediately to evaluation: this is a good culture, or this is a bad culture. Artifacts are deceptive, however. They cannot be evaluated in isolation, but must be attached to their roots. You have to look behind the artifacts to really understand the culture. Otherwise, managers can wind up as misguided as Carly Fiorina, CEO of Hewlett-Packard (HP), who professed the "HP Way," but failed to really understand it.

The Leadership Development Journey

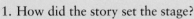

Leaders use storytelling as a tool to reinforce cultural assumptions. Storytelling can be an effective leadership practice when it paints a clear picture of the organization's values, and how these values enable members to achieve goals. Recall a time when you heard a leader tell a story to align values with goals.

1. How did the story set the stage?
2. Did the story have heroes or heroines?
3. What examples were used to communicate values?
4. Did the story call for certain types of actions?
5. What was the moral of the story?

Hewlett-Packard

Few organizations have had a more pronounced culture than HP. The company's founders focused their business model on profit and people and were famous for the culture that became known as the "HP Way." This company culture included "a focus on profits more than revenue growth, teamwork, open-door management, full employment, egalitarian pay practices, and flexible work hours."[35] By 2000, HP had grown to become one of the top technology companies in the world and the HP Way had led the company onto Fortune's list of "100 Best Companies to Work For."

In the mid-1990s, HP had become "a market leader in both printers and UNIX computers and a rising force in PCs."[36] Consistent growth brought new challenges for the company, and the retirement of both founders by 1993 placed a new leader, Lew Platt, in charge of the company. Platt was a firm believer in the HP Way, but some thought he lacked the tough business edge that both founders possessed. Platt recognized the need for change, and, with the strategic guidance of McKinsey & Company, HP spun off its instrument and related businesses to focus on printers and computers. The spin-off company became Agilent Technologies.

iStockphoto.com/GYI NSEA

Despite this change, the company continued to struggle in the late 1990s to meet its profit goals, and the board began to look for new leadership to help move the company forward. The board was looking for someone with "charisma, an ability to increase the company's profile, a marketing and sales background, and the strength to challenge the HP culture."[37] Carly Fiorina had earned a strong reputation at Lucent Technologies, and she was hired to take HP in a new direction. Fiorina quickly began changing the culture of HP and rewriting the HP Way. At a meeting one month after her arrival, she interrupted a division head discussing challenges by saying, "Let me make something very clear. You will make your numbers. There will be no excuses. And if you can't make your numbers, I will find someone who can."[38]

Fiorina also quickly brushed aside HP's egalitarian ideals by purchasing an executive jet. This was not unusual for many CEOs at the time, but it was in stark contrast to Lew Platt, who flew 200,000 miles annually in coach class on regular airlines.[39] Despite these changes, Fiorina continued to emphasize the importance of the HP Way and its continued influence on the company. Behind the scenes, however, Fiorina began to institute drastic strategic and organizational changes by focusing on selling solutions rather than products. Some employees and board members were resistant to these changes, but the most drastic change came with Fiorina's decision to acquire Compaq Computer Corporation.

HP had rarely used acquisitions as a business strategy, but Fiorina believed that combining forces with Compaq would give HP the ability to compete with rival IBM. The acquisition was met with great opposition by David Packard, son of the cofounder, who sat on the company's board of directors. After the merger, Packard filed a lawsuit against Fiorina for attempting to deceive shareholders, but the case was dismissed. The results of the acquisition were mixed. The new company was able to cut costs by $3.5 billion and head count by almost 20,000.[40] While HP retained its competitiveness in the printer area, it did not improve significantly in its sales of personal computers (PCs).

The area of greatest change after the acquisition was that of culture. The company that was once known for being employee-centric, even in the pursuit of profitability, had lost its way. More than half of HP's employees after 2003 had worked there fewer than 5 years, and when HP applied for Fortune's list of "100 Best Businesses to Work For" in 2003, it did not rank. In addition, an HP internal memo "indicated that employees gave low marks on management credibility, respect, and fairness."[41]

A DIFFERENT View

Culture in a Crisis

Extreme challenges and adversity can bring out the best in human beings. This is especially true of the 33 miners who fell victim to a mine collapse in Chile in 2010. They survived an astonishing 69 days underground before they were all safely rescued. As a means of survival, the 33 organized their own democracy. Leaders were assigned to manage the group, facilitate food rationing, lead prayer, monitor health, organize communication with rescuers, and facilitate contact with family and the outside world. All 33 miners had a vote in decisions that were made as they patiently waited to be rescued. Through these rules and guidelines emerged a group culture that, in turn, influenced their behavior, which was shaped by a set of beliefs and assumptions. Observers of this remarkable survival story suggest that their survival can be directly attributed to the organizational culture they created for themselves in a crisis.

1. What lessons can be learned in business from a crisis like the Chilean mine collapse?
2. Identify a company that has survived its own challenges. What similarities are there in organizational culture between that company and the miners?
3. Identify a company that has not survived challenging times. What could they have learned from the miners and their rescuers?

HOW DOES CULTURE DEVELOP?

Culture begins to develop quickly in any group of people as they spontaneously interact with each other and establish norms of behavior. In many organizations, the backbone of culture begins with its founder.[42] A founder usually comes to his or her organization with a strong set of assumptions, based on previous experiences, and infuses them into the group. Often it was these ideas that sparked the founder's desire to create something new.

For example, Home Depot's original founders built their organization on the idea of serving the customer above all else; this affected how they divvied out resources and structured their stores, but also how they interacted with customers. When Bob Nardelli took over as CEO of Home Depot, he tried to radically change the entrepreneurial, customer-facing culture with one focused on top-down driven operational performance. The result was a cultural disconnection, and Nardelli was soon replaced as CEO.[43]

Role of Founders

Founders have a variety of ways in which they embed a particular culture into their organization and exert their influence, including the following:

- *Their capacity to absorb the anxiety associated with risk.* Because they take the most risk, they also have the strongest belief in what the company is doing and, in times of stress, can ease the pressure employees may feel.
- *Their capacity to make assumptions stick.* They can insist on decisions that aren't in the company's financial interest but that uphold cultural values. In allowing values to trump economics, founders can have a strong influence on a company's culture and what is valued in the organization. In the early days of Apple Computer, Steve Jobs pursued many paths that were deemed financially imprudent in his search for a new path to personal computing.
- *Their encouragement of innovation.* A founder is the only person who can make risky decisions and who isn't accountable to anyone. Therefore, founders are uniquely situated to be innovative and to model innovation for their employees.[44]

Cisco's culture, for example, started with Sandy Lerner and Leonard Bosack's focus on the customer. From the beginning, they worked to infuse their own set of beliefs into their business. Based on their experiences, they believed that the customer was the key to success. The challenge, of course, is to keep the culture alive long after the founders are gone and this is something that subsequent leadership at Cisco has worked hard to do.

When he became CEO of Southwest Airlines, Herb Kelleher infused the company with a strong culture of humor and fun. While Southwest's strategy is built on the premise of providing low-cost point-to-point air travel, it does so in a culture characterized by a sense of humor and ongoing excitement. A fun culture does not mean that employees at Southwest do not work hard. On the contrary, they work harder than most other airline employees to help the firm provide the lowest-cost airfare. Employees are hired based on their ability to fit into this fun, service-oriented culture.[45]

Role of Organizational Leaders

By the nature of their role in the organization, leaders are held responsible for results. They also significantly influence the manner in which those results are achieved as well as the values that are upheld.[46] Employees at all levels look to leaders for guidance about what is important, what is measured, and what is rewarded in the organization. Given that employees look to leaders for clues about appropriate behavior, leaders at all levels in an organization must comprehend the implications of what they say and do.[47] In other words, as role models, leaders must be vigilant that their actions do not result in adverse consequences. The leaders of an organization often have the responsibility to ensure that the culture reinforces positive behavior.[48]

A leader can use culture to impact performance in a multiplicity of ways. For starters, they can hold employees in the organization to high standards and use public forums to reward exceptional behavior. In addition, leaders can play a key role in reinforcing a company's culture by ensuring that the firm's vision and direction are aligned with the changing contextual environment.[49] In a study of companies that have been successful over a long period of time, the following aspects of a leader's role in relation to culture were deemed critically important:[50]

- Inspire all managers and employees to do their best.
- Empower employees and managers to make independent decisions and to find ways to improve operations.
- Reward achievement with pay based on performance and continue raising the bar.
- Reward achievement with nonpay perks such as new assignments and employee recognition.
- Create a challenging work environment.
- Establish and abide by a clear set of values.

Role of Teams

As we have seen throughout this chapter, an organization's culture can be profoundly shaped by its founders and by its formative experiences. However, culture is rarely static and usually continuously changes. Some would say that an organization's culture is being reinvented and reshaped on an ongoing basis as its leaders and employees take actions and make decisions. In this way, culture can be an emergent phenomenon—one that bubbles up from the way individuals interact and operate with each other. These interactions eventually become part of the organization's shared beliefs and values.[51]

Teams directly impact culture by the manner in which they encounter big problems, solve them, and perceive the effects of their solutions. Early in its existence, every organization encounters some problem and has to come together, make decisions, and find a solution.[52] If the solution is unsuccessful, the company will likely find a different way to do things the next time a similar problem crops up. If the solution is successful, however, the company will probably choose to do things the same way the next time—and the next time and the next time. In doing so, they create "organizational routines" that are reapplied on an ongoing basis. At some point in the organization's history, however, people stop asking how they're going to solve a particular problem and apply that routine. The solution becomes unconscious and is, therefore, no longer debatable; neither is the process for making this decision nor the priorities that have developed as a result. This is the birth of a group or team-based culture. Even a course of action prescribed by a founder has to be tried and tested by employees before it becomes an integral part of an organization's culture.[53]

Cultural Socialization

So how are cultural elements embedded? How do new employees become assimilated in the culture of an organization? A company has many tools at its disposal for embedding culture. For instance, all Toyota team members attend culture training when hired. During their first year with United Parcel Service (UPS), new managers are required to work in various parts of the business, including sorting and delivering packages. This process of understanding how work gets done and how individuals

should interact is called **socialization**. The process of cultural socialization can take the following forms:

- *Formal statements of philosophy, creeds, and values.* Google, for example, has sketched out its culture in various documents, including a cover letter attached to the company's initial public offering prospectus and an operating philosophy called "Ten Things." "Google is not a conventional company," the cover letter reads. "We do not intend to become one."[54] The operating philosophy lists the company's values, including "You can be serious without a suit" and "You don't need to be at your desk to need an answer."[55]

- *Design of physical spaces.* The feeling that is conveyed in a group by the physical layout and the way in which members of the organization interact with each other, with customers, or with other outsiders can convey an important message about the culture. When Google's founders, Larry Page and Sergey Brin, moved their growing company into its new head-quarters in Mountain View, California, they called it the Googleplex. They also began establishing a set of values and characteristics they called being "googley." At the Googleplex, Google-ism first took the form of an informal atmosphere where pets were allowed and exercise balls doubled as office chairs. Video games and foosball tables lined hallways. The informal setting of the Googleplex was an important element in building Google's culture. Megan Smith, former Vice President of New Business Development, said "Google executives have put a great deal of thought into our physical campus. Areas are created for cross-pollination; we want people from different functions and groups to interact with each other."[56] In this way, the organization seeks to orchestrate serendipitous interactions among its employees that may, in turn, spawn new ideas and foster greater collaboration. Laszlo Bock, Senior Vice President of People Operations, says that Google pays careful attention to the all work spaces. For instance, the company "measures the length of cafeteria lines to make sure that people have to wait a while (optimally three to four minutes) and have time to talk. It makes people sit at long tables, where they're likelier to be next to or across from someone that don't know, and it puts those tables a little too close together so you might hit someone when you push your chair back—the Google bump, employees call it."[57] Google management's painstaking care of the company's physical atmosphere illustrates how seriously it takes its culture.

- *Role modeling, leader examples, teaching, and coaching.* Managers at Google want their employees to be innovative. They themselves have been innovative in the ways they encourage company values. One example of managerial innovation is the 80/20 policy, which the company endorsed from 2007 to 2013. Technical employees at Google could spend 20% of their time on projects of their own choosing. Employees reported on how they used this time and were judged by the results they achieved. Gmail, AdSense, and Google Maps all found their beginnings in this 20% arena.[58] While this program produced some impressive new products, the company sought to make the focus on innovation a core part of every employee's job. Today's leaders at Google want employees to be thinking about new ideas and innovation 100% of the time, not just 20%.[59] Role modeling was also an important driver for Jeff Charney when he joined Progressive Insurance as the Chief Marketing Officer. Charney "grabbed empty beer bottles with labels that read COMPLACENCY, GOSSIP, and ME, ME, ME and smashed them with a bat."[60] This dramatic act set a new tone for the marketing team—one that was focused on collaboration and teamwork, not infighting and turf protection.

Socialization
The process of understanding how work gets done and how individuals should interact in an organization.

- *Reward systems and norms.* Behaviors that are rewarded and recognized are key clues to what is deemed important in an organization. AdSense, a division of Google, hosts an idea contest every quarter. In addition, managers give out recognition awards for employees' ideas that speed up work processes, a tactic that also supports a company value: "Fast is better than slow."[61] By competing for these rewards, employees learn quickly what is valued: innovation and speed.

- *Stories, legends, myths, and parables.* Again, Google provides a prime example of the power of stories to influence culture. A story about one of the founders circulates throughout Google. "There's a story about how a senior executive made a big mistake that cost several million dollars, but [Google founder] Larry Page told her he was happy she made the mistake. Because if they're not making mistakes, they're not taking enough risks. They would 'rather she make a mistake in moving too fast than make no mistakes in moving too slow.'"[62] This story is told throughout the company to encourage the culture of risk-taking. The fact that it is passed around indicates its usefulness in teaching culture to team members.

- *What do leaders pay attention to, measure, and control?* Ben, of Ben & Jerry's cultivated a culture that employees often described as "caring capitalism."[63] These company values were brought home to employees in part through the things executives measured. For instance, the company's year-end reports tracked economic gain, but they also tracked how much the company had done for society that year. These policies have had the added benefit of attracting employees whose personal values are consistent with the company's values of corporate social responsibility.

- *Leader reactions to critical incidents and crises.* When a downturn in the market required major cutbacks and downsizing, Toyota cut everything but people. It refused to fire employees in spite of criticism and a general belief in the business world that it was making a poor economic decision. This response to crisis taught employees how much the company believed in its widely evangelized aphorism "people are the most significant corporate investment."[64] Other companies that profess that "people are their most valuable asset" often engage in layoffs when times are tough. Employees learn the real culture of an organization during difficult times.

- *Design of the organization.* Cisco's Customer Advocacy division is a good example of how the design of an organization influences culture. The customer being a professed value is built into the company's structure through the creation of a dedicated organizational unit with a mandate to be the advocate of the customer inside the organization.

- *Criteria for recruiting, selecting, promoting, and managing employees.* Special competences displayed by group members in accomplishing certain tasks are clues to what is valued in a particular culture. Google takes great care in who it hires. Laszlo Bock, Senior Vice President of People Operations, said, "There are many smart people that don't get hired because they don't fit culturally with the organization."[65] Google's hiring executives determine a person's cultural fit by assessing candidates for general cognitive ability who have "initiative, flexibility, collaborative spirit and evidence of being well-rounded."[66] With this kind of human resources, managers at Google believe their people "are well-intentioned, curious and aware, and most have the capacity to self-govern with the help of their peers."[67] In other words, they believe the people they hire, using the process they have in place, are more likely to fit with and contribute to the culture.

As you review the various ways in which individuals become socialized in an organization, it may become apparent that culture is determined by a few key factors, including the people who work at the company (skills and attitudes), the manner in which the company is structured (formal organization), the nature of the work that needs to be performed (task requirements), and the role of the leader. All of these elements operate in a particular context to set the stage for the development of culture (see Figure 8.2). Many of these factors are interrelated and influence one another.

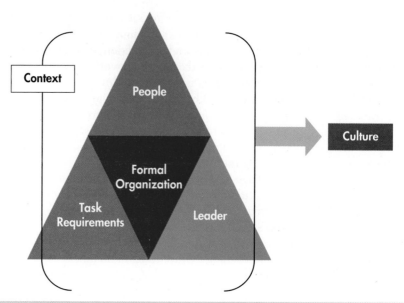

Figure 8.2 › Determinants of Culture

Source: Adapted from Michael B. McCaskey, "A Framework for Analyzing Work Groups," *Managing People and Organizations*, ed. John J. Gabarro (Boston, MA: HBS Press, 1992), pp. 241–262.

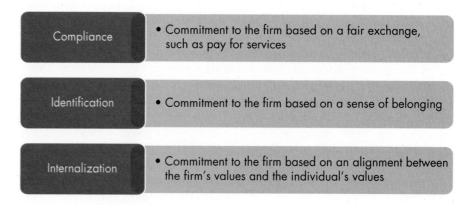

Figure 8.3 › Building Organizational Commitment

Source: "Building Organizational Commitment," in Charles O'Reilly, "Corporations, Culture and Commitment: Motivation and Social Control in Organizations, *California Management Review*, Vol. 31, No. 4, Summer 1989, pp.9–25. © 1989 by the Regents of the University of California. Reprinted by permission of the University of California Press.

Over time, the process of cultural socialization can lead to a stronger level of employee commitment. The process by which **organizational commitment** is achieved typically evolves over three stages—from compliance to identification to internalization (see Figure 8.3). Organizational commitment is the desired end result of socialization, whereby employees become committed to the organization and its goals. An internalized culture can lead to stronger overall performance as employees feel like owners of the firm. As such, they are willing to go above and beyond to ensure that the firm delivers on its commitments to customers as well as other employees.[68]

CULTURE AND CRUCIAL MOMENTS

While understanding an organization's culture is generally very important, there are a few times in an individual's career when it becomes even more critical, such as when someone joins a new organization or takes charge of a new team in

Organizational commitment
The desired end result of socialization whereby employees become committed to the organization and its goals.

an organization.[69] Culture is particularly important to understand in the merger and acquisition process. One study of mergers identified that 90% of them never live up to their expectations. The culprit: a clash of corporate cultures between the merging organizations.[70]

Evaluating Culture in Mergers and Acquisitions

When one company acquires another, the acquiring company obtains the other's "resources, its processes, and its business model, with the priorities embedded therein."[71] While the resources are easily observable, the company's processes and business model are largely embedded in the unwritten, unarticulated assumptions that make up the group's culture. Before an acquisition takes place, managers of acquiring companies must understand their own company's culture, including its strengths and weaknesses. They must also understand the culture of the company that is to be acquired. Where are the similarities and differences? What needs to change? How do we ensure that we maximize the value of both cultures? Which elements of which culture will we retain and which elements will we let go?

In extreme cases, the end result of the incorporation of one company into another is that the culture of the acquired company gets completely replaced by the culture of the acquiring firm; or, in some rare cases, the acquired firm's culture becomes the dominant culture of the new entity. The most challenging instances are those where the aspired goal is to truly merge the two cultures into a new one. In this instance, leaders must carefully assess which elements of each organization's culture to incorporate into the new culture and then proceed to do it in a deliberate and thoughtful way. Regardless of which approach to culture is followed, it is important to make sure that the two entities have broadly compatible cultures such that employees of both organizations can be brought together under a common banner.

In its early years, Cisco was one of the most prolific acquirers in the technology sector. It was successful in acquiring companies by carefully ensuring that the companies it acquired fit the fabric of its culture. When the fit was not as strong as anticipated, Cisco was not apologetic about walking away from an attractive target. In most instances, Cisco was clear that the acquired entity had to embrace the Cisco way. This forcible process can be feasible when the acquired company is small and has a less-developed culture. When the acquired company is bigger or when a key part of the company's value is embedded in its culture, it is not always feasible or advisable to force such integration. By doing so, the acquirer often squanders a key value component. In essence, it can forfeit the very reason the company was valuable to begin with.

SUMMARY

LO1 An organization's culture provides the parameters by which individuals interact and work. Anyone joining a new firm needs to understand what behaviors and activities are rewarded or punished, what conduct is expected, and how work is completed. Some elements of an organization's culture are obvious—its physical layout and climate, its focus on customer service, or its commitment to innovation, for instance. Other aspects of an organization's culture are less obvious, including the unstated way in which employees interact with and solve problems.

LO2 Culture can be a strong driver of performance. Companies such as Cisco and Ritz-Carlton have built cultures based on customer advocacy and support. Google and 3M have built cultures that value and reinforce innovation. In many ways, their cultures have been key drivers of their successes. However, culture can be a double-edged sword. Given its embedded nature, it is often difficult to change. Companies that have strongly entrenched cultures often have more difficulty adapting to environmental changes. In these cases, new leadership is often required.

LO3 : The three levels of culture include (1) artifacts (what is visible), (2) beliefs and values (what is known by members of the organization), and (3) assumptions (what is embedded in and unique to a firm). Businesses that try to copy another company's culture without fully understanding its hidden elements often fail. They can replicate the visible aspects of the culture but not the underlying processes.

LO4 : Culture arises as an organization develops a shared concept of how work should be accomplished and how individuals should interact with each other. An organization's culture is often initially influenced by the actions, beliefs, and assumptions of the founder. Over time, culture becomes more embedded in the organization through a variety of reinforcing mechanisms such as formal statements and creeds, the design of physical space, coaching and mentoring by senior leaders, and reward systems.

LO5 : Paying attention to culture is particularly important when a firm is acquired or when two firms merge. If the two firms have similar cultures, there is a greater likelihood that there will be less disruption as the firms outline post-merger processes and procedures. When the culture of one firm differs dramatically from another firm, it can be very hard to combine processes and procedures especially when both firms are of similar size. Sometimes, the acquired firm is allowed to operate independently to enable the combined entity to obtain the greatest possible advantage. In most cases, one culture tends to become dominant and influences the overall firm.

KEY TERMS

Artifacts

Assumption

Beliefs and values

Culture

Organizational commitment

Socialization

Subcultures

ASSIGNMENTS

Discussion Topics

1. In what ways are organizational design and culture aligned? How does or should culture impact organizational design decisions?

2. How can you assess an organization's culture? What clues should you investigate?

3. Why are an organization's assumptions so hard to change?

4. What aspects of an organization's or group's culture are most important to you? Why?

5. If an organization seeks to foster a culture of risk-taking, creativity, and innovation, what organizational design choices should they make? How should they think about rewards and reinforcements?

6. If an organization seeks to foster a culture of efficiency and low cost, what design elements should they embrace? Consider Southwest Airlines; they have been able to build a fun, supportive culture while remaining fiscally conservative and cost efficient. How are they able to build this type of culture?

7. Why do companies seek to build organizational commitment from employees? What is the downside to a compliance-based culture?

8. In what ways can culture impact the performance of a firm? How can a strong culture be both an advantage and a disadvantage for a firm?

9. Should an organization be concerned about the development of subcultures? When can subcultures be beneficial for an organization?

10. Why is culture so important to consider when two firms merge?

Management Research

1. Think about an organization or group you joined recently. How would you describe its culture? What is the organization's process of cultural socialization? What did the leaders do to reinforce the culture?

2. Select a company that has transitioned from being led by a founder to a new CEO. What was the culture under the founder? What aspects of

that culture continued with the new CEO? What aspects are no longer relevant?

3. Evaluate a company that has been acquired. In what ways did it absorb the culture of the acquirer? In what ways was the company able to retain aspects of its own culture?

4. Find two or three people with several years of work experience. Ask them about their work history. Has the culture and attitude in business changed from when they started to today? If so, how?

In the Field

Assume the role of cultural anthropologist for your college by completing the following tasks.

1. Collect artifacts and stories that represent your college's culture.

2. Describe the basic beliefs and values of your college's culture. How do these values reinforce basic assumptions of the culture?

3. Research how the founders have influenced the culture.

4. Identify contemporary heroes and heroines on your campus.

5. Categorize the different subcultures on your campus.

Use your research to create a presentation for your class to describe your findings.

ENDNOTES

1 Joseph A. Michelli, "Be the New Gold Standard," *Industrial Management*, Vol. 51, No. 2, 2009, p. 26, www.proquest.com, accessed July 2010.

2 Chip Jarnagin and John W. Slocum, Jr., "Creating Corporate Cultures through Mythopoetic Leadership," *Organizational Dynamics*, Vol. 36, No. 3, 2007, p. 288.

3 Ibid.

4 Christopher A. Bartlett and Afroze Mohammed, "3M: Profile of an Innovating Company," Harvard Business School Case No. 9-395-016 (Boston, MA: HBS Publishing, 1995), pp. 4–5.

5 Ralph H. Kilmann, Mary J. Sexton, and Roy Serpa, "Issues in Understanding and Changing Culture," *California Management Review*, Vol. 28, No. 2, Winter 1986, p. 89.

6 Danny Miller and John O. Whitney, "Beyond Strategy: Configuration as a Pillar of Competitive Advantage," *Business Horizons*, 1999, pp. 5–17.

7 Clayton M. Christensen and Kirsten Shu, "What Is an Organization's Culture?," Harvard Business School Note No. 9-399-104, rev. August 2, 2006 (Boston, MA: HBS Publishing, 1999), p. 2.

8 John Theroux, "Ben & Jerry's Homemade Ice Cream Inc.: Keeping the Mission(s) Alive," Harvard Business School Case No. 9-392-025, rev. December 15, 1993 (Boston, MA: HBS Publishing, 1993), p. 18.

9 Ibid., p. 9.

10 Edgar H. Schein, *Organizational Culture and Leadership,* 3rd edition (San Francisco, CA: Jossey-Bass, 2004), p. 17.

11 Charles O'Reilly, "Corporations, Culture, and Commitment: Motivation and Social Control in Organizations," *California Management Review*, Vol. 31, No. 4, Summer 1989, pp. 9–25.

12 Ralph H. Kilmann, Mary J. Sexton, and Roy Serpa, "Issues in Understanding and Changing Culture," *California Management Review*, Vol. 28, No. 2, Winter 1986, p. 90.

13 Jennifer A. Chatman and Sandra Eunyoung Cha, "Leading by Leveraging Culture," *California Management Review*, Vol. 45, No. 4, Summer 2003, p. 23.

14 Chip Jarnagin and John W. Slocum, Jr., "Creating Corporate Cultures through Mythopoetic Leadership," *Organizational Dynamics*, Vol. 36, No. 3, 2007, p. 291.

15 John P. Kotter and James L. Heskett, *Corporate Culture and Performance* (New York: Free Press, 1992); Jeff Rosenthal and Ann Masarech, "High-Performance Cultures: How Values Can Drive Business Results," *Journal of Organizational Excellence*, Spring 2003, pp. 3–18; and Nitin Nohria, William Joyce, and Bruce Roberson, "What Really Works," *Harvard Business Review*, July 2003.

16 Paul Meehan, Darrell Rigby, and Paul Rogers, "Creating and Sustaining a Winning Culture," Harvard Management Update, Reprint No. U0801C, January 2008.

17 Jesper B. Sorensen, "Note on Organizational Culture," Stanford Graduate School of Business Note No. OB-69 (Stanford, CA: Stanford Graduate School of Business, 2009), p. 2.

18 Jennifer A. Chatman and Sandra Eunyoung Cha, "Leading by Leveraging Culture," *California Management Review*, Vol. 45, No. 4, Summer 2003, p. 21.

19 Jesper B. Sorensen, "Note on Organizational Culture," Stanford Graduate School of Business Note No. OB-69 (Stanford, CA: Stanford Graduate School of Business, 2009), p. 2.

20 Eric Van den Steen, "Culture Clash: The Costs and Benefits of Homogeneity," *Management Science*, Vol. 56, No. 10, 2010, pp. 1718–1738.

21 Clayton M. Christensen and Kirsten Shu, "What Is an Organization's Culture?," Harvard Business School Note No. 9-399-104, rev. August 2, 2006 (Boston, MA: HBS Publishing, 1999), p. 4.

22 Tom Tyler, John Dienhart, and Terry Thomas, "The Ethical Commitment to Compliance: Value-Based Cultures," *California Management Review*, Vol. 50, No. 2, Winter 2008, pp. 31–51.

23 Chip Jarnagin and John W. Slocum, Jr., "Creating Corporate Cultures through Mythopoetic Leadership," *Organizational Dynamics*, Vol. 36, No. 3, 2007, p. 289; and Charles O'Reilly, "Corporations, Culture, and Commitment: Motivation and Social Control in Organizations," *California Management Review*, Vol. 31, No. 4, Summer 1989, pp. 9–25.

24 Ronald R. Sims, "Linking Groupthink to Unethical Business Practices," *Journal of Business Ethics*, Vol. 11, No. 9, 1992, p. 651.

[25] Ronald R. Sims and Johannes Brinkmann, "Enron Ethics (or Culture Matters More Than Codes)," *Journal of Business Ethics*, Vol. 45, No. 3, 2003, pp. 243–256.

[26] Dean McFarlin, "Strong Culture Can Be a 'Double-Edged Sword'," *Dayton Business Journal*, October 14, 2012.

[27] Jennifer A. Chatman, David F. Caldwell, Charles A. O'Reilly, and Bernadette Doerr, "Parsing Organizational Culture: How the Norm of Adaptability Influences the Relationship between Culture Consensus and Financial Performance in High-Technology Firms," *Journal of Organizational Behavior*, Vol. 35, No. 6, August 2014, pp. 785–808.

[28] Charles O'Reilly, "Corporations, Culture, and Commitment: Motivation and Social Control in Organizations," *California Management Review*, Vol. 31, No. 4, Summer 1989, p. 14.

[29] Michael L. Tushman and Charles A. O'Reilly, III, "Shaping Organizational Structure," *Winning through Innovation: A Practical Guide to Leading Organizational Change and Renewal* (Boston, MA: HBS Press, 2007), p. 2.

[30] Edgar H. Schein, "Three Cultures of Management: The Key to Organizational Learning," *Sloan Management Review*, Fall 1996.

[31] Edgar H. Schein, *Organizational Culture and Leadership*, 3rd edition (San Francisco, CA: Jossey-Bass, 2004), pp. 25–26.

[32] Ibid., p. 28.

[33] Ibid., p. 30.

[34] Ibid., p. 31.

[35] Michael Beer, Rakesh Khurana, and James Weber, "Hewlett-Packard: Culture in Changing Times," Harvard Business School Case No. 9-404-087, rev. January 25, 2005 (Boston, MA: HBS Publishing, 2004), p. 2.

[36] Ibid.

[37] Ibid., p. 6.

[38] Peter Burrows, *Backfire: Carly Fiorina's High-Stakes Battle for the Soul of Hewlett-Packard* (Hoboken, NJ: John Wiley & Sons, 2003), pp. 141, 153.

[39] Michael Beer, Rakesh Khurana, and James Weber, "Hewlett-Packard: Culture in Changing Times," Harvard Business School Case No. 9-404-087, rev. January 25, 2005 (Boston, MA: HBS Publishing, 2004), p. 11.

[40] Roy Harris, "Doubly Blessed?," *CFO*, September 1, 2003, www.proquest.com, accessed August 2010.

[41] Dean Takahashi, "Hewlett-Packard's Failure to Make Best-Employer's List Raises Questions," *San Jose Mercury News*, January 27, 2004, www.proquest.com, accessed August 2010.

[42] Clayton M. Christensen and Kirsten Shu, "What Is an Organization's Culture?," Harvard Business School Note No. 9-399-104, rev. August 2, 2006 (Boston, MA: HBS Publishing, 1999), p. 4.

[43] Chip Jarnagin and John W. Slocum, Jr., "Creating Corporate Cultures through Mythopoetic Leadership," *Organizational Dynamics*, Vol. 36, No. 3, 2007, p. 289.

[44] Edgar H. Schein, "The Role of the Founder in Creating Organizational Culture," *Organizational Dynamics*, Summer 1983, p. 27, www.proquest.com, accessed August 2010.

[45] Anthony J. Mayo, Nitin Nohria, and Mark Rennella, *Entrepreneurs, Managers and Leaders: What the Airline Industry Can Teach Us About Leadership* (New York: Palgrave-MacMillan, 2009), pp. 155–172.

[46] Paul McDonald and Jeffery Gandz, "Getting Value from Shared Values," *Organizational Dynamics*, Winter 1992, pp. 64–76.

[47] Harrison M. Trice and Janice M. Beyer, "Cultural Leadership in Organizations," *Organization Science*, Vol. 2, No. 2, May 1991, p. 150.

[48] Ralph H. Kilmann, Mary J. Sexton, and Roy Serpa, "Issues in Understanding and Changing Culture," *California Management Review*, Vol. 28, No. 2, Winter 1986, p. 89.

[49] John J. Sherwood, "Creating Work Cultures With Competitive Advantage," *Organizational Dynamics*, Winter 1988, pp. 5–27.

[50] Nitin Nohria, William Joyce, and Bruce Roberson, "What Really Works," *Harvard Business Review*, July 2003.

[51] Jesper B. Sorensen, "Note on Organizational Culture," Stanford Graduate School of Business Note No. OB-69 (Stanford, CA: Stanford Graduate School of Business, 2009), p. 1.

[52] Clayton M. Christensen and Kirsten Shu, "What Is an Organization's Culture?," Harvard Business School Note No. 9-399-104, rev. August 2, 2006 (Boston, MA: HBS Publishing, 1999), p. 3.

[53] Edgar H. Schein, *Organizational Culture and Leadership*, 3rd edition (San Francisco, CA: Jossey-Bass, 2004), pp. 28–29.

[54] Larry Page and Sergey Brin, "2004 Founders' IPO Letter," http://investor.google.com/corporate/2004/ipo-founders-letter.html, accessed August 2010.

[55] Google Inc., "Our Philosophy: Ten Things We Know to Be True," www.google.com/corporate/tenthings.html, accessed August 2010.

[56] Boris Groysberg, David A. Thomas, and Alison Berkley Wagonfeld, "Keeping Google 'Googley'," Harvard Business School Case No. 9-409-039, rev. July 7, 2011 (Boston, MA: HBS Publishing, 2009), p. 6.

[57] Geoff Colvin, "Personal Bests," *Fortune*, March 15, 2015.

[58] Bala Iyer and Thomas H. Davenport, "Reverse Engineering Google's Innovation Machine," *Harvard Business Review*, April 2008.

[59] Miguel Helft, "Larry Page Looks Ahead," *Fortune*, January 14, 2013.

[60] "Jeff Charney, CMO, Progressive Insurance: How to Keep a Work Culture Fresh," *Fast Company*, June 2012, p. 110.

[61] Google Inc., "Our Philosophy: Ten Things We Know to Be True," www.google.com/corporate/tenthings.html, accessed August 2010.

[62] Boris Groysberg, David A. Thomas, and Alison Berkley Wagonfeld, "Keeping Google 'Googley'," Harvard Business School Case No. 9-409-039, rev. July 7, 2011 (Boston, MA: HBS Publishing, 2009), p. 10.

[63] John Theroux, "Ben & Jerry's Homemade Ice Cream Inc.: Keeping the Mission(s) Alive," Harvard Business School Case No. 9-392-025, rev. December 15, 1993 (Boston, MA: HBS Publishing, 1993), p. 7.

[64] Steven Spear, "Decoding the DNA of the Toyota Production System," *Harvard Business Review*, September–October 1999, p. 9.

[65] Boris Groysberg, David A. Thomas, and Alison Berkley Wagonfeld, "Keeping Google 'Googley'," Harvard Business School Case No. 9-409-039, rev. July 7, 2011 (Boston, MA: HBS Publishing, 2009), p. 5.

[66] Ibid.

[67] Ibid., pp. 6–7.

[68] James L. Heskett, W. Earl Sasser, and Jon Wheeler, *The Ownership Quotient: Putting the Service Profit Chain to Work for Unbeatable Competitive Advantage* (Boston, MA: HBS Press, 2008); and Daniel R. Denison and Aneil K. Mishra, "Toward a Theory of Organizational Culture and Effectiveness," *Organization Science*, Vol. 6, No. 2, 1995, pp. 204–223.

[69] Clayton M. Christensen and Kirsten Shu, "What Is an Organization's Culture?," Harvard Business School Note No. 9-399-104, rev. August 2, 2006 (Boston, MA: HBS Publishing, 1999), p. 5.

[70] Chip Jarnagin and John W. Slocum, Jr., "Creating Corporate Cultures Through Mythopoetic Leadership," *Organizational Dynamics*, Vol. 36, No. 3, 2007, p. 289.

[71] Clayton M. Christensen and Kirsten Shu, "What Is an Organization's Culture?," Harvard Business School Note No. 9-399-104, rev. August 2, 2006 (Boston, MA: HBS Publishing, 1999), p. 6.

CHAPTER

9

Managing Human Capital

Learning Objectives

After reading this chapter, you should be able to:

LO1 Describe how human resources management can be a strategic asset to an organization.

LO2 Outline the processes by which an organization plans for, recruits, and selects employees.

LO3 Explain what organizations do to nurture and cultivate employees.

LO4 Describe how various contextual forces impact the management of human capital.

LO5 Explain the role that individuals can and do play in shaping their own careers and personal development.

SELF-REFLECTION

Strategic People Management

Finding and retaining key talent is an increasingly important component of a firm's strategy. Without talented and motivated employees, a firm cannot hope to deliver on the promise of its strategic objectives. What is the best way to ensure that new and existing employees will function at their potential? How can a strategic approach to human resources ensure success? As you consider these questions, please answer True or False to the following statements:

1. Most people overestimate how well they perform on the job.

2. Conversations about employee feedback and compensation should be separate.

3. Once employees have mastered a task, they perform better when they are told to "do their best" than when they are given specific, direct performance goals.

4. Mentoring programs have no effect on individual career success.

5. Companies that screen job applicants for values have better retention and success than companies that screen job applicants for intelligence.

6. The best predictor of a new employee's success in a company is his or her past experiences.

7. A star performer is less likely than a nonstar performer to change jobs.

8. Team-based compensation programs are better than individual-based compensation programs.

9. Most companies carefully plan their human resource needs well in advance.

10. Voluntary employee departures hurt the company's bottom line.

Based on your responses, what is your conception of strategic human resource management? What is your conception of human nature?

Source: Adapted from Boris Groysberg and David Lane, "People Management," Harvard Business School Exercise No. 9-406-034, rev. August 3, 2006 (Boston, MA: HBS Publishing, 2005).

INTRODUCTION

During most of the twentieth century, the management of human resources (HR) was about hiring employees to perform a task, compensating them fairly, and providing job security. Today, HR management still supports these functions, but its scope has greatly expanded. In an increasingly competitive marketplace, firms compete not only for customers but also for the best talent. There is a growing recognition that employees can be key to business success. For some businesses, their collective reservoir of human capital is even more important than their financial capital. Retaining these critical human assets can be challenging in a context where employees frequently change employers. How do companies get their most valuable talent to stay with them as long as possible, and how do they get the most out of those who stay only for a short while? Progressive organizations view HR not as a cost to be minimized but as a valuable resource that can be optimized and can become a key differentiator and competitive advantage.[1] Just like financial capital, human capital can reap tremendous rewards through investment, nurturing, and cultivation. In a similar way, without nourishment and care, human capital can wither.

Companies that invest in human capital often appear on *Fortune* magazine's "Great Places to Work" list. Each year employees from over 400 companies participate in a survey cosponsored by the magazine and the Great Places to Work Institute. The survey measures employee engagement and satisfaction as well as the overall conditions in the work environment. Employees who complete the questionnaire provide information related to their attitudes about their management team's credibility, their job satisfaction, and workplace camaraderie. Companies also provide information about their culture, including their demographic makeup, pay and benefit programs, philosophies, methods of internal communications, opportunities, compensation practices, and diversity efforts.[2] Two-thirds of each company's score is based on employees' responses on the questionnaire, and one-third is based on the company's responses to a cultural audit. The companies with the top 100 scores are designated as the "100 Best Companies to Work For" (see Table 9.1).

Companies such as Google and Wegmans Food Markets routinely appear on the top of this list because they recognize the strategic value of HR. Google provides its employees with first-class dining facilities, gyms, laundry rooms, massage rooms, haircuts, car washes, and dry cleaning services.[3] The company is often cited not only because it offers competitive pay and numerous benefit programs but also because it supports unique programs. For instance, CEO Larry Page donates $50 for every five hours an employee volunteers for a not-for-profit organization. The company even sponsored a group of employees to work on community projects in India and Ghana in 2012.[4]

Wegmans also rewards employees with opportunities for growth. Each year the company provides nearly $4.91 million in tuition assistance to enable employees to expand their repertoire of skills and knowledge. As of 2014, the company awarded $95 million in scholarships to over 30,000 employees.[5] The company states, "At Wegmans, we believe that good people, working toward a common goal, can accomplish anything they set out to do . . . . We also believe that we can achieve our goal only if we fulfill the needs of our own people."[6] Similarly, Edward Jones has

	2015	2014	2013	2012	2011
1.	Google	Google	Google	Google	SAS
2.	Boston Consulting	SAS	SAS	Boston Consulting	Boston Consulting
3.	ACUITY	Boston Consulting	CHG Healthcare	SAS	Wegmans Foods
4.	SAS Institute	Edward Jones	Boston Consulting	Wegmans Foods	Google
5.	Robert W. Baird	Quicken Loans	Wegmans	Edward Jones	NetApp
6.	Edward Jones	Genentech	NetApp	NetApp	Zappos.com
7.	Wegmans	Salesforce	Hilcorp Energy	Camden Property Trust	Camden Property Trust
8.	Salesforce	Intuit	Edward Jones	REI	Nugget Market
9.	Genentech	Robert W. Baird	Ultimate Software	CHG Healthcare	REI
10.	Camden Property Trust	DPR Construction	Camden Property Trust	Quicken Loans	DreamWorks

Table 9.1 〉 Top 10 Best Companies to Work For, 2011–2015

Source: Data compiled from Top 100 lists from Great Places to Work Institute website, http://www.greatplacetowork.com/best-companies/100-best-companies-to-work-for, accessed March 24, 2015.

appeared on the list several years because of its commitment to employee development and growth. Even in the midst of the financial crisis, Edward Jones has focused on retaining employees and investing in personal development. In fact, during the height of the Great Recession, Edward Jones continued to provide profit sharing and did not close any of its offices.[7]

In this chapter, we outline the ways in which companies build their strategic HR capabilities through planning, recruiting, and selecting. In planning, a company compares its human resources strategy with its financial resources and organizational structure to forecast how many employees it will need and what roles they will fill.[8] Once human capital has been acquired, a firm must then turn its attention to the management of its human capital. To that end, this chapter discusses the various ways in which firms manage their human capital including the design and delivery of training programs, the utilization of performance management systems, and the need to constantly monitor the internal and external environments to ensure that the right resources are deployed in the right way.

Ultimately, the responsibility for an individual's career rests with himself or herself. The time an employee spends with a single company is getting shorter and shorter, and you will most likely have multiple jobs at different organizations across your entire career. It will be important for you to know how to manage yourself so that you can pursue a career that's best for you. One company that has created interesting career paths for its employees and has fully embraced the notion of HR management as key to their success is Zappos.com.

Zappos.com

Having sold his first company to Microsoft for $265 million in 1999, 25 year-old Tony Hsieh launched Venture Frogs, a venture capital investment fund. One of his most promising investments was a little-known, but growing online shoe retailer called Zappos. Created in 1999 by 27-year-old Nick Swinmurn, Zappos was originally named shoesite.com, but Swinmurn quickly changed it to Zappos because he thought that it would be easier to remember and was similar to the Spanish word for shoes, zapatos. When he launched the company, there were more than 1,500 retailing sites that sold shoes, but within 2 years, Zappos, with Hsieh's investment and managerial advice, had taken the lead as the largest online shoe retailer.[9] Zappos's success was attributed to two primary factors—its unrelenting focus on customer service and its deeply rooted, employee-centric culture. In fact, the two were intertwined.

Since its inception, Zappos sought to mitigate some of the potential disadvantages of buying shoes online. Fit, style, functionality, and price were the four common factors that consumers considered in buying shoes. To address these concerns, Zappos offered next day shipping and free returns on all its shoes, which allowed consumers to try on their purchase in the comfort of their own homes. Zappos also offered more shoe styles than any other online or offline retailer. Most important, Zappos provided relevant, timely, and effective customer service through its website and call center. Zappos's wide product selection, fast shipping, and expert customer service allowed them to charge full prices for its products, which was a key advantage in supporting a cost structure that was focused on high touch customer service and extensive employee development.

Hsieh decided to formally join Zappos as co-CEO in 2001 and became the sole CEO by 2003. Swinmurn stayed on as Chairman for a few years but eventually decided to move on to other entrepreneurial ventures. As CEO, Hsieh championed the company's focus on employees with a special emphasis on happiness. Alfred Lin, Zappos's Chief Operating Officer, agreed, "We only hire happy people and we try to keep them happy. You can't have happy employees without having a company where people are inspired by the culture. We view this as a strategic asset. We have 1,200 to 1,500 brand relationships and a good head start against the competition, but that can be copied. Our websites, policies—all can be copied, but not our special culture."[10] Hsieh believed that the company's special culture enabled it to provide the type of customer service that set Zappos apart from other online and offline retailers.

To solidify his commitment to employees, Hsieh promoted the development of Zappos's ten core values by soliciting input from everyone in the company. While its first core value is "Deliver WOW through service," other values include "Build a positive team and family spirit," "Be passionate and determined," and "Be humble." Hsieh believed that there was a direct correlation between employee happiness and productivity. To that end, he encouraged his employees "to spend 10% to 20% of their time socializing with team members outside work."[11] Hsieh believed that if employees built personal emotional connections with their coworkers, they would model that behavior with customers as well. By building these connections, he hoped that employees would be more willing to collaborate, to solve problems, and to brainstorm new ways of serving the customer. Employees were expected to "bring their full selves" to work, not to separate their home life from their work life.

Ronda Churchill/Bloomberg v/Getty Images

Zappos's third core value is "create fun and a little weirdness." This value was reinforced in the company's hiring practices starting with the employee application, which included a crossword puzzle, maze, and cartoon graphics. During the interview, applicants were asked to name their personal theme song and rate themselves on weirdness and lucky scales. Zappos sought employees who considered themselves somewhat weird (not too weird) and very lucky. The recruiting manager noted, "If someone rates herself as being on the high end of the lucky scale, then she is probably going to be the type of person that we're looking for, who will be creative, adventurous, and can think outside the box."[12] One sure deal breaker in the hiring process was the core values. The core values were not just words on a document; they were embedded deeply in the culture, and prospective applicants were expected to embrace them. Hsieh commented, "We are willing to hire and fire based on whether people are living up to [our] core values, independent of whether they're doing their specific job function well enough."[13]

In 2014, Zappos scrapped the traditional process of posting job openings on such career management sites like Monster.com and CareerBuilder.com. Instead, job applicants must join Zappos's private social network called Zappos Insider to be considered for a possible new position. Zappos employees interact with potential job applicants through this social network to better understand if they will fit with the culture of the company, and if so, what type of role would make sense. The Insider network also allows the applicant to have a better sense of who they will be working with and what will be expected of them.[14]

Regardless of the position an individual was hired to fill, all new employees underwent an extensive orientation program that required them to spend time answering customer service calls. In fact, this was one way of assessing a candidate's humbleness. If a finance manager or high-level supervisor balked at answering the phone, it was an indication that the cultural fit with the company may not be right. Zappos was so committed to hiring the right employees that it offered them $2,000 (no questions asked) at the end of the four-week orientation program to leave the company if they so desired. While very few individuals took the offer, it was a quick way to assess new employee commitment to the company and its core values. Once an individual passed through the four-week orientation program, they were required to take an additional 200+ hours of training each year. Some of this training included new skill development on topics such as communication, conflict management, and coaching, and some of this training focused on softer topics such as happiness and the search for meaning in work and life.[15]

Zappos's deep commitment to employees produced strong results. The company grew to over $1 billion in retail sales in less than 10 years and 75% of its business came from satisfied repeat customers. Amazon was so impressed with Zappos's results and focus on customer service that it acquired the company in 2009 for approximately $847 million. Hsieh has stayed with the company through the transition and has been allowed to operate independently. Since the acquisition, Zappos has continued to be listed on *Fortune's* "Best Companies to Work For" list.

Case in Point   Zappos.com

1. What is the secret to Zappos's success?
2. What is your assessment of Zappos's recruiting practices?
3. What type of employee would be successful at Zappos?
4. Can the Zappos approach be copied by other companies?

ACQUIRING HUMAN CAPITAL

As Zappos learned, success often starts with who you have on your team. Hiring the right people for the right positions is critical to building a sustainable competitive advantage. Before recruiting a pool of qualified applicants, HR managers must work alongside company leadership to define and plan for their current and future talent needs. This entails both anticipating internal organizational needs and considering the impact of the external business environment.[16] Clearly the employees who are ideal for an organization like Zappos, where customer service is key, may not be appropriate for another organization where this is less important.

Managers must align HR practices with the company's stage of growth and its strategic objectives. A company may be in one of five stages of growth, and each stage is likely to have very different HR/capital needs. Stage I is the initiation phase, when a company is characterized as highly entrepreneurial and informal.[17] When a company enters stage II, it reaches functional growth and is characterized by technical specialization and increased formality.[18] In stage III, the company concentrates on controlled growth, develops more formal procedures, and increases its focus on professional management. It is in this stage that firms also begin to diversify their product lines. Stage IV is characterized by functional integration where a company develops multiple product groups or divisions and integrates various functional aspects like accounting and marketing to give divisions more autonomy.[19] And finally, in stage V, strategic integration, management focuses on flexibility, adaptability, and integration across business functions.[20] HR management is most effective when it matches the stage of development of the company (see Table 9.2). In stage I, employees are hired for their flexibility and willingness to do whatever it takes to get the job done. As the company matures, different skills take on more importance. For instance, during stage IV, the company should seek employees who can engage in cross-functional planning and analysis and who can see connections between different product and service offerings.

Another way to think about this fit between a firm's strategy and its HR practices is in terms of some of the strategic frameworks we discussed earlier in the book. As we discussed in Chapter 5, the competitive strategy that a company pursues (cost leadership, differentiation, or focus) influences the culture of an organization and the type of individuals who are most suited to that culture.[21] The cost leadership

Stage I Initiation	Stage II Functional Growth	Stage III Controlled Growth	Stage IV Functional Integration	Stage V Strategic Integration
Loose, informal management; Basic salary and benefits; Flexible job definitions	Responding to business needs in compensation and benefits; Add training and development programs; Recruit specialists	Formalized control measurements and goals; Routine performance appraisals; More formal control mechanisms; More well-defined job roles and functions	Long-range planning; Generate interdisciplinary training programs; Succession planning; More formal planning and hiring cycles	HR fully integrated with strategic direction; Long-range planning; Training and development focused on strategic issues

Table 9.2 ⟩ Human Resource Practices Matched to Organizational Stage of Growth

Source: Lloyd Baird and Ilan Meshoulam, "Two Fits of Strategic Human Resource Management," *Academy of Management*, Vol. 13, No. 1, 1988, pp. 116–128.

strategy is characterized by tight controls, low overhead, and economies of scale and, as a result, HR practices should focus on cost-effectively increasing productivity. Such practices might include hiring part-time employees or subcontractors, providing flexibility in job assignments, or simplifying tasks to reduce training time. In companies pursuing a differentiation strategy focused on improving quality relative to competitors, HR practices should include constant feedback systems, collaboration across functions, and employee participation in decision making and responsibility. With a focused innovation strategy, HR practices should allow for greater autonomy and room for experimentation as well as provide ample opportunities for development and training.[22] If the organization is like Zappos and believes that customer service is a key differentiator for them, then they need to hire service-oriented professionals.

Human Resource Planning

Before hiring anyone, a company must consider internal resource needs and potential changes as well as the external business environment. Human resource planning is particularly important as firms expand into new regions (both domestically and abroad). Planning is also important when firms decide to produce new products and services, deploy new technologies, acquire a company, or contemplate potential downsizing.

Even if the company is not anticipating major organizational changes, HR departments must still plan how to meet current human capital needs. Target, for example, invests in planning to ensure that it is positioned to meet its potential growth needs. The company uses data such as employee turnover by position, month, and department as well as future business projections to determine specific hiring requirements. For some critical positions such as business analysts, Target hires and trains employees well in advance of actual openings. This allows the new employees to be in a position to add value at the right moment. Target also expects its team leaders and managers to develop their bench strength. At any point in time, managers at Target should have one or two direct reports who are being groomed for their positions. This allows vacancies to be filled with speed and conviction.[23]

Successful HR planning, like the approach used at Target, requires **job analysis**, which is the process of analyzing information about specific job tasks in order to provide a more precise job description and define the characteristics of the ideal candidate for the position. Job analysis can be conducted in a number of ways, including interviews with management and current jobholders, observations in the

Job analysis
Analyzing information about specific job tasks in order to provide a more precise job description and define the characteristics of the ideal candidate for the position.

workplace, and self-administered questionnaires.[24] The absence of an accurate job analysis can lead to problems such as increased recruiting costs, inequities among employees, inadequate job preparation, and wasted training resources.[25]

Lynn Watson/Shutterstock.com

Having assessed a firm's resource needs, a HR manager can then turn his or her attention to the competitive landscape in order to benchmark its compensation and benefits offerings. Most positions are compensated based on the required combination of education, experience, and potential talent expected to perform a particular job. Firms often set compensation levels based on an external analysis of comparable positions in the marketplace. If a firm chooses to hire a worker from a competitor or another firm, it should expect to offer compensation that meets or exceeds the worker's current level. We address additional details about compensation and benefits later in this chapter.

An assessment of the business environment is also important in understanding the availability of workers with specific skill levels. For example, during recessions, there are more unemployed workers, so it may be easier to find appropriate workers for open positions, but this does not always translate into successful hiring. In the last recession (2008–2009), many workers were unemployed, but many of them were low-skilled workers with little or no college education. While the peak unemployment rate for college educated workers in the United States was 5.0%, the peak unemployment rate for high-school graduates was 11.1%, and the peak unemployment rate for those with less than a high school diploma was 15.6%.[26] Firms that seek to hire specific skill levels may still find it difficult to find qualified individuals even during tough economic times.

Recruiting Talent

Once HR managers have discussed anticipated internal changes with the company's leadership, considered how external factors will impact their hiring, done a careful job analysis, developed job descriptions, and determined the desired characteristics in job candidates, it is time to recruit a pool of applicants. Recruiting can take place both internally and externally. Internal recruitment involves choosing qualified applicants for a position from workers currently at the firm, while external recruitment involves finding qualified applicants anywhere else. There are several benefits of hiring internally. First, internal candidates know the company's culture, background, and products, which often allow them to make a quicker and more meaningful impact in the new role. In addition, by hiring internal candidates, the company demonstrates that employees have access to a potential career path that allows for growth and development. The presence of a career path is helpful in attracting high-quality candidates who hope to stay at a company for a significant period of time. Finally, by hiring internally, companies know much more about the skills and potential of the candidate for the position. This knowledge allows the company to be more proactive in properly supporting the individual's transition to the new role. Nordstrom, a company that has been consistently named one of the "100 Best Companies to Work For," has sustained its reputation for high-end customer service, in part, by recruiting and developing managers from within its employee base. Promising new sales clerks are often promoted within 1 year, and the ones with the greatest potential are invited to participate in the company's 6-month job rotation training program.[27]

Another firm that is especially successful at internal recruiting is General Electric (GE).[28] They focus on providing jobs that foster talent so that employees will be prepared to take on leadership roles after working a number of years at the

Bizu Tesfaye/Sipa USA/Newscom

firm. To that end, GE has a number of internship and job rotation programs that allow new employees to experience different functions in the firm. These programs provide new employees with broad exposure to GE as well as provide GE with a fuller sense of the employee's capabilities and skills. This knowledge is used to help place individuals into permanent positions that are aligned with their skills and the needs of the company.

HR managers sometimes seek external applicants who went to specific universities or worked at certain firms. In this process, they will sometimes leverage HR consulting firms, online job boards, and trade shows. Some firms are even using mobile applications to enhance their recruiting efforts. PepsiCo, for instance, realized that many job seekers used their phone to search for new positions while standing in a line, waiting at a restaurant, or watching a sporting event. The company is going a step further by creating the capability for job seekers to not only search but to also apply for jobs using their phone.[29]

There are advantages and disadvantages to hiring externally. If the worker is already employed elsewhere, the firm may have to offer higher compensation than planned to encourage the worker to leave his or her current job. If higher compensation is offered, this can lead to equity issues within the firm if employees of similar skill levels are at a lower rate than the newly recruited employee.[30] In fact, recent research shows that workers hired externally are paid 18% more than those in the same job who were hired internally. The extra pay does not always result in better performance. One study noted that workers hired externally had worse job performance marks and were 61% more likely to be fired than internal hires.[31]

Despite some of the issues with hiring externally, many firms have no choice, especially when they need to fill critical new roles in the company. Paul English, founder and CEO of Kayak, an online aggregator of travel information, believes in hiring great people wherever and whenever he can, even if there is no immediate job opening. Commenting on his appetite for recruiting, English said: "I am pretty obsessed with [recruiting]. The joke at Kayak is, if we have a business trip out to San Francisco, when the plane lands, my colleagues will say, 'How many people did you hire on this flight?'"[32] When a promising candidate is identified, English tries to close the deal in 7 days, regardless of whether or not there is an open position. For English, finding key talent is a critical strategic objective for Kayak.[33] The company's growth is predicated on its ability to build a pipeline of capable technology specialists.

Many employers find new talent through referrals by existing employees. In this way, the company is able to mitigate some of the unknowns from hiring externally. For instance, the existing employee can act as a primary reference point for the company. Since the employee knows the company well, he or she is also in a better position to describe the actual nature of the position and the company culture to the prospective applicant. In essence, this type of description is called a **realistic job preview (RJP)**. An RJP is the process of providing information to job candidates, which highlights the most important conditions of a job, including its positive and negative aspects.[34] Traditional job descriptions generally do not include the negative aspects of the position. Although it may seem strange that a recruiter would reveal the unappealing aspects of a job to a potential candidate, RJPs have been shown to decrease turnover.[35] In essence, job candidates obtain a more comprehensive understanding of the expectations and nature of the position before they make a formal commitment. The firm must also consider that in some cases RJPs can lead to a smaller pool of applicants if the negative aspects of the position discourage some individuals from continuing in the recruiting process.[36] Once the HR managers have

Realistic job preview (RJP)
When an organization provides information to job candidates that highlights the most important conditions of a job, including its positive and negative aspects.

recruited a pool of applicants and informed them of both the positive and negative aspects of the job, the next task is to select the best candidates.

Selecting Talent

Today's companies utilize a wide variety of information to select the best job candidates. The process is similar to the process universities and colleges use to select students. In college admissions, schools collect a variety of both quantitative data such as test scores and grades and qualitative information such as recommendations, lists of activities and achievements, and notes from interviews with alumni and school representatives. Companies also collect a variety of quantitative and qualitative information from their job candidates. This may include results from cognitive ability and personality tests, college GPA, standardized test scores, basic background information provided by the candidate, and information gathered from interviews and references. Companies are also beginning to use social media to learn more about potential new hires. While it is not without controversy, some employers even ask prospective employees to provide them with their password to Facebook. Seeing how applicants present themselves in a social setting can be very informative to employers, especially those that espouse a certain set of values and expect employees to adhere to them.

Since most job applications include a broad array of information, it can be a formidable task for companies to sort through it all and find the best candidates to screen for an interview. This problem has become worse in recent years since on-line job boards have made it easier to find jobs and apply for them, leading to very large numbers of applicants. Many firms sort through resumes to look for key information, and then pick a few candidates that stand out. Other firms add another layer to the application process and utilize ability tests to sort through all of the job applications. Some researchers believe that ability tests have a better track record than sorting through resumes for predicting future performance.[37] Ability tests usually consist of a series of both quantitative and qualitative problems that must be completed in a set period of time. These tests provide the employer with a standard measure of performance for each candidate, which can be beneficial when faced with a diverse applicant pool. Although ability tests are quite common for low and medium-skill jobs, they are rarely used in selecting candidates for senior positions within a company.

In a similar way, employees also evaluate companies. They use websites such as glassdoor.com to assess a potential employer. This website includes information about pay rates as well as ratings of managers by current employees.

While reviewing a candidate's past work history is important, situational interviews tend to provide a better predictor of future behavior.[41] A situational interview is an interview in which a candidate is asked to explain how he or she would respond in various scenarios that are likely to occur on the job. Situational interviews allow the company to better understand how a candidate uses his or her analytical skills to dissect the situation and present a series of possible action steps. In some situations, the candidate will be able to draw upon previous experience, but in many cases, he or she will be asked about a completely novel situation. Situational interviews are very commonly used for on-campus interviews where students have limited work experience.

The final stage in the selection process often tends to be reference checks. While most employers contact the three or four references that are typically supplied by the job candidate, some firms go further by trying to contact former colleagues to vet a prospect. The more senior the position, the more references are checked. A key question in the reference check process is usually "would you hire this individual again?" If there is even a slight pause in the response, the employer will often think twice about making a potential job offer.[42]

A DIFFERENT View

Looking for the Right Hire

More and more firms are turning to personality tests to identify potential new hires. Xerox, for example, has abandoned its previous approach of hiring new call center employees based on prior experience. Instead, the company relies on a personality test that assesses a candidate's creativity and curiosity. Xerox found that employees who were more inquisitive were more likely to stay at the company at least long enough for the firm to recoup its $5,000 investment in new employee training. Instead of asking candidates about past experiences, Xerox's personality test asks candidates to choose between statements like: "'I ask more questions than most people do,' and 'People tend to trust what I say.'"[38] Xerox is working with the start-up Evolv to design its employment test. Through its data modeling activities, Evolv has found that the "ideal Xerox call center employee" is someone who "lives near the job, has reliable transportation, and uses one or more social networks, but not more than four."[39] While tests such as this one can help companies to lower employee turnover, they can also open the company up to more potential lawsuits, especially if the data modeling seems to systematically discriminate against a certain type of individual. In these cases, a company needs to demonstrate that the criteria are "proven to predict success in the job."[40]

1. What are the advantages and disadvantages of using personality tests to select new employees?
2. If you were developing a personality test for a nonprofit organization, what characteristics of a job candidate would you try to assess?
3. How much weight should a company place on personality tests? What other hiring criteria would you rank as more important? Why?

Once the interviews have taken place, the various interviewers often meet to discuss the candidates, making sure to focus on specific characteristics that are pertinent to the position. Although it is ideal if all of the interviewers agree on the best candidate for the job, the immediate supervisor is usually given the final say in hiring decisions, since he or she will be working most closely with the candidate.[43]

MANAGING HUMAN CAPITAL

Once a company has acquired its human capital, it must focus on managing it. While this entire section of the book is dedicated to managing others, in this chapter, we focus on the specific aspects of management that deal with employee development and employee transitions. Managing human capital is ultimately about putting people in the best position to help a company by giving them what they need—whether it is compensation or skills—to perform their job well. First, we discuss how companies develop and train their talent. When employees first arrive, companies spend considerable time and money bringing them up to speed and giving them the skills to perform their specific jobs. Zappos, for instance, requires all new hires to complete 4 weeks of training, including spending a substantial amount of time on the phone with customers. This interaction allows new Zappos employees to better understand what is important to customers and, ultimately, to the performance of the company as a whole. Employee development does not stop with the initial training processes. Formal and informal feedback is used to encourage or discourage certain behaviors. In the following section, we will discuss how companies provide feedback, including the use of performance appraisals, to support and guide employee behavior.

Training and Developing Employees

For a long time, employee training mostly consisted of on-the-job training, where employees learned how to perform a specific task and then they were evaluated on how well they did that task. In today's environment, ongoing development is crucial to keeping employees up to date on the latest skills and technological innovations. The investment in training programs is also a long-term investment in the company as a whole as it helps to build skills and capabilities for the future.

Organizations train employees for a variety of reasons including the need to orient them on business practices, to teach them skills with a new piece of equipment, or to educate them on new product or service offerings. For the training to be effective, it must fit internally with the structure and culture of the organization and externally with the strategic, competitive landscape. Before an organization invests in training, however, it should understand what type of training needs to be done and who is best positioned to deliver it. This is referred to as a **needs assessment**.[44] Unfortunately, many companies do not regularly assess their training needs. They often react to the environment or follow another company's lead. One survey found that only 27% of organizations assess training needs systematically.[45]

Managers can use a series of steps to determine how to best proceed with training. First, managers should be clear about their goals for training, and those goals should be informed by the strategy of the organization. Second, managers should identify the organization's training needs and determine the appropriate audience for those needs. The identification of training needs can come from a gap assessment, whereby the HR function conducts an audit of the current skill set in the organization and compares that skill set to the future needs of the organization. For instance, if a company is launching a new product line that requires a particular type of customer support, the training should be designed to address this support. Once training needs and target audiences have been determined, managers, in conjunction

Needs assessment
A process by which an organization outlines what type of training needs to be done and who is best positioned to deliver it.

with HR professionals, can design the training curriculum, deliver it to employees, and assess its effectiveness. The assessment of the effectiveness of the training is usually apparent in the manner in which employees apply (or do not apply) the new skills. As with any intervention, it is useful to evaluate the overall outcomes of the program to determine possible improvements to the training experience.[46]

Types of Training

There can be as many types of trainings as there are job functions in an organization, but most training is typically focused on helping new employees get acquainted with the processes and procedures of the organization. In addition, many organizations conduct training programs that are focused on employee development, legal compliance, or safety. Table 9.3 provides a list of various types of training used in companies with more than 100 employees along with the percentage of companies that use them.[47] While this list is extensive, not all employees in an organization, and not all organizations, will use them. It is important to consult the company's strategy to decide which trainings are relevant. For example, the R&D division of the company may benefit from training on creativity and computer programming, but not necessarily on purchasing. On the other hand, the entire company may need to undergo diversity training or sexual harassment training to mitigate any potential legal issues in the future.

Training Program	% Providing	Training Program	% Providing
New employee orientation	92	Information technology	60
Performance appraisal	79	Motivation	60
Personal computing	78	Computer programming	58
Team building	75	Finance	57
Leadership	75	Stress management	54
Sexual harassment	74	Planning	54
Hiring/selection process	71	Writing skills	54
Train-the-trainer	71	Strategic planning	53
New equipment operation	71	Diversity	52
Safety	69	Negotiation skills	51
Delegation skills	66	Creativity	48
Product knowledge	66	Ethics	46
Conducting meetings	66	Marketing	43
Goal setting	65	Purchasing	40
Listening skills	64	Financial literacy	40
Decision making	64	Substance abuse	39
Managing change	63	Outplacement/retirement	39
Quality improvement	63	Smoking cessation	32
Time management	62	Reengineering	30
Problem solving	61	Foreign language	22
Public speaking	61	Other topics	4

Table 9.3 › Typical Training Programs in Companies with More than 100 Employees

Source: Zandy B. Leibowitz, "Designing Career Development Systems: Principles and Practices," *Human Resource Planning*, Vol. 10, No. 4, 1987, pp. 195–207.

While training topics vary widely, the methods by which employees are trained are more limited; they can be divided into formal and informal training. The most common formal training is on-the-job training, which is conducted on the work site and often led by an employee's supervisor.[48] For certain positions, especially those that require adherence to specific regulations such as heavy equipment operation or the use of dangerous materials, tests are often administered to confirm employee knowledge and compliance.[49] Formal training can also be done off-the-job such as at a facility that is specifically designed to teach certain skills.[50] For example, the airline industry has long used simulators to train pilots, and NASA has developed a virtual control tower that can simulate day or night at any airport in the world, any weather pattern, and the movement of up to 200 aircraft.[51] Formal education programs are another example of off-the-job training. Many companies team up with community colleges and universities to provide specially tailored corporate education that supports their specific training agenda.[52] Other companies go even further and create their very own private universities. One example is McDonalds' Hamburger University, where employees can learn about the specific operations of the McDonalds franchise.[53] Boeing and GE also have their own training campuses and use a combination of internal and external resources to deliver targeted programs to their employees.

Although formal training can be valuable to an employee's learning, informal training can often be much more effective.[54] Informal training may include coaching or mentorship, by which employees get matched up with a more experienced member in their field or department. In the best cases, these relationships become valuable resources for employees to develop their understanding of the company and their skills. As we will see in Chapter 20, these relationships can also be a vital part of an individual's network.

A key challenge for a company is to assess the value and impact of various training programs. This assessment is generally easier for specific skill-based training of repetitive or safety tasks where employees are expected to adhere to a set of rules or guidelines. In this case, the company can administer a test to assess the competency levels of new employees. In other cases, assessing the impact of the training can be more difficult. This is especially true for training that is focused on broader areas of leadership or management.

Development

Development
A long-term process designed to build greater self-awareness, enhance managerial capabilities, and enable an individual to reach his or her potential.

Training is typically focused on the acquisition of specific skills, tasks, or knowledge. While personal development often includes training on specific skills, it encompasses much more. **Development** is a long-term process designed to build greater self-awareness, enhance managerial capabilities, and enable an individual to reach his or her potential. A developmental plan for a high-potential employee may include a roadmap for achieving a higher level within the company. This roadmap or development plan could include a leadership assessment to enhance self-awareness, a job rotation program to experience multiple areas of the firm, or formal class sessions to build specific leadership competencies. Focusing on personal development has become a more valuable practice for employers because it attracts higher quality employees and keeps them more engaged in the company.[55]

Employee development initiatives are most effective when the organization's needs are aligned with the individual's career needs. To ensure alignment, one must have a strong understanding of the company's strategy as well as a strong understanding of an individual's capabilities, skills, and aspirations. With this understanding, the HR department can work with managers to find developmental opportunities that are challenging, match individual interests, and support the overall direction of the company.[56] A crucial part of employee development is providing feedback.

Feedback and Performance Reviews

There are many ways to conduct feedback, but the method that is by far the most popular in *Fortune 1000* companies is **360-degree feedback**, a system that enables employees to conduct a self-assessment and then compare their responses to others. With this approach, employees receive feedback from their superiors (the only source in a traditional system), their peers, their subordinates, and, in some cases, even their customers or clients.[57] The origins of 360-degree feedback can be traced to the human relations movement of the 1950s and 1960s, but it gained traction and popularity in the last two decades as organizational hierarchies have flattened, work has become increasingly cross-functional, and employees have become more empowered.[58] The process of soliciting feedback from others generally includes a Web-based survey or questionnaire that asks respondents to rate or evaluate an individual on various competencies that are important to the organization. Some of these competencies may include managing and developing teams, interpersonal skills, communication abilities, and strategic management. In most cases, 360-degree feedback respondents are selected by the individual employee and his or her manager.

There are numerous advantages to using the 360-degree feedback system. First, it includes a component of self-assessment, which has been shown to help individuals with career planning and decision making. But pure self-assessment can lead to unrealistically high ratings. This brings us to the second benefit of 360-degree feedback: a more realistic view of the employee's skills, capabilities, and behaviors.[59] It's easy to paint your own actions in the most glowing terms, so it's important to compare your views to the anonymous feedback from those who work closely with you.[60] Third, 360-degree feedback is an effective tool in the leadership development process since it identifies potential areas for improvement.[61]

In some cases, 360-degree feedback has been so effective that companies also use it for performance appraisals. That is, they use the feedback to evaluate an employee's merit and use it to make decisions regarding promotions or raises.[62] This practice has exposed some drawbacks of the 360-degree feedback tool. For example, one study has shown that up to 35% of raters change their ratings when 360-degree feedback is used for evaluation and pay.[63] Some raters report holding back because they don't want to penalize their coworker.[64] Even worse, deals may be struck among employees to provide artificially high ratings for each other.[65] Conversely, raters may provide particularly harsh criticism in response to poor leadership or to get back at a coworker for some perceived or alleged transgression.[66] Because of the drawbacks to 360-degree feedback, it is best used for developmental discussions, not to determine raises or other matters relating to compensation. In this way, the supervisor and the employee can have a productive conversation that celebrates an individual's strengths and highlights some opportunities for improvement.

Given the time and effort to conduct 360-degree feedback, companies generally only engage in this form of feedback on an annual or bi-annual basis. In the interim, more and more companies are focusing on real-time opportunities for feedback provided by immediate managers. High-potential employees, in particular, crave ongoing feedback about their performance and potential in the company.[67] By providing quick, actionable feedback, employees are in a much better position to accentuate what they do well and address their developmental weaknesses in a timely fashion.

Performance Appraisal

While 360-feedback is useful for developing and mentoring employees, formal performance appraisals are used to assess and measure an employee's performance over a certain period of time (generally 1 year). Specifically, **performance appraisal** is the identification, measurement, and management of individual performance in

360-degree feedback
A system in which employees conduct a self-assessment of key competencies and then compare their responses to others in the organization including managers, peers, direct reports, and clients.

Performance appraisal
The identification, measurement, and management of individual performance in organizations.

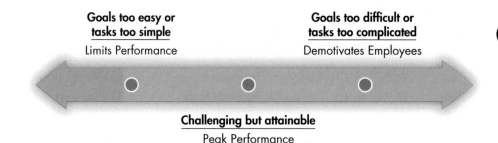

Source: Adapted from Robert N. Anthony, John Dearden, and Norton M. Bedford, *Management Control Systems*, 6th edition (Homewood, IL: R. D. Irwin, 1989), pp. 55–57.

organizations. It usually takes the form of a formal process in which an employee meets with his or her immediate manager and discusses his or her performance over the past year while also outlining expectations for the following year. The subject of the discussion for this meeting is usually a formal performance assessment form that has been completed by both the manager and the employee.

One tool that can be used in performance appraisals is **management by objectives (MBO)**. MBO derives its content from scientific management, one of the earliest theories on organizational control. MBO is the process of managing employees by outlining a series of specific objectives or milestones that they are expected to meet in a defined time period.[68] The main components of MBO are derived from goal setting and participation in decision making.[69]

Goal setting involves defining objectives or targets for individual or firm performance. Quantitative measurements should be used whenever possible because they clearly define the expectations of employees and communicate the most important objectives of an organization.[70] Because goal setting is the most direct and simplest way to motivate employees, managers must be aware of its drawback: setting goals in one area can lead to neglect of performance in other areas.[71] For simple tasks, managers should choose specific and measurable goals because they show employees that plans have substance and specificity.[72] But for more complex tasks, "do your best" goals are often more appropriate.[73]

Employees must accept goals in principle to be motivated to work toward them. To that end, goals must seem fair, challenging, and legitimate (see Figure 9.1).[74] When goals are slightly beyond employees' expectations, employees will work hard to achieve them, but if goals are too difficult, they can become detrimental to morale.[75] If goals are too easy, employees reach their target, become satisfied, and often stop trying to improve their performance.[76]

Goal setting, driven by senior leaders at the top of the organization, is common in many companies and is a reflection of twentieth-century style management. In this style, senior managers set budgets and performance targets for lower levels of the organization, expecting them to fully accept and comply with the numbers.[77] While top-down management is effective in times of crisis, it rarely works in most situations and often leads to a lack of commitment.[78] Instead, a bottom-up approach generates commitment by using employee knowledge about how to get things done, where opportunities lie, and which weaknesses to address.[79] When employees have an opportunity to share their opinions and expertise, they are more likely to be actively engaged in the achievement of specific goals.

Reward Systems

Performance appraisals are used to evaluate past performance and to determine potential salary increases and bonus opportunities. Compensation plans and reward

Management by objectives (MBO)
The process of managing employees by outlining a series of specific objectives or milestones that they are expected to meet in a defined period of time.

systems are an integral part of the ongoing employee relationship. So how do companies compensate their employees? While there are many variations of compensation, the baseline is structured as either an hourly wage (assigned to most low-level positions in an organization) or a salaried wage (assigned to higher-level supervisory or management-level positions in the organization). Beyond this basic structure, many jobs also include a bonus potential. Some jobs are almost entirely based on a bonus structure (e.g., commission-based sales positions). Other forms of compensation include group-based pay structures and benefits. Another common form of compensation is stock options. Sometimes individuals are willing to take less pay in exchange for a certain number of stock options. For the most part, salary is determined on an individual level while bonuses can be determined by the achievement of both individual and group-based goals.

Compensation

A common form of individual compensation is **job-based pay**, which means that pay is attached to a particular job; the only way to increase pay is to switch jobs.[80] These pay policies are usually mechanistic, predetermined, and standardized. They are most often used in hierarchical organizations where job tasks are narrowly defined and managers closely monitor behavior.[81] An example would be a customer service call center where employees are monitored closely through phone recordings. In this type of scenario, rewards may be tied to how many calls an individual successfully handles during his or her shift. Job-based pay systems are most suited for companies that pursue cost leadership strategies.[82]

A second common form of individual compensation is **skill-based pay**, where an individual's compensation is determined by his or her personal skills and knowledge, not by the specific job. In these cases, compensation is tied to the skills, experience, knowledge, and insights that an individual brings to a company. Skill-based compensation systems are most appropriate for organizations with lower hierarchical structures, more decentralized authority, and a high degree of ambiguity.[83] These types of environments often require an individual to use his or her personal judgment to make a decision.

To encourage greater teamwork and collaboration, firms often use group-based pay systems such as **gain-sharing** or **profit-sharing** to supplement an employee's compensation package. Both are similar in that they reward group performance and seek to improve productivity by aligning interests between the organization and a group of employees.[84] One advantage of using these team-based pay approaches is that they can be fully customized to a particular division, department, or team. Gain-sharing rewards teams based on the achievement of certain metrics associated with productivity, efficiency, or quality.[85] The metrics used to calculate gain-sharing rewards tend to be somewhat complicated and are generally specific to a team or a department. As such, several different metrics tend to be used within a single organization. Profit-sharing programs do exactly that—share rewards based on improving the profitability of the group.[86] Profit-sharing programs are generally easier to measure and monitor.

Like individual-based pay systems, group-based pay can have advantages and disadvantages. Gain-sharing programs allow managers to modify their targets and formulas as production evolves.[87] Additionally, group-based systems provide a layer of protection to employees that can free them to take more risks and be more innovative.[88] Being a member of a group can provide a strong performance incentive, especially when all members are contributing their best. However, instead of creating employee freedom, group-based pay systems can also lead to a diffusion of responsibility because no individual employee is ultimately responsible for results.[89] Consequently, some members of the group may not contribute their fair share, yet still receive the benefits of the overall team. This can lead to heightened tensions in the team if it is not properly addressed. In some cases, the overall performance

Job-based pay
Pay that is determined by the nature of a particular job.

Skill-based pay
Pay that is determined by an individual's personal skills and knowledge.

Gain-sharing
A team-based compensation structure that rewards teams based on the achievement of certain metrics associated with productivity, efficiency, or quality.

Profit-sharing
A team-based compensation structure that shares rewards based on improvements in profitability.

of the group regresses to the average ability of the group, not to its highest ideal.[90] When this happens, the group is less likely to benefit from the group compensation structure. Furthermore, shirked responsibility can alienate star performers, and they may be more inclined to look for another job.

Benefits

Benefits are another form of compensation, and they can include health coverage such as medical, dental, and disability as well as long-term planning programs such as life insurance and retirement accounts. A recent survey of over 6,000 American workers demonstrated the importance of benefits. More than 70% of the respondents said that a company's benefits package would influence their decision to look for a new opportunity, and 61% commented that they would consider a slightly lower salary in exchange for a strong benefits package.[91] Many companies include the costs of benefits when they outline an individual employee's total compensation package. In some cases, the company can pay upwards of 30% of an employee's salary toward benefits (see Table 9.4). According to the U.S. Bureau of Labor Statistics, private industry employers spent an average of $30.32 for employee compensation in September 2014 of which $9.16 (or 30.2%) was attributed to the costs of benefits. The largest cost component of these benefits was for health care coverage.[92] Many positions offer retirement plans or pensions, which help to ease the financial transition to not working. For example, public service professions such as firefighters and policemen receive a pension that grows in relation to their number of years of service. For public sector employers, the cost of these retirement plans can be quite significant and are often borne by the state and local governments. Private sector workers may also receive retirement benefits in the form of 401(k) savings plans. In some cases, companies contribute to these savings plans, but generally most of the contribution comes from employees.

The most popular way for companies to offer benefits to employees is through the use of **cafeteria plans**. A cafeteria plan is an arrangement that allows employees to make their own choices from a wide array of benefit options. Employees can choose between taxable benefits (such as retirement savings) and nontaxable benefits (such as health coverage). Cafeteria plans can dramatically reduce the costs of providing benefits because they allow individual employees to select what is most important to them. In this way, the company and the employee do not have to pay for benefits that do not provide value. Placing selection in the hands of employees through automated benefit selection programs has also helped to significantly reduce the administrative costs and burden on HR departments.[93] Different

Cafeteria plans
An arrangement that allows employees to make their own choices about benefit options.

Compensation Component	Civilian Workers (%)	Private Industry (%)	State and Local Government (%)
Wages and salaries	68.7	69.8	64.0
Benefits	31.3	30.2	36.0
Paid leave benefits (vacation and sick pay)	7.0	6.9	7.3
Health benefits	8.5	7.8	11.7
Retirement benefits	5.2	4.1	10.0
Other benefits	10.6	11.4	7.0

Table 9.4 ⟩ Component's Percent of Total Compensation Costs Paid by Employers

Source: Adapted from "Employer Costs for Employee Compensation—September 2014," Bureau of Labor Statistics, U.S. Department of Labor, December 10, 2014, http://www.bls.gov/news.release/pdf/ecec.nr0.htm, accessed March 10, 2015.

generations in the workforce place different levels of emphasis on compensation and benefits. For some, compensation is a key motivator while others are driven by interesting and diverse work assignments.

Managing a Multigenerational Workforce

Many of today's organizations include at least three and sometimes four generations in the workforce: (1) Baby Boomers, born between 1946 and 1964; (2) Generation X, born between 1965 and 1978; (3) Generation Y (also called Millennials), born between 1979 and 1994; and (4) Re-Generation (Re-Gens), born after 1994. Generational groups are said to share similar historical or social life experiences, and these experiences shape their perceptions of the world. For instance, Baby Boomers were impacted by the Vietnam War, civil rights, Watergate, and the sexual revolution. On the other hand, Millennials are the first generation to be born into a fully wired world that impacts the way in which they interact at home and at work.[94] Re-Gens have been shaped by the 9/11 attacks, Hurricane Katrina, the wars in Iraq and Afghanistan, the proliferation of social media, and the impact of the post-2008 recession.

Effective organizations are able to tap into the unique qualities and skills that each group provides. The challenge of leadership is that the motivational drivers of each group are not always consistent, and these drivers tend to change as a person gains more experience.[95] For instance, recognition is a motivational driver that is generally considered universal, but the form of recognition that is valued by each generation can be different. One recent study found that Generation X employees are more motivated by financial rewards and job security, while Baby Boomers and Generation Y employees value job flexibility and the opportunity to give back to society.[96] This motivational difference may be attributable to the fact that Baby Boomers and Gen Ys tend to be at a stage in their careers where they can experiment more— at either the late or early stage of their careers. Gen Xs, alternatively, are entering the peak of their careers and tend to value stability and financial security. Having experienced rapid technological change, significant layoffs, and massive organizational restructuring in the late 1990s, Gen Xs tend to be more individualistic than other groups. On average, they also tend to be less loyal to their organizations.[97]

Interestingly, a study of what motivates Baby Boomers and Gen Ys indicated that these groups have much in common (see Figure 9.2). When asked what they

Baby Boomers	Generation Y
• High-quality colleagues	• High-quality colleagues
• Flexibility	• Flexibility
• Access to new challenges	• Access to new challenges
• Recognition from one's company or boss	• Recognition from one's company or boss
• Intellectually stimulating workplace	• Prospects for advancement
• Autonomy	• Steady rate of advancement
• Opportunity to give back to the world	

Figure 9.2 〉 What Motivates Baby Boomers and Gen Ys

Source: Adapted from Sylvia Ann Hewlett, Laura Sherbin, and Karen Sumberg, "How Gen Y and Boomers Will Reshape Your Agenda," *Harvard Business Review*, July–August 2009.

value as much or more than compensation, many of the motivational drivers over-lapped between Baby Boomers and Gen Ys, including high-quality colleagues, flex-ibility, recognition, and challenge. The primary differences seem to involve life stage issues. Baby Boomers seek greater autonomy and stimulation, while Gen Ys seek career advancement. For managers, the information is striking—both groups value aspects other than compensation as key motivators.

In 2008, UBS tapped into this sentiment for Generation Y by offering new hires the opportunity to pursue a "gap year" before joining the organization. Recent college graduates were offered the opportunity to defer their offer to UBS to pur-sue a socially responsible initiative such as teaching English as a second language, rebuilding homes devastated by natural disasters, or supporting microfinance en-trepreneurship in developing economies. During this sabbatical year, the company provided a stipend for health insurance and one-half the new hire's base salary. At the other end of the spectrum, CVS has initiated a program for some of their senior workforce that relocates from south to north in the summer and north to south in the winter. Employees can transfer their position from one store to another without losing seniority or benefits.[98] Both organizations have pursued creative ways to tap into the preferences and motivations of key employee groups.

Flexible Work Options

Because different generations in the workforce prefer to balance professional and personal goals, organizations have sought creative ways to structure the work environment.[99] For some employees, working a typical 8-hour day or one that encourages overtime is a demotivator. For these employees, opportunities to participate in alternative work arrangements that provide greater flexibil-ity in how and when they work can be more motivating.[100] Some of the most popular alternative work arrangements are variable work schedules, flexible work schedules, job sharing, and telecommuting.[101] IBM has been using technol-ogy for years to support employees who choose to use flexible work options. After creating a global work/life flexibility project office, IBM has increased offers for compressed workweeks, individualized work schedules, telecommu-nication work, part-time reduced work schedules, and the opportunity to work from home. By 2011, more than 160,000 employees had engaged in some form of flexible work arrangement, which enabled the company to save over $100 million in real estate costs.[102]

- *Variable work schedules*. Traditional work schedules that start at 9 a.m. and end at 5 p.m. five days a week can make it difficult for employees to attend to routine personal business (e.g., doctor appointments and parent-teacher conferences). To address this, a variable work schedule that includes work-ing 10-hour days for 4 days or working more than 8 hours for 4 days and less than 8 hours on a fifth day might be appropriate. At Hewlett-Packard, field technicians need to be on call to respond to customer problems 24 hours a day, 7 days a week. To satisfy this need, some employees volunteer to work three 12-hour shifts on Friday, Saturday, and Sunday, followed by a 4-hour shift on Monday. The rest of the employees work regular 8-hour shifts during the week.[103]
- *Flexible work schedules*. Like variable work schedules, flexible work sched-ules can affect the times that employees begin and end work each day. Yet unlike varied work schedules, flexible work schedules are less structured and give employees more control over their work times. Usually, flexible work schedules account for flexible time and core time. During core time, employees must be at their workstation, but during flexible time, they can choose their own schedule. For example, employees can start work early and leave in the middle of the afternoon; start late morning and work

until late afternoon; or start early in the morning, take a long lunch break, and work until late afternoon.[104] To retain their mid-career and mature workers, Home Depot allows its employees to participate in flexible work schedules. This attracts long-term employees whose knowledge and experience translate into excellent customer service.[105]

- *Job sharing.* Employees may seek part-time work for many reasons, including the need to attend to childcare responsibilities or to care for an elderly or sick parent. By sharing the responsibilities of one job with an additional person, both parties can achieve the balance they need. Abbott Laboratories, a global healthcare company devoted to the discovery, development, and marketing of pharmaceuticals, uses programs such as job sharing to generate an extremely low turnover rate of 8%. Job sharing is particularly important for new parents who often need to reduce the amount of time they work to take care of their children. By offering flexible work environments, Abbott has improved its productivity and ability to retain highly skilled workers.[106]

- *Telecommuting.* Given the increased sophistication of technology, telecommuting is becoming a more feasible option for many employees, and more than 8 in 10 of *Fortune's* "100 Best Companies to Work For," allowed employees to telecommute for some portion of their job.[107] Through telecommuting, employees spend part of their time working off-site (at home) and use e-mail and the Internet to stay in contact with the organization. Telecommuting appeals to all generations. One study found that over 50% of college graduates had in interest in telecommuting. For some, this interest stemmed from their desire to reduce their carbon footprint.[108] It is no surprise that AT&T, one of America's oldest communications companies, is one of the biggest supporters of telecommuting. By 2013, 24% of its workforce telecommuted.[109] A recent study of the impact of telecommuting on call center productivity was conducted on a Chinese travel agency. The productivity of the telecommuters was 12% higher than those working in the office. A majority of the increase in productivity was a result of fewer breaks and sick days.[110]

Employee Separations

The final stage of the employment lifecycle comes when there is a separation of the employee from the employer. Sometimes these separations are voluntary such as when an employee finds a better opportunity at another firm or decides to exit the workforce to pursue education or concentrate on personal matters. The other common form of voluntary separation is retirement, in which case an employee comes to the end of his or her career.

With voluntary separations, a company needs to spend money on the entire HR cycle again, from recruitment to selection to training to development.[111] Sometimes the voluntary separation is a result of not effectively performing these vital HR activities in the first place. For instance, one study found that 80% of voluntary separations could be avoided by improving recruitment, selection, training, or development.[112] In today's environment, where competition is incredibly fierce, losing a valuable employee can be costly in other ways, especially if the employee takes his or her knowledge, expertise, and insights to a competitor. To prevent the leakage of trade secrets and other proprietary information, many companies ask employees to sign nondisclosure and noncompete agreements both when they are hired and when they leave the firm.

Involuntary separations are a result of terminations or layoffs and are often the most difficult part of a manager's job. When an employee is not performing to the standards of a position, he or she is a candidate for termination. Conversely, layoffs are often the result of changes in a company's competitive positioning (e.g., a loss of market share or a more intense competitive threat). In these cases, the termination may not be a result of an individual's performance, but rather a consequence of a downturn in the market. In either case, getting fired can be a traumatic experience, and managers should review and adhere to both company policies and legal requirements.

Involuntary separations are also costly for the firm. Involuntary separations often entail the payment of severance that can be quite substantial. Severance pay varies from one company to another, but it generally consists of paying a lump-sum of money to a fired or laid-off employee. While 2 weeks pay is generally the minimum severance payment, many firms opt to pay an employee 1 or 2 weeks of salary for every year that he or she has been with the company.

Despite some of the downsides, there can be considerable upsides to involuntary employee separations, even from the employee's point of view. Most of the time employees are let go because they are not performing well. From the employee perspective, he or she has an opportunity to find a position that is more aligned with his or her skill set and expectations. From the company perspective, releasing employees provides an opportunity to increase diversity, reduce labor costs, or bring in a more talented individual.[113] Even when employee separations are done in great numbers, like in the case of layoffs, the organization is often realigning itself for future strategies. Though it can be painful, this process can provide an organization with the opportunity to hit a metaphorical restart button.[114]

Downsizing

Downsizing is a process of reducing the employee base of the company in an effort to be more competitive. Downsizing tends to be a natural part of an organization's developmental life cycle and is often conducted to bolster revenue, cut costs, or improve competitiveness.[115] As part of the globalization process in the 1980s and 1990s, many companies engaged in downsizing efforts to compete more effectively. In fact, during the first half of the 1990s, more than 85% of *Fortune 500* companies downsized.[116] More recently, the 2008 global financial crisis has again brought downsizing into the limelight. The primary manifestations of downsizing are layoffs, plant closings, and consolidations. Each of these activities is very difficult to manage. Organizations that conduct downsizing in a fair and transparent manner are better positioned to reap the potential advantages of a lower cost structure and more streamlined operations.

Managing the victims of downsizing is a challenging process, but there are guidelines that can be useful. The first is that management should notify employees of their departure well in advance, at least 60 days, according to law, for employers with more than 100 employees.[117] Letting employees know early gives them a chance to come to terms with the separation and also gives them time to find a new job. Second, employees should hear the news individually from their immediate supervisor, not through some impersonal announcement. The news should be brief, to the point, and should include an appreciation for the time and effort an employee has spent with the company.[118] In the best cases, a company will help an employee transition by providing lead time, financial benefits, counseling, retraining, or outplacement services.[119] These types of services are most often available only to very senior executives.

Downsizing is a traumatic experience for everyone involved, but the individuals who are often overlooked are the ones who continue in the organization—the survivors. The attitude of survivors can have a dramatic impact on the ongoing culture of the organization. Employees put their faith in the organization and trust in the intangible contract that if they do good work, they will be able to keep their jobs and progress in their careers. Downsizing can destroy this

Downsizing
A process of reducing the employee base of the company in an effort to be more competitive.

trust.[120] Furthermore, downsizing can cause resentment toward the organization and guilt among the surviving employees. Within this context, the work still needs to get done, and it must often be performed by fewer people, which can impact productivity.[121] This may cause survivors to become narrow-minded, self-absorbed, resentful, or risk-averse. This has become such a pervasive problem that the term **survivor syndrome** has been coined to describe it.[122] While downsizing is extremely challenging for survivors, many studies find that survivors react more positively when they believe that layoffs were necessary, that they were administered fairly, and that victims were treated with dignity throughout the process.[123]

CONTEXTUAL FORCES IMPACTING HUMAN CAPITAL

Managing human capital is a dynamic endeavor that can be impacted by a number of contextual forces including legislation, labor mobilization, and globalization. While many of these forces are outside a manager's control, the manner in which he or she responds to them can be the difference between success and failure.

The Legal Environment

In Chapter 3, we explored some of the legal frameworks that affect the business environment. In this section, we focus on specific laws that have an impact on managing human capital in the United States. Throughout the twentieth century, a series of laws were enacted to improve both the access to and the conditions in the workplace. One of the most important pieces of legislation that transformed the working environment was the Fair Labor Standards Act of 1938, which established minimum conditions for health, safety, and general well-being of workplaces. In addition, it established a federal minimum wage, set maximum hours for a workweek, and officially banned child labor. Violators were subject to severe fines and possible imprisonment.[124]

While this was a major victory for employees, there was still a huge disparity in the treatment of women and minorities. This changed dramatically when the Civil Rights Act of 1964 was passed, and specifically Title VII of the bill, which made sweeping changes in the legal environment for HR practices. The most important provision of this Act is that it "prohibits employment discrimination based on race, sex, color, religion, and national origin . . . The Act prohibits discrimination in recruitment, hiring, wages, assignment, promotions, benefits, discipline, discharge, and layoffs."[125] The Civil Rights Act of 1964 was the first of many laws known as Equal Employment Opportunity (EEO) laws. The Act also established the Equal Employment Opportunity Commission (EEOC) to ensure compliance with the law.[126] Since then, there have been numerous laws passed to enhance the coverage of Title VII as well as laws to cover other aspects of employment such as compensation, health, and safety (see Table 9.5). In some states the law has been expanded to prevent discrimination based on sexual orientation.

Labor Relations

The labor movement in the United States during the twentieth century had an important impact on early labor legislation especially in the aftermath of the Great Depression when unemployment peaked at 25% of the workforce. One of the most important labor laws that emerged during this period was the Wagner Act of 1935, which granted employees the right to organize and fight for better wages, working

Survivor syndrome
A condition that can occur when certain employees who survive a downsizing become narrow-minded, self-absorbed, resentful, or risk-averse.

Federal Law	Year	Provisions
Equal Pay Act	1963	Men and women who do the same job in the same organization should receive the same pay.
Civil Rights Act, Title VII	1964	Prohibits discrimination based on sex, race, religion, or national origin.
Age Discrimination in Employment Act (ADEA)	1967	Protects individuals between ages 40 and 65 from discrimination in employment.
Occupational Safety and Health Act	1970	Outlines minimum standards of safety in the workplace.
Vocational Rehabilitation Act	1973	Prohibited discrimination against people with disabilities, but only applied to the federal government.
Americans with Disabilities Act	1990	Prohibits discrimination against people with disabilities. The world's first civil rights law for people with disabilities.
Civil Rights Act	1991	Amended the original Civil Rights Act to make it easier for employees to win in their discrimination lawsuits.
Family and Medical Leave Act	1996	Entitles employees to take unpaid leave of absence for family and medical reasons without losing their job.

Table 9.5 > Major U.S. Laws Affecting Human Capital

Source: U.S. Department of Labor, "Equal Employment Opportunity," http://www.dol.gov/dol/topic/discrimination/index.htm, accessed August 2012.

conditions, and job security. The passage of the Wagner Act resulted in a surge of union membership which peaked at 35% of the U.S. workforce by the mid-1950s. Subsequent laws, such as the Taft-Hartley Act of 1947, reigned in some of the power that unions gained but membership continued to rise for a few decades. By the 1980s, however, unions began to lose some of their clout, and union membership has retreated significantly, dipping to 11.1% in 2014 (see Figure 9.3).[127] While union membership in the United States has declined in recent times, many industries (e.g., airline, automobile, and film production) are still heavily influenced by unions.

Unions typically fall into two categories: industrial unions and craft unions. Industrial unions tend to be very large and encompass a vast array of employees within an organization. For example, the United Auto Workers is a single union that accounts for most manufacturing positions in companies such as Ford, General Motors, and other automakers. Craft unions, on the other hand, are composed of workers who are all practicing the same craft or specialty and may gravitate from one job to another.[128] In Hollywood, for example, there are unions representing each of the functions of a film set—screenwriters, editors, directors, cameramen, animators, and so on. Each union represents members of their craft and aims to secure consistent employment and comprehensive benefits for their workers.

Employees may join a union for a number of reasons, but the most typical reason is to secure fair compensation and benefits for a particular job. Employees who are unhappy with their wages, experience low job satisfaction, and distrust the management of a firm are more likely to see the advantages of union membership.[129] Unions are valuable to members because they offer many benefits that may not be obtainable without **collective bargaining**, the process by which union representatives negotiate with the management of a firm to secure certain concessions on wages, benefits, job security, or seniority. On average, wages and benefits are higher in unionized organizations. In certain cases, the threat of unionization alone can cause an increase in compensation. Unions also provide members with the opportunity to express grievances in a more formal manner. One recent high-profile labor dispute occurred between the players and owners of the National Basketball Association prior to the 2011–2012 season. The early negotiations resulted in a lockout

Collective bargaining
The process by which union representatives negotiate with the management of a firm to secure certain concessions on wages, benefits, job security, or seniority for union members.

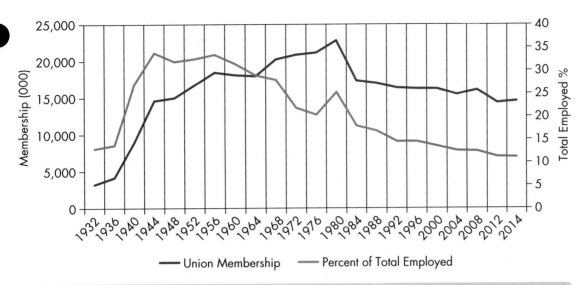

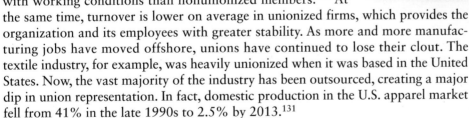

Figure 9.3 Union Membership in the United States, 1932–2014

Sources: Table 8-9-Series D 946-951: "Labor Union Membership as a Percent of Total Employment, 1930–2002," in George Kurian, ed., *Datapedia of the United States*, (Lanham, MD: Bernan Press, 2004), p. 123. Barry T. Hirsch and David A. Macpherson, "Union Membership and Coverage Database from the CPS," available at http://www.unionstats.com/, accessed April 8, 2015.

where the owners prevented the players from doing their job. Through collective bargaining, a new contract was eventually reached and the lockout ended.

While a union can provide greater job protection and better benefits, the decision to become a member is not always easy. Joining a union can sometimes represent a larger commitment than someone is willing to make. Union members must pay a certain portion of their wages to support the administrative functioning of the union. In addition, the career path of a union member is often predetermined with little room for change which has resulted in some unionized workers expressing a lower job satisfaction and greater discontent with working conditions than nonunionized members.[130] At the same time, turnover is lower on average in unionized firms, which provides the organization and its employees with greater stability. As more and more manufacturing jobs have moved offshore, unions have continued to lose their clout. The textile industry, for example, was heavily unionized when it was based in the United States. Now, the vast majority of the industry has been outsourced, creating a major dip in union representation. In fact, domestic production in the U.S. apparel market fell from 41% in the late 1990s to 2.5% by 2013.[131]

The Offshoring Trend

If you've watched national news programs over the last few years, you've probably heard many discussions about the outsourcing (see Chapter 6) and offshoring trend among U.S. firms (see Figure 9.4). Some news programs and politicians have made outsourcing their dominant issue. Such commentators have railed against the practice of outsourcing certain corporate functions overseas. And while the topic logically inspires political discussion, managers need to understand what the basics of this practice are and why firms pursue it.

As global competition has increased, many firms have searched for new ways to lower costs in their value chain. In so doing, they have tried to move certain jobs

"Outsourcing Is the Source of Another Lawsuit"
• *Business Week*, February 3, 1992

"Need to Cut Costs? Order Out; Outsourcing Saves Money, but Labor Is Frustrated"
• *The New York Times*, April 11, 1996

"U.S. to Speed Up Job 'Outsourcing'; Rule Change Could Affect Up to 425,000"
• *The Washington Post*, November 15, 2002

"Survey Says: Boost Productivity by 'Outsourcing' Payroll"
• *Business Wire*, November 17, 2009

"Small Business, Joining a Parade of Outsourcing"
• *The New York Times*, February 15, 2014

Figure 9.4 ⟩ Newspaper Headlines about Outsourcing

Sources: Sunita Wadekar Bhargava, "Outsourcing Is the Source of Another Lawsuit," *Business Week*, February 3, 1992; Keith Bradsher, "Need to Cut Costs? Order Out; Outsourcing Saves Money, but Labor Is Frustrated," *The New York Times*, April 11, 1996; Christopher Lee, "U.S. to Speed Up Job 'Outsourcing'; Rule Change Could Affect Up to 425,000," *The Washington Post*, November, 15, 2002; "Survey Says: Boost Productivity by Outsourcing Payroll: 2,000+ Accounting Pros Share Practices and Attitudes on Payroll Processing," *Business Wire*, November 17, 2009, via LexisNexis, accessed January, 2010; and Phyllis Korkki, "Small Business, Joining a Parade of Outsourcing," *The New York Times*, February 15, 2014.

overseas where they can find local talent who can sometimes do the same work cheaper and even better than the company can get done in its home market. For example, many firms have decided to outsource customer service and information technology functions to outside vendors such as Wipro and Infosys in India. In addition, firms have also begun outsourcing other noncore functions such as accounting, HR, and facilities management. When a company outsources a business activity to a contractor in a foreign country, it is called **offshoring**.[132] The outsourcing of business functions does not necessarily guarantee higher profits for a business. In many cases, the success of outsourcing is driven by a firm's ability to effectively manage people in different locations.[133]

Labor cost savings are often the major incentive for companies that outsource activities. In services, for example, a financial analyst who earns $35 an hour in the United States might receive only $10 an hour in India. In the manufacturing sector, workers who earn $15 an hour in the United States can often be replaced by people who are willing to work for as little as $1 an hour in places such as China and Mexico.[134]

Many firms make common mistakes with respect to their offshoring activities. First, they spend too much time identifying cities, countries, and vendors for their offshoring needs and not enough time deciding which activities should be offshored in the first place. For example, managers often fail to designate core processes that the firm must keep in-house for competitive reasons. Second, managers do not account for the inherent risks in offshoring a process. Some managers fail to realize that offshoring can give a vendor the upper hand in the relationship, which can increase the vendor's negotiating power in later transactions.[135] Finally, many managers fail to realize that instead of offshoring, they can outsource locally or even set up an alliance with a partner.

Offshoring
Outsourcing a business activity to a contractor in a foreign country.

Outsourcing is a complicated issue. While the practice can lower a firm's cost structure, it can also create growing unrest about the loss of jobs and concerns over working conditions and standards in foreign countries. One company that encountered such challenges was IKEA. IKEA is one of the most recognizable and popular companies in the world. With a management philosophy that wanted "to create a better everyday life for people," IKEA's founder, Ingvar Kamprad, constantly redesigned activities to drive costs lower. With this focus, IKEA looked to outsource production to low-cost facilities throughout the world. This became a problem when IKEA discovered that its carpet suppliers in India were part of an industry that used approximately 200,000 child laborers.[136] Following the incident, IKEA added a strongly worded clause to all of its supplier contracts stipulating the right to terminate the contract if any child labor was used in production. Following another incident involving child labor, IKEA adopted even more rigorous internal controls and audits to ensure that it avoided child labor issues.[137] Nonetheless, these incidents have hurt IKEA's global reputation.

MANAGING YOURSELF

In the past, it was not uncommon for workers to stay in the same job or in the same town where they grew up for decades. Those days are over. In fact, the U.S. Bureau of Labor Statistics reports that, on average, each American worker only stays in a job for 4.6 years.[138] This means that for most people, job changes and even career changes will be a normal part of life. Employees can also no longer depend on their employer for guiding their career path. As the workforce becomes more complex, it is up to workers to manage their own careers and take charge of developing themselves to create greater opportunities.

Before considering different career options, it is valuable to do some soul-searching. First, you must determine your strengths and your values. What do you like to do? What are you good at? What are your interests? You cannot build your career without having a solid understanding of what value you bring to the table. Companies often search for candidates who bring a unique skill set to help them succeed. Consider not only what you know but also your natural talents; you will need both to be successful.

You should always try to find a job that takes advantage of your strengths. If you feel that you don't actually know your strengths, you are not alone. In fact, most people don't know what sets them apart from other job applicants. One strategy for discovering your strengths is called feedback analysis.[139] Feedback analysis is the process of tracking the results of your key actions and decisions. By comparing the results with your expectations, you can get a better idea of what you do well and what you do poorly. This process is better than a standard process of reflecting on what you "feel" you do well, because often your emotions will mislead you. By comparing tangible results with your expectations you will be able to better quantify your strengths and weaknesses. You may want to use the 360-degree feedback method with your friends and parents to obtain some insight into your strengths.

In addition to knowing your strengths, you need to know how you work with other people. Do you prefer having close contact with your manager or do you prefer being left alone? Do you prefer working in teams or individually? Do you communicate best via e-mail, phone, or in person? Interpersonal relationships at the office can make or break your experience in a job, so it is important to think about your preferences. If your relationship with your boss is poor, is it because you have different communication styles? Setting up a meeting to discuss your preferred communication style can go a long way in improving your working relationship. Your preferences for how you work with other people may also impact your career

The Leadership Development Journey

Making career transitions can be both very beneficial and very risky. Switching jobs may lead you to the job of your dreams, but it could also put you on a dead-end career path. Your goal should be to make steady progress in your career with each job change. Although a new job involves some uncertainty, there are plenty of things you can do to improve your career transitions. The first step is to do your research before making a switch. You should know the basics about the industry. What differentiates the company you are interviewing with from its competitors? Is the industry growing, shrinking, or stable? The answers to these questions will enable you to present yourself in a more knowledgeable way. In addition, the research should enable you to confirm your interest in the position and the company. Consider your ideal job after graduation:

1. What type of industry is most appealing to you?
2. What lifecycle stage of a business do you think would enable you to thrive— a start-up, a mature business, or a turnaround?
3. What are your longer-term goals? Do you want to stay at one firm for many years or do you want to explore a variety of potential opportunities?
4. How important is geographic location in your choice of potential employers?

decisions. For example, if you prefer to work individually, a consulting firm might not be a good career option for you since most consulting projects are completed in teams. Almost all jobs in business require some level of teamwork, but there are some positions that have less interpersonal interaction, such as jobs in research and development as well as financial management and accounting.

Knowing how you work with others may guide your career direction, but knowing how you learn is important no matter what direction you take, because increasing your knowledge, understanding, and skills are the keys to solid career development. Knowing how you learn is especially important early in your career. Some people learn by reading—they are visual learners. Others learn by listening— they are auditory learners. Still others learn by writing, taking notes, or some other action—they are kinesthetic learners. Knowing how you best learn can improve your productivity, especially over the long term. To determine how you learn best, try utilizing just one way of learning for a set period of time. Then switch to a different method and see whether you are more or less successful.

Knowing your values is also important when making decisions about your career. To determine your values, you must consider all the things you care about in your life and identify which of those things are most precious to you. Note that determining your values is different from determining what is ethical. While ethics consist of general rules that apply to everyone, your values are specific to you—you can decide what you value. For example, if you value spending a lot of time with your extended family, you may want to limit yourself to jobs that will not require travel or relocation to different areas of the country. If you value a specific political cause, you may want to look for a job that will grant you the flexibility to take time off during elections to volunteer with a campaign.

In switching jobs, you should always be going "to" rather than "from."[140] In other words, taking a different job just because you want to get out of your current one is not always the best decision. It can lead you to accept a job that is less than ideal, and sometimes trying to fix the issues at your current job is a better choice.

Whenever you are under pressure to leave, stop and consider your alternatives. If there is an awkward social situation, is there someone you could reach out to that could help with the situation? If you dislike the tasks you are working on, could you ask to be reassigned to a different department? Asking these questions helps to clarify whether your unease and unhappiness is related to the job and company as a whole or whether it is a symptom of a component of the job. In some cases, fixing the component can lead to a renewed sense of engagement and satisfaction in the job.

Career transitions can be stressful, but it is important to keep things in perspective. Setbacks are part of life, and most careers are not linear. If you know yourself well enough, a setback (or two or three) will not deter you from meeting your goals in the long term. If you do suffer a setback—you lose a job or you don't like your job— go back to the basics. Consider your strengths, how you work with others, how you learn, and what you value. Knowing yourself is a key to managing your career.

SUMMARY

LO1 The management of HR is a critical component of any organization's strategy, and organizations that approach their employees as strategic assets are better positioned to achieve long-term success. While in the past, human resources were considered a cost to be minimized, today, organizations are investing in the cultivation and development of their talent. These organizations realize that a firm's strategy is enacted by the people in the organization, and that success depends on a highly motivated and engaged workforce.

LO2 Like an organization's strategy, the first step in developing an effective and defensible approach to HR begins with planning. Organizations should assess the internal and external environments to predict the types of resources that will be needed to meet future challenges. Effective planning incorporates a gap analysis whereby the firm assesses its capabilities compared to what it needs. The gaps in this assessment form the foundation for HR needs. Having assessed its needs, an organization must then turn its attention to the recruitment and selection of employees. Most firms approach recruitment from an internal and external perspective. Internal hires are generally more productive in the short-term than external hires. A focus on hiring internally also demonstrates that the firm is committed to an employee's development and potential. Despite its advantages, internal hiring is not always an option, especially for jobs that require unique skill sets. Regardless of the approach to recruitment, firms must assess a candidate's abilities in light of the job requirements. This assessment can be based on a number of factors including ability and personality tests, general interviews, reference checks, and situational interviews.

LO3 The strategic approach to HR management does not stop when an employee is hired; it just begins. Cultivation and development are critical to ensure that the firm realizes the full potential of all its employees. Many firms have extensive training and development programs that enable both new and existing employees to build their skills and capabilities. As employees continue their career within a firm, they should have access to ongoing professional development programs to enhance their performance and potential for increased responsibilities. Through constant feedback and performance appraisals, an organization can assess how its employees are performing in relation to specific goals, milestones, and objectives. These interventions can also inform the types of training and development that would be most useful in the future. Performance appraisals, in particular, form the basis for decisions regarding raises, promotions, bonuses, and even terminations.

LO4 The management of HR does not happen in a vacuum. Organizations must comply with various employment laws to ensure that their HR practices are fair, legal, and consistent. Over the years, employees and members of society have influenced the legislative landscape for business. Unions, in particular, have played a large role in setting standards for fair wages and good working conditions. Though the union movement has waned in recent decades, it is still a viable and influential entity in many critical industries. Two of the most pressing contextual factors today are globalization and increased competitiveness. To compete more effectively in the global landscape, many firms have opted for offshoring some noncore functions. While this approach can save costs, it can also increase complexity as managers need to oversee a globally diverse and dispersed workforce.

LO5 Although organizations can help individuals to maximize their potential, the ultimate responsibility for personal development rests with the individual. Individuals should take ownership of their own careers by seeking employers whose values and culture are aligned with their own. Individual career success is often a result of careful planning and analysis. The unit of analysis in this case is not the organization, but the individual. Individuals who better understand what motivates them will be more likely to pursue career paths that are meaningful and satisfactory.

KEY TERMS

360-degree feedback
Cafeteria plans
Collective bargaining
Development
Downsizing
Gain-sharing

Job analysis
Job-based pay
Management by objectives (MBO)
Needs assessment
Offshoring
Performance appraisal

Profit-sharing
Realistic job preview (RJP)
Skill-based pay
Survivor syndrome

ASSIGNMENTS

Discussion Topics

1. In what ways can HR become a strategic asset for a firm?

2. Why is it important for a company's HR department to be aligned with a firm's stage of growth? How does and should the role of HR change as a company expands (see Table 9.2)?

3. What are effective ways in which a firm can plan its HR needs? What information is most important in the planning process?

4. Explain the advantages and disadvantages of recruiting internally and externally.

5. When selecting a new employee, what criterion about the candidate would you consider to be the most important? What would you consider to be the most accurate predictor of success—job tests, interview performance, reference checks, or some other aspect?

6. What is the difference between training and development?

7. What are the benefits and drawbacks of 360-degree feedback systems?

8. What piece of employment legislation has had the greatest impact on HR management? Why?

9. Why has the union movement in the United States declined so much in the last few decades? What potential businesses or industries may be ripe for unionization?

10. In what ways has offshoring made a manager's job easier? Harder?

Management Research

1. Identify a company that has appeared on the "Great Places to Work For" List (http://www.greatplacetowork.com/best-companies/100-best-companies-to-work-for) for at least two years and outline why you believe that it was placed on this list. Find a competitor of the company that is not included on the list. Compare and contrast the two companies. How does the company on the list stand out?

2. More and more companies are relying on flexible job options to attract and retain employees. Identify two or three companies that actively promote flexibility. What do they offer? In what ways, if any, does this flexibility provide the company with a competitive advantage? Are there any potential downsides?

In the Field

1. Visit your college campus's career center or online job bank and review some of the job descriptions. Which ones, if any, present a RJP? If a company decided to post a RJP, what would it include?

2. Interview a HR executive at a local company. Ask him or her to explain the company's planning, recruiting, and selection processes. How is the HR function aligned with the needs of the business?

3. Interview a family member about his or her career. How many jobs did he or she have? Why did they change jobs? Knowing what they know now, would they manage their careers any differently?

ENDNOTES

[1] Brian E. Becker and Mark A. Huselid, "High Performance Work Systems and Firm Performance: A Synthesis of Research and Managerial Implications," *Research in Personnel and Human Resources Management*, Vol. 16, 1998, pp. 53–101.

[2] R. Levering and M. Moskowitz, "100 Best Companies to Work For," *Fortune*, February 4, 2008.

[3] "Google, Inc.," www.google.com/support/jobs/bin/static.py?page=benefits.html, accessed October 1, 2008.

[4] Milton Moskowitz and Robert Levering, "The 100 Best Companies to Work For," *Fortune*, February 3, 2014.

[5] "Wegmans Employees Scholarship Program Announces 1,766 New Recipients in 2014," Press Release May 27, 2014, www.wegmans.com, accessed March 24, 2015.

[6] "Wegmans, 2008, Company Overview," www.wegmans.com, accessed October 1, 2008.

[7] Laurie Burstein, "St. Louis Companies Rank High on Best Places to Work Lists," *St. Louis Commerce*, July 1, 2010.

[8] Patrick M. Wright and Scott A. Snell, "Toward an Integrative View of Strategic Human Management," *Human Resource Management Review*, Vol. 1, No. 3, 1991, pp. 203–225; Brian E. Becker and Mark A. Huselid, "High Performance Work Systems and Firm Performance: A Synthesis of Research and Managerial Implications," *Research in Personnel and Human Resources Management*, Vol. 16, 1998, pp. 53–101; Patrick M. Wright and Gary C. McMahan, "Theoretical Perspectives for Strategic Human Resource Management," *Journal of Management*, Vol. 18, No. 2, 1992, pp. 295–320; and Randall S. Schuler and Susan E. Jackson, "Linking Competitive Strategies with Human Resource Management Practices," *The Academy of Management Executive*, Vol. 1, No. 3, 1987, pp. 207–219.

[9] Frances X. Frei, Robin J. Ely, and Laura Winig, "Zappos.com 2009: Clothing, Customer Service and Company Culture," Harvard Business School Case No. 9-612-701 (Boston, MA: HBS Publishing, 2011).

[10] Ibid.

[11] Ibid.

[12] Ibid.

[13] Ibid.

[14] Adam Auriemma, "Zappos Zaps Job Postings, Seeks Hires on Social Media," *Wall Street Journal*, May 27, 2014.

[15] Frances X. Frei, Robin J. Ely, and Laura Winig, "Zappos.com 2009: Clothing, Customer Service and Company Culture," Harvard Business School Case No. 9-612-701 (Boston, MA: HBS Publishing, 2011).

[16] R. H. Miles and K. S. Cameron, *Coffin Nails and Corporate Strategy* (Englewood Cliffs, NJ: Prentice-Hall, 1982); Raymond E. Miles and Charles C. Snow, "Designing Strategic Human Resources Systems," *Organizational Dynamics*, Vol. 13, No. 1, 1984, pp. 36–52; Larry Greiner, "Evolution and Revolution as Organizations Grow," *Harvard Business Review*, May–June 1998; and Paul Milgrom and John Roberts, "Complementarities and Fit Strategy, Structure, and Organizational Change in Manufacturing," *Journal of Accounting and Economics*, Vol. 19, No. 2–3, 1995, pp. 179–208.

[17] R. C. Davis, *The Fundamentals of Top Management* (New York: Harper, Row, and Brothers, 1951); A. C. Filey and R.J. Aldag, "Organizational Growth and Types: Lessons from Small Institutions," *Research in Organizational Behavior*, B. M. Straw and L. L. Cummings, eds. (Greenwich, CT: JAI Press, 1980), pp. 279–321; Larry Greiner, "Evolution and Revolution as Organizations Grow," *Harvard Business Review*, May-June 1998; and B. R. Scott, *Stages of Corporate Development* (Cambridge, MA: Intercase Clearing House, Harvard Business School, 1971).

[18] A. C. Filey and R. J. Aldag, "Organizational Growth and Types: Lessons from Small Institutions," *Research in Organizational Behavior*, B. M. Straw and L. L. Cummings, eds. (Greenwich, CT: JAI Press, 1980), pp. 279–321; H. Mintzberg, *The Structuring of Organizations* (Englewood Cliffs, NJ: Prentice-Hall, 1979); M. S. Salter, "Stages of Corporate Development, Implication for Management Control," Unpublished doctoral dissertation, Harvard University, 1968; and B. R. Scott, *Stages of Corporate Development* (Cambridge, MA: Intercase Clearing House, Harvard Business School, 1971).

[19] M. S. Salter, "Stages of Corporate Development, Implication for Management Control," Unpublished doctoral dissertation, Harvard University, 1968.

[20] Larry Greiner, "Evolution and Revolution as Organizations Grow," *Harvard Business Review*, May–June 1998.

[21] Michael E. Porter, *Competitive Strategy* (New York, NY: The Free Press, 1980); and Michael E. Porter, *Competitive Advantage* (New York, NY: The Free Press, 1985).

[22] Randall S. Schuler and Susan E. Jackson, "Linking Competitive Strategies with Human Resource Management Practices," *The Academy of Management Executive*, Vol. 1, No. 3, 1987, pp. 207–219.

[23] Sunil J. Ramlall, "Strategic HR Management Creates Value at Target," *Journal of Organizational Excellence*, Spring 2006, pp. 57–62.

[24] Edmund Heery and Mike Noon, "Job analysis," *A Dictionary of Human Resource Management* (Oxford: Oxford University Press, 2008).

25 Frederick P. Morgeson and Michael A. Campion, "Social and Cognitive Sources of Potential Inaccuracy in Job Analysis," *Journal of Applied Psychology*, Vol. 82, No. 5, 1997, p. 628.

26 Data from Current Population Survey, U.S. Bureau of Labor Statistics.

27 Christopher Tkaczyk, "Nordstrom," *Fortune*, October 18, 2010.

28 John Sullivan, "The Top 25 Benchmark Firms in Recruiting and Talent Management," *Ere.net*, February 28, 2005, http://www.ere.net/2005/02/28/the-top-25-benchmark-firms-in-recruiting-and-talent-management/, accessed September 2012.

29 Jennifer Alsever, "Objective: Hire Top Talent," *Fortune*, February 3, 2014.

30 Robert G. Eccles, Boris Groysberg, and Ann Cullen, "A Note on Compensation Research," Harvard Business School Note No. 9-408-114 (Boston, MA: HBS Publishing, 2011), p. 1.

31 Susan Adams, "Why Promoting From Within Usually Beats Hiring from Outside," *Forbes*, April 5, 2012, http://www.forbes.com/sites/susanadams/2012/04/05/why-promoting-from-within-usually-beats-hiring-from-outside/, accessed September 2012.

32 Geoff Colvin, "Kayak Takes on the Big Dogs," *Fortune*, October 8, 2012.

33 Ibid.

34 Edmund Heery and Mike Noon, "Realistic Job Preview," *A Dictionary of Human Resource Management* (Oxford: Oxford University Press, 2008).

35 Jean M. Phillips, "Effects of Realistic Job Previews on Multiple Organizational Outcomes: A Meta-Analysis," *The Academy of Management Journal*, Vol. 41, No. 6, 1998, p. 673.

36 John W. Boudreau and Sara L. Rynes, "Role of Recruitment in Staffing Utility Analysis," *Journal of Applied Psychology*, Vol. 70, No. 2, 1985, p. 673.

37 Robert M. Guion and Wade M. Gibson, "Personnel Selection and Placement," *Annual Review of Psychology*, Vol. 39, 1988, p. 363.

38 Joseph Walker, "Companies Trade In Hunch-Based Hiring for Computer Modeling," *Wall Street Journal*, September 20, 2012.

39 Ibid.

40 Ibid.

41 Jeff A. Weekley and Joseph A. Gier, "Reliability and Validity of the Situational Interview for a Sales Position," *Journal of Applied Psychology*, Vol. 72, No. 3, 1987, p. 486.

42 Vickie Elmer, "Avoid Hiring the Unexpected," *Fortune*, September 24, 2012.

43 Claudio Fernández-Aráoz, Boris Groysberg, and Nitin Nohria, "The Definitive Guide to Recruiting in Good Times and Bad," *Harvard Business Review*, May 2009.

44 Irwin L. Goldstein, *Training in Organizations* (Pacific Grove, CA: Brooks Cole Publishing, 1993).

45 K. Galvin, "Texaco Settlement with Female Staff to Cost $3 million," *Arizona Republic*, January 7, 1999, p. D-1.

46 Cynthia D. Fisher, Lyle F. Schoenfeldt, and James B. Shaw, *Human Resources Management*, 4th edition (Boston, MA: Houghton Mifflin, 1999), p. 394.

47 Zandy B. Leibowitz, "Designing Career Development Systems: Principles and Practices," *Human Resource Planning*, Vol. 10, No. 4, 1987, pp. 195–207.

48 J. E. A. Russell, "Career Development Interventions in Organizations," *Journal of Vocational Behavior*, Vol. 38, 1991, pp. 237–287.

49 R. A. Noe, "An investigation of the determinants of successful assigned mentoring relationships," *Personnel Psychology*, Vol. 41, 1988, pp. 457–479.

50 Cynthia D. Fisher, Lyle F. Schoenfeldt, and James B. Shaw, *Human Resources Management*, 4th edition (Boston, MA: Houghton Mifflin, 1999), p. 411.

51 Luis R. Gómez-Mejia, David B. Balkin, and Robert L. Cardy, *Managing Human Resources*, 5th edition (Upper Saddle River, NJ: Pearson, 2007), p. 251.

52 Jeanne C. Meister, "The Brave New World of Corporate Education," *The Chronicle of Higher Education*, February 9, 2001, http://chronicle.com.ezp-prod1.hul.harvard.edu/article/The-Brave-New-World-of/17032/, accessed October 30, 2012.

53 McDonald's, "Hamburger University," http://www.aboutmcdonalds.com/mcd/corporate_careers/training_and_development/hamburger_university.html, accessed September 2012.

54 Georgia T. Chao, "Unstructured Training and Development: The Role of Organizational Socialization," *Improving Training Effectiveness in Work Organizations*, J. K. Ford et al., eds. (Mahwah, NJ: Lawrence Erlbaum Associates, 1997), pp. 129–151.

55 K. Tyler, "Do the Right Thing," *HR Magazine*, Vol. 50, No. 2, February 1, 2005.

56 T. G. Gutteridge, Z. B. Leibowitz, and J. E. Shore, *Organizational Career Development: Benchmarks for Building a World-Class Workforce* (Silver Springs, MD: Conceptual Systems, 1993).

57 Manuel London and Richard W. Beatty, "360-Degree Feedback as a Competitive Advantage," *Human Resource Management*, Vol. 32, No. 2–3, Summer/Fall 1993, pp. 353–372; and Walter W. Tornow, "Editor's Note: Introduction to Special Issue on 360-Degree Feedback," *Human Resource Management*, Vol. 32, No. 2–3, Summer/Fall 1993, pp. 211–219.

58 David A. Waldman, Leanne E. Atwater, and David Antonioni, "Has 360 Degree Feedback Gone Amok?," *The Academy of Management Executive*, Vol. 12, No. 2, 1998, pp. 86–94; and Ginka Toegel and Jay A. Conger, "360-Degree Assessment: Time for Reinvention," *Center for Effective Organizations CEO Publication G 03-17(445)*, May 2003.

59 William L. Mihal and Janet L. Graumenz, "An Assessment of the Accuracy of Self-Assessment for Career Decision Making," *Journal of Vocational Behavior*, Vol. 25, 1984, pp. 245–253.

60 Manuel London and Richard W. Beatty, "360-Degree Feedback as a Competitive Advantage," *Human Resource Management*, Vol. 32, No. 2–3, Summer/Fall 1993, pp. 353–372; and Walter W. Tornow, "Editor's Note: Introduction to Special Issue on 360-Degree Feedback," *Human Resource Management*, Vol. 32, No. 2–3, Summer/Fall 1993, pp. 211–219.

61 David A. Waldman, Leanne E. Atwater, and David Antonioni, "Has 360 Degree Feedback Gone Amok?," *The Academy of Management Executive*, Vol. 12, No. 2, 1998, pp. 86–94; and H. J. Barnardin and R. W. Beatty, "Subordinate Appraisals to Enhance Managerial Productivity," *Sloan Management Review*, Vol. 28, 1987, pp. 63–74.

62 William W. Tornow, "Editor's Note: Introduction to Special Issue on 360-Degree Feedback," *Human Resources Management*, Vol. 32, No. 2–3, Summer/Fall 1993, pp. 211–219; D. M. Pollack and I. J. Pollack, "Using 360 Degree Feedback in Performance Appraisal," *Public Personnel Management*, Vol. 25, 1996, pp. 507–528; J. E. Jones and W. L. Bearley, *360 Degree Feedback: Strategies, Tactics and Techniques for Developing Leaders* (Amherst, MA: HRD Press, 1996); M. Dalton, "When the Purpose of Using Multi-Rater Feedback is Behavior Change," *Should 360-Degree Feedback be Used Only for*

Developmental Purposes?, D. Bracken, M. Dalton, R. Jacko, C. McCauley, and V. Pollman, eds. (Greensboro, NC: Center for Creative Leadership, 1997); V. Pollman, "Some Faulty Assumptions that Support Using Multi-Rater Feedback for Performance Appraisal," *Should 360-Degree Feedback be Used Only for Developmental Purposes?*, D. Bracken, M. Dalton, R. Jacko, C. McCauley, and V. Pollman, eds. (Greensboro, NC: Center for Creative Leadership, 1997); and A. DeNisi and A. Kluger, "Feedback Effectiveness: Can 360-degree Feedback Appraisals be Improved?," *Academy of Management Executive*, Vol. 14, No. 1, 2000, pp. 129–139.

[63] M. London and J. Smither, "Can multisource feedback change perceptions of goal accomplishment, self-evaluations and performance related outcomes? Theory-based applications and directions for research," *Personnel Psychology*, Vol. 48, 1995, pp. 803–839.

[64] Mark R. Edwards and Ann J. Ewen, "How to Manage Performance and Pay With 360-Degree Feedback," *Compensation and Benefits Review*, Vol. 28, May/June 1996, pp. 41–46; and Lauren Keller Johnson, "The Ratings Game: Retooling 360s for Better Performance," *Harvard Management Update*, January 2004, pp. 3–5.

[65] David A. Waldman, Leanne E. Atwater, and David Antonioni, "Has 360 Degree Feedback Gone Amok?," *The Academy of Management Executive*, Vol. 12, No. 2, 1998, pp. 86–94.

[66] Ginka Toegel and Jay A. Conger, "360-Degree Assessment: Time for Reinvention," *Center for Effective Organizations CEO Publication G 03–17(445)*, May 2003; and David A. Waldman, Leanne E. Atwater, and David Antonioni, "Has 360 Degree Feedback Gone Amok?," *The Academy of Management Executive*, Vol. 12, No. 2, 1998, pp. 86–94.

[67] Deloitte, "Global Human Capital Trends 2015," Deloitte University Press, available at http://www2.deloitte.com/us/en/pages/human-capital/articles/introduction-human-capital-trends.html, accessed March 26, 2015.

[68] Edwin A. Locke, "The Ubiquity of the Technique of Goal Setting in Theories of and Approaches to Employee Motivation," *Academy of Management Review*, July 1978, pp. 594–601.

[69] Barnard (1938), Drucker (1954), and Odiorne (1976, 1986) quoted in Robert Rodgers and John E. Hunter, "Impact of Management by Objectives on Organizational Productivity," *Journal of Applied Psychology Monograph*, Vol. 76, No. 2, 1991, pp. 322–336.

[70] Robert N. Anthony, John Dearden, and Norton M. Bedford, *Management Control Systems*, 5th edition (Homewood, IL: R. D. Irwin, 1984), p. 387.

[71] Edwin A. Locke, "The Ubiquity of the Technique of Goal Setting in Theories of and Approaches to Employee Motivation," *Academy of Management Review*, July 1978, pp. 594–601, www.proquest.com, accessed May 2010.

[72] E. A. Locke, L. M. Saari, K. N. Shaw, and G. P. Latham, "Goal Setting and Task Performance, 1969–1980," *Psychological Bulletin*, Vol. 90, No. 1, 1980, pp. 125–1, quoted in Michael Goold and John J. Quinn, "The Paradox of Strategic Controls," *Strategic Management Journal*, Vol. 11, No. 1, 1990, pp. 43–57, www.proquest.com, accessed June 2010.

[73] Anat Drach-Zahavy and Miriam Erez, "Challenge Versus Threat Effects on the Goal-Performance Relationship," *Organizational Behavior and Human Decision Processes*, Vol. 88, 2002, pp. 667–682.

[74] Edwin A. Locke, "The Ubiquity of the Technique of Goal Setting in Theories of and Approaches to Employee Motivation," *Academy of Management Review*, July 1978, pp. 594–601, www.proquest.com, accessed May 2010.

[75] Neil C. Churchill, "Budget Choice: Planning vs. Control," *Harvard Business Review*, July–August 1984.

[76] Robert N. Anthony, John Dearden, and Norton M. Bedford, *Management Control Systems*, 5th edition (Homewood, IL: R. D. Irwin, 1984), p. 392.

[77] Ibid, p. 391.

[78] Neil C. Churchill, "Budget Choice: Planning vs. Control," *Harvard Business Review*, July–August 1984.

[79] Neil C. Churchill, "Budget Choice: Planning vs. Control," *Harvard Business Review*, July–August 1984; and Robert N. Anthony, John Dearden, and Norton M. Bedford, *Management Control Systems*, 5th edition (Homewood, IL: R. D. Irwin, 1984), p. 391.

[80] James P. Guthrie, "Alternative Pay Practices and Employee Turnover: An Organization Economics Perspective," *Group & Organization Management*, Vol. 25, No. 4, 2000, pp. 419–439.

[81] Luis R. Gomez-Mejia, "Structure and Process of Diversification, Compensation Strategy, and Firm Performance," *Strategic Management Journal*, Vol. 13, 1992, pp. 381–397.

[82] Edilberto F. Montemayor, "Congruence Between Pay Policy and Competitive Strategy in High-Performing Firms," *Journal of Management*, Vol. 22, No. 6, 1996, pp. 889–908.

[83] James P. Guthrie, "Alternative Pay Practices and Employee Turnover: An Organization Economics Perspective," *Group & Organization Management*, Vol. 25, No. 4, 2000, pp. 419–439; Edilberto F. Montemayor, "Congruence Between Pay Policy and Competitive Strategy in High-Performing Firms," *Journal of Management*, Vol. 22, No. 6, 1996, pp. 889–908; and Luis R. Gomez-Mejia, "Structure and Process of Diversification, Compensation Strategy, and Firm Performance," *Strategic Management Journal*, Vol. 13, 1992, pp. 381–397.

[84] James P. Guthrie, "Alternative Pay Practices and Employee Turnover: An Organization Economics Perspective," *Group & Organization Management*, Vol. 25, No. 4, 2000, pp. 419–439.

[85] James P. Guthrie, "Alternative Pay Practices and Employee Turnover: An Organization Economics Perspective," *Group & Organization Management*, Vol. 25, No. 4, 2000, pp. 419–439; and Luis R. Gomez-Mejia, Theresa M. Welbourne, and Robert M. Wiseman, "The Role of Risk-Sharing and Risk Taking under Gainsharing," *The Academy of Management Review*, Vol. 25, No. 3, 2000, pp. 492–507.

[86] James P. Guthrie, "Alternative Pay Practices and Employee Turnover: An Organization Economics Perspective," *Group & Organization Management*, Vol. 25, No. 4, 2000, pp. 419–439.

[87] Theresa M. Welbourne and Luis R. Gomez Mejia, "Gainsharing: A Critical Review and a Future Research Agenda," *CAHRS Working Paper #95-10* (Ithaca, NY: Cornell University, School of Industrial and Labor Relations, Center for Advanced Human Resource Studies, 1995).

[88] Luis R. Gomez-Mejia, Theresa M. Welbourne, and Robert M. Wiseman, "The Role of Risk-Sharing and Risk Taking under Gainsharing," *The Academy of Management Review*, Vol. 25, No. 3, 2000, pp. 492–507.

[89] Ibid.

[90] Luis R. Gomez-Mejia, Theresa M. Welbourne, and Robert M. Wiseman, "The Role of Risk-Sharing and Risk Taking under Gainsharing," *The Academy of Management*

Review, Vol. 25, No. 3, 2000, pp. 492–507; and James P. Guthrie, "Alternative Pay Practices and Employee Turnover: An Organization Economics Perspective," *Group & Organization Management*, Vol. 25, No. 4, 2000, pp. 419–439.

91 Lauren Weber, "Benefits Matter," *Wall Street Journal*, April 4, 2012.

92 "Employer Costs for Employee Compensation–September 2014," Bureau of Labor Statistics, U.S. Department of Labor, December 10, 2014, http://www.bls.gov/news.release/pdf/ecec.nr0.htm, accessed March 23, 2015.

93 Frank E. Kuzmits, "Communicating Benefits: A Double-Click Away," *Compensation & Benefits Review*, Vol. 30, 1998, pp. 60–64.

94 Karen Wey Smola and Charlotte D. Sutton, "Generational Differences: Revisiting Generational Work Values for the New Millennium," *Journal of Organizational Behavior*, Vol. 23, 2002, pp. 363–382.

95 Teresa M. Amabile, "The Motivation for Creativity in Organizations," Harvard Business School Note No. 9-396-240 (Boston, MA: HBS Publishing, 1996).

96 Sylvia Ann Hewlett, Laura Sherbin, and Karen Sumberg, "How Gen Y and Boomers Will Reshape Your Agenda," *Harvard Business Review*, July–August 2009.

97 Karen Wey Smola and Charlotte D. Sutton, "Generational Differences: Revisiting Generational Work Values for the New Millennium," *Journal of Organizational Behavior*, Vol. 23, 2002, pp. 363–382.

98 Sylvia Ann Hewlett, Laura Sherbin, and Karen Sumberg, "How Gen Y and Boomers Will Reshape Your Agenda," *Harvard Business Review*, July–August 2009.

99 Karen Wey Smola and Charlotte D. Sutton, "Generational Differences: Revisiting Generational Work Values for the New Millennium," *Journal of Organizational Behavior*, Vol. 23, 2002, p. 380.

100 B. W. Graham, "The Business Argument for Flexibility," *HR Magazine*, May 1996, pp. 104–110.

101 Ibid.

102 Lucy M. Chan, "Work/Life Integration at IBM," PowerPoint Presentation, May 2, 2011, IBM available at http://webcache.googleusercontent.com/search?q=cache:JsGnSsQyjusJ:globewomen.org/summit/2011/ppt%2520-%2520Lucy%2520Chan.ppt+&cd=4&hl=en&ct=clnk&gl=us, accessed March 24, 2015.

103 Ken Dychtwald, Tamara J. Erickson, and Robert Morison, "Flexible Work Arrangements: Why You Need Them and How to Make Them Work," *Workforce Crisis: How to Beat the Coming Shortage of Skills and Talent* (Boston, MA: HBS Publishing, 2007), p. 7.

104 R. W. Griffen, *Management*, 9th edition (New York, NY: Houghton Mifflin, 2008).

105 Ken Dychtwald, Tamara J. Erickson, and Robert Morison, "Flexible Work Arrangements: Why You Need Them and How to Make Them Work," *Workforce Crisis: How to Beat the Coming Shortage of Skills and Talent* (Boston, MA: HBS Publishing, 2007), p. 7.

106 "Abbott Laboratories Recognized as One of the Top 10 Best Places to Work for Mothers Nationwide," *PR Newswire*, September 24, 2002; and Ken Dychtwald, Tamara J. Erickson, and Robert Morison, "Flexible Work Arrangements: Why You Need Them and How to Make Them Work," *Workforce Crisis: How to Beat the Coming Shortage of Skills and Talent* (Boston, MA: HBS Publishing, 2007), pp. 13–14.

107 J. P. West, "Employee-Friendly Policies and Development Benefits for Millennials," in *Managing Human Resources for the Millennial Generation* eds. William I. Sauser, Jr. and Ronald R. Sims (Charlotte, NC: Information Age Publishing, 2012), p. 209.

108 Ibid.

109 AT&T, "Work/Life Balance," available at http://about.att.com/content/csr/home/issue-brief-builder/people/work-life-balance.html, accessed March 24, 2015.

110 Nicholas Bloom, James Liang, John Roberts, and Zhichun Jenny Ying, "Does Working from Home Work? Evidence from a Chinese Experiment," Stanford University Draft Research Paper, July 2012.

111 Luis R. Gómez-Mejia, David B. Balkin, and Robert L. Cardy, *Managing Human Resources*, 5th edition (Upper Saddle River, NJ: Pearson, 2007), p. 185.

112 J. Taylor, "Avoid Avoidable Turnover," *Workforce*, April 1999.

113 Luis R. Gómez-Mejia, David B. Balkin, and Robert L. Cardy, *Managing Human Resources*, 5th edition (Upper Saddle River, NJ: Pearson, 2007), p. 187.

114 Steven H. Appelbaum, Claude Delage, Nadia Labib, and George Gault, "The Survivor Syndrome: Aftermath of Downsizing," *Career Development International*, Vol. 2, No. 6, 1997, pp. 278–286.

115 Kim S. Cameron, "Strategies for Successful Organizational Downsizing," *Human Resource Management*, Vol. 33, No. 2, 1994, pp. 189–211.

116 Ibid.

117 R. G. Ehrenberg and G. H Jakubson, "Advance Notification of Plant Closing: Does it Matter?," *Industrial Relations*, Vol. 28, No. 1, 1989, pp. 60–71.

118 Luis R. Gómez-Mejia, David B. Balkin, and Robert L. Cardy, *Managing Human Resources*, 5th edition (Upper Saddle River, NJ: Pearson, 2007), p. 196.

119 Rocki-Lee DeWitt, "The Structural Consequences of Downsizing," *Organization Science*, Vol. 4, No. 1, 1993, pp. 30–40.

120 Joel Brockner, "Managing the Effects of Layoffs on Survivors," *California Management Review*, Vol. 34, No. 2, 1992, pp. 9–28; and Steven H. Appelbaum, Claude Delage, Nadia Labib, and George Gault, "The Survivor Syndrome: Aftermath of Downsizing," *Career Development International*, Vol. 2, No. 6, 1997, pp. 278–286.

121 R. Henkoff, "Cost-Cutting: How to Do It Right," *Fortune*, April 9, 1990.

122 Steven H. Appelbaum, Claude Delage, Nadia Labib, and George Gault, "The Survivor Syndrome: Aftermath of Downsizing," *Career Development International*, Vol. 2, No. 6, 1997, pp. 278–286; and William McKinley, Carol M. Sanchez, Allen G. Schick, and A. Catherine Higgs, "Organizational Downsizing: Constraining, Cloning, Learning (and Executive Commentary)," *The Academy of Management Executive*, Vol. 9, No. 3, 1995, pp. 32–44.

123 J. Brockner, R. L. DeWitt, S. Grover, and T. Reed, "When it is Especially Important to Explain Why: Factors Affecting the Relationship between Managers' Explanations of a Layoff and Survivors' Reactions to the Layoff," *Journal of Experimental Social Psychology*, Vol. 26, 1990, pp. 389–407; and J. Brockner, B. M. Wiesenfeld, T. F. Reed, S. Grover, and C. Martin, "Interactive Effect of Job Content and Context on the Reactions of Layoff Survivors," *Journal of Personality and Social Psychology*, Vol. 64, 1993, pp. 187–197.

124 U.S. Department of Labor, "Fair Labor Standards Act of 1938," http://www.dol.gov/whd/regs/statutes/FairLaborStandAct.pdf, accessed August 2012.

125 National Archives, "The Civil Rights Act of 1964 and the Equal Employment Opportunity Commission," http://www.

archives.gov/education/lessons/civil-rights-act/, accessed September 2012.

126 U.S. Equal Employment Opportunity Commission, "Laws & Guidance," http://www.eeoc.gov/laws/index.cfm, accessed September 2012.

127 U.S. Bureau of Labor Statistics, "Union Members—2014," January 23, 2015 available at http://www.bls.gov/news.release/union2.nr0.htm, accessed March 23, 2015.

128 James N. Baron and David M. Kreps, *Strategic Human Resources: Frameworks for General Managers* (Hoboken, NJ: Wiley and Sons, 1999), p. 121.

129 Steven L. Premack and John E. Hunter, "Individual Unionization Decisions," *Psychological Bulletin*, Vol. 103, No. 2, 1998, pp. 223–234.

130 Richard B. Freeman and James L. Medoff, *What do Unions Do?* (New York: Basic Books, 1984).

131 "Suddenly, Made in USA Looks Like a Strategy," *Bloomberg Businessweek*, March 28–April 3, 2011; and Andrew Ward, "Made in America? Why More of Your Clothes Soon Might Be," *Daily Finance*, August 25, 2014 available at http://www.dailyfinance.com/2014/08/25/made-in-america-why-more-of-your-clothes-soon-might-be/.

132 Steven Tadelis, "The Innovative Organization: Creating Value Through Outsourcing," *California Review Management*, Vol. 50, 2007, p. 264.

133 Richard H. K. Vietor and Alexander Veytsman, "American Outsourcing," Harvard Business School Case No. 9-705-037, rev. February 2, 2007 (Boston, MA: HBS Publishing, 2005), p. 2.

134 Ibid.

135 Ravi Aron and Jitendra V. Singh, "Getting Offshoring Right," *Harvard Business Review*, December 2005.

136 U.S. Department of State, "2000 Country Reports on Human Rights Practices," www.state.gov/g/drl/rls/hrrpt/2000, accessed October 2005.

137 Christopher A. Bartlett, Vincent Dessain, and Anders Sjöman, "IKEA's Global Sourcing Challenge: Indian Rugs and Child Labor (B)," Harvard Business School Case No. 9-906-414, rev. November 14, 2006 (Boston, MA: HBS Publishing, 2006), p. 1.

138 U.S. Bureau of Labor Statistics, "Employee Turnover in 2014," September 18, 2014 available at http://www.bls.gov/news.release/pdf/tenure.pdf, accessed March 24, 2015.

139 Peter F. Drucker, "Managing Oneself," *Harvard Business Review*, January 2005.

140 Boris Groysberg and Robin Abrahams, "Five Ways to Bungle a Job Change" *Harvard Business Review*, January 2010.

CHAPTER

10

Performance Management

Learning Objectives

After reading this chapter, you should be able to:

LO1 Describe the four stages of the control cycle and how the control cycle is used to assess the performance of a firm.

LO2 Explain how the balanced scorecard and its associated components are used in performance management systems.

LO3 Outline the various ways in which a firm can set performance targets.

LO4 Describe how a firm can monitor and measure its performance across multiple dimensions.

LO5 Explain the corrective actions that managers can make to improve organizational performance.

SELF-REFLECTION

How Do You Manage Your Performance?

Effective management entails knowing the results you want to produce and creating a plan to yield those results. Assess your ability to use performance management to produce results. Please respond True or False to the following statements:

1. When starting a project, I begin with the end in mind.

2. When setting goals, I identify targets that may stretch my abilities but develop my skills.

3. I use tools, dashboards, or scorecards to manage my performance.

4. When working on an assignment, I have internal control systems that I use to stay on task and monitor my progress.

5. I believe that focusing on quality is an important aspect of managing my performance.

6. When setting a goal, I create linkages between my vision, strategy, and performance.

7. When working on a task, I benchmark best practices so that I can learn how to improve my performance.

8. When managing my personal performance, I adapt to the situation or the environment.

9. I use a diversity of metrics to measure performance.

10. I seek feedback to evaluate and improve my performance.

If you responded True to most of the statements, you have the ability to produce results by focusing on performance management.

INTRODUCTION

While an organization's strategy is usually formulated by top executives, others in the organization are responsible for its implementation. It may seem like a daunting task to take simple ideas, summarized in just a few sentences, and use them to generate activity for an entire organization. But in business, as in life, measurements are the most effective way to understand if you are accomplishing the right goals. The underlying linchpin to success is choosing the correct measurements. If done well, performance measures will support an organization's strategy by allowing managers to understand the implications of their actions and tactics.[1]

To understand how performance management works, we must understand it in the context of the organization, which can be conceptualized as an engine. A car engine undergoes a complex series of actions including the orchestration of moving parts that, when timed to perfection, propel a vehicle down the road. But if you look at a car from a distance, it is simply a metal object that takes an input—gasoline—and transforms it into an end product—motion. A business operates in the same way and can be broken down into three parts: inputs, transformation, and outputs.

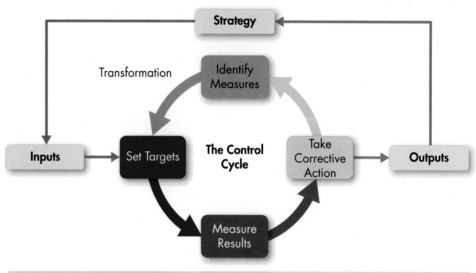

Source: Reprinted from *Accounting, Organizations and Society*, Vol. 8, 1983, pp. 153–169. Eric G. Flamholtz, "Accounting, Budgeting, and Control Systems in Their Organizational Context: Theoretical and Empirical Perspectives," with permission from Elsevier.

While businesses look simple from a macro view, they consist of complex systems that work together to transform inputs into outputs. The **control cycle**, a four-stage process (see Figure 10.1), provides the mechanisms and systems that monitor the transformation process, ensuring that outputs are produced to the desired quality, quantity, and specifications of an organization and its customers.

The control cycle includes four key activities: (1) identifying measures that track the right information to assess the performance of the company; (2) setting targets for the selected measures; (3) monitoring performance against the selected measures; and (4) taking corrective action when performance does not meet expectations. Corrective actions often influence the future measures that are identified to assess the performance of the organization. Each section of this chapter is dedicated to one of the four stages of the control cycle. Like most concepts described in this book, management control and performance management are not prescriptions for well-defined plans: no universal system can be applied to all organizations. Approaches will differ based on specific local and organizational cultures.[2] Managers must be thoughtful and creative to understand their organization and use the correct tools that fit their context. As managers design control systems, it is important that they ask the following questions: Is it relevant? Does it work? How well does it work?[3]

The following case shows how Shell reevaluated and reconceptualized its strategy and used techniques of the control cycle to implement it.

Control cycle
The four-stage process that provides the mechanisms and systems to monitor the transformation process, ensuring that outputs are produced to the desired quality, quantity, and specifications of an organization and its customers.

Creating a New Strategy: Sustainable Development at Shell

For years, Royal Dutch Shell was proud of its financial performance and core set of business principles, which outlined a comprehensive road map for serving a variety of constituents. But during the mid-1990s, Shell experienced two major controversies that contributed to a collapsing public image.[4] The first occurred in early 1995. Shell was going to retire one of its oil storage buoys, the Brent

Spar, by sinking it in the North Atlantic Ocean. Just before executing the plan, it received significant public criticism from Greenpeace, sparking international media attention. Activist criticism turned into public protests, including the destruction of several Shell service stations in Germany.

Shortly after the Brent Spar incident, Shell found itself in the middle of another public controversy. The company operated heavily in oil-rich Nigeria. At the time, a human rights activist, environmentalist, and leader of a local tribe was detained by the government and eventually executed. Because Shell continued investment and operations in the region, it was again criticized by the public and the media. These two incidents forced Shell to reassess its business practices, its relationship with its stakeholders, and, ultimately, its strategy.[5]

Determined to define a new strategy, Shell conducted a widespread survey of key stakeholders from around the world, including nongovernmental organizations (NGOs), academics, local community leaders, and government bodies from 14 countries. Shell followed up with a survey of 7,500 people from the general public in 10 countries, 1,300 opinion leaders in 25 countries, and 600 Shell employees in 55 countries. Results showed that customers expected the company to move from a "trust me" attitude to a "show me" attitude, as stakeholders wanted to see that Shell was living up to high environmental and social standards as well as financial metrics.[6]

By 1997, a new strategy emerged. Shell created the Sustainability Development Group (SDG), which was focused on attaining sustainability and delivering three components to the company: an annual Shell report that described economic, social, and environmental performance; the Sustainable Development Management Framework (SDMF), which promoted sustainability practices and described how to implement the SDMF in business units worldwide; and the definition of key performance indicators (KPIs) to monitor performance.

Photofusion Picture Library/Alamy

Shell's 1998 annual report provided information on sustainability initiatives to key stakeholders, and it was sent to shareholders, NGOs, academics, governments, employees, and the socially responsible investment community. The 1998 report restructured the content to focus on the three pillars of its sustainable development strategy: financial, environmental, and social performance. It also included a 5-year strategy for certain targets and explained how the company would achieve those targets.[7] As the years went by, Shell improved its measures and processes. By 2001, Shell gathered reliable data from all of its core businesses in all parts of the world and verified it with third-party organizations.

The annual report was the most important instrument for transparency between Shell and its stakeholders.[8]

The SDMF was a tool used to introduce strategy objectives to all business units. Senior managers created manuals with an interactive guide to implement the framework and sent SDG employees as consultants, promoting communication between managers and higher level strategists. But upper-level management understood that it could not push the framework from the top and introduced the SDMF to each of its 3,500 managers worldwide, allowing them to use their own methods to incorporate it into their businesses. By giving each manager the autonomy to adapt and implement the framework, each manager was allowed to balance all of his or her resources to achieve strategic objectives.[9] To facilitate adoption across businesses, senior executives encouraged managers to share best practices.[10]

The KPIs served as a platform to set targets, measure performance, and drive continuous improvement. Focused on strategic success, the KPIs were quantitative and qualitative measurements that balanced short-term goals with long-term needs and were critically important to both internal priorities and external concerns.[11] After an iterative process of narrowing down KPIs, Shell created a set of 16 KPIs, 11 of which were completely new measurements for the company.[12] While Shell continued to measure return on capital, total shareholder return, and greenhouse gas emissions, it introduced new KPIs such as reputation, social and environmental performance, and integrity to address its new strategic direction.

When all was said and done, senior managers at Shell had successfully undertaken one of the largest initiatives by a major energy company to balance financial, environmental, and social performance; incorporate it into its strategy; implement the strategy throughout the company; and track the implementation with a comprehensive performance management system.[13]

Case in Point   Creating a New Strategy: Sustainable Development at Shell

1. Why did the Brent Spar incident redefine Shell's strategy?
2. What stakeholders did Shell engage with to redefine its strategy?
3. How did the process of redefining Shell's strategy link to performance management?
4. How does Shell monitor and communicate the attainment of performance objectives?

IDENTIFYING MEASURES

Shell identified several KPIs that, when implemented correctly, helped the organization become the first in the industry to succeed in incorporating environmental and social aspects into its strategy. Managers have long known that "if you can't measure it, you can't manage it," and measurements serve a dual purpose.[14] Although they help managers assess past performance, they also guide future **behavior**.[15] In business, only two things can be observed, measured, and monitored: behavior and **outputs**. While behavior refers to the actions and decisions of individual employees, outputs are the products and/or services that an organization produces. Outputs can be specified for an entire organization, such as the number of laptops manufactured by Apple, or for departments of an organization, such as the number of software updates for the iTunes division. While outputs are quantifiable and controlled from a central office, behavior is more flexible and diverse; therefore, it is controlled and measured at the unit or department level.[16] As such, most organizations identify both high level corporate measures of success as well as department, function, or team measures of success. Sometimes corporate measures need to be translated into team measures. In other instances, teams have their own unique measures.

For much of the twentieth century, businesses relied heavily on financial numbers to measure success, such as return on investment and profit. These financial metrics are still important today, but so are other measures (e.g., quality, rate of innovation, customer satisfaction, and employee engagement). More recently, executives have emphasized nonfinancial measures (e.g., sustainability and social impact) to complement financial measures and encourage a more balanced perspective.[17] Despite its value, measuring data such as employee attitudes or research and development (R&D) activity can be challenging; as a result, they often do not get measured.[18] But companies are now developing meaningful metrics to assess their performance in light of their strategic goals. By far, the most popular metric is the balanced scorecard with a reported 60% of *Fortune 1000* companies experimenting with one.[19]

Behavior
The actions and decisions of individual employees.

Outputs
The products and/or services that an organization produces.

The Balanced Scorecard

The **balanced scorecard** was created to help businesses translate strategy into action by identifying the most critical measures to drive business success and by linking long-term strategic goals with short-term operational actions.[20] The primary advantage of using a balanced scorecard, however, is that it helps managers create a set of quantitative and qualitative measurements that are related and mutually reinforcing, known as **cause–effect relationships**. It allows companies to quickly look at failures and isolate what may be their root cause. At the same time, it also allows them to understand the source of their successes. With 25–30 measurements, the balanced scorecard is often a complement to the traditional measures that companies use to monitor their health.

Depending on the size and scope of the company, the balanced scorecard can be used to assess the performance of the company as a whole, or it can be used to assess one business unit or division. For example, GE operates in many businesses, ranging from aircraft engines to healthcare imaging, each with a different strategy. If GE chooses to adopt the balanced scorecard, it would need to create a unique scorecard for each of its business units. A smaller company, on the other hand, may have a single strategy for the entire firm, thus needing only one balanced scorecard. Using four different perspectives—financial, customer, business process, and learning and growth—the balanced scorecard aligns the goals of an organization with the day-to-day action of individual employees (see Figure 10.2).

Financial Perspective

The **financial perspective** involves choosing the financial measurements that are most important for reaching strategic goals. Key financial measurements include net income, cost of goods sold, administrative expenses, inventory management, accounts receivable, return on equity, and return on assets.[21]

New financial measurements have been developed to complement conventional measures including **activity-based costing (ABC)**, which provides a more accurate view of the costs to develop products. ABC is the accounting system used to assess the specific cost components of producing a product or service. ABC links production to a series of activities and assigns a cost to each activity,[22] providing a more accurate picture of how to minimize these expenses.[23] We will review some of the most important financial measures in greater detail in the section on Monitoring and Measuring Performance.

Balanced scorecard
A method created to help businesses translate strategy into action by identifying the most critical measures to drive business success and linking long-term strategic goals with short-term operational actions; it uses four perspectives (financial, customer, business process, and learning and growth).

Cause–effect relationships
A set of quantitative and qualitative measurements that are related and mutually reinforcing.

Financial perspective
Choosing the financial measurements that are most important for reaching strategic goals.

Activity-based costing (ABC)
The accounting system used to assess the specific cost components of producing a product or service.

Figure 10.2 Four Perspectives of the Balanced Scorecard

Source: Adapted from Robert S. Kaplan and David P. Norton, "Linking the Balanced Scorecard to Strategy," *California Management Review*, Vol. 39, No. 1, Fall 1996, p. 54.

Al Freni//Time Life Pictures/Getty Images

Customer Perspective

The **customer perspective** links key customer-based metrics such as market share and customer retention to the financial performance of a firm. The customer perspective of the balanced scorecard is used by managers to identify the most important customers of the business and to measure how well the company is doing in meeting or exceeding these customers' needs. For the balanced scorecard to be valuable, measurements from the customer perspective must link directly to financial results or strategic goals. While the list included in Table 10.1 is not exhaustive, it covers the most important customer-based measurements.

In addition to the general customer metrics, firms should also understand customer **value propositions**, which drive many of the outcomes described in Table 10.1. Value propositions refer to the quantitative or qualitative aspects of products or services that customers value most.[24] Each major customer segment will value different things, and it is up to the company to determine those core drivers of success. Companies should try to understand what customers most value, and how well they are delivering that value.

Sometimes the implications of making specific marketing and operational choices are clear. For instance, it didn't take long for the management at Coca-Cola to learn that the introduction of New Coke was based on an imperfect understanding of consumer preferences. For nearly a century, Coca-Cola was not just the market leader of soft drinks, it was an American icon. The original formula for Coca-Cola, conceived in the nineteenth century, was the backbone of its worldwide reputation, and company leaders vowed never to change it, regardless of local tastes and cultures. But during the 1980s, Pepsi ran a successful marketing campaign, known as "The Pepsi Challenge," that slowly chiseled away at Coca-Cola's market leadership. After Pepsi commercials showed that consumers preferred Pepsi in blind taste tests, Coca-Cola confirmed the findings with its own nationwide taste test.

Believing that it was working with solid data, Coca-Cola changed its formula to mimic Pepsi with a smoother and sweeter taste. Many consumers were outraged, and the company received thousands of angry phone calls and letters. The public outrage lasted for 3 months and transcended nations and cultures. The opposition to the change was so strong that Coca-Cola brought back the old formula and renamed it "Classic Coke." It took years before Coca-Cola was able to regain its status as a market leader and worldwide icon.[25] This incident illustrates the importance of using and analyzing the right measures to make significant strategic choices as well as the importance of drawing the right conclusions from the data.

As Coca-Cola learned, organizations must excel at implementing their strategy, analyzing the business environment, and adjusting tactics when new threats or opportunities are discovered.[26] Meanwhile, they must continuously improve their operational performance to ensure that their organizational design choices match their strategic objectives.[27]

Internal Business Process Perspective

The **business process perspective** focuses on the manner in which the company runs its operations. For instance, does the manufacturing operation run smoothly? Is

Customer perspective
Linking key customer-based metrics such as market share and retention to the financial performance of a firm.

Value propositions
Quantitative and qualitative aspects of products or services that customers value most.

Business process perspective
Focuses on the manner in which a company runs its operations.

Market Share	The percent of the target market who are customers of a firm.
Account Share	This is a share of the target customer's wallet. Consumers spend money on many different items spanning several industries to support their needs. Some companies find it valuable to monitor the amount customers spend on their products relative to all other products.[29]
Customer Retention	An easy way to maintain or increase market share is to retain existing customers. Many companies also track customer loyalty by measuring the percentage growth of business with existing customers.[30]
New Customer Acquisition	This metric is measured in two ways: the number of new customers and the total sales to new customers.[31]
Customer Satisfaction	This is one of the most important metrics, but also the most subjective and qualitative. Customer satisfaction is often measured with feedback surveys.[32] Recent research has shown that customers perform repeat purchases only when they rate their experience as extremely satisfying.[33]
Customer Profitability	Although it is good to have happy and satisfied customers, they should also be profitable for a business. Newly acquired customers can seem unprofitable due to high acquisition costs, but measures of lifetime profitability can be used to decide whether to acquire a specific set of customers.[34]

Table 10.1 > Various Customer Metrics

the company meeting product quality standards in an efficient and cost-effective way? Are customer service calls handled expeditiously? The company can't produce strong financial results or deliver value to customers if they cannot run their operations effectively and efficiently. With the balanced scorecard, managers identify the most important business processes to achieve the best results.[28]

Learning and Growth Perspective

The final component of the balanced scorecard, the **learning and growth perspective** identifies the infrastructure and skills needed to carry out business processes, interact with customers, and achieve long-term financial growth. It also helps to identify gaps in capabilities or resources.[35] Organizational learning and growth stem from employee measurements, information systems, and employee motivation. Managers often measure employee satisfaction, productivity, and retention to better understand employee issues or concerns.[36] Information systems stimulate learning and growth by giving employees the necessary information to be effective and innovative. The key to this perspective is fostering an environment that is conducive to learning. Managers must make time for reflection and analysis and train employees in brainstorming, problem solving, and evaluating experiments.[37]

Implementing the Balanced Scorecard

Implementing a balanced scorecard can often require a company to change the way it operates. Because each company has a different history, culture, mission, vision, and strategy, the employees look at the balanced scorecard through a different lens. One aspect of the scorecard may be more important than another for specific businesses. For example, a company that is focused on innovation and new product introduction may heavily emphasize the learning and growth perspective. A different company that is in an entrenched, highly competitive market for commodities may emphasize the business process perspective to drive production efficiency. The following case study illustrates how one company has chosen to implement the balanced scorecard.

Learning and growth perspective
Identifies the infrastructure and skills needed to carry out business processes, interact with customers, and achieve long-term financial growth; it also helps to identify gaps in capabilities or resources.

The Sustainability Scorecard at Amanco

Water is the world's most abundant resource, and yet it is still elusive to many people in the world. As of 2005, there were still 1.1 billion people without access to drinking water and 2.6 billion who had insufficient sanitation. Water is critical for more than just human health. It also drives long-term economic development and environmental sustainability.[38] As a result, water services presented a multibillion dollar global market, and the Latin American company Amanco was in the ideal position to capitalize on it.[39]

Amanco was a major producer of plastic piping and accessories for water systems throughout South America.[40] The company worked with clients to manage the complete water cycle—from extraction and distribution to collection and waste management. Although Amanco obtained the highest market share in the industry and operated on a global scale, it had to constantly improve its operations to remain competitive. While it developed new materials, production prices increased and local companies offered substitutes for its products.[41] Amanco wanted to be known as a socially responsible company that provided economic value, ecological efficiency, and strong ethics. As a result, it adopted a "triple bottom line" strategy to promote the following goals.[42]

1. Create economic sustainability in the long run.
2. Generate value through a system of corporate social responsibility.
3. Generate value through environmental management.

To achieve its goals, Amanco adopted the balanced scorecard and modified it to fit its unique company vision. The scorecard had all of the elements of a traditional balanced scorecard, including the financial, customer, business process, and learning perspectives, but it also included a fifth perspective—an environmental and social dimension.

When looking at its business from a financial perspective, Amanco wanted to produce economic value and sustainable revenue. The company achieved this by increasing its sales each year and reducing operating costs.[43] Through the customer perspective, Amanco measured customer satisfaction and product innovation.[44] Through the business process perspective, the company focused on four main areas: branding, customer management, product innovation, and financial management. It identified multiple measurements to improve each of these processes, including measuring the communication between marketing and consumers, ensuring quality deliveries, improving creativity in R&D, and optimizing the purchase of raw materials.[45] The fourth perspective of the balanced scorecard, learning and growth, focused on leadership development, succession planning for managers, and collaboration among employees with different competencies.[46]

Amanco's social and environmental perspective encompassed a broad definition, including employees, local communities, and the industries in which the company competed. Amanco conducted employee satisfaction surveys, measured time lost due to injury, and kept tabs on the percentage of women employed.[47] For environmental effect, it measured per unit inputs and waste from its processes.[48] To improve communities, it measured water savings and increased income from communities that used its products.[49]

During the first 3 years of introducing the new system, Amanco experienced success in all areas of its vision. Each year, profitability, return on net assets, and environmental efficiency improved. Despite the fact that Amanco made sacrifices for social and environmental purposes, its financial earnings still increased by 44% during the first 3 years.[50]

Eyal Nahmias / Alamy

SETTING PERFORMANCE TARGETS

After using the balanced scorecard or another system to identify key measurements, the next step is to set performance targets for those measures. Setting goals and measuring their achievement is a strong motivational force in itself, which becomes more powerful when targets are meaningful and serve a greater purpose.[51] One way that companies set performance targets is by comparing their performance to other companies that are considered best in class in their respective industries.

Benchmarking

The concept of **benchmarking** broadens a manager's perspective to look outside the company, primarily at competitors, to assist with target setting. Benchmarking is the process of collecting data from the industry's best players and using their measures as a goal or guideline. While the goal is to learn how an organization compares to others on specified measures, it has industry-wide benefits. Benchmarking promotes competition and reveals best practices so that they can be analyzed, adopted, and implemented throughout an industry.[52]

Benchmarking also has benefits within an organization. It stimulates an unbiased review of internal operations, reveals problems for which others have found solutions, and provides objective data and targets for improvement.[53] When implemented appropriately, benchmarking includes the following:

- Identifying the processes to benchmark
- Choosing measurement criteria and collecting data
- Finding the best companies for each process
- Analyzing data
- Creating plans for improvement

If a company adopts a rigorous benchmarking program, members of an organization apply all of their energy and ingenuity to improve their performance, in hopes of matching or exceeding their competitors.[54] The most difficult hurdle to overcome is finding other companies to share their processes and data. Few companies regularly collect and share data, making it costly to find useful benchmarking partners.[55] Still, any effort to look outside the company for best practices is useful. While it may be difficult to implement a full benchmarking program, elements can be used effectively with other systems described in this chapter.

One novel technique that some managers are using to benchmark their operations is job swaps. In a job swap, one executive switches jobs with another executive at a different company for a day or a few days. For instance, Dharmesh Shah, the chief technology officer (CTO) of HubSpot.com, an Internet marketing firm, traded jobs with Paul English, the CTO of Kayak.com, an online travel pricing company. Shah hoped to understand how to recruit top engineers to his firm and how to improve customer service. He walked away from the experience with several insights for improving his start-up.[56] Of course, job swaps must be carefully selected. They tend to be useful when there is a lot of trust between the two executives, and the companies are in different, noncompeting industries.

Budgets

For most of the twentieth century, the **budgeting process** was the central control mechanism for organizations because of its ability to integrate all aspects of an organization's activity into a single, coherent summary.[57] It still continues to be used in many organizations today. Budgets are generally created at both the corporate and department or business unit level. A budget typically includes revenue and cost projections for each unit, and these projections are used to allocate resources (e.g., human resources, capital equipment,

Benchmarking
The process of collecting data from the industry's best players and using their numbers as a goal or guideline for evaluating company performance.

Budgeting process
The process for allocating financial resources and measuring expected quantitative and qualitative outcomes of a firm.

and R&D funding) throughout the company. Once approved, budgets are used to measure the performance of a particular unit or department. These measurements generally occur monthly and include a comparison of actual revenue achieved and costs incurred against budgeted expectations. Units that do not perform as expected often must outline the reasons for their underperformance and define a corrective plan of action.

The budgeting process also plays an important role in providing an annual financial yardstick with which to measure progress. Although recent research suggests that some aspects of budgeting can hamper organizational potential, it still remains the primary management system for setting short-term targets, allocating resources, and reviewing performance.[58] Because budgeting is so central to many organizations, and has been used by them for a very long time, managers who want to use contemporary measurement systems such as the balanced scorecard must link the new systems with the old ones. By combining the budget with the balanced scorecard, organizations translate their strategy into scorecard measures and set targets for each measure.[59]

MONITORING AND MEASURING PERFORMANCE

After measures are identified and performance targets are set, the next step in the control cycle is to monitor activity and evaluate performance. **Measurement** is the process of evaluating behaviors and outputs to see whether standards have been met or objectives have been obtained.

The process of measuring can take many forms—from complex systems involving computer programs and databases to simple systems that use Excel spreadsheets. One new approach to measurement is open-book management, a concept in which management shares all of the financial data of a company with all of its employees. In a transparent company, employees have access to accurate information, helping to improve their individual performance. They can also update figures with their own measurements, ensuring speedy and accurate data collection.[60] HCL Technologies, an India-based systems integration firm, uses a vibrant intranet to share financial results and goals throughout the organization.

More common are monthly and quarterly review sessions with senior managers where actual performance results are compared to forecasts, plans, and budgets. As we discussed earlier, these meetings enable the company to track its progress against expected goals. Managers are often expected to explain variances in performance and to outline recommendations for closing gaps. Other measurement systems such as total quality management and Six Sigma are comprehensive processes for monitoring large-scale operations.

Financial Management

The long-term success or failure of a business is determined by its ability to sustain profitability, especially as the business environment changes. As such, it is very important for managers to continually assess the financial performance of the company. Two important financial statements, the **balance sheet** and the **income statement**, are very useful in helping managers monitor and measure the health of the company.

The balance sheet highlights the company's financial position by identifying the assets that the firm controls and the manner in which those assets are financed. In essence, the balance sheet is a summary of the firm's assets and liabilities at a point in time, typically one year. Figure 10.3 shows an example of a balance sheet for the Party in a Box Company, a company that sells prepackaged thematic party supplies. An analysis of the balance sheet can provide insight into how effectively the company utilizes its assets and manages its liabilities.[61]

Measurement
The process of evaluating behaviors and outputs to see whether standards have been met or objectives have been obtained.

Balance sheet
Highlights the company's financial position by identifying the assets that the firm controls and the manner in which those assets are financed.

Income statement
Summarizes the financial performance of the company over a specific period of time, usually monthly, quarterly, or yearly.

	2015	2014	Increase (Decrease)
Assets			
Current Assets			
Cash	$225,000	$192,000	$33,000
Accounts Receivable	218,000	180,000	38,000
Inventory	270,000	210,000	60,000
Prepaid Expenses	55,000	40,000	15,000
Total Current Assets	**768,000**	**622,000**	**146,000**
Fixed Assets			
Plant and Equipment	1,000,000	950,000	50,000
Less Depreciation	145,000	125,000	20,000
Total Fixed Assets	**855,000**	**825,000**	**30,000**
Total Assets	**$1,623,000**	**$1,447,000**	**$176,000**
Liabilities and Owners Equity			
Current Liabilities			
Accounts Payable	$214,000	$180,000	$34,000
Accrued Expenses	67,000	60,000	7,000
Income Taxes Payable	19,000	13,000	6,000
Total Current Liabilities	**300,000**	**253,000**	**47,000**
Long-term Debt	465,000	400,000	65,000
Total Liabilities	**765,000**	**653,000**	**112,000**
Owners Equity			
Contributed Capital	200,000	200,000	-
Retained Earnings	658,000	594,000	64,000
Total Owners Equity	**858,000**	**794,000**	**64,000**
Total Liabilities and Owners Equity	**$1,623,000**	**$1,447,000**	**$176,000**

Figure 10.3 Party in a Box Balance Sheet as of December 31, 2015

A company's assets are classified as either current assets or fixed assets. A company's cash, inventory, and accounts receivables (monies owed to the company from customers or other parties) are examples of current assets. The company's building and equipment are examples of fixed assets. A company's liabilities are classified as either short-term or long-term. Examples of short-term liabilities (also called current liabilities) are accounts payable (monies that the company owes to suppliers and others for items that it has agreed to purchase), income taxes payable, and other accrued expenses. Long-term liabilities include long-term debt or mortgages on property and equipment.

The final major component of the balance sheet is owners' equity, which is the difference between assets and liabilities, and is comprised of retained earnings (monies earned from operations and reinvested in the business) and contributed capital, which is the value of stock of various stockholders in the company. In a balance sheet, assets must be equal to liabilities plus owners' equity. The balance sheet for Party in a Box for 2015 included total assets of $1,623,000, total liabilities of $765,000, and owners' equity of $858,000. To assess the ongoing health of a company, it is often useful to compare balance sheets over time. Figure 10.3 includes the balance sheet for 2014 and 2015 and indicates that the company has been able to increase its retained earnings by $64,000 in one year.

The income statement, often called a profit and loss statement, summarizes the financial performance of the company over a specific period of time, usually monthly, quarterly, or yearly. Unlike the balance sheet, which highlights a company's financial position at one point in time, the income statement reflects cumulative

	2015 Actual	2015 Budget	Variance to Budget	2014 Actual	% Change 2015 v. 2014
Retail Sales	$1,050,000	$975,000	$75,000	$900,000	16.7%
Corporate Sales	650,000	635,000	15,000	575,000	13.0%
Total Sales	1,700,000	1,610,000	90,000	1,475,000	15.3%
Less: Cost of Goods Sold	1,100,000	1,050,000	50,000	1,000,000	10.0%
Gross Profit	600,000	560,000	40,000	475,000	26.3%
Less: Operating Expenses	399,000	405,000	(6,000)	340,000	17.4%
Less: Depreciation	20,000	20,000	–	17,500	14.3%
Earnings Before Interest and Taxes	181,000	135,000	46,000	117,500	54.0%
Less: Interest Expense	65,000	65,000	–	55,250	17.6%
Earnings Before Income Tax	116,000	70,000	46,000	62,250	86.3%
Less: Income Tax	52,000	28,000	24,000	29,500	76.3%
Net Income	**$64,000**	**$42,000**	**$22,000**	**$32,750**	**95.4%**

Figure 10.4 Party in a Box Income Statement for Period Ending December 31, 2015

business results during a specific time frame.[62] The basic elements of an income statement can be simplified into one equation:

$$Revenues - Expenses = Net\ Income\ (or\ Net\ Loss)$$

The basic income statement has three primary components (1) sales or revenue; (2) costs to produce those sales; and (3) other expenses. Figure 10.4 includes an income statement for the Party in a Box Company. The company has two sources of sales—retail sales and corporate sales. Cost of goods sold includes the costs associated with producing the material for the company's sales. For Party in a Box, these costs include the cost of the box as well as the material inside the box. Operating expenses include nonmaterial costs such as expenses for marketing, rent, and accounting services. After deducting expenses for depreciation and taxes, the company is left with either a positive or negative income. Party in Box produced $64,000 in net income in 2015.

To assess the health of a business, managers compare actual profit and loss results to both budgeted expectations and company performance in previous years. As noted in Figure 10.4, Party in a Box exceeded the budgeted sales and income figures for 2015. In fact, the company generated $22,000 more in net income than expected. In addition, the company grew sales by 15% from 2014 and net income by 95%, mostly as a result of reducing its costs of goods sold. This type of analysis helps managers determine how effective the company has been in trying to achieve specific financial and operational objectives.

Key Financial Ratios

While the balance sheet and income statement are good starting points for measuring the financial performance of a company, there are several key financial ratios that can provide a manager with even greater insight. These ratios are also useful in comparing the performance of one company against competitors, which can support the benchmarking process. Some of the most useful ratios are liquidity ratios, profitability ratios, and leverage ratios (see Table 10.2).

Liquidity ratios
Ratios used to assess a firm's ability to meet its current or short-term financial obligations.

Liquidity ratios are used to assess a firm's ability to meet its current or short-term financial obligations. The most common liquidity ratio is the current ratio, which is current assets divided by current liabilities. The higher the ratio, the more protection the company has against liquidity problems.[63] The current ratio for Party in a Box is 2.56 for 2015, which means the company is capable of paying off its

Ratio	Definition	Category
Current Ratio	Current assets / Current liabilities	Liquidity
Profit Margin	Net income / Sales	Profitability
Gross Margin	Gross income / Sales	Profitability
Return on Assets	Net income / Total assets	Profitability
Debt Ratio	Total debt / Total assets	Leverage

Table 10.2 ⟩ Common Financial Ratios

immediate debts 2.56 times. In general, this ratio seems to indicate that Party in a Box is in a relatively strong position to fulfill its short-term debt obligations. Comparing the 2014 and 2015 ratios also shows that the company has improved its performance on this metric.

Profitability ratios are used to assess the firm's profits in relation to the source of those profits including sales and assets. The profit margin ratio, calculated by dividing net income by sales, measures the operating and financial ability of management. For Party in a Box, the profit margin for 2015 was 3.8%, which is relatively low but is an improvement from 2.6% in 2014. To assess the overall financial health of the company, it is often important to understand its performance in relation to other competitors in its industry. While a 3.8% profit margin may seem low, it could be above average for a highly competitive industry or could be appropriate for the lifecycle stage of the company.

Managers need to understand what metrics are important at each stage in their business's lifecycle. For instance, companies often expect to lose money in the start-up phase. Their primary objectives are based on market reach and product or service adoption. In this case, financial metrics take a backseat to consumer metrics. Consider Facebook. Since 2004, Facebook membership has skyrocketed. By 2014, over 890 million individuals accessed Facebook each day. During its first 6 years of operation, the company focused on building membership, not on financial performance. In fact, the company was not able to cover the bulk of its operating costs until 2009.[64] In more mature businesses, however, the tolerance for financial loss is virtually nonexistent. Process and profitability metrics take center stage.

Another important profitability ratio is return on assets (ROA), which measures how well the management of the company is using the company's assets to generate income. Both the balance sheet and the income statement are needed to calculate this ratio, which is net income divided by total assets. The ROA ratio for Party in a Box in 2015 was 3.9% ($64,000 in net income divided by total assets of $1,623,000).

Leverage ratios are used to evaluate a company's debt levels. Debt is typically used to finance a company's core assets, including its facilities. Debt can also be used to fund ongoing operations in a firm, including the buildup of inventory. Generally, companies that have a lot of debt are riskier investments than those with limited debt. One quick assessment of a company's leverage is the debt ratio, which is total debt divided by total assets. The debt ratio for Party in a Box for 2015 was 47%. Almost half the company's assets are being funded by short- and long-term debt. Is this high or low? Again, comparing companies within similar industries helps to assess the relative strengths or weaknesses of different financial ratios.

Total Quality Management

While financial metrics are very important in assessing a company's performance in meeting its sales, growth, and profitability goals, other metrics are useful in assessing a company's operations, manufacturing, and customer delivery processes. With the ultimate goal of fulfilling customer needs, **total quality management (TQM)** has gained

Profitability ratios
Ratios used to assess the firm's profits in relation to the source of those profits, including sales and assets.

Leverage ratios
Ratios used to evaluate a company's debt levels.

Total quality management (TQM)
A comprehensive and structured approach to identifying ways to improve the quality of a company's products and services.

popularity not only in the United States but also around the world over the past several decades.[65] TQM is a comprehensive and structured approach to identifying ways to improve the quality of a company's products and services. Higher quality is one of the most important requirements for long-term success in many industries because it reduces errors; thus, rework and costs are also reduced.[66] While it satisfies customers (which translates to higher market share, better customer retention, more loyal customers, and higher prices), high quality also allows companies to easily move into new markets and acquire new customers.[67] For example, Apple began as a producer of desktop computers, but its focus on high quality and user experience enabled the company to move into markets for laptops, music devices, cell phones, and watches.

The goal of TQM is to ensure that the company produces high-quality products and services that fulfill specific customer needs. To do so, company's often review and enhance their internal operational processes with a focus on building a learning organization through continuous improvement.[68] When looking back at the balanced scorecard, we see a similar linkage between the learning and growth, business process, and customer perspectives, making TQM a suitable complement to enforce the measures that were chosen.

One of the more important measurements of TQM is **total cycle time**, defined as the amount of time required to develop and deliver products and services to the customer.[69] Reducing cycle time improves quality in three fundamental ways. First, as companies use flow charts, cause–effect diagrams, and statistical tools to reduce cycle time, deficiencies in materials and processes are revealed, providing more opportunities to improve quality. Second, reducing cycle time often reduces the number of steps involved from production to delivery. As a result, the number of handoffs, parts, and delays decrease and there are fewer chances for mistakes. Third, labor and overhead costs decrease, inventories are cut, and rework is reduced.[70]

Continuous improvement, one of the most important aspects of TQM, means a commitment to examining processes in pursuit of better methods.[71] It relies on employees actively engaging in scientific experimentation and problem solving.[72] During the experimentation process, employees work in teams to design and execute a series of small experiments to produce incremental gains. Using the scientific method known as "plan, do, check, act" to diagnose problems, employees rely on hard data rather than assumptions to make decisions for improvement.[73] As teams work to reduce waste, improve cycle time, and increase efficiency of resources, incremental adjustments can accumulate to mimic broad, sweeping improvements.[74]

Six Sigma

Six Sigma was originally developed in the 1980s at Motorola as a method for reducing defects during the manufacturing process. More and more companies have turned to Six Sigma to quickly reduce operating costs in search of a competitive advantage.[75] **Six Sigma** is a disciplined, quantitative approach to improve cycle time, reduce costs, and eliminate waste with a technical goal of 3.4 defects per million (six standard deviations from the mean).[76]

In practice, Six Sigma uses a method known as DMAIC, which stands for define, measure, analyze, improve, and control. It entails defining a problem precisely, measuring to clarify the process, analyzing the process to identify root problems, improving the process by considering several solutions, and controlling through ongoing measurements to ensure the problem does not recur. Companies train employees who become "black belts" and are responsible for applying DMAIC to specific projects over a predetermined span of time.[77] After identifying and measuring the key problems of a process, black belts ask "Why is that?" over and over again until they find the underlying problems.[78]

Since its conception, Six Sigma has abandoned its precise definition and become a more generic term, meaning the pursuit of higher quality and

Total cycle time
The amount of time required to develop and deliver products and services to the customer.

Six Sigma
A disciplined, quantitative approach to improve cycle time, reduce costs, and eliminate waste with a technical goal of 3.4 defects per million (six standard deviations from the mean).

Joan Kerrigan/Shutterstock.com

The Leadership Development Journey

Six Sigma is one approach that leaders use to continuously improve quality and reduce cost. Think about a job you have, or have had, that you would like to improve. Apply the Six Sigma methodology to develop an improvement plan.

1. Write a description of the job.
2. Create a flow chart that outlines each task associated with the job.
3. Analyze the flow chart to identify root problems with your performance.
4. Based on your analysis, what are several solutions for improving your performance?
5. Consider how you will control, monitor, and measure your performance so that you can improve.

lower costs.[79] While the efforts started in manufacturing, Six Sigma concepts have been transferred to other business areas such as human resources, customer service, and R&D, where "defects" are more subjective.[80] In recent years, two-thirds of *Fortune 500* companies have used Six Sigma.[81] But it is not the answer for all companies in all situations. Six Sigma assumes that the current product design and process are fundamentally sound and need only minor improvements.[82] While Six Sigma can isolate and solve problems in a current framework, it fails to challenge that framework and create a new one.[83] As such, it is most appropriate in manufacturing, where products and processes are mass customized and mass standardized.[84]

ISO 9000

Another major program that has become popular in recent years is called ISO 9000, an international control mechanism that pursues high-quality products by ensuring high-quality processes. While TQM and Six Sigma focus on improving products, ISO 9000 concentrates on the process of production. It does not provide a method to improve the end product, but requires organizations to document and measure every part of the process that contributes to the quality of an end product. To become ISO 9000 certified, a company (and its suppliers) must meet the ISO standards of quality. Consequently, companies that obtain certification are able to do business with other certified companies.[85] But many critics believe it is too costly and diverts company attention from pursuing quality to pursuing quality certificates. Beyond the complexity, ISO 9000 can cost companies from thousands to millions of dollars in training, consultants, registration, and time.[86]

Improvement programs such as total quality management, and cycle time reduction can overtake managers' priorities to the point that they become ends in themselves. While these programs often begin by serving customer needs and improving economic results, managers must keep an eye on tangible results, maintaining a strong linkage between these activities and financial objectives to ensure that they remain relevant.[87]

TAKING CORRECTIVE ACTION

After an organization has identified measures, set targets, and monitored results, the next step is focused on corrective action and is often considered the most

A DIFFERENT View

Lost in Translation

Development and implementation are keys to the success of performance management. But a lapse in or lack of communication between the development of a strategy and its implementation can cause even the best strategies to fail. The goals established by leaders of an organization can be lost in translation before or during execution of the strategy. Leaders at companies like Southwest Airlines have been very successful in communicating their goals to all employees across their organization. Their goals are focused, and their employees understand them.

1. What can organizations learn from Southwest Airlines?
2. What organization has failed in implementing a strategy because it's been lost in translation? What could they have done differently?

important part of the control cycle. As people gain experience, they learn from their achievements and mistakes; the same is true for organizations. Managers must review all aspects of their organization, assess their past successes and failures, and record the lessons in a forum that employees can access.[88] By doing so, managers create the possibility for employees to participate in the learning process and to improve all aspects of the control cycle. With accessible information, better measurements are chosen, more informed standards are set, and improved methods of monitoring are used.

In addition, through understanding the driving forces behind failures, companies turn mistakes into productive mistakes: in many cases, the lessons learned from failures can be more important than those learned from successes. When companies adopt a learning mindset, employees are focused on increasing their ability to reach preferred results, and they also learn how to learn collectively.[89] An organization skilled at creating, acquiring, and transferring this knowledge fosters continuous improvement in processes, products, and services.[90]

Leaders generally take corrective action in two primary areas. First, they take corrective action to validate their company's strategy. The control cycle enables leaders to better assess how the company is responding to changes in the environmental landscape. Annual business reviews can be used by leaders to recommit to a certain strategy or to outline a plan for change. The second area in which leaders use measurements and corrective action is to ensure that employees are engaging in the right type of activities and producing the right results for the company.

Validating the Strategy

As we have discussed throughout this text, companies must continuously adapt to the business environment and revise their management control systems in light of new threats and opportunities.[91] Because environmental changes can occur spontaneously or steadily, a business should set up a dual process to account for different possibilities. First, businesses should conduct an annual review of their strategy, comparing the organization's performance to standards and assessing the assumptions, opportunities, and threats in the market. Second, businesses should continually collect and analyze data from the environment in order to implement timely changes.[92] The first method accounts for slow, steady changes in the market and helps managers compare business performance to standards. Managers can answer the question, "Are we meeting our strategic goals?" The second method accounts for quick, sporadic changes and identifies new threats or opportunities. Managers can answer the question, "Are we pursuing the best strategy?"[93]

Aligning People

As strategy is implemented and the control cycle takes place, giving feedback to employees is commonly used to correct, sustain, or improve performance. Feedback in itself improves future performance because it heightens employees' awareness of what is expected of them.[94] As we saw in Chapter 9, if employees are maintaining or surpassing standards, managers may reward them with a pay raise, provide new opportunities, or challenge them to acquire new skills. However, if employees are performing poorly, managers tend to use punitive measures such as warnings, probation, and even termination. More effective managers take a problem-solving approach: they discuss performance with the employee, redesign the employee's job, or transfer the employee to a position that is better suited to his or her skills.[95] Ultimately, achieving strategic objectives depends on a manager's ability to motivate employees in their work and promote cooperation between teams.

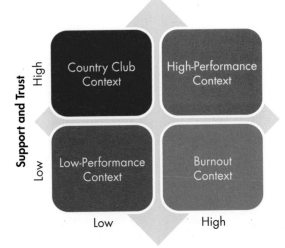

Figure 10.5 ⟩ Balancing Performance and Support

Source: Adapted from Julian Birkinshaw and Cristina Gibson, "Building Ambidexterity Into an Organization," *Sloan Management Review*, Vol. 45, No. 4, Summer 2004, p. 51.

For organizations to achieve certain strategic objectives, they must create a context that is performance based and supportive (see Figure 10.5). High-performance organizations are created in a manner that emphasizes performance metrics as well as support and trust. Organizations that focus solely on performance tend to lead to burnout environments. Success in these situations can be achieved in the short term, but high turnover and poor morale eventually undermine progress. At the other end of the spectrum, too much emphasis on support and development without a counterbalancing focus on performance can result in a country club context. Without a performance focus, employees tend to worry more about social interaction and less about results, eventually becoming complacent. Organizations that lack both a performance focus and supportive environment are not likely to survive very long.

SUMMARY

LO1 Performance management encompasses the tools and processes that managers use to ensure a company is meeting its strategic objectives. The control cycle provides one way to measure and assess the performance of a company. The control cycle encompasses four key activities: (1) identifying key measures of analysis; (2) setting performance targets; (3) monitoring and measuring results; and (4) taking corrective action.

LO2 The balanced scorecard provides a comprehensive way to identify measures of performance. The balanced scorecard includes a financial perspective, a customer perspective, a business process perspective, and a learning and growth perspective. Each of these perspectives, in turn, includes key metrics that help a manager better understand the performance of the firm on a number of dimensions. Certain perspectives are more important at specific points in a firm's lifecycle.

LO3 A company sets performance targets through both external and internal mechanisms. A key external mechanism to set performance targets is to benchmark the firm's performance against competitors or other firms that are "best in class" in their respective industries. Internal performance targets can be derived and monitored through budgets and forecasts.

LO4 To ensure that a firm meets its targets, a manager must monitor and measure performance. A number of tools exist, which enable a manager to assess performance, including financial management, total quality management, Six Sigma, and employee evaluations. Managers need to understand that every organization is unique, whether in size, history, culture, or industry. As a result, managers must not rely on a single method of performance management. Rather, they should consider the methods as tools to use under appropriate conditions. For example, Six Sigma is most appropriate for manufacturing processes while budgeting is most appropriate for resource allocation.

LO5 When a firm is not meeting its targets or objectives, a manager needs to take corrective action. Corrective action can take many forms. If the issue is employee performance, a manager may need to reexamine incentives to ensure that they are aligned with desired results. If the issue is a misaligned strategy or process, the manager may need to reevaluate the firm's goals and objectives. As a manager examines the performance of a company, he or she may also need to recalibrate the control systems that are in place. Are they measuring what needs to be measured? Are managers getting the information that they need in a timely fashion? If not, these control systems may need to be revised. Performance management systems help a manager to assess how well a firm is pursuing its strategic, financial, and operational objectives.

KEY TERMS

Activity-based costing (ABC)
Balance sheet
Balanced scorecard
Behavior
Benchmarking
Budgeting process
Business process perspective
Cause–effect relationships

Control cycle
Customer perspective
Financial perspective
Income statement
Learning and growth perspective
Leverage ratios
Liquidity ratios
Measurement

Outputs
Profitability ratios
Six sigma
Total cycle time
Total quality
    management (TQM)
Value propositions

ASSIGNMENTS

Discussion Topics

1. What does it mean when a manager says, "if you can't measure it, you can't manage it?" Why can't you manage it?

2. Describe how the lifecycle stage of a business informs the types of performance metrics that a manager should pay attention to.

3. When a business is in a turnaround situation, what performance measures are most critical?

4. If you were the CEO of Facebook, what measures would you pay attention to? Why? What if you were the CEO of Microsoft?

5. Why would a company benchmark its performance against companies in different industries? What value can be derived from considering completely different contexts?

6. If you were the head of a nonprofit organization, what performance metrics would you consider to be most important? How would you apply the balanced scorecard to your organization? How would you measure success?

7. How can an organization develop a learning and growth perspective?

8. In the previous chapter, we discussed how feedback and performance appraisal systems are used to manage human capital. In what ways are these approaches connected to the overall performance management of the firm?

9. What tools can companies use to make their performance against key metrics transparent to all employees? What are the advantages of being transparent?

10. Shell and Amanco both included sustainability metrics in their balanced scorecards. When and how should companies think about including metrics on social responsibility in their business evaluation processes?

Management Research

1. Identify a company and conduct research to understand its strategy. Given your analysis, which tools of performance management would you use in this company if you were the CEO? What tools would you use if you were a lower level manager with direct supervision of a team?

2. Now imagine that a new competitor enters the market with the same strategy as your company.

Keeping the same performance tools, what is the sequence of events that would take place in the company? Should the strategy change? If so, how?

In the Field

Create a 30-minute training session on performance management for a local organization. Use the following steps to design your training session.

1. Create learning objectives for the training session.

2. Develop content that is aligned with the learning objectives and include material from this chapter.

3. Incorporate "real-world" examples into the training session that illustrate the performance management concepts.

4. Create an exercise that assesses the organization's performance management system.

5. Conclude the training session by discussing how the organization can improve its performance management system.

ENDNOTES

[1] William J. Bruns, "Responsibility Centers and Performance Measurement," Harvard Business School Note No. 9-193-101, rev. May 13, 1993 (Boston, MA: HBS Publishing, 1993), p. 1.

[2] David Otley, "Performance Management: A Framework for Management Control Systems Research," *Management Accounting Research*, Vol. 10, 1999, pp. 363–382.

[3] Eric Flamholtz, "Organizational Control Systems as a Managerial Tool," *California Management Review*, Winter 1979, pp. 50–59, www.proquest.com, accessed May 2010.

[4] Jane Wei-Skillern, "Sustainable Development at Shell (A)," Harvard Business School Case No. 9-303-005, rev. July 6, 2004 (Boston, MA: HBS Publishing, 2004), p. 1.

[5] Ibid., p. 2.

[6] Ibid., p. 3.

[7] Ibid., p. 4.

[8] Ibid., p. 5.

[9] Ibid., p. 6.

[10] Ibid., p. 7.

[11] Ibid., p. 8.

[12] Ibid., p. 9.

[13] Ibid., p. 3.

[14] David A. Garvin, "Building a Learning Organization," Harvard Business Review, July–August 1993.

[15] William J. Bruns, "Responsibility Centers and Performance Measurement," Harvard Business School Note No. 9-193-101, rev. May 13, 1993 (Boston, MA: HBS Publishing, 1993), p. 1.

[16] William G. Ouchi, "The Transmission of Control through Organizational Hierarchy," *Academy of Management Journal*, Vol. 21, 1978, pp. 173–192, www.proquest.com, accessed May 2010.

[17] Andy Neely and Mohammed Al Najjar, "Management Learning Not Management Control: The True Role of Performance Measurement," *California Management Review*, Vol. 48, Spring 2006, pp. 101–114.

[18] David Otley, "Performance Management: A Framework for Management Control Systems Research," *Management Accounting Research*, Vol. 10, 1999, pp. 363–382, www.idealibrary.com, accessed May 2010.

[19] Ibid.

[20] Gerhard Speckbacher, Juergen Bischof, and Thomas Pfeiffer, "A Descriptive Analysis on the Implementation of Balanced Scorecards in German-Speaking Countries," *Management Accounting Research*, Vol. 14, 2003, pp. 361–387.

[21] Nils-Göran Olve, Carl-Johan Petri, Jan Roy, and Sofie Roy, "Twelve Years Later: Understanding and Realizing the Value of Balanced Scorecards," *Ivey Business Journal*, May–June 2004, pp. 1–7.

[22] Robin Goldwyn Blumenthal, "Tis the Gift to Be Simple," *CFO Magazine*, January 1, 1998, www.cfo.com/printable/article.cfm/2990236, accessed June 2010.

[23] Michael Contrada, "Using the Balanced Scorecard to Manage Value in Your Business," *Balanced Scorecard Report*, Article Reprint No. B0001C, http://hbsp.harvard.edu/product/cases, accessed July 2010.

[24] Robert S. Kaplan and David P. Norton, "Linking the Balanced Scorecard to Strategy," *California Management Review*, Vol. 39, No. 1, Fall 1996, p. 59.

[25] Elizabeth Candler Graham and Ralph Roberts, *The Real Ones: Four Generations of the First Family of Coca-Cola* (Fort Lee, NJ: Barricade Books, 1992), pp. 293–204.

[26] Lawrence M. Fisher, "Inside Dell Computer Corporation: Managing Working Capital," *Strategy + Business*, January 1, 1998, www.strategy-business.com/article/9571?gko=d8c29, accessed May 2010.

27 Michael Hammer, "Process Management and the Future of Six Sigma," *MIT Sloan Management Review*, Winter 2002, pp. 26–32.

28 Robert S. Kaplan and David P. Norton, "Linking the Balanced Scorecard to Strategy," *California Management Review*, Vol. 39, No. 1, Fall 1996, pp. 59–60.

29 Ibid., p. 60.

30 T. O. Jones and W. E. Sasser, "Why Satisfied Customers Defect," *Harvard Business Review,* November–December 1995.

31 Robert S. Kaplan and David P. Norton, "Linking the Balanced Scorecard to Strategy," *California Management Review*, Vol. 39, No. 1, Fall 1996, p. 61.

32 Ibid.

33 Ibid., p. 62.

34 Ibid., p. 63.

35 Ibid.

36 Robert S. Kaplan and David P. Norton, *The Balanced Scorecard: Translating Strategy Into Action* (Boston, MA: HBS Press, 1996), pp. 130–131.

37 David A. Garvin, "Building a Learning Organization," *Harvard Business Review*, July–August 1993.

38 "Water policy 'fails world's poor,'" BBC News, http://news.bbc.co.uk/2/hi/science/nature/4787758.stm, accessed October 7, 2011.

39 Robert S. Kaplan and Ricardo Reisen de Pinho, "Amanco: Developing the Sustainability Scorecard," Harvard Business School Case No. 9-107-038, rev. January 29, 2008 (Boston, MA: HBS Publishing, 2007), p. 2.

40 Ibid., p. 3.

41 Ibid., p. 4.

42 Ibid., p. 5.

43 Ibid., p. 19.

44 Ibid., p. 9.

45 Ibid., p. 23.

46 Ibid., p. 19.

47 Ibid., p. 9.

48 Ibid., p. 10.

49 Ibid., p. 11.

50 Ibid., p. 19.

51 Neil C. Churchill, "Budget Choice: Planning vs. Control," *Harvard Business Review*, July–August 1984.

52 Robert C. Camp, *Benchmarking: The Search for Industry Best Practices that Lead to Superior Performance* (Milwaukee, WI: ASQC Quality Press, 1989), p. 12.

53 Jac. Fitz-enz, "Benchmarking Best Practices," *Canadian Business Review*, Vol. 19, No. 4, Winter 1992, p. 28, www.proquest.com, accessed July 2010.

54 Jeremy Hope and Robin Fraser, "Who Needs Budgets?," *Harvard Business Review*, February 2003.

55 Jac. Fitz-enz, "Benchmarking Best Practices," *Canadian Business Review*, Vol. 19, No. 4, Winter 1992, p. 28, www.proquest.com, accessed July 2010.

56 Jennifer Alsever, "Job Swaps: Are They for You?" *Fortune*, October 29, 2012.

57 David Otley, "Performance Management: A Framework for Management Control Systems Research," *Management Accounting Research*, Vol. 10, 1999, pp. 363–382, www.idealibrary.com, accessed May 2010.

58 Robert S. Kaplan and David P. Norton, "Linking Strategy to Planning and Budgeting," *Balanced Scorecard Report*, Article Reprint No. B0005A, http://hbsp.harvard.edu/product/cases, accessed July 2010.

59 Ibid.

60 Perry Pascarella, "Open the Books to Unleash Your People," *Management Review*, Vol. 87, No. 5, May 1998, pp. 58–60, www.proquest.com, accessed July 2010.

61 "Understanding Financial Statements: Making More Authoritative Decisions," in *Manager's Toolkit: The 13 Skills Managers Need to Succeed* (Boston, MA: HBS Press, 2006).

62 Ibid.

63 David Hawkins, "Financial Statement Analysis," Harvard Business School Note No. 9-195-177, rev. November 24, 2010 (Boston, MA: HBS Publishing, 1994).

64 "Facebook, Inc. Company Profile," Hoover's, www.hoovers.com, accessed November 1, 2012.

65 A. Blanton Godfrey, "Section 14: Total Quality Management," Joseph M. Juran, ed. *Juran's Quality Handbook*, 5th edition (New York, NY: McGraw-Hill, 1999), p. 14.2.

66 James W. Dean, Jr., and David E. Bowen, "Management Theory and Total Quality: Improving Research and Practice through Theory Development," *Academy of Management Review*, Vol. 19, No. 3, 1994, pp. 392–418, www.proquest.com, accessed July 2010.

67 A. Blanton Godfrey, "Section 14: Total Quality Management," Joseph M. Juran, ed. *Juran's Quality Handbook*, 5th edition (New York, NY: McGraw-Hill, 1999), p. 14.5.

68 Peter Murray and Ross Chapman, "From Continuous Improvement to Organizational Learning: Developmental Theory," *The Learning Organization*, Vol. 10, 2003, pp. 272–282.

69 Richard M. Hodgetts, *Blueprint for Continuous Improvement: Lessons from the Baldridge Winners* (New York, NY: American Management Association, 1993), pp. 39–50.

70 Ibid., pp. 70–71.

71 James W. Dean, Jr., and David E. Bowen, "Management Theory and Total Quality: Improving Research and Practice through Theory Development," *Academy of Management Review*, Vol. 19, No. 3, July 1994, pp. 392–418, www.proquest.com, accessed July 2010.

72 Peter Murray and Ross Chapman, "From Continuous Improvement to Organizational Learning: Developmental Theory," *The Learning Organization*, Vol. 10, 2003, pp. 272–282.

73 David A. Garvin, "Building a Learning Organization," *Harvard Business Review*, July–August 1993.

74 A. Blanton Godfrey, "Section 14: Total Quality Management," Joseph M. Juran, ed. *Juran's Quality Handbook*, 5th edition (New York, NY: McGraw-Hill, 1999), pp. 14–20.

75 "True Six Sigma Leads to Performance Improvements beyond Manufacturing; Top Performers Slash Costs, Improve Quality and Reduce Cycle Times," *Marketwire*, November 10, 2009, available at Lexis-Nexis, accessed July 2010.

76 A. Blanton Godfrey, "Section 14: Total Quality Management," Joseph M. Juran, ed. *Juran's Quality Handbook*, 5th edition (New York, NY: McGraw-Hill, 1999), p. 14.32.

77 Dr. Michael Hammer and Jeff Goding, "Putting Six Sigma in Perspective," *Quality*, October 2001, pp. 58–62.

78 Jim Biolos, "Six Sigma Meets the Service Economy," *Harvard Management Update*, Article Reprint No. U0211A, http://hbsp.harvard.edu/product/cases, accessed July 2010.

79 Hal Plotkin, "Six Sigma: What It Is and How to Use It," *Harvard Management Update*, Article Reprint No. U9906C, http://hbsp.harvard.edu/ product/cases, accessed July 2010.

80 Ibid.

81 "Six Sigma Certification Booms as Employment Busts," *Marketwire*, December 22, 2008, available at LexisNexis, accessed July 2010.

82 Michael Hammer, "Process Management and the Future of Six Sigma," *MIT Sloan Management Review*, Winter 2002, pp. 26–32.

83 Dr. Michael Hammer and Jeff Goding, "Putting Six Sigma in Perspective," *Quality*, October 2001, pp. 58–62.

84 Jim Biolos, "Six Sigma Meets the Service Economy," *Harvard Management Update*, Article Reprint No. U0211A, http://hbsp. harvard.edu/product/cases, accessed July 2010.

85 Frank C. Barnes, "ISO 9000 Myth and Reality: A Reasonable Approach to ISO 9000," *Sam Advanced Management Journal*, Spring 1998, pp. 23–30.

86 Thomas H. Stevenson and Frank C. Barnes, "Fourteen Years of ISO 9000: Impact, Criticisms, Costs, and Benefits," *Business Horizons*, May–June 2001, pp. 45–51.

87 Robert S. Kaplan and David P. Norton, "Linking the Balanced Scorecard to Strategy," *California Management Review*, Vol. 39, No. 1, Fall 1996, p. 67.

88 David A. Garvin, "Building a Learning Organization," *Harvard Business Review*, July–August 1993.

89 Ibid.

90 James W. Dean, Jr., and David E. Bowen, "Management Theory and Total Quality: Improving Research and Practice through Theory Development," *Academy of Management Review*, Vol. 19, No. 3, 1994, 392–418, www.proquest.com, accessed July 2010.

91 Y. Li, L. Li, Y. Liu, and L. Wang, "Linking Management Control System With Product Development and Process Decisions to Cope with Environment Complexity," *International Journal of Production Research*, Vol. 43, No. 12, 2005, pp. 2577–2591.

92 Eric Flamholtz, "Organizational Control Systems as a Managerial Tool," *California Management Review*, Winter 1979, pp. 50–59, www.proquest.com, accessed May 2010.

93 Ibid. and Peter Lorange, Michael F. Scott Morton, and Sumantra Ghoshal, *Strategic Control Systems* (St. Paul, MN: West, 1986).

94 Kenneth A. Merchant, *Control in Business Organizations* (Marshfield, MA: Pitman, 1985), p. 50.

95 N.R.F. Maier, *The Appraisal Interview* (New York: Wiley, 1958), quoted in Mark B. Gavin, Stephen G. Green, and Gail T. Fairhurst, "Managerial Control Strategies for Poor Performance over Time and the Impact on Subordinate Reactions," *Organizational Behavior and Human Decision Processes*, Vol. 63, No. 2, 1995, pp. 207–221.

CHAPTER

11

Organizational Change

Learning Objectives

After reading this chapter, you should be able to:

LO1 Outline the key drivers of change including those stemming from the external and internal environments of an organization.

LO2 Understand the different aspects of organizational change including proactive and reactive change, planned and organic change, and incremental and transformative change.

LO3 Describe the change process and the key elements that comprise it.

LO4 Explain how organizations and change leaders combat resistance to change.

SELF-REFLECTION

Are You a Change Agent?

A change agent embraces change. Do you think of yourself as a change agent? On a scale of 1 to 5, rate your approach to change and then analyze your areas for improvement.

1 = never 2 = rarely 3 = sometimes 4 = usually 5 = always

1. I am good at combining knowledge from different sources. _____

2. I am flexible and adapt to new situations. _____

3. In change situations, I can build consensus. _____

4. I am willing to take risks in order to learn and make progress. _____

5. I know how to work through the emotional aspects of change. _____

6. I leverage my strengths in change situations. _____

7. In change situations, I work hard to create positive energy. _____

8. When confronting change, I focus on the result that I want to create. _____

9. Change excites and energizes me. _____

10. When confronting change, I first create an action plan. _____

11. I am tolerant of ambiguity and can function in uncertain conditions. _____

12. I am able to convince others why change is important. _____

13. I am reflective in change situations and use them as opportunities to learn. _____

14. I know how to navigate the politics of change. _____

15. I have a futuristic orientation when I think about solutions for problems. _____

Based on your scores, are you a change agent? In what areas? Where do you still need to focus?

INTRODUCTION

The interplay of globalization, regulatory changes, and the growing speed of technological innovation continue to transform the world at an unprecedented pace. It has been happening for so long now that to say we live in chaotic and changing times has become cliché. Yet the rate of change in the world marketplace hasn't slowed; it continues to intensify and the implications are clear. Organizations must develop the capacity to adapt, innovate, and transform if they are going to remain competitive and viable. Slow hierarchical management approaches must give way to responsive and agile ways of operating. As the pursuit of greater market share, higher

A DIFFERENT View

Social Movements

We often only think of organizational change from the perspective of for-profit corporations. However, all types of organizations manage change. In the nonprofit sector, leaders often collaborate to create social change through movements. Social movements are groupings of individuals or organizations focused on a specific political or social issue. Their actions can result in, resist, or undo societal practices. Examples of social movements include the French Revolution, the Civil Rights Movement in the United States, the global environmental movement, and the labor movement.

• Identify an example of a successful social movement. Why did it succeed?
• Why do you think some social movements fail? What is an example of a social movement that failed?
• What can managers learn from social movements?

*Organizational change
The processes and activities that organizations go through to align themselves with the internal and external business environment and to prepare for future potential opportunities.*

profits, lower costs, and innovation continues, leaders must remain vigilant about gauging their environment and ensuring that they are adapting quickly to it.

Our journey through this textbook has led us to a greater understanding of organizations—how they act and how they are acted upon. To this point, we have discussed the business environment, business- and corporate-level strategy, and the ways a firm can maintain a competitive advantage in an increasingly global marketplace. We have also looked at the role that organizational structures, human resources, culture, and performance management systems play in influencing performance. To sustain their relevance and viability, organizations need to constantly evolve. Unfortunately, change is hard not only for individuals but also for organizations. To do so, leaders must be well versed in the change management process. The inability to change can result in the demise of even the most well-known brands. A quick comparison of the best brands in 1990, 2000, 2010, and 2014 highlights the need for change (see Table 11.1).

For over 20 years, Coca-Cola has been able to retain its relevance as an important and respected brand. Despite shifting tastes (especially the prevalence and demand for energy drinks and various types of water), Coca-Cola has been able to successfully tap into the social consciousness of consumers—ensuring that its products are still in high demand. Since 1990, Coca-Cola has been a top three world brand. More recently, Apple and Google have built strong brands through a continuous process of reinvention. Other firms have not fared as well. For instance, by 2014, Pepsi-Cola, Sony, and Nestle had dropped from being a top 10 brand to numbers 24, 52, and 54, respectively. Kodak, which was considered the fourth best brand in 1990, fell out of the top 100 list completely in 2008. Kodak failed to keep pace with the changes in digital photography, resulting in a quick and painful loss of competitive relevance.

Corporations, nonprofits, governments, and even sports teams engage in organizational change to better fulfill their purposes, achieve their objectives, and implement their strategies. When their strategy becomes misaligned with the environment or the organization's capabilities fail to keep pace with new competitive realities, organizations must embark on organizational change. **Organizational change** consists of the processes and activities that organizations go through to align themselves with the internal and external business environment and to prepare for future potential opportunities.

Rank	1990	2000	2010	2014
1	Coca-Cola	Coca-Cola	Coca-Cola	Apple
2	Sony	Microsoft	IBM	Google
3	Mercedes-Benz	IBM	Microsoft	Coca-Cola
4	Kodak	Intel	Google	IBM
5	Disney	Nokia	General Electric	Microsoft
6	Nestlé	General Electric	McDonald's	General Electric
7	Toyota	Ford	Intel	Samsung
8	McDonald's	Disney	Nokia	Toyota
9	IBM	McDonald's	Disney	McDonald's
10	Pepsi-Cola	AT&T	HP	Mercedes-Benz

Table 11.1 ⟩ Best Global Brands, 1990, 2000, 2010, and 2014

Source: Interbrand, "Best Global Brands, 2014," available at Interbrand Web site, http://www.bestglobalbrands.com/2014/ranking/#?sortBy=name&sortAscending=true&listFormat=ls, accessed April 6, 2015.

In this chapter, we will explore why change is necessary, the various approaches to initiating change, the reasons change is resisted, and the role leaders play in orchestrating the overall process. To help illustrate the value of change, let's look at the case of IBM, a company that could have suffered the same fate as Kodak, which filed for bankruptcy, but was able to transform itself to retain and even enhance its competitive positioning in a turbulent market setting.

Stability, Crisis, and Revolution at IBM

When IBM was formed in 1896, its first major client was the U.S. Census Bureau. Originally called the Tabulating Machine Company, IBM worked with the government to reduce the time and complexity of the census process. After the census in 1900, the company led a stable existence by applying its existing products to businesses that wanted automatic tabulating machines. Its first major change occurred when it merged with three other companies in 1911. Three cultures and product lines were brought together. The result was a company that manufactured everything from weighing scales to tabulating machines to automatic meat slicers.

Thomas J. Watson joined the company in 1911 and led the company for almost 40 years. He instigated the "dark suited . . . culture of corporate pride and loyalty" and led the company through a long stretch of growth and continuity.[1] After helping manufacture weapons during World War II, IBM began to change once again. The company secured a contract to build computers for the Air Force and developed cutting-edge technology with the assistance of the Massachusetts Institute of Technology. This jump to computers was an extension of IBM's tabulation business; yet the stage was set for a more significant move.

That unprecedented and revolutionary move came from Watson's son, Thomas J. Watson, Jr., who took the helm of the company in 1955. Watson Jr. invested $5 billion to "develop the System/360 computer, the first family of products based on an integrated semiconductor chip and offering interchangeability of components."[2] Watson Jr. revolutionized IBM with this move to mainframe computers. He abandoned incremental changes to gamble on an entirely new platform. The gamble paid off, and the now transformed company used this quantum change to produce an unprecedented number of information technology (IT) innovations, including the hard disk and floppy disk. IBM reconfigured its sales force, research and development (R&D), and corporate structure to further its new IT direction and came to dominate the IT field to such an extent that, in the 1960s, the U.S. Justice Department tried unsuccessfully for 13 years to bring an antitrust action against the company.

The introduction of the mainframe led to another long stretch of stable growth and incremental change. IBM continued to dominate the market and was considered one of the best places to work.[3] In the 1980s, IBM's solidified culture and constricted grip on its mainframe business led to a crisis period that almost destroyed the company. In 1981, IBM entered the personal computer (PC) market. Despite its success, the PC was pushed aside by the larger organization as it continued to pursue its traditional focus on the mainframe business.

The focus on mainframes and the inertia against growing into the PC business came to a head in 1991. The company's earnings plummeted 146% to a loss of $2.8 billion.[4] Revenues continued to fall by 60% for each of the next 2 years, and the once-paragon of Wall Street almost became a laughing stock. Warning signs had appeared earlier, yet inertia held the company back. Costs had risen to crushing levels, different business units (including the PC business) were more interested in fighting each other than cooperating, the culture reinforced complacency, and management was insulated from the growing critical reality by huge staffs and complicated levels of bureaucracy. In the midst of the crisis, Lou Gerstner was brought in as CEO.

Describing what he found when he came to IBM, Gerstner said, "I found a group of employees literally frozen in place. They didn't know what had hit them. In 1990, the company had had record profits. For two decades, it was listed as the best-run company in the world, most admired company in the world, and all of a sudden people are talking about breaking it up, calling it a dinosaur . . . "[5]

Gerstner immediately set about transforming IBM by breaking out of past traditions and reconfiguring the company's strategy. The first thing Gerstner did was to shift the company's focus to its customers. Executives were assigned to certain customers and were held accountable for helping those customers succeed and for solving any issues they had. Gerstner traveled constantly his first few months on the job, visiting customers to find out how IBM was serving them.[6] This emphasis on customers shocked the technology-intensive IBM culture that had previously taken customers for granted.

While driving the customer-centric focus, Gerstner also sought to unify IBM into one company with one mission. "One IBM" became Gerstner's mantra and the impetus for organizational transformation. He consolidated structures and flattened hierarchies to facilitate this move. The mantra also became the basis for decision making, as executives consolidated or cut products and services to bring them under one group.

Gerstner's support for emergent change set the stage for another critical initiative that helped radically redefine IBM. Gerstner sought to make "network-centric computing" the backbone of the company's e-business strategy. He surmised that all the data collected on the Internet would need to be analyzed and evaluated with sophisticated computing power, and he believed that IBM's mainframe technology was well poised for the task. Though IBM's approach to the Internet was "far less sexy than the high-flying Internet initial public offerings (IPOs) at the time," it became a significant source of new revenue.[7]

By focusing on data collection and analysis, IBM not only survived the bursting of the Internet bubble but also prospered as other companies scrambled to identify their real assets. In the process, IBM regained its reputation as a technology leader and had several years of steady growth.[8]

Gerstner's successor Sam Palmisano, who took the helm in 2002, continued the change process by divesting unprofitable or low margin businesses and further focusing the company on providing services to customers instead of just hardware solutions. To that end, Palmisano made the difficult choice to sell IBM's low margin, relatively low-growth PC business to Lenovo in 2004. To significantly increase

Nattul/Shutterstock.com

the company's service offerings, Palmisano oversaw the acquisition of PriceWaterhouseCoopers's consulting business, which added a significant new strategic capability to the firm. In addition, Palmisano continued Gerstner's initial investments in Internet-based data analytics by acquiring several companies that specialized in sophisticated analytical services. These investments allowed IBM to help businesses make sense of the increased complexity, volume, and interconnectedness of their customer data.[9]

In addition to moving toward a service orientation, Palmisano also sought to increase IBM's global footprint, especially in emerging markets. He created the Global Integrated Enterprise to signify the company's focus on global opportunities, and he split the enterprise into two distinct groups—one focused on mature markets and was based in New York, the other focused on growth markets and was based in Shanghai.[10]

To support these business changes and to reinforce a focus on innovation and customer service, Palmisano also sought to recharge the cultural values of the company, and he decided to focus on cultural change from the bottom-up. Palmisano used IBM's technology to reach out to all 300,000 employees in what he called a "values jam," where employees could discuss and debate the nature of the company's values. The result was an intense and vibrant debate that coalesced on three core values: (1) dedication to every client's success; (2) innovation that matters—for our company and the world; and (3) trust and personal responsibility in all relationships.[11]

IBM's focus on innovative services and solutions for global customers was part of the company's new overall strategy called "Smarter Planet." By the end of his tenure as CEO, Palmisano had succeeded in changing the business mix and focus of the company. The majority of the company's sales were driven by solutions and services and an increasingly larger sales volume originated from emerging markets.[12]

When Palmisano stepped down as CEO in 2012, the reins were handed to Ginni Rometty who is overseeing her own efforts to grow and develop IBM. As Rometty noted: "Every generation of IBMers has the opportunity, and, I believe, the responsibility—to invent a new IBM. This is our time."[13] Similar to her prior two predecessors, Rometty is pursuing a combination of incremental and transformative change by continuing to focus on data-driven solutions for clients while also investing in new innovative services. This process of continual reinvention will be critical to sustaining the relevance of IBM.

Case in Point   Discussion Questions: Stability, Crisis, and Revolution at IBM

1. Construct a timeline of IBM's strategic change process. Based on your analysis of the timeline, was IBM proactive or reactive to change?
2. What external conditions were impetuses for change at IBM?
3. How did IBM's corporate culture support change?
4. What was the role of leadership in managing change at IBM?

THE CASE FOR CHANGE

IBM has moved from a case study of change to an enabler of change for many of its clients. IBM's Global Business Intelligence group recently interviewed more than a thousand CEOs around the world to better understand their concerns and challenges. Not surprisingly, the report highlights the enhanced need for organizational change as more than half of the CEOs stated that they plan to "deeply change their organizations' capabilities, knowledge and assets."[14]

Organizations change to better compete, thrive, and bring value to their various stakeholders. In a survey of corporate leaders, three of the most cited reasons for beginning a change initiative were the following:

1. To compete more effectively—68% indicated that they were experiencing a high level of competition, which they saw as only increasing in the future.
2. To improve performance—82% stated that without engaging in some form of change, they would see a significant drop in their performance.
3. To survive—15% indicated that their organization would cease to exist in the next few years without a serious change initiative.[15]

As discussed in Chapter 10, many organizations use the balanced scorecard and the control cycle to continuously reassess their strategic priorities, especially in light of changes in the external environment. Some of these changes require companies to invest more in R&D to ensure that their products and services continue to fit consumer preferences and tastes. Other changes in government policies may require companies to adopt new processes and procedures to comply with regulations. For example, governments can have an obvious direct effect on the levels of regulation and competition within their borders. Raising taxes, regulating banks, restricting trade, demanding high tariffs, providing subsidies, and utilizing other economic controls directly impact the environmental landscape. As such, organizations need to be vigilant about the manner in which the environment changes and then remain agile in their response to those changes. Sometimes, organizations need to be ahead of their environment. They may either initiate those environmental changes or may simply anticipate them and prepare their organization for the changes to come.

The Role of the External Environment in Driving Change

Organizations now compete in an increasing number of countries against a dizzying array of global and local competitors. At the same time, they must confront a variety of local government regulations that may be constantly changing in their different markets. Customer demands vary dramatically across markets and also change more quickly. Jean Fang of Fang Brothers Holdings, a textile company, noted that consumers in China have an insatiable appetite for certain lifestyle products but that they lose their interest quickly. Companies that remain successful in China must constantly reinvent themselves to ensure that they stay relevant.[16]

Technological advances escalate these changes. For instance, the amount of new technical information doubles every 2 years, and it is predicted to double every 72 hours in the future.[17] New entrants in the marketplace, substitute products, increased competitive intensity, and growing bargaining power of customers and suppliers, all have a dramatic influence on the competitive landscape. As these forces evolve, they necessitate that organizations transform the way they conduct business. Among the many drivers of change, two of the most prominent are globalization and technological innovation.

Globalization

In the last several decades, we have seen a decline of trade barriers and concomitant increase in the extent of cross-border trade. For businesses, this has meant unprecedented opportunities to both buy from overseas suppliers and to sell their goods and services in those markets. Not only are companies venturing far from their home markets but they are also facing foreign rivals coming into their home markets. Operating in a diverse array of markets has meant that organizations can no longer rely upon a few variations of their offerings that are then sold around the world. Instead, they have to tailor their products and services to local preferences. A washing machine that is desirable in the United States may not be desirable in India. The features, price points, and look and feel all may differ in different markets. Customization can prove to be difficult for many of these companies because they are, at the same time, seeking economies of scale, which is easiest when a company produces a small number of variants of a product in very large quantities. Georg Bauer, CEO of BMW, has stated, "Products have to be local with a global brand. I see us as a globally integrated organization with a local presence and localized products."[18] One way in which organizations meet this demand is to build foundational products that can be produced efficiently and can be easily reconfigured to fit local preferences.

Globalization has also changed the dynamics of the workforce in many organizations. Organizations that employ local leadership or engage in partnerships can gain a competitive advantage through their extensive knowledge of the local culture, political environment, and available resources. At the same time that they retain local leadership, those multinationals also have to find the right balance of control and autonomy for those local managers to respond quickly to shifts in their local market. A venture capitalist doing business in China noted, "Multinational corporations have good products and services, but their disadvantage is they are not flexible. Their decision making procedures are long . . . In certain industries where the competitive landscape can change every few months, Chinese entrepreneurs can make decisions very fast and that gives them an advantage."[19]

Technology

The ability to communicate and send massive amounts of data around the world has allowed globalization to move from something that affects countries and corporations to something that affects individuals in more significant ways than first imagined. Companies can reach for customers, resources, and talent from all over the world. They can reach into people's lives through the Internet and mobile phones, as well as through newspapers, radio, television, and movies. Indeed, technology has allowed for more than adaptation; it has driven complete transformations.

Technology may well be the greatest driver for change in today's new competitive landscape, having "become a strategic part of most businesses, enabling the redefinition of markets and industries and the strategies and designs of firms competing within them."[20] In the best seller, *The World Is Flat*, Thomas Friedman points to three major technological changes that drastically affected the world's competitive environment:

1. The "massive installation of undersea fiber-optic cable and bandwidth . . . that have made it possible to globally transmit and store huge amounts of data for almost nothing."
2. The "diffusion of PCs around the world."
3. "The convergence of a variety of software applications—from e-mail, to Google, to Microsoft Office, to specially designed outsourcing programs— that, when combined with all those PCs and bandwidth, made it possible to create global work-flow platforms."[21]

Technology has influenced almost every aspect of business. Inventory systems, manufacturing processes, human resource systems, and financial controls were redesigned using technology that could drastically improve productivity, predictability, speed, and accuracy. For example, Walmart's ability to adapt technology sooner and integrate new technological systems more effectively than its competitors greatly added to the company's growth and competitive prowess. The company introduced electronic scanning of uniform product codes at the point of sale years ahead of most of its competitors (2 years ahead of Kmart). In addition, Walmart was one of the first retail stores to launch its own satellite system, which allowed sales data to be gathered and analyzed continuously and in real time. Later, this system proved crucial as Walmart continued to adapt its processes and systems, using it for everything from credit card authorizations to inventory control to automated distribution.[22]

Nintendo was a victim and later a beneficiary of technological innovation. The company dominated the video gaming industry in the early 1990s with a 60% market share; yet in the early years of the new millennium, it lost two-thirds of its market share. New technology and the infiltration of higher end gaming consoles pushed Nintendo out of the market lead.

In 2005, Nintendo transformed its organization through a $220 million investment in R&D and a realignment of its operating strategy. Nintendo used the Internet and networking technology to create an online community (called "sages"), which offered the company advice on new products and design features. These sages were given exclusive rewards (e.g., previews of new games) in exchange for helping users and providing community support.[23] By interfacing with its core customers through its online environment, Nintendo deepened loyalty, learned more about the market, and gained crucial ideas it could leverage to obtain the most from its capital commitment to R&D. In recent years, we have seen the results of that investment with the very successful introduction of the Wii.[24]

The need for constant innovation affects organizations in other ways as well. For example, product life cycles can no longer take years to complete. In fact, by introducing new models or variations on existing models, companies often move so quickly that they can cannibalize their own products.[25] Short cycles offer less opportunity to recuperate major expenditures in R&D and product marketing efforts. As such, organizations must adapt and find ways to keep pace with the changes and yet manage their business effectively. Such parameters have led organizations to consider partnering on innovation to share some of the costs.

Some companies are even looking outside their employee base to drive innovation. One approach that has become popular is

Jason Wambsgans/MCT/Newscom

open source innovation, a process where companies invite "the community" to help solve certain challenges. Linux, OpenIDEO, and Wikipedia have built their businesses by developing a collaborative community where individuals from all over the world contribute ideas, solutions, and new challenges. By using open source innovation, many companies have been able to tap into technical resources that would be impossible to hire on their own.[26]

Open source innovation is one form of crowdsourcing, where a company sources new ideas and contributions from a community that is far larger than their employee base. Crowdsourcing is not confined to technology companies. Threadless, a Chicago-based fashion company, has used crowdsourcing as the basis of their design business. The company began by inviting designers from anywhere to submit T-shirt designs on the Threadless website. The design submissions (usually 100 per week) are reviewed by an internal Threadless team and the top 10 designs are showcased on the Threadless website for one week. The designs that generate the greatest number of votes from the broader Threadless community (including its customers, fans, and other designers) are offered for sale. The winning designer receives a small payment, as financial incentive, as well as recognition from the design community. In essence, Threadless has outsourced both its design and production planning to the broader community. They rely on the Threadless community to both supply the idea for the product as well as buy the product. Using this approach, Threadless has been able to cost-effectively manage their business, innovate with new designs, and give customers what they want.[27]

As we discussed in Chapter 7, those few organizations that are successful for long periods of time are able to champion innovation and experimentation while simultaneously reinforcing efficiency and cost effectiveness in traditional business lines.[28] They are able to anticipate and/or react to the demands of the changing external environment while preserving the aspects of internal operations that have enabled them to achieve success in the past. To accomplish this dual task, organizations sometimes need to drive change in their internal environments. Their biggest challenge is not in the marketplace and lies instead within their own organizations. They need to mobilize their own people to embrace change and, in turn, adapt their organization to allow those changes to thrive. Agility is the mantra for survival and success but it only comes to fruition in an organization that embraces change.

The Role of the Internal Environment in Navigating Change

External change drivers such as globalization and technological innovation can impact the competitive landscape so dramatically that it is easy to overlook the role of the internal environment. Organizations often resist change; this resistance is referred to as **inertia**, or the "inability of organizations to change as rapidly as the environment."[29] This implies that the greater the inertia, the greater the distance between the environment and organizational practices.

Sometimes, organizations only wake up to change when they begin to perform poorly. Necessity is indeed sometimes the precursor to change. As stated earlier, misalignment between an organization and its strategy often drives the need for change. The strategy may have adjusted to the market context, but to actually implement it, the company may need to make organizational adjustments. The balanced scorecard discussed in Chapter 10 can be a useful tool for understanding some of the performance gaps that arise from such implementation failures. When organizations are faced with dysfunctional internal processes or when internal operations no longer keep pace with competitive pressures, the need for change is heightened. Internal

Inertia
The inability of organizations to change as rapidly as the environment.

changes may include restructuring the organization, the development of training programs, or the need to add resources with particular skill sets.

Over the last few years, Google has taken over Microsoft's once unassailable perch atop the computer/Internet world. Google's rise to power illustrates an important key to internally motivated change. While firms often have limited control over the external environment, they can greatly affect their internal environment. This, in turn, allows them to respond to and even shape their external conditions. Some observers argue that much of Google's success has come through a relentless commitment to fostering innovation and organizing its business around the idea of developing internal agility. As discussed in Chapter 8, successes such as Gmail and Google Maps started as innovation communities rather than through a top-down investment in R&D. These innovations have the power to change Google's direction by creating new lines of business.

Innovation requires more than technology and open structures, of course. Developing and managing the individuals who form the Google family is a top priority. As such, hiring and on-boarding at Google remain critical to its success. New employees must go through a rigorous interview schedule, meeting with potential teammates, managers, and executives. They are vetted in these interviews to see if they have the skill, drive, and attitude to thrive in Google's innovative environment. This practice has proven critical as Google maintains its culture by hiring individuals who can effect change in the organization. In other words, Google prepares the organization for change by hiring people who are always looking for change and have the ability to adjust when necessary. Through its efforts, Google has created a culture that celebrates change and pushes contributors to innovate. Google thrives by asking employees to take risks, to follow their passions, and to not be afraid of failure.[30]

As organizations grow, adapt, and even transform, different drivers intensify at different times. Sometimes change initiatives are focused on cost cutting or process improvement. In other situations, the nature of the change initiative is more culturally focused. The objective of the change process often dictates the most appropriate approach.

KEY ASPECTS OF ORGANIZATIONAL CHANGE

Understanding the need for change and where it originates is only part of the equation. The more difficult aspect of the change process is often the way in which it is channeled in an organization. Companies often need to find the right balance between reactive and proactive change, between planned and organic change, and between incremental and transformative change (see Figure 11.1). Balancing these approaches is a key role of leadership in an organization.

Triggers of Change: Reactive versus Proactive

Organizations receive constant feedback from both inside and outside the organization. When those signals portend a "growing misalignment," the best organizations act quickly to analyze the nature of the phenomena, design the most effective changes to be made, and then execute them.[31]

Reactive change is a process where change is initiated in response to some known external threat or opportunity. For instance, when oil prices drop, oil companies often react by changing their activities, focusing less on exploration and more on cost management. Reactive change programs are generally rolled out from the top-down. Leaders tend to notice lagging performance indicators first and then seek to identify the problem. Once they diagnose the problem, they analyze the issue

Reactive change
A process in which change is initiated in response to some known external threat or opportunity.

Peter Morgan/Reuters/Landov

and seek to find its underlying causes. Often the initial problem turns out to be a symptom of greater, more fundamental issues. Once leaders understand the full scope of the problem, the next phase requires them to design different options for closing the gap or solving the problem. Typically, the plan includes not only the steps to be taken but also the identification of individuals who will be accountable for each of them. Deadlines and checkpoints are also created and agreed upon.

Of course, the capacity to react effectively to environmental shifts is crucial; yet the greater ability, in terms of leverage for higher levels of performance, comes through the capacity to engage proactively with change. **Proactive change** has the potential to thrust an organization forward in the marketplace, thus creating the opportunity for greater competitive success. Proactive change is a process in which change is initiated based on some anticipatory event or opportunity on the horizon.[32] Where the nature of reactive change forces organizations to focus almost exclusively on closing some strategic or performance gap, proactive change encourages the search for new opportunities.

Proactive change leaders often engage in envisioning new possibilities for an organization. This envisioning leads to designing what should be, rather than simply focusing on what is. The exploration of what should be leads to implementing a plan to create what will be.[33] This collectively held image is used by individuals and teams to find ways to proactively move an organization in that direction.

One of the final initiatives that Jack Welch championed before stepping down as CEO at GE personifies proactive change. Looking to leave the organization moving into the future even more strongly than before, he launched a program called "destroyyourbusiness.com." When speaking of his reasoning, he succinctly stated, "Change means opportunity. And this is our greatest opportunity yet."[34] In doing so, he wanted to force managers to look beyond the current state of the company to a future desired state. He also wanted them to identify changes or competitors on the horizon that could supplant their role in their respective industries.

Origination of Change: Planned versus Organic

Proactive change
A process in which change is initiated based on some anticipatory event or opportunity on the horizon.

Planned change
A process where change efforts are predetermined and driven from corporate strategy departments or top-down directives.

When we think of change, we most often think of planned change—interventions where organizational leaders plan to affect a few or all of the following: organizational structures, processes, and culture as well as the behaviors, beliefs, and emotions of their employees. **Planned change** is a process where change efforts are predetermined and driven from the top-down. Organizations often initiate this type of change through a planned program based on a scan of the competitive horizon, an analysis of their control cycle, or through a strength, weakness, opportunity, threat (SWOT) analysis. As we discussed in Chapter 4, many organizations employ strategic planning functions to help ensure that they remain competitive and relevant in the marketplace. Organizations engage in planned change to "create a better fit between the organization's capabilities and its current environmental

Triggers of Change	Origination of Change	Magnitude of Change
• Reactive • Proactive	• Planned • Organic	• Incremental • Transformative

Figure 11.1 ⟩ Balancing the Different Approaches to Change

Source: Wal-Mart Stores, Inc. annual reports for 1999, 2004, 2010, and 2014

demands, or promote changes that help the organization to better fit predicted future environments."[35]

Although planned change surfaces from organizational leaders who perceive gaps in alignment or potential future opportunities and then design and implement distinct change initiatives in a top-down approach, **organic change** emerges from lower in the organization from individuals or teams as they innovate, solve problems, seek more effective ways to accomplish their work, react to large environmental shifts, or interact with others in cross-functional positions.[36] Note that change in an organization can be both top-down and also organic at the same time.

Organic change gains its "distinctive quality" from the precept that "continuous adjustments . . . can cumulate and create substantial change."[37] Often organic change begins through employee empowerment in areas that place value on having problems solved at the level of those who do the work. Individuals as well as managers are trusted and asked to identify opportunities for improvement. When the answers or best practices do emerge, a manager can institute changes and share them across the organization where necessary. Organic change can be slow, but it also can lead to increased organizational buy-in.

The empowering nature of organic change offers space for unleashing the creative drives in individuals and teams. Organic change is about "harnessing the collective genius" of teams and individuals and using it to make a difference for an organization.[38] Unfortunately, in authoritative top-down organizations, organic change is difficult if not impossible to initiate. Even in organizations that are more open, the uncertainty inherent in organic change can generate unease.

Magnitude of Change: Incremental versus Transformative

Another facet of change to consider is the magnitude of change. During stable times, most organizations engage in **incremental change**, a process in which small improvements or changes are made to processes and approaches on an ongoing basis. Incremental change is often part of a planned process and could include improvements in the quality of operations, supply chain processes, or product or service features.

In many organizations, incremental changes are focused on what are called **sustainable technologies**, which are designed to "improve the performance of established products, along the dimensions of performance that mainstream customers in major markets have historically valued."[39] While improvements in sustainable technologies are important, success on this dimension can lead to complacency and prevent new ideas or approaches from filtering into the company.[40] These new ideas can sometimes take the form of **disruptive technologies**, which usually include a different set of attributes than those valued by mainstream customers. These attributes generally appear to satisfy only a small subset of the market and often do not initially appear to be very compelling or valuable.[41]

Leaders who focus solely on sustainable technologies may hurt their organizations in the long term. Focusing solely on sustainable technologies drives managers to make resource allocation decisions based on their current customers and ignore future potential markets. Xerox's failure to capitalize on the small tabletop photocopier market is a case in point. Xerox had so dominated the photocopier industry with large copy centers that its name became synonymous with copying. The company's management and sales practices were considered the best in the industry. Yet when the idea of developing small tabletop photocopiers emerged, Xerox did nothing. When the small copiers appeared on the market, the demand was so low that Xerox continued building the large copiers it believed its best customers wanted. For the most part, these customers did not want the smaller copiers, but a much larger customer base was on the horizon. By not going after the small copier market, Xerox missed out on a massive profit opportunity. Ultimately, their joint venture with Fuji, which was focused on the Japanese market and most vulnerable to

Organic change
A process by which change emerges from individuals or teams as they innovate, solve problems, seek more effective ways to accomplish their work, react to large environmental shifts, or interact with others in cross-functional positions.

Incremental change
A process in which small improvements or changes are made to processes and approaches on an ongoing basis.

Sustainable technologies
Innovative forces that improve the performance of established products, along the dimensions of performance that mainstream customers in major markets have historically valued.

Disruptive technologies
Innovative forces that include a different set of attributes than those valued by mainstream customers.

iStockphoto.com/Shaun Lowe

this gap in their product line, found a solution. A small team collaborated to build a new smaller product themselves, without the permission of the parent company. This unanticipated innovation allowed Xerox to shore up their position in the small copier market.

When organizations perceive disruptive technologies in the marketplace or ones that will create entirely new markets, they must react, adapt, and even transform to keep or increase market share and profitability. With enough foresight, they may be able to engage in proactive changes and prepare themselves to lead in disruptive arenas. As we mentioned in the Introduction, Kodak is one firm that failed to innovate in its industry even after it saw the changes coming.

Kodak's fall from grace came with the rise of digital technology, a disruptive innovation that kept eating away at the photographic film market. From 1996 to 2007, digital imaging "hollowed out Kodak's core film business."[42] The irony is that Kodak had invested in digital cameras as early as 1970. Yet Kodak's problem was typical of sustainable technology thinking: many individuals in the company did not want to take the company in the digital direction because they felt threatened by the new technology and were concerned about cannibalizing their core film business.[43] Ever since Kodak began to lose market share in the early 1990s, it searched for a way to get back to its market leader position. The company changed structures, fired thousands of employees, brought in new management, and invested in massive retraining programs. In spite of all its efforts, success was unattainable. A similar story unfolded at Polaroid that clung to its instant picture film model right until the company shut down.

Many organizations face significant inflection points in their history, sometimes called "frame-breaking changes."[44] These inflections can be triggered by disruptive technologies; new competitive threats; shifts in internal dynamics, including the loss of key resources; new government regulations; or other factors. The airline industry in the United States experienced such a frame-breaking jolt when it was deregulated in 1978. Deregulation changed all of the industry's rules. Before deregulation, the Civil Aviation Board dictated air fares, routes, new airlines, and many other aspects of air travel. After deregulation, competition intensified as new airlines entered the industry and fares were sharply cut.[45] The entire economics of doing business changed, which called for **transformative change**, a process where change is radical or disruptive, typically in response to a major competitive threat and/or significant change in a firm's external or internal environment.

Transformational change often accompanies dramatic shifts not only in processes, systems, and people but also in strategy and mission. The changes are so drastic that creating alignment requires breaking the old paradigms and introducing completely new ones. Needless to say, while incremental change is welcomed by most individuals in an organization, transformational change faces much greater resistance. We will address ways to confront resistance to change later in this chapter.

Transformative change
A process in which change is radical or disruptive, typically in response to a major competitive threat and/or significant change in a firm's external or internal environment.

THE CHANGE PROCESS

Change is not an easy process for many organizations. While some in a company may see a need for change, many others will be satisfied with the status quo, fearing that any change may lessen their credibility or status in the organization. One universal truth that everyone will agree upon, no matter how good of an idea you may have for any change, you will always encounter resistance to it.

Figure 11.2 A Change Process

Leaders who seek to lead change often can't simply announce a plan and hope it will stick. Making change a reality requires concerted effort and a methodical approach to overcome resistance that could derail the initiative. For starters, leaders must make the case for change by creating dissatisfaction with the status quo and presenting a new model for the organization that is realistic, compelling, and appealing. In addition, for change to be successful, leaders need to lessen employees' fears about and resistance to the change process. The major components of the change process can be summarized in a simple formula (see Figure 11.2) where D is dissatisfaction with the status quo, M is a new model for the organization, and P is the process for change. The combination of these forces for change must be greater than the resistance to change (Rc) and cost of change (Cc) that employees experience.[46]

Creating Dissatisfaction

In this formula, **dissatisfaction** (D) provides the energy necessary for breaking organizational inertia and helps create the motivation for change. Creating dissatisfaction with the status quo helps to free people and organizations from complacency. In a crisis situation, dissatisfaction is generally high and many employees understand the need for change. In this case, the leader doesn't have to do much. The real challenge comes when leaders see potential forces for change on the horizon that are not impacting the firm's performance today but could be major influences in the future. How does a leader create a case for change in this situation? How does he or she jolt an organization out of complacency? How does he or she create a sense of dissatisfaction with the status quo within their organization?

Some researchers have likened the creating of dissatisfaction to "unfreezing" an organization.[47] Unfreezing can be very difficult because most people gravitate toward patterned behavior, especially when they have been successful in the past. One way to build dissatisfaction is to appeal to the rational instincts among employees and show them a quantitative assessment of the need for change. This can be done by disseminating a benchmarking or internal and external performance/opportunity gap analysis that clearly shows the challenges ahead for their firm. As we discussed in Chapter 10, with benchmarking, organizations compare their performance to that of other companies in the same or different industries that are "best in class." This can sometimes showcase a looming gap with key competitors on important dimensions and can serve as a motivation for change.[48] Other external triggers can be identified by scanning the competitive horizon—looking for ways in which the context is likely to change and benchmarking an organization's ability to meet the new contextual realities. Employee attitude surveys are a means to better understand employee concerns and issues, and the results of those surveys can also provide the foundation for a change process.

To ensure traction, organizational dissatisfaction must extend beyond a few scattered individuals to include influential leaders. It is particularly important to identify those who are essential to the change process and to solicit their support. Without the support of key individuals, change can be easily derailed or minimized.

Developing a New Model for the Future

Once dissatisfaction has been aroused, it needs to be channeled. One way that leaders channel dissatisfaction is through the development and communication of a compelling **model** (M) or vision for change. The model should present a portrait

Dissatisfaction
A component of the change process in which creating dissatisfaction with the status quo helps to free people and organizations from complacency or inertia. It often creates the spark needed to begin the change process.

Model
A vision for change.

> **Desirable**
> • Satisfies stakeholders
> • Motivates employees

> **Feasible**
> • Opportunity for short-term wins
> • Realistic stretch

> **Relevant**
> • Contextually sensitive

Figure 11.3 ⟩ Characteristics of Effective Models

of what is being changed and why. It should present a description of a future end state—where an organization wants to go and what it needs to do to get there.

A compelling model offers employees hope and a higher sense of meaning as they band together to achieve the desired goal. Effective models are desirable, feasible, and relevant (see Figure 11.3). Change often requires organizations to stretch in significant ways, but the desired change should not be so radical that employees can easily discount it. If the model appears to be beyond the realm of possibility, it can be easily resisted in an organization. The model also should fit with the expected contextual landscape in which the company will work.

In communicating the model for change, leaders need to appeal to both logic and emotions. They must present a compelling case for change based on benchmarking or other assessments. In addition, leaders need to tap into an emotional connection with employees. They often do so by demonstrating passion and excitement for the desired change. This passion can become contagious if leaders understand and respond to employees' concerns and issues. As we will see, change can be easily resisted if employees do not feel a sense of emotional engagement in the process.

The Implementation Process

Process
A series of plans (communication, measurement, etc.) and approaches to implement a change effort.

Dissatisfaction with the current situation and a model for a high-performing future state will come to nothing if people do not know how to get there. The most important next step is to develop an effective process for implementing change. An effective **process (P)** includes a detailed implementation plan, a communication process, and a mechanism for measuring progress. This often includes a combination of kickoff events or meetings coupled with training sessions focused on implementing the desired changes in the organization. The process serves as the map to building organizational change.

Many organizational leaders fail to create lasting changes by mistakenly seeing organizational change as an event rather than a process. After years of studying the

The Leadership Development Journey

The premise of this book is that leadership is a continuous learning journey. Reflect upon an example of managing change as it applies to your personal life.

• How did you manage change successfully?
• What was the impetus for managing change?
• Did change management in your personal life include a new mode of behavior?
• When have you resisted change and why?

difference between organizations that create real change and those that generate only fleeting progress, John P. Kotter developed an eight-step process that outlines many of the keys to success.[49] The first few steps of his process are aligned with creating dissatisfaction with the status quo and crafting a model for a better future. Kotter found that most significant changes occur in sequence as follows:

1. *Establish a sense of urgency.* Change leaders must build enough momentum to overcome any inherent organizational or individual inertia. This is part of the process of raising dissatisfaction in an organization and galvanizing people into action.

2. *Form a powerful guiding coalition.* Once a sense of urgency is heightened, it is important to build a team or coalition of support. This must include individuals who have both the authority and responsibility for ensuring that change can be successfully cultivated. The support of the senior management team is particularly important if the change process is being championed by lower level employees in the organization.[50]

3. *Develop a vision.* The vision includes the model of the desired future state of an organization. This vision must move beyond numbers to give direction and impetus for the organization to move.

4. *Communicate the new vision.* Communication is vital to ensuring buy-in throughout an organization. A vision can provide a source of motivation and excitement for employees.[51] As mentioned previously, communication must speak to both the mind and heart of employees. That is, employees must logically understand the case for change as well as have the passion to engage in the change process.

5. *Empower others to act on the vision.* After creating and sharing the vision, the guiding coalition must work to empower an organization to act. The communication plan should reinforce empowerment, but the coalition also must remove the organizational structure, systems, and process obstacles.

6. *Plan for and create short-term wins.* The change implementation process can be a long one. To sustain momentum and excitement, it is important to set short-term goals and, when you achieve them, to celebrate. Otherwise, having only a long-term plan plays into the hands of cynics who can easily tout the lack of progress.

7. *Consolidate improvements and produce more changes.* While the initial push to move a change program forward is often the most difficult, the program can fail at other crucial junctures. One of these occurs after some initial momentum when the tendency is to think "we have arrived." Reinvigorating the change process requires constant vigilance and the full involvement of organizational leaders, especially in the heat of pushing the wheel forward or, if the wheel has begun to move forward, when people want to stop pushing to rest their arms.

8. *Institutionalize changes in the culture.* The new processes, systems, and values have to become institutionalized for success to be sustained. This institutionalization requires management to share how the new system has accomplished its goal, to explain how performance has improved because of it, and to instill those norms and values into the next generation of leaders.

Freezing the changes in place is often overlooked. As any personal coach or person who has tried and failed at dieting will explain, embedding the new behaviors into common practice is difficult. Many individuals will fall back into old patterns once the anxiety is no longer strong enough to move the system toward change. Refreezing makes change sustainable. To refreeze organizational change requires paying attention to the environment. Structures, systems, and culture have to be aligned to the desired change.[52]

In leading change, it is also important to think about timing and pace. In situations where there is high dissatisfaction, a heightened sense of urgency, and a large

- Urgency or crisis
- High dissatisfaction
- Low resistance
- High level of support
- Leadership has relevant information
- Changes are clear

Top-Down, Directive Process

- Not a crisis
- High need for commitment to engage in change
- Change is not clear
- Change is complex
- Leadership needs support of key constituents

Collaborative Process

Figure 11.4 ⟩ Process for Implementing Change

Sources: Rosabeth Moss Kanter, Barry A. Stein, and Todd D. Jick, *The Challenge of Organizational Change: How Companies Experience It and Leaders Guide It* (New York: Free Press, 1992), pp. 489–519; and Rosabeth Moss Kanter, "Leadership for Change: Enduring Skills for Change Masters," Harvard Business School Note No. 9-304-062, revised November 17, 2005 (Boston, MA: HBS Publishing, 2003), pp. 15–16.

base of support, change can be implemented in a more top-down, directive fashion. This is particularly true for organizations facing a deep crisis. Under this pressure, "bold strokes" may be the best initial implementation plan. In situations where the change process is complex, the outcomes/benefits of change are not immediately clear, and there is a need to galvanize followers, a slower, more collaborative approach may be appropriate. Leaders need to assess the situation that is driving change and engage in the right type of leadership approach (see Figure 11.4).

The ultimate goal or objective of the change process also impacts the nature of the implementation. When the goal is strictly focused on improving shareholder value or cash flow, a more directive, authoritarian approach is often utilized. When the goal is broader cultural change, a more participatory and collaborative process is typically adopted. Effective and sustainable change actually requires a combination of both approaches. In many cases, leaders need to make some quick bold moves to improve financial performance or overall competitiveness. Sustainability and long-term success, though, hinge on an engaged and enthusiastic employee base, which requires leaders to be less dictatorial and more participatory. As such, successful change leaders need to find the right balance between these approaches.[53]

Together, the first three variables in the change equation (dissatisfaction, model, and process) form the driving forces, while the cost of change and resistance to change represent the restraining forces. The equation is a good representation of what happens in change environments, and it has been observed that, without one of these variables, change initiatives often fail. Therefore, all three variables are necessary to ensure success. Let us now briefly turn to the other side of the equation and look at the derailers of change so we can properly anticipate and tackle them.

Costs of and Resistance to Change

If there is one critical fact to understand about organizational change, it is that change is difficult to implement and even more difficult to sustain.[54] Multiple articles, books, conferences, and educational programs are created every year to help executives implement change, yet more change programs fail than succeed every year. Even a cursory glance through *The Wall Street Journal* or the *Harvard Business Review* highlights that implementation of organizational change programs has a poor record of success.[55] One study found that "of 100 companies that attempted to make fundamental changes in the way they did business, only a few were very successful."[56] Another study noted that 70% of all change initiatives fail.[57]

Complacency does not simply unravel organizational transformation efforts; it can also prevent the momentum from ever beginning.[58] Complacency comes from the natural predilection of people to resist change and seek out what they are familiar with. This opposition often grows exponentially when pooled into larger communities. Storytelling, group rationalization, and shared experiences of failed organizational alignment to the new direction can spread and deepen complacency and greatly hinder efforts to transform the old organization. In some organizations where many past change efforts have failed, there is broad cynicism about any new change. The general belief is that these new ideas come and go, and the best approach is to duck for cover and hope the new change will go away like the ones before.

The excitement, model, and process for change must be greater than the cost of and resistance to change. Resistance to change originates at an individual level and then amplifies when you aggregate groups of people who are all hesitant about change. At an individual level, the costs may be social, psychological, emotional, political, or financial. Most of us don't like change once we are comfortable with a certain way of doing things. Change often requires a reevaluation of roles, priorities, and processes. As part of the change process, employees could lose their positions, sense of identity, or friends. Employees may also need to learn new competencies, build new relationships, and invest significant time and energy in "reinventing" themselves. This can be a scary process. As such, people may legitimately fear a loss of influence or status in an organization. Everything they had previously worked toward may now be irrelevant.

Gripped by fear or uncertainty, employees can resist change by either overtly refusing to engage in the process or through passive/aggressive actions—acting as if they support the process, but doing nothing to move it forward. As one researcher noted, all employees possess a "silent veto power" that they can exercise at any time if they disagree with a change initiative.[59] This type of veto power is very difficult to overrule.

Employees may also resist change if they believe the change is not right for the organization or if they do not understand the reasons behind the change process.[60] In these situations, leaders need to do even more to communicate the reasons for change and to build trust throughout the organization.

COMBATING RESISTANCE TO CHANGE

One way to better understand resistance to change is to assess an organization's resources, processes, and values.[61] An organization's resources can dramatically affect the difficulty of engaging the organization in change. Resources include people, equipment, and capital, but they also include intellectual property, brand identity, R&D designs, and relationships with customers, distributors, and suppliers. Organizations that have "access to abundant high-quality resources" face a double-edged sword. At one level, they are in a better position to successfully confront resistance to change but, at another level, the abundance of resources means greater attachment to the status quo and a lack of urgency in the organization.[62] Organizations with poor brand images, lack of cash, or people without the necessary skills to drive change can have lots of urgency within the organization but simply lack the resources to drive change efforts.

While resistance to change ultimately resides within individuals, it is exacerbated by organizational systems. Over time, organizations develop formal processes such as workforce planning and informal processes such as those that determine how decisions are made to allocate resources. The very nature of these processes invites employees to act the same way every time. Their sameness brings greater speed and efficiency. Yet these routines and systems become ingrained in the organizational practices and can produce a massive amount of resistance when organizations begin a transformation initiative.[63] Breaking these processes can be extremely difficult.

The values of an organization are another key factor to consider in managing resistance to change. In the change process, values refer to the manner in which employees work together and set priorities about what is important.[64] In essence, values are reflected in the culture of an organization and impact the way people think and act.[65] What people believe; what they value; what their expectations are for the ways things should be done; and what actions they take because of those predispositions often are the most crucial part in determining whether an organizational change effort will succeed. As noted in Chapter 8, a strong set of values combined with a strong culture can be a formidable barrier to change.

Engaging Hearts and Minds

Organizational leaders often try to help their employees' reason through the necessity of change, but they forget to engage employees' hearts and emotional commitment.[66] They enact change as if structural and procedural changes, or knowledge creation itself, will bring about the desired transformation. Without an emotional engagement that goes beyond analytical reason or structural redesign, inertia will break down any transformational efforts. In the same vein, many change programs falsely equate increased knowledge with improved performance. While improved action may be correlated to increased knowledge, education alone will not improve performance, much less produce change.

Gail McGovern learned the importance of engaging the heart of her organization when she oversaw the transformation of the American Red Cross. When she took over the organization in 2009, it was suffering from a number of problems, including a large financial deficit and a slow, bureaucratic, and confusing organiza-

tional structure. McGovern and her senior team developed a creative and logical restructuring plan that they thought would be an easy sell to the board and the employees. It was not. While the plan was solid, it did not engender passion.

McGovern decided to alter the process of change and reached out to a number of lower level executives to help reshape and reframe the plan. She also decided to share the plan with all 30,000 employees and hundreds of thousands of volunteers. Their input made the plan better and allowed employees to feel a sense of purpose and emotional (not just logical) understanding. Recalling her presentation of the final plan to the chapters of American Red Cross, McGovern stated: "I found myself delivering a deeply emotional talk. I pointed to recent disasters, described how local chapters responded, and implored the group to save the Red Cross. Earlier in my career, I would have considered that kind of speech sappy. But in the room I saw people's skepticism change to belief."[67]

New structures and processes can only provide avenues for change to be implemented; they cannot enforce it. Explaining analytical reasoning for change or delivering programs designed to increase participant knowledge can only build the potential for change, not produce it. Successful organizational change efforts, therefore, build a coalition of believers in the need for change (as McGovern did at the American Red Cross), and they address the key questions that employees have about the impact of change, including the following:

- What is in this change for me?
- What will I have to give up?
- Will I get credit for past achievements?

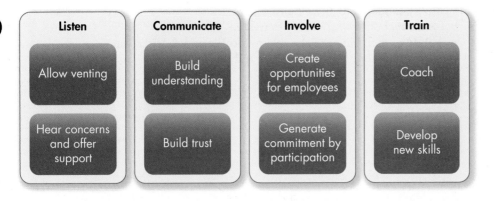

Figure 11.5 Combating Resistance to Change

- Will I know how to do . . . ?
- How does this change affect my career prospects?
- Do I have the energy to make this change?
- Am I really in a position to make a difference?

Some of these questions will be explicitly stated, but others will remain beneath the surface. Successful change leaders help employees answer these questions. The keys to addressing resistance to change are to listen, communicate, involve, and train (see Figure 11.5). Leaders must allow employees impacted by change to vent their frustrations and concerns. If there is no valid outlet for these issues, anger will bubble below the surface and become a strong barrier.[68] As noted, leaders need to constantly communicate the benefits of change and the costs associated with not changing. Effective communication helps build greater trust and understanding throughout an organization. Creating opportunities for key individuals to be a part of the change process often enables leaders to generate a greater level of buy-in and commitment, not just compliance. One common form of involvement includes the establishment of task forces with specific assignments.[69] Finally, employees need to know that there is a path for success that will be facilitated through training and development opportunities; employees won't be left to fend for themselves.

Without an understanding of the factors that cause inertia and resistance to change, change initiatives are unlikely to succeed. In certain circumstances, leaders may need to force employees to engage in the change process. The use of coercion can be effective in times of crisis or turmoil, but it cannot serve as a long-term approach to institutionalizing change.

Characteristics of Change Leaders

The high failure rate of change initiatives points to the difficulty that most individuals and organizations encounter when they try to adapt to internal or external drivers of change. As noted, the forces of resistance can seem insurmountable. To become a change leader requires the drive for change but demands much more than just that. If you are to drive change in your future job what might you need to do aside from having great enthusiasm and commitment to change? To better understand what it takes to successfully lead change, a team of researchers studied over two dozen change initiatives. Through their analysis, they discovered that successful change leaders share the following characteristics:

- Commitment to a better way
- Courage to challenge existing power bases and norms
- Personal initiative to move beyond defined boundaries

- Ability to motivate oneself and others
- Concern about how people are treated
- Ability to maintain a relatively low profile and share credit
- Sense of humor about themselves and the situation[70]

SUMMARY

Organizational change can be driven by external or internal forces and may be focused on operational processes, strategy, people, skills, culture, structure, or a combination of factors. Change is not easy and, in many cases, change efforts fail. Firms that hope to remain relevant must constantly monitor the business environment and adapt their strategies, organizational design choices, or processes on an as-needed basis.

LO1 The need for change can come from both the external environment as well as the internal environment of a firm. In recent years, the external environment of a firm has been impacted by globalization, technology, and disruptive innovation. Firms that succeed for long periods of time are able to adapt or respond to these environmental changes. As a firm responds to external environmental factors, it must also consider its internal resources to determine if it is able to compete effectively in the changed landscape. Sometimes present success can lead to organizational inertia or complacency, which makes future-oriented change even more difficult.

LO2 Some of the most important aspects of change are its triggers, origination, and magnitude. The triggers of change are driven by the marketplace and the external environment. Some organizations simply react to the changes in the environment. Others engage in proactive or preemptive change to ensure that they are continually relevant and innovative. Change can originate through a planned or organic process. Planned change is generally driven from the top of an organization while organic change emerges at lower levels. The final aspect of change is its magnitude. Most organizations pursue incremental change on an ongoing basis in an effort to continuously improve, but there are certain times when transformational change is needed. Transformational change can be driven by the organization in an effort to gain a competitive advantage or it can be driven in response to a fundamental shift in the environmental landscape.

LO3 Identifying the cause or need for change is just the first step. The process of leading change is often very difficult. Leaders need to create a sense of urgency to galvanize a group of influential followers toward a model or vision of the future. This is particularly important when the need for change is not obvious. The model or vision is realized through the implementation process, which may include different leadership approaches. Restructuring processes, removing excess costs, firing employees, or selling off pieces of the business are often performed in a top-down leadership style to secure quick wins. While these approaches are often necessary in the short term, especially in times of crisis, long-term change is sustainable only with a more collaborative approach. This is particularly true when the nature of change is more cultural than structural. In this circumstance, employees need to be involved in the change process. Change leaders need to assess the situation and deploy an appropriate process and style.

LO4 Resistance to change is generally very high in organizations. A key role of leadership is to combat this resistance. Leaders can combat resistance by engaging employees on both cognitive and emotional levels. In addition, leaders need to listen to employee concerns as well as communicate the need and benefits of change. Involving key employees in the change process and providing training opportunities can be effective mechanisms to combat resistance.

KEY TERMS

Disruptive technologies
Dissatisfaction
Incremental change
Inertia
Model

Organic change
Organizational change
Planned change
Proactive change
Process

Reactive change
Sustainable technologies
Transformative change

ASSIGNMENTS

Discussion Topics

1. Why have certain brands like Coca-Cola, Disney, and McDonald's been able to remain relevant for so long? How have they changed with the times?

2. In what ways will Google and Facebook need to evolve to ensure that they continue to be relevant brands in the next 10 years?

3. Why is organizational change so hard?

4. How should a business balance what it does well, today, with what it will need to do in the future? Can a firm do both activities well?

5. What tools can a manager use to scan the external environment in an effort to anticipate potential organizational changes?

6. Consider the various approaches to organizational change. What are the advantages and disadvantages of each approach? Under what conditions is one approach more suitable than another?

7. What is your approach to change? Do you embrace change or avoid it? In what circumstances are you more amenable to change?

8. Why is creating dissatisfaction with the status quo so difficult? In what ways can a manager create dissatisfaction?

9. How is change derailed in organizations? What can managers do to prevent the failure of change processes?

10. Why is building an emotional connection so important in solidifying the change process?

Management Research

1. Select a company that is at least 25 years old. How has that company changed over time? How have they remained relevant?

2. Identify a technological innovation that you believe will impact an industry. How will it impact the competitive landscape? Which company is likely to thrive? To struggle?

In the Field

1. Conduct a podcast interview with a change agent and post this interview on the course's website or YouTube. Ask questions about how the change agent managed the change process and the key implementation components. Ask the change agent to share stories about how he or she exhibited the characteristics of change leaders by engaging hearts and minds through the following:

   • Commitment to a better way

   • Courage to challenge existing power bases and norms

   • Personal initiative to move beyond defined boundaries

   • Ability to motivate oneself and others

   • Concern about how people are treated

   • Ability to maintain a relatively low profile and share credit

   • Sense of humor about themselves and the situation

2. Conduct a change intervention on your campus. For example, create a recycling program in your dormitory. Use the change equation as your roadmap for this intervention and document how you accomplished the following:

   • Created dissatisfaction with the status quo

   • Developed a new mode of behavior

   • Created a change process that supports and institutionalizes the new mode of behavior

ENDNOTES

[1] Lynda M. Applegate and Elizabeth Collins, "IBM's Decade of Transformation: Turnaround to Growth," Harvard Business School Case No. 9-805-130, rev. July 8, 2009 (Boston, MA: HBS Publishing, 2005).

[2] Ibid.

[3] Ibid.

[4] Ibid.

[5] Anthony Wilson-Smith and Berton Woodward, "The Customer Drives Everything," *Maclean's*, Vol. 115, No. 50, 2002, pp. 40–41.

[6] Lynda M. Applegate and Elizabeth Collins, "IBM's Decade of Transformation: Turnaround to Growth," Harvard Business School Case No. 9-805-130, rev. July 8, 2009 (Boston, MA: HBS Publishing, 2005).

[7] Anthony J. Mayo and Nitin Nohria, *In Their Time: The Greatest Business Leaders of the 20th Century* (Boston, MA: HBS Press, 2005), p. 346.

[8] OneSource® Business BrowserSM, www.onesource.com, accessed August, 2010.

[9] Joseph L. Bower and Sonja Ellingson Hout, "Leaders Who Make a Difference: Sam Palmisano's Smarter IBM: Day 1," Harvard Business School Case No. 9-311-030, rev. January 5, 2012 (Boston, MA: Harvard Business School Publishing, 2010).

[10] Ibid.

[11] William W. George, "Leading by Values: Sam Palmisano and IBM," Harvard Business School Case No. 9-411-097, rev. July 21, 2011 (Boston, MA: Harvard Business School Publishing, 2011).

[12] Joseph L. Bower and Sonja Ellingson Hout, "Leaders Who Make a Difference: Sam Palmisano's Smarter IBM: Day 1," Harvard Business School Case No. 9-311-030, rev. January 5, 2012 (Boston, MA: Harvard Business School Publishing, 2010).

[13] Larry Dignan, "IBM CEO Rometty Tales Reinvention, Strategy," *Between the Lines*, March 2014, accessed at http://www.zdnet.com/article/ibm-ceo-rometty-talks-reinvention-strategy/, accessed April 6, 2015.

[14] IBM Global Business Services, "Global CEO Survey," 2008.

[15] Teresa J. Colvin and Ralph H. Kilmann, "A Profile of Large Scale Change," *An Experiential Approach to Organization Development*, Donald F. Harvey and Donald R. Brown, eds. (Upper Saddle River, NJ: Prentice Hall, 2001), p. 202.

[16] Jean Fang quoted in Felix Oberholzer-Gee, Michael Chen, Nancy Dai, and G.A. Donovan, "Doing Business in China," Harvard Business School Case No. 9-713-428 (Boston, MA: HBS Publishing, 2012).

[17] Michael A. Hitt, "The New Frontier: Transformation of Management for the New Millennium," *Organizational Dynamics*, Vol. 28, No. 3, Winter 2000, pp. 6–17.

[18] IBM Global Business Services, "Global CEO Survey," 2008.

[19] Ray Yang quoted in Felix Oberholzer-Gee, Michael Chen, Nancy Dai, and G. A. Donovan, "Doing Business in China," Harvard Business School Case No. 9-713-428 (Boston, MA: HBS Publishing, 2012).

[20] Lynda M. Applegate, Robert D. Austin, and F. Warren McFarlan, *Corporate Information Strategy and Management: Text and Cases* (Boston, MA: McGraw-Hill/Irwin, 2003).

[21] Thomas L. Friedman, *The World Is Flat: A Brief History of the Twenty-First Century* (New York: Farrar, Straus and Giroux, 2005).

[22] Stephen P. Bradley, Pankaj Ghemawat, and Sharon Foley, "Walmart Stores, Inc.," Harvard Business School Case No. 9-794-024, rev. November 6, 2002 (Boston, MA: HBS Publishing, 1994), p. 1.

[23] IBM Global Business Services, "Global CEO Survey," 2008.

[24] Ibid.

[25] Michael A. Hitt, "The New Frontier: Transformation of Management for the New Millennium," *Organizational Dynamics*, Vol. 28, No. 3, Winter 2000, pp. 6–17.

[26] Kevin J. Boudreau and Karim R. Lakhani, "How to Manage Outside Innovation," *MIT Sloan Management Review*, Summer 2009; and Gary P. Pisano and Roberto Verganti, "Which Kind of Collaboration is Right for You?" *Harvard Business Review*, December 2008.

[27] Karim Lakhani and Zahra Kanji, "Threadless: The Business of Community," Harvard Business School Case No. 608-719 (Boston, MA: HBS Publishing, 2008).

[28] Charles A. O'Reilly, III, and Michael L. Tushman, "The Ambidextrous Organization," *Harvard Business Review*, April 2004.

[29] Jeffery Pfeffer, *New Directions for Organization Theory: Problems and Prospects* (New York, Oxford University Press, 1997).

[30] Bala Iyer and Thomas H. Davenport, "Reverse Engineering Google's Innovation Machine," *Harvard Business Review*, April 2008.

[31] Karl E. Weick and Robert E. Quinn, "Organizational Change and Development," *Annual Review of Psychology*, Vol. 50, No. 1, 1999, pp. 361–386.

[32] J. Stewart Black and Hal B. Gergersen, *It Starts With One: Changing Individuals Changes Organizations* (Upper Saddle River, NJ: Wharton School Publishing, 2008).

[33] David L. Cooperrider, Diana Whitney, and Jacqueline M. Stavros, *Appreciative Inquiry Handbook* (Brunswick, OH: Crown Custom Publishing, 2008).

[34] Christopher A. Bartlett, "GE's Two-Decade Transformation: Jack Welch's Leadership," Harvard Business School Case No. 9-399-150, rev. May 3, 2005 (Boston, MA: HBS Publishing, 1999).

[35] Jerry I. Porras and Robert C. Silvers, "Organization Development and Transformation," *Annual Review of Psychology*, Vol. 42, No. 1, 1991, p. 51.

[36] Wanda J. Orlikowski, "Improvising Organizational Transformation Over Time: A Situated Change Perspective," *Information Systems Research*, Vol. 7, No. 1, 1996, pp. 63–92.

[37] Karl E. Weick and Robert E. Quinn, "Organizational Change and Development," *Annual Review of Psychology*, Vol. 50, No. 1, 1999, pp. 361–386.

[38] Linda A. Hill, "Leadership as Collective Genius," *Management 21C: New Visions for the New Millennium*, Subir Chowdry, ed. (New York: Financial Times Publishing, 1999).

[39] Clayton M. Christensen, "Why Great Companies Lose Their Way," *Across the Board*, Vol. 35, No. 9, 1998, pp. 36–42.

[40] Clayton M. Christensen, *The Innovator's Dilemma: When New Technologies Cause Great Firms to Fail* (Boston, MA: HBS Press, 1997).

[41] Joseph L. Bower and Clayton M. Christensen, "Disruptive Technologies: Catching the Wave," *Harvard Business Review*, January–February 1995.

[42] Clayton M. Christensen, "Will Kodak's New Strategy Work?," *Forbes*, February 26, 2007.

[43] Jeremy Dann, "Interview: Focusing on the Next Big Thing," *Strategy and Innovation* (Boston, MA: HBS School Publishing and Innosight, 2003).

44 Michael L. Tushman, William H. Newman, and Elaine Romanelli, "Convergence and Upheaval: Managing the Unsteady Pace of Organizational Evolution," *California Management Review*, Vol. 20, No. 1, Fall 1986, pp. 29–44.

45 Anthony J. Mayo, Nitin Nohria, and Mark Rennella, *Entrepreneurs, Managers, and Leaders: What the Airline Industry Can Teach Us about Leadership* (New York: Palgrave MacMillan, 2009), pp. 149–153.

46 Michael Beer, "Leading Change," Harvard Business School Note No. 9-488-037, rev. January 12, 2007 (Boston, MA: HBS Publishing, 1988).

47 Kurt Lewin, "Frontiers in Group Dynamics: Concept, Method and Reality in Social Science; Social Equilibria and Social Change," *Human Relations*, 1947, pp. 5–41.

48 "Are You Change-Ready? Preparing for Organizational Change," *Managing Change and Transitions* (Boston, MA: HBS Publishing, 2003).

49 John P. Kotter, "Leading Change: Why Transformation Efforts Fail", *Harvard Business Review*, March–April 1995; and John P. Kotter, *Leading Change* (Boston, MA: HBS Press, 1996).

50 Arnoud Franken, Chris Edwards, and Rob Lambert, "Executing Strategic Change: Understanding the Critical Management Elements That Lead to Success," *California Management Review*, Spring 2009.

51 Rosabeth Moss Kanter, "Moving Ideas into Action: Mastering the Art of Change," Harvard Business School Note No. 9-388-022, rev. October 10, 1989 (Boston, MA: HBS Publishing, 1987).

52 Kurt Lewin, "Frontiers in Group Dynamics: Concept, Method and Reality in Social Science; Social Equilibria and Social Change," *Human Relations*, 1947, pp. 5–41.

53 Michael Beer and Nitin Nohria, "Cracking the Code of Change," *Harvard Business Review*, May–June 2000; and Kerry A. Bunker and Michael Wakefield, "The Balance Needed to Lead Change," *Harvard Management Update*, November 2008.

54 John P. Kotter and Leonard A. Schlesinger, "Choosing Strategies for Change," *Harvard Business Review*, March–April 1979.

55 Michael Beer, "Why Total Quality Management Programs Do Not Persist: The Role of Management Quality and Implications for Leading a TQM Transformation," *Decision Sciences*, Vol. 34, No. 4, Fall 2003, p. 626.

56 John P. Kotter, "Leading Change: Why Transformation Efforts Fail," *Harvard Business Review*, March–April 1995.

57 Michael Beer and Nitin Nohria, "Cracking the Code of Change," *Harvard Business Review*, May–June 2000.

58 Freek Vermeulen, Phanish Puranam, and Ranjay Gulati, "Change for Change's Sake," *Harvard Business Review*, June 2010.

59 Rosabeth Moss Kanter, "Leadership for Change: Enduring Skills for Change Masters," Harvard Business School Note No. 9-304-062, rev. November 17, 2005 (Boston, MA: HBS Publishing, 2003).

60 John P. Kotter and Leonard A. Schlesinger, "Choosing Strategies for Change," *Harvard Business Review*, March–April 1979.

61 Clayton M. Christensen and Michael Overdorf, "Meeting the Challenge of Disruptive Change," *Harvard Business Review*, March–April 2000.

62 Ibid.

63 Michael L. Tushman and Charles A. O'Reilly, "Ambidextrous Organizations: Managing Evolutionary and Revolutionary Change," *California Management Review*, Vol. 38, No. 4, Summer 1996, p. 8.

64 Clayton M. Christensen and Michael Overdorf, "Meeting the Challenge of Disruptive Change," *Harvard Business Review*, March–April 2000.

65 Roger Connors and Tom Smith, *Journey to the Emerald City: Achieve a Competitive Edge by Creating a Culture of Accountability* (Paramus, NJ: Prentice Hall, 1999).

66 John P. Kotter and Dan S. Cohen, *The Heart of Change: Real-Life Stories of How People Change Their Organizations* (Boston, MA: HBS Press, 2002).

67 Gail McGovern, "Lead from the Heart," *Harvard Business Review*, March 2014.

68 Jayne Alexandre Dias de Lima, "Managing Change: Winning Hearts and Minds," *Balanced Scorecard Report*, January–February 2009.

69 Rosabeth Moss Kanter, "Moving Ideas into Action: Mastering the Art of Change," Harvard Business School Note No. 9-388-022, rev. October 10, 1989 (Boston, MA: HBS Publishing, 1987).

70 Jon R. Katzenbach and The RCL Team, *Real Change Leaders: How You Can Create Growth and High Performance at Your Company* (New York: Times Books, 1995).

P A R T **4**

INDIVIDUAL PERSPECTIVE

CHAPTER

12

Chapter Outline

Leadership in Organizations

Learning Objectives

After reading this chapter, you should be able to:

LO1 Explain why the study of leadership is so complicated and identify some of the various debates about leadership.

LO2 Describe the different theories of leadership that emerged from analyzing individual leaders.

LO3 Describe how leaders are influenced by followers and describe the theories of leadership that have been derived from analyzing the leader–follower dynamic.

LO4 Explain how the situational context influences the exercise of leadership.

SELF-REFLECTION

What Are Your Leadership Strengths?

Leaders excel when they can leverage their strengths. Do you know your leadership strengths? Read the following statements and assess your leadership strengths on a scale of 1 to 5.

1 = never 2 = rarely 3 = sometimes 4 = usually 5 = always

1. I lead by building cohesive teams. _____

2. I lead by innovating and generating new ideas. _____

3. I lead by using my expertise. _____

4. I lead by emphasizing relationships that are built upon trust and effective communication. _____

5. I lead by empowering others. _____

6. I lead by mentoring and teaching others. _____

7. I lead by focusing on systems and processes. _____

8. I lead by creating a vision and inspiring others to enact the vision. _____

9. I lead by focusing on the end goal or task. _____

10. I lead by encouraging others to experiment and take risks. _____

Based on your responses, what did you learn about your leadership strengths?

INTRODUCTION

Up to this point, we've discussed strategy and organizational design and one of the common threads throughout these chapters has been the role of the individual leader or manager. To fulfill the objectives of strategy, leaders design the organization, motivate their subordinates, and monitor activity to ensure that groups work together to achieve goals. But how does a person lead? What do individuals need to know and do to be effective in their leadership roles?

Ultimately, leadership is about bringing out the best in oneself and in others in order to achieve a collective goal. Some people have mastered the concepts of leadership and make it look easy, while others struggle to motivate people toward a collective goal. Pinpointing what accounts for this difference is difficult because, in many ways, leadership is as mysterious as a well-performed magic trick. But for years, researchers have sought to crack the magician's code and describe the processes that make some leaders so powerful and inspirational.

Leadership research has not provided all of the answers. In fact, much of the research has produced conflicting theories, but it is from these disagreements that key questions about the essence of leadership have emerged.[1] One recurring question is whether leaders are born or made. While it is easy to say that leaders are born to lead, many believe that anyone can become a leader. Those who support that line of thinking believe that if a person understands what to do and how to do it, it is possible to consciously develop leadership skills and behaviors.

Another polarizing topic in the research is the question of whether leadership is universal or contingent. This debate raises such questions as: Is there such a person as a transcendent leader who can lead any group of people in any situation? Or does effective leadership result from the right person with the right skills pursuing the right project at the right time? Would Henry Luce, founder of *TIME*, *Life*, and *Sports Illustrated* magazines, succeed in today's culture of social media? Would Elisabeth Claiborne's conception of fashion for the working woman resonate with the new generation of women in the workforce? Could Ray Kroc, founder of McDonald's, succeed today in the crowded marketplace for health-oriented fast food? Or are these leaders simply reflections of their time?

The final point of contention that plays out in leadership theories is the debate between satisfaction and performance. Is the leader's primary role to ensure superior performance, even if it comes at the cost of their employees' well-being? Or should a leader do everything possible to ensure that his or her followers are happy?

Although these theories seem to oppose each other, they are actually different sides of the same coin. In reality, leadership is a combination of all of these aspects. Leaders are born and made. While some people may have more innate skills, leadership potential exists in everyone, and this potential is realized through practice and experience. Successful leaders are also versatile. They have many different styles and approaches to apply to various situations. And leaders must produce results as well as satisfy employees.

This chapter discusses performance, satisfaction, traits, behaviors, and contingent theories and presents information that is complex and, at times, contradictory. By reading this chapter, you can build your own intellectual framework about leadership. The following case study on Kazuo Inamori highlights many facets of successful leaders. As you read this case, consider his approach to leadership. Is it universal or is it specific to the context of Japan? What can be learned from studying historical and contemporary business leaders?

Kazuo Inamori, a Japanese Entrepreneur

Kazuo Inamori was one of Japan's most successful entrepreneurs during the second half of the twentieth century. Born in southern Japan in 1932, he was the second of seven children. While his parents owned and operated small businesses to support their family, the devastation of World War II and an 8-year war with China deeply affected their business and their ability to survive. Inamori's father encouraged him to begin working after junior high school, but Inamori insisted on completing high school and even persuaded his father to let him attend college. He was given permission as long as he wasn't a financial burden on the family. Despite various obstacles, Inamori persevered; he graduated from high school and college and then worked for a ceramics company before setting out to start his own company, Kyocera, in 1959 at the age of 27.[2]

To start Kyocera, he tried to secure capital by speaking with investors and selling his idea, but his youth made them skeptical. He persisted, however, and eventually gained their confidence, even inspiring one to comment, "I see possibility in you, some potential. You have your own philosophy. That is why I am investing in you."[3] Kyocera manufactured its first product, a ceramic U-shaped tube used in televisions, in 1959, and was profitable in its first year.[4] Being an outsider, Inamori and Kyocera often had to take on projects and work that other more established Japanese firms did not want. Inamori turned these leftovers into a vibrant enterprise through perseverance, dedication, and commitment. By 2014, the company earned more than $14.0 billion in sales and had grown to more than 69,000 employees.[5] Twenty-five years after founding his first company, Inamori founded DDI (later named KDDI), a venture into the telecommunications industry. Many companies entered the industry to compete against Japan's monopolistic Nippon Telegraph and Telephone (NTT), but KDDI outpaced all competitors and, within 10 years, became one of the top alternative long-distance providers in Japan. By 2014, KDDI employed more than 28,000 people and generated $42.1 billion in sales.[6]

With such success, it seemed that Inamori was destined for greatness, regardless of the contextual factors that affected his businesses. His allure became so strong that thousands of people sought his advice and mentorship. So what enabled him to overcome such hardships and succeed? What drew so many to seek his influence and involvement? The core of his success was his management philosophy, a set of ideals that laid out the foundation of his companies' practices. Not only did it drive all business operations, but it also reflected his core beliefs about life.

Beginning in the early days of Kyocera, Inamori knew he had to create a management philosophy that would serve as the pulse of his company. He started cultivating his views in his twenties and continued to refine them throughout his life. Inamori always believed three things: (1) to be happy, people should lead their lives by a guiding philosophy or attitude; (2) people should do the right thing as human beings; and (3) people are in control of their own destiny. He wanted his company to foster such values, and he wanted all of his employees to share these views.[7]

To propagate his philosophies, Inamori developed a culture that cultivated them, including symbols, traditions, and memorable phrases. One of the most influential pieces of the philosophy was his formula for success: The result of your life = Ability × Effort × Attitude. While ability and effort could be scored from 0 to 100, attitude was scored between −100 and 100, which emphasized the weight of attitude. Neither hard work nor capability could overcome a negative attitude.[8] Employees found comfort in the formula because it showed that they did not

Toshifumi Kitamura/AFP/Getty Images

need extraordinary abilities to succeed. As long as they worked hard and had a good attitude, they believed they could lead a happy and fulfilling life—that they could control their destiny. Inamori also adopted a personal motto for his company: "Respect the Divine and Love People."[9] As time passed, he consolidated his views and composed them in a booklet, distributing it to every employee in his company. During compa, weekly employee gatherings of drinks and discussion, Inamori openly read and discussed the Kyocera Philosophy.[10]

These practices were a reflection of Kyocera's overarching goals: to stimulate the material and intellectual growth of its employees and to contribute to advancing society and mankind.[11] Inamori believed that providing such opportunities would naturally lead to business success, and it did. Executives in the company embraced the philosophy because it continued to produce good performance. The chairman of the board even claimed, "If we must choose which comes first [good performance or a philosophy], I would say that we have the philosophy first, and this leads to [the] good performance of our company."[12]

The philosophy worked so well in Kyocera that Inamori used a more concise and compact version of it when launching his new company, DDI. As the philosophy continued to produce results, Inamori believed more and more in its power. During the merger between DDI and another company (to create KDDI), Inamori compromised on many facets of the business, but he refused to concede the Kyocera Philosophy.[13] Even when executives from the partner company doubted its influence and power, Inamori remained resolute and negotiated the Kyocera Philosophy into the new company's culture.

Inamori was clearly a unique business leader. His philosophy had such a profound impact on his companies primarily because it tapped into the motivation of each employee. As you read about the different facets of leadership in this chapter, think about how Kazuo Inamori reflects the qualities of a leader.

Case in Point

Kazuo Inamori, a Japanese Entrepreneur

1. How did Inamori's childhood and adolescent experiences influence his leadership style?

2. What are the pillars of Inamori's management philosophy? Is this an effective management philosophy?

3. Why was creating an organizational culture an important aspect of Inamori's leadership actions?

4. Would you consider Inamori a resilient leader? Why?

THE LEADER

When thinking about leadership, it seems intuitive to first identify great leaders and observe their characteristics. For example, if we look at business leaders such as Oprah Winfrey, Richard Branson, Li Ka-shing, Bill Gates, Steve Jobs, and Kazuo Inamori, it seems they are endowed with capabilities to produce extraordinary results and influence others in order to achieve a common purpose. Such leaders also inspire several questions: What are these leaders like? What do they do? What makes them so influential? If we focus on the traits, skills, and behaviors of great leaders and try to find a common pattern, perhaps we will be able to distill the qualities and styles that are effective in all situations. This was the strategy used by the first group of leadership researchers.

Who Is a Leader? Traits and Skills

For nearly a century, researchers have pursued answers to leadership questions by focusing solely on leaders and examining their traits (innate personal characteristics) and skills (learned capabilities). Using this narrow lens, researchers have attempted to build a theory that not only explains observed leadership patterns but also identifies the characteristics of a universal leader—one who is capable of leading in any situation. While this line of research has been controversial, it does offer some insights into the qualities of individual leaders.

This approach was first called the **"Great Man" theory**, a theory that explained leadership by examining the traits and characteristics of individuals considered to be historically great leaders. This theory posited that the events of human history could be explained by the leadership of people such as Niccolò Machiavelli, George Washington, Abraham Lincoln, and Napoleon Bonaparte, who captured the imagination of followers and deeply influenced millions of individuals.[14] At first, researchers believed that these leaders were born with extraordinary qualities and that they descended from genetically superior family lines. While those theories did not last long, they led to the widely popular **traits-based leadership theory**, a theory of leadership that tries to reveal a set of universal traits and skills that are relevant in all leadership situations.[15]

One of the most common traits identified in leaders is self-confidence. With a strong belief in their abilities and skills, these leaders are more likely to take on responsibility and gain trust from others.[16] Times of crisis cause a great deal of stress and uncertainty about the future of an organization. For example, when the consumption of Tylenol resulted in several deaths in the Chicago area in 1982, Johnson & Johnson (J&J) experienced tremendous public outrage and government pressure to remove all bottles of Tylenol from store shelves.[17] Throughout this crisis, J&J's chief executive officer (CEO), James Burke, was steadfast in his belief in the company's credo, a document

"Great Man" theory
A theory of leadership that explained leadership by examining the traits and characteristics of individuals considered to be historically great leaders.

Traits-based leadership theory
A theory of leadership that tries to reveal a set of universal traits and skills that are relevant in all leadership situations.

iStockphoto.com/Anthony Seebaran

professing a commitment to patients, doctors, communities, and stockholders. By remaining confident and abiding by the company's core values, Burke made crucial decisions in order to navigate J&J through a potential catastrophe. He recalled all Tylenol products and was transparent with the public during the entire investigation. Now J&J is one of the most trusted brands in the world. Self-confident leaders, like James Burke, can overcome such crisis situations and make decisions in the face of uncertainty.[18]

Another common trait found in effective leaders is the drive to take initiative. By exhibiting persistence and a willingness to take risks, leaders persevere in the face of obstacles.[19] It is interesting to note that leaders who take initiative most likely have a high level of self-confidence as well. Taking initiative requires a leader to be confident in his or her abilities to both analyze a situation and devise a sound solution. Other traits that have been attributed to great leaders include high levels of physical energy and motivation to complete tasks.[20] While traits are one important element to consider in the examination of leaders, by themselves, they are not sufficient to assess effective or ineffective leadership. As we will discuss throughout this chapter, there are many other factors that are important to consider when defining leadership.

Leadership Skills

In addition to leadership traits, researchers have identified a core set of learned skills or capabilities that are relevant to effective leadership: **cognitive skills, technical skills,** and **interpersonal skills.** Cognitive skills enable a leader to gather and process large amounts of information, create suitable strategies, solve problems, and make correct decisions.[21] For instance, when the chairman of Samsung electronics visited an electronics store in Los Angeles during the early 1990s, he recognized that Americans viewed Korean electronics as cheap commodities. Upon returning to Korea, he started investing in innovative design and simultaneously began a marketing campaign to bolster the image and reputation of Samsung as a progressive manufacturer of electronics. His small realization mobilized an entire industry to

Cognitive skills
A leader's ability to gather and process large amounts of information, create suitable strategies, solve problems, and make correct decisions.

Technical skills
A leader's knowledge about an organization and job-related activities.

Interpersonal skills
A leader's ability to interact with others.

invest in innovation and eventually resulted in Samsung winning 32 innovation and design awards in 2008.[22] This example shows that, once a leader makes sense of the environment, he or she can then direct subordinates toward activities that result in organizational success.[23]

Technical skills refer to a leader's knowledge about an organization and job-related activities. Technical skills fall into two categories: expertise in a field or activity, and knowledge about an organization or industry. For leaders to be effective, particularly at the lower levels of an organization, they need to be proficient in the methods, processes, and equipment that their subordinates use.[24] This is particularly important in highly technical environments where trust and credibility depend heavily on technical expertise.[25] While technical skills are typically obtained through education, experience can be more important than formal training.[26] A leader's knowledge about an organization, including its rules, structure, and management systems, improves his or her ability to prioritize information and make decisions.[27]

In addition to possessing strong cognitive and technical skills, leaders must develop their interpersonal capabilities. Interpersonal skills refer to a leader's ability to interact with others. Interpersonal skills that have been observed consistently in good leaders include effective communication and social competency. A leader's ability to use symbolic, verbal, and nonverbal communication to make influential presentations improves his or her ability to develop strong coalitions with subordinates, peers, superiors, and those outside the organization.[28] Social competency includes a leader's ability to be aware of how other people's attitudes, assumptions, and beliefs are related to their behaviors and motivation. By understanding these complex interpersonal dynamics, leaders are more effective at empathizing with others, facilitating teamwork, and improving team spirit.[29]

The competence and legitimacy of a leader is often based on a combination of his or her cognitive, technical, and interpersonal skills. In addition to evaluating competence, followers also consider a leader's **character**. Referring to core values and fundamental beliefs, character is a constant factor that drives behavior in variable situations. While this topic is more thoroughly discussed in other chapters, two of the most important character traits in leaders are personal integrity and accountability.[30] Leaders with high personal integrity adhere to a strong set of principles and, by doing so, they inspire confidence, earn respect, and gain loyalty.[31] In many ways, the Kyocera philosophy enabled Inamori to demonstrate his commitment to and respect for his employees. It also functioned as a touchstone for other leaders throughout the organization. For Inamori, leadership is a responsibility that transcends profitability; it has a higher purpose: to improve lives. With the multitude of corporate scandals, controversial bailouts, and political misdeeds in recent years, the importance of character and integrity has been magnified in the public's eye. Inamori's approach stands in stark contrast to that of the leaders who were engaged in these scandals.

What Does a Leader Do? Behaviors

While traits refer to who leaders are, behaviors refer to what leaders do. Beginning in the 1950s, behavior theories emerged from the traits-based theories and added a new perspective with which to consider leadership. This new viewpoint examined the actual work and activities of leaders. By correlating particular behaviors with effectiveness, behavior theories contribute to a more complete understanding of leadership. A popular concept in leadership discourse is that each leader expresses a dominant **leadership style**, which is the pattern of behaviors that leaders use in situations. For example, drill sergeants are said to exhibit a military style of leadership, while humanitarians are often described as servant leaders.

Books and mainstream sources seem to discuss countless types of leadership styles, but researchers have found that leadership styles stem from just two categories of behavior. Leaders can engage in behavior that facilitates task achievement or

Character
The core values and fundamental beliefs that drive behavior in variable situations.

Leadership style
The pattern of behaviors that leaders use in situations.

in behavior that fosters a productive relationship. However, it would be a mistake to assume that these areas are completely independent from each other or that leaders can express only one set of behaviors; these categories interact with each other in complex ways.[32] In reality, leaders must balance the performance standards of their organization with the relational needs of their subordinates.[33]

Focusing on the Task

Individuals who focus on accomplishing a task in an efficient and reliable way exhibit **task-oriented behavior**.[34] Leaders who are purely task-oriented are concerned with group goals and the means of achieving those goals.[35] Primary task-oriented behaviors include the following:[36]

- *Doing short-term planning:* Leaders are responsible for deciding what needs to get done, who is going to do it, and when it needs to be completed. To ensure that an organization does its work efficiently, leaders must prioritize objectives and strategies, assign responsibilities, schedule activities, and allocate resources. Useful tools include written plans, budgets, and staff meetings.
- *Clarifying roles and objectives:* Leaders must ensure that their subordinates fully understand what is expected of them and how to accomplish their tasks. To coordinate work activity, leaders communicate plans and set expectations for specific tasks.
- *Monitoring operations and performance:* In business, leaders are ultimately responsible for the quantity and quality of work produced by their unit. To ensure that subordinates are pursuing the correct path and performing at a high standard, leaders observe workers, read reports, and inspect quality. This category includes many of the functions described in Chapter 10.

While research shows that task-oriented behaviors are strongly correlated with the performance of subordinates, those behaviors do not always contribute to a subordinate's job satisfaction and may even detract from it.[37]

Focusing on the People

The complement to task-oriented behavior is **relations-oriented behavior**, characterized by the concern for interpersonal relationships, the value of workers as humans, and a strong commitment to the unit and its mission.[38] Three main categories account for the most influential behaviors:

- *Supporting subordinates:* By fostering the needs and feelings of others, leaders can build and maintain effective relationships, increase satisfaction, and form emotional ties with their subordinates. When leaders show consideration, acceptance, friendliness, and concern for others, they can influence subordinates' self-confidence, trust in the leader, and commitment to the organization.[39]
- *Developing subordinates:* To elevate an employee's ability and position within a company, leaders can coach, mentor, or offer career counseling to subordinates. Another way to develop subordinates is to treat them as equals and encourage them to take initiative in solving problems.[40] When leaders exhibit these behaviors, they foster mutually cooperative relationships, more job autonomy, and faster career advancement.[41]
- *Recognizing work:* Employees need to feel appreciated for their hard work; therefore, leaders must give praise and show appreciation for subordinates' contributions to the organization or group.[42]

Other benefits of relations-oriented behaviors include lower turnover, higher motivation to work, more creativity, more self-regulation, more long-term success, deeper commitment, and stronger loyalty.[43]

Task-oriented behavior
Behaviors that prioritize the accomplishment of a task in an efficient and reliable way.

Relations-oriented behavior
Behaviors that prioritize interpersonal relationships, the value of workers as humans, and a strong commitment to the unit and its mission.

High-Relationship, Low-Task	**High-Relationship, High-Task**
These individuals are most concerned about the needs and feelings of others. They operate under the assumption that as long as people are happy and secure, they will work hard.	These individuals integrate production and people concerns in a mutually reinforcing effort where all behaviors enhance each other. This is a goal-centered, team approach.
Low-Task, Low-Relationship	**High-Task, Low-Relationship**
These individuals do not have a high regard for creating systems, getting the job done, or developing relationships with others.	These individuals believe that work is simply a means to an end. They believe that employees' needs are secondary to the need for efficient and productive workplaces.

Figure 12.1 The Managerial Grid

Source: Adapted from Mindtools, Ltd., "Blake Mouton Managerial Grid," 2008, www.mindtools.com/pages/article/newLDR_73.htm, accessed September 10, 2008.

The Managerial Grid

Developed in the 1960s, the **managerial grid** (see Figure 12.1) tries to reconcile task-oriented and relations-oriented behaviors.[44] While some researchers believed that task-oriented and relations-oriented behaviors existed at opposite ends of the same spectrum, the prevailing theory was that leaders could exhibit different levels of each category of behaviors, thereby producing different leadership styles. Under this premise, the quality of leadership style depends on the level of each behavior portrayed.

Many factors may affect or limit the style a leader is capable of exhibiting. For instance, an organization may impose rules and requirements that restrict certain behaviors. Other constraints include the manager's values and beliefs, which influence his or her ideals about how to treat others and how to manage results. For example, if a leader believes that quality is more important than meeting deadlines, he or she will not exhibit behaviors that increase the urgency to deliver and, as a result, may decrease overall performance. Finally, a leader's personal history and knowledge can influence his or her style. While most leaders exhibit various styles depending on the situation and task at hand, each leader has a single dominant style, one that he or she feels most comfortable with and defaults to in the majority of situations, especially when under pressure.

The traits and behavior perspectives include a comprehensive set of characteristics about a leader. Still, these theories do not explain why some leaders are revered, even worshipped. This is where the traits and behavior theories end and the charismatic theory of leadership begins.

The Charismatic Leader

Originally, **charismatic leaders** were thought to be people with an inspirational vision who emerged from a crisis situation because of special personal

Managerial grid
A two-dimensional grid showing leaders' different levels of task-oriented and relations-oriented behavior, which results in particular styles of leadership.

Charismatic leaders
Individuals who arouse strong followership through inspirational visions and/ or compelling personal attributes.

characteristics. Using their extraordinary qualities and capabilities, charismatic leaders aroused a strong emotional attachment from followers.[45] Rather than offering material incentives or threatening punishment, these leaders gave meaning and moral purpose to people's lives.[46] However, a modern perspective takes a more pragmatic approach. According to the refined theory, charismatic leaders are not superhuman individuals who have indescribable effects on followers; instead, they exhibit a specific set of traits and behaviors that work together to create the impression that they are endowed with ineffable capabilities.[47] Charisma is not an innate quality; rather, it is the creation of social milieu.[48] In other words, charisma is a source of power that is ascribed to an individual by others; it is socially constructed.

iStockphoto.com/Justin Sullivan/EdStock

According to this line of research, leaders are considered charismatic if they elicit performance beyond expectations from followers, change the fundamental beliefs of followers, instill devotion and loyalty, arouse excitement, and convince followers to sacrifice personal interests for the sake of the collective goal.[49] Steve Jobs was one leader who passionately articulated a future state of interconnection that at once galvanized his employees as well as customers of Apple. His focus on both the technical sophistication and artful, innovative design of Apple products enabled the company to perform beyond anyone's expectations. Commenting on Apple's unique formula, *Time* columnist, Lev Grossman noted: "While most high-tech firms focus on one or two sectors, Apple does them all at once. Apple makes its own hardware, it makes the operating system, and it makes programs that run on the operating system. It also makes the consumer-electronic devices that connect to all of these things. Would anyone run a business like that? If you follow conventional wisdom, Apple is doing it wrong. Try to do everything at once, and you won't do anything well . . . And yet, this is the company that gave us three of the signature innovations of the past 30 years: the Apple II, the Macintosh, and the iPod."[50] The iPhone has also joined that list of iconic products. Apple's success, in large part, was driven by Jobs's vision and charisma. He motivated his employees to reach far beyond what they thought they were capable of, and he motivated customers to expect more from Apple.

Patterns in Charismatic Leaders

Charismatic leaders are extremely self-confident in their abilities, possess a willingness to take personal risks, and usually adhere to a strong moral conviction to exercise their power positively for social benefit.[51] These traits manifest themselves through behaviors, the most important of which is creating a compelling vision. After creating a vision, charismatic leaders communicate this vision to others by using powerful imagery, symbolism, and metaphor. They are adept at using eye contact, fluent gestures, energy, and tone of voice to inspire others.[52] Communicating through speeches and more intimate contact, leaders challenge followers to take initiative. And if leaders express high confidence in followers' abilities, followers feel more capable of accomplishing tasks and achieving the vision.[53] Martin Luther King, Jr.'s "I Have a Dream" speech is one of the most famous expressions of a vision in modern history.[54]

But there is also a darker side to charismatic leadership. Not all charismatic leaders are positive role models. Rather than espousing positive social influence, these leaders are characterized as narcissistic, self-aggrandizing, and exploitive. Rather than developing their followers, they exert power over others and hold them back. Rather than appealing to ideological values that are socially valuable, they promote corrupt ideals to gain power and serve a separate personal agenda. Despite these negative attributes, they still rise to power.[55] An obvious question is, how do these leaders attract followers? Shouldn't rational humans recognize the underlying motives of a leader and reject his or her cause if it poses a threat or is fundamentally immoral? While the answer may seem like a resounding yes, the context of the situation plays a strong role in allowing such leaders to rise to power.

Charismatic leaders often rise to power during times of crisis. When followers suffer from psychological distress and disenchantment with the status quo, it becomes easier for a leader to garner support for a vision that is radically different from, and seemingly better than, the current environment.[56] In a sense, followers can be blinded by the promise of a better future. Under these circumstances, some leaders take advantage of the situation to promote their own agenda.

THE LEADER AND THE FOLLOWERS

The first section of this chapter presented theories that focused primarily on the leader. While the traits, skills, and behaviors of a leader explain some aspects of leadership, they overlook a crucial aspect of the leadership construct: the follower. Even if someone has the formal position of a leader, they can only truly function as a leader if their followers accept them as a leader. After all, you are only a leader if you have followers. In reality, leadership is a dynamic interaction between those who lead and those who are led, in which leaders are influenced by followers as much as followers are influenced by leaders.[57]

Transformational Leadership Theory

One of the most popular and heavily researched concepts in this area is **transformational leadership**, which is defined as a set of behaviors that leaders use to transform or change their organization and individuals for the better. Guided by a strong moral compass and a sense of duty, transformational leaders influence followers to work toward a common vision and achieve results that exceed expectations. Scholars developed this theory through observational studies of highly successful CEOs and managers. While transformational leadership sounds similar to charismatic leadership, there are important differences. For instance, scholars insist that transformational leadership is applicable to all levels of an organization, not just the top.

Components of Transformational Leadership

Transformational leadership focuses on the process of change, assuming that effective leadership is performed under conditions of rapid technological, social, and cultural change. Based on interviews with successful change agents, scholars identified a common pattern that they claim is relevant to all leaders at all levels of organizations. Transformational leaders appeal to followers' higher level needs by motivating them to sacrifice self-interests and personal goals for the group's interests and goals.[58] Transformational leaders are characterized by the following:

- *Charisma and vision:* Charisma is necessary for transformational leadership, but charisma alone is not sufficient to create a transformational process.[59] Charisma refers to the same set of traits and behaviors as described previously, but transformational leadership places a stronger emphasis on providing a vision, instilling pride, and garnering the respect and trust of followers, which results in a strong emotional attachment to the leader.[60] Inspiring a shared vision is considered one of the most important aspects of leadership because it adds meaning to activities, arouses emotions, and intellectually stimulates followers.[61]
- *Inspirational motivation:* To inspire followers to pursue a vision, leaders must gain a great deal of trust. This is accomplished by upholding strong moral and ethical standards and acting as a role model for the vision. People trust leaders

Transformational leadership
A set of behaviors that leaders use to transform or change their organization and individuals for the better.

The Leadership Development Journey

Robert Quinn coined the term "fundamental leaders" to describe individuals who optimize organizational performance through transformational leadership.[72] In the fundamental state, leaders are

- Results-centered by pursuing ambitious new outcomes
- Internally directed by behaving according to their values
- Other-focused by putting the good of the collective first
- Externally open to learning from their environment and adapting to change

Reflect upon a time when you entered a fundamental state of leadership.

1. What was the impetus for your fundamental state of leadership?
2. How was your performance optimal in the fundamental state of leadership?
3. How do you think you can more frequently enter a fundamental state of leadership?

who communicate their values and maintain integrity in the face of pressure. In essence, they trust leaders who are predictable.[62] The more people trust their leader, the more willing they are to take personal risks, make changes, and improve the organization.[63]

- *Intellectual stimulation:* Respect for a leader is very important, and one of the best ways to earn respect is to give it. Within the context of intellectual stimulation, this means that leaders challenge their followers to think for themselves and to be creative in solving problems that may be beyond their current capabilities; as a result, the follower's ability to interpret problems and generate solutions improves.[64] Most importantly, leaders encourage others to challenge ideas. With more autonomy to challenge the beliefs of the group, transformational leaders stimulate creativity and innovation. But this can happen only in an environment of mutual trust and respect.[65] To promote this kind of environment, leaders should openly question their own assumptions, reframe problems, and approach old situations in new ways.[66]

- *Individualized consideration:* Like the traits- and behavior-based theories, one of the most important aspects of transformational leadership is individualized consideration, which is a leader's effort to understand each follower's needs for achievement, growth, and support and to continuously develop the followers' abilities.[67] By actively listening, delegating tasks, and monitoring results, leaders help individuals grow and achieve results.[68]

Transformational leaders are capable of producing effects that are rarely seen in groups led by other types of leaders. Perhaps the most striking and consistent result is that transformational leaders can influence their followers to transcend self-interests and dedicate themselves to accomplishing more than they thought possible.[69]

Transactional Leadership Theory

While charismatic and transformational leadership theories describe leadership in the context of emotional arousal and in motivating followers to exceed their expectations, transactional leadership describes a simple process that is more common in management of organizations. **Transactional leadership** is a style of leadership in which a leader provides something to subordinates in return for something the subordinates want.[70] The underlying model here is that the relationship between the leader and the follower is a form of exchange or transaction in which each provides

Transactional leadership
The process by which a leader provides something to subordinates in return for something the subordinates want.

the other something they want. For example, managers provide the promise of a raise or a promotion in return for hard work and quality products. In politics, bureaucrats make campaign promises in exchange for votes.[71] Recall from Chapter 10 that these types of transactions are strong components of performance management.

Components of Transactional Leadership

The two most important approaches to deploying transactional leadership are **contingent reward** and **management-by-exception** (MBE), which is further divided into active MBE and passive MBE.[73] MBE is a method of leadership, engaged either passively or actively, that dictates when leaders should intervene to increase a subordinate's effort to meet standards. Other activities associated with transactional leadership include many task-oriented behaviors, such as setting organizational goals, outlining detailed steps, allocating resources, organizing and staffing jobs, and monitoring results to solve problems.[74]

- *Contingent reward:* Known as the carrot-and-stick method, contingent reward is the exchange process between leaders and followers in which leaders offer rewards to subordinates in exchange for their services.[75] Leaders will offer a range of things from tangible items such as compensation, votes, and promotions to psychological items such as trust, commitment, and respect. However, the latter are rarer and more characteristic of transformational leadership.[76] To use contingent rewards effectively, leaders should understand what followers want most from their work, whether it is compensation, career advancement, or more subtle desires, and do their best to provide those things. For example, some employees care more about their salary, while others care more about the people they work with and the culture of the company. We will discuss motivational drivers in more detail in Chapter 18.
- *Active management-by-exception:* When managers use active MBE, they constantly monitor employees to make sure they are meeting standards and avoiding mistakes. If subordinates deviate from their desired performance, managers can take immediate action to correct performance.[77] Forms of active MBE range from positive reinforcement, which improves self-esteem and long-term achievement, to negative criticism. Before employees begin their work, leaders should clarify expectations for performance, which helps the subordinate avoid confusion and build confidence.[78]
- *Passive management-by-exception:* While active MBE promotes constant monitoring, passive MBE dictates that managers should take corrective action only when subordinates fall below expectations.[79] Passive MBE avoids micromanaging and allows subordinates to work more autonomously. Thus, subordinates learn from mistakes and become more functionally independent. While this may be a riskier strategy in the short term, it is more effective in the long term. Managers should balance each style of MBE based on the urgency of the situation and the skill level of their subordinates. For example, active MBE is more appropriate in high pressure situations or when managing workers who are less skilled.

Combining Transactional with Transformational Leadership

By negotiating an exchange of rewards and effort, employees work hard to achieve goals, but effort and commitment can decline once employees reach targets. Only when employees are emotionally invested in their work will they continue to perform beyond expectations. In these situations, they no longer work for material rewards, but for self-satisfaction and personal pride.[80] Put simply, transactional leadership does not go far enough to motivate followers to achieve their full potential.[81] This is not to say that transactional methods should be ignored; in fact, they are a necessary part of any organizational leadership.[82]

Contingent reward
The exchange process between leaders and followers in which leaders offer rewards to subordinates in exchange for their services.

Management-by-exception
A method of leadership done passively or actively that prescribes when leaders should intervene to increase a subordinate's effort to meet standards.

The best leaders display both transactional and transformational leadership behaviors.[83] While transactional leaders create order, maintain efficiency, and produce consistent results, transformational leaders elevate performance by introducing an emotional element. Transactional leaders use the existing framework to get results, but transformational leaders will change the framework to pursue new opportunities and avoid crises.[84] Transformational leaders also have better relationships with their subordinates because they instill a sense of duty, articulate a vision of a higher social cause, and stimulate followers' intellects, consequently improving satisfaction and performance.[85] Henry Ford, for example, was both transactional and transformational. While he gave workers a high wage ($5 per day) and controlled activity with rigid rules and procedures, he transformed the automobile industry by using the assembly line and hiring the disabled and illiterate.[86]

Leader–Member Exchange Theory

While the transformational and transactional theories of leadership focus on the way in which leaders use inspiration or rewards to motivate followers to pursue organizational goals, the **leader–member exchange** (LMX) theory dives deeper into the actual relationship between a leader and a follower. Before the LMX theory, all leadership theories assumed that leaders exhibit the same traits, behaviors, and styles toward all members of the group they lead—that they use the same style of leadership with all of their followers. The LMX theory challenged this assumption. According to this theory, leaders treat each member differently; as a result, they develop unique relationships with each follower.[87]

As leaders work with subordinates to define each individual's role, they develop a high-exchange or a low-exchange relationship.[88] Owing to time constraints and job responsibilities, leaders are capable of developing a high-exchange relationship with only a few key members. The rest of the group is subjected to formal authority, rules, and policies. As a result, two groups form: the in-group and the out-group.[89]

In-Groups and Out-Groups

A leader's relationship with members of the in-group compared to that with members of the out-group echoes the duality we have seen throughout much of the chapter: some leaders prioritize a close personal relationship, while others maintain a structured environment to get work done. But rather than exhibiting one consistent style, the leader exhibits both behaviors. Much like transformational leadership and relationship-oriented behavior, high-exchange relationships are most strongly characterized by mutual trust, respect, and commitment.[90] A leader invokes commitment by offering more autonomy, influence, and support to followers.[91]

When subordinates are part of the in-group, they are assigned more interesting tasks, gain greater responsibility and authority, and receive more tangible rewards such as raises and promotions.[92] They also receive more resources to complete their work, which further enables them to advance their influence and career. This strongly contrasts with the characteristics of an out-group relationship, which suffers from a low level of mutual influence. Subordinates simply comply with formal rules and do what is required of them; as a result, they receive the standard benefits of the job.[93]

Followers are not the only ones to gain in the high-exchange relationship; leaders also benefit from the interaction. They can accomplish more work more efficiently because their members are willing to go above and beyond the duties of their position. Under high-exchange relationships, subordinates look for innovative ways to achieve the group's goals and spend more time communicating; overall, they are more dependable than out-group members.[94] Because these

Leader–member exchange theory
A method of leadership in which leaders treat each follower differently, and as a result, develop unique relationships with each member.

subordinates work harder and are more committed to the task, the relationship transforms into one marked by high mutual dependence, loyalty, and trust.[95] The organization also experiences less employee turnover, better job attitudes, and greater participation.[96]

While the advantages of a high-exchange relationship are clear, usually a leader can develop this relationship with only a small number of people. As a result, subordinates compete for the leader's time as they seek access to the in-group. Table 12.1 describes the actions that help followers gain that access.[97] On the surface, this approach to leadership can appear to be unfair or discriminatory.[98] For this reason, LMX evolved to include the relationship life cycle, a concept that promotes equal treatment and opportunity for all subordinates.

The Relationship Life Cycle

The **relationship life cycle** was created by LMX researchers to promote a more equitable leadership style and improve overall performance in organizations.[99] After observing the different relationships that leaders cultivate, researchers discovered that LMX relationships are products of a role-making process. While a leader provides opportunities to subordinates to advance their responsibilities and skills, the leader also evaluates the extent to which these roles are accepted or rejected. The evaluation of the leader, in addition to the characteristics and behaviors of members, drive the type of relationship in the LMX process.[100] This role-making process involves the following three phases:[101]

1. *Stranger phase:* During the first phase, leaders and subordinates are getting to know each other, and their interactions are formal and based on organizational policies. Leaders rely on rules and contractual obligations to motivate performance. As this phase is dominated by transactional leadership, subordinates comply with the leader in exchange for economic rewards. If leaders see potential during the stranger phase, they elevate the relationship to the acquaintance phase.

2. *Acquaintance phase:* The second phase is a testing phase that begins when a leader offers the subordinate a chance to increase his or her responsibility in the group; the subordinate must accept the new role for the relationship to enter into this phase. With more responsibility, subordinates engage with the leader in sharing information and resources, at both the personal and work level. While each side evaluates the other's motives and interests, the leader tests the subordinate's ability to cope with more responsibility, and the subordinate decides whether the leader is worth the extra effort and commitment. As the quality of the leader–subordinate relationship improves, members begin exchanging self-interests with group interests. They begin developing mutual trust, respect, and loyalty. While in the acquaintance phase, one of two things

Relationship life cycle
A concept marked by the stranger, acquaintance, and mature partnership phases in which a leader and follower undergo a process that dictates whether followers become part of the in-group or out-group.

Find out what is expected of you	Support the leader's effort to make changes
Take the initiative to deal with problems	Show appreciation when appropriate
Keep the boss informed of decisions	Challenge flawed plans by being specific
Verify the accuracy of information with the boss	Provide upward coaching when appropriate
Encourage honest feedback from the boss	Negotiate ways to expand responsibilities

Table 12.1 > Actions that Promote Access to In-Groups

can happen: followers don't meet the expectations of the leader, or followers gain enough credibility and reliability to get promoted to the mature partnership phase.

3. *Mature partnership phase:* Marked by strong mutual trust, respect, and obligation, leaders and followers know they can depend on each other; subordinates perform additional assignments, and leaders provide extra support. Interactions are no longer formal or contractual, and members participate in a high level of exchange marked by mutual influence and reciprocity. Each side abandons his or her self-interests and becomes committed to the mission of the organization. With strong emotional attachment for each other, leaders and followers engage in transformational leadership.

The progression of the relationship life cycle occurs at different rates and with different end results. As the relationship advances, followers take on more responsibilities and leaders provide consistent, honest, and constructive feedback. Followers move beyond their own self-interests to focus on mutual interests, and hierarchical relationships are not emphasized. For these reasons, scholars have strongly advocated that leaders should attempt to cultivate such a relationship with all of their subordinates. Rather than selecting in-group members based on time constraints, favoritism, and convenience, leaders should provide the opportunity to develop a high LMX relationship with everyone.[102] Doing so will not only improve job performance, satisfaction, and innovation but also will be perceived as more equitable, which enhances a leader's credibility.[103]

THE LEADER, THE FOLLOWERS, AND THE SITUATION

The theories discussed so far have focused on the leader and the relationship between leaders and followers. While the roles of leaders and followers are crucial pillars for understanding leadership, the situation in which they interact is equally, if not more, important. Contingency theories are based on the way situations affect leadership interactions and outcomes. In other words, different situations call for different styles of leadership. We have learned that, for the most part, leadership is composed of two functions—directing and supporting—but each is applied differently depending on the situation.[104] Would the CEO of a major corporation be effective in a technology start-up? Could an entrepreneur successfully lead a large, bureaucratic organization? How transferable are leadership skills? Contingency theories build on previous theories to address these questions and reveal the nuances of situational leadership by suggesting that the most appropriate leadership style is contingent on the situation. The goal of such theories then was to articulate a taxonomy of leadership styles. With this taxonomy, appropriate leadership styles could be mapped to specific situations.

Fiedler's Contingency Model

As trait-based and behavioral theories failed to consistently explain leadership interactions, organizational psychologist Fred Fielder proposed one of the first contingency theories of leadership during the 1960s, called the **Fiedler contingency model**.[105] According to his model, each situation is characterized by certain variables that make the situation either favorable or unfavorable for leadership. Depending

Fiedler contingency model
A contingency theory in which leaders are more effective depending on the favorability of a leadership situation, which is described by leader–member relations, task structure, and positional power of the leader.

on the favorability of the situation, a different style of leadership is required. Before going into the details, it is important to note that this particular theory proposed that leaders are incapable of changing their styles to adapt to a situation. Rather than leaders adapting, Fiedler suggests that the situation should be changed to match the leader, or the leader should be replaced to match the situation.

Three variables make up the favorability of a leadership situation: leader–member relations, task structure, and positional power of the leader. The leader–member relations, which can be good or bad, refer to the quality of relationships between leaders and followers, including the extent to which subordinates are loyal to the leader. Task structure, which can be structured or unstructured, refers to the extent to which standard procedures are in place to complete a task. For example, a manufacturing facility has many standard procedures, while a design firm is more flexible and requires creativity for tasks to be completed. The last variable, positional power, which can be strong or weak, refers to the extent to which a leader has the authority to evaluate performance and administer rewards or punishments.

Favorable leadership conditions include good leader–member relations, structured tasks, and strong positional power.[106] When relationships are good, there is a high level of group confidence, trust, and loyalty to the leader; as a result, subordinates are more likely to comply with the leader's requests and not subvert them. With structured tasks, leaders can more easily give instructions and monitor performance because tasks are simple and repetitive, they can be clearly demonstrated, and there are a limited number of correct solutions, which increases a leader's ability to measure and monitor results. Strong positional power means that leaders have the formal authority to hire, fire, promote, and punish and therefore have more tools to motivate subordinates.

Hersey and Blanchard's Situational Theory

As Fiedler's contingency model struggled to gain acceptance among leadership scholars, Paul Hersey and Kenneth Blanchard devised a different approach to contingency theory. Rather than conceiving of leaders as fixed in their leadership style, Hersey and Blanchard believed that leaders have the flexibility and range of skills to adapt their behavior to the maturity of their subordinates.[107] **Situational leadership** is based on the interplay among (1) the amount of task-related behaviors a leader exhibits; (2) the amount of relationship-related behaviors a leader exhibits; and (3) the level at which followers are mature enough to perform a specific task, function, or objective.[108]

While the first two categories have been thoroughly discussed in this chapter, the third has not. Maturity level refers to a follower's competence and commitment to accomplishing a task or an activity. High maturity indicates self-confidence and the ability to perform a task; low maturity indicates a lack of ability and low self-confidence.[109] Leaders must evaluate each employee to assess his or her level of confidence and commitment and adjust their direction and support to match that employee's maturity. Over time, leaders should look for opportunities to build the confidence and skills of subordinates and adjust their leadership style as subordinates mature.[110]

Hersey and Blanchard examine the behaviors of leaders and the characteristics of followers to create a sliding scale of behaviors and maturity. Followers can exhibit four levels of maturity, and leaders should respond to each level with an appropriate leadership style. Figure 12.2 provides a visual representation of two different factors in which followers can vary—their skill to perform and their will to achieve superior results—and maps them to the most effective leadership style.

With employees who are highly skilled and very motivated, a leader should focus on delegation, essentially stepping aside and letting these employees do their

Situational leadership
A leadership theory based on the interplay among (1) the amount of task-related behaviors a leader exhibits; (2) the amount of relationship-related behaviors a leader exhibits; and (3) the level at which followers are mature enough to perform a specific task, function, or objective.

Path–goal theory of leadership
A theory that states that the most important aspect in leadership is the follower's expectation that a task can be accomplished and that it will lead to rewards.

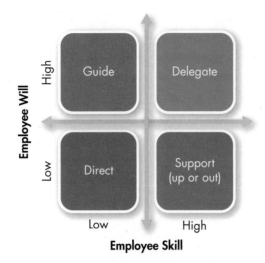

Figure 12.2 Leadership Styles Mapped to Subordinates' Characteristics

Source: Adapted from Paul Hersey, Kenneth H. Blanchard, and Dewey E. Johnson, *Management of Organizational Behavior: Leading Human Resources*, 8th edition (Upper Saddle River, NJ: Prentice Hall, 2001), pp. 174–187.

jobs. At the other end of the spectrum, with new employees who are not yet skilled and have not developed a strong sense of motivation for the job, a leader needs to be directive. In situations where an employee is excited and passionate about the position but has not developed the necessary skills to be successful, a leader should act as a guide, helping the individual to increase his or her skill level.

The most difficult leadership position tends to occur when an employee is very skilled yet lacks the motivation to function at his or her best. An employee may be in this state because he or she has been asked to do the same thing over and over again. As such, the employee may not feel that he or she has the opportunity to continue to learn and develop. In this situation, a leader should offer support to help rekindle a sense of passion for the job or company. One way to motivate such an employee is to provide new opportunities and challenges. If this does not result in better performance, the leader should support the individual in searching for a new position. Individuals who lack passion and commitment can significantly detract from the culture of an organization. As such, it is imperative that a leader takes quick action to address this situation by moving those employees to the upper right quadrant or out of the organization.

House's Path–Goal Theory

While other contingency theories try to match leadership behaviors with specific situations, the **path–goal theory of leadership** takes a different approach. According to organizational theorist Robert House, the most important aspect of leadership is the followers' belief that they can complete a task and that, upon completion, they will gain rewards and satisfaction. If followers believe they can complete a task, they will do so and therefore gain rewards and satisfaction. If there is uncertainty about their ability to complete a task, they will not. This may seem similar to transactional leadership, where leaders offer rewards in exchange for a subordinate's effort. However, the path–goal theory identifies a situational variable with a sliding scale—a follower's belief in his or her ability to complete a task—as an explanation of how leaders can invoke the best performance from the transactional relationship.

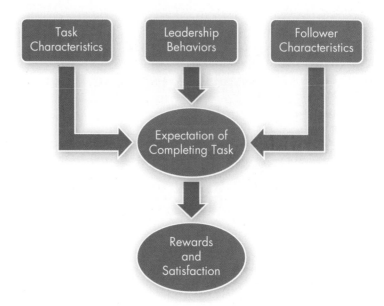

Figure 12.3 Visual Representation of the Path–Goal Theory

The degree to which followers feel certain of their ability to complete a task and gain rewards depends on three factors: (1) the characteristics of the task; (2) the characteristics of the followers; and (3) the behaviors of the leader. While the nature of the task and characteristics of the follower can provide some of that certainty, a leader must supplement what is missing with emotional support or guidance (see Figure 12.3).[111]

Tasks can be structured or unstructured, repetitive or diverse, simple or complex. Different followers may seek any of these variables, and the leader must guide them toward what they seek.[112] Subordinates' characteristics are based on preferences for structure, desire for control, and confidence in ability. Some followers prefer supportive leadership, while others prefer more task structuring.

By engaging in directive, participative, supportive, or achievement-oriented styles, leaders complement the work environment. However, it is unlikely that a leader will be able to practice all of these behaviors simultaneously. Effective leaders choose the behaviors that are most natural to their personality and abilities. For example, a leader who always focuses on "getting the job done" may seem awkward if he or she is suddenly interested in your family life and personal issues. If a situation calls for behaviors that lie outside a leader's comfort zone, he or she can delegate responsibility to others in the group.[113]

Leadership Substitutes and Neutralizers

Leadership substitutes
Aspects of a situation that render leadership unnecessary.

Leadership neutralizers
Aspects of a situation that hinder a leader's ability to act a particular way.

Some scholars believe that task structure, follower characteristics, and other aspects of the environment can satisfy the functions of a leader. Other scholars go one step further: they claim that leadership can be replaced by work design, reward systems, and self-management. They separate these concepts into **leadership substitutes** (aspects of a situation that render leadership unnecessary) and **leadership neutralizers** (aspects that hinder a leader's ability to act a particular way).[114] In addition, these scholars claim that leadership is not a real phenomenon: it is only an attribution made by followers. Those who assume a particular responsibility and exhibit particular behaviors are simply given the title of leader by subordinates but don't actually contribute to the performance and satisfaction of groups.[115]

Category	Substitute or Neutralizer	Relationship-Oriented Behavior	Task-Oriented Behavior
Subordinate characteristics	Experience, ability, training	N/A	Substitute
	Professional orientation	Substitute	Substitute
	Indifference toward rewards	Neutralizer	Neutralizer
Task characteristics	Structured, routine tasks	N/A	Substitute
	Feedback provided by task	N/A	Substitute
	Intrinsically satisfying task	Substitute	N/A
Organization characteristics	Cohesive work group	Substitute	Substitute
	Low position power	Neutralizer	Neutralizer
	Formalization (roles, procedures)	N/A	Substitute
	Inflexibility (rules, policies)	N/A	Neutralizer
	Dispersed subordinate work sites	Neutralizer	Neutralizer

Table 12.2 > List of Leadership Substitutes and Neutralizers

Source: Reprinted from Steven Kerr and John M. Jermier, "Substitutes for Leadership: Their Meaning and Measurement," *Organizational Behavior and Human Performance*, Vol. 22, 1978, pp. 375–403 with permission from Elsevier.

Leadership substitutes and neutralizers extend path–goal theory to provide more insight into how leaders should behave to complement a certain situation. Substitutes are aspects of a situation that allow subordinates to operate at optimal levels without leaders. For example, if subordinates have significant knowledge and prior experience that is relevant to a task, they are capable of performing the task without the help of a leader. Likewise, an organization with strict rules of conduct already provides a clear path to achieving results; thus, a worker can easily figure out the optimal work level within the given constraints.

Conversely, leadership neutralizers are constraints that prevent or discourage leaders from having influence. For example, organizational rules may prevent a leader from performing certain behaviors such as giving raises or authorizing resources.[116] Physical distance can limit the interaction between leaders and their subordinates. For example, regional managers at FedEx, which provides professional copying services at locations nationwide, get frustrated about their limited ability to provide guidance and personal support for new store managers.[117] A list of possible leadership substitutes and neutralizers is shown in Table 12.2.

SUMMARY

LO1 Leadership is a difficult topic to grasp. Despite more than 100 years of focused research, few can agree about how to approach leadership, how to explain it, and particularly how to determine what the best form of leadership is. Despite its complexity, leadership is vital to the success of organizations, and it is critical to understand what makes leaders effective or ineffective.

LO2 Many studies of leadership have attempted to examine the characteristics of a leader. Traits- and

behavior-based leadership theories contribute the most to an understanding of leadership, as the balance between relationships and task structure are evident in nearly all other theories. While these two theories provided the foundation on which others have been built, charismatic leadership was the first theory to include an emotional aspect to driving superior results.

LO3 Another influential group of leadership theories examines the relationship between leaders and followers. Two primary theories of leadership emerged from this analysis: (1) transformational leadership and (2) transactional leadership. Transformational leaders tend to focus on inspiration to motivate followers, while transactional leaders tend to focus on a reward system to motivate followers. The LMX theory revealed that leaders do not exhibit a generic style of leadership; instead, they cultivate unique relationships with each of their subordinates. From this line of research, it became clear that leaders should strive for a transformational relationship with all subordinates while maintaining transactional behaviors, which are necessary for basic group performance.

LO4 : Finally, contingency theories of leadership provided the most complete but also the most complex perspective, as they encompassed aspects about the leader, the followers, and the situation. According to these theories, approaches to leadership vary depending on the characteristics of the work environment. Some situations require leaders to be more involved, while others require less influence. Although these theories do not build a consensus, they provide interesting perspectives with which to evaluate the complexity of a situation.

KEY TERMS

Character	Leadership neutralizers	Situational leadership
Charismatic leaders	Leadership style	Task-oriented behavior
Cognitive skills	Leadership substitutes	Technical skills
Contingent reward	Management-by-exception	Traits-based leadership theory
Fiedler contingency model	Managerial grid	Transactional leadership
"Great Man" theory	Path–goal theory of leadership	Transformational leadership
Interpersonal skills	Relationship life cycle	
Leader–member exchange theory	Relations-oriented behavior	

ASSIGNMENTS

Discussion Topics

1. Consider the three aspects of leadership that have been discussed in this chapter—the leader, the follower, and the situation. Do you believe that one aspect is more important than another? Why?

2. Why is the "Great Man" theory of leadership so compelling? Why do many people still believe that leaders are born, rather than made?

3. Consider the primary leadership skills—cognitive, technical and interpersonal. As an individual moves up in his or her career, which skills become more important? Why?

4. How do you assess the character of a leader? What do you look for in his or her traits and behaviors?

5. In times of crisis, is it more important for a leader to be focused on task-oriented or relations-oriented behaviors? What about in a start-up?

6. Explain the dark side of charisma. How can leaders abuse charisma?

7. How do the transformational and transactional approaches to leadership complement each other?

8. What can individuals do to ensure that they move from the stranger phase to the mature partner phase in their relationship with their leaders?

9. Why is having a versatile leadership style so important?

10. Compare and contrast the three primary contingency approaches to leadership—Fiedler, Hersey and Blanchard, and House.

Management Research

1. Choose an activity in which you are involved—anything that includes a group of people who collaborate to achieve common goals and ideas. Who is the leader? Who are the followers? Use the concepts in this chapter to analyze the nature of the situation. Describe the interactions between the followers and the leader. Describe the tasks you participate in, and then identify the traits and behaviors of the leader. Do they match the

situation? What kind of leader would be best for the situation? Is a leader even necessary? Why or why not?

2. Choose a leader who fits the charismatic or transformational description of leadership. What are this person's specific traits? What behaviors does he or she exhibit? How would you describe the situation in which this person leads? Explain how the situation aligns with other concepts in the chapter. Explain if there is anything the leader exhibits that cannot be explained by other theories.

In the Field

Observe and analyze an effective leader you have known from work or activities outside of work. This leader could be a peer, a project team leader, a senior executive you worked with closely, a teacher, a member of your community, and/or someone you know from a volunteer organization.

Name of effective leader: _____

Make a list of five to ten behaviors and characteristics that you believe make this person an effective leader.

1. _____
2. _____
3. _____
4. _____
5. _____
6. _____
7. _____
8. _____
9. _____
10. _____

Based on your experience, put each of these behaviors/characteristics into one of the following categories:

Can be learned in a few months	Can be learned in a few years	Cannot be learned

What aspects of leadership cannot be learned? Why?

ENDNOTES

[1] Nitin Nohria and Rakesh Khurana, *Handbook of Leadership Theory and Practice* (Boston, MA: HBS Press, 2010), p. 7.

[2] Anthony J. Mayo, Masako Egawa, and Mayuka Yamazaki, "Kazuo Inamori, A Japanese Entrepreneur," Harvard Business School Case No. 9-408-039, rev. April 7, 2009 (Boston, MA: HBS Publishing, 2008), pp. 2–3.

[3] Ibid., p. 6.

[4] Ibid.

[5] Kyocera Corporation, Inc., "Company Overview," www.hoovers.com, accessed April 13, 2015.

[6] KDDI Corporation, Inc., "Company Overview," www.hoovers.com, accessed April 13, 2015.

[7] Anthony J. Mayo, Masako Egawa, and Mayuka Yamazaki, "Kazuo Inamori, A Japanese Entrepreneur," Harvard Business School Case No. 9-408-039, rev. April 7, 2009 (Boston, MA: HBS Publishing, 2008), p. 9.

[8] Ibid., p. 10.

[9] Ibid.

[10] Ibid., p. 11.

[11] Ibid., p. 30.

[12] Ibid., p. 11.

[13] Ibid., pp. 21–22.

[14] Peter G. Northouse, *Leadership: Theory and Practice* (Thousand Oaks, CA: Sage Publications, 1997), p. 13.

[15] Ralph M. Stogdill, *Stogdill's Handbook of Leadership: A Survey of Theory and Research* (New York: Free Press, 1981), p. 26.

[16] Shelley A. Kirkpatrick and Edwin A. Locke, "Leadership: Do Traits Matter?," *The Executive*, Vol. 5, 1991, pp. 48–60.

[17] Thomas R. Piper, "Johnson & Johnson's Corporate Credo," Harvard Business School Case No. 9-304-084, rev. May 9, 2008 (Boston, MA: HBS Publishing, 2004), pp. 1–4.

[18] Gary A. Yukl, *Leadership in Organizations,* 6th edition (Upper Saddle River, NJ: Pearson/Prentice Hall, 2006), p. 189.

[19] Peter G. Northouse, *Leadership: Theory and Practice* (Thousand Oaks, CA: Sage Publications, 1997), pp. 17–18.

[20] Shelley A. Kirkpatrick and Edwin A. Locke, "Leadership: Do Traits Matter?," *The Executive*, Vol. 5, 1991, pp. 48–60.

[21] Ibid.

[22] "Samsung Receives CES Innovations Awards for 2008," *Business Wire*, November 14, 2007.

[23] Gary A. Yukl, *Leadership in Organizations*, 6th edition (Upper Saddle River, NJ: Pearson/Prentice Hall, 2006), p. 185; and Robert L. Katz, "Skills of an Effective Administrator," *Harvard Business Review*, September–October, 1974.

[24] Gary A. Yukl, *Leadership in Organizations*, 6th edition (Upper Saddle River, NJ: Pearson/Prentice Hall, 2006), p. 198; and Robert L. Katz, "Skills of an Effective Administrator," *Harvard Business Review*, September–October, 1974.

[25] Bernard M. Bass, *The Bass Handbook of Leadership: Theory, Research, and*

Managerial Applications (New York: Free Press, 2008), pp. 112–114.

26 Shelley A. Kirkpatrick and Edwin A. Locke, "Leadership: Do Traits Matter?," *The Executive*, Vol. 5, 1991, pp. 48–60.

27 Gary A. Yukl, *Leadership in Organizations,* 6th edition (Upper Saddle River, NJ: Pearson/Prentice Hall, 2006), p. 198.

28 Gary A. Yukl, *Leadership in Organizations,* 6th edition (Upper Saddle River, NJ: Pearson/Prentice Hall, 2006), p. 185; Robert L. Katz, "Skills of an Effective Administrator," *Harvard Business Review,* September–October, 1974; and Bernard M. Bass, *The Bass Handbook of Leadership: Theory, Research, and Managerial Applications* (New York: Free Press, 2008), p. 103.

29 Gary A. Yukl, *Leadership in Organizations,* 6th edition (Upper Saddle River, NJ: Pearson/Prentice Hall, 2006), p. 185; and Bernard M. Bass, *The Bass Handbook of Leadership: Theory, Research, and Managerial Applications* (New York: Free Press, 2008), p. 103.

30 Gary A. Yukl, *Leadership in Organizations,* 6th edition (Upper Saddle River, NJ: Pearson/Prentice Hall, 2006), pp. 192–193; Shelley A. Kirkpatrick and Edwin A. Locke, "Leadership: Do Traits Matter?," *The Executive,* Vol. 5, 1991, pp. 48–60; and Ralph M. Stogdill, *Stogdill's Handbook of Leadership: A Survey of Theory and Research* (New York: Free Press, 1981), pp. 81–82.

31 Peter G. Northouse, *Leadership: Theory and Practice* (Thousand Oaks, CA: Sage Publications, 1997), p. 18.

32 Teresa M. Amabile, Elizabeth A. Schatzel, Giovanni B. Moneta, and Steven J. Kramer, "Leader Behaviors and the Work Environment for Creativity: Perceived Leader Support," *The Leadership Quarterly,* Vol. 15, 2004, pp. 5–32.

33 Daniel Katz and Robert L. Kahn, *The Social Psychology of Organizations,* 2nd edition (New York: Wiley, 1978), p. 543.

34 Gary Yukl, Angela Gordon, and Tom Taber, "A Hierarchical Taxonomy of Leadership Behavior: Integrating a Half Century of Behavior Research," *Journal of Leadership and Organizational Studies,* Vol. 9, No. 1, 2002, pp. 15–32.

35 Ralph M. Stogdill, *Stogdill's Handbook of Leadership: A Survey of Theory and Research* (New York: Free Press, 1981), p. 498; and Edwin A. Fleishman, "The Description of Supervisory Behavior," *Journal of Applied Psychology,* Vol. 37, No. 1, 1953, pp. 1–6.

36 Gary A. Yukl, *Leadership in Organizations,* 6th edition (Upper Saddle River, NJ: Pearson/Prentice Hall, 2006), pp. 68–71; and Bernard M. Bass, *The Bass Handbook of Leadership: Theory, Research, and Managerial Applications* (New York: Free Press, 2008), p. 498.

37 Bernard M. Bass, *The Bass Handbook of Leadership: Theory, Research, and Managerial Applications* (New York: Free Press, 2008), pp. 507–511; and Timothy A. Judge, Ronald F. Piccolo, and Remus Ilies, "The Forgotten Ones? The Validity of Consideration and Initiating Structure in Leadership Research," *Journal of Applied Psychology,* Vol. 89, No. 1, 2004, pp. 36–51.

38 Gary A. Yukl, *Leadership in Organizations*, 6th edition (Upper Saddle River, NJ: Pearson/Prentice Hall, 2006), p. 51; Peter G. Northouse, *Leadership: Theory and Practice* (Thousand Oaks, CA: Sage Publications, 1997), p. 35; and Gary Yukl, Angela Gordon, and Tom Taber, "A Hierarchical Taxonomy of Leadership Behavior: Integrating a Half Century of Behavior Research," *Journal of Leadership and Organizational Studies,* Vol. 9, No. 1, 2002, pp. 15–32.

39 Gary A. Yukl, *Leadership in Organizations*, 6th edition (Upper Saddle River, NJ: Pearson/Prentice Hall, 2006), pp. 71–72.

40 Gary Yukl, Angela Gordon, and Tom Taber, "A Hierarchical Taxonomy of Leadership Behavior: Integrating a Half Century of Behavior Research," *Journal of Leadership and Organizational Studies,* Vol. 9, No. 1, 2002, pp. 15–32.

41 Ibid.

42 Gary A. Yukl, *Leadership in Organizations,* 6th edition (Upper Saddle River, NJ: Pearson/Prentice Hall, 2006), pp. 74–75.

43 Bernard M. Bass, *The Bass Handbook of Leadership: Theory, Research, and Managerial Applications* (New York: Free Press, 2008), pp. 505–508; Teresa M. Amabile, Elizabeth A. Schatzel, Giovanni B. Moneta, and Steven J. Kramer, "Leader Behaviors and the Work Environment for Creativity: Perceived Leader Support," *The Leadership Quarterly,* Vol. 15, 2004, pp. 5–32; and Timothy A. Judge, Ronald F. Piccolo, and Remus Ilies, "The Forgotten Ones? The Validity of Consideration and Initiating Structure in Leadership Research," *Journal of Applied Psychology,* Vol. 89, No. 1, 2004, pp. 36–51.

44 Robert R. Blake and Jane S. Mouton, *The Managerial Grid III: A New Look at the Classic That Has Boosted Productivity and Profits for Thousands of Corporations Worldwide* (Houston, TX: Gulf Publication Co., 1985), pp. 12–13.

45 Gary A. Yukl, *Leadership in Organizations,* 6th edition (Upper Saddle River, NJ: Pearson/Prentice Hall, 2006), p. 249; and Maxwell Weber, *The Theory of Social and Economic Organizations* (New York: Free Press, 1947).

46 Boas Shamir, Robert J. House, and Michael B. Arthur, "The Motivational Effects of Charismatic Leadership: A Self-Concept Based Theory," *Organization Science,* Vol. 4, No. 4, 1993, pp. 577–594.

47 Robert J. House, "A 1976 Theory of Charismatic Leadership," *Leadership: The Cutting Edge,* James G. Hunt and Lars L. Larson, eds. (Carbondale, IL: Southern Illinois University Press, 1977), pp. 189–207; and Jay A. Conger and Rabindra N. Kanungo, "Toward a Behavioral Theory of Charismatic Leadership in Organizational Settings," *Academy of Management Review,* Vol. 12, No. 4, 1987, pp. 637–647.

48 Robert J. House, William D. Spangler, and James Woycke, "Personality and Charisma in the U.S. Presidency: A Psychological Theory of Leader Effectiveness," *Administrative Science Quarterly,* Vol. 36, 1991, pp. 364–396; and Rakesh Khurana, "The Curse of the Superstar CEO," *Harvard Business Review,* September 2002.

49 Robert J. House, William D. Spangler, and James Woycke, "Personality and Charisma in the U.S. Presidency: A Psychological Theory of Leader Effectiveness," *Administrative Science Quarterly,* Vol. 36, 1991, pp. 364–396.

50 Lev Grossman, "How Apple Does It," *Time,* October 16, 2005.

51 Boas Shamir, Robert J. House, and Michael B. Arthur, "The Motivational Effects of Charismatic Leadership: A Self-Concept Based Theory," *Organization Science,* Vol. 4, No. 4, 1993, pp. 577–594; and Katherine J. Klein and Robert J. House, "On Fire: Charismatic Leadership and Levels of Analysis," *Leadership Quarterly,* Vol. 6, No. 2, 1995, pp. 183–192.

52 Alan Bryman, *Charisma and Leadership in Organizations* (Newbury, CA: Sage Publications, 1992), pp. 116–118.

53 Jaepil Choi, "A Motivational Theory of Charismatic Leadership: Envisioning, Empathy, and Empowerment," *Journal of Leadership and Organizational Studies,* Vol. 13, No. 1, 2006, pp. 24–43.

54 Jay A. Conger and Rabindra N. Kanungo, "Toward a Behavioral Theory

of Charismatic Leadership in Organizational Settings," *Academy of Management Review*, Vol. 12, No. 4, 1987, pp. 637–647.

55 Gary A. Yukl, *Leadership in Organizations*, 6th edition (Upper Saddle River, NJ: Pearson/Prentice Hall, 2006), p. 259; and Robert J. House and Jane M. Howell, "Personality and Charismatic Leadership," *The Leadership Quarterly*, Vol. 3, No. 2, Summer 1992, pp. 81–108.

56 Robert J. House, "A 1976 Theory of Charismatic Leadership," *Leadership: The Cutting Edge*, James G. Hunt and Lars L. Larson, eds. (Carbondale, IL: Southern Illinois University Press, 1977), pp. 189–207; and Robert J. House, William D. Spangler, and James Woycke, "Personality and Charisma in the U.S. Presidency: A Psychological Theory of Leader Effectiveness," *Administrative Science Quarterly*, Vol. 36, 1991, pp. 364–396.

57 James MacGregor Burns, *Leadership* (New York: Harper Perennial, 1978), p. 244.

58 Peter G. Northouse, *Leadership: Theory and Practice* (Thousand Oaks, CA: Sage Publications, 1997), p. 134.

59 Gary A. Yukl, *Leadership in Organizations*, 6th edition (Upper Saddle River, NJ: Pearson/Prentice Hall, 2006), p. 264; and Alan Bryman, *Charisma and Leadership in Organizations* (Newbury, CA: Sage Publications, 1992), p. 128.

60 Gary A. Yukl, *Leadership in Organizations*, 6th edition (Upper Saddle River, NJ: Pearson/Prentice Hall, 2006), p. 263; James MacGregor Burns, *Leadership* (New York: Harper Perennial, 1978), pp. 243–244; Warren G. Bennis and Bert Nanus, *Leaders: The Strategies for Taking Charge* (New York: Harper & Row, 1985), pp. 27–33; and Bernard M. Bass, *Leadership and Performance Beyond Expectations* (New York: Free Press, 1985), pp. 37–48.

61 James M. Kouzes and Barry Z. Posner, *The Leadership Challenge*, 4th edition (San Francisco, CA: Jossey-Bass, 2008), p. 16; and Noel M. Tichy and Mary Anne Devanna, *The Transformational Leader* (New York: Wiley, 1986), pp. 30–31.

62 Warren G. Bennis and Bert Nanus, *Leaders: The Strategies for Taking Charge* (New York: Harper & Row, 1985), pp. 43–55; and James M. Kouzes and Barry Z. Posner, *The Leadership Challenge*, 4th edition (San Francisco, CA: Jossey-Bass, 2008), p. 26.

63 James M. Kouzes and Barry Z. Posner, *The Leadership Challenge*, 4th edition (San Francisco, CA: Jossey-Bass, 2008), pp. 20–21.

64 Bernard M. Bass, *Leadership and Performance beyond Expectations* (New York: Free Press, 1985), p. 99.

65 Peter G. Northouse, *Leadership: Theory and Practice* (Thousand Oaks, CA: Sage Publications, 1997), p. 136; and Bruce J. Avolio, Bernard M. Bass, and Dong I. Jung, "Re-Examining the Components of Transformational and Transactional Leadership Using the Multifactor Leadership Questionnaire," *Journal of Occupational and Organizational Psychology*, Vol. 72, 1999, pp. 441–462.

66 Bernard M. Bass, *Transformational Leadership: Industrial, Military, and Educational Impact* (Mahwah, NJ: Lawrence Erlbaum, 1998), pp. 5–6.

67 Bernard M. Bass, *The Bass Handbook of Leadership: Theory, Research, and Managerial Applications* (New York: Free Press, 2008), p. 622; and Bruce J. Avolio, Bernard M. Bass, and Dong I. Jung, "Re-Examining the Components of Transformational and Transactional Leadership using the Multifactor Leadership Questionnaire," *Journal of Occupational and Organizational Psychology*, Vol. 72, 1999, pp. 441–462.

68 Bernard M. Bass, *Transformational Leadership: Industrial, Military, and Educational Impact* (Mahwah, NJ: Lawrence Erlbaum, 1998), p. 6.

69 Alan Bryman, *Charisma and Leadership in Organizations* (Newbury, CA: Sage Publications, 1992), p. 97; Bernard M. Bass, *Leadership and Performance Beyond Expectations* (New York: Free Press, 1985), p. 20; and Bernard M. Bass, *Transformational Leadership: Industrial, Military, and Educational Impact* (Mahwah, NJ: Lawrence Erlbaum, 1998), p. 4.

70 Alan Bryman, *Charisma and Leadership in Organizations* (Newbury, CA: Sage Publications, 1992), p. 95.

71 Peter G. Northouse, *Leadership: Theory and Practice* (Thousand Oaks, CA: Sage Publications, 1997), p. 131.

72 Robert E. Quinn, "Moments of Greatness: Entering the Fundamental State of Leadership," *Harvard Business Review*, July–August 2005.

73 John J. Hater and Bernard M. Bass, "Superiors' Evaluations and Subordinates' Perceptions of Transformational and Transactional Leadership," *Journal of Applied Psychology*, Vol. 73, No. 4, 1988, pp. 695–702.

74 John P. Kotter, *A Force for Change: How Leadership Differs from Management* (New York: Free Press, 1990), p. 4.

75 Peter G. Northouse, *Leadership: Theory and Practice* (Thousand Oaks, CA: Sage Publications, 1997), p. 137; Bernard M. Bass, *Leadership and Performance beyond Expectations* (New York: Free Press, 1985), p. 14; and Bruce J. Avolio, Bernard M. Bass, and Dong I. Jung, "Re-Examining the Components of Transformational and Transactional Leadership Using the Multifactor Leadership Questionnaire," *Journal of Occupational and Organizational Psychology*, Vol. 72, 1999, pp. 441–462.

76 Karl W. Kuhnert and Philip Lewis, "Transactional and Transformational Leadership: A Constructive/Developmental Analysis," *Academy of Management Review*, Vol. 12, No. 4, 1987, pp. 648–657; and Bernard M. Bass, "From Transactional to Transformational Leadership: Learning to Share the Vision," *Organizational Dynamics*, Vol. 18, No. 3, 1990, pp. 19–31.

77 Gary A. Yukl, *Leadership in Organizations*, 6th edition (Upper Saddle River, NJ: Pearson/Prentice Hall, 2006), p. 138; Bruce J. Avolio, Bernard M. Bass, and Dong I. Jung, "Re-Examining the Components of Transformational and Transactional Leadership Using the Multifactor Leadership Questionnaire," *Journal of Occupational and Organizational Psychology*, Vol. 72, 1999, pp. 441–462; and Bernard M. Bass, *Transformational Leadership: Industrial, Military, and Educational Impact* (Mahwah, NJ: Lawrence Erlbaum, 1998), p. 7.

78 Bernard M. Bass, *Leadership and Performance Beyond Expectations* (New York: Free Press, 1985), pp. 147–148.

79 Gary A. Yukl, *Leadership in Organizations*, 6th edition (Upper Saddle River, NJ: Pearson/Prentice Hall, 2006), p. 138; and Bernard M. Bass, *Leadership and Performance beyond Expectations* (New York: Free Press, 1985), p. 135.

80 Alan Bryman, *Charisma and Leadership in Organizations* (Newbury, CA: Sage Publications, 1992), p. 98; and Bernard M. Bass, "From Transactional to Transformational Leadership: Learning to Share the Vision," *Organizational Dynamics*, Vol. 18, No. 3, 1990, pp. 19–31.

81 Bruce J. Avolio, Bernard M. Bass, and Dong I. Jung, "Re-Examining the Components of Transformational and Transactional Leadership Using the Multifactor Leadership Questionnaire," *Journal of Occupational and Organizational Psychology*, Vol. 72, 1999, pp. 441–462; and Jane M. Howell and Bruce J. Avolio, "Transformational Leadership, Transactional Leadership, Locus of Control, and Support for

Innovation: Key Predictors of Consolidated-Business-Unit Performance," *Journal of Applied Psychology*, Vol. 78, No. 6, 1993, pp. 891–902.

[82] John P. Kotter, *A Force for Change: How Leadership Differs from Management* (New York: Free Press, 1990), p. 3.

[83] Bruce J. Avolio, Bernard M. Bass, and Dong I. Jung, "Re-Examining the Components of Transformational and Transactional Leadership Using the Multifactor Leadership Questionnaire," *Journal of Occupational and Organizational Psychology*, Vol. 72, 1999, pp. 441–462.

[84] Bernard M. Bass, *Leadership and Performance Beyond Expectations* (New York: Free Press, 1985), pp. 24–28; and John P. Kotter, *A Force for Change: How Leadership Differs from Management* (New York: Free Press, 1990), p. 3.

[85] Bernard M. Bass, "From Transactional to Transformational Leadership: Learning to Share the Vision," *Organizational Dynamics*, Vol. 18, No. 3, 1990, pp. 19–31.

[86] Bernard M. Bass, *Leadership and Performance Beyond Expectations* (New York: Free Press, 1985), p. 28.

[87] George B. Graen and Mary Uhl-Bien, "Relationship-Based Approach to Leadership: Development of Leader-Member Exchange (LMX) Theory of Leadership Over 25 Years: Applying a Multi-Level Multi-Domain Perspective," *Leadership Quarterly*, Vol. 6, No. 2, 1995, pp. 219–247; Richard M. Dienesch and Robert C. Liden, "Leader–Member Exchange Model of Leadership: A Critique and Further Development," *Academy of Management Review*, Vol. 11, No. 3, 1986, pp. 618–634; and Fred Dansereau, Jr., George Graen, and William J. Haga, "A Vertical Dyad Linkage Approach to Leadership within Formal Organizations: A Longitudinal Investigation of the Role Making Process," *Organizational Behavior and Human Performance*, Vol. 13, 1975, pp. 46–78.

[88] Gary A. Yukl, *Leadership in Organizations*, 6th edition (Upper Saddle River, NJ: Pearson/Prentice Hall, 2006), p. 117; and Peter G. Northouse, *Leadership: Theory and Practice* (Thousand Oaks, CA: Sage Publications, 1997), p. 109.

[89] Richard M. Dienesch and Robert C. Liden, "Leader-Member Exchange Model of Leadership: A Critique and Further Development," *Academy of Management Review*, Vol. 11, No. 3, 1986, pp. 618–634; and Fred Dansereau, Jr., George Graen, and William J. Haga, "A Vertical Dyad

Linkage Approach to Leadership within Formal Organizations: A Longitudinal Investigation of the Role Making Process," *Organizational Behavior and Human Performance*, Vol. 13, 1975, pp. 46–78.

[90] George B. Graen and Mary Uhl-Bien, "Relationship-Based Approach to Leadership: Development of Leader-Member Exchange (LMX) Theory of Leadership Over 25 Years: Applying a Multi-Level Multi-Domain Perspective," *Leadership Quarterly*, Vol. 6, No. 2, 1995, pp. 219–247; and Charlotte R. Gerstner and David V. Day, "Meta-Analytic Review of Leader-Member Exchange Theory: Correlates and Construct Issues," *Journal of Applied Psychology*, Vol. 82, No. 6, 1997, pp. 827–844.

[91] Fred Dansereau, Jr., George Graen, and William J. Haga, "A Vertical Dyad Linkage Approach to Leadership within Formal Organizations: A Longitudinal Investigation of the Role Making Process," *Organizational Behavior and Human Performance*, Vol. 13, 1975, pp. 46–78.

[92] Gary A. Yukl, *Leadership in Organizations*, 6th edition (Upper Saddle River, NJ: Pearson/Prentice Hall, 2006), pp. 117–120; and Robert C. Liden and George Graen, "Generalizability of the Vertical Dyad Linkage Model of Leadership," *Academy of Management Journal*, Vol. 23, No. 3, 1980, pp. 451–465.

[93] Gary A. Yukl, *Leadership in Organizations*, 6th edition (Upper Saddle River, NJ: Pearson/Prentice Hall, 2006), pp. 118–120; and Peter G. Northouse, *Leadership: Theory and Practice* (Thousand Oaks, CA: Sage Publications, 1997), p. 115.

[94] Fred Dansereau, Jr., George Graen, and William J. Haga, "A Vertical Dyad Linkage Approach to Leadership within Formal Organizations: A Longitudinal Investigation of the Role Making Process," *Organizational Behavior and Human Performance*, Vol. 13, 1975, pp. 46–78.

[95] Gary A. Yukl, *Leadership in Organizations*, 6th edition (Upper Saddle River, NJ: Pearson/Prentice Hall, 2006), p. 118.

[96] Peter G. Northouse, *Leadership: Theory and Practice* (Thousand Oaks, CA: Sage Publications, 1997), p. 112.

[97] Gary A. Yukl, *Leadership in Organizations*, 6th edition (Upper Saddle River, NJ: Pearson/Prentice Hall, 2006), p. 136; and Peter G. Northouse, *Leadership: Theory and Practice* (Thousand Oaks, CA: Sage Publications, 1997), pp. 110–111.

[98] Peter G. Northouse, *Leadership: Theory and Practice* (Thousand Oaks, CA: Sage Publications, 1997), p. 117.

[99] George B. Graen and Mary Uhl-Bien, "Relationship-Based Approach to Leadership: Development of Leader-Member Exchange (LMX) Theory of Leadership Over 25 Years: Applying a Multi-Level Multi-Domain Perspective," *Leadership Quarterly*, Vol. 6, No. 2, 1995, pp. 219–247.

[100] George B. Graen and Mary Uhl-Bien, "Relationship-Based Approach to Leadership: Development of Leader-Member Exchange (LMX) Theory of Leadership Over 25 Years: Applying a Multi-Level Multi-Domain Perspective," *Leadership Quarterly*, Vol. 6, No. 2, 1995, pp. 219–247; and Robert C. Liden, Sandy J. Wayne, and Dean Stilwell, "A Longitudinal Study on the Early Development of Leader-Member Exchanges," *Journal of Applied Psychology*, Vol. 78, No. 4, 1993, pp. 662–674.

[101] Gary A. Yukl, *Leadership in Organizations*, 6th edition (Upper Saddle River, NJ: Pearson/Prentice Hall, 2006), p. 118; Peter G. Northouse, *Leadership: Theory and Practice* (Thousand Oaks, CA: Sage Publications, 1997), pp. 113–115; and George B. Graen and Mary Uhl-Bien, "Relationship-Based Approach to Leadership: Development of Leader-Member Exchange (LMX) Theory of Leadership Over 25 Years: Applying a Multi-Level Multi-Domain Perspective," *Leadership Quarterly*, Vol. 6, No. 2, 1995, pp. 219–247.

[102] Gary A. Yukl, *Leadership in Organizations*, 6th edition (Upper Saddle River, NJ: Pearson/Prentice Hall, 2006), p. 121; Peter G. Northouse, *Leadership: Theory and Practice* (Thousand Oaks, CA: Sage Publications, 1997), p. 113; and George B. Graen and Mary Uhl-Bien, "Relationship-Based Approach to Leadership: Development of Leader-Member Exchange (LMX) Theory of Leadership Over 25 Years: Applying a Multi-Level Multi-Domain Perspective," *Leadership Quarterly*, Vol. 6, No. 2, 1995, pp. 219–247.

[103] George B. Graen and Mary Uhl-Bien, "Relationship-Based Approach to Leadership: Development of Leader-Member Exchange (LMX) Theory of Leadership Over 25 Years: Applying a Multi-Level Multi-Domain Perspective," *Leadership Quarterly*, Vol. 6, No. 2, 1995, pp. 219–247; and Charlotte R. Gerstner and David V. Day, "Meta-Analytic Review of Leader-Member Exchange Theory: Correlates and Construct Issues," *Journal of Applied Psychology*, Vol. 82, No. 6, 1997, pp. 827–844.

[104] Peter G. Northouse, *Leadership: Theory and Practice* (Thousand Oaks, CA: Sage Publications, 1997), p. 53.

105 Gary A. Yukl, *Leadership in Organizations*, 6th edition (Upper Saddle River, NJ: Pearson/Prentice Hall, 2006), pp. 215–218; and Peter G. Northouse, *Leadership: Theory and Practice* (Thousand Oaks, CA: Sage Publications, 1997), pp. 74–77.

106 Gary A. Yukl, *Leadership in Organizations*, 6th edition (Upper Saddle River, NJ: Pearson/Prentice Hall, 2006), pp. 215–218; and Peter G. Northouse, *Leadership: Theory and Practice* (Thousand Oaks, CA: Sage Publications, 1997), p. 76.

107 Paul Hersey, Kenneth H. Blanchard, and Dewey E. Johnson, *Management of Organizational Behavior: Leading Human Resources,* 8th edition (Upper Saddle River, NJ: Prentice Hall, 2001), p. 171.

108 Ibid., p. 172.

109 Gary A. Yukl, *Leadership in Organizations*, 6th edition (Upper Saddle River, NJ: Pearson/Prentice Hall, 2006), p. 223.

110 Gary A. Yukl, *Leadership in Organizations*, 6th edition (Upper Saddle River, NJ: Pearson/Prentice Hall, 2006), p. 225; and Peter G. Northouse, *Leadership: Theory and Practice* (Thousand Oaks, CA: Sage Publications, 1997), p. 54.

111 Gary A. Yukl, *Leadership in Organizations*, 6th edition (Upper Saddle River, NJ: Pearson/Prentice Hall, 2006), pp. 218–219; Peter G. Northouse, *Leadership: Theory and Practice* (Thousand Oaks, CA: Sage Publications, 1997), pp. 88–89; Robert J. House, "Path-Goal Theory of Leadership: Lessons, Legacy, and a Reformulated Theory," *Leadership Quarterly*, Vol. 7, No. 3, 1996, pp. 323–352; and Robert J. House, "A Path-Goal Theory of Leader Effectiveness," *Administrative Science Quarterly*, Vol. 16, No. 3, 1971, pp. 321–339.

112 Gary A. Yukl, *Leadership in Organizations*, 6th edition (Upper Saddle River, NJ: Pearson/Prentice Hall, 2006), pp. 219–221; and Peter G. Northouse, *Leadership: Theory and Practice* (Thousand Oaks, CA: Sage Publications, 1997), p. 93.

113 Gary A. Yukl, *Leadership in Organizations*, 6th edition (Upper Saddle River, NJ: Pearson/Prentice Hall, 2006), pp. 219–221; and Robert J. House, "Path-Goal Theory of Leadership: Lessons, Legacy, and a Reformulated Theory," *Leadership Quarterly*, Vol. 7, No. 3, 1996, pp. 323–352.

114 Steven Kerr and John M. Jermier, "Substitutes for Leadership: Their Meaning and Measurement," *Organizational Behavior and Human Performance*, Vol. 22, 1978, pp. 375–403.

115 Gary A. Yukl, *Leadership in Organizations*, 6th edition (Upper Saddle River, NJ: Pearson/Prentice Hall, 2006), p. 228.

116 Ibid., pp. 225–227.

117 Bernard M. Bass, *Transformational Leadership: Industrial, Military, and Educational Impact* (Mahwah, NJ: Lawrence Erlbaum, 1998), p. 160.

CHAPTER

13

Becoming a Leader: Knowing Yourself

Learning Objectives

After reading this chapter, you should be able to:

LO1 Explain why self-awareness is an important aspect of becoming a leader.

LO2 Outline the different forms of intelligence and describe how they can influence an individual's personality and leadership style.

LO3 Explain how personality impacts an individual's likelihood of success in certain roles.

LO4 Describe the role that self-monitoring can play in learning to adapt behaviors and becoming a more versatile leader.

SELF-REFLECTION

Are You Aware of Your Leadership Style?

A key aspect of self-discovery is being aware of your leadership style and its impact on others. This demands knowledge of your strengths and weaknesses. On a scale of 1 to 5, respond to the following statements to assess your leadership style.

1 = never 2 = rarely 3 = sometimes 4 = usually 5 = always

1. I rely upon my intelligence—the sum of my experiences, acquired knowledge, and adaptive skills - when making a decision. _____

2. I excel at creativity. _____

3. I apply common sense and practical analysis to situations. _____

4. I am a big picture thinker. _____

5. I can sense environmental opportunities and predict threats. _____

6. I understand and respond appropriately to different cultural situations. _____

7. I have the capacity to recognize the emotions of others. _____

8. I lead by example. _____

9. I am open to feedback and advice. _____

10. I seek input of many people before making a decision. _____

Based on your responses, how aware are you of your leadership style? How do you capitalize on the strengths of your leadership style? What are your areas of opportunity?

INTRODUCTION

In the previous chapter, we discussed the interplay between a leader, his or her followers, and the situation. Effective leaders are able to adjust their leadership style to fit the unique aspects of a specific situation.[1] For instance, in times of crisis, leaders often must be authoritarian. In less stressful situations when an organization is focused on innovation and creativity, a leader can be more successful by adopting a participatory or democratic style. A similar level of flexibility and adaptability in leadership style and approach must be applied to different followers. With some employees, a leader needs to be supportive and encouraging; with other employees, the leader must be challenging. And with still other employees, the leader must be directive and controlling. Applying different styles to different employees often enables a leader to tap into unique motivational drivers, which, in turn, can result in increased job satisfaction as well as productivity.

The process of adapting one's leadership style to specific situations and with different individual employees is easier for some than others. A person's leadership style and approach can be likened to a rubber band; it can be stretched and manipulated in

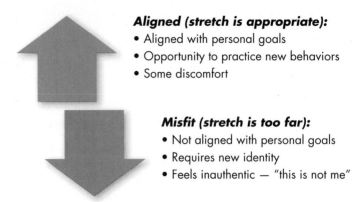

Aligned (stretch is appropriate):
- Aligned with personal goals
- Opportunity to practice new behaviors
- Some discomfort

Misfit (stretch is too far):
- Not aligned with personal goals
- Requires new identity
- Feels inauthentic — "this is not me"

Figure 13.1 › Calibrating Your Leadership Style

Source: Anthony J. Mayo.

multiple ways, but at some point, it will break. For certain leaders, the pliability of their style is wide; for others, it is very narrow. If leaders stretch too far outside their comfort zone and try to lead in a way that does not resonate with their values or experiences, they will likely feel uncomfortable and may be viewed as inauthentic. As such, while it is important that leaders be able to stretch their style, they also must be aware of their limitations (see Figure 13.1).

Even individuals who can adopt a variety of leadership styles have a default position or approach that they tend to rely upon in most situations. This is especially true when an individual is stressed; he or she often reverts to a comfortable style regardless of what the situation dictates.[2] An individual's default style is driven by his or her personality, skills and abilities, values, and experiences.

Throughout this chapter, we build on the tenet that understanding your default leadership style is an important starting place for building more effective relationships, completing tasks, and achieving organizational goals. To that end, this chapter is focused on **self-awareness**, an understanding of one's thoughts, feelings, and behaviors. Individuals with greater self-awareness are able to understand their own tendencies and preferences. As a result, they are better able to calibrate their leadership style and approach.[3] This understanding of self is often a prerequisite for the cultivation and development of effective relationships with others.

The ability to acknowledge and take responsibility for one's role in cultivating relationships and in communicating effectively with others is called **interpersonal effectiveness**. There is an interesting reciprocal relationship between self-awareness and interpersonal effectiveness whereby a greater awareness of others can, in turn, lead to a greater awareness of oneself.[4] The reverse is also true; greater self-awareness can lead to a better understanding of others.

The following case, Wolfgang Keller at Königsbräu-TAK, provides an example of why self-awareness is so important to the development of effective and productive working relationships.

The Wolfgang Keller case demonstrates that differences in personality can create interpersonal tensions. When these differences arise, individuals often challenge, avoid, or become irritated with one another. Despite the inherent complications and difficulties, working with people who have different personalities can be valuable. In fact, different personality traits may be more suitable to certain job functions. For example, someone who is highly extroverted and conscientious may have a successful career in marketing or sales, like Keller. Someone who is less extroverted may have a successful career managing information technology systems or conducting research.

Self-awareness
An understanding of one's thoughts, feelings, and behaviors.

Interpersonal effectiveness
The ability to acknowledge and take responsibility for one's role in cultivating relationships and in communicating effectively with others.

Wolfgang Keller at Königsbräu-TAK[5]

A graduate of Harvard Business School, 34-year-old German national Wolfgang Keller was named general manager of the Ukrainian subsidiary of Königsbräu, a large German brewery. His tenure had been remarkable for a successful turnaround effort at Königsbräu-TAK, which many believed placed him in line for a senior position at the corporate offices. Yet he continued to have difficulty managing the behavior of Dmitri Brodsky, Königsbräu-TAK's commercial director and Keller's subordinate.

Since hiring Brodksy, a Ukrainian national 10 years older than him, Keller had reservations about his skills and management style. As commercial director, Brodsky had done a great job redesigning the sales force organization and developing a comprehensive set of information and control systems. Although these were successes, Brodsky's methodical and analytical approach to the redesign efforts took more time than expected. While he was pleased with the new systems, Keller believed that Brodsky had neglected to build effective and productive working relationships with customers and the sales team. Brodsky's management style, described as "formal and distant," seemed to prevent him from developing close relationships with his peers. Brodsky rarely talked about his family with colleagues, nor did he participate in social outings with other managers. Brodsky also refrained from visiting sales representatives and distributors whom Keller believed were critical to Königsbräu's future in the Ukraine. All of these factors were issues for Keller, who believed that loyalty and enthusiasm were cultivated through personal relationships.

In contrast to Brodsky, Keller enjoyed being involved with the sales team and working with customers. Keller was described as a "hands-on" manager who was action oriented when dealing with problems, but also impatient, jumping quickly to solve problems as they arose. Many believed that Keller did not know how to delegate authority. Believing that Brodsky did not manage with the level of urgency that was required, Keller regularly intervened with Brodsky's team. After one performance evaluation, Keller's boss cautioned that if he wanted to advance, Keller would have to learn to step back from functional responsibilities and be more of a team player.

When it came time to review Brodsky's performance, Keller indicated to Brodsky that he had "a low level of leadership and no personality" and that Brodsky was "not a leader for the sales force." Brodsky vehemently refuted Keller's characterization of him and claimed that Keller's micromanaging style prevented Brodsky from being successful. He felt that his own behavior was in reaction to Keller's interventions.

The leadership styles of Keller and Brodsky were fundamentally different, and each had difficulty appreciating the value the other person brought to the business. For example, each person thought differently about workplace relationships. Keller, a highly extroverted individual, believed that personal relationships and contact with peers, subordinates, and customers cultivated loyalty and enthusiasm. Therefore, he thrived on creating a collegial environment at Königsbräu-TAK. Brodsky, on the other hand, did not actively seek close workplace relationships. In fact, he tended to avoid them. Despite being less extroverted than Keller, however, Brodsky was successful at the company. Redesigning the sales force organization and developing the information and control systems were positive contributions to the company.

Case in Point   Wolfgang Keller at Königsbräu-TAK

1. Compare and contrast Keller's and Brodsky's leadership styles.
2. Why was Keller concerned about Brodsky's performance?
3. How can Brodsky improve his management skills?
4. How should Keller manage Brodsky?

A recent study concluded that extroverted leaders perform better when their team consists of many introverts. The reverse is also true; an introverted leader tends to produce better results with a team of extroverts. The extroverted team members help to draw out the introvert. If a team consisted of all extroverts, there would be many ideas but little follow-through. With a team of all introverts, few novel or innovative ideas would surface. While we often prefer to work with people who are more like us, the collective performance of the group may be inhibited by similarity.[6] So how do we begin to work through these differences so that our interactions with others are more effective? To do this, we must learn more about our own tendencies and predispositions.[7]

FORMS OF INTELLIGENCE

Differences in skills and abilities can affect how work gets done and how people interact with one another. Skills and abilities are the aptitudes that are acquired or developed through education, training, and/or experience. Skills and abilities tend to be associated with **intelligence**, which is defined as a person's ability to profit from experience, acquire knowledge, think abstractly, and adapt to changes in the environment. Typically, we think of intelligence in terms of the **intelligence quotient (IQ)**, which represents the overall quality of an individual's mental abilities, and which can be plotted on a standard normal distribution, or bell curve.[8] Sixty-eight percent of the population has an average IQ score between 85 and 115 (see Figure 13.2). As we will discuss below, IQ only identifies one form of intelligence. Humans have other facets of intelligence, beyond what is measured on an IQ scale, that can shape performance and success in the workplace.

The IQ test was initially designed by Alfred Binet in the early 1900s to identify children who could benefit from remedial work or other forms of modified instruction. It was later adapted to help identify candidate readiness for various armed services professions. The modern version of the test was created in 1939 by David Wechsler, who continued to revise it through the late 1960s. Since that time, the IQ test has been used to classify students throughout the world. The notion of IQ as an inherited trait has sparked bitter controversy and endless debate as it has been used to describe group differences, to determine educational placements, and to assign employees to particular jobs.

Those who oppose the use of IQ scores in these situations focus on perceived bias against individuals who come from lower socioeconomic classes. They argue

Intelligence
A person's ability to profit from experience, acquire knowledge, think abstractly, and adapt to changes in the environment.

Intelligence quotient (IQ)
A measure of the overall quality of an individual's mental abilities.

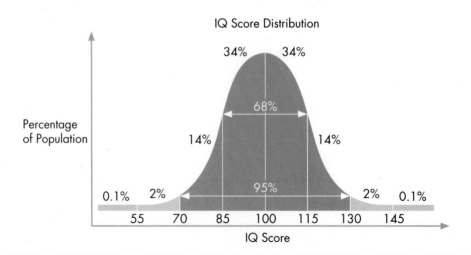

Figure 13.2 > IQ Bell Curve

that the IQ test is biased in favor of individuals who have had access to more social and economic advantages, which, in turn, enables them to take advantage of greater educational opportunities. These opponents also believe that a timed test does not accurately reflect the realities of life. To make appropriate decisions, most people need to gather information, reflect on possible options, and weigh alternatives. While some situations or occupations (e.g., air traffic controllers) call for split-second decision making, the majority of decisions are enhanced by more reflective thinking.[9] The IQ test virtually ignores the information-gathering process that would support this level of thinking.

Proponents of the use of IQ to determine educational and employment placements argue that IQ testing is fair because scores can be honed by curiosity, by studying, and through a range of experiences.[10] Other proponents note that there is a strong correlation between an individual's IQ score and his or her performance on a variety of intellectual tasks.[11] Despite its limitations, the IQ test has been considered the most accurate reflection of intelligence for decades.

However, over the last 30 years, work done by psychologists like Howard Gardner, Robert Sternberg, and Daniel Goleman has challenged IQ as the foremost measure of intelligence, paving the way for the acceptance of other models of intelligence, including multiple intelligences, creativity, contextual intelligence, and emotional intelligence. This section discusses these other models of intelligence as a way to understand why becoming cognizant of and honing one's skills and abilities is critical to building self-awareness.

Multiple Intelligences

Who was "smarter"—Albert Einstein or Johann Sebastian Bach? Many may say that Einstein was smarter because he was considered a mathematical and scientific genius. Others may say that Bach was more intelligent because he was considered a musical genius. Your decision may reflect your own biases toward which skills and abilities are "smarter"—math and science or music. When we consider Howard Gardner's approach to intelligence, however, neither man can be considered more intelligent than the other.

Library of Congress Prints and Photographs Division [LC-US262-60242]

Howard Gardner's 1983 book *Frames of Mind* rejected the notion of a single type of intelligence.[12] In it, he argued that IQ measurements, standardized test scores, and grades were relatively poor predictors of who succeeds and who does not because they do not account for all of the ways in which individuals demonstrate their intelligence.[13] While IQ tests may be predictive of academic achievement in some settings, they are not generally predictive of success in artistic, creative, or other professional endeavors.[14] Instead, Gardner proposed that there are eight kinds of intelligence that can be indicators of career success: linguistic, mathematical-logical, spatial, kinesthetic, musical, interpersonal, intrapersonal, and naturalist (see Table 13.1). Read the table and determine where your own intelligences lie.

For example, someone who is linguistically intelligent may prefer writing reports to creating spreadsheets. Someone who is spatially intelligent may prefer creating charts and slide presentations to presenting in front of an audience. Most people have a combination of intelligences that form their personality and influence their approach to various situations. Regardless of the kind of intelligence an individual possesses, aligning intelligence with career choices and job functions is especially critical to workplace effectiveness.

One internationally famous business leader who exemplifies Gardner's multiple intelligence theory is Richard Branson, founder of the Virgin Group. Although he never performed well in formal academic settings (he dropped out of school at age 16), his business savvy enabled him to create a youth culture magazine called *Student* in 1966 and turn it into a multinational conglomerate with more than

Type of Intelligence	Description	In a Company Setting, You Can Volunteer To …	Associated Careers
Linguistic	Word smart	Write reports	Lawyers, journalists, politicians
Mathematical-logical	Number/Reasoning smart	Create spreadsheets or analyze data	Scientists, mathematicians, economists, technologists, engineers
Spatial	Picture smart	Create charts or slide presentations	Artists, architects, pilots
Kinesthetic	Body smart	Organize and coach a company sports team	Dancers, athletes, personal trainers, builders
Musical	Music smart	Organize a company talent show	Musicians, singers
Interpersonal	People smart	Present to a large audience	Teachers, diplomats
Intrapersonal	Self-smart	Participate in employee satisfaction focus groups	Philosophers, psychologists, theologians
Naturalist	Nature smart	Develop a company's recycling program	Gardeners, farmers

Table 13.1 〉 Multiple Intelligences

Source: Adapted from Howard Gardner, *Frames of Mind: The Theory of Multiple Intelligences* (New York: Basic Books, 1983).

200 companies in over 30 countries. By 2009, he had been knighted in England for his contributions to entrepreneurship and was on the *Forbes* World Billionaires list. With businesses that include trains, mobile phones, a music label, airlines, and space tourism, Branson has managed to expand his business operations to six continents—all without demonstrating the traditionally valued scholastic hallmarks of intelligence.[15]

Research on the functioning of the human brain also has shed some light on an individual's intellectual proclivities. The way in which information is processed in the brain varies. According to some researchers, the left hemisphere of the brain is the processing center for logical, rational, and analytical thinking. Conversely, the right side of the brain is responsible for intuitive, spatial, and abstract thinking.[16] Some individuals are considered more left-brained, processing information in a systematic and structured manner. Others are referred to as being right-brained, processing information in a more abstract manner. These individuals tend to be more creative and innovative, are higher in spatial intelligence, and better at complex problem solving.[17]

The right-brain and left-brain labels are just that—labels. Empirical research on brain activity has not concluded that the right and left sides of the brain process information in different ways, but what is clear is that some individuals are more structured, systematic, and logical than others.[18] These predispositions, regardless of brain activity, can and do influence the types of activities and professions that lead to a greater likelihood of success.

Considering our case example of Wolfgang Keller, we can use these concepts to make some assumptions about Keller's and Brodsky's intelligence and workplace behavior. Keller's behavior shows that he is more "people smart," while Brodsky's behavior shows that he is more "reasoning smart." Keller's behavior is aligned with the needs of a general manager role, his position at Königsbräu-TAK. In contrast, Brodsky's behavior seems to contradict the needs of a position that requires interpersonal intelligence. However, his

Andrew Burton /Reuters /Landov

mathematical-logical intelligence has been useful in the aspect of the role that requires organizational redesign and system implementation.

Creativity

We often think of those with spatial, kinesthetic, or musical intelligence as being the most creative. However, **creativity** is a component of every form of intelligence and is available to all individuals. Creativity, also called divergent or lateral thinking, is defined as the ability to combine or link ideas in new ways to generate novel and useful alternatives.[19]

Creativity can affect how work gets done and how people interact with one another. Contrary to a popular opinion, being creative isn't limited to individuals working in artistic fields. For example, mathematicians and scientists constantly generate solutions to complex real-world problems. Teachers, lawyers, politicians, and psychologists spend time synthesizing data to propose alternative scenarios.

In fact, everyone has creative capacity. According to psychologist Shelley Carson, all humans do hundreds of things every day that require improvised thinking, problem solving, and creative acts. Creativity is an evolutionary trait that is wired into our brains and can be cultivated and increased through practice. Therefore, there is no distinction between a creative person and a noncreative person, but rather variations in how individuals leverage and utilize their creativity.[20]

Individuals who actively utilize their creative capacity have been shown to not only use their existing knowledge and technical skills to generate ideas, but also enlist other people and sources in the process. These people share the following four characteristics:

- Self-confidence and perseverance in the face of obstacles
- Willingness to take risks
- Willingness to grow and openness to new experiences
- Tolerance of ambiguity[21]

Creativity can also be evaluated according to three indices: fluency, flexibility, and originality.[22] Fluency is defined as the ability to generate many solutions that fit some requirement. Flexibility is the ability to change approaches to a problem, such as being able to solve a series of tasks when each task requires a different strategy. Originality is the ability to generate novel or unique propositions, ideas, or solutions.

Creativity is important to organizations because the development of new ideas and directions is critical to firms' sustainability. Some individuals who may not exhibit traditional creative traits may be adept at recognizing and unleashing the creative potential in others.[23] To that end, creativity can be cultivated by challenging normal assumptions about how problems are solved, such as identifying strategies and creating tangible solutions to problems.[24]

One company that has built a sterling reputation for creativity is Pixar, creator of such iconic and award-winning films as *Toy Story*, *Finding Nemo*, and *Monsters, Inc.* Former Chief Technology Officer of Pixar, Greg Brandeau, attributes Pixar's success to the company's ability to discover and unleash the creative power and ingenuity in all employees, which he calls finding their "slice of genius."[25] These slices of genius are not found just in the purely creative functions of animation and digital design, but in all parts of the company. The company believes that their product is the result of the collective work, from the receptionist to the director. To that

Creativity
The ability to combine or link ideas in new ways to generate novel and useful alternatives.

Lynn Watson/Dreamstime.com

end, all employees of Pixar, regardless of their position, are included on the closing film credits.

Triarchic Theory of Intelligence

A second theory of intelligence was put forth by psychologist Robert Sternberg. His theory of intelligence, like Gardner's, also is based on multiple dimensions of cognitive functioning. He believes that individuals possess three components of intelligence: (1) computational (analytic), (2) experiential (creative), and (3) contextual (practical), which he calls the **triarchic theory of intelligence**.[26] His first component of intelligence is closely aligned with the cognitive and analytical thought processing that is measured with a traditional IQ test. He differs from the traditional assessment of analytical processing by including knowledge acquisition as a central component of computational intelligence. For Sternberg, knowing what questions to ask and what information to seek to solve a problem is a key aspect of analytical intelligence.[27]

The second component of the triarchic theory of intelligence is creativity, the ability to identify and react to novel situations and stimuli and to connect with the external world. For Sternberg, creative intelligence is not being creative per se; instead, it is being open to new ideas and willing to engage in experiential learning and development. He believes that creatively intelligent people are adept at applying their existing knowledge and experience to novel or unique situations.[28]

The final component of the triarchic theory is contextual intelligence, the ability to shape and be shaped by the external environment. Some people can size up a situation and see the big picture. They seem to know what is required to accomplish tasks and the best methods for getting them done. They also seem to view setbacks as opportunities, and accomplishments as benchmarks for further improvement.

In Chapter 1, we defined an individual who possesses contextual intelligence as having a profound sensitivity to macro-level contextual factors in the creation, growth, or transformation of business.[29] Those with contextual intelligence, the "big-picture" thinkers, are able to sense opportunities and avoid threats, but several distinct personal characteristics set them apart from other individuals. They take an interest in and have an appreciation for history and are willing to learn from the past. In addition, individuals with contextual intelligence tend to be knowledgeable about trends in regulations, geopolitics, and technology, and they actively participate in cross-cultural experiences.[30] Individuals who possess contextual intelligence:

- Take time to understand the environment and its potential impact on the business landscape.
- Possess the personal characteristics to seize the opportunities that the context presents or to shape the context to fit a new possibility.
- Have the capacity to adapt their leadership style/approach as the context changes.[31]

In general, individuals who are contextually intelligent are better able to adapt to their environment. They can read and react to cues and other external stimuli in a way that others cannot.[32]

Cultural Intelligence

A key subset of contextual intelligence is **cultural intelligence**, the ability to understand and respond appropriately to different cultural contexts and situations. The increasing globalization of business has enhanced the need for cultural intelligence. An individual who is culturally intelligent can adapt to different cultural contexts without being overly influenced by his or her own background or identity.[33] Of course, a person's identity is important and cannot nor should not be suppressed, but it should not overwhelm his or her openness toward those from different cultures.

Triarchic theory of intelligence
The theory that individuals possess three components of intelligence: (1) computational (analytic), (2) experiential (creative), and (3) contextual (practical).

Cultural intelligence
The ability to understand and respond appropriately to different cultural contexts and situations.

In essence, cultural intelligence involves an understanding of oneself and one's own cultural values, an appreciation for others' culture and values, and an ability to adapt one's leadership style to a particular cultural context.[34] Individuals who have been abroad for education or employment tend to have a better appreciation for cultural differences and understand how these differences should influence behavior in negotiations as well as in management situations.[35]

Emotional Intelligence

Another stream of research on intelligence focuses on the way individuals relate to one another. Most of us have lost patience with another person at some point, perhaps while working on a team project. Or perhaps we have experienced a situation where our emotional reaction was out of proportion to what was happening, like flying off the handle when someone slightly inconveniences us. In these situations, we lacked the **emotional intelligence** to function and interact with those around us in a productive manner.

At its core, emotional intelligence is the capacity for recognizing our own feelings and those of others, for motivating ourselves, and for managing our emotions and relationships in a productive manner.[36] Made popular by Daniel Goleman, emotional intelligence emerged from a study of the difference between average and outstanding performers. Researchers found that the key differentiator between good and great managers was emotional intelligence.[37]

Emotional intelligence consists of four components that can be learned and improved over time: self-awareness, self-management, social awareness, and relationship management (see Figure 13.3). As Figure 13.3 shows, emotional intelligence has an inward (self-awareness and self-management) and outward (social awareness and relationship management) focus.[38] One side encompasses how we relate to ourselves, and the other side encompasses how we relate to others.

On the inward focus side, self-awareness encompasses the ability to recognize one's own emotions and understand how those emotions impact others. Individuals who are self-aware tend to be self-confident and to have a good sense of their personal strengths and weaknesses; as such, they are open to feedback and personal development. They also tend to have a self-deprecating sense of humor and resist taking things personally. In addition, self-aware individuals tend to make career choices that are aligned with their personal values. Finally, people who are self-aware tend to engage in personal reflection on an ongoing basis.[39]

Emotional intelligence
The capacity for recognizing our own feelings and those of others, for motivating ourselves, and for managing our emotions and relationships in a productive manner.

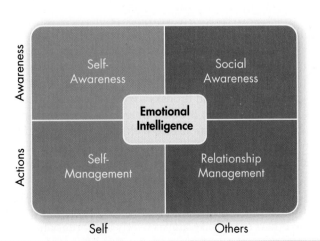

Figure 13.3 Components of Emotional Intelligence

Source: Adapted from "The Emotional Intelligence Workbook," The Hay Group, 2008.

Self-management is composed of two main components—regulation and motivation—each of which functions as a strong counterbalance to the other. Regulation includes self-control, which is the ability to keep destructive emotions in check especially during times of crisis, and adaptability, which is demonstrated through an openness to change. While regulation helps channel emotions appropriately, the motivation component of self-management functions as a source of inspiration and optimism. Motivation includes the desire for achievement and the ability to push oneself despite obstacles and setbacks. Although varying degrees of emotional intelligence can exist, individuals with high emotional intelligence know their emotions, strengths, weaknesses, needs, and drives. They are also in control of their feelings and impulses and are driven to achieve beyond typical expectations.[40]

Social awareness, part of the outward focus, is manifested on both an individual and group basis. On an individual level, social awareness is about empathy, sensing others' feelings and perspectives, and taking an active interest in their concerns. Empathy has become more important, especially as organizations increase the use of teams both domestically and internationally.[41] Empathy is particularly vital in cross-cultural teams, where it is important to understand the nuances of particular contexts. Empathy does not necessarily mean that one must agree with a different perspective, but it does mean that one can understand why someone else would have a different point of view. On a group level, social awareness is concerned with the ability to understand group dynamics and relationships. Individuals who have a strong sense of social awareness are adept at understanding the political dynamics and power structures that are often embedded in the culture of an organization.

Relationship management, the final component of emotional intelligence, includes the abilities to influence and inspire others, to constructively manage conflict, and to build and cultivate productive teams. Goleman describes relationship management as the hallmark of emotional intelligence because it demands proficiency in the other areas: self-awareness, self-management, and social awareness.[42] In other words, individuals can be more effective at managing relationships when they are better able to manage themselves. Emotionally intelligent leaders:

- Listen more than they talk.
- Emphasize the how's and why's of assignments and tasks instead of simply telling people what to do.
- Engage team members and recognize their contributions rather than criticize and correct their mistakes.
- Understand what energizes and engages people on their team and create environments that foster that creativity.[43]

In short, while skills, knowledge, and experience help an individual secure a position within an organization, emotional intelligence helps the person keep it and progress. Emotional intelligence is especially essential when working in cross-cultural situations.

How would you rate Keller's and Brodsky's levels of emotional intelligence? Keller is more emotionally intelligent than Brodsky in terms of relationship management, as evidenced by his drive to create relationships with the sales team and external customers. Brodsky is more emotionally intelligent than Keller in terms of regulation, a key component of self-management. Brodsky never seems to lose his temper at work or to act impulsively. Both men struggle with self-awareness and empathy. Neither man acknowledges how his behavior impacts his relationship with others. Brodsky does not realize that his behavior is creating social distance. Keller does not realize that his behavior is causing others to perceive him as overly authoritarian.

As we have seen throughout this section on the different forms of intelligence, successful managers need to build a level of competency or intelligence in a number of areas. Being academically smart is important, but it is just a baseline.

The Leadership Development Journey

Leaders use a diverse range of intelligences to conduct their work. Based on Gardner's Typology of Multiple Intelligences, what type of intelligence do you use when leading? Think of an example when you used this intelligence. Did it require right-brain thinking or left-brain thinking? Identify a type of intelligence you would like to improve. Develop an action plan to improve this intelligence.

Other forms of intelligence are also vitally important, especially the ability to work well with others. The nature of intelligence that is most important will depend on the values and drives of the individual and the contextual elements of the situation. Many of the intelligence factors we have discussed can be developed and enhanced through training, new experiences, practice, and determination. Although not everyone is musically gifted, artistically inclined, or logically minded, people can and should find opportunities that leverage their strengths but also provide opportunities for development. They also should look for team members who can complement their strengths. In doing so, the sum of the whole is greater than the parts. Throughout his career at Microsoft, Bill

Gates was especially adept at bringing in coleaders who complemented his leadership style and approach. As early as 1982, he hired Microsoft's first chief operating officer. Though he was the final arbitrator of Microsoft's technology investments, he often relied on co-leaders to oversee other aspects of the business in which he had less interest and experience, namely financial management and operations. This collaboration allowed Microsoft to dominate the software industry for decades.

UNDERSTANDING YOUR PERSONALITY

Understanding and then building on one's intelligences is one way of improving self-awareness. Another avenue into self-awareness is understanding one's personality. **Personality** is a system of enduring inner characteristics, tendencies, and temperaments that are inherited and shaped by social, cultural, and environmental factors. Although we tend to describe someone's personality according to the traits that person displays, personality is actually composed of two components. The first component of personality refers to the way a person is perceived by friends, family members, coworkers, and supervisors. Describing someone as "shy" or "outgoing" illustrates this concept. The second component of personality refers to someone's inner nature, or his or her underlying thought processes.

Some people work in jobs that require long periods of working alone, such as research and analysis and computer support, while others work in jobs that require substantial interpersonal contact, such as customer service and marketing. Often these positions are held by people whose personalities suit the job. Introverted, or shy, people often like to work alone and perform better when they are left to their own devices. Extroverted, or outgoing, people often perform better when their tasks relate to engaging and developing relationships with others. Neither personality type can be considered "right" or "wrong," just more suited to one type of job than another.

Personality
A system of enduring inner characteristics, tendencies, and temperaments that are both inherited and shaped by social, cultural, and environmental factors.

Trait	Description	Low versus High
Extroversion	The tendency to be sociable, assertive, and active and to experience things positively. Includes energy, liveliness, stamina, activeness, assertiveness, and dominance.[45]	Low: reserved, prefers to work alone High: sociable, prefers social interaction
Openness	Being open to experiences and willing to be original, imaginative, nonconforming, unconventional, creative, and autonomous.	Low: pragmatic, avoids risks High: creative, open to taking risks
Conscientiousness	Composed of achievement and dependability, task competence, initiative, persistence, and tenacity.	Low: flexible and spontaneous High: persistent, structured, and organized
Agreeableness	The tendency to be trusting, compliant, caring, and gentle. Overall, it refers to the friendliness and likability of a leader.[46]	Low: competitive and challenging High: compassionate and cooperative
Emotional stability (neuroticism)	The ability to remain calm and confident, especially in times of crisis.	Low: reactive and excitable High: calm and methodical

Table 13.2 › Leadership Personality Traits

Sources: Timothy A. Judge, Joyce E. Bono, Remus Ilies, and Megan W. Gerhardt, "Personality and Leadership: A Qualitative and Quantitative Review," *Journal of Applied Psychology*, Vol. 87, No. 4, 2002, pp. 765–780; and Ginka Toegel and Jean-Louis Barsoux, "How to Become a Better Leader," *Sloan Management Review*, Vol. 53, No. 3, Spring 2012.

Researchers Robert McCrae and Paul Costa tried to identify certain traits that are common in all people to explain effective and ineffective approaches to leadership. According to them, each person's personality can be broken down into five distinct factors and each factor has a sliding scale.[44] For example, people who exhibit high levels of extroversion like to be socially engaged and those who exhibit low levels are introverted (see Table 13.2).

The intensity of each of these traits varies from one individual to another, and this variability often results in differences in how work gets done and how people interact with one another. These traits influence a person's default leadership style and approach, but as we discussed, a person's style can (and should) vary greatly depending on the situation or context.

Differences in style greatly contribute to conflict in organizations. In the Wolfgang Keller case, Brodsky neglected deadlines while Keller adhered to them. Brodsky was great at creating information and control systems while Keller was better at solving problems as they arose. Brodsky refrained from developing personal relationships with peers and subordinates, while Keller actively cultivated them.

Personality Assessment

Before trying to change your leadership style to fit a particular situation, it is helpful to gain some insight into your predispositions. Where do you get your energy? How do you interact with others? How do you process information? How do you connect ideas? Carl Jung, Katherine Myers, and Isabel Briggs Myers are credited with pioneering approaches to answering those questions. As a psychologist, Carl Jung spent his career refining a theory of psychological types, suggesting that human behavior was regular and predictable. According to Jung, there are six fundamental psychological processes that impact an individual's cognitive process and ultimately influence his or her leadership style: Sensing (S), Intuition (N), Thinking (T), Feeling (F), Extraverted (E), and Introverted (I).[47]

Myers and Briggs extended Jung's research and added two other psychological processes, Judgment (J) and Perception (P), noting that some people are generally open to a continuous stream of new information while others are more interested

Description	Psychological Dimensions	Description
Extraverted (E) Concentrating on the outside world	*Where an individual receives energy*	Introverted (I) Attending to one's own thoughts and feelings
Sensing (S) Through the five physical senses; focus on here and now; concentrate on information that is real and tangible	*How data are collected*	Intuition (N) Through patterns; open to new possibilities and experimentation; focus on the connections and relationships between facts
Thinking (T) Seeing logical, analytical, impersonal, and objective links	*How ideas and concepts are connected*	Feeling (F) Based on strength of values and sense of importance
Judging (J) Through organizing and concluding activities in a structured and analytical way	*How information is processed*	Perceiving (P) Through obtaining new information; open to new ideas and possibilities; prefer not to be rushed

Table 13.3 ⟩ Psychological Dimensions of Personality

Source: Adapted from Isabel Briggs Myers and Peter B, Myers, *Gifts Differing* (Palo Alto, CA: Consulting Psychologists Press, 1980), pp. 7–11.

Dominant Function	Introverted		Extroverted	
Sensing (S)	ISTJ	ISFJ	ESTP	ESFP
Intuition (N)	INTJ	INFJ	ENTP	ENFP
Thinking (T)	ISTP	INTP	ESTJ	ENTJ
Feeling (F)	ISFP	INFP	ESFJ	ENFJ

Table 13.4 ⟩ Psychological Profiles Mapped to Dominant Functions

Source: Adapted from Isabel Briggs Myers and Peter B, Myers, *Gifts Differing* (Palo Alto, CA: Consulting Psychologists Press, 1980), p. 16.

in reaching closure.[48] From these eight processes, four personality dimensions are created: E-I, S-N, T-F, and J-P.

Continuing their research, Myers and Briggs developed the Myers-Briggs Type Indicator (MBTI) assessment to assist individuals in better understanding their personality dimensions; it has become the most widely used personality assessment tool in North America.[49] By completing the MBTI assessment, an individual can determine his or her four-letter type. The four dimensions of the MBTI assessment are considered polar opposites of each other. For instance, according to them, a person cannot be equally strong in thinking and feeling. One of the two dimensions will be stronger and will generally influence the way in which ideas are connected and the way in which an individual relates to problems (see Table 13.3).

The MBTI assessment results in 16 possible personality types, but within each personality type, there is generally one dimension that is considered dominant. The dominant process is on the S-N scale or the T-F scale, and it depends on the first and last dimensions (E-I and J-P) of a person's assessment. For extroverts (E) who are perceptive (P), the dominant function is on the S-N scale. For extroverts who are judging (J), the dominant function is on the T-F scale. The opposite is true for introverts. For introverts (I) who are perceptive, the dominant function is on the T-F scale, and for introverts who are judging, the dominant function is on the S-N scale (see Table 13.4).[50] For example, if an individual's score is INTP, thinking will be his or her dominant function, and it will generally have the strongest influence on this person's behavior. That doesn't mean the three other dimensions have no impact; they still influence the person's style, but to a lesser degree than the dominant function. It is also interesting to note that the polar opposite of the dominant function is considered the inferior function. For INTP, that would be feeling. The inferior function is underdeveloped for a dominant thinker, which could be problematic if situations or events call for more feeling than thinking.[51]

Understanding your own preferences and those of others can make you a better communicator. The way a person who scores high on intuition processes information is different from an individual who scores high on sensing. Intuitors prefer to address open questions and brainstorm, while sensers prefer facts and brevity. Thinkers prefer organized and carefully analyzed information, while feelers are more influenced by the impact of the information on others.[52] Someone who is an ENFP is considered extroverted, intuitive, feeling, and perceptive, which is considered the opposite of someone who is an ISTJ, introverted, sensing, thinking, and judging. ENFPs can be described as imaginative, capable, and persuasive improvisers who offer quick solutions. Yet an ISTJ may perceive an ENFP as unrealistic and unfocused. ISTJs are often described as quiet, thorough, logical, organized, and conventional thinkers and managers. Yet an ENFP may perceive an ISTJ as unimaginative and dull.

Different individuals thrive in different situations. For instance, a study of city managers noted that the most successful and longest-tenured candidates tended to be introverted and perceptive. Although the researchers expected that these political positions would favor individuals who were more extroverted and quick decision makers, the opposite was true. Successful city managers tend to draw attention to their jobs, not to themselves.[53]

Although there are clear distinctions in the various MBTI types that highlight the way in which individuals process information and interact with others, this personality assessment does not dictate all aspects of a person's behavior. Past experiences, personal values, and other situational elements influence an individual's leadership style. The MBTI or any other personality assessment tool is useful in providing a view into the way in which an individual acts, but human personality is multifaceted and cannot be reduced to a simple category.

Locus of Control

The manner in which individuals respond to specific events or external stimuli provides an additional window into their personality. Some believe that they can influence or control the outcome of events through their actions, personal determination, perseverance, or commitment. Others believe that the outcome of events is beyond their personal control; in essence, they believe that they cannot influence an inevitable outcome. This dichotomy of positions on the extent to which an individual believes that he or she can control the outcome of events is called the **locus of control**.[54]

In essence, different individuals attribute outcomes of events to one of four causes: personal ability, effort, task difficulty, and luck or chance (see Figure 13.4). Their attribution is impacted by two dimensions—stability and locus of control. Stability refers to the predictability of change over time. Personal ability and task difficulty are stable causes that may change from one situation to another but do so in a predictable manner. The outcome of effort and luck are less predictable and hence unstable. The second dimension is locus of control, or the extent to which an individual believes that he or she can control the outcome of events. Personal ability and effort are internally driven, and task difficulty and luck are externally generated.[55]

Individuals who believe in their ability to control events are called internals, and those who ascribe control to external events are called externals. Internals tend to

Locus of control
The extent to which an individual believes that he or she can control or influence the outcome of events.

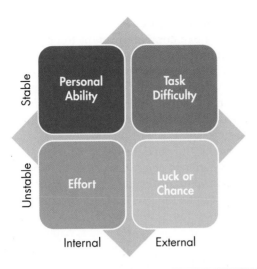

Figure 13.4 Attribution of Stability and Control on Outcomes

Source: Modified from Mark J. Martinko and William L. Gardner, "Learned Helplessness: An Alternative Explanation for Performance Deficits," *Academy of Management Review*, Vol. 7, No. 2, April 1982, pp. 195–204.

believe that their personal efforts and abilities can influence outcomes to a great degree.[56] Given their belief in self-determination, internals often seek situations or events in which they believe that they have a greater likelihood of controlling the outcome. Interestingly, when internals fail, they are willing to ascribe more control to external events or stimuli while maintaining a strong belief in personal efficacy. Conversely, when externals succeed, they do not ascribe more legitimacy to internal (self) factors; they tend to still believe that success or failure is outside their control.[57] They tend to blame others or external influences for failure and sometimes ascribe success to luck or circumstance.[58] Based on their personal sense of control or lack thereof, it is not surprising that externals tend to be more anxious about outcomes than do internals.

An individual's locus of control has some interesting implications for organizations. Individuals with a high internal sense of control are generally self-motivated and excited to take on challenging tasks at work. These individuals often possess a growth mindset whereby they "enjoy new challenges and strive to learn."[59] They also tend to exhibit higher levels of satisfaction and performance. These positive results and higher levels of motivation, however, will last only if the organization's reward system reinforces this behavior. In addition, internals and externals tend to respond differently to supervision. Based on their sense of personal control, internals prefer participatory supervisors who delegate. Externals, on the other hand, prefer more directive supervision. These preferences for different types of supervision are also evident in a person's own approach to leadership. Internals tend to be more participatory, and externals tend to be more directive.[60]

Managing Adversity

The way in which an individual confronts adversity is aligned with his or her locus of control. When individuals are confronted with struggles and roadblocks, some see these as opportunities for development while others see them as debilitating. While adversity can stimulate learning and development, it also can undermine confidence and impede an individual's ability to move forward in a productive manner. The way in which an individual confronts adversity provides another lens into understanding his or her personality and leadership style. Individuals with a high internal locus of control often believe that they can adequately address or at least control certain aspects of adverse situations.[61]

Those who confront adversity head-on are often referred to as hardy or resilient. They believe that they can control or adapt to certain events and outcomes, and they are able to bounce back from difficulty.[62] Individuals who are resilient possess some key common characteristics, including the ability to face and accept the reality of a situation, a strong set of values and confidence in their own abilities that help to guide their action, and a willingness to improvise or try new things.[63] In addition, resilient individuals tend to be very persistent; they push forward regardless of setbacks and obstacles.[64]

One individual who epitomizes **resilience** is Nelson Mandela who was imprisoned for 27 years for his activism against apartheid in South Africa. As the apartheid state of South Africa eventually crumbled, Mandela was released from prison in 1990 and went on to become the president of the country a few years later. His post imprisonment speeches and actions were filled with calls for reconciliation and forgiveness, rather than retribution and anger. While most people who had suffered as much as Mandela would be inclined to seek revenge, Mandela was able to transcend his personal feelings about his cruel treatment for the promise of a better future for the country. He channeled his adversity into moving forward, not backward.

Those who tend to shrink in the face of hardship have developed what some researchers call "learned helplessness." Based on past experiences or situations, they believe that there is nothing they can do to rectify a bad situation; consequently, they tend to do nothing. Some blame the situation and believe that no one could do anything to adequately respond; in essence, the situation is so unique or so difficult that no one could be expected to handle it in an effective manner. This is called universal helplessness. Others blame themselves, believing that there might be an appropriate personal response but that it is beyond their reach or repertoire of skills and abilities. This is called personal helplessness, and individuals who see themselves in this regard tend to have lower self-esteem, especially when they compare their skills and abilities with others.[65]

One way to understand your own tendencies is to consider the ways in which you react to difficult situations (see Table 13.5). What percent of the time do you avoid adversity? How often do you try to harness a tough situation to enhance your learning and development? Where do your tendencies lie?

How an individual understands and interprets situations shapes how he or she experiences and addresses them. Regardless of the facts of the situation, our worldview influences our response patterns, which are often automatic and subconscious.[66] Think of these common aphorisms: "The world is your oyster" or

Resilience
The belief that one can control or adapt to certain events and outcomes and be able to bounce back from difficulty.

Response Strategy	Description	% of Time Used
Avoid	Deny or dodge adversity, postpone addressing it	
Survive	Simply try to make it through and come out alive	
Cope	Find ways to work through the underlying problems and deal with the negative toll	
Manage	Actively use some tools or strategies to work with adversity	
Harness	Convert adversity into fuel to propel learning, growth, and achievement	
		100%

Table 13.5 › Adversity Response Hierarchy

Sources: Adapted from Joshua Margolis, "Leadership and Resilience," PowerPoint presentation (Boston, MA: Harvard Business School, October 2007); and Paul G. Stoltz, *Adversity Quotient @ Work* (New York: HarperCollins, 2000).

"Everyone is out to get me" or "The glass is half full" or "The glass is half empty." Those who see the glass as half full tend to confront challenges as opportunities for learning. Those who believe that everyone is conspiring against them tend to view adversity as part of this conspiracy.

Although much of a person's response to adversity is ingrained, recent research has demonstrated that an individual can increase his or her abilities to effectively address adversity by thinking through four key dimensions—control, ownership, reach, and endurance.[67]

- *Control:* The extent to which you think you can influence whatever happens next. Are there components of the situation you can control?
- *Ownership:* The level of accountability or responsibility that you assume to improve the situation. Can or should you work on certain aspects of this situation?
- *Reach:* The extent to which the adversity impacts other aspects of your professional or personal life. Is it contained in one area? Does it influence your personal behavior? How large of a shadow does it cast over your activities?
- *Endurance:* The expected length of the adversity. What can you do to lessen the length?

Control and ownership are mutually reinforcing. The more control you feel, generally, the more difficulty you have deflecting accountability and responsibility. Similarly, the more ownership you feel, the greater level of control you will have over a situation. Although certain situations or events may at first seem unwieldy, individuals can enhance their sense of control and ownership (and hence their adversity response) by breaking down components of the situation they can control. It is often easier to make progress on small aspects of a problem rather than trying to tackle the entire problem at once, which can be overwhelming and frightening.[68]

Reach and endurance are also interdependent. If you believe that the adversity is far-reaching, it is likely to endure. Similarly, the longer you believe that an adversity will last, the greater the likelihood it will impact other aspects of your life. The key is to limit the impact of adversity and to shorten its duration.[69]

An understanding of one's adaptive capacity or resilience is important. It has implications for the types of environments and level of risk that a person might be willing to assume. Developing one's ability to effectively face adversity has become increasingly relevant, especially in light of the economic downturn and increased global competition. In addition, the nature of leadership is increasingly about what Ronald Heifetz refers to as "adaptive challenges," the ability to respond effectively to anticipated and unanticipated incidents.[70] This ability to respond productively to hardships or crucibles was a key finding in a recent study of successful business leaders.[71] Those who succeeded addressed their adversity as a learning and developmental opportunity.

SELF-MONITORING

Like differences in personality, skills and abilities, and style, differences in **self-monitoring** can affect how work gets done and how people interact. Self-monitoring is the act of reading and using cues from the environment to assess one's behavior. When your ability to self-monitor differs from that of others, your workplace behavior may differ and your relationships can be affected.

At the movie theater, you are told to turn off your cell phone and not to talk while the movie is running. Later you hear the couple in front of you talking. You wonder, "Weren't they listening?" As you reflect on their rudeness, you look around and see other people motioning toward the couple, whose conversation is getting

Self-monitoring
The ability of individuals to read cues from their environment to assess their behavior. People can vary from being high self-monitors to being low self-monitors.

A DIFFERENT
View

Authentic Leadership

Authentic leaders are true to themselves and to others. They lead with trustworthiness, passion, values, and self-discipline. Wendy Kopp is an authentic leader who persevered despite many challenges. She recognized the inequities of public education and established Teach for America in which recent college graduates commit to 2 years of teaching in public schools. After 5 years of relentless hard work, Teach for America was on the verge of shutting their doors. Determined not to let that happen, Kopp refocused her efforts and recommitted to her core values. Through her renewed and dedicated focus, she was able to transform and significantly grow Teach for America. Identify another authentic leader of a for-profit or nonprofit organization.

1. What value does the leader add to his or her organization? How does his or her leadership style influence employees at the organization?
2. How is his or her leadership style unique from leaders at competitive organizations?
3. What could you learn from the authentic leader?

louder. Yet the disruptors seem oblivious and carry on anyway. One person leaves the movie theater and returns with an usher who quietly tells the couple to stop talking. The couple looks around, unaware of the effect they were having on their fellow moviegoers and abashedly sink lower in their seats. So why did the couple need someone to tell them that they were being rude? Couldn't they judge this for themselves?

We tend to describe individuals as high self-monitors or low self-monitors. High self-monitors read environmental and social cues regarding norms and accepted behaviors and use those cues to adjust their own behaviors.[72] They may be able to mirror others' behaviors so that they get along and are more adaptive to change than are low self-monitors. High self-monitors also may be described as chameleons. They are able to change their style according to the dictates of the situation.[73] Conversely, low self-monitors do not read environmental and social cues, nor do they use them to change their behavior. They may be more internally focused and exhibit behavior that stays consistent in different situations.[74] As such, low self-monitors are often described as rigid and inflexible.

As you have learned, work environments include individuals with different personalities, skills and abilities, and styles, all of which must be leveraged to create effective and productive working relationships. Therefore, a certain degree of adaptability is necessary to create collaborative and productive work environments.

Changing one's behavior does not necessarily mean that certain approaches are always better. On the contrary, there is no one right approach or style. There are successful people of all kinds in all types of careers. Finally, while we tend to think that someone who does things differently from us may be ineffective, that person may just be behaving in ways that are different from our own preferences. In these situations, it is important not to jump to conclusions about a person's intent. Instead, you should inquire about the differences and try to come to some form of mutual understanding.

Managing Oneself

Much like building self-awareness, becoming more interpersonally effective is an iterative process. Interpersonal effectiveness requires feedback and continuous development. While you have learned that knowing yourself and managing yourself is critical to interpersonal effectiveness, you have also learned how knowing yourself and managing yourself is integral to developing a fulfilling and satisfying career.

Peter Drucker proposed that to remain engaged and productive during the course of a work life that may span 50 years, individuals need to cultivate a deep understanding of themselves. In this respect, Drucker proposes that individuals ask themselves the following questions:[75]

- *What are my strengths?* People are often more familiar with what they are not good at doing relative to what they are good at doing. Yet knowing your strengths is especially helpful in deciding where you belong. To uncover this, it is helpful to obtain feedback. Drucker proposes that individuals understand their strengths and focus on improving them. He also suggests that individuals understand and improve upon their weaknesses, but only to the extent that those weaknesses are inhibiting the individuals' effectiveness and performance on a large scale.
- *How do I perform?* People should focus on achieving results by working in ways they best perform. For example, individuals should know whether they prefer to learn new information by reading or by listening. They should also understand whether they prefer to work alone or as a team member, whether they prefer to be a decision maker or an adviser, whether they perform well under stress or need structure and predictability, and whether they prefer working in small or large organizations.

- *What are my values?* For an individual to be effective in an organization, his or her values must be aligned with the organization's values. Although the values need not be exactly the same, they should be close enough that individuals do not become frustrated, disenfranchised, and ultimately, less productive.
- *Where do I belong?* Just as individuals are challenged with knowing their strengths and understanding how they perform, so too are individuals challenged with knowing where they belong. To answer this question, however, individuals must know how they fare on the first three questions. By understanding their strengths, performance drivers, and values, they can determine where they belong and, by extension, where they do not belong.
- *What should I contribute?* To answer this question, people should ask themselves (1) what the situation requires? (2) given my strengths, performance, and values, how can I make the greatest contribution to what needs to be done? and (3) what results have to be achieved to make a difference?

By answering these questions, Drucker proposes that a course of action will become clear for each individual. They will be able to determine what to do, where and how to start, and what goals and deadlines to set in order to remain engaged and productive over the course of a long work life.

SUMMARY

LO1 A successful leader is able to adapt his or her style to different situations and contexts. This adaptive capability is honed and developed with greater self-awareness and insight. This insight, in turn, can lead to developmental opportunities and experiences that help to reinforce the leader's strengths and shore up the leader's weaknesses.

LO2 Different individuals have different levels and kinds of intelligence. The theory of multiple intelligences expands the classical notion of "book smarts," or traditional academic aptitude, as measured by the IQ test. There are, in fact, a variety of intellectual domains, including artistic, musical, interpersonal, and spatial. These other forms of intelligence are often more important than traditional measures of intelligence for certain professions and in specific situations.

Being able to understand macro-level environmental factors and being in a position to shape the context are both important when competing in an increasingly global landscape. Two keys to success in this global environment are contextual and cultural intelligence. On a more personal level, emotional intelligence enables leaders to build stronger and more productive working relationships. Emotionally intelligent leaders are adept at knowing their personal strengths and weaknesses and are able to manage their emotions and motivations in a constructive manner.

LO3 A person's personality and predispositions are strongly connected to the manner in which different forms of intelligence are manifested. By understanding his or her personality, an individual is given clues and insights into how and why he or she acts a certain way. Some prefer introspection and reflective thinking, while others prefer vibrant interaction and quick action. A person's leadership style and approach is influenced by these tendencies as well as by his or her locus of control, the extent to which the person believes that he or she can control a situation or influence the outcome of an activity.

A person's sense of control also has implications for his or her reaction to adversity or hardships. Leadership is fraught with considerable unforeseen obstacles and challenges. Some individuals are able to confront adversity head-on and use the challenge as a way to build personal learning and development. Others shrink in the face of adversity, believing that they can do very little to control the outcome of events. A person's predispositions with regard to control and adversity can be adapted and changed over time with practice and experience.

LO4 Ultimately, to become effective leaders, people need to know who they are. Are they able to change their style and approach in different situations (high self-monitors), or do they use the same techniques regardless of the circumstance (low self-monitors)? Those who can and do change are more versatile and are likely to be successful in a greater variety of situations.

KEY TERMS

Creativity
Cultural intelligence
Emotional intelligence
Intelligence

Intelligence quotient (IQ)
Interpersonal effectiveness
Locus of control
Personality

Resilience
Self-awareness
Self-monitoring
Triarchic theory of intelligence

ASSIGNMENTS

Discussion Topics

1. Why is self-awareness so important to being an effective leader?

2. Research on emotional intelligence has consistently demonstrated that as individuals advance in their careers, their self-awareness tends to decrease. Why do you think self-awareness decreases as individuals gain positions of greater authority?

3. As companies seek to recruit new employees, should they evaluate candidates based on multiple intelligences? If so, how should they assess them? If not, why not?

4. How important is academic intelligence to success in business?

5. Innovation has become an increasingly important way in which a company distinguishes itself in the marketplace. If a company is seeking to hire individuals who are innovative, what should they look for in candidates?

6. How do the various elements of emotional intelligence connect to each other? Think of a leader who was emotionally intelligent. How would you describe him or her?

7. Look at the two approaches to assessing an individual's personality that are included in this chapter—Tables 13.2 and 13.3. What aspects do you think are most important for successful leaders? How would you assess your own personality? What areas do you need to develop?

8. How are locus of control and resilience connected?

9. One's leadership style and personality tend to be stable for long periods, but they can be impacted by certain crucible or life-changing events. Think about your own style. What experiences have influenced your leadership style? Have you learned more from your successes or your failures? Why?

10. Explain the connection between contextual intelligence and self-monitoring.

Management Research

1. Think of the best and worst leaders that you have worked with or for. How would you describe their personalities? What are the major differences between them? How did you feel about yourself when you worked with them? What did you learn about yourself?

2. Now think about a leader you admire—someone you have worked with or an historical figure. What forms of intelligence did they tap in to? Was the leader versatile? If so, in what ways?

In the Field

Spend some time with a family member or a role model and learn more about their leadership style. Based on this interaction, create a portrayal of their leadership style that describes how he or she leads when performing at his or her best. This portrayal may discuss the person's personality, multiple intelligences, cultural competencies, social awareness, creative skills, or other aspects of their leadership strengths.[76]

ENDNOTES

[1] George L. Hanbury, Alka Sapat, and Charles W. Washington, "Know Yourself and Take Charge of Your Own Destiny: The 'Fit Model' of Leadership," *Public Administration Review*, Vol. 64, No. 5, 2004, pp. 566–576; William Taggart and Daniel Robey, "Mind and Managers: On the Dual Nature of Human Information Processing and Management," *Academy of Management Review*, Vol. 6, No. 2, 1981, pp. 187–195.

[2] Scott W. Spreier, Mary H. Fontaine, and Ruth L. Malloy, "Leadership Run Amok: The Destructive Potential of Overachievers," *Harvard Business Review*, June 2006.

[3] Jeffrey Polzer and Hillary Anger Elfenbein, "Identity Issues in Teams," Harvard Business School Note No. 9-403-095 (Boston, MA: HBS Publishing, 2003).

[4] Anthony G. Athos and John J. Gabarro, "Understanding Another Person, Part 1: The Individual Frame of Reference," Harvard Business School Note No. 9-473-009, rev. September 1, 1976 (Boston, MA: HBS Publishing, 1972).

[5] John J. Gabarro, Alison Comings, and Jennifer M. Suesse, "Wolfgang Keller at Königsbräu-TAK (A)," Harvard Business School Case No. 9-498-045, rev. October 17, 2008 (Boston, MA: HBS Publishing, 1997); John J. Gabarro, Alison Comings, and Jennifer M. Suesse, "Wolfgang Keller at Königsbräu-TAK (B)," Harvard Business School Case No. 9-498-046, rev. May 20, 2008 (Boston, MA: HBS Publishing, 1997).

[6] Adam M. Grant, Francesca Gino, and David A. Hofmann, "Stop Stealing the Spotlight: The Perils of Extraverted Leadership," *European Business Review*, 2011; and Carmen Nobel, "Introverts: The Best Leaders for Proactive Employees," *HBS Working Knowledge*, October 4, 2010.

[7] Robert Benfari and Jean Knox, *Understanding Your Management Style: Beyond the Myers-Briggs Type Indicators* (Lexington, MA: Lexington Books, 1991).

[8] S. K. Whitbourne, "Language, Problem Solving and Intelligence," *Adult Development and Aging: Biopsychological Perspectives*, 3rd edition (Hoboken, NJ: John Wiley & Sons, 2008), p. 175.

[9] Robert J. Sternberg, "What Should Intelligence Tests Test? Implications of a Triarchic Theory of Intelligence for Intelligence Testing," *Educational Researcher*, Vol. 13, No. 1, 1984, pp. 5–15.

[10] J. G. Clawson, "Leadership and Intelligence," *Level Three Leadership: Getting below the Surface*, 2nd edition (Upper Saddle River, NJ: Prentice Hall, 2003), p. 112.

[11] Dennis Garlick, "Integrating Brain Science Research with Intelligence Research," *Current Directions in Psychological Science*, Vol. 12, No. 5, 2003, pp. 185–189.

[12] Howard Gardner, *Frames of Mind: The Theory of Multiple Intelligences* (New York: Basic Books, 1983).

[13] J. G. Clawson, "Leadership and Intelligence," *Level Three Leadership: Getting below the Surface*, 2nd edition (Upper Saddle River, NJ: Prentice Hall, 2003), p. 111.

[14] Justin Menkes, "Hiring for Smarts," *Harvard Business Review*, November 2005.

[15] Biography.com, "Sir Richard Branson Biography," www.biography.com/articles/Sir-Richard-Branson-9224520.

[16] William Taggart and Daniel Robey, "Mind and Managers: On the Dual Nature of Human Information Processing and Management," *Academy of Management Review*, Vol. 6, No. 2, 1981, pp. 187–195.

[17] Edward M. Bowden and Mark Jung Beeman, "Getting the Right Idea: Semantic Activation in the Right Hemisphere May Help Solve Insight Problems," *Psychological Science*, Vol. 9, No. 6, 1998, pp. 435–440.

[18] Terence Hines, "Left Brain/Right Brain Mythology and Implications for Management and Training," *Academy of Management Review*, Vol. 12, No. 4, 1987, pp. 600–606.

[19] A. Nahavandi, *The Art and Science of Leadership* (Upper Saddle River, NJ: Prentice Hall, 2006), p. 125.

[20] Shelley Carson, *Your Creative Brain* (San Francisco, CA: Jossey-Bass, 2010), p. 9.

[21] A. Nahavandi, *The Art and Science of Leadership* (Upper Saddle River, NJ: Prentice Hall, 2006), p. 125.

[22] L. Thompson, "Creativity: Mastering Strategies for High Performance," *Making the Team: A Guide for Managers* (Upper Saddle River, NJ: Prentice Hall, 2000), p. 151.

[23] Mihaly Csikszentmihalyi, "Creativity," *Encyclopedia of Leadership*, eds. George R. Goethals, Georgia J. Sorenson, and James MacGregor Burns (Thousand Oaks, CA: Sage Publications, 2004), pp. 286–288.

[24] Lynne C. Levesque, *Breakthrough Creativity: Achieving Top Performance Using the Eight Creative Talents* (Palo Alto, CA: Davies-Black Publishing, 2001).

[25] Linda A. Hill, "Leadership: Leading from Behind," Harvard Business Review Blog, http://blogs.hbr.org/imagining-the-future-of-leadership/2010/05/leading-from-behind.html, accessed November 9, 2012.

[26] Robert J. Sternberg, *The Triarchic Mind: A New Theory of Human Intelligence* (New York: Viking, 1988).

[27] Robert J. Sternberg, "What Should Intelligence Tests Test? Implications of a Triarchic Theory of Intelligence for Intelligence Testing," *Educational Researcher*, Vol. 13, No. 1, 1984, pp. 5–15.

[28] Robert J. Sternberg, *The Triarchic Mind: A New Theory of Human Intelligence* (New York: Viking, 1988).

[29] Anthony J. Mayo and Nitin Nohria, *In Their Time: The Greatest Business Leaders of the Twentieth Century* (Boston, MA: HBS Press, 2005), p. xv.

[30] Ibid., pp. 359–360.

[31] Anthony J. Mayo and Nitin Nohria, *In Their Time: The Greatest Business Leaders of the Twentieth Century* (Boston, MA: HBS Press, 2005).

[32] Dennis Garlick, "Integrating Brain Science Research with Intelligence Research," *Current Directions in Psychological Science*, Vol. 12, No. 5, 2003, pp. 185–189.

[33] Ronald E. Riggio, "Intelligences, Other," *Encyclopedia of Leadership*, eds. George R. Goethals, Georgia J. Sorenson, and James

MacGregor Burns (Thousand Oaks, CA: Sage Publications, 2004), pp. 733–735.

34 Lynn R. Offerman and Ly U. Phan, "Culturally Intelligent Leadership in a Diverse World," *Multiple Intelligence in Leadership*, eds. R. E. Riggio, S. E. Murphy, and F. J. Pirozzolo (Mahwah, NJ: Lawrence Erlbaum Associates, 2002), pp. 187–214.

35 Kerri Anne Crowne, "What Leads to Cultural Intelligence?," *Business Horizons*, Vol. 51, 2008, pp. 391–399.

36 Daniel Goleman, *Emotional Intelligence: Why It Can Matter More Than IQ* (New York: Bantam Book, 1995).

37 Barbara Mandell and Shilpa Pherwani, "Relationship Between Emotional Intelligence and Transformational Leadership Style: A Gender Comparison," *Journal of Business and Psychology*, Vol. 17, No. 3, Spring 2003, pp. 387–404; and Daniel Goleman, "What Makes a Leader?," *Harvard Business Review*, November–December 1998.

38 The Hay Group, "The Emotional Intelligence Workbook," 2008.

39 Daniel Goleman, Richard Boyatzis, and Anne McKee, *Primal Intelligence: Realizing the Power of Emotional Intelligence* (Boston, MA: Harvard Business Review Press, 2002), p. 40.

40 Daniel Goleman, "What Makes a Leader?," *Harvard Business Review*, November–December 1998.

41 Michael Maccoby, "Chapter 5," *The Leaders We Need: And What Makes Us Follow* (Boston, MA: HBS Press, 2007).

42 Daniel Goleman, "What Makes a Leader?," *Harvard Business Review*, November–December 1998, p. 9.

43 The Hay Group, "Being Clever Isn't Everything: Making the Business Case for Emotional and Social Intelligence," PowerPoint presentation, 2008.

44 Robert R. McCrae and Paul T. Costa, Jr., *Personality in Adulthood: A Five-Factor Theory Perspective*, 2nd edition (New York: Guilford Press, 2003).

45 Shelley A. Kirkpatrick and Edwin A. Locke, "Leadership: Do Traits Matter?," *The Executive*, Vol. 5, 1991, pp. 48–60.

46 John M. Digman, "Personality Structure: Emergence of the Five-Factor Model,"

Annual Review Psychology, Vol. 41, 1990, pp. 417–440.

47 G. Jung, *Psychological Types* (New York: Harcourt, Brace & Company, 1923).

48 J. G. Clawson, J. P. Kotter, V. A. Faux, and C.C. McArthur, *Self-Assessment and Career Development* (Upper Saddle River, NJ: Prentice Hall, 1992), p. 72.

49 Jamie L. Franco and Greg Reaume, "Personality and Group Roles," *Encyclopedia of Leadership*, eds. George R. Goethals, Georgia J. Sorenson, and James MacGregor Burns (Thousand Oaks, CA: Sage Publications, 2004), pp. 1187–1192.

50 Isabel Briggs Myers and Peter B. Myers, *Gifts Differing* (Palo Alto, CA: Consulting Psychologists Press, 1980).

51 Robert Benfari and Jean Knox, *Understanding Your Management Style: Beyond the Myers-Briggs Type Indicators* (Lexington, MA: Lexington Books, 1991).

52 Anne Field, "Intuitor, Thinker, Feeler, Senser: Which One Are You Talking To?" *Harvard Management Communication Letter*, July 2003.

53 George L. Hanbury, Alka Sapat, and Charles W. Washington, "Know Yourself and Take Charge of Your Own Destiny: The 'Fit Model' of Leadership," *Public Administration Review*, Vol. 64, No. 5, 2004, pp. 566–576.

54 J. B. Rotter, "Generalized Expectancies for Internal versus External Control of Reinforcement," *Psychological Monographs*, Vol. 80, No. 1, 1966.

55 Mark J. Martinko and William L. Gardner, "Learned Helplessness: An Alternative Explanation for Performance Deficits," *Academy of Management Review*, Vol. 7, No. 2, 1982, pp. 195–204.

56 Herbert M. Lefcourt, "Personality and Locus of Control," *Human Helplessness: Theory and Applications*, eds. Judy Garber and Martin F. Seligman (New York: Academic Press, 1980), pp. 245–259.

57 Paul E. Spector, "Behavior in Organizations as a Function of Employee's Locus of Control," *Psychological Bulletin*, Vol. 91, No. 3, 1982, pp. 482–497.

58 Micha Popper, "Psychological Substructures," *Encyclopedia of Leadership*, eds. George R. Goethals, Georgia J. Sorenson, and James MacGregor Burns (Thousand

Oaks, CA: Sage Publications, 2004), pp. 1265–1270.

59 Carol Dweck, "How Companies Can Profit from a 'Growth Mindset,'" *Harvard Business Review*, November, 2014.

60 Paul E. Spector, "Behavior in Organizations as a Function of Employee's Locus of Control," *Psychological Bulletin*, Vol. 91, No. 3, 1982, pp. 482–497.

61 Herbert M. Lefcourt, "Personality and Locus of Control," *Human Helplessness: Theory and Applications*, eds. Judy Garber and Martin F. Seligman (New York: Academic Press, 1980), pp. 245–259.

62 Karen Reivich and Andrew Shatte, *The Resilience Factor: 7 Keys to Finding Your Inner Strength and Overcoming Life's Hurdles* (New York: Broadway Books, 2002); and Suniya S. Lithar, Dante Cicchetti, and Bronwyn Becker, "The Construct of Resilience: A Critical Evaluation and Guidelines for Future Work," *Child Development*, Vol. 71, No. 3, 2000, pp. 543–562.

63 Diane Coutu, "How Resilience Works," *Harvard Business Review*, May 2002.

64 Jeffrey Pfeffer, *What Were They Thinking? Unconventional Wisdom about Management* (Boston, MA: HBS Press, 2007).

65 Lyn Y. Abramson, Judy Garber, and Martin E. P. Seligman, "Learned Helplessness in Humans: An Attributional Analysis," *Human Helplessness: Theory and Applications*, eds. Judy Garber and Martin F. Seligman (New York: Academic Press, 1980), pp. 3–34.

66 Carol Dweck, *Self-Theories: Their Role in Motivation, Personality, and Development* (Philadelphia, PA: Psychology Press, 2000), pp. 138–141.

67 Paul G. Stoltz, *Adversity Quotient @ Work* (New York: HarperCollins, 2000).

68 Joshua D. Margolis and Paul G. Stoltz, "How to Bounce Back from Adversity," *Harvard Business Review*, January–February 2010.

69 Paul G. Stoltz, *Adversity Quotient @ Work* (New York: HarperCollins, 2000).

70 Ronald A. Heifetz and Marty Linsky, *Leadership on the Line: Staying Alive through the Dangers of Leading* (Boston, MA: HBS Press, 2002).

[71] Warren G. Bennis and Robert J. Thomas, *Geeks & Geezers: How Era, Values, and Defining Moments Shape Leaders* (Boston, MA: HBS Press, 2002).

[72] A. Nahavandi, *The Art and Science of Leadership* (Upper Saddle River, NJ: Prentice Hall, 2006) p. 134.

[73] V. J. Derlega, B. A. Winstead, and W. H. Jones, *Personality: Contemporary Theory and Research*, 3rd edition (Belmont, CA: Wadsworth, 2005), p. 285.

[74] A. Nahavandi, *The Art and Science of Leadership* (Upper Saddle River, NJ: Prentice Hall, 2006), p. 134.

[75] Peter F. Drucker, "Managing Oneself," *Harvard Business Review*, January 2005.

[76] L. M. Roberts, J. Dutton, G. Spreitzer, and E. D. Heaphy, "Composing the Reflected Best Self-Portrait: Building Pathways for Becoming Extraordinary in Work Organizations," *Academy of Management Review*, Vol. 30, No. 4, 2005, pp. 712–736.

CHAPTER

14

Power and Influence

Learning Objectives

After reading this chapter, you should be able to:

LO1 : Explain how leaders use power and influence to realize an organization's vision and achieve strategic goals.

LO2 : Describe the various forms of interpersonal power and how they are developed and used.

LO3 : Outline how individuals react to the exercise of power.

LO4 : Describe how interdependence, resource scarcity, and disagreement on priorities can escalate organizational conflict and heighten the need for exercising power.

LO5 : Outline the different influence styles and explain how these styles should be applied to specific situational contexts.

SELF-REFLECTION

What Are Your Sources of Power?

How do you use power to influence individuals or groups? What is the source of that power? On a scale of 1–5, rate the following statements to explore how you use power.

1 = never 2 = rarely 3 = sometimes 4 = usually 5 = always

1. I rely on my formal position or title as a source of power. _____

2. I use power to reward people for their behavior. _____

3. I use power to punish people for their behavior. _____

4. I use my expertise as a source of power. _____

5. My power sources are rooted in personal relationships. _____

6. I rely on my access to unique information as a source of power. _____

7. I empower others by treating them equitably and working collaboratively.
   _____

8. I influence others by securing credible information and using data. _____

9. My power comes from reciprocity for favors that are being repaid. _____

10. I build power by creating coalitions of individuals that have common interests or perspectives.
   _____

Based on your responses, what did you learn about your sources of power? How do you use this power? How can you expand your sources of power?

INTRODUCTION

Being a leader requires working with and through others to achieve a set of objectives or goals. As we have discussed, effective leadership does not happen in a vacuum; it requires the ability of the leader to appropriately size up a situation and to appeal to the desires, needs, or aspirations of followers.[1] Appealing to the needs of followers, in turn, means that leaders must learn to persuade others to join them on their journey. Sometimes that persuasion involves appealing to someone's personal motives or aspirations. Other times, it means using someone's formal position to enforce a certain activity or behavior.

Leadership is often defined as the exercise of **power** and the effective use of **influence**.[2] In fact, many researchers believe that a person cannot lead without power.[3] Power is the potential of one individual or group to influence the behavior, thinking, or attitudes of another individual or group.[4] In turn, influence is the means or vehicle by which power is exercised. The distinction between power and influence is often quite subtle. In essence, power is something that one may possess by virtue of his or her position, expertise, or relationships while influence is something that one does.[5]

Power
The potential of one individual or group to influence the behavior, thinking, or attitudes of another individual or group.

Influence
The means or vehicle by which power is exercised.

While "all influential managers have power, not all powerful managers have influence."[6] Ultimately, the exercise of power is required to build coalitions of support for a company's vision and strategy. In other words, power can transform individual interests into coordinated activities that accomplish common goals and objectives.[7]

Two organizational researchers, John P. Kotter and Jeffrey Pfeffer, have individually studied power in organizations extensively. Each has found that when few people are involved in the decision-making process and when differences among people are small, working cooperatively and collaboratively is fairly simple.[8] The parties can convene, confront the issues in a straightforward way, and search for a solution that satisfies the needs of all people involved. In these types of situations, power is not as important.

In most organizations, however, many people tend to be involved in the decision-making process. Their work depends on that of others, and the differences among these individuals tend to be great. With high interdependency and the potential for conflict, power is more important.

An individual who aspires to or uses power, despite its strong and vital interconnection to leadership, is often misunderstood and even feared.[9] Unfortunately, you don't need to search far for compelling evidence of the abuse and misuse of power. Think for a moment about the reigns of Adolf Hitler in Germany and Josef Stalin in the Soviet Union. Each used power to control and manipulate others. Business also has been wrought with abuses of power.

Given these abuses, it is not surprising that there is widespread disdain for power. Many people think of power in terms of having control over others. Likewise, many think of influence as a behavior that is manipulative rather than as the capacity to change the attitudes and/or values of another individual or group to create mutually beneficial outcomes. While there is certainly a dark side of power, a person cannot lead without it. The effective use of power requires that a person learn about its sources and manifestations.

To that end, this chapter will introduce the role of power in interpersonal relationships and in organizations as well as the consequences of using it effectively and ineffectively. This chapter will also present strategies for managing with power at both the interpersonal and organizational levels to create more cooperative, collaborative, and high-performing work environments. Building a greater understanding of power is especially critical as you consider how your relationships with others are becoming ever more interdependent and interconnected. Increasing your awareness in this respect can help you develop sufficient sources of power that you can leverage throughout your career. To illustrate these concepts, we will introduce several protagonists beginning with Keith Ferrazzi.

Keith Ferrazzi: "One-of-a-Kind"[10]

Keith Ferrazzi's colleagues described him as "one-of-a-kind." He was good looking and dressed impeccably in custom suits and Prada shoes. Ferrazzi believed that people respected him for his drive and work ethic. Years of effort allowed Ferrazzi to obtain plum consulting and senior executive positions at prestigious firms such as Deloitte & Touche and Starwood Hotels & Resorts Worldwide.

Even at the outset of his career, Ferrazzi sought to make connections with people who could help him along the way. After graduating from Harvard Business School, he was offered a position at Deloitte, but he insisted on seeing "the head guys" before he accepted. Pat Loconto, former head of Deloitte, agreed to meet Ferrazzi at an Italian restaurant in New York City. After a few drinks, Ferrazzi told Loconto that he would accept the offer on the condition that Loconto have dinner with Ferrazzi once a year at the same restaurant. Many thought his request was extremely bold and risky. Loconto, however, was impressed by Ferrazzi's assertiveness and agreed. Ferrazzi used these annual dinners with Loconto to obtain critical career guidance and coaching, and as the years went by, the two became friends.

Not everyone at Deloitte cared for Ferrazzi, though. He acted differently than everyone else and was not shy about sharing his accomplishments. He also liked to talk about what he wanted to do next. In his consulting role, Ferrazzi tried to do many things at once and didn't necessarily finish them all. He did not do what he did not want to do, including the analysis that was generally required of all consultants. Loconto said, "He was both ambitious and impatient, and he didn't want to go through the steps to get where he wanted to be . . . He was definitely difficult to manage, but he made up for all of that with the great ideas he came up with."[11] However, Tom Friedman, a Deloitte partner, thought people were jealous of Ferrazzi because he had accomplished so much. Attracted to Ferrazzi because he was different, Friedman decided to become his mentor.

Just before he was to become a partner at Deloitte, Ferrazzi left the firm for a position as chief marketing officer at Starwood Hotels and Resorts. Loconto revealed, "When I spoke with Keith about Starwood, I told him that he needed to slow down and get experience at a big company before running something himself. I told him to walk before you run and don't have so many ideas."[12] After spending less than 2 years at Starwood Hotels, during which time he reported to four different presidents and CEOs, Ferrazzi resigned. Many believed that his lack of patience regarding the changes that were happening in the organization were to blame. Ferrazzi remarked that he just needed time to figure out how to get to where he wanted to be. While contemplating his options, Ferrazzi wondered what else he should be doing to build his bases of influence so that he could someday run a company.

Why did Keith Ferrazzi's peers consider him a powerful manager—because he dressed well or maybe because he worked hard and was promoted to several high-level positions early in his career? Was his forthright personality and clear sense of where he was headed unique? Or was the fact that he maintained a successful career but tended to rub people the wrong way enviable? While we cannot propose that any one of these factors was the sole criterion for Ferrazzi's success, we can conclude that having all of these personal characteristics allowed him to gain substantial interpersonal power.

INTERPERSONAL POWER

The increasing decentralization of organizations and the need to work with a variety of people to accomplish goals enhance the need for increased levels of interpersonal power. Interpersonal power can be derived from a number of sources, including an individuals' formal authority, ability to deliver rewards or enforce punishments, level of knowledge or expertise, and personal attractiveness. Power is used by leaders to set goals, prioritize activities, and decide who should be given certain assignments, how work should be allocated, how disputes will be resolved, and when tasks should be completed.[13]

Forms of Interpersonal Power

In 1959, John R. P. French and Bertram Raven, two American social psychologists, developed a typology for describing interpersonal power that has been used by many researchers to study group behavior: "The Social Bases of Power." It includes five bases of power: **legitimate power, reward power, coercive power, expert power,** and **referent power.**[14] An individual may rely on one or multiple bases of power to influence others.

At the end of the Ferrazzi case, we learned that he is contemplating the bases of power he should build so that he can someday run a company. To explore this question, we first define French and Raven's typology and then identify how each base of power can apply to Ferrazzi's experiences:

- *Legitimate power is based on the formal position that an individual holds in an organization.* It is the perception that someone has the right and legitimacy to influence behavior by the nature of his or her organizational position.

Legitimate power
A type of interpersonal power that is based on the formal position an individual holds in an organization.

Reward power
A type of interpersonal power that gives someone the ability to reward another for his or her behavior.

Coercive power
A type of interpersonal power that gives someone the ability to punish another for his or her behavior.

Expert power
A type of interpersonal power based on an individual having specialized knowledge or skills.

Referent power
A type of interpersonal power based on the personal liking an individual has for another.

An individual can have more legitimate power when their subordinates respect his or her position in the organization, but can have less legitimate power when his or her authority is questioned. When Keith Ferrazzi's peers at Deloitte remarked, "Who is this guy, why is he here, and why would I want to have anything to do with him," they were indicating their disbelief in his legitimate power. Over time, however, Ferrazzi acquired more legitimate power as he attained higher positions of leadership and gained the backing of senior executives.

- *Reward power exists when one person has the ability to reward another for his or her behavior.* It is the perception that someone can provide positive consequences or remove negative ones for certain behavior. An individual who has the authority to recognize others for their performance by giving raises, promotions, or praise has high reward power. A key to effectively using reward power is to understand what motivates others. With this understanding, rewards can be individually and collectively administered. We will further discuss the specific drivers of motivation in Chapter 18. Ferrazzi knew that Pat Loconto had high reward power as evident in Ferrazzi's request that Loconto meet with him once a year. This relationship paid off for Ferrazzi in the form of critical guidance and coaching.

- *Coercive power exists when one person has the ability to punish another for his or her behavior.* The opposite of reward power, coercive power, is the perception that someone can punish another for nonconformity and noncompliance. An individual who has the authority to punish or recommend punishment for someone who fails to act according to his or her expectations has high coercive power. Coercion can lead to more rapid short-term results and can be effective in a crisis situation, but overuse of this form of power can lead to disenfranchisement and low morale.[15] Although coercive power was not illustrated in the case of Keith Ferrazzi, it can be assumed that Pat Loconto had high coercive power that could have been used when others at Deloitte complained that Ferrazzi was difficult to manage. It appears that coercive power was not used toward Ferrazzi because he made up for his lack of follow-through on projects by coming up with great ideas.

- *Expert power is based on a significant difference in the knowledge level of two or more individuals in a particular area.* An individual who has specialized knowledge, abilities, or skills and is highly regarded because of his or her expertise has expert power. As an extension of expert power, Raven has subsequently added access to information as an additional source of interpersonal power. Information power is derived from having access to key data sources that can influence important decisions.[16] Through his experiences in consulting and marketing, Ferrazzi increased his expert power, which is evidenced by the offers to become partner at Deloitte and to become chief marketing officer at Starwood Hotels.

- *Referent power is based on the personal liking an individual has for another.* An individual who others would like to emulate has high referent power and others do things for him or her out of personal appeal. Although Ferrazzi tended to rub some people the wrong way initially, others were attracted to him, especially those in senior-level positions.

Positional and Personal Power

Similar to French and Raven, David Whetten and Kim Cameron, two organizational researchers, developed a method for classifying and explaining interpersonal power. While they identify many of the same bases of power as French and Raven, Whetten and Cameron extend the bases of power from five to nine, which they then classify as either position characteristics or personal attributes.[17] Whetten and Cameron

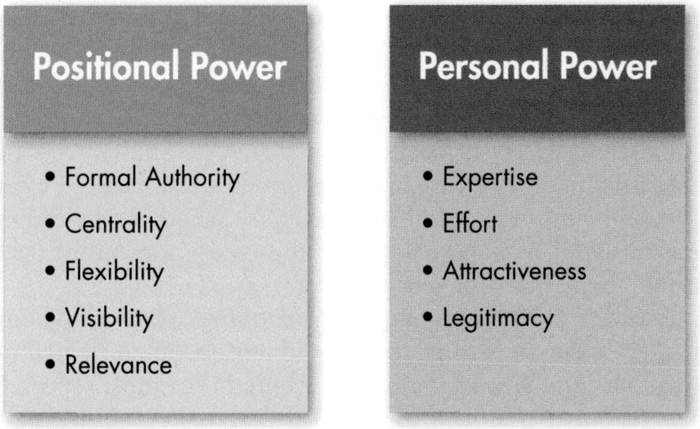

Positional Power	Personal Power
• Formal Authority	• Expertise
• Centrality	• Effort
• Flexibility	• Attractiveness
• Visibility	• Legitimacy
• Relevance	

Figure 14.1 › Sources of Positional Personal Power

propose that **positional power** is obtained from an individual's formal place within an organization's structure, which can be described in terms of the position's centrality, flexibility, visibility, and relevance. **Personal power**, in contrast, is obtained from having personal attributes that others desire, including expertise, attractiveness, effort, and legitimacy (see Figure 14.1). We can use the characteristics associated with positional and personal power that are described next to make inferences about Ferrazzi.

Positional Power

Positional power is usually the first image that comes to mind when we think about power. Where does a person stand in the hierarchy of an organization? How many people report to that person? How big is his or her budget? What resources and information does the person control? The answers to these questions generally define an individual's formal position or authority in an organization or a group and often act as a proxy for defining his or her power.[18]

By the nature of their formal positions, top executives in organizations are often considered powerful. Subordinates defer to them out of respect for their high standing and authority. In addition, their positions confer certain privileges, including the ability to determine the distribution of resources. While senior executives often request input and information about resource allocation, the final determination often rests with them. In addition, top management plays a significant role in setting the organization's mission, strategy, and operational roles.[19]

Beyond being deferential or respectful, many employees prefer to work with individuals who have a strong base of organizational power, sometimes called political clout. This political clout often leads to greater opportunities for visibility and the potential for upward mobility. In addition, a powerful boss can create an aura of status or respect for his or her subordinates, which can increase satisfaction and enhance motivation. In contrast, individuals who work for managers who are less powerful or who do not embrace power tend to experience less satisfaction.[20]

The extent to which positional power is important depends on a number of other aspects beyond formal authority. These other aspects include centrality, flexibility, visibility, and relevance. Centrality refers to how pivotal an individual's role is in an organization. Centrality is gained by those individuals who occupy central positions with regard to important tasks and interpersonal networks in organizations. These individuals are depended on by others for getting access to resources or for getting tasks done because they have information that others need. While

Positional power
Power that comes from an individual's formal place within an organization's structure.

Personal power
Power that is obtained from having personal attributes that others desire.

Keith Ferrazzi's initial position within Deloitte was not considered central, his relationships with senior executives at the company enabled him to benefit from their centrality. Their coaching and general advice helped him make decisions that were critical to his career success and protected him from discord with peers.

Another important aspect of positional power is flexibility, which refers to the freedom to exercise judgment. A flexible position has few rules or established routines that dictate how work should be done. Those who have flexible positions do not have to seek a senior manager's approval to make a nonroutine decision. In this way, they have the power to decide how to act.

Visibility accounts for the number of influential people with whom an individual normally interacts in an organization. Therefore, people-oriented positions can be thought of as more powerful than task-oriented positions, especially when the position fosters frequent contact with key decision makers. While centrality gives individuals access to information, visibility allows them to interact with influential people, making an individual's accomplishments more evident to them. Ferrazzi made visibility a priority by insisting on meetings with senior executives and seeking out mentors.

Finally, relevance is specific to those individuals who are engaged in activities that are closely aligned with an organization's priorities. An individual who seeks influential positions must be aware of the relevance of his or her department's activities for the company. Based on the information given in the case, we can assume that Ferrazzi's consulting and marketing experience was relevant to his pending appointment to partner at Deloitte and his chief marketing officer position at Starwood Hotels.

Personal Power

Although positional power is a very important source of power, it can sometimes be less effective than personal power. Sometimes, even if a person's formal position in an organization is at a relatively low level, that person can still wield tremendous power and influence. A primary source of personal power is expertise, which is gained from having task or organizationally relevant competencies. Expertise can be technical (having necessary task-related skills), human (managing relationships), or conceptual (seeing the organization as a whole). Think back to the multiple intelligences section in Chapter 13. Different situations call for different types of intelligence. To the extent that an individual's skills match the situation, he or she will have greater personal power.

Expertise is gained from both formal education and on-the-job experiences. Establishing a track record is part of an individual's expertise. A track record refers to an individual's task and organizationally relevant experiences and accomplishments, including what he or she has done well or not so well. Having expertise and a good track record implies that an individual is reliable. Important decisions are often deferred to individuals with specific expertise. In this way, an individual's expertise can be leveraged as a source of power. Ferrazzi's consistent successes enabled him to build a strong track record, which reinforced his expertise.

Early career professionals can influence others who hold decision-making responsibility through access to critical information. For instance, a technology specialist may have some unique insight or skill set that is critical to a strategic decision even though he or she is in a relatively low-level position in the firm. While low-level professionals lack formal authority and many other aspects of positional power, they can cultivate their sources of personal and relational power by developing their expertise and increasing their access to influential senior executives.

The second source of personal power is effort, which relates to working hard and being committed to success. Someone who devotes higher-than-expected effort

The Leadership Development Journey

Recent research into body posture has demonstrated that striking a power pose before a job interview or a presentation can result in greater personal confidence and better performance. As part of this research, subjects were asked to hold a low or high power pose for just five minutes. High power poses included leaning back and placing one's feet on a desk top or expansively opening up limbs by stretching one's arms out. Low power poses included shrinking one's body by crossing one's arms and legs in a closed way or folding one's arms in front of his or her chest. Those subjects that engaged in a high power pose performed significantly better in a number of interpersonal interactions including interviews, presentations, and negotiations. This simple act changed a person's hormone levels (higher levels of testosterone and lower levels of the stress hormone cortisol) and subsequently, his or her behavior.[21] During the next few weeks, experiment with a few of these power poses. Keep a journal of your experiments and assess the effectiveness of them.

to their work can be viewed as more committed and more dependable. This dependability can lead to more interesting assignments or access to unique information, which can also be leveraged as a source of power. We know from the case that Ferrazzi was ambitious and driven. However, these characteristics were not always viewed positively by others in the company. Many of Ferrazzi's managers had difficulty in managing him because of his aggressive approach.

An individual's attractiveness, which stems from having attributes that others identify with and would like to emulate, including physical appearance, charisma, and likability, is another source of personal power. An attractive person may be perceived as open, honest, loyal, and empathetic. Ferrazzi's physical dress, good looks, and networking ability made him attractive to others, but his ambition and drive were sometimes less attractive to those who did not understand his motives.

Finally, personal power can be enhanced if a person is viewed as legitimate. While French and Raven defined legitimacy as a source of positional power that is aligned with an individual's position within the formal hierarchy of an organization, the notion of legitimacy as a source of personal power is not based on a person's position but on his or her credibility. Legitimacy is gained from acting in ways that are consistent with the prevailing value system and are viewed as credible by other organizational members. Having legitimacy increases acceptance, which is key to personal influence.

Relational Power

As a means of further defining types of interpersonal power, researchers have classified **relational power** as the power that is gained from the types of networks to which an individual belongs, the types of people in those networks, and the strength of the relationships within the networks. In essence, relational power is a form of informal power that is based on the nature of an individual's various relationships in an organization.[22] To understand relational power, we first need to think of a network as the set of relationships critical to a person's ability to get things done, get ahead, and develop personally and professionally.[23] We will discuss networks in greater detail in Chapter 20, but for now, it is important to understand the role that networks can play in a person's ability to influence others.

Once you map an individuals' network of contacts, there are many ways to compute who is most influential in that network using their position in the network

Relational power
Power gained from the types of networks to which an individual belongs, the types of people in those networks, and the strength of the relationships within the networks.

as an indicator of influence. The social networks you map can be a network of communication (who you speak to), advice (who you go to for advice), or trust (who you trust). Centrality, or where one is located in a network of connections into which one is placed, is one factor that affects an individual's ability to effectively wield power. As outlined in the previous section, it can also be considered an indicator of positional power. Breadth of the network is another indicator of a person's positional power.

The breadth of an individual's network refers to the types of networks to which an individual belongs and the diversity of contacts within those networks. Herminia Ibarra, an organizational researcher, claimed that an individual can be positioned in three different types of networks—task networks, career networks, and social networks.[24] Task networks involve the exchange of specific job-related resources such as information, expertise, advice, political access, and material resources. Career networks include people who provide career direction and guidance, exposure to top management, help in obtaining challenging and visible assignments, and advocacy for promotions. Social networks consist of people who you communicate with, who you go to for advice, or who you trust more than those in other networks. Social networks may or may not be related to work assignments, but they do provide a role in mobilizing resources, transmitting information, and providing peer coaching.

Ibarra also proposed that all ties are not equal and that the depth or strength of a person's network can depend on how long an individual has known someone in the network and how often they interact. The strength of relationships affects the type of resources that are exchanged.[25] These factors often relate to whether someone is part of an individual's core network or extended network. A core network includes relationships that are characterized by close bonds and reciprocity. These relationships are generally long term. In contrast, an extended network includes distant acquaintances that may provide connections between an individual and other people or groups. The relationships within an extended network are generally weaker than the relationships within a core network.

Another facet of a person's network is its portability, that is, his or her ability to carry it with them if he or she leaves his or her job. In a study of successful stock analysts, Boris Groysberg found that female and male analysts differed in their approach to developing relationships with others. The majority of women built their reputations and success by cultivating relationships with clients and companies they covered.[26] On the other hand, male analysts focused on developing relationships within their organizations. When women switched firms, their performance remained strong. In contrast, when men switched firms, their performance dropped dramatically. So what accounts for this phenomenon? First, Groysberg proposed that the extent of the female analysts' networks allowed for the critical career support that made them "stars" and that made their skills highly effective in other companies. Second, Groysberg speculated that female stars adopted these career strategies as a way to overcome barriers in their organizations. These barriers often excluded women from key assignments or access to important resources. For the most part, men did not confront these barriers. As a result, the female analysts' external relationships were more portable and the male analysts' internal relationships were more firm specific.[27]

Challenges of Interpersonal Power

Although individuals may have initially spent a great deal of time building relationships and cultivating networks, they may find themselves becoming complacent as they reach higher levels in organizations. Research shows that those who lack insight into the dynamics of power are susceptible to losing it.[28] This lack of awareness makes individuals vulnerable to organizational changes. Consider, for example, the following discussion of Robert Moses.

Robert Moses: Fall from Power

As a government official in New York City from 1924 to 1968, Robert Moses played a dominant role in creating and reshaping numerous roads and parks in the metropolitan area.[32] Throughout his career, Moses was appointed to many public offices by elected officials he had helped. They relied on him to get things done. He was described as "dominating, sometimes tyrannizing" and as an "arrogant, manipulative man with a constant craving for power," but also as someone who "devoted his life to reshaping the city."[33] Among other accomplishments, Moses oversaw the development of more than two dozen parkways and bridges including the Brooklyn-Queens Expressway, the Henry Hudson Parkway, the Cross Bronx Expressway, the Van Wyck Expressway, the Throgs Neck Bridge, and the Triborough Bridge. In addition, Moses secured funding and developed considerable amounts of green space in New York City and Long Island,

Library of Congress Prints and Photographs Division [LC-USZ62-136079]

including Massapequa State Park and Jones Beach State Park.

During the final years of his career, the vast number of projects in which he was involved (and his pride and arrogance) caught up with him.[34] Moses grew busier but refused to accept ideas from others. His lack of openness left him without access to critical knowledge that would have allowed him to continue to do his job effectively. Eventually, despite his vast contributions to New York City, he lost his job.

Although by many standards Robert Moses was a powerful figure, he lost sight of what was important. In the beginning, he realized that building relationships with prominent officials was critical to being appointed to public offices in which he could make an impact. As he grew busier and became more of an expert, however, he refused the input of others. This critical mistake was a significant factor in his termination.

As a person gains power, he or she should be cognizant of the potential danger of letting power overwhelm his or her perceptions of reality. This danger intensifies as an individual moves into senior management roles, especially if subordinates and peers are afraid to offer constructive criticism and feedback. In the previous chapter, we discussed the importance of self-awareness in long-term career success. As individuals advance in their careers, it is important to constantly monitor their strengths and weaknesses.

Power is often lost when individuals are resistant to change and closed to new information. Sustaining power requires that an individual focus on a continued sense of relevance.[29] Researchers have proposed several other patterns of behavior that can enable individuals to sustain power or that might place individuals at risk of losing power (see Table 14.1).

The context of a situation also can influence a person's level of power. Some researchers even believe that power comes from being in the right position at the right time.[30] As we discussed, power is derived from a person's position, relationships, and experience. Each of these sources can be influenced by the context of an organization. For instance, when two companies merge and combine similar departments, the sources of historical power are changed. In this case, only one manager may survive. It is important to consider the context in assessing potential opportunities for increased power as well as limits to power.[31] How much of an individual's power is context specific? Would an individual in one context be as powerful in another context?

Sustaining Power	Losing Power
Energy, endurance, and physical stamina	Ruthlessness
Ability to focus energy, strong attention to detail	Willing to use and exploit others
Flexibility	Inflexibility
Sensitivity, ability to read others	Lack of empathy for others
Willingness to engage in constructive conflict	Sense of entitlement
Ability to subordinate ego when necessary	Inflated view of self

Table 14.1 › Sustaining and Losing Power

Sources: Nina W. Brown, *Coping with Infuriating, Mean, Critical People: The Destructive Narcissistic Pattern* (Westport, CT: Praeger Publishers, 2006); A. Delbecq, "'Evil' Manifested in Destructive Individual Behavior: A Senior Leadership Challenge," *Journal of Management Inquiry*, Vol. 10, 2001, pp. 221–226; Jeffery Pfeffer, *Managing with Power: Politics and Influence in Organizations* (Boston, MA: HBS Press, 1992); and Manfred. F. R. Kets de Vries, *Leaders, Fools, and Imposters: Essays on the Psychology of Leadership* (San Francisco, CA: Jossey-Bass, 1993).

REACTIONS TO POWER

People react differently to the exercise of power throughout an organization. The three primary responses to managerial decisions are resistance, commitment, and compliance (see Figure 14.2). Resistance can be active (refusing to do what is asked) or passive (pretending to agree but doing nothing). In these cases, managers tend to rely on coercive power to force individuals to do what is asked, which can result in even greater resistance. This use of power cannot go on indefinitely. It generally signals a significant disconnect between managers and employees and is indicative of a dysfunctional unit.

Compliance involves completing tasks that have been assigned but without a sense of excitement or personal buy-in. With this response, employees do the work because they have to, not because they want to. Managers who only rely

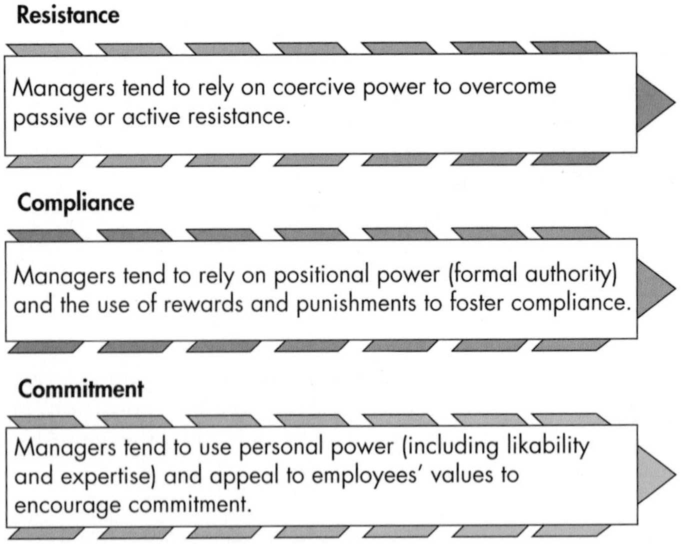

Resistance

> Managers tend to rely on coercive power to overcome passive or active resistance.

Compliance

> Managers tend to rely on positional power (formal authority) and the use of rewards and punishments to foster compliance.

Commitment

> Managers tend to use personal power (including likability and expertise) and appeal to employees' values to encourage commitment.

Figure 14.2 › Three Responses to the Exercise of Power

Source: Adapted from Gary A. Yukl, *Leadership in Organizations* (Englewood Cliffs, NJ: Prentice-Hall, 1981).

Leadership Techniques Affecting Empowerment	Organizational Factors Affecting Empowerment
Creating a positive emotional atmosphere	Using a decentralized structure
Setting high performance standards	Appropriately selecting and training leaders and employees
Encouraging initiative and responsibility	Removing bureaucratic constraints
Rewarding employees openly and personally	Rewarding empowering behaviors
Practicing equity and collaboration	Carefully monitoring and measuring
Expressing confidence in subordinates	Using fair and open organizational policies

Table 14.2 ⟩ Factors That Impact Empowerment

Source: Adapted from A. Nahavandi, *The Art and Science of Leadership* (Upper Saddle River, NJ: Prentice Hall, 2006).

on positional power and use rewards or formal authority tend to engender responses that are compliant. This exercise of power is generally appropriate for routine tasks, but is less effective with more complex problems, which require creativity.

Commitment is the most preferred outcome and occurs when employees fundamentally agree with management's decisions and work hard to ensure that they are implemented properly. In this case, employees' values and perspectives are aligned with those of management, and they often put in extra effort to ensure success. Commitment is often derived from aspects of personal power, including expertise and likability.[35]

One increasingly popular way in which organizations are seeking to increase commitment is through **empowerment**. Empowerment involves sharing power with subordinates and pushing decision making and implementation to the lowest possible level.[36] Empowerment also is a way to develop leaders throughout an organization. As an employee accomplishes new tasks and takes on greater responsibility, his or her sense of self-confidence and self-worth increases, which, in turn, enhances his or her repertoire of skills.[37] Several leadership techniques and organizational factors can affect empowerment (see Table 14.2).

Empowerment is an important concept because sharing decision-making power can motivate employees to take ownership of an organization's performance, which can ultimately enhance cooperation, collaboration, and productivity as well as promote strategic organizational change. Empowerment also changes the role of the leader by forcing him or her to delegate more. When more work is delegated, managers are freed up to pursue other opportunities, which further supports development.[38]

When employees are empowered, they rightly believe that their opinions and perspectives on decisions will be heeded. If their decisions are not respected, empowerment can backfire, causing disenfranchisement and low morale.[39] Employees do not want to be asked their opinion and then be ignored when they give it.

Black & Decker has been innovative in the way in which it has empowered its sales team. Rod Sharpe, Director of Sales Training, gave each member of his sales team a Flip video camera and free video editing software so that they could film and edit quick videos of competitors' products—showing both strengths and weaknesses. Besides providing some interesting competitive intelligence, the videos also determined the way in which future sales team members would be trained, enabling them to highlight the comparative benefits of Black & Decker products.[40] We will return to the discussion of empowerment in Chapter 18 when we review the drivers of motivation.

Empowerment
The process of sharing power with subordinates and pushing decision making and implementation to the lowest possible level, increasing the influence and autonomy of all employees.

Victor J. Blue/Bloomberg/Getty Images

POWER AND CONFLICT

Power plays an important role in the resolution of conflict in organizations. The interdependence of relationships in organizations, the scarcity of resources, and disagreement about priorities all can contribute to conflict. Each of these factors can influence the manner in which decisions are made in an organization. To explore the notion of competition and conflict, we will analyze Dr. Esserman's situation. We will use a framework designed to evaluate conditions in organizations that induce competition and that can derail strategic organizational change. These conditions include: interdependence, resource scarcity, disagreement, and level of importance.[43]

Interdependence

Organizational power is rooted in the notion of dependent relationships. Relative power between two individuals depends upon who is more dependent on the other for ongoing tasks and information. The greater the asymmetry of dependence, the greater power one has over the other. At the same time, the greater the overall intensity of mutual dependence between them, the closer the relationship is likely to be. Ranjay Gulati and Maxim Sytch, two organizational researchers, studied some of the dynamics of power and dependence that exist between individuals in the context of organizations and their suppliers.[44] As part of their research, they looked at manufacturers' and suppliers' dependence on each other, taking into account a variety of factors. The authors found that a phenomenon called **dependence asymmetry** exists when a firm is more dependent on a business partner than a business partner is on a firm. When a firm is more dependent on a partner, the difference in dependencies reflects the degree of power the business partner potentially has over the firm. By the same token, when a firm is less dependent on a partner, the degree of difference in dependence shows the firm's power over the partner.

While asymmetry in dependence generates potential power dynamics among the partners, there is another facet of dependence that has to do with the extent to which actors are mutually dependent on each other. Instead of the difference in dependence, this is about the sum of dependence of each on the other. When both firms are more dependent on the other, **joint dependence** exists. As a result,

Dependence asymmetry
A phenomenon that exists when a firm is more dependent on a business partner than a business partner is on a firm.

Joint dependence
A phenomenon that exists when two firms are equally dependent on the other.

Dr. Laura Esserman at the Carol Franc Buck Breast Cancer Center[41]

Dr. Laura Esserman, breast cancer surgeon, associate professor of surgery and radiology, and director of the Carol Franc Buck Breast Cancer Center at the University of California, San Francisco (UCSF), envisioned an information systems project that could change patient care not only for breast cancer, but also for medicine in general. Esserman hoped to create a full-service, one-stop treatment process for women diagnosed with breast cancer. All diagnostic tests and treatments would be handled in a coordinated and efficient manner. In doing so, she hoped to lessen the anxiety and concern of the patients.[42]

She had come up with the idea for this project more than a decade before, but the project had not moved forward as quickly as she had hoped. Despite having raised significant external funds, Esserman still needed to attract resources from outsiders as well as other units and hospitals at UCSF. She also needed to overcome internal resistance from key hospital administrators who were critical to the project's success. Unfortunately, Esserman had historical conflicts with key administrators who thought she was a troublemaker who went against the status quo and who wanted to invest in projects that did not consider the competencies of the individuals who would need to see them through. How would she get the rest of the resources she needed to make the Breast Cancer Center successful?

a higher degree of involvement in terms of higher-quality information flows, and trust is established between business partners (see Figure 14.3).

Similar to Gulati and Sytch's joint dependence, Pfeffer proposed **interdependence** as a quality that exists whenever one individual requires another individual's assistance to achieve a goal.[45] In the case of Dr. Esserman, she needed to enlist the support of outsiders and key hospital administrators to achieve her vision for a

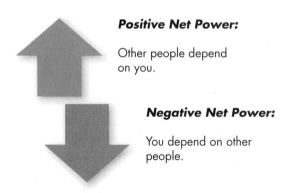

Positive Net Power:

Other people depend on you.

Negative Net Power:

You depend on other people.

Figure 14.3 Nature of Dependencies

Source: R. Gulati and M. Sytch, *Administrative Science Quarterly*, (Vol. 52, Issue 1), *"Dependence Asymmetry and Joint Dependence in Organizational Relationships,"* pp. 32–69. © 2007 by SAGE Publications. Reprinted by Permission of SAGE Publications.

Interdependence
A quality that exists whenever one individual requires another individual's assistance to achieve a goal.

Resource scarcity
The lack of sufficient resources, such as money and staff, that forces individuals in organizations to make critical decisions about how to best allocate the available resources throughout the company.

coordinated care system. Without this support, the information systems project could not be implemented. In this situation, she was more dependent on the support of these outsiders than they were on her.

Resource Scarcity

Resource scarcity is the lack of sufficient resources, such as money and staff, which forces individuals in organizations to make critical decisions about how to best allocate the available resources throughout the company. In times of scarcity, different departments may share resources such as office space and office equip-ment. At other times, organizations may decide to give more resources to one department or team than another. This can result in competition. When people or departments compete for scarce resources, power is often used to determine outcomes.[46]

As an academic medical institution, UCSF provided care that was more expensive than private hospitals because its practices involved teaching interns, residents, and surgical fellows as well as doing trials of new drugs, equipment, and procedures. UCSF also treated a larger proportion of uninsured and government-insured patients with limited reimbursement plans. As a result, UCSF had to rely on external grants to fund some of its operations, but the institution still faced a sig-nificant budget deficit. UCSF was experiencing resource scarcity. Although Dr. Es-serman had successfully raised $7 million for her project from external sources, she still had to attract physical and human resources from other units at UCSF and its hospitals. This forced her to compete with others—an action that could prevent the project from being implemented.

Disagreement about Priorities

In an increasingly heterogeneous workplace, differences of opinion become more apparent and overt disagreement is more likely to take place.[47] Disagreement becomes especially problematic when it serves as a barrier to decision making and task completion. Under these circumstances, individuals often use their ability to influence others to secure agreement.

Many top administrators at UCSF viewed Dr. Esserman's information systems project as radical and unnecessary.[48] Therefore, to move forward with the project, Dr. Esserman needed to obtain critical support from key administrators. To do this, she had to minimize the areas of disagreement and appeal to a set of common or mutually held perspectives. Reaching agreement often requires prioritizing requirements and sifting through a series of trade-offs. We will explore the process of negotiation in greater detail in Chapter 16.

Disagreement often arises when people have different priorities. The priorities, goals, and aspirations of one individual may not correspond with those of another. The importance of an issue depends not only on what it is, but also on how it is viewed by those involved. For example, the future of the information systems proj-ect was of high importance to Dr. Esserman but the other administrators believed it was both unnecessary and too expensive. To garner more resources for her center, Dr. Esserman needed to convince others of the value and importance of the initiative and to make it a higher priority for them.

USING INFLUENCE

As noted throughout this chapter, power can be derived from a number of differ-ent bases (position, personal attributes, and relationships). While having a base of power is important, the use of that power is even more so. Influence is the mechanism through which power is exercised. As individuals consider different situations and contexts, they should look for ways to effectively influence others. The following steps can be useful: (1) choose an influence style and influence tactics; (2) use specific influence principles; (3) build sources of power; and (4) assess performance.

Step 1: Choose an Influence Style and Influence Tactics

The influence style that individuals choose should correspond to the situation they are facing and to how important the issue is to them. Situation Management Systems, Inc., a management training and professional development organization, created the situational influence model, which classifies individual influence styles according to different categories and proposes associated influence tactics. The three primary styles of influence in this model are pushing, pulling, and moving away. Each style defines how energy moves from one person to another (see Figure 14.4).

Pushing styles are directed from one person to others; these styles include persuading and asserting. With these approaches, a person attempts to "push" his or her opinions and perspectives on others through reasoning and/or the application of incentives or pressures. Pulling styles involve bridging and attracting. In this approach, an individual attempts to draw information from others in order to find some common ground. The moving away style, as the name implies, involves disengaging from a situation and opting out of the influence process for a period of time.[49] Managers tend to use the pull strategies when managing up and laterally, and the push strategies when managing down.

Pushing Styles

- *Persuading.* Using this style may be helpful when requestors are viewed as credible, when they have exclusive information, and when they can use data to support their position. Associated influence tactics include creating solutions and making strong arguments. For example, Dr. Esserman can create a cost–benefit analysis to show each hospital administrator from whom she seeks support how the Breast Cancer Center's technology project will benefit his or her department.
- *Asserting.* Using this style may be helpful when both parties have a personal stake in the matter at hand. Associated influence tactics include setting expectations, providing feedback, and exchanging assistance. A key to the success of this tactic is identifying what motivates or inspires the

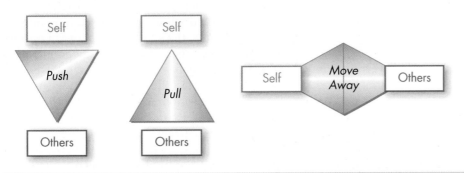

Figure 14.4 > Influence Styles

Source: Adapted from SMS, Managing Influence (Nashua, NH: Situational Management Systems, 1998).

other party.[50] For example, Dr. Esserman may appeal to the professional oaths taken by healthcare practitioners by suggesting that without the technology project, they will not be able to serve patients to the best of their abilities.

Pulling Styles

- *Bridging*. This style can be beneficial when another person's contributions may be helpful to the requestor, when the requestor is open to influence, and when the other person involved will not lose something by working with the requestor. Associated influence tactics include engaging others, listening, and sharing personal information. For example, Dr. Esserman can convene with several of the other hospital administrators in a social setting, talk to them about the challenges they face in their departments, and look for common themes or links.
- *Attracting*. Associated influence tactics include creating common ground and communicating goals. Using this style may be helpful when the requestor and the other person share common values, goals, and aspirations; the other person trusts and admires the requestor; or the other person is not sure what to do.

Moving Away Style

- *Disengaging*. Using this style may be helpful when requestors want to reduce or diffuse conflict, when they are not prepared, when new information has surfaced, or when another person's behavior prevents the requestor's success. Associated influence tactics include postponing, changing the subject, taking a break, or avoiding interaction altogether.

Step 2: Use Specific Influence Principles

Robert Cialdini, a psychologist and organizational researcher, proposed a number of principles that he called "weapons of influence" as a model that can be used to influence others.[51] The first principle, called the reciprocation principle, is based on the premise that by doing something for someone now, a future obligation will be created. In other words, "one good deed deserves another." Called the **law of reciprocity**, it demands that every favor must be repaid at some time. Repayment can include favors, gifts, invitations, and information. For example, Dr. Esserman can negotiate with administrators who aren't currently in agreement with her proposal by suggesting that she will support one of their projects in the future.

The next two principles—liking and authority—are based on personal and positional power. Liking, an element of personal power, suggests that someone will be more willing to say yes to an individual whom they like. Liking may be influenced by a person's physical attractiveness, the similarities between two individuals, exchanged compliments, and the amount of contact and cooperation that exists between two individuals. Authority is based on positional power, and this influence principle assumes that someone will follow orders even when he or she doesn't agree based on the other person's position and authority in the formal organizational hierarchy. For example, Dr. Esserman can find a way to engage those who oversee the administrators who are currently dissenting. By using any of the previously mentioned influence strategies, she can attempt to mandate that they approve the technology project. This may not be the best strategy, however, because it may harm her relationships in the future. This approach should not be used very often.

Law of reciprocity
The idea that people should repay in the future what another person has done for them in the present.

The final principle is based on a source of potential conflict—scarcity. The scarcity principle asserts that opportunities seem more valuable when their availability is limited. If an opportunity feels like a "once-in-a-lifetime" situation, it may be more attractive and exciting, even to individuals who may not at first be convinced that it is worth pursuing. An individual should assess the situation and his or her base of power to determine which influencing tactics are most appropriate.

Step 3: Build Sources of Power

The third step is to take stock of one's sources of personal, positional, and relational power. Individuals can enhance personal power by building expertise (taking challenging assignments and excelling at each position), by improving their attractiveness (dressing well and being liked by others), by increasing their effort (going "above and beyond"), and by developing legitimacy over time. To build positional power, individuals seek positions that improve their centrality (position in networks), flexibility (ability to make nonroutine decisions), visibility (to influential people), and relevance (to organizational priorities). Finally, to enhance their relational power, individuals should focus on network centrality, network breadth (types of networks and people in them), and network depth (strengths of relationships).

Step 4: Assess Performance

As we discussed in Chapter 9, formal feedback from supervisors is generally given during an annual performance review. During this meeting, supervisors review the goals that individuals set the previous year (or when they were hired). Then individuals and their supervisors discuss any progress the individuals have made toward achieving his or her goals.

While this feedback is critical for understanding how individuals have performed over the last year, individuals should seek input more regularly from a variety of sources. In addition, individuals should monitor their actions. As we discussed in the previous chapter, self-monitoring also is a good way to understand performance, but it requires significant self-awareness and an understanding of environmental and social cues.

The proper influence tactics and approaches depend on the situation and the priorities of the parties involved. As such, before embarking on the preceding four-step process, it is important to assess the context. While the context is important in interpersonal interactions, it is absolutely critical at the organizational level.

Conducting an Organizational Power Audit

In addition to managing the dynamics of interpersonal power, individuals should analyze and manage the power dynamics in the organization. An important first step is for a person to decide what he or she is trying to accomplish.[52] Key questions to examine include what needs to be done and who needs to be influenced in order to achieve these goals. Once these questions have been answered, the following five-step process can be used to define how power and influence can be used to achieve the goals:[53]

1. *Identify the interdependencies.* Who is dependent on whom and for what? Whose cooperation is needed? Whose compliance matters?
2. *Determine everyone's sources of power.* Who is in a position of power and why? What are their sources of power? How are these sources maintained?

3. *Analyze differences in goals, values, stakes, and working styles.* How might these differences shape individuals' assumptions and perceptions?
4. *Analyze the broader context.* How much potential for conflict exists? Where are the major alliances and rivalries? How are key players likely to respond to conflict?
5. *Periodically update the diagnosis.*

This analysis should help an individual understand the strength or weakness of his or her position and the level of influence that will be needed to accomplish specific objectives. One way in which weaker parties can gain strength and power in organizations is through the development or formation of **coalitions**. Coalitions bring together individuals and/or groups that have common interests and perspectives. The combination of forces tends to result in a more powerful position than any one individual or group would be able to exert on its own. These common interests can span a range of issues that extend over a long period of time or can revolve around a single issue or item that brings together groups for a short-term transactional purpose.[54] For instance, the research and development group and the sales team may band together to secure organizational funding for a promising new product despite the fact that they have historically been antagonistic toward each other.

Coalitions
Individuals and/or groups that have common interests and perspectives.

SUMMARY

LO1 Power and influence play important roles in setting goals and prioritizing activities and are key levers in effective leadership. Power is the potential of one individual to influence the behavior, thinking, or attitudes of another individual, and influence is the means by which power is exercised. Power can be based on a number of factors, including a person's formal authority (legitimate power), ability to deliver rewards or enforce punishments (reward and coercive power), level of knowledge or expertise (expert power), and personal attractiveness (referent power).

LO2 Interpersonal power is derived from a number of sources, including a person's position, personal attributes, and relations. Positional power refers to an individual's role in the formal hierarchy of an organization. Individuals who have roles that are central and relevant to the goals of an organization and afford high flexibility and visibility have strong positional power. Personal power is based on a person's expertise, effort, attractiveness, and legitimacy or credibility. People who have a good track record, expertise, and credibility are perceived as having strong personal power. Relational power refers to the strength of an individual's relationships inside and outside an organization. Individuals with high relational power have wide and deep networks of support. Power is often context dependent. As

such, the ability to be self-aware and open to change is critical for long-term success.

LO3 Power plays a key role in navigating organizational politics and conflict. Power is a deciding factor in whom should be assigned to which positions, how the work should be allocated, and when tasks should be completed. Individuals throughout an organization can influence these key decisions, but senior-level executives tend to exert more power than others. Through empowerment, organizations seek to build leadership potential throughout an organization and shift certain aspects of decision making to individuals with pertinent front line experience.

LO4 Organizational conflict often emerges as a result of interdependence, resource scarcity, and disagreement about priorities. The resolution of conflict often involves the use of power and various influence tactics.

LO5 Depending on the context or situation, individuals may pursue push (exerting influence on others) or pull (drawing forth the opinions of others) influence strategies. In any use of power or influence, it is important to assess the various interdependencies that exist, as well as the different sources of power.

KEY TERMS

Coalitions	Interdependence	Power
Coercive power	Joint dependence	Referent power
Dependence asymmetry	Law of reciprocity	Relational power
Empowerment	Legitimate power	Resource scarcity
Expert power	Personal power	Reward power
Influence	Positional power	

ASSIGNMENTS

Discussion Topics

1. Describe the ways in which power is dependent on the individual leader, the reaction of followers, and the context of the situation.

2. Think back to the discussion of charismatic leaders in Chapter 12. How do charismatic leaders gain interpersonal power? In what ways can they abuse this power?

3. Consider the four primary sources of personal power—expertise, effort, attractiveness, and legitimacy. Is one aspect more important than another? Consider leaders that you respect. Which aspect of power was most appealing to you?

4. How is legitimacy a source of both positional and personal power?

5. In what ways does "who you know" influence what you do and what opportunities are presented to you?

6. The exercise of power often changes depending on the lifecycle stage of an organization. In start-ups, what forms of power should an entrepreneur rely on? What forms of power are most appropriate in a crisis or turnaround situation?

7. In what ways can a new employee build sources of power in an organization?

8. When a leader delegates and empowers others, does he or she gain or lose personal power? In what ways?

9. What are the advantages and disadvantages of the various push and pull influence strategies?

10. Sometimes coalitions are created between unlikely allies. Identify a coalition that has brought together unlikely allies. Why did they combine forces?

Management Research

1. Choose a leader who is profiled in your local newspaper and describe his or her interpersonal sources of power.

2. With a peer or a person of higher authority, practice two of the specific influence tactics you have learned. On a scale of 1 to 10, how would you rate your performance? Did you achieve the results you wanted? If yes, how did you achieve the results?

In the Field

Attend a committee, board, or council meeting. While at the meeting, take notes on the important agenda items and the objectives of that meeting. As agenda items are discussed, document how members exert power. Use the following table as a template.

Forms of Interpersonal Power	Examples from the Meeting
Legitimate Power	
Reward Power	
Coercive Power	
Expert Power	
Referent Power	

What did you learn about power from attending the meeting? How can you apply the lessons learned to your professional life?

ENDNOTES

1 Ann Frost and Lyn Purdy, "An Introductory Note on Managing People in Organizations," Richard Ivey School of Business Note No. 908C22 (London, Ontario: University of Western Ontario, 2008).

2 Joseph S. Nye, Jr., "Power and Leadership," *Handbook of Leadership Theory and Practice: A Harvard Business School Centennial Colloquium*, Nitin Nohria and Rakesh Khurana, eds. (Boston, MA: HBS Press, 2010); and Abraham Zaleznik and Manfred F. R. Kets de Vries, *Power and the Corporate Mind* (Chicago, IL: Bonus Books, 1985), p. 3.

3 Warren Bennis and Burt Nanus, *Leaders: The Strategies for Taking Charge* (New York: Harper & Row, 1985); and "The Necessity of Power: You Can't Manage Without It," *Power, Influence, and Persuasion: Sell Your Ideas and Make Things Happen* (Boston, MA: HBS Press, 2006).

4 Abraham Zaleznik and Manfred F. R. Kets de Vries, *Power and the Corporate Mind* (Chicago, IL: Bonus Books, 1985), p. xiii; and Linda A. Hill, "What It Means to Manage: Exercising Power and Influence," Harvard Business School Note No. 9-400-041, rev. February 15, 2000 (Boston, MA: HBS Publishing, 1999).

5 B. Kim Barnes, *Exercising Influence* (Berkeley, CA: Barnes & Conti Associates, 2000), p. 9.

6 Linda A. Hill, "What It Means to Manage: Exercising Power and Influence," Harvard Business School Note No. 9-400-041, rev. February 15, 2000 (Boston, MA: HBS Publishing, 1999).

7 Abraham Zaleznik and Manfred F. R. Kets de Vries, *Power and the Corporate Mind* (Chicago, IL: Bonus Books, 1985), p. 44.

8 John P. Kotter, *Power and Influence* (New York: The Free Press, 1985).

9 Jeffery Pfeffer, *Managing with Power: Politics and Influence in Organizations* (Boston, MA: HBS Press, 1992); and "The Necessity of Power: You Can't Manage Without It," *Power, Influence, and Persuasion: Sell Your Ideas and Make Things Happen* (Boston, MA: HBS Press, 2006).

10 Victoria Chang and Jeffrey Pfeffer, "Keith Ferrazzi," Stanford Graduate School of Business Case No. OB-44, November 15, 2003 (Stanford, CA: Stanford Graduate School of Business, 2003).

11 Ibid., p. 4.

12 Ibid., p. 6.

13 "The Necessity of Power: You Can't Manage Without It," *Power, Influence, and Persuasion: Sell Your Ideas and Make Things Happen* (Boston, MA: HBS Press, 2006).

14 John R. P. French and Bertram Raven, "The Bases of Social Power," *Group Dynamics: Research and Theory*, 2nd edition, D. Cartwright and A. Zander, eds. (Evanston, IL: Row, Peterson, 1960), pp. 607–623.

15 Bertram H. Raven, "Six Bases of Power," *Encyclopedia of Leadership*, George R. Goethals, Georgia J. Sorenson, and James MacGregor Burns, eds. (Thousand Oaks, CA: Sage Publications, 2004), p. 1244.

16 Ibid., pp. 1241–1248.

17 D. A. Whetten and K. S. Cameron, *Developing Management Skills*, 5th edition (Upper Saddle River, NJ: Prentice Hall, 2000).

18 "Power Sources: How You Can Tap Them," *Power, Influence, and Persuasion: Sell Your Ideas and Make Things Happen* (Boston, MA: HBS Press, 2006).

19 A. Nahavandi, *The Art and Science of Leadership* (Upper Saddle River, NJ: Prentice Hall, 2006), pp. 169–170.

20 "The Necessity of Power: You Can't Manage Without It," *Power, Influence, and Persuasion: Sell Your Ideas and Make Things Happen* (Boston, MA: HBS Press, 2006); and Ann Frost and Lyn Purdy, "An Introductory Note on Managing People in Organizations," Richard Ivey School of Business Note No. 908C22 (London, Ontario: University of Western Ontario, 2008).

21 Amy Cuddy, Caroline A. Wilmuth, Andy J. Yap, and Dana R. Carney, "Preparatory Power Posing Affects Nonverbal Presence and Job Interview Outcomes," *Journal of Applied Psychology* (in press); and Sue Shellenbarger, "Strike a Powerful Pose," *Wall Street Journal*, August 21, 2013.

22 "Power Sources: How You Can Tap Them," *Power, Influence, and Persuasion: Sell Your Ideas and Make Things Happen* (Boston, MA: HBS Press, 2006).

23 Herminia Ibarra, "Managerial Networks," Harvard Business School Note No. 9-495-039, rev. January 25, 1996 (Boston, MA: HBS Publishing, 1995).

24 Ibid.

25 Ibid.

26 Boris Groysberg, "How Star Women Build Portable Skills," *Harvard Business Review*, February 2008.

27 Ibid.

28 Jeffery Pfeffer, *Managing with Power: Politics and Influence in Organizations* (Boston, MA: HBS Press, 1992), pp. 306–307.

29 Ibid.

30 Linda L. Neider and Chester A. Schriesheim, "Power: Overview," *Encyclopedia of Leadership*, George R. Goethals, Georgia J. Sorenson, and James MacGregor Burns, eds. (Thousand Oaks, CA: Sage Publications, 2004), p. 1249.

31 Linda A. Hill, "Chapter 10," *Becoming a Manager: How New Managers Master the Challenges of Leadership*, 2nd edition (Boston, MA: HBS Press, 2003).

32 Kathleen McGinn and Alexis Gendron, "Robert Moses," Harvard Business School Case No. 9-800-271, rev. January 9, 2002 (Boston, MA: HBS Publishing, 2000).

33 Ibid., pp. 2–3.

34 Ibid., p. 16.

35 Gary A. Yukl, *Leadership in Organizations* (Englewood Cliffs, NJ: Prentice-Hall, 1981).

36 A. Nahavandi, *The Art and Science of Leadership* (Upper Saddle River, NJ: Prentice Hall, 2006).

37 Jay A. Conger and Rabindra N. Kanungo, "The Empowerment Process: Integrating Theory and Practice," *Academy of Management Review*, Vol. 13, No. 3, pp. 471–482.

38 Lynn R. Offermann, "Empowerment," *Encyclopedia of Leadership*, George R. Goethals, Georgia J. Sorenson, and James MacGregor Burns, eds. (Thousand

Oaks, CA: Sage Publications, 2004), pp. 434–437.

[39] Edwin P. Hollander and Lynn R. Offermann, "Power and Leadership in Organizations," *American Psychologist*, February 1990, pp. 179–189.

[40] Josh Bernoff and Ted Schadler, "Empowered," *Harvard Business Review*, July–August 2010.

[41] Victoria Change and Jeffrey Pfeffer, "Dr. Laura Esserman (A)," Stanford Graduate School of Business Case No. OB-42A, September 30, 2003 (Stanford, CA: Stanford Graduate School of Business, 2003).

[42] Jeffrey Pfeffer, "Power Play," *Harvard Business Review*, July–August 2010.

[43] Jeffery Pfeffer, *Managing with Power: Politics and Influence in Organizations* (Boston, MA: HBS Press, 1992), pp. 38–45.

[44] Ranjay Gulati and Maxim Sytch, "Dependence Asymmetry and Joint Dependence in Organizational Relationships," *Administrative Science Quarterly*, Vol. 52, No. 1, 2007, pp. 32–69.

[45] Jeffery Pfeffer, *Managing with Power: Politics and Influence in Organizations* (Boston, MA: HBS Press, 1992), pp. 38–40.

[46] Abraham Zaleznik and Manfred F. R. Kets de Vries, *Power and the Corporate Mind* (Chicago, IL: Bonus Books, 1985).

[47] Ibid.

[48] Victoria Chang and Jeffrey Pfeffer, "Dr. Laura Esserman (A)" Stanford Graduate School of Business Case OB-42A, September 30, 2003 (Stanford, CA: Stanford Graduate School of Business, 2003).

[49] SMS, *Managing Influence* (Nashua, NH: Situational Management Systems, 1998).

[50] Kathleen L. McGinn and Elizabeth Long Lingo, "Power and Influence: Achieving Your Objectives in Organizations," Harvard Business School Note No. 9-801-425, rev. July 5, 2007 (Boston, MA: HBS Publishing, 2001).

[51] Robert B. Cialdini, *Influence: The Psychology of Persuasion* (New York: Quill/W. Morrow, 1993).

[52] Jeffery Pfeffer, "Understanding Power in Organizations," *California Management Review*, Winter 1992.

[53] Linda A. Hill, "Power Dynamics in Organizations," Harvard Business School Note No. 9-494-083, rev. March 22, 1995 (Boston, MA: HBS Publishing, 1994), pp. 9–10.

[54] "Power Sources: How You Can Tap Them," *Power, Influence, and Persuasion: Sell Your Ideas and Make Things Happen* (Boston, MA: HBS Press, 2006).

CHAPTER

15

Decision Making

Learning Objectives

After reading this chapter, you should be able to:

LO1 Explain the step-by-step process of rational decision making.

LO2 Describe how time constraints, lack of information, and complexity influence the decision-making process.

LO3 Describe the various biases that can influence an individual's perspective and how these biases impact decision making.

LO4 Articulate how emotions and social situations impact decision making.

LO5 Compare and contrast the different ways in which decisions are made in an organization.

LO6 Describe the ways in which managers can improve their decision-making abilities.

SELF-REFLECTION

How Effective Are You at Decision Making?

The success of an organization is dependent on managers making the right decisions in a timely manner. How effective are you at decision making? Answer True or False to the following questions to assess your decision-making skills:

1. I base my decisions on research.

2. I will not make a decision until I have the evidence to support it.

3. I seek multiple perspectives before I make a decision.

4. I have a systematic process for making decisions.

5. I rely on heuristics to expedite my decision-making process.

6. I am aware of my biases when making decisions.

7. I use intuition when making decisions.

8. I realize that for certain decisions I am influenced by the opinions of my teammates or group members.

9. I recognize that some of my decisions are emotionally charged.

10. When making a decision, I analyze the risks associated with each alternative.

Based on your responses, what did you learn about your decision-making skills? How can you improve your decision-making skills?

INTRODUCTION

Decision making, the process of identifying issues and making choices from alternative courses of action, is commonly recognized as the heart of activity in every business.[1] Managers are faced with myriad decisions on a daily basis. Some can be relatively straightforward, like those regarding operational procedures, but others are more complex, like those dealing with the strategy and direction of the organization. Almost all of the concepts discussed in the first three sections of this textbook involve some kind of decision. Managers need to determine what strategies to use, what industries to compete in, how to structure the organization and allocate resources, how to best respond to or anticipate competitive threats, which performance metrics are important, and when to engage in an organizational change process.[2] In all of these decisions, managers must evaluate a variety of alternatives against a set of organizational values and objectives as well as the evolving contextual landscape. The success of an organization depends on a manager's ability to make the right decisions at the right time with the right information.[3]

How do you make decisions? Do you rely on past experiences? Do you assess the context and try to determine the best course of action based on the

Decision making
The process of identifying issues and making choices from alternative courses of action.

information in front of you? Do you seek advice from others, or do you rely on gut instinct? Think about the college you decided to attend. What criteria did you use to make the decision—cost, location, size, athletic programs, social organizations, college guidebooks, or academic reputation? Each of these criteria probably assumed a specific weight in the decision process based on your financial situation; your social preferences; your family's and friends' opinions; and your past academic, athletic, or artistic pursuits. In addition to these considerations, you probably tried to assess whether the college was a good "fit" for you. Did you feel a sense of belonging? Could you picture yourself on the campus? Did it feel right? In many cases, these intangible considerations outweigh the more rational and objective elements.

While it is easy to construct a list of pros and cons for each criterion, it is often more difficult to make the leap from the list to a decision. Even when we attempt to make a rational decision by creating a list of criteria and then weighting each one, we often are not entirely sure about the criteria or the weights. While this methodical approach may create an aura of rationality, the final decision may not, in fact, be rational. Not only do we have selective filters that focus our attention on certain information over others, but the way we assess our choices, the criteria, and the weights we apply to them, can also be systematically biased. Think back to your criteria and the weights you applied to them when making your college choice. Looking back now, does your criteria and the weights you placed on them look right? Did you make a reasoned, rational choice, or did you go with your gut instinct?

Generally, we tend to assume that we are rational decision makers, but if we look closely at our decision-making behaviors, we may find that we are not completely rational in the way we make decisions. As we will discuss in this chapter, even when one thinks he or she is making a rational decision, he or she is often influenced by a number of factors. The ambiguity of the situation, our judgments and biases, and our previous decisions can greatly affect our future decisions. This applies to the daily decisions we make in our personal lives as well as the decisions we make in the workplace. The question then becomes, how can we better understand the decision-making process so that we can become better decision makers? To understand some of the factors that affect decisions, let's take a look at a pivotal decision of one of the most successful college basketball coaches, Roy Williams.

Roy Williams and Kansas University

"As a kid, I dreamed of playing at North Carolina, and as a young high-school coach I dreamed of coaching at North Carolina."[4] From early in his life, Roy Williams had a strong emotional connection to the University of North Carolina (UNC), and in 2003 he had the opportunity to become the head coach for the basketball team. With such an affinity for his alma mater for so many years, it seemed that the decision to become the head coach at UNC would be an easy one. However, many factors made it one of the most difficult of his life.

Williams grew up in Spruce Pine, North Carolina, about 200 miles from the UNC, Chapel Hill. He went to school in Asheville and was twice named to the all-county and all-state basketball teams. He attended UNC and played his freshman year but did not continue with the team because he wasn't promoted to the varsity squad. Instead, he served in a team manager role tracking statistics and attending practices, which became an opportunity to cultivate his basketball knowledge. After graduating with a bachelor's degree in education in 1972 and a master's degree in 1973, Williams began his coaching career at a high school in Swannanoa, North Carolina.[5]

Williams got the first big break of his coaching career in 1978, when he was hired as an assistant coach for UNC under the legendary Dean Smith. Smith coached UNC for 35 years and amassed an impressive 879–224 record (0.797 win percentage).[6] While working with Smith, UNC played in the NCAA Tournament for ten consecutive seasons, won six ACC Conference titles, and won a national championship in 1982 with future NBA stars James Worthy and Michael Jordan. For Williams, things could not get much better than coaching under his mentor at his beloved alma mater. Then, in 1988 it did: he was offered the head coaching job at Kansas University, a school with such high expectations that a season was only considered successful if it ended in a championship. In fact, several other high-profile coaches with significant head coaching experience were passed over in favor of Williams.[7]

With a mountainous challenge ahead of him, Williams accepted the position. Kansas had won the national championship the previous year and was on probation for NCAA violations made during the previous coach's tenure. During his first season, Williams led Kansas to a 19–12 record. While it seemed like a slow start, it far outpaced the expectations of both fans and school officials. That season inaugurated one of the most successful coaching careers in the history of the NCAA: Williams went on to coach Kansas for 15 years, making fourteen consecutive NCAA Tournament appearances. Over that time, Kansas went to the Final Four four times and finished in second place twice. He was also named National Coach of the Year in 1990, 1991, 1992, and 1997 and was awarded the John R. Wooden Legends of Coaching Award in 2003.[8]

When UNC offered the head coaching job to Williams at the end of the 2003 season, it was one of the most difficult decisions he ever had to make. At Kansas University, Williams had accumulated a 418–101 record, which was the highest win percentage for any coach in Kansas's history, and the University was competing for the national

championship in 2003. Thanks to his hard work building the program, Kansas would be contending for the title for the next several years. In contrast, the 2003 UNC team did not even qualify for the tournament. Additionally, Williams valued his legacy as a coach and knew that his place in basketball history might be compromised if he left Kansas: "People look at guys differently if they only coach at one school for their entire career. It's viewed with more respect . . . coaching at Kansas for my entire career would definitely be a positive."[9] While these were strong factors in his decision, perhaps the most influential one was his coaching philosophy.

On Roy Williams's desk sits an engraved plaque from his daughter reading, "Statistics are important but relationships last a lifetime." This can be seen in everything he does, from recruitment to coaching to keeping in touch with former players. When he recruits high school players, he visits their homes, gets to know them on a personal level, and builds relationships with both the players and their families. On the court, he emphasizes relationships to help team members not only become great players, but also to become well-rounded, respectable young men. He believes that just as there is a right way to play basketball, there is a right way to carry oneself off the court, a right way to communicate, and a right way to deal with problems.[10] He felt so strongly about this philosophy that when UNC first offered him the coaching job in 2000, he declined because he felt a commitment to his players.

However, by 2003, the situation had changed and turning down the UNC position was not as easy. Interestingly, the very reason that drove him to stay at Kansas in 2000 was the reason driving him to leave in 2003. In early 2001, Bob Frederick, Kansas University's Athletic Director, resigned. This was devastating because both Williams and Frederick shared a similar philosophy about athletics and a mutual commitment to the players' best interests. The new Athletic Director, Al Bohl, focused more on fund-raising and the financial side of Kansas athletics. He didn't understand the relationships that Williams valued so dearly and frequently exploited

Kansas players to appease donors. As a result, Williams felt less fulfilled, less happy, and less satisfied with his job.[11]

To help him make a decision, Williams compiled a list—one column for North Carolina and one column for Kansas. By the time he finished there were more than 100 factors, but it was simply too broad.

Rather than relying on a list of pros and cons, Williams decided to identify the most important one or two things and go with his gut feeling.[12] While he had as much love for Kansas as he did for North Carolina, he ultimately chose to switch schools, continuing his fabled career as the head coach of North Carolina.

Case in Point   Roy Williams and Kansas University

1. What information was important to Roy Williams in his decision to move to UNC?
2. How would you characterize the way that Roy Williams evaluated the two options? Did he rely more on facts or emotions?
3. What could Kansas have done to convince Roy Williams to stay?

In this chapter, you will learn about the multitude of factors that can influence the decision-making process as well as what you can do to make decisions that are more productive. Personal biases, for instance, can significantly influence our thought processes and, by extension, the decisions we make. As such, it is very important to become aware of our biases to ensure that they do not negatively influence key decisions. To that end, this chapter will provide an overview of some of the key biases that can impact decision making. We begin this chapter by examining how individuals should make decisions compared to how decisions are actually made. With an understanding of how and why individuals make certain decisions, we will turn our attention to the organizational context to examine how decisions are made in an organizational setting. Finally, we will review ways in which an individual can improve his or her decision-making abilities.

RATIONAL DECISION MAKING

Early research on decision making focused on ways in which individuals seek to maximize an outcome or achieve a personal benefit. Researchers believed that individuals would often make decisions based on a rational thought process that optimized self-interest. This was called the **theory of rational choice**. It was developed from the work of mathematicians, statisticians, and economists, including John von Neumann and Oskar Morgenstern. In their seminal work and the first book on game theory, *Theory of Games and Economic Behavior*, von Neumann and Morgenstern explored the role that utility, or payoff, plays in decision making, arguing that when individuals are confronted with a choice, they try to make the best possible decision and the one that maximizes their expected utility.[13]

Theory of rational choice
The theory that individuals make decisions based on a rational thought process that optimizes self-interest.

In this expected utility model, individuals assign a numerical value to each alternative and select the one that offers the highest payoff or profit. This model also presumes that decision makers are vigilant and calculating in their efforts to assess alternatives and determine the probable payoff associated with each choice, then choose the option that maximizes or optimizes value.[14] Rational decision making generally follows a set process (see Figure 15.1).

Step 1 • A problem or opportunity is defined.

Step 2 • Objectives and goals are identified.

Step 3 • Objectives are weighted according to the importance of each.

Step 4 • Possible courses of action or alternatives are considered.

Step 5 • Each objective is rated according to how well it will achieve the desired course of action.

Step 6 • The optimal decision is chosen.

Figure 15.1 Rational Decision-Making Process.

Source: Adapted from Max Bazerman, *Judgment in Managerial Decision Making*, 6th edition (Hoboken, NJ: John Wiley & Sons, 2006), p. 4.

To better understand the rational decision-making process, let's look at a fictional company called ABC Corporation. ABC Corporation is seeking to gain a competitive advantage over rival firms. While there are many ways to address this goal, the organization has decided to focus on three objectives (listed below in order of priority):

1. Cut costs
2. Grow revenue
3. Improve existing operational capabilities

Rank ordering, which is used in this example, is just one of many value metrics that can be helpful in assessing alternatives. Three courses of action have been proposed, and your role is to decide which of the three options is best to pursue at this time based on the rank-ordered objectives.

- Action 1: Increase funding for new ventures
- Action 2: Implement a program to improve operational efficiency
- Action 3: Hire creative people

Which course of action would you choose? If you made your decision based on the rational model, it might look like the one presented in Table 15.1. Based on the rating system used in this scenario, the optimal and rational choice would be to implement a program to improve operational efficiency.

HOW MANAGERS MAKE DECISIONS

While this process is systematic and structured, it is not practical for all decisions. This rational process may capture the goal of the decision-making process, but it does not reflect the manner in which all people make decisions. Managers often do

Step	Example
1. Define the problem or opportunity.	The organization wants to gain a competitive advantage.
2. Identify the objectives.	Objective 1: Cut costs Objective 2: Grow revenue Objective 3: Improve existing operational capabilities
3. Weight the objectives according to importance (1 being the least important).	Cut costs = 3 Grow revenue = 2 Improve existing operational capabilities = 1
4. Identify a few possible courses of action (alternatives).	Action 1. Increase funding for new ventures Action 2. Implement a program to improve operational efficiency Action 3. Hire creative people
5. Rate each course of action on each of the objectives (1 being the worst).	Objective 1: Cut costs Action 1. Increase funding for new ventures = 1 Action 2. Implement a program to improve operational efficiency = 3 Action 3. Hire creative people = 2 Objective 2: Grow revenue Action 1. Increase funding for new ventures = 2 Action 2. Implement a program to improve operational efficiency = 1 Action 3. Hire creative people = 3 Objective 3: Improve existing operational capabilities Action 1. Increase funding for new ventures = 2 Action 2. Implement a program to improve operational efficiency = 3 Action 3. Hire creative people = 1
6. Compute the optimal decision. • Multiply ratings in Step 5 by weights in Step 3. • Add weighted ratings across all of the objectives for each course of action. • Choose the solution with the highest sum of the weighted ratings.	Multiply ratings in Step 5 by weights in Step 3. Objective 1: Cut costs Action 1. Increase funding for new ventures $\rightarrow 1 \times 3 = 3$ Action 2. Implement a program to improve operational efficiency $\rightarrow 3 \times 3 = 9$ Action 3. Hire creative people $\rightarrow 2 \times 3 = 6$ Objective 2: Grow revenue Action 1. Increase funding for new ventures $\rightarrow 2 \times 2 = 4$ Action 2. Implement a program to improve operational efficiency $\rightarrow 1 \times 2 = 2$ Action 3. Hire creative people $\rightarrow 3 \times 2 = 6$ Objective 3: Improve existing operational capabilities Action 1. Increase funding for new ventures $\rightarrow 2 \times 1 = 2$ Action 2. Implement a program to improve operational efficiency $\rightarrow 3 \times 1 = 3$ Action 3. Hire creative people $\rightarrow 1 \times 1 = 1$ Add weighted ratings across all of the objectives for each course of action. Action 1. Increase funding for new ventures $\rightarrow 3 + 4 + 2 = 9$ Action 2. Implement a program to improve operational efficiency $\rightarrow 9 + 2 + 3 = 14$ Action 3. Hire creative people $\rightarrow 6 + 6 + 1 = 13$

Table 15.1 › Rational Decision-Making Model in Action

Source: Adapted from Max Bazerman, *Judgment in Managerial Decision Making*, 6th edition (Hoboken, NJ: John Wiley & Sons, 2006), p. 4.

not have time to go through this process, or they lack the relevant information to make accurate assessments or conclusions. As such, in most situations, managers make decisions based on a host of other influential factors. The busier people are, the more likely they are to rely on less rational approaches to decision making.[15]

The complexity and consequences of the decision can also impact the way managers approach it. For example, a manager at a small venture capital company must make decisions about everything from ensuring his team can carry out their work to executing business deals with start-up companies. Some decisions (e.g., which office supplies to order) are simple and straightforward. The options are limited and the consequences of choosing one supplier over another are minimal.

However, other decisions don't lend themselves to easy quantification nor to concrete evaluation of alternatives. For instance, choosing one out of a dozen start-up companies to fund is much more complex. Not only are the consequences for making a wrong decision much greater, but also identifying measures for success is often ambiguous. In addition, different start-up companies may create completely different products and compete in different industries, making comparisons more like apples to oranges rather than apples to apples. Such complex decisions are subject to numerous conditions, including the following:

- Incomplete, imperfect, or even misleading information
- Limited ability or background to process information (i.e., lack of experience)
- Limited time to make a decision
- Conflicting preferences, incentives, or goals of various organizational players[16]

These conditions tend to complicate the rational decision-making process, and as such, decisions tend to be made within a set of boundaries or constraints called **bounded rationality**. Owing to lack of information or time or both, decision makers tend not to exhaustively evaluate all of their options; instead, they only search for a course of action until an acceptable solution is found.[17] By "bounding" what they need to consider, decision makers attempt to accelerate and simplify the overall process. While the best option would be to optimize the decision by exploring all possible contingencies and outcomes, there is rarely time to do this, so people will narrow their options to come up with a solution that is good enough—80% accuracy is a common rule of thumb in business. This act of choosing a solution that is "good enough" is called **satisficing**.[18]

While the rational framework presumes that individuals make decisions under **conditions of certainty**, in which individuals have all the information they need to make the best possible decision, the notion of bounded rationality contends that individuals make decisions in the midst of **ambiguity**, situations that are characterized by uncertainty and risk, and where the optimal decision is not obvious. In so doing, they opt for solutions that may not be perfect but are practical. **Conditions of risk** and **conditions of uncertainty** are two such conditions of ambiguity that influence the rational decision-making process and cause decision-making behaviors to deviate from rationality. Under conditions of risk, individuals have information about objectives, priorities, and potential courses of action, but they do not have all the information about the possible outcomes for each course of action. Under conditions of uncertainty, individuals have information related to objectives and priorities, but they do not have complete information about alternative courses of action or about the possible outcomes of each one.

When the speed of a decision is vitally important or when an individual is faced with a difficult ambiguous situation, he or she often defers to intuition. Intuition can emerge as a form of "automated expertise" if it is drawn from linkages or connections to past experiences.[19] Our brains create patterns and look for connections to our past decisions. One study found that 45% of executives rely on intuition, or gut feeling, for decision making instead of rational analysis.[20]

Intuitive decision making often emerges from subconscious activity, and the insights that are tapped through intuition are not always fully understood by the

Bounded rationality
A set of boundaries or constraints that tend to complicate the rational decision-making process.

Satisficing
The act of choosing a solution that is good enough.

Conditions of certainty
Conditions in which individuals have all of the information they need to make the best possible decision.

Ambiguity
Situations that are characterized by uncertainty and risk and where the optimal decision is not clear or obvious.

Conditions of risk
Conditions in which individuals have information about an organization's goals, objectives, priorities, and potential courses of action, but they do not have complete information about the possible outcomes for each course of action.

Conditions of uncertainty
Conditions in which individuals have information related to an organization's objectives and priorities, but they do not have complete information about alternative courses of action or about the possible outcomes for each one.

Intuitive decision making
Insights that are tapped through intuition and are not always fully understood by the decision maker.

A DIFFERENT View

Blink

Is it right to judge a book by its cover? Malcolm Gladwell's *Blink* maintains that snap judgments and conclusions made in the blink of an eye are powerful, important, and can be very good. In some situations, less is more. For instance, firefighters responded to a house fire in a residential neighborhood. As they entered the home to fight the fire, the lieutenant felt something was wrong. In a snap decision, he ordered his men out of the house. Moments later, the floor that they had been standing on collapsed. This decision made in the blink of an eye and based on intuition saved his fellow firefighters. Critical decisions like this one are made every day, in both our personal and professional lives. *Blink* challenges its readers to listen to instant conclusions rather than waiting to gather all possible information before making a decision.

1. Describe a situation in which you made a thoughtful, informed decision but your snap judgment would have been better.
2. What snap decisions or judgments in your professional life have been correct? When have they been wrong?
3. What can leaders learn from making decisions based on their initial reactions?

decision maker. The decisions or choices just seem to feel right. Sometimes they are called hunches.

In his 2005 best seller *Blink*, Malcolm Gladwell calls intuitive decision making "The Power of Thinking Without Thinking."[21] Gladwell refers to "thin-slicing" as the ability of the subconscious mind to find patterns in situations and behavior based on very narrow slices of experience.[22] Gladwell argues that when our subconscious engages in thin-slicing, it rapidly and automatically draws a conclusion about a complex situation. This enables snap judgments to be made, and many of these snap judgments appear to be accurate.

One way in which snap judgment has received traction has been in speed dating.[23] In this social activity, two dozen men and women gather at a bar to determine whether there are any potential sparks or connections between them. In the speed dating process, each man and woman engages in 6 minutes of conversation; the women remain in the same seat for the duration of the evening, and the men rotate from woman to woman, moving to the next one when the coordinator rings a bell. The daters are given a badge, a number, and a short form to complete, with the instruction that if they liked someone after 6 minutes, they should check the box next to that person's number. If the person whose box they checked also checked his or her box, both daters are given the other's e-mail address within 24 hours. Speed dating has become very popular around the world because it boils down dating to a simple snap judgment to a very simple question: "Do I want to see this person again?"[24] The answer to this question tends not to be based on any deep knowledge of the individual, but rather on one's first impression, or "gut feeling."

Intuition also plays a significant role in how individuals make moral judgments. Research has shown that moral judgment results from quick moral intuitions and is followed by slow moral reasoning. While moral reasoning is deliberate, effortful, and rational, moral intuition appears suddenly and effortlessly in the consciousness, without the person's awareness.[25] When moral intuitions conflict or when the social situation demands a thorough examination of all facets of a scenario, the moral reasoning process is called upon (see Table 15.2).

Although research has revealed that intuitive decision-making can be appropriate in many contexts, there are instances when using "gut instinct" can be problematic. This is especially true when a manager uses intuition based on past situations that occurred in vastly different contexts.[26] While pattern recognition (how the brain synthesizes information from the past and uses it to understand the present and anticipate the future) serves us well for simple conditions or in similar contexts, our instinctive tendency to apply patterns to situations becomes more misleading in complex circumstances where cause and effect is not always absolute. Some researchers believe that intuition does not even assess complexity, but instead ignores it.[27]

For instance, if a lit candle is knocked over and starts to burn nearby papers, instinct tells you to extinguish the fire. Based on past experiences (pattern recognition),

Intuition	Reasoning
Fast and effortless	Slow and effortful
Process is unintentional and automatic	Process is intentional and rational
Context dependent	Context independent
Depends on individual	Process can be conducted by any individual or machine

Table 15.2 › Intuitive versus Reasoning Systems in Moral Judgments

Source: J. Haidt, "The Emotional Dog and Its Rational Tail: A Social Intuitionist Approach to Moral Judgment," *Psychological Review*, Vol. 108, No. 4, 2001, p. 820.

you are fairly certain that water will put out the small fire; so you pour a glass of water on the fire (the cause). As a result, the fire is extinguished (the effect). You may then project that future small fires should be handled the same way (pattern recognition). This is a simple situation in which the problems, actions, and solutions are obvious. Yet we face more complex situations in business. For instance, if you are facing a pressing decision about investing millions of dollars in a new product for a rapidly changing market, patterns, causes, and effects are not as easy to see. You may think that comparing a similar investment would help to shape your judgment (pattern recognition), but there are usually many other influences at play, including your company's present risk tolerance, resources, and market conditions. Moreover, various investment strategies (causes) may result in significantly different outcomes that could be positive or negative (effects). Therefore, the same pattern of thinking that was used for the previous investment may not work as well in the new situation.

All in all, what is important to know about intuition in decision making is that it has the power to help you consider your options and to shape your decisions, but relying on intuition alone can cause your decisions to be more biased and constrained. Therefore, balancing intuition with analytical processes is a more effective way of considering all of your options and it helps you make the most appropriate decisions.[28]

HOW BIASES IMPACT DECISION MAKING

Many decision makers believe that they are better able to predict success and choose the right approach than results would otherwise suggest.[29] Whether we use our intuition or engage in a deliberate and methodical decision-making process, we are all likely to deviate from rationality due to pervasive biases that influence each of us to varying degrees. These biases are usually hidden from us and we often don't realize when we are influenced by them. And yet, individuals are subject to myriad judgment biases that can result in suboptimal decisions. Biases sometimes arise from our use of **heuristics** or quick judgments that enable decision makers to act with speed and efficiency. The growing complexity of business often necessitates this speed, but with speed comes potential dangers in the decision-making process.

Heuristics

We use heuristics, or rules of thumb, for quick and inconsequential decisions as well as important and deliberate decisions. And their pervasive use leads many of our decisions to deviate from rationality. These rules of thumb are typically based on our recall of information, our assessment of its relative salience, and our evaluation of our perceived choices. The point to note here is that we make our assessment of the information at hand with a distinct set of filters that are not entirely objective. These filters not only slant what we see, but also our assessment of its relative importance, and ultimately our judgment of the best course of action. These filters are handy because they allow us to come to quick decisions as we saw in the case of speed dating, but at the same time they are not entirely objective and colored by our past experiences and the way the information was presented to us. The good news for us is that a rich body of research has studied these filters and shows us patterns in the way we sometimes distort things when we use heuristics to make decisions. The primary rules of thumb that most people use are availability, representativeness, and adjustment heuristics.

Availability

When you think about some of your childhood memories, you probably remember specific details about birthdays, vacations you took with your family, arguments you had with friends or family members, or social events you attended. You

Heuristics
Rules of thumb or short-cuts that individuals use to save time when making complex decisions.

probably do not as easily recall what you wore last Tuesday or what you ate for breakfast 3 weeks ago unless these episodes were especially memorable. The reason you can easily recall the details of your childhood rather than the details of episodes that happened in the last few weeks is because your childhood memories tend to be more emotional and vivid. Research shows that emotional and vivid events are more memorable than unemotional or vague events and are thus "available" to use in decision making.[30] At the same time, more recent events are also more vivid and easy to recall.

Recalling the details of emotional and vivid events, along with more recent ones, influences decision making when a new situation resembles one from the past. For example, when it comes time to review an employee's performance this year, a manager may put more weight on the most recent and vivid events, like a disagreement, than more distant and less vivid moments. And so, while the manager is supposed to provide an objective assessment of an employee's performance over the entire year, he or she is likely to be more influenced by what happened toward the end of the year than by what happened earlier in the year. At the same time, he or she will have more vivid recall of charged moments and weigh those more heavily in the assessment. If those charged moments were positive ones, then the result will be beneficial to the employee, and if they were negative, they could have disadvantageous repercussions. These examples illustrate a manager's use of the **availability heuristic**, which contends that individuals assess the frequency, probability, or likely cause of an event by the degree to which instances or occurrences of that event are readily "available" in memory.[31] The more emotional or vivid the event, the more readily available it is. Individuals then use this availability as an important input in their decision making.

The availability heuristic can be extremely valuable for managers as they evaluate information to make decisions. It is likely that previous experiences that evoked a strong emotional reaction were those that had a significant impact, either positive or negative, on the success of the manager or the business. When making a decision, a manager should draw on those vivid memories to make a decision in the present. In fact, the accumulation of these experiences is what makes experienced managers so much more effective than inexperienced managers. They are able to draw on more positive and negative experiences to formulate more accurate judgments and thus make better decisions.

However, managers must be careful not to overly rely on their recall to inform decisions. Often times, individuals remember experiences differently than they actually happened, so seeking additional concrete information can be valuable when forming judgments. Likewise, managers cannot depend on their emotional reactions and memories to be completely rational, although they may believe that they are. By focusing on select information based on its recall availability means that we are, at the same time, neglecting other information that may not be easy to recall. Not only might we end up with unfair decisions, but we may also end up deviating from rationality and making suboptimal decisions. To avoid this, it can be useful to ask others for their opinions and feedback about a situation to help provide additional context. Others may recall events or situations in a different way and allow us to overcome our blind spots and make a more informed decision.

Representativeness

The **representativeness heuristic** contends that individuals tend to look for traits in another person or situation that correspond with previously formed stereotypes.[32] In some cases, individuals look for supporting evidence to confirm their initial impression or stereotype. For example, some managers may predict the success of a new product based on that product's similarity to past successful and unsuccessful products. Similarly, some managers predict a

---

Availability heuristic
The rule of thumb that contends that individuals assess the frequency, probability, or likely cause of an event by the degree to which instances or occurrences of that event are readily "available" in memory.

Representativeness heuristic
The rule of thumb that contends that individuals tend to look for traits in another person or situation that correspond with previously formed stereotypes.

Ismagilov/Shutterstock.com

person's performance or behavior based on the observed performance or behavior of a category of people to which that person belongs or if that person reminds them of someone else they knew before. They then project future expectations of that situation or person based on the past experiences that are triggered. Sometimes our reasoning works and other times it does not.

The representativeness heuristic can be used positively to approximate performance when insufficient information or time is available. However, it can also result in strongly biased judgment especially when it is used to affirm negative biases we may have in the form of prejudices against people of certain types. For example, a study on the U.S. labor market was performed by two researchers, Marianne Bertrand and Sendhil Mullainathan in the early 2000s. They wanted to determine if people still received differential treatment based solely on race. To do so, they sent fictitious resumes to job postings in Boston and Chicago. The credentials and pedigree of the candidates were the same. The only difference was that some had names that sounded African American while others had names that sounded Caucasian. Caucasian names received 50% more callbacks for interviews. The racial gap was uniform across occupation, industry, and employer size. Such biased judgment is not only detrimental to equality, but it can also be detrimental to a business as viable candidates may be overlooked.[33]

Adjustment

The third rule of thumb that can lead decision makers to deviate from rational decisions is called the **adjustment heuristic**, which contends that individuals make estimates or choices based on a certain starting point.[34] Individuals generally give greater weight to the first information they receive about a problem or potential solution and then don't adjust away from it even when they receive information to the contrary. As such, many people fail to consider alternatives in the decision-making process.[35] The adjustment heuristic is one of the primary reasons that making a good first impression is vitally important. We tend to judge others based on our first impressions. For instance, an individual with tattoos and piercings may be perceived as a rebel or nonconformist even though he or she may hold conservative opinions and perspectives. If we receive subsequent information that defies our initial impressions, we will tend to discount it.

This concept was recently tested with new airport security personnel. Security screeners were asked to review a collection of test bags. When the screeners were told that 50% of the bags included a dangerous object such as a knife, their error rate was about 7%. When screeners were told that only 1% of the bags included a dangerous object, their failure rate jumped to 30%. Because they did not expect to see many dangerous objects, they in fact did not see them even when they were there.[36]

Despite some of the potential downsides, the adjustment heuristic can be helpful in accelerating the decision-making process and can also lead to accurate judgments. For example, the budget and sales results for a company from the previous year can be great starting points for the current year. Those results were based on previous projections, which were based on previous results, which were based on previous projections, and so on. In other words, those numbers come from a long line of reliable data and can therefore be trusted to be fairly accurate.

Cognitive heuristics can be both helpful and harmful in making decisions. They help to speed up the decision-making process and may provide some context for the judgments that we make, but that speed can often result in a less than ideal decision. As we have seen, decisions

Adjustment heuristic
The rule of thumb that contends that individuals make estimates or choices based on a certain starting point.

AP Images/Jeff Roberson

that are based on cognitive heuristics (availability, representativeness, and adjustment) can be biased. Individuals are also susceptible to the other forms of bias, including confirmation, escalation of commitment, status quo, and framing.

Confirmation Bias

Confirmation bias can be a powerful factor not only in the decisions we make but in how we perceive decisions after they have been made. According to researchers, confirmation bias occurs when people have already made up their mind about a decision and then seek information that confirms a decision and ignore or neglect to seek information that may disconfirm the decision, even if the disconfirming information is more powerful and important.[37] In other words, an individual who succumbs to confirmation bias will focus on information that makes him or her feel that he or she made the right choice and will look away from information that may suggest otherwise.

Escalation of Commitment

Escalation of commitment is a bias that arises when we are in situations where we have already invested a lot and are faced with a choice of continuing to invest or exit.[38] Even when it makes rational sense to exit, we are unable to do so and rationalize our choice to continue by focusing on the past investments we have made. In these situations, we often place far greater weight than is warranted on the investments we have made and continue to add to that investment, despite evidence that suggests that this continued investment is not prudent. Consider the following scenario:[39]

You accept a job with a prestigious consulting firm, believing that the job offers a promising career opportunity with room for growth. Two years later you have not been promoted, although you think you deserve it. Anxious to demonstrate your worth to the company, you decide to work a lot of overtime (unpaid) to get ahead. After a few more years with the company, you still fail to get the recognition you think you deserve, but if you leave, you will lose numerous benefits, including a vested interest in the company's pension plan. Do you quit?

You have invested a great deal of time, effort, and resources, but things are not working out the way that you would have liked. Escalation of commitment becomes a factor when decision makers commit themselves to an irrational course of action as a means of justifying previous commitments. In the preceding example, escalation of commitment would exist if you decided to stay at the job to keep your benefits even though the job does not support your original goal of developing your career.

The sense of commitment to past investment decisions can unduly weigh on your future decisions. As a result, you may make a series of "bad" decisions that have required a greater investment than you originally anticipated. Ironically, attempting to avoid admitting a mistake by continuing to invest in a losing proposition can result in a far greater error.

Status Quo Bias

In its extreme form, confirmation bias can lead individuals to be resistant to change and to favor the status quo. Most individuals are more comfortable with what they know and have experienced than with the unknown, which is one reason why organizational change, discussed in Chapter 11, can be so difficult. This resistance to change is often ingrained in companies where risk-taking is discouraged and failure is publicly punished. In these situations, individuals often prefer to do nothing rather than risk being publicly embarrassed or, worse, being fired. This tendency

Confirmation bias
A bias in which people tend to seek information that confirms a decision before seeking information that disconfirms a decision, even if the disconfirming information is more powerful and important.

Escalation of commitment
Occurs when decision makers commit themselves to a particular course of action beyond the level suggested by rationality as a means of justifying previous commitments.

to favor the "here and now" is called the **status quo bias**.[40] In such situations, we tend to overweight the information that supports what we know and neglect any information that supports beneficial changes.

Mutual fund companies often struggle to convince individuals to save for their retirement, especially when the actual retirement can be decades away. Even though there is considerable data to support the benefits of retirement savings, individuals are often reluctant to participate. Some of the resistance is due to the plethora of information and choices about investment options; too many choices can be paralyzing. Another form of resistance is time. Many individuals can't picture their retirement years and thus choose not to focus on it. To combat this issue, one group of researchers showed individuals a computer-generated photo of them at age 70. When individuals saw the 70-year-old version of themselves, they were more likely to consider retirement investing.[41] The simple act of seeing a version of themselves in the future was helpful in breaking through the status quo bias. Without this trigger, it is often hard for individuals to conceptualize themselves in retirement, and this lack of conceptualization leads to inaction.

Framing

Framing refers to a decision-making bias that arises from alternative presentations of the same information that in turn can significantly alter a decision.[42] In particular, it starts with the idea that when we examine two choices as choosing between possible losses, we take the riskier option. But when we frame those same choices as choosing between possible gains, we take the risk-averse option. Many situations can be framed as either a set of gains or losses and that, in turn, can impact our willingness to take risks. As a result, how we frame the choice in our mind or how it's presented to us can impact how much risk we are willing to take. Acknowledging the framing bias is important because it suggests that decision making and the associated risk can be affected by the way we frame those choices.

For example, a sales manager may consider an acquisition decision in terms of the perceived gains it might provide; however, a risk manager may consider an acquisition in terms of the perceived losses it might generate. Because these two managers use different frames, each individual's opinion on the prospective acquisition differs. Although differences between frames should have no effect on a rational decision, research shows that it can. Consider the following scenario of a possible disease outbreak.[43]

Imagine that the United States is preparing for the outbreak of a rare disease that is expected to kill 600 people. Two alternative programs to combat the disease have been proposed. Assume that the exact scientific estimates of the consequences of the programs are as follows:

Program A: If Program A is adopted, 200 people will be saved.
Program B: If Program B is adopted, there is a one-third probability that 600 people will be saved and a two-thirds probability that no people will be saved.

Which of the two programs would you favor?

To think through this decision, you might select the alternative that provides the best overall outcome. In the preceding scenario, however, the expected values of the two programs are equal. Program A will definitely save 200 lives, and Program B has a one-third chance of saving 600 lives, or 200 lives on average. Research has shown that most people choose Program A, a risk-averse choice. Note that the choices were framed as "gains" and this framing in turn triggers us to typically choose the risk-averse option, which is what you typically see in the experiments done with these choices.

Status quo bias
The tendency to favor the "here and now" and to reject potential change.

Framing
Alternative presentations of the same information that can significantly alter a decision.

Consider, though, a second version of the problem where we frame the identical choices above as possible losses. Note that the two choices are identical to those above except they have been phrased as losses instead of as gains.

Imagine that the United States is preparing for the outbreak of a rare disease that is expected to kill 600 people. Two alternative programs to combat the disease have been proposed. Assume that the scientific estimates of the consequences of the programs are as follows:

Program C: If Program C is adopted, 400 people will die.
Program D: If Program D is adopted, there is a one-third probability that no one will die and a two-thirds probability that 600 people will die.

Which of the two programs would you favor?

Whereas most people choose the risk-averse Program A in the first scenario, they tend to choose the risk-seeking Program D in the second scenario. Researchers have explained that individuals treat risks concerning perceived gains (i.e., saving lives) differently from risks concerning perceived losses (i.e., losing lives). When people make decisions regarding losses, they are risk-seeking, but when they make decisions regarding gains, they are risk-averse. Research has shown that decision makers are twice as likely to avoid losses as they are to favor gains.[44] If the choice between programs in the scenario were made based on the rational maximization of expected utility model, the framing of choices should not affect decisions.

Knowledge of biases is important because it allows us to begin to understand why our decisions are less rational than we assume or than they appear. This discussion also opens the door for understanding a number of other factors that can influence decision making and detract from rationality, namely emotions and social pressures.

THE IMPACT OF EMOTIONS AND SOCIAL SITUATIONS ON DECISION MAKING

In the past, behavioral decision research had focused primarily on the ways in which bias impacts decision makers without devoting much attention to the role that emotion plays in the decision-making process. New research on decision making reveals that decisions can be driven by an unconscious emotional evaluation even before any cognitive reasoning takes place.[45]

Emotions

Although researchers are just beginning to understand the role of emotions in decision making, some of the most conclusive studies have shown how specific positive and negative emotions can affect judgment. As we noted previously, emotionally charged situations are often easier to recall and can have a disproportionate impact on one's decision making. Emotions are also a key determinant in the hiring process. One recent study of hiring managers for consulting firms found that 80% of hiring managers "spontaneously reported using their own emotions to evaluate job candidates."[46]

Creating a context that helps to channel certain emotions has been useful for specific businesses. Some studies have even shown that people in good moods are more optimistic and that people in bad moods are more pessimistic.[47] Companies that rely on the mood of their customers to buy more have paid careful attention to this research. Casinos, for example, play on emotional manipulations to put their customers in a good mood, which encourages them to feel more optimistic and bet more money. Casinos pay acute attention to décor, music, and ambiance. The lack of visible clocks and simulated natural daylight in casinos also produce a steady, euphoric feeling 24 hours per day.[48]

Other research has found that fear and anxiety can create risk-averse behaviors and that feelings of regret associated with action versus inaction can differ. One study investigated why an investor who sells his stock and finds out he would have done better had he not sold regrets his decision more than another investor who considers selling her stock, but does not sell it and later finds out she would have made more money had she sold. Although both investors lost out on the same potential earnings, people feel greater regret for their choices to act rather than their choices not to act.[49]

Social Situations

Although the rational framework emphasizes the process that individuals should use to make decisions, it downplays the impact that social influences have on those individuals when they are making choices. Anthropologists, psychologists, and sociologists have argued that since decision making tends to occur in social settings, it is important to consider how social situations can influence individuals and their decisions. By investigating decisions in this way, we find that social situations do influence individuals and that we may systematically deviate from rationality.

Solomon Asch, a social psychologist, conducted a famous experiment that highlighted an individual's tendency to conform to the majority. During the study, the experimenter told a series of groups of eight male college students (one subject and seven others who pretended to be subjects) that they would be participating in a psychological experiment. The experiment informed them that they would be comparing the lengths of lines and showed them two large white cards—one with a single vertical black line and the other with three vertical lines of various lengths. The group's charge was to match one of the three lines on the second card to the single line on the first card. One of the three lines actually matched the single line, but the other two were slightly larger or smaller.

In the first two rounds, every person in the group chose the same matching line, but in the third round, disagreement began. In rounds three and four, one person, who made his choice after most of the rest of the group, looked surprised when he disagreed with all of the others and became more worried when he disagreed with the others who were unanimous in their choice. What the subject did not know was that the others had been instructed by the experimenter to give incorrect answers in unanimity at certain points in the experiment. Occasionally, however, the majority reported correct answers so that the subject would not be suspicious. The final results showed that some subjects remain convinced of their own responses while others conformed to the erroneous majority.

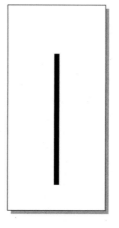

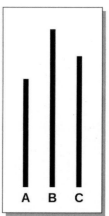

After debriefing each of the subjects, Asch discovered that those who were confident in their convictions had the capacity to recover from self-doubt. Others who continued to disagree with the majority began to believe that the majority was correct, but they kept dissenting because they felt obligated to reveal what they actually saw. The individuals who gave in to the majority believed that they were wrong and the majority was right. Some did not want to "spoil" the results of the experiment; they believed that the majority was a victim of an optical illusion, but despite this conviction, they did not want to be a contrarian voice.

The Asch experiments reveal an interesting perspective about consensus and conformity.[50] When individuals rely less on their experience and insight and more on "majority rule," conformity dominates. This supremacy of conformity can cause reasonably intelligent people to make decisions that go against their own assessment. In extreme situations it can also lead us to go against our values. While the Asch experiments show how social conformity can lead us to deviate from our own beliefs and even engage in nonrational decision making, there are also situations where following social norms can produce more optimal outcomes. Researchers have argued that social decisions involving norms are generally shaped by an **appropriateness framework** in which people ask themselves questions like, "What does a person like me do in a situation like this?" or "How do other people understand this kind of situation?"[51] These questions imply that to make decisions that are prescriptive in nature, individuals should be aware of how society views potential outcomes.

Research has also shown that individuals who are confronted with situations involving social norms tend to compromise by "splitting the difference" or by defecting. For example, individuals often divide a restaurant bill 50–50, even when one individual ordered more. In essence, an individual will cooperate as long as he or she is assured that his or her partner will cooperate as well. Trust becomes a key issue. Yet, if one individual decides not to pay his or her fair share, another individual may make the same decision to defect. Thus, the bill is short and none of the individuals can legitimately leave the restaurant until the bill is settled. As a result, decision makers may not view compromising as the best option, but as the option that provides the least hassle.[52]

This discussion on the ways in which social factors can influence decisions is important. It supports researchers' theories that a number of factors, including ambiguous information, biases, emotion, and intuition, can cause individuals to deviate from the rational decision-making process. This evidence has not only shaped how decision making is studied at the individual level but also paved the way for how decisions are investigated in an organizational setting.

DECISION MAKING IN ORGANIZATIONS

We now know that because individual decision making is subject to a number of influences, it can deviate from rationality. This notion holds true in organizations as well, but in an organizational context, the fact that there are multiple decision makers creates its own set of dynamics and complexity. In this section we will explore how the process of making decisions in organizations can vary substantially and become even less rational.

Programmed versus Nonprogrammed Decisions

Decisions in organizations vary widely based on the extent to which the decision-making process is programmed.[53] **Programmed decisions** are applied to repetitive, well-defined problems with a set of preestablished alternatives. If a problem recurs often enough, a routine procedure will usually be worked out to solve it. Examples of programmed decisions include pricing regular customers' orders and reordering office supplies. Programmed decisions generally do not require a manager or higher-level employee to execute. They also do not require social consensus.

In contrast, **nonprogrammed decisions** are made in response to novel, poorly defined, or unstructured situations. Nonprogrammed decisions are made under conditions of risk and uncertainty in which limited information exists. As a result,

Appropriateness framework
The process of making decisions based on societal norms or expectations.

Programmed decisions
Decisions that are made in response to recurring organizational problems that require individuals to follow established rules and procedures.

Nonprogrammed decisions
Decisions that are made in response to novel, poorly defined, or unstructured situations that require managers to use their best judgments.

managers may need to rely on their best judgments to make a decision. Examples of nonprogrammed decisions are whether to relocate company headquarters to a new market and how to integrate a newly acquired firm.[54] Many of the strategic choices discussed in the first three parts of this book fall under the category of nonprogrammed decisions.

It is important to distinguish between programmed and nonprogrammed decisions because different techniques are used to make each type of decision. Programmed decisions require managers to rely on habit, standard operating procedures, common expectations, and well-defined information channels to make the most appropriate decisions.[55] In general, these types of decisions are best made through rational analysis that explicitly prespecifies how those decisions will be made, leaving little discretion or doubt on what is to be done. In contrast, nonprogrammed decisions require managers to rely on rational thought processes as well as heuristics and intuitive judgment. Nonprogrammed decisions are also highly susceptible to social and political influences. All the decision processes we described come into play for the individuals involved in those decisions. This is further complicated by the fact that there are multiple decision makers who come to the decision process with their own set of biases.

Models of Organizational Decision Making

Decision making in organizations depends on whether the decision is programmed or nonprogrammed and the extent to which the decision is characterized by information ambiguity—in other words, how clear the objectives are, how accessible the information is, and how certain the risk is. In organizations, managers approach decision making using one of four models: the **classical model**, the **administrative model**, the **political model**, or the **garbage can model**. The first two models are generally applied to individual decision making within organizations, while the other two models are used in broader group decision-making situations within organizations.

The Classical (Rational) Model

The classical model of decision making seeks to maximize economic or other outcomes using a rational choice process. This process generally includes the various steps outlined in Figure 15.1:

- The decision maker aims to accomplish organizational goals.
- The decision maker strives for conditions of certainty by gathering complete information, defining all possible alternatives, and calculating the potential results of each.
- The decision maker uses logic to assign values, prioritize, evaluate alternatives, and make decisions that will maximize the attainment of organizational goals.[56]

This model is used when managers have enough time and have access to the relevant information needed to make an informed, logical decision.

The Administrative Model

In contrast to the classical model, the administrative model describes how managers make nonprogrammed decisions. This model acknowledges that managers may be unable to make economically rational decisions even if they want to because they lack sufficient information on which to base their decisions. Bounded rationality and satisficing are central to the administrative model, meaning managers, due to time constraints, will opt for the first option that appears to solve the problem, even though better options may exist. The administrative model also accounts for

Classical model
A model of decision making that seeks to maximize economic or other outcomes using a rational choice process.

Administrative model
A model of decision making that acknowledges that managers may be unable to make economically rational decisions even if they want to because they lack sufficient information on which to base their decisions.

Political model
A model of decision making that acknowledges that most organizational decisions involve many managers who have different goals and who have to share information to reach an agreement.

Garbage can model
A model of decision making whereby problems, solutions, participants, and choices flow throughout an organization. This decision process is not viewed as a sequence of steps that begins with a problem and ends with a solution.

the fact that managers often rely on their base of knowledge and experience, or intuition, to make decisions. They tend to look for patterns that resemble something familiar to accelerate the decision-making process.

The Political Model

Like the administrative model, the political model of decision making is also valuable for making nonprogrammed decisions. The political model departs from the administrative model in that it acknowledges that most organizational decisions involve many managers who have different goals and who have to share information to reach an agreement.[57] Because interests, goals, and values differ, managers may disagree about problem priorities and may not understand or share in the goals and interests of other managers.[58] As a result, managers using the political model need to bargain and build coalitions with other managers in order to get decisions made or implemented. Therefore, a manager's inability to bargain or build coalitions often results in poor or less informed decisions. We will learn more about negotiation in Chapter 16.

The Garbage Can Model

Whereas the classical, administrative, and political models focus on how a single decision is made, the garbage can model focuses on multiple decisions being made throughout an organization. In the garbage can model, the decision-making process is not viewed as a sequence of steps that begins with a problem and ends with a solution. Rather, a solution may be proposed when no problem is specified or a problem may exist without a plausible solution. Under this model, organizational decision making takes on a random, unpredictable quality that can seem disorderly.[59]

Though most managers tend to consider goal setting to be important and reward it accordingly, this adherence to strict goals can prevent one from seeing the value in doing things for which there is no good reason immediately apparent. Although the act of doing things without clear goals can be considered "foolish," it can also help organizations explore possibilities that they might not otherwise consider. James March calls this encouraging **playfulness**. According to March, playfulness is the deliberate, temporary relaxation of rules to explore as many possible alternatives as possible.[60] Playfulness is particularly important when organizations are attempting to spark innovation or creativity. The relaxation of rules, however, must be temporary. Eventually, a decision needs to be made. The goal of playfulness is to encourage the consideration of alternatives and approaches that may not otherwise be identified and evaluated.

IMPROVING DECISION-MAKING SKILLS

At the beginning of this chapter, we introduced the notion that individuals can consciously choose to make decisions that result in optimal outcomes but that most choices are shaped by a variety of factors. How do managers prepare for inevitable problems? How do they ensure that they make the best possible decisions with limited information? Managers can use different tools to develop their decision-making skills. A common way to make better decisions, regardless of the situation, is to carefully consider several alternatives and perspectives. But even before that, managers must be aware that they may be susceptible to biases.

Playfulness
The deliberate, temporary relaxation of rules to explore many possible alternatives.

Managing Your Biases

The only way to prevent biases from impacting decision making is to better understand them. The following actions can help to "de-bias" your judgments:[61]

- *Acquire experience and expertise.* Develop awareness for what constitutes rational decision making and learn to recognize biases that limit your rationality (e.g., escalation of commitment and adjustment).
- *Reduce bias in your judgment.* Reduce or eliminate your biases by first "unfreezing" ingrained thinking and behaviors. This step will help you consider alternative information. Then "change" your decision-making process by explaining why your bias exists and what underlies it. Accept that everyone is subject to judgment biases. Finally, "refreeze" your new thoughts by examining your decisions for bias on an ongoing basis.
- *Engage in analogical reasoning.* Engage in training that uses cases, simulations, and real-world experiences to solve problems and make decisions. This training should allow you to improve your ability to conceptualize situations. Taking away an abstract message can increase the likelihood that you will be able to generalize these lessons and apply them to different decision-making contexts.
- *Take an outsider's view.* When making a decision, invite an outsider to share his or her insight or thoughts about the situation. This process allows you to challenge your existing perspective and consider an issue from a different vantage point.
- *Implement statistical models.* Use statistical or other computer software to build models that analyze and evaluate future decisions.
- *Understand biases in others.* Understand the biases that others have shown across a wide range of decisions and adjust your actions so that you do not follow in their footsteps.

Preparing for Tough Calls

Tough calls or high-stakes decisions often include situations in which information is ambiguous, values conflict, and experts disagree. In these cases, there are often no right or easy answers. One way in which managers can prepare for these inevitable decisions is to follow a process that a team of researchers has called SCRIPTS:[62]

1. *Search for signals of threats and opportunities.* Identify threats and opportunities when they are small and manageable.
2. *Find the causes.* Conduct a root-cause analysis. Determine the sequence of events that led to the incident. Seek answers to the "why" question. Recognize that a single cause can generate many symptoms and may share symptoms with other causes. Understand that there may be more than one root cause.
3. *Evaluate the risks.* Consider the consequences and the probabilities of the mistake and the missed opportunity. Acknowledge losses that occurred in the past to be "sunk" costs that should not impact current decisions.
4. *Apply intuition and emotion.* Use intuition and emotion when you want to double-check rational decisions, when crisis situations develop, and when a rational process cannot help you choose between two options.
5. *Consider different perspectives.* Challenge your biases. Ask for other opinions.
6. *Consider the time frame.* Minimize the negative effects of time pressure on crisis decisions by preplanning and rehearsing.
7. *Solve the problem.*

The Leadership Development Journey

High-reliability organizations (HROs) are organizations with systems that are aligned with the goal of avoiding potentially catastrophic errors. By virtue of their services, organizations such as airlines, nuclear power plants, and hospitals must be HROs. HROs are always ready to confront the unexpected, and they excel at consistency and effectiveness. Leaders in HROs make decisions by:

- not becoming preoccupied with their successes and instead focusing on analyzing failures;
- relying on the experts who work on the front line;
- learning from the unexpected;
- embracing complexity and not simplifying facts; and
- anticipating that there are limits to cognitive and operational capacity but committing to being resilient if failure occurs.[63]

Reflect upon a time when you applied, or should have applied, the decision-making practices of HROs. What type of situation demanded that you use the decision-making practices of HROs? Based on this experience, what did you learn about the importance of reliability when making a decision?

Using SCRIPTS may allow you to increase the flexibility and speed of your decisions as well as send a signal that you can effectively manage crises and make risky decisions, thus improving your confidence and the confidence that others have in your decision-making abilities.

SUMMARY

LO1 Decision making includes a process of identifying issues and choosing between alternative courses of action. The rational decision-making process generally includes six steps: (1) defining the problem or opportunity, (2) identifying the goals and objectives, (3) weighting the objectives based on the level of importance of each, (4) outlining possible courses of action, (5) rating each alternative according to the objectives and goals, and (6) determining an optimal solution.

LO2 In reality, managers often do not have all the necessary information to make the best decisions. As a result, rationality is constrained. Managers generally need to make decisions based on incomplete or ambiguous information. In many cases, managers have to opt for a solution that is "good enough," called satisficing, because they do not have the time or resources to consider every possible option. Sometimes individuals rely on their intuition to make a decision. While intuition can be helpful in making quick judgment calls, it can also be dangerous in complex situations, when relying on intuition may result in discounting new information or perspectives.

LO3 Decisions are often influenced by a number of biases. One group of biases is called cognitive heuristics, which include availability, representativeness, and adjustment. The availability heuristic contends that an individual makes a decision based on his or her recall of similar events or situations. The representativeness heuristic denotes decisions based on previously formed stereotypes. The adjustment heuristic refers to decisions being based on a certain starting point. Individuals are also susceptible to other forms of bias, including confirmation, escalation of commitment, status quo, and framing. With the confirmation bias, individuals place greater weight on information that confirms or favors his or her point of view and discounts any evidence that contradicts it. With escalation of commitment, individuals become emotionally committed to a course of action even when continued investment in that action is counterproductive. Individuals who succumb to the status quo bias are reluctant to change; they prefer what they already know. Finally, the way a decision is framed can significantly influence the choices that are made.

LO4 Although individuals should strive to make rational decisions, emotion can impact the decision-making process. Specific situations or contexts also play a role in decision making as they can provide cues to what is or is not socially appropriate. Individuals may choose to do what is socially expedient instead of exploring all alternatives.

LO5 Rational decision making is especially challenging at the organizational level because many individuals can affect the decision-making process. To make effective decisions in the context of an organization, it is important to understand how decisions are made in these environments. Thus, four decision-making models are used to analyze how decisions are made in organizations: the classical (rational) model, the administrative model, the political model, and the garbage can model.

LO6 Because decision making is subject to a number of influences that can enable it to depart from rationality, managers need to understand these influences. It is important to balance rational and intuitive decision-making processes to ensure that alternatives and choices are evaluated in an expedient, yet complete manner. Understanding biases and ways to limit their impact contributes to a more effective decision making process.

KEY TERMS

Adjustment heuristic
Administrative model
Ambiguity
Appropriateness framework
Availability heuristic
Bounded rationality
Classical model
Conditions of certainty
Conditions of risk

Conditions of uncertainty
Confirmation bias
Decision making
Escalation of commitment
Framing
Garbage can model
Heuristics
Intuitive decision making
Nonprogrammed decisions

Playfulness
Political model
Programmed decisions
Representativeness heuristic
Satisficing
Status quo bias
Theory of rational choice

ASSIGNMENTS

Discussion Topics

1. Think about the decisions of your past managers, teachers, or coaches. How rational were they in their decision-making process? How much did they succumb to their emotions?

2. Think about the decisions that you have made regarding your course of study or career. What has guided your decisions? Do you rely more on rational decision-making processes or intuition? Are there certain decisions for which intuition has been more valuable?

3. Why do people think that they are more rational in their decision making than they actually are?

4. When making decisions that are constrained by time or information, what can managers do to

ensure a better outcome? What are the potential dangers of satisficing?

5. How do heuristics help or hinder the decision-making process? Which heuristic do you tend to rely on the most? Why? Do you think one heuristic is more problematic than another?

6. In *Blink*, Malcolm Gladwell encourages individuals to listen to their gut to make quick decisions. What are the advantages and disadvantages of this approach? When individuals rely on gut instinct, what biases are they susceptible to?

7. Think of a time when you have been caught up in the escalation of commitment. How did the commitment escalate? What did you do to reverse the cycle of commitment? What signs could you look for in the future?

8. How do social situations and peer pressure impact decision making? Why are certain individuals more likely to be influenced by peers or social situations than others?

9. Under what conditions should an organization use the garbage can model of decision making?

10. Biases can often result in suboptimal decisions. Are there, however, certain decisions or situations in which biases can be constructive?

Management Research

1. Think about the way you selected which college to attend. What criteria did you consider? How did you make your decision? What percentage of the decision was based on rational analysis? What percentage was based on nonrational factors?

2. Identify a decision that you view as unethical. Explain why you think this decision is unethical. Do you think any of the following biases negatively influenced this decision-making process? If so, which ones?
   - Confirmation
   - Availability
   - Representativeness
   - Adjustment
   - Escalation of commitment
   - Framing

In the Field

Consult with a person who would like to start a business. Take notes while you guide that person through the rational decision-making process by having that person perform the following tasks:

1. Define the business opportunity.
2. Identify the business objectives.
3. Weight the business objectives according to importance.
4. Identify a few possible courses of action.
5. Evaluate each course of action based on each of the business objectives.
6. Decide upon the optimal course of action for that person to start a business.

Be prepared to share your notes about the decision-making process with your classmates.

ENDNOTES

[1] Richard M. Cyert, Herbert A. Simon, and Donald B. Trow, "Observation of a Business Decision," *Management Decision Making*, L. A. Welsch and Ronald M. Cyert, eds. (Harmondsworth, England: Penguin Books, 1970).

[2] R. Duane Ireland and C. Chet Miller, "Decision-Making and Firm Success," *Academy of Management Executive*, Vol. 18, No. 4, 2004, pp. 8–12; and Kathleen M. Eisenhardt, "Strategy as Decision Making," *Sloan Management Review*, Spring 1999, pp. 65–72.

[3] Elbanna Said and John Child, "The Influence of Decision, Environmental and Firm Characteristics on the Rationality of Strategic Decision-Making," *Journal of Management Studies*, Vol. 44, No. 4, 2007, pp. 561–591.

[4] Thomas J. DeLong, Christopher Chang, and Scott Schweitzer, "Coach Roy Williams; What's Next? (A)," Harvard Business School Case No. 9-405-070, rev. October 25, 2005 (Boston, MA: HBS Publishing, 2005), p. 3.

[5] Ibid., p. 11.

[6] Ibid., p. 8.

[7] Ibid., p. 3.

[8] Ibid.

[9] Ibid., pp. 6–7.

[10] Ibid., p. 4.

[11] Ibid., p. 5.

[12] Ibid., p. 7.

[13] John von Neumann and Oskar Morgenstern, *Theory of Games and Economic Behavior* (Princeton, NJ: Princeton University Press, 1944).

[14] James G. March and J. P. Olsen, "Organizational Choice under Ambiguity," *Ambiguity and Choice in Organizations*, James G. March and J. P. Olsen, eds. (Oslo: Universitetsforlaget, 1976), p. 67.

[15] Katherine Milkman, Dolly Chugh, and Max Bazerman, "Intuition vs. Deliberation: How Decision Making Can Be Improved," *Rotman Magazine*, Winter 2010, pp. 23–27.

[16] Herbert A. Simon, *Administrative Behavior: A Study of Decision-Making in Administrative Organizations*, 3rd edition (New York, NY: The Free Press, 1976).

[17] K. J. Radford, *Managerial Decision Making* (Reston, VA: Reston Publishing Company, 1975).

[18] Ibid.

[19] Erik Dane and Michael G. Pratt, "Exploring Intuition and Its Role in Managerial Decision Making," *Academy of Management Review*, Vol. 32, No. 1, 2007, pp. 33–54; C. Chet Miller and R. Duane Ireland, "Intuition in Strategic Decision Making: Friend or Foe in the Fast-Paced 21st Century?," *Academy of Management Executive*, Vol. 19, No. 1, 2005, pp. 19–30; and Weston H. Agor, "The Logic of Intuition: How Top Executives Make Important Decisions," *Organizational Dynamics*, Winter 1986, pp. 5–18.

[20] Eric Bonadeau, "Don't Trust Your Gut," *Harvard Business Review*, May 2003, pp. 116–121.

[21] Malcolm Gladwell, *Blink: The Power of Thinking Without Thinking* (Boston, MA: Back Bay Books, 2005).

[22] Ibid., p. 23.

[23] Ibid., pp. 61–62.

[24] Ibid., p. 63.

[25] J. Haidt, "The Emotional Dog and Its Rational Tail: A Social Intuitionist Approach to Moral Judgment," *Psychological Review*, Vol. 108, No. 4, 2001, pp. 814–834.

[26] C. Chet Miller and R. Duane Ireland, "Intuition in Strategic Decision Making: Friend or Foe in the Fast-Paced 21st Century?," *Academy of Management Executive*, Vol. 19, No. 1, 2005, pp. 19–30.

[27] Eric Bonadeau, "Don't Trust Your Gut," *Harvard Business Review*, May 2003, pp. 116–121.

[28] Herbert A. Simon, "Making Management Decisions: The Role of Intuition and Emotion," *Academy of Management Executive*, February 1987, pp. 57–64.

[29] S. Trevis Certo, Brian L. Connelly, and Laszlo Tihanyi, "Managers and Their Not-So Rational Decisions," *Business Horizons*, Vol. 51, 2008, pp. 113–119.

[30] Max H. Bazerman, *Judgment in Managerial Decision Making*, 6th edition (Hoboken, NJ: John Wiley & Sons, 2006), pp. 8–9.

[31] Ibid.

[32] Ibid., p. 9.

[33] Marianne Bertrand and Sendhil Mullainathan, "Are Emily and Greg More Employable than Lakisha and Jamal? A Field Experiment on Labor Market Discrimination," *The American Economic Review*, September 2004, pp. 991–1013.

[34] Amos Tversky and Daniel Kahneman, "Judgment under Uncertainty: Heuristics and Biases," *Science*, New Series, Vol. 185, No. 4157, 1974, pp. 1124–1131.

[35] John S. Hammond, Ralph L. Keeney, and Howard Raiffa, "The Hidden Traps in Decision Making," *Harvard Business Review*, January 2006, pp. 118–126.

[36] Max H. Bazerman and Dolly Chugh, "Decisions Without Blinders," *Harvard Business Review*, January 2006, pp. 88–97.

[37] Max H. Bazerman, *Judgment in Managerial Decision Making*, 6th edition (Hoboken, NJ: John Wiley & Sons, 2006), p. 36.

[38] B. M. Staw, "Knee-Deep in the Big Muddy: A Study of Escalating Commitment to a Chosen Course of Action," *Organizational Behavior & Human Decision Processes*, Vol. 16, No. 1, 1976, pp. 27–44.

[39] Max H. Bazerman, *Judgment in Managerial Decision Making*, 6th edition (Hoboken, NJ: John Wiley & Sons, 2006), pp. 81–82.

[40] John S. Hammond, Ralph L. Keeney, and Howard Raiffa, "The Hidden Traps in Decision Making," *Harvard Business Review*, January 2006, pp. 118–126.

[41] Geoff Colvin, "Retirement Guide 2011: Take Control and Win," *Fortune*, June 13, 2011.

[42] Max H. Bazerman, *Judgment in Managerial Decision Making*, 6th edition (Hoboken, NJ: John Wiley & Sons, 2006), p. 43.

[43] Ibid., p. 41.

[44] S. Trevis Certo, Brian L. Connelly, and Laszlo Tihanyi, "Managers and Their Not-So Rational Decisions," *Business Horizons*, Vol. 51, 2008, pp. 113–119.

[45] Nitin Nohria and Bridget Gurtler, "Note on Human Behavior: Reason and Emotion," Harvard Business School Note No. 9-404-104 (Boston, MA: HBS Publishing, 2004).

[46] Lauren Rivera, "Go with Your Gut: Emotion and Evaluation in Job Interviews," *American Journal of Sociology*, Vol. 120, 2015.

[47] G. V. Bodenhausen, S. Gabriel, and M. Lineberger, "Sadness and Susceptibility to Judgmental Bias: The Case of Anchoring," *Psychological Science*, Vol. 11, No. 4, 2000, pp. 320–323.

[48] Megan Lane, "The Psychology of Super-Casinos," *BBS News Magazine*, May 25, 2006, http://news.bbc.co.uk/2/hi/uk_news/magazine/5013038.stm

[49] Daniel Kahneman and Amos Tversky, "Psychology of Preferences," *Scientific American*, Vol. 246, 1982, pp. 161–173; and M. Spranca, E. Minsk, and J. Baron,

"Omission and Commission in Judgment and Choice," *Journal of Experimental Social Psychology*, Vol. 27, 1991, pp. 76–105.

[50] Solomon Asch, "Opinions and Social Pressure," www.panarchy.org/asch/social.pressure.1955.html, accessed August 18, 2008.

[51] J. March, *A Primer on Decision-Making: How Decisions Happen* (New York: Free Press, 1994).

[52] Max H. Bazerman, "The Mind of the Negotiator: The Dangers of Compromise," *Negotiation*, February 2005, p. 3.

[53] James G. March and Herbert A. Simon, *Organizations* (Hoboken, NJ: John Wiley & Sons, 1958).

[54] Ibid.

[55] Ibid.

[56] Ibid., p. 275.

[57] Paul J. H. Shoemaker, "Strategic Decisions in Organizations: Rational and Behavioral Views," *Journal of Management Studies*, Vol. 30, No. 1, 1993, pp. 107–129.

[58] James G. March and Herbert A. Simon, *Organizations* (Hoboken, NJ: John Wiley & Sons, 1958), p. 280.

[59] R. Daft, *Organization Theory and Design*, 4th edition (New York, NY: West Publishing Company, 1993), p. 364.

[60] James G. March, "The Technology of Foolishness," *Ambiguity and Choice in Organizations*, James March and J. P. Olsen, eds. (Oslo: Universitetsforlaget, 1972), pp. 69–81.

[61] Max H. Bazerman, *Judgment in Managerial Decision Making*, 6th edition. (Hoboken, NJ: John Wiley & Sons, 2006), pp. 189–206.

[62] J. K. Murnighan and J. C. Mowen, *The Art of High-Stakes Decision-Making: Tough Calls in a Speed-Driven World* (New York, NY: John Wiley & Sons, 2002), pp. 64–65.

[63] K. E. Weick and K. M. Sutcliffe, *Managing the Unexpected: Resilient Performance in an Age of Uncertainty*, 2nd edition (San Francisco, CA: Jossey-Bass, 2007).

CHAPTER

16

Conflict and Negotiation

Learning Objectives

After reading this chapter, you should be able to:

LO1 Explain the difference between interpersonal conflict and intergroup conflict.

LO2 Describe the most common sources of conflict.

LO3 Outline ways in which managers can respond to or manage conflict.

LO4 Differentiate between distributive and integrative negotiations and describe situations in which these two approaches are used.

LO5 Outline the steps involved in preparing to negotiate, explain the difference between creating and claiming value, and describe ways in which biases can influence the negotiation process.

LO6 Describe how cross-cultural differences influence the way negotiations are conducted.

SELF-REFLECTION

What Is Your Conflict Management Approach?

Conflict is an emotional or cognitive response that occurs when the interests, perspectives, and behaviors of one person or group differ from another person or group. Although most people dislike conflict, it can be managed effectively, and it can be constructive. Conflict management styles develop over time based on diverse factors such as life experiences, values, and training. Reflect upon your approach to managing conflict by responding True or False to the following statements:

1. I learned how to manage conflict through familial interactions.

2. I am a competitive person and my conflict management style emphasizes winning.

3. I enjoy engaging in heated arguments.

4. My conflict management style is guided by religious or spiritual beliefs.

5. I rely on collaborative problem solving to resolve conflict.

6. My cultural heritage has influenced my conflict management style.

7. I learned from my childhood and adolescence to avoid conflict.

8. I tend to procrastinate when faced with a difficult conflict.

9. Through my life experiences, I have learned that compromising is the best way to resolve conflict.

10. I try to appease everyone in a conflict situation.

Based on your responses, how would you characterize your conflict management approach? What life experiences influenced your conflict management style? What can others learn from your conflict management approach?

INTRODUCTION

When you disagree with someone, do you address the issue head-on? Do you try to find common ground? Or do you avoid the issue, not wanting to cause a problem or escalate the situation? Some people enjoy the excitement and thrill that comes from arguing their point of view and convincing others to support their perspective. They are energized by debate. Many politicians and pundits fall into this category. So too do effective sales executives. At the other end of the spectrum are people who would rather smooth over problems or pretend they don't exist to avoid direct confrontation. Most of us, however, operate somewhere in the middle. On certain issues and with some people, we are passionate, engaged, and willing to fight for our agenda. At other times, we tend to hold back, not wanting to hurt someone's feelings or to be hurt ourselves. Regardless of your tendency, you will be faced with many uncomfortable situations. In fact, given the diversity of individuals, functions, and interests in an organization, disagreement is inevitable. As such, learning how to effectively navigate conflict and how to manage negotiations is vitally important.

Encyclopaedia Britannica, Inc. / NASA/Universal Images Group Limited/Alamy

Conflict is an emotional or cognitive response that occurs when interests, perspectives, and behaviors of one individual or group explicitly differ from those of another individual or group. In many cases, conflict can negatively affect a relationship, especially if it escalates and remains unresolved.[1] Conflict can also lead to suboptimal decisions, especially when it prevents new ideas and perspectives from emerging.

While most people dislike conflict because of its negative consequences, avoiding and suppressing conflict is not always appropriate.[2] Suppressing conflict can lead to extreme consensus in decision making that can be dangerous. The Challenger space shuttle explosion on January 8, 1986 is one example of a situation in which consensus led to a disastrous outcome. Despite warning signs, concerns, and indications that a potential disaster existed, the team at NASA suppressed conflicting opinions and launched the space shuttle, which exploded less than a minute after liftoff.[3]

When managed properly, conflict can be constructive and can be stimulated to promote mutual understanding, enhanced performance, greater levels of creativity, and higher-quality decisions.[4] Conflict, however, cannot be allowed to run free indefinitely. At some point, conflict needs to be resolved, and one common approach to resolving conflict is through **negotiation**. Negotiation is a process by which two parties attempt to reach agreement on an issue by offering and reviewing various positions or courses of action.

Every day, people in organizations negotiate to obtain resources, to resolve issues, and to build support for a new idea or concept. Managers negotiate budgets with the finance department. Employees negotiate with team members to divide up tasks. Individuals also negotiate to attain resources and rewards. Working hard and doing a good job should earn recognition and reward, but in many situations, people must negotiate to receive salary increases, change their work schedules, or receive a promotion.[5] In any of these situations, interests can conflict. The key is to find a negotiated and mutually agreeable settlement to the conflict.

In this chapter, we discuss the nature and sources of conflict as it occurs between individuals and groups, as well as the strategies that are used to manage conflict effectively. Because conflict can be both destructive and constructive, understanding the factors that support and inhibit these distinct types of conflict is especially important. Understanding the nature of conflict will also enable you to be a better negotiator. This is significant because the outcomes of negotiations can have a considerable impact on personal motivation and overall business performance. The following case study about Thomas Green illustrates the common conflicts that can occur in a company.

Conflict
An emotional or cognitive response that occurs when interests, perspectives, and behaviors of one individual or group explicitly differ from those of another individual or group.

Negotiation
A process by which two parties attempt to reach agreement on an issue by offering and reviewing various positions or courses of action.

LEVELS OF CONFLICT

Regardless of the organization in which you are a member, you will be working in a group to complete activities and working across groups to accomplish organizational goals. For instance, you may join the sales organization and need to work with other sales professionals to complete duties such as marketing and public relations. You may also need to work with nonsales-related groups such as manufacturing and service teams to ensure that what you sell can be delivered.

Thomas Green at Dynamic Displays[6]

Five months after he had been promoted to his dream job at Dynamic Displays, Thomas Green felt that his job was in jeopardy. He couldn't understand why it had come to this point. He had worked hard since he had joined Dynamic Displays in March 2007. It was his second job after graduating from college 6 years earlier. He had previously worked for National Business Solutions as a sales person, focused on selling automated teller machines (ATMs) solutions to regional banks in the southeast. His success and experience at National Bank Solutions seemed to be a perfect match for Dynamic Displays.

Dynamic Displays was founded as a provider of self-service options for banks via ATMs. As the ATM market became saturated, Dynamic Displays applied their technical expertise to the travel and hospitality sector and developed a line of self-service kiosks used at airports, hotels, and rental car agencies throughout the United States. These self-service kiosks enabled airlines, in particular, to streamline and significantly reduce the cost of the flight check-in process. By 2007, the vast majority of Dynamic Displays' revenues were derived from its hospitality solutions. The company provided full service including hardware, software, engineering, and maintenance.

When Green joined the company, he was based in Atlanta, and he aggressively attacked his role as an account executive. Within a few months, he was able to close a major deal with a large regional airline. At the time, he told a close friend, "I want to come in and dazzle them at Dynamic Displays. I want to be more than an account executive. I had heard that there was a lot of opportunity for fresh talent at corporate headquarters."[7] When he attended a corporate training session in July, he made it a point to get noticed. And he succeeded. Green established quick rapport with Shannon MacDonald, the division vice president, and a fellow alumnus of the University of Georgia.

During the week, Green met with MacDonald on a number of occasions and impressed her with his knowledge of the market opportunities for the company. Through these interactions, Green learned about an open position for a senior market specialist in the corporate office in Boston. Though the position was two levels above his current role, over the next several weeks Green aggressively lobbied for the position. MacDonald agreed to take a chance on Green and offered him the position after being convinced that he had some innovative ideas for the company. In doing so, she said, "Tom, you are obviously a bright and ambitious account executive. You have great rapport with clients. However, I do have a couple of reservations about your lack of managerial experience. You will have to think strategically as well as tactically, and you will have to coordinate between several different functions. I hope you will compensate for your lack of experience by seeking out guidance from some of our more seasoned managers."[8]

The senior market specialist role was responsible for identifying industry trends, evaluating new business opportunities, establishing sales goals, and helping account executives develop appropriate client strategies. In his new role, Green would supervise two account executives and report to Frank Davis, the marketing director. Davis, age 45, had been recently promoted to his position from the role that Green, age 28, now occupied. Green was the company's youngest market specialist by over 10 years.

On his first day in his new role, MacDonald stopped by Green's office and said, "Tom, you are walking into a tricky situation with Frank Davis. Frank had expected to choose the new senior market specialist and it would not have been you. You will have to deal with any fall-out from that. You are getting an unusual opportunity with this promotion. Don't let me down."[9]

During the first few weeks, Davis and Green meet with a number of clients. Davis told Green, "We had some good meetings and the clients responded well to your ideas. However, I think we would have been more effective if we had been able to provide the clients with some market data. When you are on your own, I expect you to spend a significant amount of time preparing for client meetings and developing supporting details for your proposals."[10] Davis's initial impression of Green was that his style was too loose with clients; he was personally persuasive but he did not do the detail work to back up his arguments.

A month into the new role, Green attended a budget review meeting in which Davis presented the revenue targets for the following year including a 10% growth rate for Tom's area. Though Davis had been in Green's role previously, Green felt that the growth rate was inflated. He decided to publicly challenge Davis in the meeting. Green did not want his performance review to be based on what he considered unrealistic expectations. Davis was upset with Green for challenging him and did not back down on the projections. Since Davis had personally achieved the 10% growth target in the previous five years, he saw no need to revise it. Still reeling from the meeting, Davis approached MacDonald and said, "Thomas's negative attitude is not what we need on this team. He is thinking like an account executive who is only concerned with the sales target. In a senior specialist position, he has to think outside the box and develop strategies to capture that aggressive growth target."[11]

A few weeks after the budget meeting, Davis met with Green to hold a quick performance check-in, which was a customary practice in the company. Though Green knew that Davis was upset about the budget meeting, he felt that the rest of his performance was on track. He had a number of productive client meetings and was pursuing some promising new business opportunities. Davis did not feel the same way. Davis was upset that Green had several meetings with clients and had not prepared the necessary supporting materials. In addition, Davis was concerned that he did not actually know who Green was meeting with and how he was spending his time. Green rarely checked-in and was often late in responding to Davis's inquiries. For his part, Green did not feel he needed to run everything by Davis, and he resented being told what to do. It was clear from the meeting that both parties disagreed on how the job should be performed, how clients should be managed, and how they should interact with each other.

After the meeting, Davis wrote to MacDonald outlining some of his concerns about Green and articulating a plan to improve performance. For his part, after the meeting Green immersed himself in a promising new software application that he believed could enable clients to up-sell and cross-sell

additional services to their customers. In addition, he continued to meet with clients. One of his account executives commented, "Thomas is great when it comes to selling clients his ideas. He is very charismatic and can think quickly on his feet. I really like working for him. However, the clients are starting to ask me for hard data to back up his claims of cost savings. Thomas doesn't really work that way. He would rather talk through the issues face to face."[12]

Over the next few months, Green worked independently on his projects and avoided Davis whenever he could. He realized that avoiding Davis was not a productive way to address the conflict between them, but he felt he had no other choice. Instead of trying to build a relationship with Davis, Green sought support from other managers who were sympathetic to Green's perspective on the growth projections.

When Davis and Green met for their second performance discussion in late January, Davis indicated that he had seen no real progress in Green's performance. He felt that Green was spending too much time complaining about problems and sympathizing with client issues and not enough time developing solutions and documenting his ideas for improvement. Green resented Davis's continued micromanagement. Davis felt that he had no choice, since Green was not delivering on his expected commitments.

After the meeting, Green debated what he should do. Avoiding Davis only seemed to make the situation worse. He still believed that Davis was wrong about the budget but did not know what to do. He could face their conflict in a competitive fashion and look for ways to prove his point of view by gathering data and managerial support from other departments. Another option was to simply accommodate the situation and do what Davis asked even if he thought it was wrong. He was not sure that he could stomach that approach. He hoped that they could find some way to manage the conflict, but was not sure how to go about it.

Case in Point

Thomas Green at Dynamic Displays

1. What is the nature of the conflict between Green and Davis?
2. What are the work styles and personalities of Davis and Green? How have these differences impacted their relationship?
3. How would you assess Green's approach so far?
4. What should Green do?

While working in these groups, conflict can emerge, sometimes between members of the same group (**interpersonal conflict**) and sometimes between groups (**intergroup conflict**). Each has its own set of dynamics.

Interpersonal Conflict

Being part of a group can be rewarding and exciting, especially when each member contributes to the group's activity as well as enhances his or her own learning and development.[13] Groups such as sports teams and activity-based clubs are often unified under a common set of issues, beliefs, and values, which can build group pride. This pride can lead to exceptional outcomes that far surpass what each individual member could accomplish on his or her own.

In group situations, members are dependent on one another for achieving common goals. As a result, there is an increased need to coordinate the team's actions, and team members often need to learn to effectively influence one another. Cooperation arises when individuals perceive that they are working toward common goals and interests. Competition and conflict arise when individuals perceive that one individual's goals come at the expense of another's ability to attain his or her goals.[14]

As discussed in Chapter 14, interdependence exists when two or more individuals must work together to achieve a common goal. The need for interdependence has increased as organizations have moved from formal centralized structures to decentralized network-type structures.[15] In these environments, no one individual or team can accomplish the organization's goals. They must depend on each other, often without formal reporting relationships.

When interdependence exists, incompatible goals and interests are often the basis of interpersonal conflict.[16] Because of this interdependency and pressure to perform, members of less effective groups often blame one or two members for the group's inability to perform rather than place blame on the actions of the group as a whole.[17] While this process leads to the awareness that a conflict exists, it can be divisive, especially when negative emotions such as frustration and anger lead to retaliation.[18]

Interpersonal conflict is often evident in the way in which group members communicate. Conflict can escalate when disagreements become personal and participants spend more time either attacking others or defending themselves. In these contexts, communication is often disrespectful. Avoiding conflict can also ultimately lead to its escalation, especially when the lack of communication leads to assumptions about the motives and intentions of others.

Intergroup Conflict

Groups that are unified under a common set of issues, beliefs, or values can provide members with a sense of pride and can encourage them to develop a sense of loyalty to their specific group or team.[19] As loyalty grows, members unite around in-group positions. While this can be beneficial in promoting cohesion within the group, it can sometimes have a negative impact on the relations of that group with other groups. In particular, the differences between one group and another group can become exaggerated.[20] This can lead to an increase in intergroup conflict.

In many cases, intergroup conflict arises when there is competition among groups over scarce resources.[21] This is especially true when different groups seek funding for capital-intensive projects or other activities. When resources are limited, one group inevitably loses.[22] Staff groups like corporate information technology (IT) teams often find themselves at the center of this type of conflict. With limited time and resources, corporate teams like IT often need to prioritize and rank technology projects. For instance, the marketing group that hoped to unveil a new website may need to wait until the manufacturing department receives a new inventory control system.

Interpersonal conflict
Conflict that occurs between two or more individuals who are members of the same group.

Intergroup conflict
Conflict that occurs between two or more groups.

Intergroup conflict emerges when the other group is viewed as "the enemy." For instance, employees who work on the manufacturing line may view the sales team as "the enemy" if they believe that products have been sold and promises have been made without their input. This is especially true when the promises made to customers require significant changes to the manufacturing process.

While belonging to a group with common interests can increase a person's pride in and loyalty to the group, group members can exaggerate differences between groups, which may lead to rigid stereotypes. Competition, exaggeration of differences, and stereotypes all induce intergroup conflict. **Social identity theory** and **realistic conflict theory** help explain the dynamics underlying some of this intergroup conflict.

Social Identity Theory

Social identity theory proposes that group members of an in-group (a social group that a person identifies with) will seek to find negative aspects of an out-group (a social group that a person does not identify with) to enhance their self-image.[23] In other words, group members develop greater cohesion among themselves by finding an external common enemy, but that enhanced cohesion can escalate conflict with external groups. Researchers have defined the behaviors of in-group members using a three-step process: social categorization, social identification, and social comparison.[24] Social categorization is an attempt to define the norms of the in-group in a way that favors the in-group at the expense of the out-group. "Black," "white," "student," and "professor" are examples of social categories used to understand and identify people. Social identification is an attempt to adopt the identity of the group we have categorized ourselves as belonging to. We do this by conforming to the norms of the group, a behavior that increases pride in the group, increases loyalty to the group, and binds a person's self-esteem with group membership. Social comparison occurs when we define our group in opposition to another. This usually comes about as a response to rivalry and competition between groups. Once two groups identify themselves as rivals, they compete for resources. Through this three-step process, an in-group fosters greater within-group cohesion, which can lead to an increase of intergroup conflict.

Realistic Conflict Theory

Realistic conflict theory was pioneered by social psychologists Muzafer and Carolyn Sherif who proposed that limited resources will lead to conflict between groups and that this is one reason why discrimination and stereotypes exist in society.[25] The research was conducted at a summer camp in Oklahoma. Twenty-two 11-year-old boys with similar backgrounds were divided into two groups in which preexisting friendships were broken up so that each boy's identification in his new group could happen faster. Neither group was aware of the other group's existence. To facilitate this, the groups were assigned to two different living areas that were far apart. Sherif and Sherif observed that intergroup conflict intensified from in-group formation to friction to integration.[26]

During the in-group formation phase, each group was asked to choose a name. One group chose the name "The Rattlers"; the other group chose "The Eagles." These names served as a basis of team affiliation. In addition, the groups spontaneously developed internal social hierarchies in which a leader was designated, group norms (including sanctions for deviating behavior) were developed, and in-group friendships were established.[27] We will discuss more about team process and development in Chapter 17.

Social identity theory
A theory that proposes that group members of an in-group will seek to find negative aspects of an out-group to enhance their self-image.

Realistic conflict theory
A theory that proposes that limited resources will lead to conflict between groups.

The Leadership Development Journey

Issue selling is the process by which an individual influences another person's understanding of a situation, event, or trend. As part of issue selling, individuals collaborate with others to develop their ideas, then effectively present, package, and market the ideas. Issue-selling skills help leaders manage conflict and negotiate. Emergent leaders can issue sell by adhering to the following guidelines:

1. Respect hierarchy.
2. Realize that timing is important.
3. Build a case for their ideas.
4. Present their ideas logically.
5. Propose their ideas continually.
6. Package ideas as incremental.
7. Align ideas with the goals, values, and concerns of other constituents.
8. Involve a diverse group of stakeholders that will contribute to the process or influence its outcome.[28]

Reflect upon a time when you engaged in issue selling or observed another leader engage in this process. What issue selling strategies were used, or could have been used, in that situation for managing conflict or negotiating?

During the friction phase, the two groups were brought together in competitive situations. These competitive situations tended to reinforce identity within the teams. Specifically, the interactions built greater in-group solidarity, supported more respectful in-group interaction, and enhanced in-group friendships. In addition, the competitive situations resulted in greater levels of hostility, name-calling, and fights with the other group. As the groups became more antagonistic toward each other, they also became more cohesive among themselves.

During the final phase, the integration phase, the researchers introduced "superordinate goals." The attainment of the goals required the two teams to work together to find the cause of a drinking water shortage, for example. The researchers discovered that an overarching goal could transcend group identity and create an opportunity for more collaboration and cooperation between groups. Intergroup conflict was essentially reduced when the two groups were forced to work together.

SOURCES OF CONFLICT

Affective Conflict

The very nature of group work requires that individuals with different experiences, backgrounds, and personalities come together to achieve a common goal.[29] **Affective conflict,** also called personal conflict, occurs when disagreements between individuals are attributed to personal differences instead of differences in how to approach a task or problem. When affective conflict emerges, individuals tend to attack each other's personalities through personalized criticism, threats, and insults.[30]

Affective conflict
Conflict occurs when disagreements between individuals are attributed to personal characteristics instead of differences in how to approach a task or problem.

Individuals who are goal- and success-driven report a higher frequency of affective conflict with others like them and also with those who are less goal- and success-driven.[31] Any obstacle to achieving the goal is met with frustration, and sometimes that frustration turns into a personal attack instead of a disagreement about tactics. Similarly, someone with high aspirations because of past achievements, perceived power, or competition is more apt to be susceptible to affective conflict with those who have different backgrounds and motivations.[32]

In many cases, conflict arises when inequality exists in the relationship between two people. For example, when one individual has more power or a higher status in the hierarchy than the other, the weaker person may resist the stronger person's influence or they may see conflict as a way to increase power.[33] Both of these actions can lead to greater levels of affective conflict.

Coworkers experiencing affective conflict tend to be less satisfied with the group in which they are working and tend to feel more negative about their group when they dislike or are disliked by others in the group.[34] Such conflict can cause those involved to lose perspective about the task being performed, which can result in ineffective working relationships, poor individual performance, and suboptimal group productivity.[35]

Cognitive Conflict

While affective conflict results from interpersonal friction, **cognitive conflict**, also called task-related conflict, results from disagreements over work-related issues such as meeting schedules, work assignments, processes, or the task itself. The focus of the conflict here is not about the person; it is about the task at hand.

While affective conflicts are usually destructive, cognitive conflicts can actually have a positive influence on the team. As long as the focus of the conflict remains on task-related differences, teams are more likely to look for ways to reconcile their differences in an effort to reach a better solution. In such instances, the leader should try to foster cognitive conflict while mitigating affective conflict.

A key leadership challenge is that cognitive conflicts can be interpreted as personal attacks, especially by those who have a hard time separating cognitive disagreement from personal conflict. In other words, some people may think that other individuals disagree with them because they dislike them rather than because they simply have different approaches to completing a task. In these instances, cognitive conflict turns into affective conflict. These situations cause tension and unhappiness among group members.[36] A leader's job then is to foster task conflict while ensuring that it doesn't spillover into personal conflict.

As indicated above, a certain level of cognitive conflict can be constructive, especially when it is promoted in situations where groups might be likely to experience **groupthink** or extreme consensus during a decision-making process.[37] Groupthink is the tendency to conform to the consensus viewpoint in group decision making.[38] In these situations, divergent perspectives and approaches that might be extremely important are not adequately considered. Groupthink occurs when team members place consensus above all other criterion, even when the consensus can reflect poor judgment and stymie creativity.[39] Researchers have established the following three key symptoms of groupthink:[40]

- *Overestimation of the group's opinion:* believing that the group is invulnerable to outside influences
- *Close-mindedness:* not soliciting differing perspectives
- *Pressures toward uniformity:* suppressing differing perspectives to maintain harmony

To avoid groupthink in team decision making, leaders should stimulate intellectual debate among team members and reduce concerns about how the team and

Cognitive conflict
Conflict that results from disagreements over work-related issues such as meeting schedules, work assignments, processes, or the task itself.

Groupthink
Extreme consensus during a decision-making process.

Affective Conflict May Lead to:	Cognitive Conflict May Lead to:
• Anger	• Creativity
• Distrust	• Challenge of the status quo
• Frustration	• Personal development
• Stress	• Learning
• Low morale	• Increased motivation
• Withdrawal	• Greater awareness of the problem
• Decreased satisfaction	

Figure 16.1 ⟩ Consequences of Affective and Cognitive Conflict

Source: Adapted from K. Jehn, "Affective and Cognitive Conflict in Work Groups," *Using Conflict in Organizations,* Carsten K. W. De Dreu and Evert Van de Vliert, eds. (London: Sage Publications, 1997).

team members will be viewed by others if they disagree with or reject the status quo. In these cases, it may be appropriate to appoint a devil's advocate to challenge the group's assumptions.[41] While too little conflict can result in groupthink, too much conflict can create stress and disengagement among team members. Successful teams are able to foster moderate levels of cognitive conflict while minimizing affective conflict (see Figure 16.1).

Any conflict, whether it arises from individual characteristics, interpersonal factors, or tasks, can escalate or de-escalate. Conflict **escalation** occurs when one person's negative behaviors encourage or foster another person's negative behaviors. Escalation can also occur when one party perceives the other as the enemy. Research has demonstrated that conflict has a predisposition to escalate in diverse teams or when there is a history of antagonism between individuals.[42] Conflict **de-escalation** occurs when conflict is reduced or eliminated.[43] Conflicts often de-escalate when individuals who are in conflict perceive a common enemy, are at a stalemate, or when time elapses, which allows individuals to reflect on the reasons for the conflict in the first place.[44]

MANAGING CONFLICT

People respond to conflict in different ways. Some avoid it, while others actively embrace it. Some people address conflict by accommodating others' requests at the expense of their own interests, while others try to achieve mutual gains for each person involved. Still others respond to conflict by attempting to force the other person to accommodate their interests (see Table 16.1).

An individual must assess a situation to determine the most appropriate response. While avoiding conflict can provide some short-term benefits, it should not become a default response. Regardless of the motivation, avoidance is generally associated with weak leadership.[45]

To manage conflict effectively, individuals must engage in a two-step process: one step draws awareness to the nature of the disagreement, and the other takes discrete steps to resolve the disagreement.

Escalation
An increase in conflict that occurs when one person's negative behaviors encourage or foster another person's negative behaviors.

De-escalation
The reduction or elimination of conflict.

Response	Description	When Appropriate
Avoidance	Avoid conflict because disagreements are perceived to create tension. Interpersonal problems do not get resolved, which causes long-term frustration.	When the issue is trivial or when a delay will enable the individual to gather more information or will enable both sides to cool down.
Accommodating	Try not to upset the other person because maintaining a harmonious relationship is a top priority. In some cases, those who accommodate are taken advantage of by the people they accommodate.	When an issue is more important to the other party, when a person seeks to build some social capital for the future, or when it is important to preserve friendly relationships.
Compromising	Reach an agreement quickly because prolonged conflicts can distract people from their work and cause bitter feelings. Using this approach can result in less-effective solutions.	When goals of both sides are equally important or when a temporary, expedient solution is needed.
Forcing	Reach an agreement that satisfies your needs rather than the needs of the other person because staying committed to an issue is more important than upsetting someone else.	When faced with a crisis or a need to enact an unpopular decision.
Collaborating	Solve a problem together because the positions of both individuals involved are perceived as equally important. Often this approach is the only approach that will resolve a problem because both parties are committed to the solution and are satisfied that they have been treated fairly.	When both parties' views are too important to abandon and when commitment from both sides is needed.

Table 16.1 ⟩ Responses to Conflict

Sources: T. Ruble and K. Thomas, "Support for a Two-Dimensional Model of Conflict Behavior," *Organizational Behavior and Human Performance*, Vol. 16, 1976; and D. Whetten and K. Cameron, *Developing Management Skills* (Upper Saddle River, NJ: Prentice Hall, 2002).

Diagnosing the Disagreement

When attempting to resolve a conflict, three important issues must be addressed: (1) the nature of the difference among the people involved; (2) the factors that may underlie this difference; and (3) the extent to which the difference has evolved.[46] Initially, it is important to determine whether the disagreement is related to facts, goals, methods, or values. Disagreements that are related to facts often occur when individuals have different definitions of a problem, have different information, or have different impressions of their respective power and authority.[47]

The second step in diagnosing the disagreement is to identify the factors that may underlie the disagreement. To do this, you should determine whether those involved have access to the same information, whether they perceive the information differently, and whether each person involved is significantly influenced by his or her role in the organization.[48] Informational factors are sources of conflict when various perspectives have been developed on the basis of different sets of facts. Perceptions are sources of conflict when those involved interpret the information differently. Finally, roles are sources of conflict when individuals use their position and status to influence the other person involved.

The final step in diagnosing the disagreement is to identify the state to which the disagreement has evolved. Is conflict simply anticipated, or has it escalated to full-blown dispute? Conflict is more easily addressed as a disagreement emerges. As tensions increase and disagreement builds, individuals tend to lock themselves into a position, which makes resolution more complicated.[49]

Resolving the Disagreement

After you have diagnosed a disagreement, it is time to take specific actions to resolve it.[50] Productive resolution requires effective communication, which involves separating the people from the problem. It also involves focusing on interests, not on positions that individuals have taken with respect to the issues.

An **issue** is the subject of discussion, but a **position** is the perspective a person takes on the issue. Positions tend to differ because relative **interests**, or the underlying needs of each party involved in the issue, also differ. A teenager may believe that the curfew set by his or her parents is too strict because of the social time the teen is missing with friends. The teenager's parents may believe that enforcing an early curfew will keep their son or daughter safe. In this scenario, the issue is the curfew, the positions are early versus late, and the interests are socialization versus safety. To communicate effectively, individuals should begin by maintaining ownership of the problem by not placing blame entirely on the other person. Next, individuals should encourage two-way discussion, seeking additional information when necessary. Ultimately, success depends on both parties going beyond trying to convince the other of the merits of their position on the issue, and instead trying to understand the underlying goals and interests of the other party. Interests often remain hidden to the other party, and when this happens, it is very hard to resolve the conflict.

TYPES OF NEGOTIATIONS

Ultimately, the goal of conflict resolution is to work toward a mutually agreed-upon decision. Reaching a decision that is acceptable to both sides often means engaging in some form of negotiation. Some negotiations occur during a conflict while others are simply efforts by two parties to find a way to work together. Regardless of the antecedents of negotiations, there are some general principles of effective negotiation that can have a huge impact on the outcome. Some negotiations involve a single issue, such as price or salary, in which one person gains something at the expense of the other person. In these scenarios, a "fixed pie" is assumed because one person's gain is the other person's loss. Much of what is negotiated in these types of situations involves taking away "slices of the pie" so that the other party will not be able to consume those pieces. To appeal to each side's relative interests, negotiating parties in single-issue negotiations tend to carefully bargain (or haggle) within a range that is acceptable to each party's interests.

In an effort to create more value for each negotiator, additional issues might be added to the negotiation. This creates an exchange opportunity whereby one party gives up on one issue in exchange for receiving more on another issue. During these negotiations, the two parties should attempt to assess each side's relative interests across multiple issues, believing that each party's interests and priorities may differ for each issue. During this process, each party may "trade off" his or her stake in one issue to better preserve his or her stake in a higher-priority issue. This type of negotiation can allow each party to reach an agreement in which each person would be better off than if he or she had not reached the agreement. For instance, some negotiations, such as a salary negotiation, seem like a "fixed pie" at first. But underlying interests often lead to value creation. For example, an employee may be interested in longer vacations, flexible hours, or higher benefits. The employer may be interested in higher motivation or higher quality or may be willing to pay for training, which helps both the employee and the employer. By putting more pieces on the table, each side has more flexibility and creativity to reach an agreement by trading issues with each other.

Issue
The subject of a discussion.

Position
The perspective a person takes on an issue.

Interests
The underlying reasons or needs of each party involved in an issue.

Prodakszyn/Shutterstock.com

Distributive Negotiations

Distributive negotiations, or single-issue negotiations, involve a complex system of activities focused on the attainment of one party's interests.[51] A "fixed pie" is assumed in distributive negotiations with each side seeking to gain the larger "slice of the pie." In essence, what one person wins, the other person loses. These are also called "zero-sum" negotiations. These can engender competitive or adversarial behaviors such as haggling or concealing information. These types of negotiations are common when one party does not expect to interact with the other party in the future; there is no perceived benefit to trying to build or maintain a long-term relationship.

A negotiation in which the sole issue is price (e.g., buying or selling a car) is an example of a purely distributive negotiation. The customer may perceive that the value of a car is one amount, while a car salesperson may insist that the car is worth much more. Their positions tend to differ because their relative interests differ. The customer wants to purchase the car for a "good price," one that is low and within his or her allocated budget. The car salesperson wants to sell the car for a high price, one that maximizes the dealership's revenues and his or her commission on the sale. Buying a car at a "good price" for the customer could mean that a car dealer loses potential revenue and the car salesperson loses potential commission. Because each party's relative interests in the sale differ, they may haggle over price during the negotiation, leaving them at an impasse.

Distributive negotiations have four defining characteristics: (1) the distribution of resources, (2) a focus on winning, (3) the notion of limits, and (4) a bargaining zone framework.

Distribution of Resources

All negotiations involve the distribution of resources, whether those resources are physical, human, or financial. In construction negotiations, contractors and landowners are concerned with the distribution of space. In domestic situations, roommates are concerned with the distribution of effort with respect to the completion of household chores. In salary negotiations, employees and their managers are concerned with the distribution of money. An employee wants higher compensation, but a manager wants to limit departmental expenses. In each scenario, each party negotiates to receive the resources that he or she wants and believes that he or she deserves.

Focus on Winning

Ultimately, the primary objective in distributive negotiations is winning even at the expense of the other person.[52] In construction negotiations, contractors and landowners may have different perspectives on how much space is necessary to complete a project. Both may perceive that space is a limited resource, so each may try to "win" his or her terms. The landowner may believe that having limited space available allows him or her to sell that space for a high price. The contractor may believe that he or she should be able to purchase the leftover space at a bargain price.

In domestic situations that involve household chores, each roommate wins by getting the other roommate to take on more of the household chores or by getting the other to take on the less desirable chores. The "fixed pie" that is to be divided up in this case is twofold: the number of people available to do the chores and the types of chores that must be completed.

Distributive negotiations
Single-issue negotiations that are assumed to be part of a "fixed pie" where one person's gain is the other person's loss.

To "win," either party may conceal his or her interests during the negotiation, especially when revealing these interests may cause the party to lose. In this case, each party believes that if the other party discovers his or her primary interest, this information can be used against him or her. To "win," either party may also bargain during the negotiation, especially when certain alternatives are more or less desirable than others. For example, roommates may prefer some household chores to others, but both may detest the same tasks. Each roommate may dislike cleaning bathrooms; therefore, each will try to bargain for chores that do not include bathroom duty.

Notion of Limits

In a distributive negotiation, the terms that need to be negotiated are experienced as limits by both parties. Neither party has an interest in knowingly going above the higher or below the lower of these terms. Within this range, there may be benefits to both parties, but the higher the terms, the more gain for one party.

When negotiating the sale of a house, both the buyer and the seller have limits. The maximum price a buyer is willing to pay may be the minimal price a seller is willing to accept, or it may be a price that is unacceptable to the seller altogether. The maximum price a buyer is willing to pay may also be within the range of prices that are acceptable to the seller. Therefore, each party will try to negotiate within that range. For example, a seller may list a house for $300,000 but may be willing to go as low as $275,000. A buyer may prefer to purchase a house for $260,000 but may have the flexibility to spend $285,000. In this case, each dollar value is perceived as a limit to each party and neither party has an interest in knowingly going above the higher or below the lower of these terms. The seller does not want to sell the house for less than $275,000, and the buyer does not want to purchase a house for more than $285,000. Within this range, there are still benefits to both parties, but if the seller receives more than $275,000 or the buyer pays less than $285,000, the more gain there is for that party.

Bargaining Zone Framework

The bargaining zone framework assumes that each party has some point or number that the negotiator will not go above or below (i.e., above $275,000 or below $285,000).[53] This point is called the reservation point or the walk-away point after which the party is willing to withdraw from the negotiation. Each party's reservation point becomes an input to the **bargaining zone**, which includes the range of settlements within which it is better for both parties to agree than not to agree. It shows the overlap, if any, of each side's acceptable price ranges.[54] The final agreement should fall somewhere between each party's price range.

In some cases, the bargaining zone may be positive. In a **positive bargaining zone**, negotiators' acceptable positions overlap. For example, if your salary increase bargaining range is 3%–6% and your company's salary increase bargaining range is 1%–5%, your positive overlap is between 3% and 5%. In a **negative bargaining zone**, there is no overlap.[55] Therefore, there is no settlement that will be acceptable to both parties (see Figure 16.2). For example, if your salary increase bargaining range is 3%–6% and your company's salary increase bargaining range is 0%–2%, there is no positive overlap and negotiators should pursue other alternatives.

Integrative Negotiations

While distributive negotiations focus on a single issue such as the price of a car, **integrative negotiations** focus on multiple issues, such as the price of a car, service support, and financing. During an integrative negotiation, negotiating parties attempt to assess each side's relative preferences or interests with respect to a number

Bargaining zone
The range of settlements within which it is better for both parties to agree than not to agree.

Positive bargaining zone
The zone that exists when negotiators' acceptable positions overlap.

Negative bargaining zone
The zone that exists when negotiators' acceptable positions do not overlap and no settlement will be acceptable to both parties.

Integrative negotiations
Negotiations that focus on multiple issues to "expand the pie" and actively seek alternative solutions that satisfy both parties.

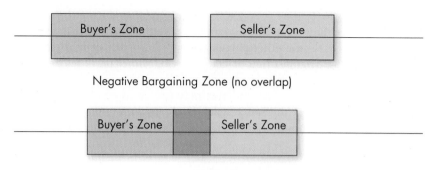

Figure 16.2 〉 Bargaining Zones

of different issues that have been put on the table, believing that each party's interests and priorities for each issue may differ. During this process, each party makes trade-offs in an effort to add or create more value for each negotiator, and the final agreement is one in which each party is believed to be better off than if they had not reached the agreement. As a result, integrative negotiations include a system of activities in which the attainment of one party's objectives is not necessarily in conflict with the other party's objectives.[56]

Like distributive negotiations, integrative negotiations are concerned with the distribution of resources, winning, limits, and a bargaining zone, yet they also emphasize ways to actively "expand the pie" and are known as non-zero-sum negotiations. Successful integrative negotiations tend to rely on trust between parties and a willingness to cooperate.[57]

Although a customer and a salesperson may disagree over the price of a car, adding other issues to the negotiation (e.g., down payment, service support, and terms of financing) may create more agreement and may be less likely to result in an impasse. For instance, a customer with a tight budget may agree to pay a higher price for the car if less of a down payment is required, if a loan is financed at a low interest rate, and if an extended service warranty is provided. A car salesperson who would like to receive a healthy commission from the sale may agree to sell the car at a lower price if the customer is willing to purchase an extended service warranty or finance the loan through the manufacturer. By adding a down payment, service support, and financing terms to the negotiation, the negotiation pie has been expanded and more opportunities for reaching an agreement have been created.

To add issues to a negotiation, negotiators must share information and communicate their interests, not just the issues and their relative positions on the issues. An employee must be willing to reveal that his or her salary is no longer proportionate to his or her living expenses. A manager must be willing to admit that the department's budget is limited. Disclosing this type of information helps each party brainstorm ways to create value for him or herself, all while keeping in mind his or her interests. As you can see, integrative negotiation doesn't necessarily mean splitting each issue in half, but rather it sometimes involves a willingness to give up certain issues in order to get other ones. This can only come about if we know what issues are most important to one another and are willing to engage in active trading across these issues.

During integrative negotiations, each party also makes trade-offs. Making a trade-off does not mean that either party should concede his or her interests. Rather, it proposes that each party prioritize his or her interests for a number of issues while maintaining an environment of joint problem solving. For instance, an employee may be willing to accept a smaller salary increase if he or she is given a more flexible work schedule.

NEGOTIATING EFFECTIVELY

Effective negotiators don't just jump into the bargaining process; they prepare.[58] They evaluate the interests, priorities, and alternatives of all parties involved before the negotiation begins. For example, for negotiations that involve a salary increase, a negotiator may ask himself or herself these questions: "Am I a valued employee? What are my manager's interests? What will I do if I don't receive a raise?"

Preparing to Negotiate

Negotiators prepare by conducting an assessment of the course of action they will pursue if the current negotiation ends in an impasse, as well as the lowest offer they are willing to accept from the other party. Negotiators also prepare by conducting an assessment of what they believe the other party would do if the current negotiation ends in an impasse, as well as what they believe would be the highest amount the other party would be willing to pay.

In the case of an integrative negotiation, this value should encompass the entire package of issues. Negotiators should also identify their multiple interests, as well as those of the other party. At some point in your career, you will receive a performance evaluation and will participate in a discussion about a salary increase. While the majority of these discussions go well, at times, you may believe that you deserve a higher increase than your company is willing to give. It is important to prepare for these situations, and the following nine steps can be critical to the success of this process.[59]

Step 1: Assess Your BATNA

The first step in preparing to negotiate is to assess your **best alternative to a negotiated agreement (BATNA)**. Ask yourself what you will do if the current negotiation ends in no deal. This is your BATNA, and it is the course of action you will take if the current negotiation ends in an impasse.[60] Knowing your BATNA will help you decide to accept a final offer or to walk away and pursue other options. To assess your BATNA, you should follow three steps:

- Identify all possible alternatives you might be able to pursue if you are unable to reach an agreement with the other party. Do you have other offers? Can you survive for long without a job?
- Estimate the value associated with each alternative.
- Select the best alternative.

Step 2: Calculate Your Reservation Value

The second step in preparing to negotiate is to calculate your **reservation value**. Ask yourself what the lowest offer is that you would be willing to accept. Your reservation value is based on a realistic assessment of your alternatives. It is the point at which you are indifferent between accepting a proposed offer and rejecting it in favor of pursuing your BATNA. For instance, in a salary negotiation, if you realistically believe that you could negotiate a 3%–6% salary increase, your reservation value should fall within this range. If you are risk-averse, your reservation value might be 3%. If you are risk-seeking, your reservation value might be 5%.

Step 3: Assess the Other Party's BATNA

The third step in preparing to negotiate is to assess the other party's BATNA. Ask yourself what the other party will do if the negotiation ends in an impasse. If no agreement on a salary increase can be reached and you decide to seek employment

---

Best alternative to a negotiated agreement (BATNA)
The course of action that a person will take if a negotiation ends in an impasse.

Reservation value
The lowest offer a negotiator is willing to accept. It is the point at which a negotiator is indifferent between accepting a proposed offer and rejecting it in favor of pursuing his or her BATNA.

elsewhere, your company could put your project or position on hold until they find a qualified replacement for you. However, your company may also have trouble finding a suitable candidate to finish a project that is facing a tight deadline. As a result, your employer may be more interested in negotiating a salary increase with you.

Step 4: Calculate the Other Party's Reservation Value

The fourth step in preparing to negotiate is to calculate the other party's reservation value. To assess your company's reservation value, you could investigate the range of increases normally given to employees and determine the midpoint of this range. If, for example, the normal range of increases is 1%–5%, you would determine that the midpoint and your company's reservation value is most likely 3%.

Step 5: Evaluate the ZOPA

The fifth step in preparing to negotiate is to evaluate the **zone of possible agreement (ZOPA)**. The ZOPA is the space between both parties' reservation values. It contains all possible agreements because any point in this range is a possible final deal to which both parties could agree, while any point outside this range will be rejected by one of the parties. Therefore, it is important for you to make a deal that is as high and close to the other party's reservation value as possible, while the other party will want the deal to be as low as possible. An example ZOPA for the salary increase scenario is highlighted in Figure 16.3.

The next four steps in preparing to negotiate involve assessing whether there is integrative potential in the negotiation.

Step 6: Identify Your Multiple Interests

Ask yourself what you value that the other party might be able to provide. For example, in addition to negotiating salary, you could also negotiate compensatory time off or a promotion. The goal is not to be demanding but to give the other party many different ways to compensate you. If your company cannot increase your salary but it can make you equally happy by giving you more vacation days or a promotion, you both stand to gain. Your company retains a motivated and talented employee without making an exception to the company's rules, and you get a compensation package that makes you happy. To achieve this, each party may have to look beyond the initial negotiating positions and instead try to understand the interests that may be guiding those positions. This understanding should provide a window into possible tradeoffs the other side may be willing to make.

Zone of possible agreement (ZOPA)
The set of all possible deals that would be acceptable to both parties. The ZOPA is the space between one party's reservation value and the other party's reservation value.

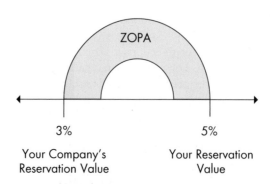

3%	5%
Your Company's Reservation Value	Your Reservation Value

Figure 16.3 › Zone of Possible Agreement

Step 7: Create a Scoring System

A scoring system allows you to list each issue and weight it according to its importance. You might start with 100 points and distribute them among salary, vacation days, and promotion in proportion to relative importance. The important factor is that the metric you use across all issues should help you evaluate the package offers the other party will make and help you structure your counteroffers more strategically.

Step 8: Calculate a Package Reservation Value

Ask yourself what the lowest value is that you would be willing to accept for a package offer that includes multiple issues simultaneously. If you have a minimum threshold of acceptability on each issue, the combination of those thresholds is your **package reservation value**. Instead of having a reservation value for each issue (e.g., salary, vacation days, and promotion), you can calculate a package reservation value that accounts for the total value of the offer you have assessed using your scoring system.

Step 9: Identify the Other Party's Multiple Interests

The final step in preparing to negotiate is to identify the other party's multiple interests. In every negotiation, there may be issues you do not care about but are very important to the other party. You may be indifferent about a new project the company is developing, but your company may want you to lead it. This is valuable information because you are now in a position to offer your company something and get something valuable in return.

Reaching an Agreement

Once the preparation is complete, it is time to begin negotiating. As previously discussed, the negotiation can be purely distributive or it can be integrative, depending on the tactics you and the other party choose to use. As you have learned, every negotiation has distributive components (i.e., distribution of resources, focus on winning, limits, and bargaining zone) but not every negotiation has to appeal solely to self-interests. To reach an agreement, negotiation partners should work not only to **claim value** for themselves but also to **create value** for each negotiator.

Claiming Value

Claiming value is a distributive process. Therefore, negotiators continually look for ways to "slice the pie." To claim value in negotiations, negotiators need to examine how they can achieve the most for themselves. To answer that question, negotiators need to be aware of their limits and their bargaining zone.

To claim value, each party tries to imagine the other's perceptions of where agreement is possible. The parties may also try to convey the impression that the proposed agreement is no better than no agreement at all. To claim value, each party may aim high (or low for that matter), hoping that the final agreement will maximize his or her interests. Each party may also try to lower the other party's aspirations, citing the challenges associated with achieving such high demands.

During a salary negotiation, an employee may propose a 10% salary increase as a means of claiming value at an "aspirational level." A manager, unable to meet that demand given budget constraints, may propose a 2% salary increase as a means of claiming value at his or her aspirational level. Each party will then try to claim value by bargaining within a 2% and 10% range, acknowledging that an agreement that appeals to either limit is more of a win for one party.

Package reservation value
The lowest value that a negotiator would be willing to accept for a package offer.

Claim value
The process by which a negotiator attempts to gain benefits or concessions for his or her position.

Create value
The process of expanding the opportunities or issues that can be evaluated in a negotiation. By expanding the issues, there is a greater likelihood that each party will achieve some level of satisfaction.

A DIFFERENT View

Difficult Conversations

Procrastinating the inevitable. We have all tried to avoid uncomfortable conversations that we ultimately need to have. In business, perhaps an employee needs to be told that he needs to dress more professionally, a customer needs to be told that a product they need is late, or a supplier needs to be told that their business is no longer required. As difficult as these conversations are, there are strategies and approaches that you can use to make them easier. Some of these strategies include giving bad news first, focusing on problem solving, and keeping your feedback simple.

1. What strategies would you use to make a difficult conversation easier?

2. Describe a difficult conversation that you have had. What strategies did you implement to make that conversation easier for you or the receiver? What did you do right? What would you change about that conversation? Was the outcome successful?

3. Describe a difficult conversation that you have observed. How did the recipient react? What strategies did the conversation starter use? What would you have done differently?

Knowing when to make the first offer or how to respond to it is another important aspect of claiming value. The primary benefit of making a first offer in negotiation is that it establishes a number that focuses the other negotiator's attention and expectations, and it can influence the final outcome. As we discussed in Chapter 15, the first offer can act as an anchor—forcing counteroffers to be based on this initial position. Should you decide to make the first offer, you should consider the following guidelines:[61]

- Set high but realistic aspirations by establishing the outcome you hope to achieve before the negotiation begins. Those who have more aggressive targets tend to achieve more favorable outcomes than those with more modest aspirations.
- Make an offer that falls outside the ZOPA, meaning a proposition that you know the other side will not accept. Your goal is to make the other party negotiate his or her way into the ZOPA. Asking for a 10% raise when 4% is standard and your target is 6% is done in the hopes that the other party will negotiate closer to 6%.
- Provide a justification for your offer. During a salary negotiation, for example, you could say, "I would like to propose that I receive a 10% salary increase because the quality of my work has gone above and beyond the demands of the job and the requirements of the position."
- Get the best deal you can while strengthening your relationship with the other party. During a salary negotiation you could say, "Although I know my request may impact the budget somewhat, I do believe that the additional value I bring to this department and to the company would outweigh the expense."

Sometimes, a first offer is made prematurely and can be costly as a result. Therefore, you should make the first offer only when you believe you have sufficient information about the other party's reservation value. If you suspect you may not have enough information about the ZOPA, wait to make an opening offer until you have collected more information.[62]

In other cases, the other party will make the opening offer. Should this happen, you can use any of the following strategies:[63]

- Ignore the other party's offer because it can act as an anchor. Instead of addressing the anchor, shift the conversation to an entirely different topic, one that allows you to reassert control of the discussion.
- Find out if there is any information that would help you understand the other party's opening offer. Are there budget constraints? Does the other person disagree with how well you believe you performed?
- Make a high counteroffer; then suggest that you need to work together to bridge the gap between the other party's offer and your own.
- Reject the offer and give the other party more time to reconsider his or her offer.
- Accept the offer if it meets your requirements and fits your reservation value.

Creating Value

While claiming value involves bargaining over interests, creating value involves a careful assessment of each side's preferences or interests to identify all possible opportunities. Creating value is an integrative process that involves negotiating over multiple issues. The potential to create value exists in most negotiations.

Agreements that create value can strengthen the relationship between negotiators.[64] For instance, your company may not be able to increase your salary at this time, but it can make you equally happy by increasing the number of vacation days you receive. Similarly, you could make your company equally happy by accepting a different compensation package, one that does not ask your employer to make an exception to the rules. To create value, individuals can apply the following strategies:[65]

- *Build trust and share information.* To accomplish this, each side should explain to the other the rationale for his or her demands in terms of the real interests that underlie them. Then, together, the negotiators can explore alternative ways to meet those needs. Because some concealment is typical during negotiations, negotiators may want to emphasize the value of open discussion in strengthening their future relationship.
- *Ask questions.* Simple questions might be, "How much would you lose?" or "How much would it cost you?" In some cases, parties will not fully share their interests; in that case, you must assess what you need from the other side before starting the negotiation, and then ask the questions necessary to collect the information.
- *Strategically disclose information.* If the other party is not answering your questions in a useful way, give away some information of your own, but not your BATNA. By strategically disclosing information, you focus discussion on the trades you are willing to make.
- *Make package offers and multiple offers simultaneously.* When negotiators put only one offer on the table and it is subsequently turned down, they know little more about the other person's priorities than they did before they made the initial offer. Therefore, negotiators should focus on discussing every issue and comparing relative preferences.

Avoiding Common Mistakes

Despite preparation, many negotiators make several costly mistakes that prevent them from negotiating effectively. While you may give away information about your interests, the other party may not necessarily be as revealing. In essence, the other party may be focusing more on claiming value than on creating value. Such behaviors can lead to a breakdown in trust. Therefore, it is important to remember that the most effective negotiations focus on both claiming and creating value.

The same lessons regarding biases and assumptions discussed in Chapter 15 apply to the negotiation process (see Table 16.2). It is important to understand your frame of reference before beginning the negotiation process so that you can avoid making common mistakes.

Common Mistakes in Negotiations	Description
Irrational escalation of commitment	In some negotiations, one party ineffectively stays committed to an initial course of action. This behavior biases perception and judgment, causing negotiators to make irrational decisions to avoid admitting failure or to appear consistent.[66]
Anchoring and adjustment	In every negotiation, one party must make the first offer. In most cases, negotiators with good alternatives or higher power are more likely to make the first offer than those with poor alternatives or lower power.[67] First offers have the power to anchor the negotiation and determine the outcomes.
Framing	The manner in which options are presented can alter the ways in which negotiators perceive the value of the alternatives.
Availability of information	The availability of information can overwhelm a person's ability to analyze a negotiation effectively.[68] As a result, negotiators sometimes use available, not reliable, information when assessing alternatives, interests, and priorities and wind up with a less than satisfying deal.
Negotiator overconfidence	Negotiators have an inflated sense of confidence in their judgments and choices.

Table 16.2 Common Mistakes in Negotiations

In some situations, negotiators assume that one person's interests conflict with the other's interests. In essence, they believe that both are fighting for the biggest "piece of the pie" even when there is more than one issue at stake and each party values the issues differently.[69] Some negotiations fail to become integrative because of an overemphasis on winning and an under emphasis on searching for mutually beneficial trade-offs. In these cases, the parties fail to realize that their interests may be more compatible than competitive.[70]

In other instances, negotiators make a low offer that is immediately accepted by the other party. This is called the "winner's curse." While the negotiator who made the first offer may be excited that his or her offer was accepted, the other side may have had much better information and, as a result, received a better deal than expected.

Knowing When to Exercise Your BATNA

Sometimes parties cannot come to an agreement. If this is the case, negotiators must determine whether a BATNA is better than any offer the other party can make and whether exercising a BATNA is the best strategy. To determine whether no deal is the best outcome, you should look for the following signs:[71]

1. You have told the other party about other offers, and he or she is unable to match or beat the value that these alternatives offer you.
2. Instead of trying to meet your needs, the other party is trying hard to convince you that your interests are not what you think they are.
3. The other party seems more interested in stretching the negotiation than in exchanging information, building a relationship, or structuring an agreement.
4. Despite your best efforts, the other party will not answer your questions, nor will he or she ask about your needs or interests.

Negotiating effectively requires that you consider each of the factors that support and inhibit negotiation effectiveness. To negotiate effectively, you must consider not only your own interests, but also those of the other party. Likewise, the other party should consider your interests. Unless there is a mutual exchange of reliable information, it will be difficult to reach agreement. Under the previously mentioned conditions, no ZOPA exists. When there is no ZOPA, instead of "getting to yes," you should exercise your BATNA.[72]

Mediation and Arbitration

Mediator
An individual who does not make a final decision but works with each party to find some common ground on which both parties can agree.

Arbitrator
An individual who listens to both sides of a disagreement and makes a final decision based on the arguments.

In some cases, these methods fail and the high emotions of a negotiation require each party to consult a neutral third party: a **mediator** or an **arbitrator**. A mediator is someone who does not make a final decision but works with each party to find some common ground on which both parties can agree.[73] Effective mediators build rapport and trust with both parties, engage in creative brainstorming, and refrain from jumping to a conclusion too quickly.[74]

An arbitrator generally does make the final decision when two parties are at an impasse. Acting like a judge, the arbitrator listens to both sides of the disagreement and makes a final decision based on the arguments.[75] In most cases, arbitration is binding. That is, the two parties agree that they will support and abide by the arbitrator's decision.

NEGOTIATING ACROSS CULTURES

When two parties negotiate, they bring their interests, priorities, and alternatives to the table. They also bring their culture. Cross-cultural differences in negotiation can be significant and can affect why the negotiators have taken the position they have, why they prioritize certain issues over others, and what strategies they use.[76] Negotiation strategies, in particular, can vary according to two primary cultural values: egalitarianism versus hierarchy and low- versus high-context norms for communication.[77]

Egalitarianism versus Hierarchy

Egalitarianism versus hierarchy distinguishes between hierarchical cultures that emphasize differentiated social status from egalitarian cultures that do not. As a result, people in hierarchical cultures (e.g., China, Turkey, Japan, and Brazil) may be less willing to confront the other party directly in a negotiation because this behavior implies a lack of respect for those with higher social status. People in egalitarian cultures (e.g., Italy, Spain, France, Denmark, and Greece) are more comfortable with confrontation, as well as the concept of BATNA, which implies that negotiators can improve their status if they so choose.[78]

Low- versus High-Context Norms for Communication

Low- versus high-context norms for communication distinguishes between low-context cultures that prefer to communicate directly from high-context cultures that prefer to communicate indirectly. In low-context cultures (e.g., Germany, Scandinavia, Switzerland, and the United States), information is explicit and meaning is clear. In other words, people tend to say what they mean. In high-context cultures (e.g., the United Arab Emirates, France, Japan, India, and Russia) information is embedded in the context of the message, and its meaning must be inferred.[79] In these situations, individuals may not be explicit about what they mean. One party may need to ask questions to ensure that he or she fully understands the intent of the message.

When negotiating cross-culturally, negotiators should proceed slowly, test their assumptions about what strategy will be effective with the other party, and be willing to adjust their strategy to achieve their goals. The following key questions may be helpful in identifying how best to negotiate with different cultures:[80]

- Is the goal to build a relationship or to establish a contract?
- What is the nature of communication—direct or indirect?
- What styles are most effective—formal or informal?
- How time sensitive is the decision?
- Are agreements expected to be general guidelines or specific mandates?
- Is decision making top-down or bottom-up?

SUMMARY

Conflict is an emotional or cognitive response that occurs when interests, perspectives, and behaviors of one individual or group explicitly differ from those of another individual or group. Because conflict can be both destructive and constructive, understanding the factors that support and inhibit both types of conflict is especially important. By understanding the nature of and the factors that underlie differences, by communicating effectively, and by formulating an action plan that considers the interests of the individuals and groups involved in the conflict, a manager can more effectively manage any type of conflict.

LO1 Conflict that occurs between members of the same group is called interpersonal conflict. Interpersonal conflict often emerges because of interdependence, when two or more individuals must work together to achieve a common goal. When their interests or perspectives are not aligned, conflict can emerge. Conflict that occurs between members of different groups is called intergroup conflict. Two theories help explain why intergroup conflict can escalate—social identity theory and realistic conflict theory. According to social identity theory, members of one group try to enhance their self-image by finding negative aspects of the other group, which leads to conflict. According to realistic conflict theory, access to limited resources can lead to conflict and can cause one group to more strongly coalesce against the other group.

LO2 : Cognitive (or task-related) conflict can lead to more positive or productive outcomes, especially when individuals leverage their different interests, perspectives, and beliefs. If left unresolved, however, conflict can be detrimental and can limit the effectiveness of decision-making, creativity, and communication. Conflict that is directed at individuals rather than the task is called affective conflict, and it tends to impede the ability of the group to work together.

LO3 : There are various ways to manage conflict from avoidance to compromise to collaboration. Managers must assess the situation to determine the most appropriate course of action. One way to try to resolve disagreements between individuals or groups is to outline the positions and interests of both parties. By doing so, the individuals in the dispute may be able to find some common ground.

LO4 : Sometimes disagreements cannot be solved easily, and the two parties must turn to more formal processes such as negotiation. The two primary forms

of negotiation are distributive and integrative negotiation. Distributive negotiations are single-issue negotiations that assume that one person's win is the other person's loss. Integrative negotiations focus on multiple issues that have the potential to allow both parties to achieve some level of victory or satisfaction.

LO5 : To negotiate effectively, negotiators must evaluate each party's alternatives, interests, and priorities before the negotiation begins. Effective negotiators understand how to claim value and how to create value. They also understand the power of negotiating multiple issues simultaneously and exploring all opportunities so that no resources are left on the table. An effective negotiator avoids making mistakes including unnecessarily committing to his or her original stance, prematurely accepting a first offer, or becoming overconfident in the value he or she brings to the negotiation.

LO6 : The form of and approach to negotiations will vary based on the cultural values that are important within a specific region or country. For instance, individuals in egalitarian cultures are more open to confrontation while individuals from hierarchical cultures tend to be less comfortable with direct confrontation. In cross-border negotiations, negotiators need to take time to understand any cultural implications that can influence the process.

KEY TERMS

Affective conflict
Arbitrator
Bargaining zone
Best alternative to a negotiated
    agreement (BATNA)
Claim value
Cognitive conflict
Conflict
Create value
De-escalation

Distributive negotiations
Escalation
Groupthink
Integrative negotiations
Interests
Intergroup conflict
Interpersonal conflict
Issue
Mediator
Negative bargaining zone

Negotiation
Package reservation value
Position
Positive bargaining zone
Realistic conflict theory
Reservation value
Social identity theory
Zone of possible agreement (ZOPA)

ASSIGNMENTS

Discussion Topics

1. Why is conflict avoidance so common?

2. Explain the difference between interpersonal conflict and intergroup conflict. What are the primary causes of each type of conflict?

3. Think about ways in which you have become susceptible to the social identity theory. What activities or behaviors did you engage in that strengthened your allegiance to your group or team? What are the dangers of this type of identification?

4. How can teams spark task-related conflict without engaging in affective conflict? What are ways in which a group can de-escalate affective conflict?

5. Outline the differences between distributive and integrative negotiations.

6. What are the advantages and disadvantages of being the first one to outline his or her position in a negotiation?

7. A key to effective negotiations is the understanding of the other party's position and alternatives. What are the ways in which one party can learn about the other party's positions and alternatives?

8. In negotiations, how does one strike the right balance between creating and claiming value?

9. How could overconfidence impact the outcome of a negotiation?

10. How can and do emotions impact the outcome of negotiations?

Management Research

1. Think about the best and worst teams of which you were a member. What were the differences between the teams? How was conflict handled? What could have been done to improve the worst team?

2. Think about a situation in which you disagreed with a roommate, teammate, friend, or sibling. What is your default position when faced with conflict? Do you accommodate, or do you try to force your way?

3. Think about a major purchase or decision you recently made—for instance, the purchase of a new car, a new computer, or a new phone service. What were important aspects of the decision to you— price, service, features, etc.? What trade-offs were you willing to make? How did you reach an agreement or make a decision?

In the Field

Observe a conflict management resolution process on your campus or at an organization in your community. Prepare notes on the following aspects of the conflict management process:

- Who are the parties involved?
- What is the issue causing the conflict?
- Why is the issue causing a conflict?
- How was the conflict managed?
- Did the parties involved negotiate to resolve the conflict? If so, which negotiation strategies were effective?
- How was the conflict resolved?
- How did stakeholders react to the resolution of the conflict?
- Share your notes with your classmates and discuss which concepts from this chapter you observed.

ENDNOTES

[1] Carsten K. W. De Dreu, "Productive Conflict: The Importance of Conflict Management and Conflict Issue," *Using Conflict in Organizations*, K. Carsten K. W. De Dreu and Evert Van de Vliert, eds. (London: Sage Publications, 1997).

[2] Ibid.

[3] M. E. Turner and A. R. Pratkanis, "Mitigating Groupthink by Stimulating Constructive Conflict," *Using Conflict in Organizations*, Carsten K. W. De Dreu and Evert Van de Vliert, eds. (London: Sage Publications, 1997).

[4] Carsten K. W. De Dreu, "Productive Conflict: The Importance of Conflict Management and Conflict Issue," *Using Conflict in Organizations*, Carsten K. W. De Dreu and Evert Van de Vliert, eds. (London: Sage Publications, 1997).

[5] Linda Babcock and Sara Laschever, *Women Don't Ask: Negotiation and the Gender Divide* (Princeton, NJ: Princeton University Press, 2003).

[6] The case study is derived from W. Earl Sasser and Heather Beckham, "Thomas Green: Power, Office Politics, and a Career in Crisis," Harvard Business School Brief Case No. 2095 (Boston, MA: Harvard Business Publishing, 2008).

[7] Earl Sasser and Heather Beckham, "Thomas Green: Power, Office Politics, and a Career in Crisis," Harvard Business School Brief Case No. 2095 (Boston, MA: Harvard Business Publishing, 2008), p. 2.

[8] Ibid., p. 3.

[9] Ibid.

[10] Ibid.

[11] Ibid., p. 4.

[12] Ibid., p. 5.

[13] J. Richard Hackman, *Leading Teams: Setting the Stage for Great Performances* (Boston, MA: HBS Press, 2002).

[14] M. A. Korsagaard, S. S. Jeong, D. M. Mahony, and A. H. Pitariu, "A Multilevel View of Intragroup Conflict," *Journal of Management*, Vol. 34, No. 6, 2008, pp. 1222–1252.

[15] Nitin Nohria and Carlos Garcia-Pont, "Global Strategic Linkages and Industry Structure," *Strategic Management Journal*, Vol. 12, Summer 1991, pp. 105–124.

[16] Richard E. Walton, *Managing Conflict: Interpersonal Dialogue and Third-Party Roles*, 2nd edition (Boston, MA: Addison-Wesley, 1987), p. 3.

[17] M. A. Korsagaard, S. S. Jeong, D. M. Mahony, and A. H. Pitariu, "A Multilevel View of Intragroup Conflict," *Journal of Management*, Vol. 34, No. 6, 2008, pp. 1222–1252.

[18] Ibid.

[19] Carsten K. W. De Dreu and Evert Van de Vliert, "Using Conflict in Organizations," *Using Conflict in Organizations*, Carsten K. W. De Dreu and Evert Van de Vliert, eds. (London: Sage Publications, 1997).

[20] Ibid.

[21] Martin N. Davidson, "Managing Conflict in Organizations," University of Virginia Case No. UV0416 (Charlottesville, VA: Darden Business Publishing, 2001), p. 2.

[22] Richard E. Walton, *Managing Conflict: Interpersonal Dialogue and Third-Party Roles*, 2nd edition (Boston, MA: Addison-Wesley, 1987), p. 68.

[23] H. Tajfel and J. C. Turner, "The Social Identity Theory of Intergroup Behavior," *Psychology of Intergroup Relations*, Stephen Worchel and William G. Austin, eds. (Chicago, IL: Nelson-Hall Publishers, 1986).

[24] Ibid.

[25] M. Sherif, O. J. Harvey, B. J. White, W. R. Hood, and C. W. Sherif, *Intergroup Conflict and Cooperation: The Robbers Cave Experiment* (Boston, MA: Houghton Mifflin, 1954/1961).

[26] Ibid.

[27] Ibid.

[28] J. Dutton, S. Ashford, R. O'Neill, and K. Lawrence, "Moves that Matter: Issue Selling and Organizational Change," *Academy of Management Journal*, Vol. 44, 2001, pp. 716–736; and J. Dutton, and S. Ashford, "Selling Issues to Top Management," *Academy of Management Review*, Vol. 18, 1993, pp. 397–428.

[29] Martin N. Davidson, "Managing Conflict in Organizations," University of Virginia Case No. UV0416 (Charlottesville, VA: Darden Business Publishing, 2001).

[30] Robert A. Baron, "Countering the Effects of Destructive Criticism: The Relative Efficacy of Four Interventions," *Journal of Applied Psychology*, Vol. 75, No. 3, 1990, pp. 235–245.

[31] Ibid.

[32] D. G. Pruitt and J. Z. Rubin, *Social Conflict: Escalation, Stalemate, and Settlement* (New York, NY: McGraw-Hill, 1986).

[33] D. R. Peterson, "Conflict," *Close Relationship*, H. H. Kelley, E. Berscheid, A. Christensen, J. H. Harvey, T. L. Huston, G. Levinger, E. McClintock, L. A. Peplau, and D. R. Peterson, eds. (New York, NY: W. H. Freeman, 1983).

[34] Karen A. Jehn, "A Multimethod Examination of the Benefits and Detriments of Intragroup Conflict," *Administrative Science Quarterly*, Vol. 40, No. 2, 1995, pp. 256–282.

[35] C. Argyris, *Interpersonal Competence and Organizational Effectiveness* (Homewood, IL: Dorsey, 1962); and W. Evan, "Conflict and Performance in R&D Organizations," *Industrial Management Review*, Vol. 7, 1965.

[36] R. A. Baron, "Countering the Effects of Destructive Criticism: The Relative Efficacy of Four Interventions," *Journal of Applied Psychology*, Vol. 75, 1990; and R. S. Ross, "Conflict," *Small Groups in Organizational Settings*, R. Ross and J. Ross, eds. (Englewood Cliffs, NJ: Prentice Hall, 1989).

[37] M. E. Turner and A. R. Pratkanis, "Mitigating Groupthink by Stimulating Constructive Conflict," *Using Conflict in Organizations*, Carsten K. W. De Dreu and Evert Van de Vliert, eds. (London: Sage Publications, 1997).

[38] L. Thompson, *Making the Team: A Guide for Managers* (Upper Saddle River, NJ: Prentice Hall, 2000).

[39] Ibid.

[40] Ibid.

[41] Katsuhiko Shimizu and Michael A. Hitt, "Strategic Flexibility: Organizational Preparedness to Reverse Ineffective Strategic Decisions," *Academy of Management Executive*, Vol. 18, No. 4, November 2004, p. 52.

[42] R. J. Fisher, *The Social Psychology of Intergroup and International Conflict Resolution* (New York: Springer-Verlag, 1990).

[43] James A. Wall and Ronda R. Callister, "Conflict and Its Management," *Journal of Management*, Vol. 21, No. 3, 1995, pp. 515–558.

[44] Ibid.

[45] Martin N. Davidson, "Managing Conflict in Organizations," University of Virginia Case No. UV0416 (Charlottesville, VA: Darden Business Publishing, 2001), p. 5.

[46] W. H. Schmidt and R. Tannenbaum, "Management of Differences," *Harvard Business Review*, November–December 1960.

[47] Ibid.

[48] Ibid.

[49] Ibid.

[50] Whetten and Cameron identify four steps that should be taken to resolve conflict effectively: (1) establish super-ordinate goals, (2) communicate effectively, (3) generate solutions, and (4) formulate an action plan. D. Whetten and K. Cameron, *Developing Management Skills* (Upper Saddle River, NJ: Prentice Hall, 2002).

[51] R. E. Walton and R. B. McKersie, *A Behavioral Theory of Labor Negotiations: An Analysis of a Social Interaction System*, 2nd edition (Ithaca, NY: ILR Press, Cornell University, 1991).

[52] Roy J. Lewicki, Stephen E. Weiss, and David Lewin, "Models of Conflict, Negotiation, and Third Party Intervention: A Review and Synthesis," *Journal of Organizational Behavior*, Vol. 13, 1992, pp. 209–252.

[53] Max Bazerman, *Judgment in Managerial Decision Making*, 6th edition (Hoboken, NJ: John Wiley & Sons, 2006).

[54] Ibid.

[55] L. Thompson, *The Mind and Heart of the Negotiator* (Upper Saddle River, NJ: Prentice Hall, 2001).

[56] Max Bazerman, *Judgment in Managerial Decision Making*, 6th edition (Hoboken, NJ: John Wiley & Sons, 2006).

[57] Roy J. Lewicki, Stephen E. Weiss, and David Lewin, "Models of Conflict, Negotiation, and Third Party Intervention: A Review and Synthesis," *Journal of Organizational Behavior*, Vol. 13, 1992, pp. 209–252.

[58] Michael Wheeler, "Negotiation Advice: A Synopsis," Harvard Business School Case No. 9-905-059, rev. June 2, 2009 (Boston, MA: HBS Publishing, 2005), p. 1.

[59] D. Malhotra and Max Bazerman, *Negotiation Genius* (New York: Bantam Books, 2007).

[60] R. Fisher and W. Ury, *Getting to Yes* (New York: Penguin Books, 1981).

[61] D. Malhotra and Max Bazerman, *Negotiation Genius* (New York: Bantam Books, 2007).

[62] Ibid.

63 Ibid.

64 Max Bazerman and M. Neale, *Negotiating Effectively* (New York: The Free Press, 1992).

65 Max Bazerman and M. Neale, *Negotiating Effectively* (New York: The Free Press, 1992); and Max Bazerman, *Judgment in Managerial Decision Making*, 6th edition (Hoboken, NJ: John Wiley & Sons, 2006).

66 D. Malhotra and Max Bazerman, *Negotiation Genius* (New York: Bantam Books, 2007).

67 Ibid.

68 Max Bazerman, *Judgment in Managerial Decision Making*, 6th edition (Hoboken, NJ: John Wiley & Sons, 2006).

69 D. Malhotra and Max Bazerman, *Negotiation Genius* (New York: Bantam Books, 2007).

70 Leigh Thompson and Reid Hastie, "Social Perception in Negotiation," *Organizational Behavior and Human Decision Processes*, Vol. 47, 1990, pp. 98–123.

71 D. Malhotra and Max Bazerman, *Negotiation Genius* (New York: Bantam Books, 2007).

72 Ibid.

73 Roy J. Lewicki, Stephen E. Weiss, and David Lewin, "Models of Conflict, Negotiation, and Third Party Intervention: A Review and Synthesis," *Journal of Organizational Behavior*, Vol. 13, 1992, pp. 209–252.

74 Stephen B. Goldberg, "Beyond Blame: Choosing a Mediator," *Negotiation* (Harvard Business School Publishing and the Program on Negotiation at Harvard Law School), January 2006.

75 Roy J. Lewicki, Stephen E. Weiss, and David Lewin, "Models of Conflict, Negotiation, and Third Party Intervention: A Review and Synthesis," *Journal of Organizational Behavior*, Vol. 13, 1992, pp. 209–252.

76 Jeswald W. Salacuse, *Making Global Deals: Negotiating in the International Marketplace* (Boston, MA: Houghton Mifflin, 1991).

77 J. M. Brett, *Negotiating Globally: How to Negotiate Deals, Resolve Disputes, and Make Decisions Across Cultural Boundaries* (San Francisco, CA: Jossey-Bass, 2001).

78 Ibid.

79 Ibid.

80 Jeswald W. Salacuse, *Making Global Deals: Negotiating in the International Marketplace* (Boston, MA: Houghton Mifflin, 1991), pp. 42–71.

CHAPTER

17

Leading Teams

Learning Objectives

After reading this chapter, you should be able to:

LO1 Distinguish between a team and a work group and outline the key
elements that are essential for the establishment of a team.

LO2 Describe the characteristics of teams and how diversity can help or
hinder team performance.

LO3 Outline the stages of team development and the way in which
norms are established in teams.

LO4 Describe how teams function and how members of the team interact
to accomplish the team's goals and objectives.

LO5 Define the major aspects of team effectiveness and explain the role
that leaders play in influencing team performance.

SELF-REFLECTION

How Do You Contribute to Team Work?

Teams pursue specific tasks that require people to work together interdependently to achieve a common goal. The success of a team depends upon the members' motivation to accomplish a goal through collective actions, their ability to learn from each other, and their willingness to develop constructive work relationships. Although a team may have a formal leader, all members should contribute their talents and be accountable for the team's effectiveness. On a scale of 1 to 5, respond to the following statements to assess how you contribute to the effectiveness of a team.

1 = never 2 = rarely 3 = sometimes 4 = usually 5 = always

1. When working on a team, I am mindful of its agenda or purpose. _____

2. When working on a team, I use my unique skills and talents to enable the team to achieve its goals. _____

3. When working on a virtual team, I am effective at using technology to communicate with team members. _____

4. When I am a team member, I adhere to the working norms of the team. _____

5. When working on a team, I share my knowledge with team members. _____

6. When working on a team, I try to learn from other team members. _____

7. When working on a team, I engage in constructive conflict with team members. _____

8. When working on a team, I manage the external relationships of the team. _____

9. When working on a team, I scan the competitive environment. _____

10. When working on a team, I create positive energy by being optimistic, complimentary, or celebratory. _____

Based on your responses, how do you contribute when working on a team? Are your contributions effective and how do they benefit the team?

INTRODUCTION

"There is no I in team." Coaches and team leaders often use this phrase to establish a sense of camaraderie and to emphasize the importance of working together to achieve a common goal. In essence, they are communicating that the team cannot be successful without the collective expertise and efforts of every member. A considerable amount of research has proven that teams working together are better than individuals working alone in a variety of complex and straightforward tasks.[1] While this sentiment may resonate with many on the team, others might retort that while "there is no I in team," there is definitely a *me*. For teams to be effective, they have to satisfy the needs of the individual members as well as the collective goal or task for which the team has been brought together. There is also research showing that while teams have huge potential, many suffer from a large number of dysfunctions that can make the experience frustrating for all those on the team and at the same time, diminish the performance of the team. This sometimes leads team members to question whether it's even worthwhile working on a team.

Whether you like being on a team or not, the fact remains that teams are a dominant means by which organizations accomplish operational, strategic, and creative tasks. To that end, a **team** is a group of two or more people with complementary skills who are committed to working together to achieve a specific objective. The most effective teams develop a common purpose and have members who are aligned in their pursuit of that purpose.[2] By tapping into the collective experiences and perspectives of many individuals, organizations often compete more effectively and better adapt to changing contextual situations. The diverse skills and perspectives that individuals bring to teams enable the collective output to be much stronger than the sum of individual efforts. Teams also provide some of the first opportunities for individuals to exert leadership skills such as persuasion, negotiation, consensus building, and process management. Your ability to be an effective team member could play a significant role in your relationship with your peers as well as influence your future career prospects.

Working in teams can be crucial for organizations and the individuals in them, but at the same time, most people find such work to be difficult. Some of the frustrations experienced in teams include personal conflicts, individual agendas, lack of trust, poor communication, and ineffective leadership. And so, working in teams is at once crucial and potentially frustrating. Some of the skills needed to be an effective team player don't necessarily come naturally to most of us. And yet, when embraced, they can make all the difference toward team success and also individual satisfaction with the team.

Two companies that have been successful in achieving this balance of team member satisfaction and organizational performance are Whole Foods and Kyocera.

Team
A group of two or more people with complementary skills who are committed to working together to achieve a specific objective.

Teamwork at Whole Foods and Amoeba Management at Kyocera

Whole Foods operates more than 400 stores and generates over $14.2 billion per year in sales.[3] When measured by profit per square foot, it is America's most profitable food retailer. Whole Foods's success has been predicated on its ability to satisfy the needs of health-conscious consumers, who have made natural and organic foods the fastest-growing segment of the grocery industry in the United States.[4] One way in which Whole Foods has been able to service these consumers is by attracting and nurturing effective teams in individual stores.[5]

At each Whole Foods location, roughly eight teams oversee departments ranging from seafood to produce to baked goods. Each team is responsible for making decisions related to pricing, ordering, staffing, and in-store promotions. Each team is measured on its labor productivity, and the company

calculates the profit per labor hour for every team in the store. Teams that exceed a preset productivity goal receive a bonus in their next paycheck. Teams also compete against their own historic productivity benchmarks, against other teams in their store, and against similar teams across the company.[6] In Whole Foods, team success is a key determinant of future career opportunities.

Similarly, Japan-based Kyocera, a provider of sophisticated electronic components for cell phones, televisions, and other high-technology products, adopted a team-focused process that it calls "amoeba management" in its manufacturing operation. Kazuo Inamori, the founder of Kyocera, believed that the manufacturing process should be divided into small groups of 5 to 50 employees who operate with a self-supporting accounting system and are responsible for a particular work process and a specific component of profitability. Teams are often subdivided into smaller subteams so that the company can develop an even more accurate perspective of profitability. As the company grows, the process of subdivision continues until it no longer makes sense, just

as an amoeba changes form and divides itself. The amoeba management process has enabled Kyocera to galvanize productivity while retaining an entrepreneurial spirit, even as the company has expanded to more than 69,000 employees. Like Whole Foods, team members are rewarded for improved performance and their ability to work well with each other and other teams in the manufacturing process.[7]

Companies such as Whole Foods and Kyocera operate under the notion that working in teams is more

efficient and productive than working independently. Both companies employ teams that exhibit the three primary components of team effectiveness: (1) producing results that are meaningful and tangible; (2) building the capacity of team members to learn, adapt to change, and work together constructively in the future; and (3) creating an opportunity for personal growth and development (see Figure 17.6).[8] These organizations believe that leveraging the combined knowledge and technical skills of multiple team members to complete work tasks can result in more innovative and productive work solutions as well as better bottom line results. Despite the successful efforts of companies such as Whole Foods and Kyocera to leverage teamwork, as we highlighted above, teams are not always effective or appropriate.

Case in Point   Teamwork at Whole Foods and Amoeba Management at Kyocera

1. How are teams empowered at Whole Foods?
2. At Whole Foods, why do you think management measures the performance of teams?
3. What is "amoeba management" at Kyocera?
4. How do you think "amoeba management" influences the performance of teams at Kyocera?

This chapter will present a model for team effectiveness as well as an overview of team structures, characteristics, developmental stages, norms, and processes. We begin by describing the characteristics of teams and explain how they exist in organizations. We then describe team development and team processes, the dynamic elements that are constantly changing, which leaders must understand and to which they must adapt. Finally, we describe how managers and team members can get the most out of teams.

WHEN ARE TEAMS APPROPRIATE?

Given the complexity of managing a diverse group of individuals and trying to develop a common purpose and objective, teams are not always the best vehicle to use in organizations. Instead, work groups may be more appropriate because they

Team	Work Group
• Shared leadership roles • Individual and mutual accountability • Purpose is specific to the team • Characterized by complex and interdependent tasks • Collective work products • Open-ended discussions and problem solving are encouraged	• Clearly focused leader • Individual accountability • Group's purpose is same as organization's mission • Characterized by straightforward and independent tasks • Individual work products • Pre-determined work structure

Figure 17.1 ⟩ Teams versus Work Groups

Source: Adapted from Jon R. Katzenbach and Douglas K. Smith, "The Discipline of Teams," *Harvard Business Review,* July–August 2005.

involve a clearer structure and are still effective at achieving collective goals. Work groups share many of the characteristics of a hierarchical organization: They have clearly defined leaders, well-established group relations, and individuals who bear responsibility for contributing to the group (see Figure 17.1). But as we have seen in the previous chapters on organizational structure and leadership, well-defined roles and individual accountability can limit a group's ability to accomplish more complex tasks.

While work groups are often better than individuals working alone, teams can be even better, especially for certain types of projects or activities, including ones that are complex and require the collective expertise of multiple individuals. When a task grows in complexity, one individual is not likely to possess the required knowledge and ability to complete the task or solve the problem on his or her own. **Task complexity** refers to the amount of information that must be processed to understand the task, the degree of uncertainty about possible outcomes, the presence of many subtasks that require a range of skills and knowledge, or the absence of standardized procedures to conduct the task.[9] Tasks that are complex generally require the input of multiple individuals with diverse backgrounds and expertise. In these situations, a team can be very effective.

Teams are also defined by the interdependence of relationships between individuals. **Task interdependence** refers to the extent to which group members need to work with and rely on each other to produce the collective work of the group.[10] Task interdependence is sometimes inherent in the tasks themselves.[11] This is particularly true for tasks that involve creating something new such as product development initiatives. New product development teams generally include individuals with an understanding of the customer (marketing and sales), an understanding of the production process (manufacturing), and an understanding of new technologies or applications (research and development). Tasks like these, which require the interdependent perspectives of many individuals, are better suited for teams. In these situations, team members build on each other's unique skills.

TEAM CHARACTERISTICS

As you have learned so far, for a group of individuals to work together as a team, they need to develop successful working relationships with each other to be collectively productive and personally satisfied. Relationships can be developed by

Task complexity
The amount of information that must be processed to understand the task, the degree of uncertainty about possible outcomes, the presence of many subtasks that require a range of skills and knowledge, or the absence of standardized procedures to conduct the task.

Task interdependence
The extent to which group members need to work with and rely on each other to produce the collective work of the group.

structuring team environments in ways that foster communication among team members. In his book *The Human Group*, George C. Homans discussed how the formal design of a group can impact group effectiveness.[12] Homans suggested that teams often perform poorly when they have not been designed properly, specifically when the group composition, task design, and formal organization do not support collaboration.[13]

Well-designed teams are communities, dedicated to working together to achieve a common goal. They understand the task to which they have been assigned and the roles and responsibilities that each team member has in completing that task. **Task objectives** orient team members toward their goals and priorities and help them understand how their work fits into the bigger picture.[14] These objectives also inform members of the anticipated duration of the team's activities, which can help pace required deliverables. In some cases, teams possess the authority to set their own objectives and measurement criteria. In other cases, objectives may be set by higher management or by some other external entity. Either way, the team can define the manner in which they will work to accomplish their goals.

Teams that complete tasks with a long-term horizon sometimes set a series of shorter-term objectives to measure their progress and to maintain motivation. For example, a product development team at Eli Lilly's Peripheral Systems Division set a series of objectives for the market introduction of an ultrasonic probe to help doctors locate deep veins and arteries.[15] Because the team could measure its progress based on when each objective was achieved, the team was aware of where it stood throughout the development process. As one of the largest pharmaceutical companies in the world, Eli Lilly often engages in product development work such as its ultrasonic probe, which is very extensive and takes a considerable amount of time. By using shorter-duration milestones, Eli Lilly's product development teams can sustain momentum and enthusiasm for their work even as it evolves over a long period of time.

To achieve the task objectives, well-designed teams are also composed of the "right" team members, those who are technically adept and skilled at engaging and motivating fellow team members in the completion of the task. In this section, we discuss several team design factors that can affect teamwork and team effectiveness.

Team Composition and Size

Well-functioning teams include members who are engaged and motivated to solve a specific problem. While members may disagree on how a problem should be solved, they must have a common purpose and agenda. Teams that include members with divergent agendas or mismatched goals often struggle to come together to accomplish their assigned task. In addition to a shared purpose and objective, team members should be equally committed to the task to ensure that the team's recommendations reflect the group's collective wisdom and input.

As noted previously, teams that are assigned to complex problems and issues tend to include members with a diverse set of technical skills and capabilities. The nature of the team's task should dictate the types of individuals needed to ensure that any proposed solutions are well vetted. For instance, new product development teams should include representatives from manufacturing, engineering, marketing, product/brand management, and research. In certain cases, it may even be appropriate to include customer representatives on the team. While it is best to ensure that a team is composed of the right level and mix of technical skills at the start, it is not unusual for teams to add new members as they work through the solution or recommendation process. When new members are added to a team, care should be taken to ensure that they are properly assimilated and that they support the team's mission.

While many team members are selected for teams based on their technical skills, team members also should be selected based on their interpersonal skills. The ability to

Task objectives
Issues that orient team members toward their goals and priorities and help them understand how their work fits into the bigger picture.

work well with others, provide support, and maintain a positive attitude are all important interpersonal skills that should be considered when designing an effective team.[16] As we will discuss later in this chapter, team process is often characterized by a balance of confrontation and collaboration. Team members should be able to navigate effectively between healthy conflict and consensus. In addition to working well together, team members should be open to new ideas and should be action-oriented. Finally, effective teams include members who possess a shared sense of mutual accountability: Each one carries his or her weight and contributes to the team's objectives.

There is no optimal team size; size should reflect the nature of the task (i.e., it should include the right mix of skills and perspectives to achieve the desired objective). At Sun Microsystems, the former computer company that is now owned by Oracle, for example, teams differed in size, but each was made up of individuals with diverse specialties. Each team member was assigned to a team based on his or her talents, location, and current workload.[17] Teams typically ranged from 5 to 20 members.[18] Although some may believe that large teams can accomplish tasks faster than small teams, the opposite is usually true. As such, it is generally better to have too few members than too many.[19] Large teams can be more difficult to coordinate because communication challenges and potential for conflicts may increase with each additional member.[20] As the size of a team increases, the tendency to collaborate decreases because coordination activities increase.[21]

Manager-Led versus Self-Directed Teams

While considering team size is important in creating a well-designed team, so too is the careful assignment of team members to particular roles. Certain team members may be assigned leadership roles in which they are responsible for defining the team's goals, establishing a process to meet goals, motivating members, and reporting the team's progress to others in the organization. In some teams, this leadership role is shared among members. In all cases, being specific about individual team member roles is especially important in minimizing confusion and coordination problems.

How roles are determined may vary across teams depending on whether the team is manager-led or self-directed. For some teams, the specific team roles are assigned by a manager. When Dr. David Torchiana was a cardiac surgeon at Massachusetts General Hospital (MGH), he led a team that included a cardiologist, a surgeon, an anesthesiologist, various residents, nurses, and other personnel from multiple areas of the hospital. The team's task was to define the most effective sequencing and timing of interventions by physicians, nurses, and other staff to minimize delays, more effectively utilize resources, and most importantly, provide the highest quality of care for patients undergoing central artery bypass graft (CABG) surgeries.[22] Throughout the process, Dr. Torchiana, the manager of the team, encouraged team members to meet regularly, communicate with one another clearly, and discuss the importance of each member's role in the care path process. In addition, he set clear milestones for the team, encouraged team members to standardize procedures and share best practices, and fostered a consensus-driven decision making process. In the end, the CABG care path team led by Dr. Torchiana successfully developed a plan that supported MGH's goals for better patient care. We refer to these types of teams as **manager-led teams**. In manager-led teams, leaders have the greatest amount of control over team members and the work they perform. The manager is responsible for monitoring and managing performance processes and reporting the team's progress to the rest of the organization.[23]

In manager-led teams such as the care path team at MGH, the manager acts as the team leader and is responsible for defining the goals, methods, and functioning of the team.[24] Manager-led teams can be classified as **vertical teams** or **horizontal teams**. Vertical teams are composed of a manager and his or her subordinates in

Manager-led teams
Teams in which the manager acts as the team leader.

Vertical teams
Teams composed of a manager and his or her subordinates in the formal chain of command.

Horizontal teams
Teams composed of employees from about the same hierarchical level but from several different departments in the organization.

the formal chain of command. Everyone on the team is usually from the same function or same unit within an organization. Horizontal, or cross-functional, teams such as the MGH care path team, are composed of employees from about the same hierarchical level but from several different departments in the organization. When manager-led teams are cross-functional, a multiperspective approach to problem solving can be used.

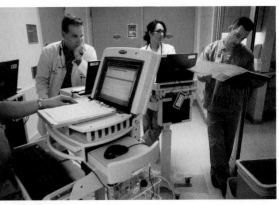

Both manager-led and self-directed teams have their respective pros and cons. While some believe that manager-led teams are most efficient because of clear direction by a leader, organizations that use **self-directed teams** also find them beneficial because they empower their workers by giving every team member authority and responsibility for team building and team progress.[25] In self-directed teams, team-building and decision-making roles are usually assigned to different team members, with each responsible for participating in processes that help the team progress. Regardless of the specific form chosen both manager-led teams and self-directed teams must encourage individual responsibility, clarity of roles, and teamwork among team members to be effective. If these standards are not promoted, disorganization can result and productivity can suffer. Without clear leadership, self-directed teams can struggle to achieve their objectives, especially when disagreement among team members reaches an impasse. If other team members cannot help to find a resolution, senior executives outside the team will most likely need to intervene.

Collocated and Geographically Distributed Teams

For manager-led or self-directed teams to be effective, team members need to work together in an environment that supports communication and interaction. **Collocated teams,** like the ones at Whole Foods, use a significant amount of face-to-face communication to make operating decisions.[26] They operate in close proximity, engage in a lot of social interaction, and provide quick feedback on the team's progress to one another.[27]

Research shows that face-to-face interaction can facilitate collaboration and teamwork.[28] When team members engage in face-to-face social interaction and informal conversation, team members feel more connected to each other. For example, team members may observe other team members' facial expressions, physical appearances, and body language to determine whether they're speaking openly. Face-to-face communication also signifies that team members are sharing experiences in a common physical space, a factor that may signal commitment to the team's experience. Establishing trust, making connections, and committing to a shared team experience are all important in developing relationships among team members.[29]

As technology improves and globalization causes team members to become separated by distance and time, more companies are creating **geographically distributed teams.** Managing geographically distributed teams is difficult as team members often work in several different countries across multiple time zones. As a result, these teams tend to rely heavily on electronic tools such as e-mail, voicemail, telephone, and videoconferencing to interact with one another.[30] These tools allow geographically distributed team members to communicate and provide feedback rapidly across physical boundaries. Team members also may have different cultural backgrounds and styles of work that impede efficient communication. To confront some of these issues, companies such as the former Sun Microsystems created programs specifically designed to support geographically distributed teams.

Top management at Sun Microsystems launched a program in 1995 to solve many of the challenges experienced by geographically distributed teams. "Open

Todd Heisler/The New York Times/Redux Pictures

Self-directed teams
Teams that determine their own objectives and the methods by which to achieve them.

Collocated teams
Teams that use a significant amount of face-to-face communication to make operating decisions. They operate in close proximity, engage in a lot of social interaction, and provide quick feedback on the team's progress to one another.

Geographically distributed teams
Teams that are made up of geographically or organizationally dispersed members who rely heavily on electronic tools such as e-mail, voice mail, telephone, and videoconferencing to interact with one another.

Work" was created to allow employees to work together across multiple time zones, function in their current workplace locations more effectively, and benefit from more flexible work schedules and a better work–life balance structure.[31] The Open Work program consisted of three components: a suite of technologies that allowed people to move between work sites and have consistent mobile access to personal computer sessions; access to "workplaces for the day" when employees were not in their permanent location; and monthly allowances that included Internet, telephone, and hardware costs for mobile employees.[32] As a result of these initiatives, Sun's geographically distributed teams experienced fewer coordination and interaction problems.

Leveraging Diversity

Geographically distributed teams tend to be more diverse, and this diversity can create both opportunities and challenges. Diversity today comes in many forms. It includes people of different genders, races, ethnicities, educational backgrounds, languages, and functions. Each of these differences, in turn, leads to fundamentally different world views but also differences in the way in which information is examined and decisions are made. Some of us are very detail oriented and want to see all the objective and subjective details before making a decision, others are much more intuitive and prefer not to get into the details. There are countless such differences some of which are culturally rooted and others are simply based on individual differences in how we explore the world and make decisions. Given the breadth and depth of their personal and professional experiences, diverse team members tend to produce more creative and innovative solutions over the long term than do teams with more homogenous members.[33] Diverse team members generally possess more complementary information and expertise as well as a broader network to draw upon, which helps facilitate the generation of numerous ideas and approaches. If, however a task is straightforward and speed and efficiency are important, a more homogenous team may be appropriate. Homogenous teams tend to possess a common language and approach that facilitate and accelerate the group process.

While diverse teams come with some advantages, they are also much more challenging to manage and when poorly managed can lead to disastrous results. As a result, you are likely to witness greater variance in performance among diverse teams than among homogenous teams. While diversity is likely to increase creativity over the long term, diverse teams tend to struggle with group identity and process in the short term as its members have a limited base of mutual knowledge and experiences. As such, diverse teams are more likely to experience conflict and misunderstandings if the team and its leader do not take the time to ensure that all team members understand each other's perspectives.[34] Whether they are manager-led or self-directed, it is critical to ensure that these leadership tasks are accomplished to make such teams work. When individuals on diverse teams do not believe that their point of view is valued, they tend to withdraw; consequently, the group squanders the value of its diversity, and its recommendations may suffer. This high variance in the performance of diverse teams makes active guidance by effective leaders critical to success.

There are a number of fundamental principles that must be followed to make a diverse team work. Along with a healthy respect and appreciation for the diversity of backgrounds of the individuals on the team, members must be comfortable with not only different points of view, but also working through those differences. While conflict may be heightened in the early stages of a diverse team's life cycle, the team's recommendations will benefit from multiple points of view in the long run. The success of diverse teams increases when its members possess a shared understanding of each other's strengths and limitations. Success also increases when a team adopts shared norms for working together and respects each other's differences. Finally, it is critical that an individual's view of himself or herself is consistent with the team's view of him or her.[35] The only way to ensure this consistency is to enable team members to express themselves freely and to share information about themselves. The goal in leading diverse teams is to unleash creativity while minimizing misunderstandings based on lack of familiarity.

TEAM DEVELOPMENT

The process of completing team tasks does not always run as smoothly as the Motorola Razr Team (described in "A Different View"), even when the team has been well designed. For example, team members may not agree on the best way to approach a task or some team members may believe other members are not putting enough effort into the task. As a result, the environment can become stressful and it may take longer for the team to finish its task. When the assignment is eventually completed, some team members may feel less than satisfied with the final product.

While a team needs to be properly designed, an effective team also is the one in which team members communicate, make decisions, and complete tasks in ways that allow each member to have a positive team experience. To achieve these outcomes, each team member should be committed equally to the team's task and to developing productive working relationships with each other.

Stages of Development

In his research on teams, Bruce Tuckman observed that teams often undergo a five-stage process of group development: forming, storming, norming, performing, and adjourning (see Figure 17.2).

In the **forming stage**, team members define what task is to be done and how that task is to be accomplished, setting the ground rules for the team. At the Royal Bank of Scotland, for example, leaders create detailed descriptions of realistic performance goals and then plan and schedule the work that needs to be done. Effort

> **Forming stage**
> *The stage that occurs when team members define the task that is to be done and how that task is to be accomplished, setting the ground rules for the team.*

The Leadership Development Journey

Leaders should be aware of some common pitfalls that have the potential to make a team dysfunctional. These pitfalls can include the following:

- Lack of trust among team members
- Fear of conflict between team members
- Uncommitted team members
- Team members who avoid accountability
- Team members who do not focus on results.[36]

Reflect upon a time when you worked on a dysfunctional team. Based upon your reflection, why was the team dysfunctional? With hindsight, how could you have improved the effectiveness of the team?

A DIFFERENT
View

Professors Deborah Ancona of MIT's Sloan School of Management and Henrik Breman of INSEAD conceived of X-teams. In an effort to drive innovation, X-teams view externally focused ideas and relationships as critical components of a successful team. X-team members are chosen for their ability to work with each other, their colleagues, and systems within their organization, but the emphasis is placed on their relationships and abilities to foster new ideas outside of the organization. The Motorola Razr cell phone was a result of an X-team.

The team started by looking at concepts that engineers had discarded and then put together a sketch that incorporated elements from different ideas. Five engineers were sent off, each charged with coming up with two different designs that would solve the problem. Three of the resulting designs had the greatest potential, but after an intense two-week process, the team settled on a single design. The result was a revolutionary new phone that sold more than one million units in six months.[37]

1. What aspects of the X-team were critical to the success of the Razr cell phone?
2. Identify a situation in your own life in which an X-team would have been valuable.
3. Identify an organization that could benefit from the innovative ideas of an X-team. How would they incorporate an X-team into their organization? What would be the goal of the X-team?

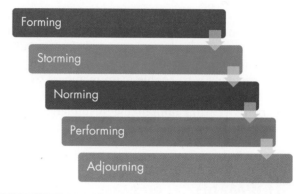

Figure 17.2 ⟩ Five Stages of Group Development

Sources: B. Tuckman, "Developmental Sequence in Small Groups," *Psychological Bulletin*, Vol. 63, No. 6, 1965, pp. 384–399; and B. Tuckman and J. Jensen, "Stages of Small-Group Development Revisited," *Group & Organization Studies*, Vol. 2, No. 4, December 1977, pp. 419–427.

is focused on providing teams with necessary resources and coordinating teams' activities. In the forming stage, team members also learn about one another's skills and competencies.[38] The team launch process can often be an important driver of future team performance. As the team forms, it is important for team members to be purposeful about the launch process, taking the time to ensure that all members agree on the team's mission. In addition, team members should take the time to learn more about each other, including what each one brings to the team and how they can best leverage their experiences to support the team's mission.[39] As noted previously, this sharing of information is especially important for diverse teams.

In the **storming stage**, team members experience conflicts about interpersonal issues and differences in perspectives. Team members can become polarized around interpersonal issues, which are exacerbated by high levels of personal conflict. Infighting and lack of unity is common, impeding the team's work on the task and the development of group members' relationships. As we saw in Chapter 16, the team leader should encourage task-related and discourage affective conflict. Refocusing the team on its purpose can help to channel conflict in an appropriate manner and can enable the team to leverage its diversity.

In the **norming stage**, team members uncover ways to create new standards that encourage more collaborative behavior. Team members adopt new group-generated standards and roles. Personal opinions are frequently shared, and group members become open to one another's input. As a result, team members accept the differences of fellow group members and group cohesion and harmony are established.

In the **performing stage**, team members have bridged their differences and work together to complete the task. In this stage, team members adopt and play roles that enhance the activities of the group. These roles are then leveraged in ways that support the completion of task activities and team problem solving. Of course, if team members are not able to overcome their personal differences and to coalesce around a mutually agreed upon purpose, they will struggle to deliver or produce an effective outcome.

Finally, in the **adjourning stage**, the team has completed its task and is disbanded. For some team members, this stage brings sadness and self-evaluation because they have become dependent on the team. For others, it brings relief because they believe that they are now able to take on the next challenge.

Several researchers have re-examined Tuckman's description of the stages of team development, and while some have different perspectives on the order and impact of the stages, there is widespread agreement that teams evolve over time. In her research, Connie Gersick found that groups initially tend to approach projects through a framework that is set during the team's first meeting. During the initial period, teams may show little visible progress because they have not yet figured out how best to work together. At the midpoint of the team's life, team members

Type of Norm	Description
Meeting norms	When, where, and how often to have meetings. Includes expectations for attendance, timeliness, and preparation.
Working norms	Standards, deadlines, distribution of work, work review process, and accountability (addressing those who do not follow through on their commitments).
Communication norms	When communication should take place, who is responsible, how it should be done, and how to discuss feelings about the team or members especially in regard to issues of conflict.
Leadership norms	What leadership structure should be used and how leadership should be exercised.
Consideration norms	Treating others with mutual respect and being considerate of members' needs.

Table 17.1 ⟩ Team Norms

Source: Adapted from A. Nahavandi, *The Art and Science of Leadership* (Upper Saddle River, NJ: Prentice Hall, 2006).

begin to search for new ideas and adopt new perspectives on their work in a push to complete the task on time.[40] It is useful for teams to reassess their priorities at this point and to reengage with external constituencies to ensure that the contextual framework has not changed the required deliverables or evaluation criteria. This transition is driven by team members' awareness of time and deadlines, not necessarily by completion of a specific developmental stage. In essence, many teams undergo a midpoint transition that allows them to start working as a productive team. Regardless of the precise stages a team may go through, it is clear that there is a formation stage, a middle stage, and then a performing stage. Team leaders play a critical role in helping to navigate teams through these various stages. This navigation process can be much more productive when teams adopt specific norms.

Team Norms

The first few team meetings are critical to establishing **team norms** that outline acceptable team behavior and processes. At the outset, the team leader should be explicit about the team's ground rules (e.g., attendance, participation, and confidentiality), team members' roles, and performance expectations. Team norms generally fall into five different categories: meeting norms, working norms, communication norms, leadership norms, and consideration norms.[41] A definition of each type of norm is included in Table 17.1.

While team members often feel uncomfortable discussing team norms, creating them can prevent some of the group conflict that arises in teams that have not set standards for acceptable team behavior. Therefore, when teams are launched, team members should spend time discussing norms to agree on a common approach to managing disruptive behaviors. In addition, team norms can hold members accountable for their contributions and discourage social loafing. **Social loafing** occurs when team members disengage from the team process and fail to contribute to the team's recommendations or other deliverables. This can lead to frustration and enhanced conflict among team members. Team norms should be revisited around the midpoint of completing a task. At this stage, team members generally know enough about each other to make a realistic assessment of what's working and what should change.

TEAM PROCESS

As each team develops across its various stages, a key to its success is the importance of establishing a productive team process, which is the way in which a team works together to accomplish its goals. Spontaneous or haphazard processes in a

Storming stage
The stage that occurs when team members experience conflicts about interpersonal issues and differences in perspectives.

Norming stage
The stage that occurs when team members uncover ways to create new standards that encourage more collaborative behavior.

Performing stage
The stage that occurs when team members adopt and play roles that enhance the activities of the group.

Adjourning stage
The stage that occurs when a team has completed its task and the team is disbanded.

Team norms
Expected team behaviors.

Social loafing
Disengaging from the team process and failing to contribute to the team's recommendations or other deliverables.

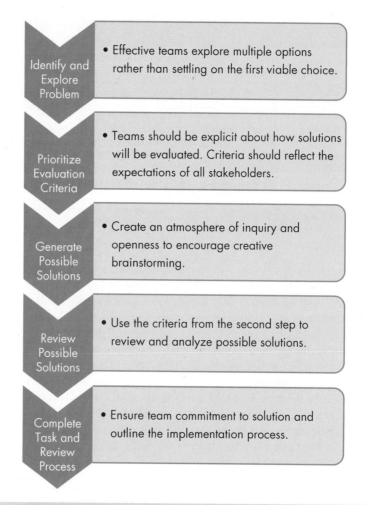

Source: These five steps are a modified version of the process discussed in Linda A. Hill and Maria T. Farkas, "A Note on Team Process," Harvard Business School Note No. 9-402-032 (Boston, MA: HBS Publishing, 2001).

team are a recipe for disaster. Hence, one of the key precepts to effective teamwork is establishing clear processes up front. There are three main components of team process: (1) purposeful and rigorous decision making, (2) effective participation and meaningful influence, and (3) constructive conflict.

Purposeful and Rigorous Decision Making

A strong team process should encourage critical thinking and debate among members.[42] As teams move through the process of making recommendations or solving problems, they generally move from divergent to convergent perspectives. That is, they consider many possibilities and open-ended alternatives before they narrow them down to a few recommendations.[43] This process of moving from a variety of possibilities to a single recommendation typically encompasses five steps (see Figure 17.3).

The first step in the process is to ensure that all team members understand the problem or issue that the team has been asked to address. A clear and agreed-upon problem definition helps to align all team members. During the second step, teams should evaluate the criteria by which possible solutions will be evaluated. In the next step, teams engage in brainstorming to generate a list of potential solutions. In well-functioning teams, team members build on each other's ideas. Steps 2 and 3 can be reversed based on the preference of the team. Some teams find it easier to generate solutions without the constraint of evaluation criteria; they believe it provides a wider canvas for the generation of ideas.

In step 4, teams analyze the possible solutions using the criteria that was defined in step 2. During the final step of the team decision-making process, the team tries to come to a final agreement on the proposed solution or recommendation. The goal of the final step is to build a level of commitment and support for the team's recommendation. Team members will generally feel more committed to the outcome if they believe that the process of reaching the recommendation was fair.

Effective Participation and Meaningful Influence

A rigorous decision-making process requires active and thoughtful participation of all team members. As such, teams should pay attention to who participates, how often and when they participate, and what impact their participation has on the team process or the possible solutions that are generated. There is generally more participation from team members who have a higher organizational status, which tends to discourage others on the team from sharing their opinions and perspectives and could force team members to withdraw from the process. Those with more knowledge of the issue or problem or those who are more talkative than others also tend to be more active participants. Finally, those who care the most about the issue participate more often than others.[44]

Recent research on team performance has shed light on two elements that contribute to more effective and productive teams. Anita Woolley and colleagues measured over 700 people on a variety of different attributes (IQ, personality, etc.) and then randomly assigned them to work alone or in teams on a number of challenging tasks, including brainstorming, moral reasoning, logistical planning, etc. They found that teams performed better than individuals on every task, but improvement was not automatic. She and her colleagues also found that while IQ did play a role in predicting team success, two other factors contributed the most to collective team performance—turn-taking and social sensitivity. They found that group performance improves when the conversation is not dominated by a single individual. While the team members did not have to have an even level of participation, they all had to have had a chance to participate in the team decisions, and they had to believe that the balance of participation was relatively fair. In addition, teams that performed better were characterized by team members who were sensitive to other team members' opinions and perspectives. In other words, these team members possessed empathy, the ability to see another person's point of view or perspective. While empathy does not mean that one person must agree with another person's position, it does mean that he or she should be open and willing to accept that someone has a different way of looking at the same information.[45]

Team leaders or members taking on a relationship-building role should encourage active participation from all individuals on the team to ensure that minority views are shared and considered. Team leaders should also actively encourage members to share their unique information. All too often, teams only discuss information that all members have in common.[46] When teams fall prey to what is called the **common information effect**, they consider commonly held information to be more important and influential than uniquely held information, and as a result, they often fail to leverage the diversity of the team.[47] In doing so, they squander the opportunity to consider more innovative and potentially stronger ideas and solutions. Imbalances in participation and/or the sharing of only common information can lead to a poor recommendation or a lack of commitment to any team recommendation.

While **participation** reflects the extent to which individuals engage in the process of generating solutions and articulating their opinions and perspectives, influence refers to the impact an individual's opinion or perspective has on the team process or solution (as defined in Chapter 14). Those who talk the most or those who are passionate about an issue can exert a disproportionate amount of influence

Common information effect
Teams that consider commonly held information to be more important and influential than uniquely held information.

Participation
The extent to which individuals engage in the process of generating solutions and articulating their opinions and perspectives.

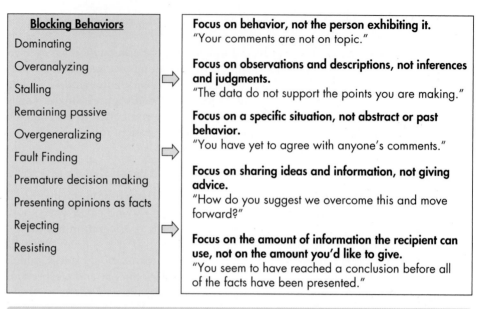

Figure 17.4 ⟩ Common Blocking Behaviors and Effective Managerial Tactics

Source: Adapted from D. A. Whetten and K. S. Cameron, *Developing Management Skills*, 5th edition (Hoboken, NJ: Prentice-Hall, 2002), pp. 467–489.

on the team. But individuals who ask pointed questions also can exert a tremendous influence. An imbalance of influence or participation can lead to behaviors that destroy morale and teamwork. These behaviors are called **blocking behaviors** because they inhibit the team and its members from achieving their objectives.[48] Effective leaders manage these behaviors by giving feedback in contexts that are appropriate and nonthreatening (generally, in private). The 10 most common blocking behaviors and methods to manage them are provided in Figure 17.4.

Constructive Conflict

Highly productive teams must develop the capacity to engage in constructive conflict and leverage their diversity. Most of us are conflict avoiders and consider all conflict to be bad and avoided at all costs. Yet, we must recall that there is task conflict that is productive and focused on the task and there is affective or relationship conflict that is personal and can be destructive. For a team to be productive, it is key for them to find a way to engage in task conflict without it spilling over into personal conflict. This isn't easy but can be done with some concerted effort. The following five strategies can help team members learn how to make the most of constructive conflict:[49]

- Make sure all team members understand the purpose of the discussion up front.
- Focus on inquiring about team members' perspectives, not on challenging them. Say, for example, "Can you explain why you think that method would help?" instead of "Well, I think we should do it this way!"
- Avoid using imprecise language that may cause confusion among team members. Instead of saying, "We just need to do more with this," say, "I think we need more quantitative data to prove our point."
- When you become confused, angry, or frustrated, raise your concerns with the group without casting blame on other team members. Say, "I'm starting to get concerned that we haven't made a decision yet and the meeting is almost over," instead of "You are stalling, and that's going to make us miss our deadline!"
- When the team is at an impasse, determine the source of disagreement by asking, "What do we agree on, and what do we disagree on?"

Blocking behaviors
Behaviors that inhibit the team and its members from achieving their objectives.

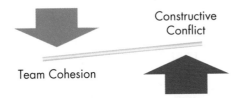

Figure 17.5 ⟩ Balancing Team Cohesion and Constructive Conflict

Teams sometimes go to one extreme or another—either avoiding conflict or embracing too much conflict that then spills over into unproductive affective conflict. When teams avoid conflict, they often encounter a pitfall, which involves conformity. **Conformity** occurs when people behave in line with a group's expectations and beliefs. Team members typically choose to conform to avoid conflict. Although conformity may speed up the decision-making process, it often results in less than ideal or even negative outcomes. Effective teams need to manage the paradox of team cohesion with the open expression of diverse perspectives (see Figure 17.5). While teams need to come to consensus at some point, they should be careful not to close out the discussion and exploration process too quickly.[50]

At the other extreme, if the level of conflict is so high that effective communication is impaired, it is usually appropriate to suspend the task and review the team process or team norms. It is especially important to halt the discussion if the conflict is too personal. As we discussed in the previous chapter, teams should encourage task-related conflict that facilitates multiple perspectives and points of view on the task and minimizes affective conflict.

Promoting Team Learning

Remember that team activities happen over time. And so, researchers looking at teams over time have also become interested in the extent to which teams learn from their experiences. Researchers have proposed that teams that focus not just on carrying out processes more efficiently but also on learning faster are more effective.[51] Yet many team leaders and members have a tendency to focus on executing tasks instead of promoting collaboration and learning. Promoting team learning requires that team members be deliberate about the value of learning and reflecting from their experiences. This takes time and effort and requires a deliberate desire to improve and learn. In addition, to do so requires creating an environment in which everyone feels safe to offer ideas, ask questions, and discuss concerns without fear of judgment, failure, or retaliation. These types of environments, which encourage an open expression of ideas and feelings without a fear of being penalized, are considered to be **psychologically safe**.[52]

To create a psychologically safe learning environment, team members should model openness and curiosity, explicitly acknowledge when the team lacks answers, ask questions showing that input is appreciated, and reward learning.[53] When environments are not psychologically safe, team members "tend to focus more on achieving their own goals rather than cooperative goals."[54] Team leaders can encourage a psychologically safe environment by the following:

- Framing the work the team does as a learning process
- Listening really well, practicing curiosity, and showing interest in others (e.g. displaying empathy)
- Practicing humility by acknowledging that you do not have all the answers
- Fostering mutual respect
- Showing appreciation for others' displays of vulnerability.[55]

Conformity
The action of people behaving in line with a group's expectations and beliefs.

Psychologically safe
An environment which encourages an open expression of ideas and feelings without a fear of being penalized.

TEAM EFFECTIVENESS

How do you determine if your team has been effective? For teams to be considered effective, they must do three things: (1) they must produce meaningful results for the organization, (2) they must satisfy team members, and (3) they must enhance the ability of team members to work well together in the future (see Figure 17.6).[56] Meaningful results could be a finished task or project or an analysis and prioritization of various recommendations for further review. The team's output (i.e., the product, service, or decision) should meet or exceed the standards of quantity, quality, and timeliness expected by the team's clients (i.e., the people who receive, review, or use the output). Some team members may use their involvement with the team to support a personal agenda.[57] Team leaders need to ensure that they achieve the proper balance between individual and team objectives and that any member's personal agenda is subordinate to the collective goal.

Effective teams also must contribute to the personal satisfaction and well-being of team members. Each member should believe that his or her role is important to the team's success and that his or her contributions are valued by other members. The most effective teams not only provide individuals with a sense of accomplishment but also provide critical developmental opportunities that enhance a team member's overall knowledge and skills in the organization. Individuals are more likely to feel connected to the team and to contribute to its mission if they believe that the experience will enhance their personal development and support the overall mission of the organization.

Finally, effective teams enhance the capabilities of members to work together in the future by building a shared sense of purpose and a strong level of mutual trust. While a team may have a limited time span for its existence, its members often have a much longer opportunity to work together in other capacities. In essence, teams help to expand an individual's personal network of relationships in the organization. This network can become a vital means by which tasks are accomplished in the organization both formally and informally.

For teams to achieve success, relationships must be skillfully managed. Member motivation must be developed and sustained, while problems with confusion and coordination are minimized.[58] As important as it is to manage these internal dynamics, it is equally important for team members to communicate effectively with external parties who rely on the team's output. The team leader plays a particularly

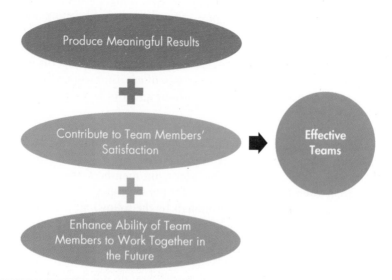

Figure 17.6 Conditions for Team Effectiveness

Source: Adapted from J. Richard Hackman, *Leading Teams: Setting the Stage for Great Performances* (Boston, MA: HBS Press, 2002).

important role in influencing the manner in which the team interacts with each other and with outsiders.

Role of a Team Leader

A team leader can be a formally designated role or it may be a role that the team assigns at the outset and then even rotates across various team members. Regardless of how a team leader role comes about, we know that it is critical to the success of a team. Effective leaders are attuned to the needs of team members and are committed to accomplishing team goals. Effective leaders also want to create high-performing teams. As a result, they motivate team members to share responsibility for the task and to trust other team members. Because you will likely be a team leader at some point in your career, it is important that you understand the specific skills that are necessary to becoming an effective team leader.

From 1996 to 2004, USA Basketball had chosen the roster for the U.S. Men's Basketball Summer Olympic team by selecting NBA All-Stars who were typically opponents during the regular basketball season.[59] While this strategy worked well in 1996 and 2000, in 2004, it fell flat as the team was plagued by personality conflicts. They were defeated by Argentina in the semifinals. For the 2008 Summer Olympic Games in Beijing, USA Basketball changed its approach to designing the U.S. Men's Basketball team, asking each prospective player to make a three-year commitment to the team for the 2006 World Championships and the 2008 Olympic Games. Mike Krzyzewski ("Coach K"), the legendary men's basketball coach at Duke University, was chosen to coach the team. As part of his "team play" approach to basketball, he focused on getting the team members to work together toward a common goal.[60] The three-year commitment allowed enough time for the team to actually become a team, not just a loose collection of All-Stars. In 2008, Coach K led the U.S. Men's Basketball team to a gold medal victory.

Leading a team effectively requires that you gain the respect and commitment of your team members. Gaining respect and commitment will allow you to be influential, and being influential will help you create a high-functioning team that can accomplish organizational goals efficiently. To gain respect, ensure commitment, and maintain credibility, researchers propose that leaders develop seven behaviors (see Table 17.2).

Behaviors of Effective Team Leaders	Description
Demonstrate integrity	Doing what you say you will do and behaving in line with your personal values. Leaders with integrity are trustworthy, have no hidden agendas, and are fair in their actions.
Be clear and consistent	Expressing certainty about what you want and how to achieve it. Your behaviors are predictable.
Create positive energy	Being optimistic, complimentary, and recognizing progress help a leader be more influential. Behaviors that are not helpful are criticizing and being cynical.
Find common ground	When addressing a group, identify the common ground before addressing areas that require compromise.
Manage agreement and disagreement	Present your point of view and support it with evidence, or present two perspectives and show ways in which one is more relevant.
Encourage and coach	Help others develop courage to tackle uncertainty and achieve more than they are currently achieving. Provide information or advice, assist members with tasks, and provide reinforcing comments when the team faces challenges.
Share information	Obtaining information from external sources and sharing it with the team makes leaders more influential. This also includes asking questions and checking with the team to assess team issues and needs.

Table 17.2 ⟩ Behaviors of Effective Team Leaders

Source: Adapted from D. A. Whetten and K. S. Cameron, *Developing Management Skills*, 5th edition (Hoboken, NJ: Prentice-Hall, 2002), pp. 460–462.

The effectiveness of a team comes not only from what happens within the team but also from the way it engages with the larger organizational context around it. When trying to understand team effectiveness, it is easy to focus on the dynamics within the team, but ignoring external parties can affect a team's ability to perform. Team leaders need to manage the team's boundaries to ensure that the team understands the contextual framework in which it operates and appreciates the perspectives and expectations of key stakeholders. While key constituents are typically individuals inside the organization, such as managers and executives, others outside the organization (customers) could be impacted by the team's final product or recommendations.

Generally, the most effective teams maintain significant contact with outsiders such as managers, executives, and customers, apprising them of the team's progress and utilizing their input when making team decisions.[61] This is important because managers and executives have the authority to allocate resources and the ability to reassign current team members or recruit new individuals. By engaging in conversations with outsiders, teams may receive a clearer indication of what is expected of them or they may receive clearer direction on what their final product should be.

Managing Boundaries

Most effective teams will have a formally appointed or informally designated boundary manager. The **boundary manager** determines how a team will work with clients, upper management, and others who have an interest in the team's performance. The team leader typically assumes this role, although others can contribute to a strong understanding of and interface with the contextual landscape. Boundary managers buffer the team from organizational infighting, persuade top management to support the team's work, and coordinate and negotiate with other groups on work deadlines.[62] Effective boundary managers identify key people who will influence or be influenced by the work of the group. In addition, boundary managers play a key role in deciding what needs to be done to ensure that the team understands the positions of others outside the team.[63] These tasks are critical to ensuring that the team's output meets or exceeds organizational expectations.

In a study of teams, Deborah Ancona found a continuum of boundary management activities—from minimal to extensive external interaction—that teams used to communicate their strategy and decisions.[64] She named these teams informing teams, parading teams, and probing teams (see Figure 17.7). The most appropriate approach depends on the nature of the team's task, the knowledge of team members, the team's access to vital information, and the team's level of autonomy regarding decision making and implementation.

Leading Geographically Distributed or Virtual Teams

Running a team whose members are not in the same location poses significant challenges to building team effectiveness.[65] Process skills are even more important for virtual teams. Therefore, in addition to deploying the strategies that you learned for leading teams, you should rely upon other approaches when leading geographically distributed teams:[66]

- *Walk before you run.* Managers should be skilled at managing a collocated team first.
- *Assume nothing; spell out everything.* Set guidelines for how the team will communicate and what the timeline will be. Effective communication skills are especially important in geographically dispersed teams because communication tends not to be face to face and there are fewer opportunities for clarification.
- *Communicate even more.* Be in touch with the team as often as possible. This may mean sending e-mails, posting information to a project website, sending faxes, and/or making telephone calls.

Boundary manager
A manager who determines how the team will work with clients, upper management, and others who have an interest in the team's product. They buffer the team from organizational infighting, persuade top management to support the team's work, and coordinate and negotiate with other groups on work deadlines.

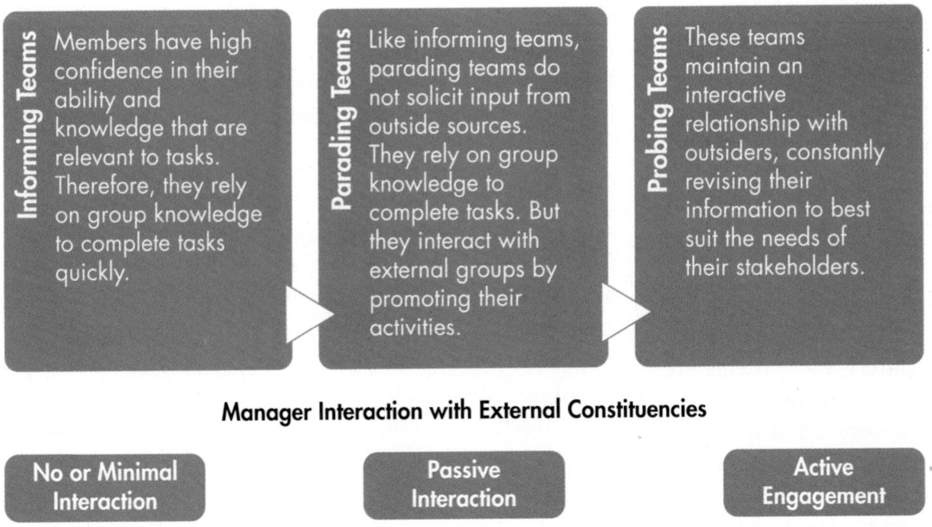

Informing Teams	Parading Teams	Probing Teams
Members have high confidence in their ability and knowledge that are relevant to tasks. Therefore, they rely on group knowledge to complete tasks quickly.	Like informing teams, parading teams do not solicit input from outside sources. They rely on group knowledge to complete tasks. But they interact with external groups by promoting their activities.	These teams maintain an interactive relationship with outsiders, constantly revising their information to best suit the needs of their stakeholders.

Manager Interaction with External Constituencies

No or Minimal Interaction	Passive Interaction	Active Engagement

Figure 17.7 Different Approaches to Boundary Management

Source: Adapted from Deborah Ancona, "Outward Bound: Strategies for Team Survival in an Organization," *Academy of Management Journal*, Vol. 33, No. 2, 1990, pp. 334–365.

- *Share background information.* If team members get to know each other, they are less likely to misinterpret actions or make incorrect assumptions about each other's motivations.
- *Find allies.* Build an alliance with someone who is high enough in the organization to sponsor the team. This person can request assistance on the team's behalf.
- *Watch for conflict—and learn to manage it.* Probe for potential problems by re-reading e-mails and asking questions such as, "Are you okay with that?" Given the lack of face-to-face communication, misunderstandings and conflict can escalate quickly in virtual teams.
- *Do better next time.* Debrief the team experience with team members when the project ends. Use this information when participating in or managing another geographically distributed team.

Teams that include members whose primary language is different have even more challenges. In these situations, team members should avoid using jargon or slang, which can lead to misinterpretations and misunderstandings. In addition, teams should arrange for multiple breaks in meetings to regularly check on the process and ensure mutual understanding. Team norms become more important in these situations as well. Team members should agree on how they will communicate, how they will engage all members in the decision-making process, and how they will deal with conflict.[67]

SUMMARY

LO1 A team is a group of two or more people with complementary skills who are committed to working together to achieve a specific objective. Teams are generally better than individuals working alone or work groups when the task is complex, when the task requires a diversity of interdependent perspectives and expertise,

and when the task requires buy-in from multiple constituencies.

LO2 There are several aspects to consider when creating a team including who should be on the team and how large the team should be. The team should be composed of members who are motivated to solve a specific objective and who have the technical skills that are relevant for this objective. Members could come from one functional area if the task is very specific to that area or teams could be cross-functional if the task requires a broader level of perspectives and expertise. For teams to be effective, the individuals on the team should possess strong interpersonal skills and should be open to new ideas and perspectives. Strong interpersonal skills are particularly important for teams that are very diverse. Diverse teams tend to struggle in the beginning, but if leveraged appropriately, these teams are often able to develop more innovative solutions.

Teams can serve different functions from information exchange to problem solving to project delivery. The nature of the team's function will determine who should be on the team as well as its duration. Some teams are short-term project teams that are established with a finite timeline and specific objective. Other teams can be ongoing. Teams that are collocated can take advantage of consistent social interaction to enhance the effectiveness of the team. Teams that are geographically dispersed must be very thoughtful about the ways in which its members communicate and disseminate information.

LO3 : Team development generally progresses through five key stages: (1) forming, when members define what task is to be done, (2) storming, when members experience conflict, (3) norming, when members create standards to guide behavior, (4) performing, when members complete the task, and (5) adjourning, when members disband and take stock of their experience. Effective teams engage in mid-point check-ins to recalibrate their norms and recommit to a common goal.

LO4 : An effective team process is composed of several components, including rigorous decision making, effective participation and meaningful influence, and constructive conflict. For team members to feel engaged, they must believe that their opinions and perspectives are valued. If team members are not able to adequately participate in the team process, they are more likely to disengage and not support the team's final recommendations.

LO5 : Effective teams develop products that are acceptable to clients, grow in their personal capabilities, and learn from one another. Several dynamics can affect the degree to which a team is effective. These dynamics include the team size, team design, and team processes and the ways in which the team members interact with those outside the team. Leaders should manage aspects that are internal to the team such as composition and process as well as manage aspects that are external to the team such as access to critical resources and buy-in from senior management. When leading a dispersed or virtual team, the leader must focus even more vigilantly on process and communication to ensure that team members are engaged and informed.

KEY TERMS

Adjourning stage	Horizontal teams	Storming stage
Blocking behaviors	Manager-led teams	Task complexity
Boundary manager	Norming stage	Task interdependence
Collocated teams	Participation	Task objectives
Common information effect	Performing stage	Team
Conformity	Psychologically safe	Team norms
Forming stage	Self-directed teams	Vertical teams
Geographically distributed teams	Social loafing	

ASSIGNMENTS

Discussion Topics

1. Under what conditions is a team better than a work group or a collection of individuals working independently?

2. Teams should include individuals with the appropriate technical and interpersonal skills. Teams with members who have a good balance of both skills are ideal, but what if you needed to choose between team members who were stronger in one

area over the other. Would you favor team members who were strong technically or interpersonally? What are the advantages and disadvantages of each approach?

3. What are the challenges and benefits of self-directed teams? Do you prefer being on manager-led or self-directed teams? Why?

4. Think of diverse teams that you have been a member of. When was diversity a help or hindrance to team performance? What can be done to ensure that diversity is leveraged in the most effective way?

5. What activities can a new team engage in to ensure that they have a successful launch?

6. When someone on a team decides to "fly under the radar" and engage in social loafing, what can be done to re-engage them? How should team members confront this behavior? Why is it so difficult to hold peers accountable for team performance?

7. What can a team leader do to encourage full participation in the team? What are the dangers of not ensuring full participation?

8. Review the three dimensions of team effectiveness in Figure 17.6. How would you rank them in terms of importance? Are they all equally important? In what situations or teams is one criterion more important than another?

9. Consider the different approaches to boundary management outlined in Figure 17.7. For each approach, how will the composition of the team and the team process need to change?

10. What are the advantages and disadvantages of geographically dispersed teams? What can a leader do to minimize the disadvantages?

Management Research

1. Research a team in the news and create a case study on that team. In your case study, document the following:

   a. Identify the team members.

   b. Identify the team type.

   c. Describe how the team is led (manager-led vs. self-directed).

   d. Provide examples of how the team leverages diversity.

   e. Describe the team norms.

   f. Analyze how the team promotes learning and manages boundaries.

   g. Evaluate the team's effectiveness.

2. Based on the information you collected for the case study, develop a visual model that depicts how the team operates.

In the Field

Identify a team on your campus and volunteer to serve as its "coach." Work with the team and help them to accomplish the following.

   a. Articulate their goals and develop performance measurements for them.

   b. Determine a strategy for managing boundaries.

   c. Develop formal decision-making processes.

   d. Learn how to manage conflict constructively.

   e. Develop practices for sharing information and creating positive energy.

At the conclusion of the coaching session, have the team comment on what aspects of the coaching they found valuable, and how they will use your coaching tips.

ENDNOTES

[1] Linda A. Hill and Maria T. Farkas, "A Note on Team Process," *Harvard Business School Note No. 9-402-032* (Boston, MA: HBS Publishing, 2001).

[2] Jon R. Katzenbach and Douglas K. Smith, "The Discipline of Teams," *Harvard Business Review*, July–August 2005.

[3] "Whole Foods, Inc. Company Profile," www.hoovers.com, accessed May 17, 2015.

[4] "Whole Foods, Inc. Company Profile," www.hoovers.com, accessed June 29, 2009.

[5] G. Hamel and B. Breen, *The Future of Management* (Boston, MA: HBS Press, 2007).

[6] Ibid.

[7] Anthony J. Mayo, Masako Egawa, and Mayuka Yamazaki, "Kazuo Inamori, A Japanese Entrepreneur," *Harvard Business School Case No. 9-408-039*, rev. April 6, 2009 (Boston, MA: HBS Publishing, 2008), pp. 8–9.

[8] J. Richard Hackman, *Leading Teams: Setting the Stage for Great Performances* (Boston, MA: HBS Press, 2002).

[9] R. J. Volkema, "Problem Complexity and the Formulation Process in Planning and Design," *Behavioral Science*, Vol. 33, pp. 292–327.

[10] Jeffrey T. Polzer, "Leading Teams," *Harvard Business School Note No. 9-403-094* (Boston, MA: HBS Publishing, 2003).

[11] Paul R. Lawrence and Jay W. Lorsch, *Organization and Environment* (Boston, MA: Graduate School of Business Administration, Harvard University, 1967); and James D. Thompson, *Organizations in*

Action: Social Science Bases of Administrative Theory (New York: McGraw-Hill, 1967).

[12] G. C. Homans, *The Human Group* (New Brunswick, NJ: Transaction Publishers, 2004).

[13] Ibid.

[14] Jeffrey T. Polzer, "Leading Teams," Harvard Business School Note No. 9-403-094 (Boston, MA: HBS Publishing, 2003).

[15] J. R. Katzenbach and D. K. Smith, "The Discipline of Teams," *Harvard Business Review*, July–August 2005.

[16] F. LaFasto and C. Larson, *When Teams Work Best* (Thousand Oaks, CA: Sage Publications, 2001).

[17] Tsedal Beyene, Thomas J. DeLong, Alison Comings, and Patricia Hernandez, "Managing a Global Team: Greg James at Sun Microsystems, Inc. (A)," Harvard Business School Case No. 9-409-003, rev. November 1, 2009 (Boston, MA: HBS Publishing, 2008).

[18] J. R. Katzenbach, and D. K. Smith, "The Discipline of Teams," *Harvard Business Review*, July–August 2005.

[19] Jeffrey T. Polzer, "Leading Teams," Harvard Business School Note No. 9-403-094 (Boston, MA: HBS Publishing, 2003), p. 7.

[20] I. Steiner, *Group Process and Productivity* (New York: Academic Press, 1972).

[21] L. Gratton and T. J. Erickson, "Eight Ways to Build Collaborative Teams," *Harvard Business Review*, November 2007.

[22] Stephen C. Wheelwright and Mikelle Fisher Eastley, "Massachusetts General Hospital: CABG Surgery (B)," Harvard Business School Case No. 9-697-021 (Boston, MA: HBS Publishing, 1997).

[23] J. Richard Hackman, *Leading Teams: Setting the Stage for Great Performances* (Boston, MA: HBS Press, 2002).

[24] L. Thompson, *Making the Team: A Guide for Managers* (Upper Saddle River, NJ: Prentice Hall, 2000).

[25] H. Seifter, "The Conductor-less Orchestra," *Leader to Leader,* Summer 2001.

[26] G. Hamel and B. Breen, *The Future of Management* (Boston, MA: HBS Press, 2007).

[27] P. J. Hinds and S. Kiesler, *Distributed Work* (Cambridge, MA: The MIT Press, 2002).

[28] Ibid.

[29] Ibid.

[30] Linda A. Hill and Maria T. Farkas, "A Note on Team Process," Harvard Business School Note No. 9-402-032 (Boston, MA: HBS Publishing, 2001).

[31] Tsedal Beyene, Thomas J. DeLong, Alison Comings, and Patricia Hernandez, "Managing a Global Team: Greg James at Sun Microsystems, Inc. (A)," Harvard Business School Case No. 9-409-003, rev. November 1, 2009 (Boston, MA: HBS Publishing, 2008).

[32] Ibid.

[33] Kathleen M. Eisenhardt, "Strategy as Decision Making," *Sloan Management Review*, Spring 1999, pp. 65–72.

[34] Linda A. Hill and Maria T. Farkas, "A Note on Building and Leading Your Senior Team," Harvard Business School Note No. 9-402-037, rev. June 6, 2002 (Boston, MA: HBS Publishing, 2002), pp. 15–17.

[35] Jeffrey T. Polzer and Hillary Anger Elfenbein, "Identity Issues in Teams," Harvard Business School Note No. 9-403-095 (Boston, MA: HBS Publishing, 2003).

[36] Patrick Lencioni, *The Five Dysfunctions of a Team* (San Francisco, CA: Jossey-Bass, 2002).

[37] S. D. Anthony, "Making the Most of a Slim Chance," *Strategy and Innovation: Breakthrough Insight and Ideas for Driving Growth* (Harvard Business School Publishing and Innosight, July–August 2005).

[38] L. Gratton, A. Voight, and T. Erickson, "Bridging Faultlines in Diverse Teams," *Sloan Management Review*, Vol. 48, No. 4, Summer 2007.

[39] Bryan L. Bonner and Alexander R. Bollinger, "Bring Out the Best in Your Team," *Harvard Business Review*, September 2014.

[40] C. J. G. Gersick, "Time and Transition in Work Teams: Toward a New Model of Group Development," *Academy of Management Journal*, Vol. 31, No. 1, pp. 9–41.

[41] Deborah Ancona, Thomas Kochan, Maureen Scully, John Van Maanen, and Eleanor Westney, *Managing for the Future: Organizational Behavior & Processes* (Boston, MA: South-Western College Publishing, 1999).

[42] L. Thompson, *Making the Team: A Guide for Managers* (Upper Saddle River, NJ: Prentice Hall, 2000).

[43] Jeffrey T. Polzer, "Leading Teams," Harvard Business School Note No. 9-403-094 (Boston, MA: HBS Publishing, 2003), p. 15.

[44] Linda A. Hill and Maria T. Farkas, "A Note on Team Process," Harvard Business School Note No. 9-402-032 (Boston, MA: HBS Publishing, 2001).

[45] Anita Williams Woolley, Christopher F. Chabris, Alex Pentland, Nada Hashmi, and Thomas W. Malone, "Evidence for a Collective Intelligence Factor in the Performance of Human Groups," *Science*, October 29, 2010.

[46] J. Richard Hackman, *Collective Intelligence: Using Teams to Solve Hard Problems* (San Francisco, CA: Berrett-Koehler Publishers, 2011), p. 15.

[47] Cass R. Sunstein and Reid Hastie, "Making Dumb Groups Smarter," *Harvard Business Review*, December 2014.

[48] D. A. Whetten and K. S. Cameron, *Developing Management Skills*, 5th edition (Upper Saddle River, NJ: Prentice Hall, 2002).

[49] R. B. Ross, "Skillful Discussion," *The Fifth Discipline Fieldbook: Strategies and Tools for Building a Learning Organization*, P. Senge, A. Kleiner, C. Roberts, R. B. Ross, and B. J. Smith, eds.(New York: Doubleday, 1994).

[50] Linda A. Hill and Maria T. Farkas, "A Note on Team Process," Harvard Business School Note No. 9-402-032 (Boston, MA: Harvard Business School Publishing, 2001).

[51] Amy C. Edmondson, "The Competitive Imperative of Learning," *Harvard Business Review*, July–August 2008.

[52] Amy C. Edmondson, *Teaming: How Organizations Learn, Innovate, and Compete in the Knowledge Economy* (San Francisco, CA: Jossey-Bass, 2012), p. 77.

[53] Amy C. Edmondson, Richard Bohmer, and Gary P. Pisano, "Disrupted Routines: Team Learning and New Technology Adaptation," *Administrative Science Quarterly*, Vol. 46, 2001, pp. 685–716.

[54] Amy C. Edmondson, *Teaming: How Organizations Learn, Innovate, and Compete in the Knowledge Economy* (San Francisco, CA: Jossey-Bass, 2012), p. 129.

[55] Ibid.

[56] J. Richard Hackman, *Leading Teams: Setting the Stage for Great Performances* (Boston, MA: HBS Press, 2002).

[57] James Ware, "Managing a Task Force," Harvard Business School Note No. 9-478-002, rev. April 6, 1995 (Boston, MA: HBS Publishing, 1995), p. 2.

[58] L. Thompson, *Making the Team: A Guide for Managers* (Upper Saddle River, NJ: Prentice Hall, 2000).

[59] J. Robinson, "U.S. Men's Basketball Roster Announced," *The New York Times*, June 23, 2008.

60 PR Newswire, "USA Basketball Coach Mike Krzyzewski (Duke University's Coach K) to Write About World-Class Team Building and the Olympic Gold Medal Quest," *MarketWatch*, September 13, 2008.

61 Deborah Ancona, "Outward Bound: Strategies for Team Survival in an Organization," *Academy of Management Journal*, Vol. 33, No. 2, 1990, pp. 334–365.

62 Deborah Ancona, Thomas Kochan, Maureen Scully, John Van Maanen, and Eleanor Westney, *Managing for the Future: Organizational Behavior & Processes*, (Boston, MA: South-Western College Publishing, 1999).

63 Ibid.

64 Deborah Ancona, "Outward Bound: Strategies for Team Survival in an Organization," *Academy of Management Journal*, Vol. 33, No. 2, 1990, pp. 334–365.

65 C. Wardell, "The Art of Managing Virtual Teams: Eight Key Lessons," *Harvard Management Update*, November 1998.

66 Jeanne M. Brett, *Negotiating Globally: How to Negotiate Deals, Resolve Disputes, and Make Decisions Across Cultural Boundaries* (San Francisco, CA: Jossey-Bass, 2001).

67 Ibid.

CHAPTER

18

Motivation

Learning Objectives

After reading this chapter, you should be able to:

LO1 Differentiate between intrinsic and extrinsic rewards and describe how they influence motivation.

LO2 Outline the five primary content theories of motivation and describe how they are similar and different.

LO3 Describe the primary process theories of motivation and what each one attempts to measure.

LO4 Explain the different ways in which desired behavior is reinforced within an organization and the role that job design plays in channeling motivation.

SELF-REFLECTION

What Motivates You?

Motivation is the desire, incentive, or stimulus to pursue a course of action. Individuals can be motivated by many different factors. Understanding what motivates you can help you with goal setting, career choices, and performance management. Reflect upon what motivates you by responding True or False to the following statements.

1. I am motivated by financial rewards.

2. I am motivated by the fear of punishment.

3. I am motivated by recognition.

4. I am motivated by challenges.

5. I am motivated by goals.

6. I am motivated by achievements.

7. I am motivated by developmental opportunities.

8. I am motivated by helping others.

9. I am motivated by affiliation or a sense of belonging.

10. I am motivated by the need to learn or master a task.

Based on your responses, what motivates you? How do you think these motivating factors will influence your selection of a career?

INTRODUCTION

To be successful, organizations must search for ways to work better, faster, or cheaper than the competition, but they cannot accomplish this without motivating employees to perform. While great leaders are adept at inspiring individuals to believe in an organization's vision or direction, the real test of leadership is the ability to stimulate actions of employees in pursuit of that vision. Success requires employee **motivation**—the desire, incentive, or stimulus to pursue a particular course of action. The underlying reasons someone is motivated to perform are not universal. Some employees are motivated to perform because their work gives them a sense of accomplishment and achievement. They may be driven by the responsibility, challenge, variety, and autonomy of the job.[1] Other employees are motivated by tangible rewards such as a competitive salary or bonus plan. Still others are more inclined to value public recognition or acknowledgment. Motivation can also be driven by a desire to avoid punishment.

Motivation that is derived from external rewards such as compensation, bonuses, recognition, and variable pay is called extrinsic. **Extrinsic rewards** are

Motivation
The desire, stimulus, or incentive to pursue a particular course of action.

Extrinsic rewards
Rewards used to facilitate or motivate task performance that include pay, promotions, fringe benefits, and job security.

specific, tangible, and easy to compare. Individuals who are extrinsically motivated have a desire to perform in a way that enables them to achieve material or social rewards. In contrast to extrinsic motivation, intrinsic motivation is derived from aspects of "doing the job," which could include interesting and challenging work, self-direction and responsibility, variety, opportunities to use one's skills and abilities, and sufficient feedback regarding one's efforts. **Intrinsic rewards** generally provide personal satisfaction and are centered on opportunities that provide learning, autonomy, meaning, challenge, and variety. The value of intrinsic rewards is based on an individual's conception of his or her worth. As such, their value tends to be harder to compare from one person to another (see Figure 18.1).

In reality, these different motivators are not mutually exclusive. For example, employees are often motivated because they enjoy doing the work and because the work pays them well and provides opportunities for recognition. The degree to which each factor (intrinsic or extrinsic) is important varies across individuals, and successful companies and their leaders must be able to determine the right balance.[2] One study found that companies that build a committed and motivated workforce outpace their counterparts by almost two to one in terms of stock price growth.[3] In line with this research, another study found that companies with engaged employees average 18% higher productivity and 49% lower turnover.[4] From these data, it is clear that building and cultivating employee engagement is important. An engaged workforce can be a significant differentiator in the marketplace especially considering that a recent analysis of major global companies found that only 13% of the workforce was highly engaged. Surprisingly, less than half of the workforce would not recommend their employer to their peers.[5]

To better understand motivation, it is important to identify what drives certain behaviors. Evaluating whether to put effort into a job requires that a person consider what the job offers, whether his or her efforts will result in better performance, and the extent to which that performance will be rewarded in ways that are considered fair and equitable. If these conditions are met, individuals are more likely to be motivated to put forth the requisite effort.[6] This chapter will explore different theories of motivation and how leaders can enhance employee motivation through reinforcement and rewards. One company that has used various motivational approaches to enhance employee engagement is HCL Technologies.

Intrinsic rewards
Rewards associated with "doing the job" that include interesting and challenging work, self-direction and responsibility, variety, opportunities to use one's skills and abilities, and sufficient feedback regarding one's efforts.

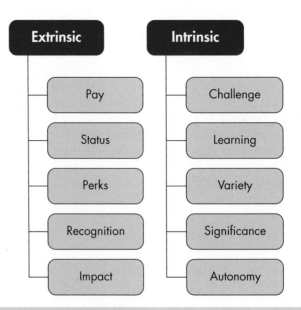

Figure 18.1 Extrinsic and Intrinsic Rewards

Vineet Nayar and HCL Technologies

HCL Technologies was founded in India in 1976 by a small group of engineers who wanted to lead the computer hardware industry. By heavily investing in research and development (R&D) and attracting India's top talent, HCL Technologies propelled itself to the forefront of the world's hardware industry: its computer systems came out before Apple, and its programming language was created before Oracle. Under the leadership of founder Shiv Nadar, HCL Technologies prospered during the "golden years" of the 1980s, and it dominated the computer industry.[7] During the 1990s, software and services began to emerge as a game changer in the industry, but HCL decided to stick to its core hardware technology. This strategy proved costly. By 1997, HCL was forced to reorganize its business and move into computer services to keep up with the competition. But it continued to lag: In 2000, HCL was no longer the most desirable place to work in India, and it suffered an attrition rate of 30%.[8] HCL's financial performance was still supported by the momentum from its hardware business.

Searching to redefine its strategy, HCL turned to Vineet Nayar in 2005. Nayar's primary strategy was to offer multiservice propositions to the midsize customers who were being ignored or poorly serviced by industry giants such as IBM and Accenture.[9] But even more important than a new strategy was company unity. As Nayar got started, he realized that many of HCL's problems were caused by the culture and values of the employees. At the time, employees were extremely talented, but they lacked unity. They were used to working in silos. Nayar knew that regardless of the strategy, employees needed to collaborate in order to identify and execute solutions together.[10] To address these problems, Nayar changed the organizational structure to focus on a few lines of business, introduced the concept of a Business Finance group, laid the groundwork for the Multi-Service Delivery Unit, and began automating processes across lines of business. But the most important change was a new slogan to drive the company's culture: "Employee First, Customer Second."[11]

Emerging from an initiative to improve employee collaboration, the Employee First campaign had four strategic objectives: to provide a unique employment environment, to drive an inverted organizational structure, to create transparency and accountability in the organization, and to encourage a value-driven culture.[12] While many employees remained skeptical, feeling the initiative seemed to lack substance, Nayar pressed ahead and emphasized that "employee first" meant that HCL was going to invest in employee development and unleash employees' potential to produce bottom line results.[13] To address these objectives, HCL Technologies launched three core initiatives.

The first initiative was to improve the existing intranet, a widely used system to connect employees. One of the new tools was the Smart Service Desk (SSD), which created a ticket-based system that employees could use to log any issue in any department that a manager would be required to address. After the transaction, the employee rated his or her level of satisfaction with the manager's resolution.[14] Nayar also implemented "U&I," a system where any employee could pose questions to him. To promote transparency and trust, Nayar answered 100 questions every week and posted them on the intranet for all to see. Both systems improved transparency.[15]

The second initiative mandated that all managers participate in 360-degree feedback, a tool in which managers seek positive reinforcement and constructive criticism about their performance from subordinates, peers, and superiors. Although these were commonly used in business environments to varying degrees of success, Nayar wanted them to transform the way people thought and the way they conducted themselves at the company. To do this, he encouraged all managers to post their reviews in a public forum. To demonstrate his faith in the system, Nayar was the first to do so.[16] While many hesitated, most managers followed suit because they did not want to seem to have anything to hide.[17]

The final initiative was called "trust pay." Rather than providing pay based on performance, which would include a monthly base pay of 14,000 rupees and a possible 6,000 rupee bonus, HCL gave the full 20,000 rupees to employees. Although this increased costs, it also increased trust. By providing full pay up front, managers were effectively expressing faith in their employees that they would deliver results. To instill even more trust, this policy was implemented for only 85% of the company: the top 15% of the company still had to hit performance targets before receiving their bonus compensation.[18]

Before the Employee First campaign was executed, Nayar admitted that he faced a difficult decision. Should he build on previous ideas or completely change them? With competitors outperforming his company by 10%–20% each year, he felt he had no choice but to take a chance by completely changing the company.[19] It proved to be successful. Within months of the structural and cultural changes, HCL beat out big players such as IBM, Accenture, and HP to win a $50 million contract with Autodesk in California, the largest deal it had ever acquired. Shortly after, in January 2006, HCL won the largest outsourcing deal in Indian history with a $330 million project for DSG International.[20] Due to his transparency and emphasis on employee development, Nayar transformed the culture and operation of HCL technologies, which, in turn, transformed its competitiveness in the market. The success of this transformation was dependent on building an engaged and motivated workforce. To that end, many of the initiatives that were championed by Nayar were designed to enhance employee motivation.

Case in Point

Vineet Nayar and HCL Technologies

1. Why did Nayar want to change the culture at HCL Technologies?
2. How do you think the objectives of the "employee first" campaign changed the culture at HCL Technologies?
3. How did he motivate employees to collaborate?
4. Why was investment in employee development an important motivator?
5. Why do you think motivating the employees improved HCL Technologies' performance?

CONTENT THEORIES OF MOTIVATION

A key to driving performance is to align employee incentives and needs with the overarching goals of the organization. Research has shown that employees often create internalized "psychological contracts" about the terms and conditions of the working relationship with their employers.[21] These are not written documents, but rather implicit understandings in the minds of the employees that, in turn, shape their motivation and behavior. These terms and conditions lay the foundation for what is expected of employees as well as what is expected of employers. In exchange for a certain performance, employees expect a commensurate level of compensation, recognition, or other forms of acknowledgment. The terms of these psychological contracts can include aspects of the culture (e.g., the open exchange of ideas and the sharing of best practices) as well as expectations for equitable pay, job security, and other associated benefits. The degree to which organizations uphold these agreements influences employees' trust in their employers, their motivation to serve customers, and their willingness to perform at their best.

Some organizations have an explicit understanding of their psychological contract with their employees and work hard to maintain it. Southwest Airlines believes that upholding its psychological contracts is critical to motivating employees. The company fulfills part of these psychological contracts by offering employees an opportunity to voice their concerns about the organization. For example, employees who have been with the company 9 months or less are randomly selected and invited to have lunch with Southwest's president and several other executives.[22] At these luncheons, the conversations focus on how well the new employees' expectations have been met and how the company can improve the recruitment, selection, training, and orientation processes.[23] Southwest believes that this process allows it to facilitate a positive emotional connection between employees and the company. This company believes that this emotional connection, in turn, motivates employees to more effectively market the airline to customers.[24]

Children's Healthcare of Atlanta, a pediatric care hospital, recognizes that employees are motivated not only by their material goals, but also to fulfill their personal needs and desires. To that end, Children's Healthcare of Atlanta created Strong4Life, an organization-wide effort to help employees achieve their personal wellness goals to create a healthier workforce to care for Atlanta's rapidly growing pediatric population. The company's senior vice president of human resources explained, "We believe that by helping our employees take better care of themselves, they are better able to take care of the kids we serve."[25]

To explain why fulfilling employees' needs (e.g., the need for a psychological contract or the desire for wellness) can motivate employees to perform better, several theories of motivation have been proposed. The study of the incentives and needs that motivate people to perform in a certain way are called **content theories**. The notion of content here refers to the precise content of what it is that motivates employees. As we will discover, there are a broad array of taxonomies each trying to unpack the distinct elements that motivates employees. One common thread across all these distinct approaches is that different people are motivated by different things. In this section, we explore five content theories: hierarchy of needs theory, ERG theory, two-factor theory, acquired needs theory, and four-drive theory.

Hierarchy of Needs Theory

The **hierarchy of needs theory**, proposed by Abraham Maslow, states that individuals have multiple needs that must be fulfilled in a specific hierarchical order to ensure the greatest level of satisfaction. When Maslow proposed this theory, it was distinctive in explicitly suggesting that workers sought to fulfill non-economic needs in the workplace. Maslow believed that individuals have five needs that they are motivated to fulfill (see Figure 18.2). Maslow postulates that there is a hierarchy across these needs in that employees look for their lower level needs to be met before they expect to receive fulfillment of their higher order needs. The first level in Maslow's hierarchy is physiological needs required for survival, such as food, water, shelter, and oxygen. According to Maslow, these are baseline needs that must be satisfied before a person can consider higher-level issues. When applied to a business situation, the baseline need is fulfilled by a person's salary. The second level encompasses safety needs. Safety refers to a secure and protected physical and emotional environment. Job security and fringe benefits are considered safety needs in organizations.

Content theories
The study of the incentives and needs that motivate people to perform in a certain way.

Hierarchy of needs theory
The theory that individuals have multiple needs that must be fulfilled in a specific hierarchical order to ensure the greatest level of satisfaction.

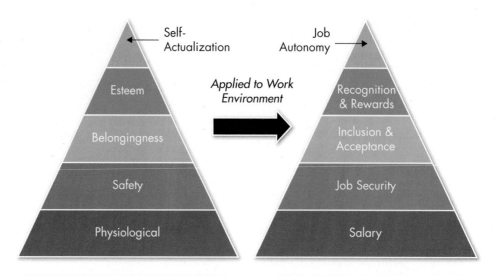

Figure 18.2 › Maslow's Hierarchy of Needs

Source: Adapted from Abraham Maslow, "A Theory of Human Motivation," *Psychological Review*, Vol. 50, 1943, pp. 370–396.

The third level includes belongingness needs such as family, friendships, and intimacy. These needs help satisfy an individual's desire for affiliation. An organization that supports open, inclusive teamwork and information sharing would fulfill a person's need for belongingness. Many of the aspects of a company's culture will increase or decrease an individual's sense of belongingness.

The two higher-order needs in Maslow's hierarchy are esteem and self-actualization. Esteem needs include self-confidence, achievement, and respect. Many of the reward systems discussed, including recognition and opportunities for advancement, fulfill the esteem needs. The final need is self-actualization, which refers to an individual's ability to grow and develop into the best person he or she can be. In essence, self-actualization is a heightened sense of being where a person has found and fulfilled his or her sense of purpose and direction.

According to Maslow, lower-order needs are the most pressing and, therefore, must be satisfied before higher-order needs can be addressed. For example, people will fulfill their physiological needs before they begin to care about fulfilling safety needs. In turn, people will fulfill their safety needs before they begin to care about fulfilling their need for belongingness. According to Maslow, most people work to fulfill their needs for belongingness and esteem while never truly arriving at self-actualization.[26]

Maslow's theory sparked a considerable amount of follow-up research on motivation and much of the subsequent research found that individuals do have a desire to fulfill a number of needs, but they are generally not fulfilled in a hierarchical manner. An individual can be motivated by higher-order needs even when lower-order needs are not satisfied. The rest of this section outlines some of the extensions and revisions of Maslow's foundational theory.

ERG Theory

ERG theory
The theory that individuals are motivated by three primary needs: existence (basic physical needs), relatedness (connection with others), and growth (personal development).

One variant on Maslow's hierarchy theory was proposed by Clayton Alderfer. He collapsed Maslow's five levels into three, which he called existence, relatedness, and growth—**ERG theory** (see Figure 18.3).[27]

- *Existence:* These are basic primary needs that enable a person to live and function productively. Maslow's physiological and safety needs are encompassed within Alderfer's existence needs.

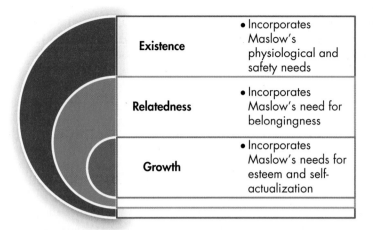

Existence	• Incorporates Maslow's physiological and safety needs
Relatedness	• Incorporates Maslow's need for belongingness
Growth	• Incorporates Maslow's needs for esteem and self-actualization

Figure 18.3 ERG Theory Mapped to Maslow's Hierarchy

- *Relatedness:* Similar to Maslow's need for belongingness, these are desires to interact with others and to be a part of a whole. Individuals seek opportunities to relate to others, share feelings, and openly express and debate thoughts and ideas.
- *Growth:* These needs refer to an individual's desire to reach his or her full potential, which results in higher esteem and a heightened sense of self-actualization.

Although Alderfer shared Maslow's belief in a hierarchical order of needs, he disagreed with Maslow on the process of achieving satisfaction. While Maslow asserted that an individual pursues the satisfaction of needs in a linear, sequential order, Alderfer believed that individuals could pursue multiple needs at once. He believed that if someone was frustrated in the achievement of a higher-order need, that person would revert to trying to satisfy a lower-order need. For instance, if an individual was frustrated with his or her ability to achieve satisfaction in seeking growth, that person would extend extra effort toward the need for relatedness or even a more aggressive pursuit of physiological needs.

Two-Factor Theory

In an effort to test Maslow's and Alderfer's theories, Frederick Herzberg surveyed employees about their job attitudes and levels of job satisfaction. His results supported the theory about higher-order and lower-order needs, but Herzberg disagreed that every need is a motivator. According to his **two-factor theory**, Herzberg believed that lower-order needs were potential dissatisfiers while higher-order needs were the true **motivators**. Fulfilling potential dissatisfiers does not cause people to become more satisfied; instead, it causes them to become less dissatisfied. Conversely, fulfilling motivators can cause people to become more satisfied and more willing to perform at a certain level. Herzberg called these two dimensions **hygiene factors** and motivators.[28]

Hygiene factors, or potential dissatisfiers, relate to physiological, safety, and belongingness needs. These factors are the primary components that comprise the makeup of the work environment. For example, employees expect their employer to provide a livable wage, a secure job, and an opportunity for teamwork and collaboration. Organizations that fall short on any of these dimensions can create the conditions for dissatisfaction. Herzberg found that the primary causes of dissatisfaction were restrictive company policies, overbearing supervision, poor working conditions, and inadequate salary. According to Herzberg, improving these aspects of the job environment does not create satisfaction, nor does it motivate people to perform better in their work. In essence, these are baseline conditions that employees expect.

Two-factor theory
The theory that two conditions, hygiene factors and motivators, simultaneously act as drivers of satisfaction and dissatisfaction. Lower-order needs are hygiene factors and a potential source of dissatisfaction, while motivators are higher-order needs and a potential source of satisfaction.

Motivators
The direct consequences of doing the job and the primary cause of satisfaction on the job.

Hygiene factors
Job factors that are potential dissatisfiers that relate to physiological, safety, and belongingness needs. These factors are the primary components that comprise the work environment.

At the other end of the spectrum are motivators, which are the direct consequences of doing the job and are the primary cause of satisfaction. Motivators correspond to Maslow's hierarchical needs for esteem and self-actualization. Maslow and Herzberg both believed that fulfilling these higher-order needs can motivate people to perform better in their work. Herzberg found that the satisfaction was derived from challenging work assignments, the opportunity for achievement and personal recognition, autonomy, and a sense of personal responsibility and accountability.

Herzberg also found that employees can be satisfied and dissatisfied at the same time. Employees can appreciate the opportunity the job offers for career advancement, but they can still be unhappy about their salary. Motivators can start at zero (no satisfaction) and increase to highly satisfied as achievement and advancement, increase. Similarly, the hygiene factors can start at zero (not dissatisfied) and increase to highly dissatisfied as expectations for a certain salary, company policy, or security are not fulfilled (see Figure 18.4). When Nayar instituted the "trust pay" policy at HCL Technologies, he was, in essence, trying to eliminate a potential dissatisfaction with pay while simultaneously rewarding employees by signaling his faith and trust in them.

Herzberg further distinguished the needs in Maslow's hierarchy as being driven by extrinsic or intrinsic motivation. Physiological, safety, and belongingness needs are essentially extrinsic in nature. Salary and security are two primary extrinsic motivators. Esteem and self-actualization are driven more by intrinsic motivation. Individuals rely on their internal thoughts, feelings, and state of mind to satisfy higher-order needs.[29]

Acquired Needs Theory

Unlike Maslow and Herzberg who asserted that individuals are born with underlying needs, David McClelland believed that certain types of needs are acquired over time and are shaped through life experiences. These needs include the need to attain success, master tasks, and surpass others. They also include the need to form relationships and avoid conflict and to exert influence and control over others. McClelland believed that early life experiences determine when and how people acquire these needs and the order in which they are prioritized.[30]

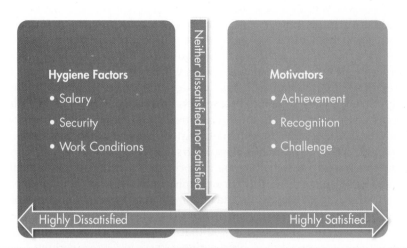

Figure 18.4 ⟩ Herzberg's Two-Factor Continua

Source: Adapted from A. B. Shani and J. B. Lau, *Behavior in Organizations: An Experiential Approach*, 7th edition (New York: McGraw Hill, 2000), pp. 242–244.

In their development of the **acquired needs theory,** McClelland and his peers examined individual differences in the workplace to determine the types of tasks people prefer to do, the kind of work they find challenging and satisfying, and how effective they are likely to be in different work environments.[31] Through their research, they discovered that individuals are motivated by three needs: the **need for achievement,** the **need for affiliation,** and the **need for power.**[32] The need for achievement includes the need to set, meet, and exceed goals. Individuals who are motivated by achievement are task-driven; they are energized by competition and the need to successfully complete a challenge. In other words, high achievers like to win. For the most part, high achievers like to work autonomously and rely only on themselves to accomplish their goals.

In contrast, those who are motivated by the need for affiliation are driven by relationships. They are motivated by the opportunity to interact, socialize, and develop friendships. High-affiliation individuals like to be part of a team, and they like to be liked. This desire for relationship building often means that high-affiliation individuals tend to dislike conflict and social disruption.

The final need that McClelland uncovered is the need for power, which can manifest in two distinct forms: personalized power and socialized power. As the term implies, those who are motivated by personalized power are concerned about their individual status and dominance in relationships. They tend to seek opportunities for personal aggrandizement. In contrast, individuals who are motivated by socialized power like to make an impact on and influence others. They seek to work with and through, not over, others. To that end, they focus on team building and the development of others as well as themselves.

Although individuals often prioritize one of the acquired needs more than the others, in general, individuals are not driven by only one of these needs. The drive to fulfill each need generally ranges from high to low. To be satisfied, a person needs to fulfill all three needs at some level. For instance, employees at SC Johnson fulfill these acquired needs in different ways. In regard to how working at the company fulfills the need for achievement, one employee said, "The culture is one that welcomes a sense of ownership and immediate contribution …"[33] Speaking about the need for power, another employee said, "I am given a sense of responsibility that lets me know my work matters …"[34] Other employees made comments about affiliation, such as, "SC Johnson is a fun place to work!" and "It's a company that cares about me."[35]

Although all individuals possess each of these needs to some degree, McClelland argued that an individual is generally motivated to fulfill one need over another. This predisposition for a certain need has implications for the way in which individuals lead (see Table 18.1). Managers who are high achievement-oriented often tend to be micromanagers. Because they are driven to succeed and win, high-achievement managers tend to struggle with delegation, especially when they believe that they can do the job better than anyone else. Not wanting to leave anything to chance, high-achievement managers tend to adopt a command-and-control leadership style, which can be discouraging for team members. Paradoxically, high achievement-oriented individuals seek continuous feedback and encouragement, yet they are reluctant to provide that same level of feedback to their team members. At the extreme, high-achievement individuals will do whatever it takes to win, even if it means cutting corners or pushing ethical boundaries.[36] Of course, most individuals who are motivated to achieve channel that energy in positive ways. Many high-achievement individuals thrive in entrepreneurial situations where their individual drive can be extremely useful.

Acquired needs theory
The theory that individuals are driven or motivated by three needs: the need for affiliation, the need for power, and the need for achievement.

Need for achievement
The need to set, meet, and exceed goals.

Need for affiliation
The need to interact, socialize, and develop friendships.

Need for power
The need to seek opportunities for personal aggrandizement (personalized power) or the need to make an impact on and influence others (socialized power).

Andrew Spiers / Alamy

	Primary Desires	Implications	When Most Effective
Achievement-Oriented Managers	• Meet or surpass self-imposed goals • Accomplish something new • Plan long-term career advancement • Outperform others	• Micromanage • Try to do things themselves • Provide little feedback • Tend to use command-and-control style of leading • Are impatient with others	• Entrepreneurial ventures
Affiliation-Oriented Managers	• Establish, restore, or maintain warm relationships • Want to be liked and accepted • Participate in group activities, socialize	• Avoid confrontation and negative feedback • Don't apply rules uniformly • Soothe rather than solve problems • Worry more about people than performance	• Service management • Human resources
Socialized Power–Oriented Managers	• Persuade people • Provide advice, coaching, and support • Generate strong positive emotions in others • Maintain their reputations inside and outside the organization	• Coach and teach • Focus on the team • Work through others • Are politically savvy and connected	• Complex organizations • Bureaucracies

Table 18.1 ⟩ Implications for Achievement-, Affiliation-, and Power-Oriented Managers

Source: Adapted from Scott W. Spreier, Mary H. Fontaine, and Ruth L. Malloy, "Leadership Run Amok: The Destructive Potential of Overachievers," *Harvard Business Review*, June 2006.

McClelland found that affiliative managers tend to make decisions based on empathy and compassion and focus on smoothing over problems rather than solving them. They also struggle with delegation if they believe that tasks will overburden their team members. In these situations, they often take on the tasks themselves. Because of their deep concern for others and intense dislike of conflict, high-affiliation managers tend to allow for many exceptions and do not apply organizational rules universally. Ironically, this lack of consistency and conflict avoidance results in less team cohesion and satisfaction, which is what high-affiliation managers seek. While high-affiliation managers tend to struggle with rules and boundaries, they are very effective in certain stressful situations and in service management roles.

Individuals who are motivated by socialized power are often good coaches and teachers. They seek to impress individuals inside and outside the organization. They like to exercise their influence through others and are effective delegators. Power-oriented managers tend to be successful in large, complex organizations where their political savvy and awareness can be put to use. Of course, power can be a double-edged sword. When a manager's power is motivated by personal gain, he or she tends to be more concerned with his or her personal reputation and interests and can focus more on manipulation than influence.

As mentioned, most individuals are motivated by all three needs—achievement, affiliation, and power. The approaches outlined above are not necessarily the way in which individuals with a particular high need will manage. They are tendencies that may be apparent. Good managers are aware of their motives and tendencies and can channel them in a useful way. In fact, each approach can be effective in certain situations.

The manifestation and strength of these motives also tend to vary by culture. For example, the achievement motive in the United States, which is considered an individualistic culture, is often focused on one individual's accomplishments and tasks. In more collectivistic cultures such as Japan, the achievement motive is driven by the collective work of the team or the group, not necessarily by the actions of one individual.[37] When considering any of the motivational drivers in this chapter, it is important to view them with a cultural lens. The culture, norms, and values of a society can and do influence what is considered important and valuable, which in turn, can influence key motivational drives.

Four-Drive Theory

More recently, Paul Lawrence and Nitin Nohria have explored motivation by integrating recent research in neuroscience, biology, and evolutionary psychology. They agreed with other motivation theorists on three specific levels: (1) that underlying needs are innate, (2) that fulfilling them creates satisfaction, and (3) that leaving them unfulfilled creates dissatisfaction. But they also believed that there was no requisite hierarchical order in which the needs must be satisfied and that the satisfaction of one need is not dependent on the satisfaction of another.[38]

From their research, Lawrence and Nohria discovered that people are driven to fulfill four basic emotional needs and that the drive to fulfill these needs is the product of a common evolutionary heritage.[39] Their **four-drive theory** includes the drive to acquire, the drive to bond, the drive to comprehend, and the drive to defend. Lawrence and Nohria proposed that fulfilling these four drives underlies human motivation and that the degree to which they are satisfied directly affects employees' emotions and behaviors.[40] To motivate employees, therefore, all four drives must be addressed at some level (see Table 18.2).

First, employees are driven to acquire scarce goods and social status. As a result, they tend to compare what they have with what others have and always want more. In the workplace, the drive to acquire is fulfilled by (1) employee reward systems that differentiate good performers from average performers, (2) employee rewards that are clearly tied to performance, and (3) salary that is commensurate with the company's competitors.[41] In essence, the drive to acquire becomes a measuring stick by which it is easy to compare one's financial rewards and status with another's.

Like Maslow's need for belongingness and Alderfer's focus on relatedness, the drive to bond manifests in an individual's desire to connect with others inside and

Four-drive theory
The theory that fulfilling four drives—the drive to acquire, the drive to bond, the drive to comprehend, and the drive to defend—underlies motivation and that the degree to which these are satisfied directly affects employees' emotions and behaviors.

Drive	Ways to Fulfill in the Workplace
The Drive to Acquire	Reward System • Differentiates good performers from average and poor performers • Ties rewards clearly to performance • Provides competitive salary and benefits
The Drive to Bond	Culture • Fosters mutual reliance and friendship among coworkers • Values collaboration and teamwork • Encourages sharing of best practices
The Drive to Comprehend	Job Design • Designs jobs that have distinct and important roles in the organization • Designs jobs that are meaningful and foster a sense of contribution to the organization
The Drive to Defend	Performance-Management and Resource-Allocation Processes • Increases the transparency of all processes • Emphasizes fairness • Builds trust

Table 18.2 Fulfilling the Four Drives

Source: Adapted from N. Nohria, B. Groysberg, and L. Lee, "Employee Motivation: A Powerful New Model," *Harvard Business Review*, July–August 2008.

A DIFFERENT View

Drive

What motivates employees? Daniel Pink discusses employee motivation in *Drive*, maintaining that today's independent thinkers are no longer motivated by external rewards such as financial incentives. Rather, they are motivated by the internal gratification of a job well done. He believes that what truly motivates people to succeed is the autonomy to direct their own lives, the mastery to continually improve, and the purpose to do something greater than themselves.

1. What rewards motivate you? Are they external or internal rewards?
2. In your business experience, what types of rewards were offered to you or your colleagues? How effective were those rewards?

Process theories
Theories that explain how employees select behavioral actions to meet their needs and then assess whether these choices were successful.

outside the workplace. Developing these types of connections can give employees pride in the organization. In the workplace, the drive to bond is fulfilled by a culture that fosters mutual reliance and friendship among coworkers, values collaboration and teamwork, and encourages sharing of best practices.[42]

In addition to seeking a sense of affiliation and connectedness, employees are driven to satisfy their curiosity and master the world around them. In the workplace, the drive to comprehend is fulfilled by designing jobs that have distinct and important roles in the organization; in essence, jobs that are meaningful and that foster a sense of contribution to the organization.[43] This drive to comprehend can be likened to an individual's intrinsic motivation; he or she seeks opportunities that present challenges, learning, and development.

Finally, employees are driven to defend themselves against external threats and to promote justice. In the workplace, the drive to defend is fulfilled through performance-management and resource-allocation processes that increase transparency, emphasize fairness, and build trust. Through this drive, employees seek a sense of fairness and equity from their employers. Employee engagement increases to the extent that employees believe that they are justly compensated, recognized, and rewarded for their contributions.[44]

The five content theories we have discussed explain the underlying needs that motivate people to perform and the ways in which these needs can be satisfied. While each of these theories is different, they all center on the individual's desire to satisfy a combination of physical, social, and psychological needs. The next section discusses theories that depart from the content of what motivates employees and instead focuses on how those rewards are delivered. These theories in turn help to explain the thought processes that people use to decide how they will act and how much effort they will put into their actions.

PROCESS THEORIES OF MOTIVATION

The content theories of motivation that we have discussed explain the human needs that underlie behavior and the factors in the workplace that can motivate certain behavior. **Process theories**, in contrast, explain how employees select behavioral actions to meet their needs and then assess whether these choices were successful.

Unlike content theories of motivation, process theories of motivation see the individual as an active decision maker (i.e., someone who engages mental processes), not as someone who satisfies needs according to a predetermined set of variables.[45] Some process theories emphasize the expectations that employees have with regard to the rewards that should result from their efforts. Other process theories emphasize the fairness of the rewards, meaning how they compare to the rewards of other employees with similar efforts, abilities, and levels of experience. Process theories also describe and analyze how behavior is energized, directed, sustained, and stopped. Finally, process theories account for the contextual and the individual factors that can influence workplace behavior.[46] For instance, when unemployment is high and the economy is suffering, individuals may give greater weight to salary and job security. In more prosperous times, opportunities for advancement or skill enhancement may take precedence. In this section, we will address three primary process theories of motivation: goal-setting theory, expectancy theory, and equity theory.

Goal-Setting Theory

Researchers Edwin Locke and Gary Latham found that setting high goals and directing employees toward meeting them is a key driver of motivation. They discovered that for some employees, the excitement and effort to reach a specific goal is as important as the tangible rewards associated with the accomplishment of that goal.[47] **Goal-setting theory** states that the mere setting of difficult but achievable goals is a significant motivator of performance. Locke and Latham proposed that setting goals can affect employee motivation and performance in the following four ways:

1. Goals direct attention and effort toward goal-relevant activities and away from goal-irrelevant activities. In other words, goals help motivate employees to pursue activities that support the overall objectives of the organization.
2. Difficult, not easy, goals make employees want to work harder, whether the goals are set by management or the employee. Difficult goals generally lead to greater effort, persistency, and focus.
3. Tight deadlines for goal completion lead to a more rapid work pace.
4. People automatically use the knowledge and skills they have attained from other activities and apply them to meet new goals.[48]

The researchers proposed that organizations that set specific, challenging goals that are acceptable to employees and that then help them track their progress by providing timely feedback, can impact motivation in positive ways.[49] Performance is enhanced when goals are clear and measurable, not vague and ill-defined, and when they have a specific time frame for completion. One acronym that has been useful in creating goals that fit these criteria is SMART (see Figure 18.5). SMART goals are specific and well-defined, can be effectively measured, and are achievable. In addition, SMART goals should be relevant to the business and should be completed within a defined time frame.

The achievement of challenging goals often leads to an increase in satisfaction with oneself as well as with the organization.[50] In fact, employee satisfaction is often the result, not the cause, of high performance.[51] This is especially true when there is a tight alignment between individual and organizational goals. Effective behavior can be motivated only when the rewards and conditions in the work environment are related to the job. Therefore, organizations must create the conditions that address employees' underlying needs and that consider the ways in which employees calculate and choose their courses of action.

When disconnects between individual and organizational goals occur or when one person's goals are vastly different from another person's goals, conflict can

Goal-setting theory
The theory that setting goals that are difficult, but achievable, is a significant motivator of performance.

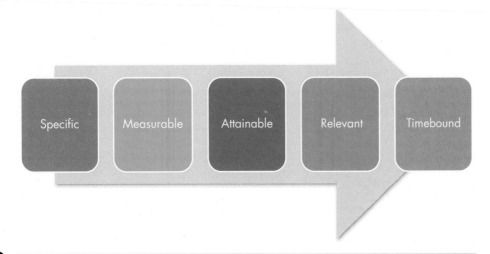

Specific   Measurable   Attainable   Relevant   Timebound

Figure 18.5 › SMART Goals

Source: Adapted from George T. Doran, "There's a S.M.A.R.T. Way to Write Management's Goals and Objectives," *Management Review*, November 1981, pp. 35–36.

ensue. This often happens when two departments have very different goals and are measured on their ability to achieve them. For instance, product development teams are often measured on the success of new product innovations or enhancements. In an effort to test their new ideas, they often need to put them into production, which can be expensive if it requires new processes or new sources of raw materials. The manufacturing unit, on the other hand, may have a goal to produce outputs at as low a cost as possible. Deviations from standard processes can impact the teams' ability to meet their goals, and they may be reluctant to engage in new activities. In these situations, organizations often design goals that combine department- or unit-specific elements with company-wide performance metrics, which may include both cost management and new product introductions. Bonuses may be designed to include individual department results as well as overall organizational performance.

The very power of goal setting can also be its downfall, especially when incentives create opportunities for inappropriate behavior. The pressure to hit specific financial targets or goals has led some individuals to make shortsighted decisions. Some individuals even cross the line into unethical behavior. This was especially true, for instance, in the case of a few chief executive officers (CEOs) in the early 2000s, when their compensation was tied directly to stock price performance. These CEOs made decisions that generated (or in some cases, just appeared to generate) short-term stock gains at the expense of longer-term stability for the organization. In some cases, the CEOs overstated revenues or underreported costs to achieve specific financial performance targets. To be effective, goals must be aligned with proper incentives, and potential pitfalls must be addressed in advance (see Table 18.3).

Expectancy Theory

Individuals often engage in a conscious evaluation of the effort–reward trade-off before deciding to work toward a specific goal. Developed by Victor Vroom, expectancy theory suggests that employees expect that two fundamental patterns to materialize in their jobs. First, high effort should lead to acknowledged good performance and second, that such good performance, in turn, should lead to appropriate reward.[52] They also expect the same to hold true for poor performers—poor effort should lead to low performance and that, in turn, should lead to no rewards. In essence, a relationship between effort, performance, and reward (or outcomes) is something that everyone expects. The research on expectancy theory was the foundation upon which the path-goal theory of leadership was developed (see Chapter 12).

At work, people expect that their accomplishments should be rewarded, especially when a good deal of energy or effort went into them. For example, people who

Pitfall	Potential Solution
Excessive risk-taking	Specify acceptable risk levels and consequences for moving beyond these levels
Increased stress	Ensure that employees have skills, provide training
Goals as ceilings rather than floors	Recalibrate goals as part of an ongoing process; reward overachievement when it is properly aligned
Ignoring nongoal areas	Make sure goals are comprehensive
Short-range thinking	Connect goals to broader mission of organization
Dishonesty and cheating	Set an example of honesty and punish dishonesty

Table 18.3 Goal-Setting Pitfalls and Potential Solutions

work long hours during the week and on weekends may believe that they should receive higher compensation. Similarly, people who take on challenging assignments that create success for the company may believe that they should be promoted.

Expectancy theory suggests that three variables enter into the thought processes of employees when trying to decide how much effort to expend: the linkage from effort to performance, the connection from performance to outcome, and valence or the perceived value of the outcomes (see Figure 18.6). The relationship between these three variables is considered multiplicative, which means that if any of these variables are absent, motivation is also absent.

Effort-to-performance (E to P) expectancy includes the evaluation of whether putting in effort will lead to commensurate performance. To make this determination, employees assess distinct elements. The first is whether they have the requisite ability, previous experience, and tools to perform. For example, to perform successfully on a difficult job assignment, employees must have appropriate education, technical abilities, and interpersonal skills. If they don't have the requisite skills for the task assigned to them, it is unlikely that their effort will translate into good performance. Employees will, in this instance, decide to withhold effort since it is unlikely that such effort would result in a favorable outcome. A second key element underlying the linkage between effort and performance expectancy is whether performance expectations have been clearly defined for employees by their manager. In many instances precise performance expectations may not be clearly delineated and employees are left to guess what is expected of them, making it hard to envision what is required of them to perform well. If they guess wrong and exert effort, they may be surprised later on to find that their assessment of what is considered good performance was wrong. This could then lead to disappointment and frustration. The lack of clarity on performance expectations is more widespread than most of us would imagine. Either managers fail to communicate those expectations clearly or subordinates fail to take note of them. Regardless of the source of this breakdown, it is important for managers to clearly and repeatedly communicate what they consider to be good performance of each of their employees. E to P expectancy is considered high if employees believe that with hard work, they will perform well. If E to P expectancy is high, employees will be highly motivated to perform.

Performance-to-outcome (P to O) expectancy includes the evaluation of whether successful performance will lead to a desired reward. For example, employees must believe that performing successfully on a difficult job assignment will lead to a

Expectancy theory
The theory that employees expect that high effort should lead to good performance and that good performance, in turn, should lead to reward.

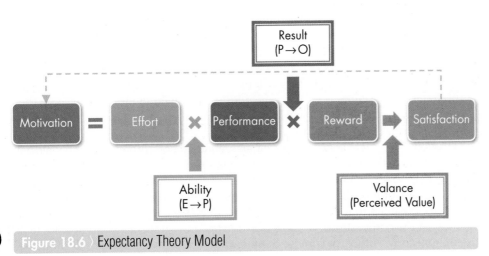

Figure 18.6 › Expectancy Theory Model

Source: Adapted from Michael Beer and Bert A. Spector, "Note on Rewards Systems," Harvard Business School Note No. 9-482-017 (Boston, MA: HBS Publishing, 1981), p. 4.

promotion or a salary increase. If P to O expectancy is high, employees will be highly motivated to perform. This too may fail if an employee is confused about the definition of what is considered good performance. It may also fail if the manager is not able to properly assess performance or live up to his or her promise to connect good performance with a desirable outcome for the employee.

Valence includes the evaluation of whether the available outcomes are attractive to the employee. To encourage high motivation, the available rewards must be valued by employees. As discussed, these rewards can be extrinsic, such as bonuses, or intrinsic, such as the opportunity to enhance one's knowledge or skill set. The timing of the rewards is important. If rewards are delivered in a timely manner, they will generally be considered more valuable.[53] There is sometimes a tendency among some managers to reward others in ways in which they themselves would like to be rewarded. This usually doesn't work because we know from much of the research discussed earlier on content theories that different individuals value different things. If managers don't incorporate valence into their thinking, they also run the risk of breaking down the connection between performance and outcome expectancy.

To increase the desired impact of expectancy theory, managers should attempt to do the following:

- Determine what rewards each employee values.
- Be clear about what behavior the organization expects of its employees.
- Ensure that desired levels of performance are challenging yet achievable.
- Link desired outcomes to desired performances.
- Analyze situations for potential conflicts.

Equity Theory

Until now we have talked about how employees react to the rewards they anticipate from their jobs. Another key element of motivation and rewards arises from the fact that employees work in a social context in which they compare their own performance to that of others. A sense of fair play and equity is central to understanding motivation. At work, employees often compare not only their compensation but also symbolic rewards such as sizes of workspaces in relation to others in similar positions as well as those above or below him or her. For instance, many employees believe that lower-ranking employees should not get a plush corner office. Instead, they believe that this reward should be reserved for higher-ranking managers. If these same employees are then promoted, they perceive that they should be rewarded with a corner office like other high-ranking managers. If their new accommodations are not equal to those of similarly ranked managers, they may perceive the organization and its leaders to be unfair.

Expectancy theory helps us understand the effort–reward trade-offs that individuals make when deciding to pursue a particular task or goal, but this is only part of the equation. Individuals do not expect just to be rewarded for their efforts; they also expect that those rewards will be fair and equitable. This motivational expectation is explained by **equity theory**.

Developed by psychologist J. Stacy Adams, equity theory proposes that people will compare their circumstances with those of similar others and that this behavior motivates them to seek fairness in the way they are rewarded for performance.[54] When they perceive a lack of fairness, they will reduce their motivation in the workplace. Equity theory also assumes that people are motivated to achieve equity. As illustrated in the example of the corner office, employees evaluate equity by a ratio of outcomes (e.g., promotion, corner office, pay, and recognition) to inputs (e.g., position, education, seniority, effort, and skills). Equity exists when the ratio of one person's outcomes to inputs equals the ratio of another person's outcomes to inputs (see Figure 18.7).

Equity theory
The theory that people will compare their circumstances with those of similar others and that this behavior motivates them to seek fairness in the way they are rewarded for performance.

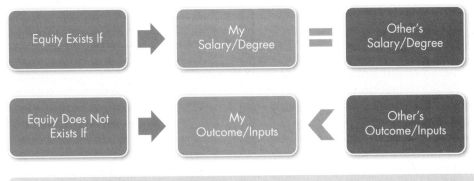

Figure 18.7 Example of Equity Theory

If one employee perceives that the ratio of his or her salary to his or her level of education is less than that of a coworker who has less education, the employee will perceive that he or she is being under-rewarded. As a result, the employee will lose motivation. They may seek to rectify this by seeking greater outcomes for themselves. If these outcomes are not available, they may decide to limit their efforts. In contrast, if the employee perceives his or her ratio to be greater than that of a coworker with less experience, the employee will be motivated to perform. If two colleagues perceive that they are fairly rewarded (essentially their output to input ratios match), both are motivated.

The key to all of these comparisons is perception, which is not always objective.[55] For instance, even though two individuals have the same terminal degree, one individual may consider his or her degree to be superior to that of the other because he or she attended a higher-tier school. Research shows that, generally, most individuals have an unduly favorable assessment of themselves compared with others.

As a result, when they engage in a comparison to others, they overweight their own inputs and underestimate the contributions of others. This can, in turn, lead to an exaggerated sense of being unfairly treated. The point to note is that this is normal behavior that is to be expected of most of us. Leaders must thus find some way to anticipate these likely concerns and provide employees with greater clarity on their own contributions while also creating a system with as much transparency as possible so that each employee can see their performance compared to others in as objective a way as possible.

Another factor that complicates this comparison is that different employees value different outcomes. As a result, organizations often need to tailor the rewards that individuals receive to ensure that the reality and perception of equity are achieved. To do so, they need to understand what is valued by each individual.

At Whole Foods, leaders have set a salary cap that limits any individual's compensation to no more than 19 times the company average, which is a considerable departure from the 400-to-1 ratio of the average *Fortune 500* company.[56] In addition, 93% of the company's stock options have been granted to nonexecutives even though 75% of the stock options are distributed to five or fewer senior executives in most companies.[57] These actions at Whole Foods have created an environment most employees consider to be fair and equitable.

REINFORCING MOTIVATION

As we have seen throughout this chapter, rewards play an integral role in motivating employees. While it is important to identify rewards that are meaningful to employees and that are aligned with the organization, it is equally important to create the organizational conditions in which motivation is continually reinforced. A considerable amount of research has been conducted to understand how to effectively reinforce behavior. One seminal study in the early part of the twentieth century on the effect of environmental stimuli on behavior was put forth by Ivan Pavlov, a Russian psychologist and physician. He found that dogs began to salivate in the presence of the lab technician who normally fed them and not in response to the presence of meat. Later, after ringing a bell on several occasions to call the dogs to their food, Pavlov found that the dogs started to salivate in response to the bell. The behavior of Pavlov's dogs revealed that when an unconditioned stimulus (i.e., the meat) is paired repeatedly with a conditioned stimulus (i.e., the bell), the two stimuli become associated and a behavioral response to the conditioned stimulus is produced (i.e., saliva).

The process of using rewards or punishments to induce behaviors or actions is central to **reinforcement theory**. B. F. Skinner, one of the most prominent reinforcement theorists, proposed that positive and negative reinforcements can increase certain behaviors while extinction and punishment can decrease them.[58] Skinner described **positive reinforcement** as rewarding a desired behavior, **negative reinforcement** as removing an aversive condition in response to a desired behavior, **punishment** as presenting an aversive stimulus in response to an undesired behavior, and **extinction** as the idea that a behavior stops because it has ceased to be rewarded or punished.[59]

In an experiment, Skinner observed that a hungry rat continued to press a bar (the behavior) in its cage as long as it received food each time. Rewarding the rat's behavior with food was a positive reinforcement. In another instance, a mild electric shock was delivered to the rat's feet. When the rat pressed the bar, the shock stopped. When the shock was delivered again, the rat continued to press the bar to stop the shock. Removing the aversive stimulus, the shock, served as a negative reinforcement. Yet when the rat pressed the bar several times and received a shock each time, the rat stopped pressing the bar. This aversive stimulus in response to the behavior was a punishment. Finally, when the rat pressed the bar repeatedly and nothing happened, the rat stopped pressing the bar. Ceasing to reward the behavior that was previously rewarded caused extinction. From this experiment, Skinner concluded that both positive and negative reinforcement increase repetitive behavior while punishment and extinction decrease such behavior. Ultimately, Skinner believed that behavior is learned and that rewards are important for encouraging employees to repeat desired behaviors and discontinue undesirable ones.[60] This notion is called the **theory of operant conditioning**.

The theory of operant conditioning can also be used to explain how workplace behavior is conditioned. Suppose an employee fails to tell his or her manager about a problem with a customer. The manager discovers that the employee was hesitant to discuss the issue because the manager tends to lose his or her temper when problems arise. So rather than be the object of that temper, the employee hides problems from the manager. In this case, telling the manager about a problem is the operant behavior that is punished when the employee becomes the object of the manager's temper. As a consequence, the employee stops letting the manager know about problems. However, if the manager stopped losing his or her temper, the employee may be more transparent with the manager about customers' problems, illustrating negative reinforcement. If the manager thanks the employee for revealing customers' problems, the employee's behavior is positively reinforced, and he or she may be more likely to bring those to the manager's attention.

Successful organizations generally build employee engagement and excitement by focusing on positive, not negative, reinforcement.[61] These organizations are

Reinforcement theory
The theory that positive and negative reinforcements can induce certain behavior.

Positive reinforcement
The act of rewarding a desired behavior.

Negative reinforcement
The act of removing an aversive condition in response to a desired behavior.

Punishment
The act of presenting an aversive stimulus in response to an undesired behavior.

Extinction
The idea that a behavior stops because it has ceased to be rewarded or punished.

Theory of operant conditioning
The theory that both positive and negative reinforcement increase behavior while punishment and extinction decrease behavior.

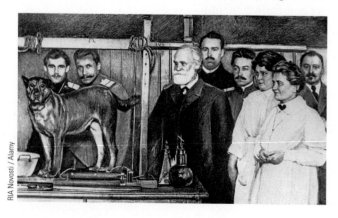

RIA Novosti / Alamy

explicit about what behaviors are expected and the associated rewards, and they are consistent in the application of rewards. For instance, at the Four Seasons Hotels, each location has an employee of the month award. The winner receives a cash award of $1,000, an all-expense paid trip for two, and an extra week's vacation.[62] Likewise, Nordstrom recognizes that by promoting from within, the company rewards employees in ways that can motivate them to work hard as they aspire to higher-level positions in the company.[63]

If not designed appropriately, however, reward systems can create undesirable, unanticipated, and unintended results.[64] For example, companies may want to create a culture that promotes teamwork but may only reward individual efforts. As a result, some team members may perform in ways that are best for their personal needs and not best for the team's goals. To prevent behavior like this, it is important to discover what behaviors are rewarded and alter the reward system to ensure that the behaviors the organization wants are reinforced (see Table 18.4).

One common mistake that many companies make is to assume that financial incentives are the most important driver of motivation. This focus on financial rewards is not surprising when you consider the way most individuals view themselves and others. Most people tend to overestimate the extent to which others are motivated by extrinsic rewards such as compensation and underestimate the role of intrinsic rewards such as meaningful work and challenge. Even individuals who say that they are more motivated by intrinsic rewards do not believe that others share the same view.[65] For instance, in a survey of prospective law school students, 64% said that they were pursuing law school because it was intellectually appealing and a meaningful profession. When asked about the motivation of their colleagues, they assumed that only 12% shared their perspective on law school. They believed that the vast majority was motivated primarily by the opportunity for financial gain.[66]

Work Design

While rewards are important, the design of the work can also be an important driver of reinforcing employee motivation. This line of research relies primarily upon the notion that employees are motivated by intrinsic rewards which in turn can be shaped by the way their tasks are set up by the organization. The original research on this was conducted by Hackman and Oldham on what they called job design. Their basic thesis was that when jobs are designed with several key attributes (variety, autonomy, and feedback), employees will be more engaged. That engagement is driven by the meaningfulness of work, a sense of personal responsibility for outcomes, and an understanding of the results of the work.

Organizations that are successful in creating a highly motivated workforce provide opportunities for employees to engage in tasks that are meaningful and

Management Hopes For ...	But Rewards ...
Long-term growth	Quarterly earnings
Teamwork	Individual effort
Setting stretch goals	Making the numbers
Commitment to total quality	Shipping on schedule, even with defects
Innovative thinking and risk-taking	Proven methods and safety
Candor and openness	Good news, agreeing with the boss

Table 18.4 › Misalignment between What Is Hoped for and What Is Rewarded

Source: Adapted from S. Kerr, "On the Folly of Rewarding A, While Hoping for B," *Academy of Management Journal*, December 1975.

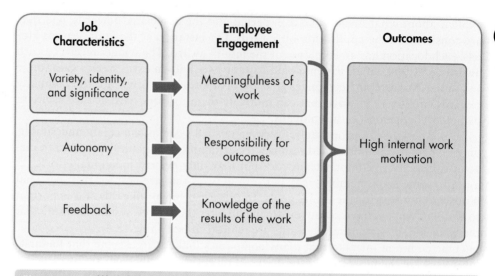

Figure 18.8 Work Design as Motivation

Source: J. Richard Hackman and Greg R. Oldham, *Work Redesign*, 1st Edition, © 1980. Reprinted by permission of Pearson Education, Inc., Upper Saddle River, NJ.

tied to overall organizational goals.[67] When employees believe that what they are doing is valued and appreciated by the organization, they will be more satisfied with their work and therefore less likely to seek alternative employment.[68] One survey of 20,000 high-potential employees by the Corporate Executive Board found that having a connection to corporate strategy was a significant job motivator.[69] In addition to experiencing work as meaningful, employees should also feel a sense of responsibility for the outcome of their work and be able to continually monitor their progress (see Figure 18.8). Employees are more likely to experience their jobs as meaningful when they use a variety of skills and have responsibility for a task from beginning to end. Piecemeal work is less appealing, especially when an employee feels disconnected to the final product. To that end, meaningfulness is enhanced when employees believe that what they are doing is significant and contributes to the organization's overall goals.

Employee engagement is also generated when individuals feel a sense of ownership and accountability for their work. Generally, jobs that provide a higher level of freedom and autonomy generate increased levels of responsibility.[70] The extent to which a manager is comfortable delegating responsibility is often a result of his or her fundamental beliefs about human nature. One way in which organizations have attempted to generate greater levels of motivation and employee engagement is through empowerment, the process of delegating responsibility and accountability to individuals in the organization for the accomplishment of certain processes, actions, or tasks. Of course, the use of empowerment assumes that managers believe that employees will do their best to support overall organizational goals and objectives.

In his study of the relationship between managers and subordinates, Douglas McGregor identified two fundamentally different approaches to managing that he called **Theory X** and **Theory Y**.[71] Managers who conform to Theory X believe that employees inherently dislike work and need to be constantly monitored and evaluated to ensure that they do what is expected. Theory X assumes that left to their own devices, employees will do the bare minimum to survive. To ensure that employees function to expected levels of performance, Theory X managers use fear, intimidation, and threats of punishment to drive motivation. In addition, Theory X managers tend to believe that employees are principally motivated by extrinsic

Theory X
The belief that employees inherently dislike work and need to be constantly monitored and evaluated to ensure that they do what is expected.

Theory Y
The belief that employees are motivated to do their best and to work to their potential.

rewards, especially compensation. In essence, these managers use a carrot-and-stick approach in management. The stick is the fear of punishment, and the carrot is the potential financial reward.[72]

Conversely, Theory Y managers believe that employees are not slackers but are motivated to do their best and to work to their potential. With this mind-set, Theory Y managers are more inclined to focus on participatory rather than command-and-control styles of leadership. They delegate more freely and believe that with increased autonomy and responsibility, employees will rise to the occasion. Theory Y managers seek consensus and try to create an open atmosphere where employees are free to experiment and innovate. Theory Y managers tend to use a blend of extrinsic and intrinsic rewards to motivate employees.

Follow-up research indicated that the attitudes and beliefs of Theory X and Y managers created self-fulfilling prophecies. For instance, if you believe that employees are irresponsible and lazy, that is what you will see. If you believe, however, that employees are self-motivated and well-intentioned, you will see those characteristics and be more inclined to focus on empowerment and participatory management.[73]

The benefits of higher employee engagement, whether through increased participation in decision making or other forms of empowerment, have been well documented. One study found that firms with high perceived levels of employee engagement experienced stronger financial performance, lower employee turnover, and increased employee morale.[74] The characteristics of organizations with high employee engagement include a climate with (1) participative decision making, (2) information sharing, (3) training and development, and (4) performance-based outcomes or rewards.[75] In other words, if employees know what is expected of them, are trained to be successful and are rewarded for their efforts, they will feel more engaged in the organization and will be more motivated to work toward its success.

This feeling of engagement creates a sense of **self-efficacy**, the belief that one has the capabilities to accomplish organizational goals.[76] Self-efficacy is often enhanced when employees are encouraged to expand their repertoire of skills and are given opportunities to grow and develop in the organization. As individuals complete more complex tasks, their self-efficacy, in turn, grows.[77] They build self-confidence and seek increasingly challenging opportunities, which further reinforces their empowered self-image.

In summary, if there is a strong fit between an individual's experiences and capabilities and the demands of the work, there will be a greater likelihood of overall organizational success. Consequently, this will result in a more satisfied and motivated employee. When employee engagement is low or performance is not what is expected, it is often useful to conduct a motivation audit to determine potential root causes (see Table 18.5). Knowing the underlying reasons for poor performance is the first step in taking corrective action.

Self-efficacy
The belief that one has the capabilities to accomplish organizational goals.

Potential Issue	Follow-up
Failure to understand new jobs or skills required	Does the individual have an appropriate role model?
Failure to see relationship between effort and performance	Does the individual have the necessary skill set?
Failure to see relationship between performance and outcomes	Are rewards and incentives aligned with expected behavior?
Failure to satisfy individual needs through organizational rewards	Has the individual been properly recognized for his or her contributions? Is the individual aware of possible rewards?

Table 18.5 Diagnosing Problems in Motivation

Prosocial Motivation

More recently, research on what is called "prosocial motivation" has indicated that employee motivation can be enhanced when an employee has the opportunity to make a positive difference in other people's lives. Jobs that are designed in a way that allows employees to see the value of their contribution through the eyes of a customer or other beneficiary tend to increase an employee's commitment to the company and satisfaction in his or her work. These opportunities allow employees to see the immediate consequences of their actions in a meaningful way. Motivation increases even more when employees have the opportunity to interact directly with the people who are benefiting from their work.[78] To that end, Medtronic, a medical technology company, hosts an annual gathering where employees are able to meet the patients who have received Medtronic pacemakers or other lifesaving devices. Former CEO Bill George called these gatherings "defining moments," because they allow employees to see the true impact of what they do every day.[79]

Reinforcing Strengths

Understanding what motivates one individual versus another is key to being an effective leader. As we have discussed, motivation can be leveraged by tailoring rewards or job design features to individual needs. A new increasingly popular stream of research takes this tailoring a step further by encouraging managers to focus almost exclusively on their employees' strengths. This research from the school of positive organizational psychology states that individuals are more motivated and productive by accentuating their strengths than by trying to address their weaknesses.[80]

Researchers who have studied the feedback process point to the fact that while most people remember criticism, they are spurred to action by praise. While constructive criticism is important, it can be paralyzing if an individual has no realistic chance to respond to it appropriately.[81] Researchers of positive psychology assert that individuals are more likely to reach their potential by focusing on what they are already good at doing. In essence, it is easier to go from a level of 80% competency to 90% than it is to go from a level of 10% to 20%. Even though the differential is the same, the effort required to build a baseline competency is more than is required to expand an existing reservoir of strength. Organizations that are able to tap into and reinforce employees' strengths produce stronger overall performance while simultaneously increasing job satisfaction.[82] Of course, organizations should not ignore the negatives; these need to be addressed, but the real leverage is in accentuating strengths.

VMware, Wayfair, and Boston Consulting Group (BCG) have all embraced the notion of reinforcing employee strengths. Managers at these companies are encouraged to "celebrate small victories and focus performance reviews around a particular worker's strengths."[83] At BCG, managers are not allowed to mention more than two areas of development during performance reviews. The company believes that it can generate much more productivity from its consultants by maximizing what they already do well.

To be successful in tailoring opportunities and rewards to employees, managers should ask three questions: (1) what are the individual's strengths, (2) what are the triggers that activate those strengths, and (3) what is the individual's learning style?[84] The answers to these questions can help drive rewards as well as career opportunities that create the foundations for a more motivated team member.

The Leadership Development Journey

One practice that leaders use to motivate their employees is to create a culture that engages them. Employee engagement is a positive emotional connection that employees have with their organization. The emotional connection motivates employees to be more involved, enthusiastic, and committed to their work. As a result, engaged employees are committed to using their talents to contribute to the goals of the organization. Leaders can do the following to engage employees:

- Create a climate of trust
- Behave with integrity
- Design jobs that are intellectually stimulating
- Provide career growth opportunities
- Invest in employee development
- Emphasize the importance of high-quality relationships
- Instill organizational pride
- Create a connection between an individual's performance and the organization's goals[85]

Think of a time when a leader engaged you. What was the leader's engagement strategy? How did the leader's ability to engage you motivate your performance?

SUMMARY

An organization without skilled and motivated employees will not be competitive very long. Successful organizations have learned to create the conditions that drive motivation and in turn employee engagement.

LO1 Employee engagement and motivation can be influenced by both intrinsic and extrinsic rewards. Intrinsic rewards are associated with "doing the job." These rewards are focused on providing an employee with interesting and challenging work, autonomy, variety, and other opportunities to exercise his or her skills and abilities. Extrinsic rewards include pay, promotions, fringe benefits, and job security. Understanding what drives specific employees enables a manager to select the right combination of intrinsic and extrinsic rewards.

LO2 Contemporary motivation theories explain the conditions that address employees' underlying needs and consider the ways in which employees calculate and choose their courses of action. Motivation theories that emphasize the underlying needs that drive people to perform are called content theories. Some theorists position individuals' underlying needs as innate or ingrained, while others believe that motivational needs and desires are acquired over time

and shaped through life experiences. As individuals change and grow, their motivational drives change as well. Early theorists also believed that employees' needs must be fulfilled in a hierarchical order. Much current research supports the notion that the satisfaction of one need is independent from the satisfaction of another and that individuals pursue multiple needs simultaneously. In summary, individuals have multiple needs—physical, social, and psychological—that must be fulfilled.

LO3 Motivation theories that focus on how workers choose among alternative actions and levels of effort are called process theories. Many researchers believe that the setting of high-performance goals can be a strong performance motivator. In addition, process theories emphasize the expectations that employees have about the rewards that should result from their efforts. An employee's assessment of the effort–reward trade-off often determines his or her level of motivation. Other process theories emphasize the fairness of the rewards, meaning how they compare to the rewards of other employees with similar efforts, abilities, and levels of experience. Employees seek equity and fairness in the distribution of rewards.

..........LO4..⋮ Companies can motivate effective employee behavior only when the rewards and conditions in the work environment and related to the job are motivating. Using rewards and punishments to induce certain behaviors or actions is called reinforcement theory. Motivation can also be increased by carefully designing the work, by engaging employees in decision making, and by reinforcing individual strengths.

KEY TERMS

Acquired needs theory
Content theories
ERG theory
Equity theory
Expectancy theory
Extinction
Extrinsic rewards
Four-drive theory
Goal-setting theory

Hierarchy of needs theory
Hygiene factors
Intrinsic rewards
Motivation
Motivators
Need for achievement
Need for affiliation
Need for power
Negative reinforcement

Positive reinforcement
Process theories
Punishment
Reinforcement theory
Self-efficacy
Theory of operant conditioning
Theory X
Theory Y
Two-factor theory

ASSIGNMENTS

Discussion Topics

1. In what ways can a company align organizational and employee goals? How can a company ensure that employees are focused on the right goals?

2. Compare and contrast the five content theories of motivation. In what ways are they similar and different? As you think about your own motivational drives, which content theory resonates with you?

3. What are the implications of the two-factor theory of motivation? How can a company effectively respond to both sides of the equation?

4. How do goals act as motivational drivers? In Chapter 13, we discussed the locus of control. How does the locus of control impact an individual's approach to the setting and achievement of goals?

5. In what ways are goal-setting theory and expectancy theory similar?

6. In what ways does an individual's conception of equity influence his or her level of motivation?

7. How does the design of a job impact an employee's motivation levels? What levers could an employer use to increase the level of motivation of its employees?

8. In what ways do cultural factors influence motivation? How should managers of global operations think about motivation?

9. Consider the Theory X and Theory Y approaches to leadership. Which one resonates with you? Think of an example of a highly successful Theory X and Theory Y leader. What did they do to achieve success?

10. Think about a time when you were at your best at work or in school. What motivated you to perform at your best? Were you motivated by extrinsic or intrinsic rewards? How does focusing on one's strengths improve his or her performance? What are the potential downsides of this approach to motivation?

Management Research

1. In Chapter 9, "Managing Human Capital," we discussed companies that have been recognized as great places to work. Look at the current list of great companies and assess how they motivate their employees. How do they recognize employees? What incentives do they use?

2. Think of a goal that you would like to accomplish this year. Describe the goal and evaluate its feasibility using the following SMART criteria.

   - Is the goal specific?
   - Can the goal be measured?
   - Is the goal attainable?
   - How relevant is the goal?
   - Have you established a timeline for achieving the goal?

In the Field

Interview both a Baby Boomer and a Gen Y. Ask each interviewee to map out how their life experiences and goals influence their motivations. What are the similarities in their motivations? What are the differences? Why do you think there are differences? What are the managerial implications of these differences?

END NOTES

[1] J. Richard Hackman and Greg R. Oldham, *Work Redesign* (Reading, MA: Addison-Wesley, 1980).

[2] Michael Beer and Bert A. Spector, "Note on Rewards Systems," Harvard Business School Note No. 9-482-017 (Boston, MA: HBS Publishing, 1981), p. 1; and Marcus Buckingham, "What Great Managers Do," *Harvard Business Review*, March 2005.

[3] James L. Heskett, W. Earl Sasser, Jr., and Leonard A. Schlesinger, *The Service Profit Chain: How Leading Companies Link Profit and Growth to Loyalty, Satisfaction, and Value* (New York: The Free Press, 1997).

[4] Rodd Wagner and James K. Harter, "When There's a Freeloader on Your Team," *Harvard Management Update*, January 1, 2007.

[5] Deloitte, "Global Human Capital Trends 2015," Deloitte University Press, available at http://www2.deloitte.com/us/en/pages/human-capital/articles/introduction-human-capital-trends.html, accessed March 26, 2015.

[6] "Motivation: The Not-So-Secret Ingredient of High Performance," *Performance Management: Measure and Improve the Effectiveness of Your Employees* (Boston, MA: HBS Press, 2006).

[7] Linda Hill, Tarun Khanna, and Emily Stecker, "HCL Technologies (A)," Harvard Business School Case No. 9-408-004, rev. July 17, 2008 (Boston, MA: HBS Publishing, 2007), pp. 1–2.

[8] Ibid., p. 3.

[9] Ibid., pp. 5–6.

[10] Ibid., p. 4.

[11] Ibid., pp. 6–7.

[12] Ibid., p. 7.

[13] Ibid., p. 8.

[14] Ibid., p. 8; and Vineet Nayar, "A Maverick CEO Explains How He Persuaded His Team to Leap into the Future," *Harvard Business Review*, June 2010.

[15] Linda Hill, Tarun Khanna, and Emily Stecker, "HCL Technologies (A)," Harvard Business School Case No. 9-408-004, rev. July 17, 2008 (Boston, MA: HBS Publishing, 2007), p. 8.

[16] Ibid., p. 9.

[17] Vineet Nayar, "A Maverick CEO Explains How He Persuaded His Team to Leap into the Future," *Harvard Business Review*, June 2010.

[18] Linda Hill, Tarun Khanna, and Emily Stecker, "HCL Technologies (A)," Harvard Business School Case No. 9-408-004, rev. July 17, 2008 (Boston, MA: HBS Publishing, 2007), pp. 9–10.

[19] Vineet Nayar, "A Maverick CEO Explains How He Persuaded His Team to Leap into the Future," *Harvard Business Review*, June 2010.

[20] Linda Hill, Tarun Khanna, and Emily Stecker, "HCL Technologies (A)," Harvard Business School Case No. 9-408-004, rev. July 17, 2008 (Boston, MA: HBS Publishing, 2007), pp. 11–12.

[21] D. Rousseau, *Psychological Contracts in Organizations: Understanding Written and Unwritten Agreements* (Thousand Oaks, CA: Sage Publications, 1995).

[22] S. J. Miles and W. G. Mangold, "Positioning Southwest Airlines through Employee Branding," *Business Horizons*, Vol. 48, 2005, pp. 535–545.

[23] Ibid.

[24] Ibid.

[25] Children's Healthcare of Atlanta, 2008, "Children's Healthcare Becomes the Only Atlanta Hospital Named Among Atlanta's Best Places to Work," www.choa.org, accessed October 17, 2008.

[26] G. Huizinga, *Maslow's Need Hierarchy in the Work Situation* (Groningen, The Netherlands: Wolters-Noordhoff, 1970).

[27] Clayton P. Alderfer, *Existence, Relatedness, and Growth: Human Needs in Organizational Settings* (New York: The Free Press, 1972).

[28] F. Herzberg, "One More Time: How Do You Motivate Employees?" *Harvard Business Review*, January 2003.

[29] Abraham Maslow, *Motivation and Personality*, 3rd edition (Reading, MA: Addison Wesley Longman, 1970).

[30] David C. McClelland, *Human Motivation* (Glenview, IL: Scott, Foresman, 1985).

[31] John J. Gabarro and Wallace Wormley, "A Brief Note on Social Motives," Harvard Business School Note No. 9-477-053, rev. November 1, 1980 (Boston, MA: HBS Publishing, 1976).

[32] David C. McClelland, *Human Motivation* (Glenview, IL: Scott, Foresman, 1985).

[33] S. C. Johnson, 2008, "Building a Career with You," http://www.scjohnson.com/en/Careers/overview.aspx.

[34] Ibid.

[35] Ibid.

[36] Scott W. Spreier, Mary H. Fontaine, and Ruth L. Malloy, "Leadership Run Amok: The Destructive Potential of

Overachievers," *Harvard Business Review*, June 2006.

[37] Abraham Sagie, Dov Elizur, and Hirotsugu Yamauchi, "The Structure and Strength of Achievement Motivation: A Cross-cultural Example," *Journal of Organizational Behavior*, Vol. 17, No. 5, 1996, pp. 431–444.

[38] Paul R. Lawrence and Nitin Nohria, *Driven: How Human Nature Shapes Our Choices* (San Francisco, CA: Jossey-Bass, 2002).

[39] N. Nohria, B. Groysberg, and L. Lee, "Employee Motivation: A Powerful New Model," *Harvard Business Review*, July–August 2008.

[40] Ibid.

[41] Ibid.

[42] Ibid.

[43] Ibid.

[44] Ibid.

[45] S. Tietze, "Motivation and the Meaning of Work," *International Journal of Applied HRM*, Vol. 1, No. 1, www.management-journals.com/journals/hrm/article19-p2.htm, accessed October 17, 2008.

[46] P. A. Gambrel and R. Cianci, "Maslow's Hierarchy of Needs: Does It Apply in a Collectivist Culture?," *Journal of Applied Management and Entrepreneurship*, Vol. 8, No. 2, April 2003; and J. B. Miner and H. P. Dachler, "Personnel Attitudes and Motivation," *Annual Review of Psychology*, 1973.

[47] E. A. Locke and G. P. Latham, *A Theory of Goal Setting & Task Performance* (Englewood Cliffs, NJ: Prentice Hall, 1990).

[48] Ibid.

[49] Edwin A. Locke and Gary P. Latham, "Building a Practically Useful Theory of Goal Setting and Task Motivation," *American Psychologist*, September 2002, pp. 705–717.

[50] Gary P. Latham and Edwin A. Locke, "Enhancing the Benefits and Overcoming the Pitfalls of Goal Setting," *Organizational Dynamics*, Vol. 35, No. 4, 2006, p. 333.

[51] Edwin A. Locke and Gary P. Latham, "Building a Practically Useful Theory of Goal Setting and Task Motivation," *American Psychologist*, Vol. 57, No. 9, September 2002, p. 712.

[52] V. H. Vroom, *Work and Motivation (Classic Edition)* (San Francisco, CA: Jossey-Bass, 1995).

[53] Michael Beer and Bert A. Spector, "Note on Rewards Systems," Harvard Business School Note No. 9-482-017 (Boston, MA: HBS Publishing, 1981), p. 5.

[54] J. S. Adams, "Injustice in Social Exchange," *Advances in Social Psychology*, 2nd edition, L. Berkowitz, ed. (New York: Academic Press, 1965), and J. S. Adams, "Toward an Understanding of Inequity," *Journal of Abnormal and Social Psychology*, Vol. 67, No. 5, November 1963, pp. 422–436.

[55] J. Stacy Adams, "Towards an Understanding of Inequity," *Journal of Abnormal and Social Psychology*, Vol. 67, No. 5, 1963, pp. 422–436.

[56] G. Hamel and B. Breen, *The Future of Management* (Boston, MA: HBS Press, 2007).

[57] Ibid.

[58] G. P. Latham, *Work Motivation: History, Theory, Research and Practice* (Thousand Oaks, CA: Sage Publications, 2007).

[59] B.F. Skinner, *Science and Human Behavior* (New York: Macmillan, 1953).

[60] Ibid.

[61] Alexander D. Stajkovic and Fred Luthans, "A Meta-Analysis of the Effects of Organizational Behavior Modification on Task Performance, 1975–95," *Academy of Management Journal*, Vol. 40, No. 5, 1997, pp. 1122–1149.

[62] *Fortune*, "100 Best Companies to Work For 2008," *Fortune*, February 2008.

[63] Nordstrom, "Nordstrom Careers," 2008, http://careers.nordstrom.com/careers/careerpaths/index.asp.

[64] S. Kerr, "On the Folly of Rewarding A, While Hoping for B," *Academy of Management Journal*, Vol. 18, No. 4, December 1975, pp. 769–783.

[65] Chip Heath, "The Social Psychology of Agency Relationships: Lay Theories of Motivation Overemphasize Extrinsic Rewards," *Organizational Behavior and Human Decision Processes*, Vol. 78, 1999, pp. 25–62.

[66] Ibid.

[67] Elizabeth J. Hawk and Garrett J. Sheridan, "The Right Staff," *Management Review*, June 1999, pp. 43–48.

[68] David E. Bowen and Edward E. Lawler, III, "The Empowerment of Service Workers: What, Why, How, and When," *Sloan Management Review*, Spring 1992, pp. 31–39.

[69] Jena McGregor, "Giving Back to Your Stars," *Fortune*, November 1, 2010.

[70] J. Richard Hackman and Greg R. Oldham, *Work Redesign* (Reading, MA: Addison-Wesley, 1980), pp. 69–98.

[71] Douglas McGregor, *The Human Side of Enterprise* (New York: McGraw-Hill, 1960).

[72] "Motivation: The Not-So-Secret Ingredient of High Performance," *Performance Management: Measure and Improve the Effectiveness of Your Employees* (Boston, MA: HBS Press, 2006).

[73] John Nirenberg, "Theories X, Y, and Z," *Encyclopedia of Leadership*, George R. Goethals, Georgia J. Sorenson, and James MacGregor Burns, eds. (Thousand Oaks, CA: Sage Publications, 2004), pp. 1538–1541.

[74] Christine M. Riordan, Robert J. Vandenberg, and Hettie A. Richardson, "Employee Involvement Climate and Organizational Effectiveness," *Human Resource Management*, Vol. 44, No. 4, Winter 2005, pp. 471–488.

[75] Edward E. Lawler, III, *High-Involvement Management: Participative Strategies for Improving Organizational Performance* (San Francisco, CA: Jossey-Bass, 1986); and Christine M. Riordan, Robert J. Vandenberg, and Hettie A. Richardson, "Employee Involvement Climate and Organizational Effectiveness," *Human Resource Management*, Vol. 44, No. 4, Winter 2005, pp. 471–488.

[76] Albert Bandura, *Self-Efficacy: The Exercise of Control* (New York: W. H. Freeman, 1997).

[77] Jay A. Conger and Rabindra N. Kanungo, "The Empowerment Process: Integrating Theory and Practice," *Academy of Management Review*, Vol. 13, No. 3, 1988, pp. 471–482.

[78] Adam Grant, "Relational Job Design and the Motivation to Make a Prosocial Difference," *Academy of Management Review*, Vol. 32, No. 2, 2007, pp. 393–417.

[79] Bill George, *Authentic Leadership: Rediscovering the Secrets to Creating Value* (San Francisco, CA: Jossey-Bass, 2003).

[80] Kim S. Cameron, Jane E. Dutton, and Robert E. Quinn, "Foundations of Positive Organizational Scholarship," *Positive Organizational Scholarship: New Foundations of a New Discipline*, Kim S. Cameron, Jane E. Dutton, and Robert E. Quinn, eds. (San Francisco, CA: Berrett-Koehler, 2003).

[81] Laura Morgan Roberts, Gretchen Spreitzer, Jane Dutton, Robert Quinn, Emily

Heaphy, and Brianna Baker, "How to Play to Your Strengths," *Harvard Business Review*, January 2005.

82 Donald O. Clifton and James K. Harter, "Investing in Strengths," *Positive Organizational Scholarship: New Foundations of a New Discipline*, Kim S. Cameron, Jane E. Dutton, and Robert E. Quinn,

eds. (San Francisco, CA: Berrett-Koehler, 2003), pp. 110–121.

83 Rachel Feintzeig, "You're Awesome! Firms Scrap Negative Feedback," *Wall Street Journal*, February 11, 2015.

84 Marcus Buckingham, "What Great Managers Do," *Harvard Business Review*, March 2005.

85 John Gibbons, "Employee Engagement A Review of Current Research and Its Implications," The Conference Board, Inc., November 2006.

CHAPTER

19

Communication

Learning Objectives

After reading this chapter, you should be able to:

LO1 : Describe how effective and ineffective communication can influence an organization.

LO2 : Outline the components of interpersonal communication and describe different styles of communication.

LO3 : Explain how managers build credibility in an organization and how communication is used to persuade teams.

LO4 : Describe the advantages and disadvantages of the different mediums and channels of communication.

LO5 : Describe the ways in which communication processes should be modified or adapted to fit different cultural situations.

SELF-REFLECTION

Evaluate Your Communication Skills

Successful managers use communication as a vehicle for planning, inspiring, and directing behavior. Managerial work involves communication with members at all levels of the organization, as well as with external stakeholders. How effective are your communication skills? On a scale of 1 to 5, respond to the following statements to assess the effectiveness of your communication skills.

1 = never 2 = rarely 3 = sometimes 4 = usually 5 = always

1. I am an active listener. _____

2. I know how to use nonverbal cues to communicate. _____

3. I excel at interpersonal communication. _____

4. I can build a compelling case through written communication and the use of data.
   _____

5. I am aware of cultural differences and adapt my communication style in cross-cultural interactions.
   _____

6. I adapt my vocal tone to the communication situation. _____

7. I communicate in a professional manner when using e-mail and social media.
   _____

8. I excel at making speeches. _____

9. I am aware of the importance of managing impressions when communicating with others.
   _____

10. I know how to ask clarifying questions when communicating with others. _____

Based on your responses, what are your communication strengths? What communication skills would you like to develop?

INTRODUCTION

In a study of great business leaders, the most often cited criterion for greatness was a leader's ability to articulate a strategy and vision that was compelling to a group of followers.[1] Long-term success depends on building and reinforcing a collective purpose or shared vision, which in turn depends on clear, persistent, and meaningful messages that energize followers. As we discussed in Chapter 11, communication is a pivotal determinant of the success or failure of change efforts. For change to be accepted and enacted, communication must appeal to both logic and emotions. Tapping into a person's emotions is extremely important in encouraging an individual to take a risk, try something new, or change his or her behavior.

Ultimately, communication is at the core of individual leadership. Think about some of the topics discussed so far in this section of the book—power, decision making, negotiation, leading teams, and motivation. All of these require skills in communication.

On a daily basis, managers must communicate at all levels of the organization and with a variety of stakeholders, many of whom have different perspectives and objectives. Managers ask questions to understand the company's goals. They discuss the choices that should be made to move the company in the right direction. They ask questions related to budgets and the company's financial health to obtain more resources. They use focus groups and surveys to ask customers what their needs are and how the company can best satisfy them. When done right, managers use communication about impending challenges and the way forward to motivate and inspire their teams. One study even found that effective communication was a key component of high performance teams.[2]

The messages that managers convey and the methods they use to communicate vary widely. To be effective, managers need to tailor their message to each audience and situational context. A successful senior executive in the music industry spoke about his need to communicate one way with his financial team, another way with the marketing staff, and yet another with the artists he managed. With the financial team, communication revolved around profitability and expenses. The marketing conversation centered on the chart position of hit records and the impact of publicity efforts. Communication with the artists was focused on the music and its inspiration. This executive noted, "With each group, I need to have a different approach.... If I were to speak with an artist in the way that I speak with his lawyer, he would probably punch me."[3] Although this executive would probably not be punched, he may have been tuned out if he did not speak the "artist's language."

At its core, **communication** consists of using sounds, words, pictures, symbols, gestures, and body language to exchange information. While we tend to think of communication as "outputs" (speaking, writing, and moving), it also consists of "inputs" (listening, observing, and reading). Communication also refers to the interpretation of information by those who have attempted or are attempting to establish a relationship. As such, communication is a two-way process of conveying, exchanging, processing, and evaluating information.

Given its level of importance, a lack of effective communication abilities can be particularly debilitating. In fact, one of the most cited reasons for dissatisfaction by direct reports is that their managers fail to keep them informed.[4] From a business perspective, managers indicate that poor workplace communication continues to be one of the greatest barriers to enhancing company performance.[5] A lack of effective communication skills can even derail an individual's career.

As companies are pressured to compete in a changing and challenging business environment, the ability to communicate effectively with employees, colleagues, customers, and other stakeholders becomes even more important. The invention of sophisticated information technology tools—teleconferencing, instant messaging, e-mail, and other social media—has helped to facilitate as well as complicate varied communication exchanges. Likewise, the growing global nature of business requires an emphasis on cross-cultural awareness and sensitivity in communication.

To create more agile, flexible, and competitive organizations, effective communication must be facilitated at all levels in an organization. Organizations must become more aware of the various ways in which people interact and convey messages and then implement communication systems that support effective dialogue. In this chapter, we will explore the various communication styles and approaches from both an individual and organizational perspective. Successful managers need to communicate effectively in one-on-one situations as well as in large group settings. One individual who is a master of individual and organizational communication is Oprah Winfrey.

Communication
The process of using sounds, words, pictures, symbols, gestures, and body language to exchange information.

Oprah Winfrey

By most estimates, Oprah Winfrey is the wealthiest woman in the entertainment industry, best known worldwide for her television show The Oprah Winfrey Show.[6] Oprah's media career began in 1971 when she was selected to attend the White House Conference on Youth. This publicity led to invitations for her to enter talent and beauty contests. During one contest sponsored by a local radio station, Oprah spoke about her career goal to be a broadcast journalist. She said, "I wanted to be a broadcast journalist because I believed in the truth. I was interested in proclaiming the truth to the world."[7]

Lisa Maree Williams/Getty Images Entertainment/Getty Images

Oprah won that contest and was offered a newscaster job after the manager of the radio station heard her read a news copy with ease and clarity. By 1984, Oprah had her own local morning television talk show. In her first year, her program won an Emmy Award, and within 2 years, it was the highest-rated talk show in Chicago. By late 1988, approximately 11 million viewers in the United States were watching The Oprah Winfrey Show each day. Her audience was captivated by her ability to relate to her guests, her passion for the subject matter, and her willingness to show vulnerability.

Through her television show, Oprah personally encouraged her viewers to take control of their lives, appreciate themselves, and develop strategies for handling life's challenges. To do this, she brought in notable authors of self-help books and various mind and body health practitioners to speak to the audience and answer their questions. Oprah was an active participant in these conversations and was candid about her personal flaws and struggles. One competing talk show host, Maury Povich, noted that Oprah had been the first to use such an intimate approach. He said, "Nobody was talking about their own problems like Oprah ... Talk show hosts didn't talk about themselves ... Oprah opened up a lot of new windows for viewers because they could empathize with her."[8] Oprah revealed that she shared these details with her audience because she had "experienced what everyone else has experienced."[9]

Through her risk-taking, Oprah transformed television into an interactive experience for audiences, connecting viewers to new ideas and to one another. Oprah was adept at creating a sense of community among viewers and spurring audiences to action. Reflecting on her success and efforts to find her voice, Oprah said: "When I first started out ... I was pretending to be somebody I was not. So I'd go to a news conference, and I was more interested in how I phrased the question, how eloquent the question sounded, as opposed to listening to the answer, which always happens when you are interested in impressing people instead of doing what you are supposed to be doing."[10] Winfrey's open, direct, and empathic style enabled her to communicate effectively with a broad array of constituents.

Case in Point   Oprah Winfrey

1. What life experiences and aspirations influenced Winfrey's communication style?
2. Why does Winfrey's communication style resonate with her audience?
3. Why was community building a core aspect of Winfrey's communication style?
4. How was Winfrey's communication style a source of innovation that transformed the viewing of television programs?

INTERPERSONAL COMMUNICATION

The core components of communication are the parties (the sender and receiver who are involved in the transmittal of information), the message (what is being conveyed both verbally and nonverbally), the medium (what format is used for communication), the interpretation (how the receiver makes sense of the message), and the response or feedback (what is conveyed in reaction to the message).[11] It is tempting to think of communication as a series of linear exchanges that move from one individual to another, but in reality, communication is an iterative and interactive process. Essentially, communication does not include just what is said or heard. It is also colored by the perceptions of those involved, including their beliefs, attitudes, and assumptions.

Communication is impacted by situational as well as personal factors.[12] In productive situations, individuals engaged in the communication process ask for clarification when they have misunderstood and provide clarification when asked. In less effective situations, because of power dynamics or other factors, individuals assume meanings and intentions without clarification, which can lead to confusion or even the dismissal of ideas. The personal aspects of communication are the style, tone, and approach of the individuals involved, which can also impact the interpretation and strength of the messages.

In addition, the message and its interpretation can be influenced by the timing of the communication, the mood and readiness of the receiver to hear the message, and other interpersonal and organizational factors. These factors are often referred to as noise in the communication process because they can distort the sender's intent or the receiver's interpretation (see Figure 19.1). The noise can be minimized through an ongoing back-and-forth process of seeking clarification. This helps ensure that the intent of the message matches the desired impact.

To address the noise in communication and ensure that a clear message is broadcast to the appropriate people, an individual must consider the following elements in communication:[13]

- *The audience.* Who is the target of the communication? What are their perspectives, and what agenda do they have? Are there other sub audiences that should be considered or will be impacted by the communication?

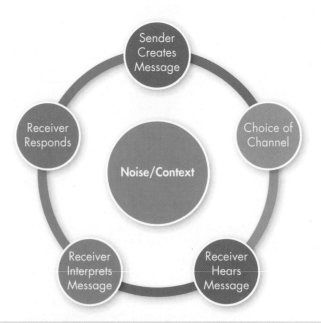

Figure 19.1 〉 Communication Process

- *The goal.* What is the objective of the communication—to generate action, to change someone's mind, to inform? How will success be measured?
- *The context.* What situational variables can impact the message or communication process? Are there power dynamics at play? What is the reporting relationship? What is the history of the parties involved?
- *The message.* What will be conveyed specifically?
- *The medium.* How will the message be conveyed, and what tool will be used to communicate—face-to-face meeting, e-mail, formal proposal, speech, and so forth?
- *The response or feedback.* How will someone react to the communication? Good communicators are good listeners; they are open to feedback and actively engage the other party.

Communication that occurs in one-on-one or small group settings is called **interpersonal communication**. Successful interpersonal communication relies on a number of personal characteristics, including the ability to be self-aware, to relate well to others, to be persuasive, to listen, and to reflect. While being an effective communicator requires that the choice of words, visual images, and body language be clear, it also requires that each communication partner perceive the other's message in the way he or she intends. This often requires the communicator to understand the perspectives and opinions of the other party. In Chapter 13, we discussed the concept of emotional intelligence, which includes a strong sense of oneself and an ability to understand others. Emotionally intelligent individuals tend to be effective in interpersonal communication.

Verbal and Nonverbal Communication

Most face-to-face communication involves a combination of verbal and nonverbal activities. With the increasing globalization of business and the growth of dispersed teams and networked organizations, there is a greater dependence on verbal forms of communication. **Verbal communication** consists of sounds, letters, words, pictures, and symbols. Although we tend to think of verbal communication as "speaking," verbal communication also includes listening, reading, and writing. Speaking and writing (e.g., e-mail, text messages, and postings) are the modes by which communication is sent. Speaking and writing are both driven by physical and cognitive behaviors. For instance, to send a message, communicators must retrieve associated sounds, letters, words, and symbols from memory and then produce that message through speech or text formats. Conversely, listening and reading are the modes by which communication is understood. Listening and reading are driven by sensing information (e.g., hearing and seeing) and thinking about the information received (e.g., comprehension and processing).

To understand a message, receivers must hear or see the associated sounds, letters, words, pictures, and symbols and process them to make the message meaningful. Part of this processing is determined by the way in which a message is framed or conveyed. Word choice is very important. Look at the difference in the following two statements:

1. The holiday party and the summer outing have been cancelled.
2. The current tough economic climate has forced us to closely manage all of our expenditures to ensure that we can sustain our dedicated workforce. Part of this cost management process involves making some sacrifices in our social activities. To that end, we have had to cancel the holiday party and summer outing this year. We appreciate your collective efforts in working with us through these difficult times, and we look forward to reinstating these events in the future.

Interpersonal communication
Communication that occurs in one-on-one or small group settings.

Verbal communication
The use of sounds, letters, words, pictures, and symbols to convey a message.

The first statement is succinct but impersonal and potentially demotivating. The second statement conveys the same content, but it also includes a rationale and an explanation for the change in company policy. Because the company outlined the context of the situation, employees reading the second message are more inclined to be supportive and understanding of the need to make sacrifices. This example highlights the importance of framing a message that helps the speaker connect with the audience in a specific and meaningful way.[14] Framing also ensures that the speaker's intent matches the desired impact on the audience.[15]

Communication also is nonverbal. **Nonverbal communication** consists of giving physical attention to a communication partner and using body language, vocal qualities, and space and objects to convey meaning. Each of these features can also affect the ways in which the message is perceived (see Table 19.1). **Body language** includes the use of posture, body movement, hand and arm gestures, facial expressions, and eye contact.[16] Even though someone may be attempting to persuade another person to consider his or her idea, crossing his or her arms and looking down when speaking can communicate a lack of confidence in that idea. Yet if a speaker uses casual gestures and looks the communication partners directly in the eye every so often, a more confident message is projected. Facial expressions can also be especially revealing; they can convey boredom, excitement, passion, or pain. Effective communicators project appropriate facial expressions and read them on others.

Vocal qualities include inflection patterns, rate of speech, fillers, and enunciation. Someone who uses fillers such as "*um*" in their speech can appear uncertain or less knowledgeable. On the contrary, someone who deliberately pauses to collect his or her thoughts may appear more thoughtful.[17] Paying attention to vocal qualities is particularly important for cross-cultural teams. These teams often need to be even more focused on clarity of communication and tone to ensure mutual understanding.

Space and objects, which can impact the delivery and interpretation of communication, include the arrangement of the seating in meetings as well as the dress and

---

Nonverbal communication
The use of body language, vocal qualities, and space and objects to convey meaning to messages.

Body language
The use of posture, body movement, hand and arm gestures, facial expressions, and eye contact to convey meaning to messages.

Vocal qualities
Inflection patterns, rate of speech, fillers, and enunciation.

Space and objects
A nonverbal form of communication that conveys meaning through the way a meeting space is arranged, objects are used, or individuals are dressed.

Body Language	Vocal Qualities	Space and Objects
Posture Sitting or standing upright, facing the audience squarely, and balancing weight on the feet, slouching, swaying, and rocking	**Inflection** Variations in speaking volume: monotone, too high	**Seating** Arrangement of chairs or tables: straight lines, curved lines, circles
Body Movement Leaning forward or backward, walking side to side, standing still	**Rate** Speed of speech: too slowly, too quickly	**Height and Distance** One person standing and the other sitting, both sitting
Hand and Arm Gestures Clasping hands, folding arms behind back, clutching the opposite arm with one hand, tugging the ear, and scratching the arm	**Fillers** Verbal pauses: uh, er, um, you know, like	**Objects** Objects between sender and receiver, no objects between sender and receiver
Facial Expressions Smiling, grimacing, frowning, deadpan	**Enunciation** Clarity of pronunciation: mumbling, running words together, dropping off consonants, being articulate, speaking crisply	**Dress** Suits, ties, dresses, skirts, darkly colored clothing, jewelry
Eye Contact Fleeting, staring		

Table 19.1 Nonverbal Communication Behaviors

Source: Adapted from M. Munter, *Guide to Managerial Communication: Effective Business Writing and Speaking* (Upper Saddle River, NJ: Prentice Hall, 1997).

appearance of the individuals. For instance, a large object such as a desk or table placed between two individuals can convey a message of power or distance. In addition, if one individual takes a seat at the head of the table, he or she may be perceived to be more powerful. Thus, his or her comments may take on greater weight than they should. For instance, in Japan, the order of seating is very important and reflects how the cultural values manifest themselves in business settings. During a presentation with three attendees, the three seats are generally lined up perpendicular to the presenter. The highest-ranking individual sits in the middle seat. The second highest-ranking individual sits closest to the presenter so that he or she can act as an intermediary between the presenter and the highest-ranking individual. The third individual sits furthest from the presenter and closest to the door in case the highest-ranking individual needs anything from outside the room.

A speaker who is underdressed for a meeting can communicate a casual air that might be inappropriate for the situation. For example, someone who wears shorts and running shoes to a job interview may signal to the interviewer that he or she is not professional enough for the job.

Communication Styles

While being an effective communicator requires that verbal and nonverbal communication be clear, it also requires each communication partner to deliver his or her message in a way that fosters a productive exchange. We call the ways in which someone interacts with and delivers information to others his or her **communication style**. The three primary dimensions of communication style are (1) the degree to which one's communication is open or self-contained; (2) the degree to which one's communication is direct or indirect; and (3) how one listens to others (see Table 19.2).

Openness defines the ease with which individuals show emotions and are emotionally accessible to other people when they communicate. Open behaviors include being animated, using facial expressions while speaking, showing and discussing

Communication style
The ways in which someone interacts with and delivers information to others when communicating.

Openness
The ease with which individuals show emotions and are emotionally accessible to other people when they communicate.

Openness	Directness	Listening
Open Behaviors • Being animated • Using facial expressions while speaking • Showing and discussing feelings • Sharing personal information • Being talkative	**Direct Behaviors** • Being assertive and outspoken in expressing opinions • Being a firm and quick decision maker • Being confrontational • Frequently contributing ideas and opinions	**Interactive** • Reacting to what others say • Actively participating in conversation • Responding with ah and uh-huh when others are speaking
		Empathetic • Being interactive • Counseling the speaker
Self-Contained Behaviors • Keeping feelings private • Being less demonstrative • Limiting discussion to business-related topics	**Indirect Behaviors** • Being accommodating and diplomatic • Using understated language • Shying away from conflict • Being reserved in choosing how to contribute ideas and opinions	**Attentive** • Consciously focusing on what the speaker is saying • Listening without performing other tasks
		Passive • Refraining from making verbal or nonverbal responses when someone else is talking • Tuning in and out of the conversation

Table 19.2 Communication Styles

Source: Adapted from M. Shapiro, "Communication Styles on Team Dynamics," Simmons School of Management Course Note: Communication Strategies, 2006.

feelings, sharing personal information, and being generally talkative.[18] Open communicators may be more likely to make eye contact with the person who is speaking to let him or her know they have that person's full attention. In the same respect, open communicators may also be more likely to interrupt the person who is speaking, sharing their own thoughts and ideas. In contrast, self-contained behaviors can include keeping one's feelings private, being less demonstrative, and limiting discussion to business-related topics.[19] Consequently, a self-contained communicator may be more likely to refrain from giving input during staff meetings or may play the role of a synthesizer, one who tries to collect and combine the perspectives of others into a coherent whole.

Directness refers to the amount of control an individual attempts to exercise in communication situations. Direct behaviors can include being more assertive and outspoken in expressing opinions, being a firm and quick decision maker, being confrontational, and frequently contributing ideas and opinions.[20] A direct communicator may be more likely to ask important clarifying questions and make quick assumptions about the meaning behind someone else's message. This person may also be more likely to make his or her suppressed feelings known in ways that make others uncomfortable. In contrast, indirect behaviors include being accommodating and diplomatic, using understated language, shying away from conflict, and being reserved in how one chooses to contribute ideas and opinions.[21] An indirect communicator may be more likely to wait until the other person has finished speaking before interjecting or asking questions. This person may never actually reveal his or her true feelings about an issue, which can be frustrating for both parties. This lack of directness can be especially problematic on diverse teams. Without the open sharing of information, the team is unable to capitalize on its diversity and therefore may produce suboptimal results.

Listening styles are also an important feature of communication. Listening is the extent to which the receiver of the message hears what the speaker or the sender meant. Listening styles are described as passive, attentive, interactive, or empathetic.[22] Passive listeners refrain from making any verbal or nonverbal responses when someone else is talking. Passive listeners tune-in and tune-out depending upon changes in their mood. Many of them use music as background noise when completing other work.[23] Attentive listeners consciously try to focus on what the speaker is saying by not letting their minds wander. Attentive listeners tend to listen to instructions, briefings, and other important information without simultaneously performing other tasks.[24] Interactive listeners react verbally and nonverbally to what they are hearing. Interactive listeners respond to speakers with vocal noises such as *ah* and *uh-huh* when speakers say things with which they agree.[25] Empathetic listeners are both reactive and participative. They attempt to share with the speaker the feelings and concerns that underlie the message by counseling the speaker.[26] They say things such as "So how did that make you feel?" in response to a comment made by a speaker.

Beyond word choice and body language, communication becomes less effective when the parties involved use different styles. Read the following two dialogues to understand how differences in style can cause communication to become more or less effective.

Dialogue A:

JENNIFER: I believe that we should go directly to Jack to find out how the problem started.

JANE: I agree. We should also e-mail everyone involved and find out what they think.

JENNIFER: Why don't you start with the e-mail and I'll find Jack?

JANE: Sounds like a good plan. Please let me know once you find out what Jack said.

JENNIFER: Sure.

Directness
The amount of control an individual attempts to exercise in communication situations.

Listening
The extent to which the receiver of the message hears what the speaker or the sender intended.

Dialogue B:

JENNIFER:	I believe that we should go directly to Jack to find out how the problem started.
SARAH:	(silence)
JENNIFER:	Well, what do you think?
SARAH:	(silence)
JENNIFER:	Don't you have an opinion?
SARAH:	Well, yes, but I'm not sure if going to Jack is the best way to start.
JENNIFER:	What do you mean?
SARAH:	Can I have some time to think about this?

The conversation between Jennifer and Jane illustrates a communication situation where both parties share a similar style. In contrast, the conversation between Jennifer and Sarah illustrates a situation where the two parties have fundamentally different communication styles. Both Jennifer and Jane use an open and direct communication style, but Sarah uses a self-contained and indirect communication style. Jennifer and Jane openly discuss their feelings and opinions and appear not to have difficulty confronting problems. They are also quick decision makers. Because of this synergy, they finish the conversation feeling as though they have agreed on a solution. Sarah, in contrast, appears to shy away from conflict, which contradicts Jennifer's open and direct style. Sarah keeps her feelings private and is reserved in expressing her thoughts and opinions. Jennifer finds it frustrating to communicate with Sarah and perceives that Sarah does not have an opinion. In fact, she may perceive Sarah as unwilling to participate. Sarah, on the other hand, may perceive Jennifer as overly aggressive and impatient.

The goal in communication, as in business, is to be as flexible as possible. It is important to understand the situational elements at play and to try to modify one's style to fit the demands of the context. In addition to understanding the situational elements, it is important to understand the style and approach of the other person.[27] While an individual may not be comfortable adopting or conforming to a particular style, the mere recognition that a difference exists can be useful in building a sense of mutual understanding and respect.

Gender Differences in Communication

Studies of communication styles and approaches of men and women have revealed some significant differences.[28] While these differences do not apply to all men and women, men are generally inclined to value status and hierarchy more than women do and tend to prefer speaking opportunities that accentuate their position of power. Men tend to avoid situations that place them at a disadvantage or in a lower-status position, which may explain why men often refrain from asking questions or seeking information from others.[29] They fear that by asking questions, they will appear weak and vulnerable. Ironically, showing vulnerability can help build a connection with team members and increase a person's effectiveness as a leader.

Conversely, women tend to pay less attention to power dynamics in their communication, preferring to focus on building rapport and collaboration among individuals. Women focus on relationship building and do so by asking questions, sharing information, and expressing interest in others. They are inclined to be more democratic in their leadership approach. Consequently, they do not always take or are not always given credit for what they do.[30] Compared to men, women also tend to spend more time communicating up in an organization. Most of this upward communication is focused on task-related issues or concerns, not personal matters. In fact, women often refrain from sharing personal information for fear that they will be taken less seriously.

Men do spend considerable time communicating upward, but they shy away from seeking advice or input from senior management because they are concerned that they will look weak or ineffective.[31] Men are more likely to focus on self-promotion, which leads to a generally more aggressive communication style and a predisposition to project a strong, unflappable image. Although women spend less time on self-promotion, they are as successful as and often more successful than men when they are advocating for the needs of their team members or partners. They are less successful than men, however, when negotiating for themselves. Men tend to be equally strong in representing their own interests and the interests of others in the negotiation process.[32]

Recent research by Yale social psychologist Victoria Brescoll sought to better understand the communication differences between men and women. In particular, she sought to understand the connection between power and communication, theorizing that people in positions of power tend to speak more than others and tend to be perceived as more powerful. Her research did confirm this finding for men in powerful positions; they tended to speak more than others. She did not find the same patterns for women. Women, regardless of their position of power, tended to speak less than men.

In a subsequent study, Brescoll found that women refrain from communicating more in meetings because of the backlash that is associated with appearing to be "too powerful." She found that both men and women held negative perceptions about women who speak more, regardless of their position of power. Neither gender reacted negatively to the men who spoke more. In fact, the opposite occurred. Men were perceived to be less effective leaders if they spoke less.[33]

Again, these general patterns of behavior are seen in most, but not all, men and women. Understanding stylistic differences in communication is important to be able to tailor messages appropriately. It is also important to understand these differences as the listener to gain insight into why or how a message is framed in a certain way.

Improving Interpersonal Communication

Creating the conditions in which messages are interpreted correctly is an important aspect of interpersonal communication. The sociologist Erving Goffman used the front and back stages of the theater as a metaphor for understanding how individuals communicate. The front stage, where the "performance" is actually given, dictates that we employ certain standards of politeness and decorum when communicating.[34] For example, we wait until the other person finishes speaking before interjecting or asking questions. We make eye contact to let the speaker know that he or she has our full attention. We consciously focus on what the speaker is saying by not letting our minds wander. In essence, we obey the rules and "play the part" that the audience expects. The rules we create, however, can also make us inflexible. In an effort to be polite, we may fail to ask important clarifying questions, meaning that we draw inaccurate conclusions or make assumptions about the meaning behind someone else's message.

At the backstage area, we do not have to pay attention to what is expected and can "break character."[35] In the back stage, we are no longer trying to make a specific impression on an audience, and we can let our guard down. When we communicate from a "back stage" arena, we may be more candid with our true feelings though we may still withhold certain perspectives or points of view. In these instances, we often tune-in and tune-out as the mood strikes. While we may believe that these types of behaviors can lead to more fruitful discussions, they can make others uncomfortable and can escalate conflict. When two individuals come to know each other better, there is more back stage and less front stage communication.

While being open to new perspectives can enhance communication, why is it so difficult? One reason is that our internal biases and expectations often make it easy to jump to conclusions about what is being communicated. Everyone has a mental model of how and why people act the way they do. These models are based on past experiences and interactions with others. The plethora of data and stimuli that individuals are confronted with on a daily basis requires individuals to access their mental model of how the world works. This model enables a person to quickly analyze situations and people.[36] Without such a model, individuals would suffer from information overload.

Unfortunately, our mental models are sometimes based on faulty logic. Chris Argyris, an organizational psychologist, suggested that people unconsciously go through a seven-step process, called the **ladder of inference**, to draw conclusions (see Figure 19.2):

1. People look at observable data (i.e., the way an individual acts in a certain situation).
2. They select and focus on some aspect of the data. An individual's past experiences can impact the data that he or she decides to hone in on.
3. They add meaning to these data based on their mental model of the world, which is informed from their past cultural or personal experiences as well as their interpersonal interactions.
4. They make assumptions about the data based on the meanings that were added.
5. They draw conclusions from these assumptions.
6. They adopt beliefs and make generalizations from these conclusions.
7. They take actions based on these beliefs and generalizations.

Individuals tend to rely on the ladder of inference when they are under stress or working in situations with significant time pressures. The ladder enables an individual to quickly process information and make connections based on past experiences or knowledge. The speed with which connections are made enables an individual to be seen as decisive. The downside, of course, is that the thought process can be based on biases. We assume that we know why people act the way they do and do not question our logic. It is these assumptions that can get a person in trouble by quickly jumping to an inaccurate or biased conclusion.

One key way to avoid the dangers associated with the ladder of inference and to improve communication is to engage in active listening and **supportive communication**. Active listening involves two primary activities: seeking to understand the perspective of the speaker and reflecting that understanding back to him

Ladder of inference
A process by which an individual uses assumptions or biases formed from past experiences to make a judgment on the intentions of another individual.

Supportive communication
A process of offering advice and suggestions (advising), relating similar experiences (deflecting), asking follow-up questions for clarification (probing), and reiterating the main points (reflecting).

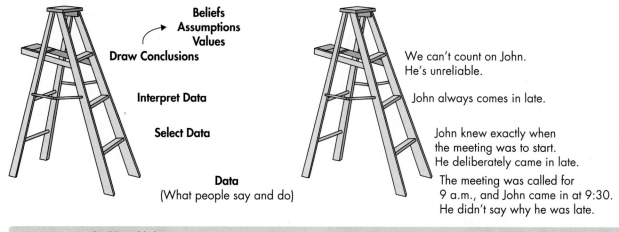

Figure 19.2 Ladder of Inference

Sources: The ladder of inference is described in Chris Argyris, *Overcoming Organizational Defenses* (Upper Saddle River, NJ: Prentice Hall, 1994), p. 88–89; and P. M. Senge, A. Kleiner, C. Roberts, R. B. Ross, and B. J. Smith, *The Fifth Discipline Fieldbook: Strategies and Tools for Building a Learning Organization* (New York: Doubleday, 1994).

Response Type	Example	Rationale
Advising	"Here's what I suggest . . ."	• Provides direction, evaluation, personal opinion, or instructions to the speaker. • Helps identify a solution to a speaker's problem. • Can provide clarity about how the speaker should interpret the problem.
Deflecting	"Let me tell you something similar that happened to me."	• Switches the focus from the speaker's problem to the listener's problem by changing the subject. • Signals that the speaker's message is not clear and uses examples that may help improve any miscommunication.
Probing	"What do you mean by that?"	• Asks a question about what the speaker has just said or about a topic the listener has selected. • Solicits additional information. • Helps the speaker say more about the topic when his or her message is unclear.
Reflecting	"If I understand correctly, you said that . . ."	• Mirrors back to the speaker what he or she just said. • Restates in a different way what the listener heard. • Communicates understanding and acceptance of the speaker's message.

Table 19.3 ⟩ Forms of Supportive Communication

Source: Adapted from D. A. Whetten and K. S. Cameron, *Developing Management Skills*, 5th edition (Upper Saddle River, NJ: Prentice Hall, 2002), p. 220.

or her. To understand the perspective of the speaker, a person must suspend his or her own judgments and beliefs. In essence, he or she must come to the conversation with an open mind.[37] Supportive communication includes offering advice and suggestions (advising), relating similar experiences (deflecting), asking follow-up questions for clarification (probing), and reiterating the main points (reflecting) (see Table 19.3).

Supportive communication emphasizes listening to what someone is trying to communicate and responding in ways that help you gain more information. This practice helps avoid reliance only on the initial "observable" data. Supportive communication also helps listeners refrain from adding meaning to what has been communicated because listeners actively solicit meaning from the speaker. As a result, listeners who use supportive communication can draw conclusions about what the speaker actually communicated, not what the listener perceived the speaker to have said.

USING COMMUNICATION TO PERSUADE

An effective approach to communication is to balance advocacy and inquiry. That is, individuals should put forth their position and objectives (advocate), but they should also seek to understand the perspectives and opinions of others by asking questions and seeking clarification (inquiry).[38] All too often, individuals focus solely on advocacy, seeking to win their point. Advocacy tends to provoke advocacy from the other side and, ultimately, results in a stalemate in communication (see Figure 19.3).[39] When individuals engage in a balanced approach to advocacy and inquiry, mutual learning can be achieved. The mutual learning that comes from balancing advocacy and inquiry is an important aspect of persuasion. **Persuasion** is a process by which an individual or a group captures an audience and influences, changes, or reinforces their perspectives, opinions, or behaviors.[40]

The art of persuasion dates back to the early days of democracy. Aristotle defined the three essential elements of communication to be logos, pathos, and ethos.[41] Logos refers to the logic used in a message or the facts that need to be conveyed. In

Persuasion

A process by which an individual or a group captures an audience and influences, changes, or reinforces their perspectives, opinions, and behaviors.

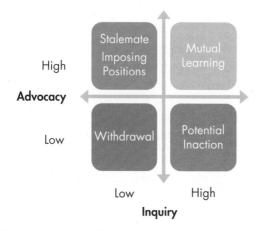

Figure 19.3 Balancing Advocacy and Inquiry

essence, it is the rationale for action. Beyond the facts, a good communicator must demonstrate passion, or pathos, for his or her argument. The goal of pathos is to make an emotional connection with the audience; it is to appeal to their hearts, not just their minds. As we discussed in Chapter 11, successful change initiatives appeal to both logic and emotions. The logic provides the rationale for change, while the pathos provides the impetus for action. The third essential component is ethos, which refers to the credibility of the speaker or communicator. Ethos is the extent to which the audience trusts and respects the person who is speaking. Ethos is derived from a person's reputation—does that person do what he or she says he or she will do? Has the person behaved in a way that can be trusted? Does he or she know what to do? Does he or she have relevant experience? Aristotle believed that ethos, or one's credibility, was the most important element of persuasion.[42] Credibility, in turn, is derived from a combination of trust and expertise (see Figure 19.4).

Effective communicators combine all of these elements. They frame their arguments by presenting and interpreting the appropriate facts; they emotionally connect with their audience; and they establish their credibility.[43] One team of researchers proposed that managers and employees use the following six principles to enhance their use of persuasion:[44]

1. Keep messages simple.
2. Make the message real and give others the information they need to make a decision.
3. Listen before speaking.
4. Transform fear into excitement by encouraging others to provide input.
5. Repeat the message personally and consistently.
6. Choose words carefully.

Persuasion has become an increasingly important management skill, especially as companies rely on more distributed forms of leadership and fewer command-and-control structures and styles. As lines of authority have been blurred with the growth of networked organizations and the pervasiveness of diverse, distributed teams, effective leaders need to rely on their ability to effectively position ideas and sway the opinions of individuals and team members. This is especially true when there are no formal reporting lines.[45]

Storytelling

An important aspect of persuasion is the ability to connect with the audience. One of the most compelling ways to build a personal connection is through storytelling.

Trust		**Expertise**		**Credibility**
• Deliver on promises • Keep confidences • Be consistent in values • Encourage exploration of ideas	**+**	• Research ideas • Get firsthand experiences • Cite trusted sources • Build on past successes • Gather endorsements	**=**	

Figure 19.4 ⟩ Building Credibility

Source: Adapted from "Persuasion I: The Basics," *Power, Influence, and Persuasion: Sell Your Ideas and Make Things Happen* (Boston, MA: HBS Press, 2006).

The use of stories, metaphors, or analogies to convey certain messages or themes is a way to build an emotional connection between the speaker and the audience.[46] Stories tend to reveal what is important to the speaker and to provide a window into his or her values.[47] In essence, stories help build trust between the speaker and the audience. If a person relates to a speaker, he or she is more likely to trust what is being communicated.[48] Compelling stories also build a connection with the audience, reminding them of what is important and why they should act a certain way.[49] This emotional connection, in turn, can be a strong driver for change or motivation for action. Oprah Winfrey is particularly adept at using stories to build a connection with her guests and her audience.

Stories have also been used to highlight important aspects of a company's culture. In Chapter 8, we discussed the ways in which Google used stories to reinforce particular behaviors and approaches. Many other companies do the same. Ed Fuller, head of international lodging for Marriott, uses stories to teach new managers about the firm's priorities for serving customers. He often likes to recount his own experience when, early in his career, he was asked to meet with Bill Marriott, the company's chief executive, at the Boston Copley Marriott where Fuller was the general manager. He assumed that Bill was going to chastise him for being off budget on catering sales. Instead, Bill was concerned about the way in which an employee had reacted to a customer's complaint about being served cold clam chowder. The customer happened to be a relative of the CEO, and the server did not handle the interaction in a professional manner. Bill was not concerned about the budget shortfall; he was worried about achieving customer service standards. Treating customers well would, in turn, lead to better sales and performance. Fuller likes to remind new managers, through this story, that it is the little things that make the difference at Marriott.[50]

andipantz/iStockphoto.com

ORGANIZATIONAL COMMUNICATION

The importance of communication is magnified at the organizational level where leaders try to make sure that their messages are appropriately conveyed to all employees, but also that employees find a way to communicate effectively with each other. An example of the latter is evident in the way in which the U.S. airspace is managed. The U.S. Air Traffic Control System Command Center (ATCSCC) is the department within the U.S. Department of Transportation Federal

The Leadership Development Journey

Storytelling is an effective leadership technique. It's a communication tool that makes information easier to remember. As a result, stories are retained longer than traditional forms of communication. They have the ability to paint a clear and vivid picture of the situation and allow listeners to learn and relate their own experiences. Reflect upon a time when you used storytelling to better communicate and respond to the following questions:

- What was the setting for the story?
- Who were the main characters?
- What was the plot of the story?
- How did you integrate the setting, characters, and plot to convey a message?
- How was the story received by your audience?

Based on this reflection, how would you use storytelling to communicate as a leader?

Aviation Administration (FAA) that manages the flow of air traffic in the continental United States. The ATCSCC reports that there are 4,000–6,000 aircraft operating in the National Airspace System (NAS) during peak periods, which amounts to approximately 50,000 aircraft operations per day. The ATCSCC also regulates air traffic when weather, equipment, runway closures, or other impacting conditions place stress on the NAS (see Figure 19.5).

The fidelity of these systems requires that voice messages be sent and received with great accuracy between air traffic controllers and pilots. To ensure a high degree of agreement about the meaning of transmitted messages, pilots must acknowledge each message sent by a controller by giving feedback (e.g., saying "Roger") and controllers must indicate whether pilots have carried out required maneuvers.[51]

Yet the challenge with air traffic control communication systems is that the controller and all pilots flying within an assigned piece of airspace are generally talking over the same voice channel. Therefore, the likelihood that one pilot will interrupt the communication of another pilot or controller is greater if the system becomes congested with more pilots entering the controller's assigned airspace.[52] As these

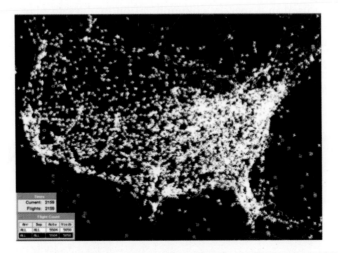

Figure 19.5 Air Traffic in the U.S. Airspace System

Source: Air Traffic Control System Command Center, 2008, www.fly.faa.gov/Products/Information/information.html, accessed October 23, 2008.

interruptions become more frequent and communication messages are delayed, misinterpreted, or lost, safety can be jeopardized and accidents can happen.

For these reasons, the Center for Advanced Aviation System Development (CAASD) created the Controller Pilot Data Link Communications (CPDLC), which has been designed to off-load non-time-critical messages from the voice channel to a data channel.[53] This change in communication has been successful in decreasing the voice channel occupancy by 75%, resulting in increased flight safety and efficiency with few missed, repeated, and misunderstood communications.[54]

Entities such as CAASD understand that communication in organizations is more effective when the **communication systems**, which are the formal and informal structures that facilitate how communication is transmitted, are efficient. The formal organization system encompasses the relationships created by the designation of rules, lines of reporting, chains of command, and physical layout.[55] These relationships generally determine whether communication should flow up, down, or across an organization. The informal organization system, in contrast, is composed of the informal and social relationships that coworkers and colleagues have developed during their tenure in the organization. Given that the transmission of information is less formal, people in different parts of an organization can have easy access to important information no matter their formal position or status.

For communication systems to work effectively, the flow of communication must be supported. In organizations, we call the features that support the flow of communication, communication media, communication channels, and communication networks. We explore each of these components in more detail in this section.

Communication Media

The media used for communication can vary widely depending on the nature, sensitivity, and importance of the message and the anticipated or desired actions of the audience. Most organizations use multiple forms of **communication media**, including oral, written, and electronic. Oral media typically include telephone conversations, face-to-face conferences, meetings, and speeches. Written media typically include letters, memos and reports, newsletters, handbooks and manuals, bulletins, and posters. Electronic media often include fax, e-mail, and videoconferencing. Different methods should be employed for different situations (see Figure 19.6).

The format used in a specific communication media can play a role in signifying the importance of the message. For instance, a face-to-face meeting to discuss an action item generally carries more weight than a voicemail message, even though both are forms of oral communication. In-person meetings are generally useful for conveying important or sensitive information. The sensitive nature of the communication often requires a back-and-forth clarification process that is

Communication systems
The formal and informal structures that facilitate how communication is transmitted throughout an organization.

Communication media
The formats used to convey messages, including oral, written, and electronic.

Oral	Written	Electronic
• Conveying personal or sensitive information	• Formal rules or policies • Following up to convey understanding or agreement	• Nonsensitive, time critical messages • Conveying company policies • Clarifying points

Figure 19.6 ⟩ When to Use Certain Communication Methods

best achieved in person. In-person meetings also provide the benefit of reading and interpreting body language and tone, which can reinforce the authority of the message. Voicemail and recorded messages are generally useful for nonsensitive information that must be communicated in a timely fashion. This can include information on new company policies or procedures. While voice messages can provide a clue to tone, they are unidirectional and not conducive to iterative clarification.

Written forms of communication are the most difficult to interpret because they generally lack a tone of voice and an opportunity for real-time dialogue. Written communication is useful for conveying formal company policies or for following up on conversations to demonstrate understanding and agreement.[56]

E-mail is a form of written communication that can be formal or informal. If e-mail is used to convey formal company policies, it is an alternative to written documents and is useful for that purpose. E-mail as part of an informal exchange can also be helpful in clarifying misunderstandings, but it can escalate misinterpretation and conflict because it lacks the components that make active listening effective—reading nonverbal clues and engaging in inquiry. Although it may seem like a fleeting form of communication, an e-mail exchange becomes part of a company's permanent record. As such, it is important to consider network etiquette, or "netiquette," in e-mail communications. In any e-mail exchange, a person should do the following:

- *Think before writing.* It may make sense to wait 24 hours to respond to a particularly emotionally charged message.
- *Avoid all capital letters in messages.* This conveys yelling at the recipient.
- *Read messages carefully before sending them.* Check grammar, spelling, and tone.
- *Be crisp and on point.* Refrain from going off on a tangent to some other issue. E-mail is most effective when it is succinct.[57]

Even though e-mail does not have the rich properties of face-to-face meetings, it is often used to convey sensitive information. E-mail's ability to simultaneously reach a multitude of people in a timely fashion is one reason for its vastly increased use. This is especially true for networked or dispersed organizations where it is not practical or feasible to traverse the globe to conduct a series of team meetings to share new developments or initiatives.[58]

Despite its increased use, e-mail is not viewed favorably by employees for all types of communication. In a recent study, face-to-face meetings were rated the most satisfactory form of communication when discussing one's job or business unit. Face-to-face meetings were also perceived to present higher quality information compared to e-mail. In essence, when the communication is directly relevant to a person's position or performance, a more interactive media format is preferred. This allows the employee to evaluate the tone and disposition of the speaker as well as the content of the message. As discussed, these nonverbal cues can convey important signals in their own right. In this same study, e-mail communication was most favorably viewed when used for distributing company policies or conveying urgent news.[59]

The nature of the task can also dictate the type of communication media that is appropriate.[60] For standard or routine tasks, e-mail and written forms of communication may suffice. These formats can provide direction and outline specific procedures that should be followed. They typically do not require an interactive level of communication. For more novel situations or less routine tasks, a face-to-face meeting or interchange may be appropriate. When launching a new project, it is often better to hold a face-to-face meeting with the parties involved to ensure that there is a common level of awareness and an understanding of the desired goals. Given the newness of the project, a key outcome of the meeting may be a

A DIFFERENT View

Crisis Communication

Organizations face public criticism every day. In the event of a damaging situation, crisis communication, a subset of public relations, is designed to help an organization maintain its good reputation and minimize long-term damage. Preparation and organization are essential to the success of crisis communication. Swift, honest, thorough responses are the preferred goals when responding to a negative situation. In 2006, Taco Bell was criticized for failing to respond quickly to an *Escherichia coli* outbreak that was caused by bacteria in their food. Johnson & Johnson, on the contrary, acted very quickly in the mid-1980s after tampered Tylenol bottles were found; they took the capsules off the market until a new bottle could be designed.

1. What steps can be taken to handle a crisis situation?
2. Identify an organization that faced negative publicity but has subsequently maintained their good reputation. What did they do right?
3. Identify an organization that failed to successfully respond to a crisis. What should they have done differently?

AP Images/Charlie Riedel

further clarification of processes or procedures and a general agreement on measures of success.[61]

American Century Investments uses various media to foster open communication throughout the company and with its customers, including the Internet, a corporate bimonthly magazine, an electronic question-and-answer database, and regularly scheduled team meetings. The company believes that these tools are important to its performance and expresses the following: "In today's competitive business world, communication is an important tool. We believe that the more informed you are about our company and our industry, the better-educated business decisions you can make. And when we listen to employees and welcome their diverse ideas, our company becomes stronger, more cohesive and better able to surpass our competitors."[62]

Communication Channels

As we have discussed, the degree of communication formality varies depending on the context. As such, communication should be tailored to the dynamics of the situation. In certain situations, such as employee company meetings and external briefings with stakeholders, a more formal communication process is appropriate. In less structured environments, open communication and back-and-forth exchanges are the norm. The degree of formality in the communication process is also a function of the culture and leadership of the organization. In strong bureaucracies with tight command-and-control leadership approaches, a top-down approach to communication is generally utilized.

While communication media function as the methods by which communication is transmitted in organizations, **communication channels** are the conduits used to deliver oral, written/print, and electronic media. The two types of communication channels in organizations today are vertical channels and horizontal channels (see Figure 19.7). Each type of communication channel is used for different purposes. In vertical channels, media are sent up and down the chain of command. Bureaucratic organizations with many levels of employees rely on downward communication to direct behaviors and influence the attitudes of employees. Typically, downward communication is used for giving instructions and training, disseminating information

Communication channels
The conduits used to deliver oral, written/print, and electronic media, including vertical channels and horizontal channels.

Figure 19.7 > Vertical and Horizontal Communication

Instructing, training, and disseminating information

Handbooks, manuals, bulletins, e-mail

Between functional departments and peer communication

Memos, reports, informal contact

Feedback from lower employees to promote employee engagement

Surveys, hotlines, e-mail

about the company, providing rationale for directions and policies, and evaluating work performance.[63] Tools such as handbooks, instruction manuals, bulletin boards, performance evaluations, department meetings, and e-mail are frequently used for this purpose.

Vertical channels also rely on upward communication to transmit messages. Some organizations encourage upward communication to provide employees with an outlet for expressing their concerns and complaints to upper management.[64] Tools such as opinion and satisfaction surveys, telephone hotlines, suggestion boxes, and e-mail are frequently used to solicit employee engagement. Employees who engage in an upward communication process tend to be more satisfied in their organization when they trust managers and believe that the managers are interested in their opinions and perspectives. In essence, this process helps facilitate employee engagement.[65] Of course, the degree of upward communication needs to be managed so that it does not overwhelm managers.

Studies of vertical communication channels have shown that employees are better able to read and understand the intent of downward communication (from upper management to subordinates) than managers are able to comprehend messages that move upward (from subordinates to upper management). This tends to be the case because downward communication is generally not filtered as it passes through the organization, while upward communication may be adjusted and analyzed by various individuals in the chain of management before it reaches the intended party.[66]

In horizontal channels, media typically flows across an organization between functional departments. Organizations that seek to save time use horizontal channels, sending a message directly to another person in another department without having to send the message up or down the hierarchy. Essentially, in horizontal channels, peers turn to one another to seek out the information they need.[67] Tools such as memos and reports, lunchtime conversations, informal and impromptu contacts and conferences, committees, task forces, and e-mail are frequently used to facilitate horizontal communication.

Children's Healthcare of Atlanta (CHOA) believes that effective communication between patients, parents, and caregivers is critical to developing the climate of collaboration and trust that is important to providing first-rate pediatric medical care.[68] Therefore, the hospital has created three initiatives to help the company meet this goal and improve its vertical and horizontal communication: the Situation Background Assessment Recommendation (SBAR) Nursing Report, Resource Nurses, and Rapid Response Teams.

- *SBAR Nursing Report.* The SBAR technique provides a framework to facilitate efficient, effective communication of critical patient information between clinicians (horizontally). SBAR guidelines help healthcare providers quickly identify and convey key patient data to ensure timely delivery of appropriate treatment.
- *Resource Nurses.* In this program, the more senior and experienced resource nurses help less experienced nurses evaluate patient conditions and relay relevant information to attending physicians. CHOA believes that this ensures that patients receive the most effective treatment possible and that the knowledge of senior nurses is passed on to less experienced nurses more effectively (vertical communication).
- *Rapid Response Teams.* One of the primary purposes of these teams is to ensure that patients are receiving the best treatment in the most appropriate unit in the hospital. If a nurse is concerned about a patient's condition, he or she can request an evaluation

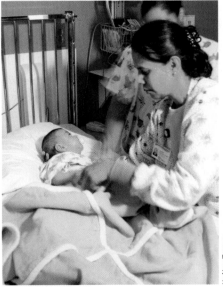

by a rapid response team. The team communicates directly with physicians or assists the primary care nurses to ensure that critical patients receive the appropriate care.

For its accomplishments with initiatives such as these, CHOA received the Joint Commission's Golden Seal of Approval for upholding national standards for healthcare quality and safety.[69]

Communication Networks

Sometimes communication does not follow a strict vertical or horizontal channel, but instead it flows through a network of contacts. At W. L. Gore, best known for its innovative Gore-Tex fabrics, there are no traditional organizational charts, no chains of command, and no predetermined channels of communication.[70] So how then do the company's employees communicate with one another? Individuals who do not rely on communication channels to communicate (and those who do) often use networks.[71] Communication networks are formal and informal connections through which individuals use their relationships with others to send and receive messages. We will discuss networks in greater detail in Chapter 20, but for now, it is important to know that communication networks differ in size, function, and centrality and dominance.[72]

- *Network size.* Some networks are very large and span an entire organization. These large networks enable one to easily and quickly send messages to all members of the organization. Other networks are small and link specific groups in the organization. These are sometimes called clique networks. Finally, personal networks are based on the personal relationships and contacts among individuals. Network size is also defined by the number of individuals required to get a message from one point to another.
- *Network function.* Different communication networks serve different purposes. In organizations, these typically include production (perform the task), maintenance (keep the structure operating), social connection (improve morale and provide support), and innovation (review and revise operations and create new opportunities).
- *Network centrality and dominance.* In dominant networks, one individual or group controls the flow of messages. Formal bureaucracies are dominant networks. All messages must go through the chain of command in a top-down fashion. In these types of networks, one person often serves as the "gatekeeper" of information. In this case, that person has network centrality.

While a bureaucratic hierarchy can be considered a formal communication network, personal networks are considered informal communication networks. A particularly strong informal personal communication network is the grapevine, which refers to the way rumors and gossip travel through an organization. One study found that 70% of organizational communication travels across the grapevine, and the vast majority of the information conveyed through it is accurate.[73] The grapevine tends to be more active when an organization is undergoing a transformation or is confronting difficult times. Grapevine activity also increases when trust in management is low. In these situations, employees look for information in a variety of places.[74]

Although the grapevine can spread gossip that might be unfounded or seemingly superficial, it can also serve a useful purpose, conveying appropriate organizational boundaries. For instance, gossip can be used to share common beliefs on how one should act in an organization. Gossip can function as a form of behavior modification if individual employees learn through the grapevine that the way they act in certain situations may not be considered appropriate (e.g., taking credit for another's idea or speaking at the wrong time). Gossip can also be used to increase a sense of belongingness to an organization.[75]

Communication Breakdowns

At any place in the organizational communication system, communication can break down. Much of this relates to how effective communication partners are in conveying and interpreting interpersonal communication. Yet more of the breakdowns in organizational communication relate to how well the communication system accommodates stress. What happens when communication media are subject to technical difficulties or when someone with centrality is missing from a communication channel or network? Can the system adapt? The U.S. federal government's response to Hurricane Katrina is an example of an inefficient and ineffective communication process.

On August 29, 2005, Hurricane Katrina hit the New Orleans, Louisiana area hard, killing over 1,800 people, cutting off phone and electricity service, breaking the levee system surrounding the city, displacing hundreds of thousands of people throughout the area, and stranding many others who did not evacuate. In the aftermath of the hurricane, the Federal Emergency Management Agency (FEMA) received harsh criticism for its failure to provide timely and adequate resources to the citizens of the devastated area.

Upon further investigation, researchers found that several communication breakdowns occurred in the emergency response system. It started with Kathleen Blanco, then Louisiana governor, who issued a state of emergency a few days before the hurricane hit and sent a letter to President George W. Bush requesting a disaster declaration for the state in an effort to receive federal assistance.[76] Before the federal government could respond, the letter traveled through several offices at FEMA.[77] By the time a significant federal response was formulated, days had passed and images of people stranded on rooftops without food or water were indelibly etched in the minds of the public.[78] Public outrage ensued, and in less than 2 weeks, Michael Brown, director of FEMA, was relieved of his duties.

An organization can employ specific strategies to prevent or productively address breakdowns in communication systems, including an audit of communication protocols. A **communication audit** allows organizations to improve the way in which they respond to routine, nonroutine, or crisis circumstances.[79] An effective communication audit includes the following:[80]

- *Employee focus groups or interviews.* Employees can discuss the ways in which they receive information related to their job and to the company. They assess whether the information they receive is helpful and whether they have any suggestions for improvements.
- *Questionnaires and surveys.* Employees rate the amount or quality of information they receive about organizational policies, job duties, technological changes, and the organization's performance.
- *Network analysis.* Managers assess the formal networks in the organization to determine whether communication flows up, down, and across the organization adequately. Employees determine where in the organization they obtain the most pertinent information.

Communication audit
The process of reviewing the communication systems in an organization.

FEMA/Alamy

- *Communication logs.* Service departments assess the record of service calls made by those in the company and the corresponding level of responsiveness.
- *Content analysis of publications, manuals, and handbooks.* Departments review printed materials to check for inaccuracies or opportunities for improvement.
- *Technology or media analysis.* Information technology departments test equipment and review records of past technology failures.

A communication audit is useful in understanding the state of communication in an organization at a given time. From the communication audit, an organization receives an objective picture highlighting the potential for real breakdowns or weaknesses in the flow of communication. For a communication audit to be useful, it should evaluate the systems of communication, not the effectiveness of those involved.

CROSS-CULTURAL COMMUNICATION

As globalization has increased, managers must often communicate with a culturally and geographically diverse set of individuals. Because of this, a person needs to be mindful of the cultural differences in cross-cultural communication. For communication to be effective, the words, pictures, and symbols must be intelligible for everyone involved. Sometimes this is problematic in jobs where workers use many acronyms or abbreviations to communicate. Someone unfamiliar with this "language" may lose track of what is being said. Body language can also impact communication effectiveness. Sometimes people say one thing and communicate another with their body movements. Someone who says, "I'm listening" but fails to make eye contact or face the person who is speaking appears to contradict himself or herself.

Chapter 16 and Chapter 17 discussed effective ways of negotiating across different cultures and leading geographically dispersed teams, respectively. The lessons addressed in those two chapters apply to cross-cultural communication. In any form of communication across geographies and cultures, it is important to take the time to learn about specific customs, norms, and approaches. For instance, in Kuwait, business meetings generally start very slowly and involve considerable talk about family and health. Unlike many Americans who are uncomfortable with long periods of silence, Kuwaitis tend to be patient and expect long pauses in conversations.[81] Conversely, in the Netherlands, the conversation about business matters begins almost immediately, with little or no small talk. Business executives doing business in the Netherlands should also refrain from showy presentations or exaggerated claims; the Dutch prefer modesty and accuracy over glitzy sales pitches.[82]

While learning the specific "rules" for every language and culture might be helpful, there are several rules people can use regardless of the language or culture of the person with whom they are communicating. To bridge linguistic and communication differences, individuals can do the following:

- Enunciate and speak slower.
- Avoid slang, colloquialisms, and profanity.
- Be careful about telling jokes that may be culturally sensitive.
- Use plenty of white space in e-mail communications.
- Use visual representations (pictures, tables, and graphs) to support what is being said.
- Use correct titles and given names (Mr. Smith) instead of familiar forms (Bob) unless granted permission to do otherwise.

- Be careful about numbers. For example, the numbers 1 and 7 are written differently in different countries.
- Be careful with dates. Some countries write the day of the month first, while others write the month first (e.g., 1 March 2016 versus March 1, 2016; 01/03/16 versus 03/01/16).
- Be sincere and communicate openly with someone you trust when you are unclear of linguistic or cultural standards.[83]

SUMMARY

LO1 Many people believe that they are effective communicators when, in fact, they are not. At work, some people have great ideas but fail to communicate them persuasively or to understand their audience. As a result, their ideas are not taken into consideration by those who make important decisions. Others may communicate their ideas well but fail to listen. When someone else is speaking, they become distracted, thinking about the tasks on their to-do lists or what their response will be after the person has finished talking. As a result, they fail to understand the issue that has been presented. Ineffective communication like this can impede productivity and performance in an organization.

LO2 The ability to communicate effectively with employees and customers is important to business performance. Communication involves using sounds, words, pictures, symbols, gestures, and body language to exchange information. Communication can be verbal or nonverbal. It is important to pay attention to the various ways in which messages are communicated—through body language, tone, pitch, and so forth. Communication styles can also impact the ways in which messages are perceived. Some individuals prefer more direct approaches, while others prefer indirect or subtle forms of communication. In communicating with different people, it is also important to keep an open mind and refrain from jumping to conclusions. Making assumptions about a person's motives or intentions can be dangerous. Successful communicators balance inquiry and advocacy and are active listeners.

LO3 Persuasion is the process by which an individual or a group captivates an audience and influences, changes or reinforces their perspectives, opinions or behaviors. At the heart of persuasion is the ability to communicate with logic, passion, and credibility. Credibility, in turn, is a function of trust and expertise. To be persuasive an individual must be considered trustworthy and must have the expertise to validate his or her perspective. One persuasion technique that is very effective is storytelling. Storytelling enables a speaker to connect with his or her audience in a more meaningful and purposeful way.

LO4 Organizations must also create the conditions under which communication can be effective. From an organizational level, it is important to consider the type of media that is appropriate for different forms of communication. For instance, a one-on-one meeting is useful for conveying sensitive or personal information, while a company-wide e-mail is effective for relaying company policies or procedures. In addition, organizations need to be concerned with the vertical and horizontal flow of information. Are messages being interpreted appropriately? Do the receivers of the information comprehend the intentions of the sender? Open channels of communication often speed the process of decision making and enhance collaboration. Closed channels can create confusion and divisiveness. Periodically, it is important for organizations to conduct a communication audit to assess the effectiveness of their communication system.

LO5 Finally, with the growing globalization of business, understanding the different cultural norms of communication is critical. Effective communicators are able to modify or adapt their style and approach to align with the cultural and contextual situation. Some situations call for a direct style of communication while others call for a more indirect style of communication.

KEY TERMS

Body language
Communication
Communication audit
Communication channels
Communication media
Communication style

Communication systems
Directness
Interpersonal communication
Ladder of inference
Listening
Nonverbal communication

Openness
Persuasion
Space and objects
Supportive communication
Verbal communication
Vocal qualities

ASSIGNMENTS

Discussion Topics

1. What can individuals do to reduce "noise" in a communication exchange?

2. How does the situational context impact the way in which messages are delivered and received? Consider different situational contexts—start-up situations, crises, business turnarounds. In what ways, if any, should a leader change his or her communication style? Under what situation is it better to be more direct or to be more self-contained?

3. What nonverbal communication tools can an individual use to convey meaning to his or her listener? On the receiving end, what can the listener do both verbally and nonverbally to signal comprehension?

4. Many studies have highlighted differences in the ways men and women communicate. What accounts for these differences? Why do both men and women hold negative perceptions about women who attempt to speak more in meetings? Why is that not the case for men? Do you think that this will change? If so, how?

5. How can the ladder of inference lead to miscommunications and misunderstandings? In what ways can an individual ensure that his or her impact (what is conveyed or interpreted by the receiver) matches his or her intent (what he or she hopes to convey)?

6. In what ways can one enhance his or her credibility as a speaker?

7. Why are stories such a powerful form of communication? Think of a story that has resonated with you. Why did it have an impact?

8. What are the advantages and disadvantages of the different mediums of communication—oral, written, and electronic? As companies rely more and more on social media, what should concern them? What are the potential communication challenges associated with social media? What are the advantages?

9. In what ways is gossip helpful in communicating a company's culture and values?

10. If you were designing a communications training program for a company that is embarking on a global strategy, how would you approach the task? What would you include in the training program? How would you measure success?

Management Research

1. Find a written speech that includes data (e.g., financial, productivity, sales, or trends) and was delivered by the leader of an organization.

   • Who was the audience for the speech?

   • How did the leader use and interpret the data?

   • What conclusions did the leader make about the data?

   • Did the leader build trust or use expertise to persuade the audience?

   • How would you evaluate the effectiveness of the speech?

2. Research a recent crisis. Assess how the leaders communicated during the crisis situation.

   - Did they take responsibility for the crisis?
   - Did they build trust with stakeholders?
   - Did they communicate a plan for resolving the crisis?

In the Field

Conduct a communication audit of your university and evaluate the following components of your university's communication practices:

- News and event notifications
- Organizational change and strategic initiative announcements
- Students, staff, and faculty inter-communication
- External stakeholder messaging
- Social media usage
- Stakeholder opinion surveys and questionnaires

What did you learn from the communication audit? Based on the information you collected from the audit, develop a set of recommendations.

ENDNOTES

[1] Anthony J. Mayo and Nitin Nohria, *In Their Time: The Greatest Business Leaders of the 20th Century* (Boston, MA: HBS Press, 2005), pp. xx–xxi.

[2] Alex "Sandy" Pentland, "The New Science of Building Great Teams," *Harvard Business Review*, April 2012.

[3] Rudi Gassner, "Rudi Gassner at BMG International," lecture and question-and-answer session, Harvard Business School, Boston, MA, June 1, 1994, available from Katherine S. Weber and Linda A. Hill, "Rudi Gassner at BMG International, Video" (Boston, MA: HBS Publishing, 1994).

[4] Carol W. Ellis, *Management Skills for New Managers* (New York: AMACOM, 2005), p. 24.

[5] M. Buckingham and C. Coffman, *First, Break All the Rules: What the World's Greatest Managers Do Differently* (New York: Simon & Schuster, 1999).

[6] Bill George and Andrew N. McLean, "Oprah!," Harvard Business School Case No. 9-405-087, rev. April 11, 2007 (Boston, MA: HBS Publishing, 2005); and Nancy F. Koehn and Erica Helms, "Oprah Winfrey," Harvard Business School Case No. 9-809-068, rev. May 13, 2009 (Boston, MA: HBS Publishing, 2009).

[7] Academy of Achievement, "Oprah Winfrey Interview," http://www.achievement.org.

[8] Paul Noglows, "Oprah: The Year of Living Dangerously," *Working Woman*, May 1, 1994, p. 52.

[9] C. Lavin, "It's All Going Oprah's Way," *Chicago Tribune*, December 19, 1985.

[10] Academy of Achievement, "Oprah Winfrey Interview," http://www.achievement.org.

[11] W. W. Neher, *Organizational Communication: Challenges of Change, Continuity and Diversity* (Needham Heights, MA: Allyn & Bacon, 1997).

[12] Michael E. Hattersley and Linda McJannet, *Management Communication: Principles and Practice* (New York: McGraw-Hill, 1997), p. 3.

[13] Ibid., pp. 4-6.

[14] David A. Garvin and Michael A. Roberto, "Change Through Persuasion," *Harvard Business Review*, February 2005.

[15] Lyle Sussman, "How to Frame a Message: The Art of Persuasion and Negotiation," *Business Horizons*, July–August 1999, pp. 2–6.

[16] M. Munter, *Guide to Managerial Communication: Effective Business Writing and Speaking* (Upper Saddle River, NJ: Prentice Hall, 1997).

[17] Gary Genard, "Leveraging the Power of Nonverbal Communication," *Harvard Management Communication Letter*, April 1, 2004.

[18] M. Shapiro, "Communication Styles on Team Dynamics," Simmons School of Management Course Note: Communication Strategies, 2006.

[19] Ibid.

[20] Ibid.

[21] Ibid.

[22] A. H. Bell and D. M. Smith, *Management Communication* (New York: John Wiley & Sons, 1999).

[23] Ibid.

[24] Ibid.

[25] Ibid.

[26] Ibid.

[27] Anne Field, "What You Say, What They Hear," *Harvard Management Communication Letter*, Winter 2005.

[28] Kathleen E. Allen, "Women's Value Orientation," *Encyclopedia of Leadership*, George R. Goethals, Georgia J. Sorenson, and James MacGregor Burns, eds. (Thousand Oaks, CA: Sage Publications, 2004), pp. 1688–1692.

[29] Deborah Tannen, "The Power of Talk: Who Gets Heard and Why," *Harvard Business Review*, September–October 1995.

[30] Linda L. Carli, "Gender Issues in Workplace Groups: Effects of Gender and Communication Style on Social Influence," *Gender and Communication at Work*, Mary Barrett and Marilyn J. Davidson, eds. (Hampshire, England: Ashgate Publishing, 2006), pp. 69–83; and Deborah Tannen, "The Power of Talk: Who Gets Heard and Why," *Harvard Business Review*, September–October 1995.

[31] Michael J. Glauser, "Upward Information Flow in Organizations: Review and

Conceptual Analysis," *Human Relations*, Vol. 37, No. 8, 1984, pp. 613–643.

[32] Dina W. Pradel, Hannah Riley Bowles, and Kathleen L. McGinn, "When Does Gender Matter in Negotiation?" *Negotiation*, November 2005.

[33] Victoria L. Brescoll, "Who Takes the Floor and Why: Gender, Power, and Volubility in Organizations," *Administrative Science Quarterly*, Vol. 56, No. 4, 2011, pp. 622–641.

[34] E. Goffman, *The Presentation of Self in Everyday Life* (New York: Doubleday Anchor, 1959).

[35] Ibid.

[36] Linda A. Hill, "Building Effective One-on-One Work Relationships," Harvard Business School Note No. 9-497-028 (Boston, MA: HBS Publishing, 1996).

[37] James G. Clawson, "Active Listening," University of Virginia Darden School Note No. UV0118, rev. December 28, 2001 (Charlottesville, VA: Darden Business Publishing, 1986).

[38] Peter Senge, *The Fifth Discipline: The Art and Practice of the Learning Organization* (New York: Doubleday, 1990).

[39] Linda A. Hill, "Building Effective One-on-One Work Relationships," Harvard Business School Note No. 9-497-028 (Boston, MA: HBS Publishing, 1996).

[40] "Persuasion I: The Basics," *Power, Influence, and Persuasion: Sell Your Ideas and Make Things Happen* (Boston, MA: HBS Press, 2006).

[41] Nitin Nohria and Brooke Harrington, "Principles of Effective Persuasion," Harvard Business School Note No. 9-497-059 (Boston, MA: HBS Publishing, 1997).

[42] Kevin W. Dean, "Rhetoric," *Encyclopedia of Leadership*, George R. Goethals, Georgia J. Sorenson, and James MacGregor Burns, eds. (Thousand Oaks, CA: Sage Publications, 2004), p. 1328.

[43] Jay A. Conger, "The Necessary Art of Persuasion," *Harvard Business Review*, May–June 1998.

[44] Nitin Nohria and Brooke Harrington, "Six Principles of Successful Persuasion," Harvard Business School Note No. 9-494-037 (Boston, MA: HBS Publishing, 1993).

[45] "Persuasion I: The Basics," *Power, Influence, and Persuasion: Sell Your Ideas and Make Things Happen* (Boston, MA: HBS Press, 2006).

[46] Beverly Kaye and Betsy Jacobson, "True Tales and Tall Tales: The Power of Organizational Storytelling," *Training & Development*, March 1999.

[47] Rob Goffee and Gareth Jones, "Chapter 7," *Why Should Anyone Be Led by You? What It Takes to Be an Authentic Leader* (Boston, MA: HBS Press, 2006).

[48] Stephen Denning, "Telling Tales," *Harvard Business Review*, May 2004.

[49] Cynthia Trapani Matthew and Robert J. Sternberg, "Intelligence, Verbal," *Encyclopedia of Leadership*, George R. Goethals, Georgia J. Sorenson, and James MacGregor Burns, eds. (Thousand Oaks, CA: Sage Publications, 2004), p. 732.

[50] Vickie Elmer, "How Storytelling Spurs Success," *Fortune*, December 6, 2010.

[51] W. W. Neher, *Organizational Communication: Challenges of Change, Continuity and Diversity* (Needham Heights, MA: Allyn & Bacon, 1997).

[52] MITRE Corporation Center for Advanced Aviation System Development, 2008, Controller Pilot Data Link Communications, www.caasd.org/work/project_details.cfm?item_id=110, accessed October 23, 2008.

[53] Ibid.

[54] Ibid.

[55] W. W. Neher, *Organizational Communication: Challenges of Change, Continuity and Diversity* (Needham Heights, MA: Allyn & Bacon, 1997).

[56] Carol W. Ellis, *Management Skills for New Managers* (New York: AMACOM, 2005), pp. 29–32.

[57] Ibid.

[58] M. Lynne Markus, "Electronic Mail as the Medium of Managerial Choice," *Organization Science*, Vol. 5, No. 4, 1994, pp. 502–527.

[59] Zinta S. Byrne and Elaine LeMay, "Different Media for Organizational Communication: Perceptions of Quality and Satisfaction," *Journal of Business and Psychology*, Vol. 21, No. 2, 2006, pp. 149–173.

[60] Ronald E. Rice, "Task Analyzability, Use of New Media, and Effectiveness: A Multi-Site Exploration of Media Richness," *Organization Science*, Vol. 3, No. 4, 1992, pp. 475–500.

[61] Richard L. Daft and Norman B. Macintosh, "A Tentative Exploration into the Amount of Equivocality of Information Processing in Organizational Work Units," *Administrative Science Quarterly*, Vol. 26, 1981, pp. 207–224.

[62] American Century Investments, "Our Culture," www.americancentury.com/careers/our_culture.jsp#1946, accessed October 28, 2010.

[63] W. W. Neher, *Organizational Communication: Challenges of Change, Continuity and Diversity* (Needham Heights, MA: Allyn & Bacon, 1997).

[64] Ibid.

[65] Michael J. Glauser, "Upward Information Flow in Organizations: Review and Conceptual Analysis," *Human Relations*, Vol. 37, No. 8, 1984, pp. 613–643.

[66] Bruce Harriman, "Up and Down the Communications Ladder," *Harvard Business Review*, September–October 1974.

[67] W. W. Neher, *Organizational Communication: Challenges of Change, Continuity and Diversity* (Needham Heights, MA: Allyn & Bacon, 1997).

[68] Children's Healthcare of Atlanta website, www.choa.org/default.aspx?id=5687, accessed October 23, 2008.

[69] Ibid.

[70] W. L. Gore & Associates website, www.gore.com/en_xx/aboutus/culture/index.html, accessed October 23, 2008.

[71] Rob Cross, Nitin Nohria, and Andrew Parker, "Six Myths About Informal Networks—and How to Overcome Them," *Sloan Management Review*, Spring 2002, pp. 67–75.

[72] W. W. Neher, *Organizational Communication: Challenges of Change, Continuity and Diversity* (Needham Heights, MA: Allyn & Bacon, 1997).

[73] Suzanne M. Crampton, John W. Hodge, and Jitendra M. Mishra, "The Informal Communication Network: Factors Influencing Grapevine Activity," *Public Personnel Management*, Vol. 27, No. 4, 1998, pp. 569–584.

[74] Ibid.

[75] Don Cohen and Laurence Prusak, *In Good Company: How Social Capital Makes Organizations Work* (Boston, MA: HBS Press, 2001), pp. 103–132.

[76] MacNeil/Lehrer Productions, Online Newshour: After Hurricane Katrina, 2005, www.pbs.org/newshour/bb/weather/july-dec05/katrina/fema_background.html, accessed October 23, 2008.

[77] Ibid.

[78] R. Abelson, A. Feuer, L. K. Altman, and S. Lohr, "10,000 Patients and Staff Members Await Evacuation from Barely Functional Hospitals," *The New York Times*, September 1, 2005.

[79] W. W. Neher, *Organizational Communication: Challenges of Change, Continuity and Diversity* (Needham Heights, MA: Allyn & Bacon, 1997).

[80] Ibid.

[81] Terri Morrison and Wayne A. Conaway, *Kiss, Bow, or Share Hands*, 2nd edition (Avon, MA: Adams Media, 2006), pp. 288–298.

[82] Ibid., pp. 322–331.

[83] David Livermore, *Leading with Cultural Intelligence* (New York: AMACOM, 2009).

CHAPTER

20

Networking

Learning Objectives

After reading this chapter, you should be able to:

LO1 : Explain how social capital is created.

LO2 : Describe the different types of interpersonal networks and the benefits associated with each type.

LO3 : Explain how centrality and brokerage impact the strength of a network.

LO4 : Differentiate between strong and weak ties in networks and explain the advantages and disadvantages of each type.

LO5 : Describe the ways in which an individual can develop strong internal and external networks.

SELF-REFLECTION

How Extensive Is Your Network?

Networks are webs of relationships that individuals can use to accomplish tasks and goals and to develop personally and professionally. Key activities of networks may include exchanging information, sharing resources, and creating new relationships. Networks can positively contribute to a person's productivity, learning, and career success. Analyze your network by responding "Yes" or "No" to the following statements. Does my network...

1. provide sources of information?

2. include people who can provide good advice, such as mentors and coaches?

3. include people with diverse backgrounds and experiences?

4. represent different generations of people?

5. provide access to opportunities?

6. help solve problems?

7. include people with connections who can help me achieve my goals?

8. consist of many people who know each other?

9. include people with whom I share interests?

10. represent memberships to organizations, clubs, or groups?

Based on your responses, who is missing from your network? How can you cultivate relationships with other people to expand your network?

INTRODUCTION

When we think of *capital*, what often comes to mind is the financial capital that an individual or an organization may possess. Every day businesses engage in activities that allow them to raise financial capital to support internal initiatives or to fund specific projects. Similarly, individuals access financial capital by tapping into their savings or by borrowing money from a bank. Another form of capital, which we discussed in Chapter 9, is human capital, which describes the talents, skills, and expertise that individuals possess and utilize in their careers. While having access to financial and human capital is important, having significant social capital is also critical for individuals and businesses alike. **Social capital** is the value that an individual can derive from his or her contacts. In fact, a study of general managers found that individuals with consistently outstanding performance had built and cultivated a strong network of relationships.[1] In essence, they had worked to create social capital.

Social networks are valuable sources of information and influence in organizations. Your social connections can provide you with access to disparate information

Social capital
The value that an individual can derive from his or her social relationships.

while also providing you with access to those who can help you take action with that information. As a result, individuals can use social capital to influence decisions about which business or project in an organization will receive financial capital. Social capital also enables individuals to leverage their human capital in organizations. New projects, jobs, and opportunities arise each day, but only those who find out about them early and are influential within the organization can take full advantage of them. An individual's ability to take advantage of such opportunities to apply and demonstrate his or her skills and talents is a function of (1) the information that individual possesses, and (2) his or her relationships with those who make decisions related to those opportunities. An individual's social networks can help with both of these elements. Not only are well-connected individuals in an organization better informed, but they also have the ability to influence those who can help them make decisions. As a result, well-connected individuals can leverage their social capital to help their organization access important opportunities as well as to develop themselves personally.[2]

The ability to build and then leverage social capital is even more important considering the changes that are increasingly prevalent in the operating structure of global organizations. Over the past several decades, the concept of the boundaryless organization has taken hold. As we learned in Chapter 7, these types of organizations promote a flat, flexible, and cross-functional approach to decision making. In such organizations, while the formal structure remains, it is no longer the only conduit through which information flows or decisions get made. Individuals increasingly work in less-structured contexts, where reporting relationships and formal authority are ambiguously defined and where rules and established procedures are less prevalent. In these contexts, people need to tap into their social capital to both gather information and get things done.

Along with making their organizations more flexible, many companies have made lower-level employees and managers accountable for executing strategy and meeting performance goals. As a result, roadblocks to information flow are being deconstructed, and informal networks of employees at all levels are making a significant impact on operations. And so, whether you are the CEO or an entry-level employee in an organization, you need to build adequate social capital in the organization to have impact.

Social capital is not only beneficial to individuals within organizations but also to organizations themselves. Although informal networks are not depicted on any formal organizational chart, they are becoming intertwined with an organization's performance and the way in which it develops and executes strategy.[3] Therefore, as this new approach to work continues to grow, managing relationships up, down, and across the organization will become even more critical. Leaders of these organizations are becoming increasingly aware of this and are beginning to look for ways to foster networking among their employees.

Networking refers to the activities associated with developing and managing relationships (or social capital) that are critical to a person's ability to accomplish tasks as well as develop personally and professionally.[4] Networking facilitates the exchange of information between those who need it, when they need it, and where they need it.[5] Networking activities may include engaging a colleague from another department in discussion about a project in which he or she may not be involved. It could mean asking an office manager for advice on the best way to gain support for a new project. It could also mean attending social gatherings with peers outside normal work hours. For most of us, networks have a great deal to do with our personal and career success. We often rely on our networks to help us accomplish a difficult task or meet a seemingly impossible deadline.[6]

Many people believe that if we know a large number of people, we have a good network. Although more contacts can mean more exposure to information, having relationships with a large number of people who have similar backgrounds and

Networking
The activities associated with developing and managing relationships that are critical to a person's ability to accomplish tasks as well as develop personally and professionally.

who know each other tends to repeatedly give you access to the same information from different sources. Some people refer to these as "echo chambers" in which you hear the same information again and again.[7]

Researchers have found that instead of having a closed network that contains the same information, it may be beneficial to cultivate a network of diverse contacts through whom you gain exposure to novel information.[8] Another way to think about your connections is in terms of your location within a larger network of interconnected individuals. It turns out that your location in a network can have a material impact on your ability to access information and also influence others. Your location in the network is a function of your connections to others but also their connections to each other and those outside the organization. You can be especially successful in creating a diverse network if you are a "broker"—the key contact that connects people who are otherwise not connected. Research has shown that brokers in organizations are far more likely to get promoted faster, gain visibility for their work, and create greater impact on their organizations. Brokers also often gain access to new and novel information in a timely manner, which they can leverage in multiple ways.[9]

The next best thing to being a broker is to make sure you are connected to brokers who provide you with access to a broad array of information. When you join a new organization, it is helpful to quickly identify the brokers within the organization and to get to know them. Ultimately, who you know is more important than how many people you know. Consider the case of Heidi Roizen.

Heidi Roizen[10]

Heidi Roizen had a reputation for using her networks wisely to develop personally and professionally. She developed her network during her years as cofounder and chief executive officer (CEO) of T/Maker, as a vice president at Apple Computer, and as an independent "mentor capitalist," a term and role that she created.[11] Through these positions, Roizen developed a network that included many of the most powerful business leaders in the technology sector.

As vice president of worldwide developer relations at Apple, Roizen's job had been to improve relationships with the company's 12,000 external software developers in order to ensure the long-term viability of the Apple platform. This required Roizen to call in favors to industry contacts with whom she had worked in the past to convince them to stay with Apple. Because these relationships were mutually beneficial, Roizen's requests for favors were usually granted. She also mastered the ability to blend her professional and social networks by hosting dinner parties at her house with prominent individuals such as Bill Gates of Microsoft and Scott McNeally of Sun Microsystems.

Later, as a "mentor capitalist," Roizen served as an active board member for start-up companies. Through this role, she helped people she liked and respected find new opportunities for career growth. As a result, Roizen was able to generate a list of contacts that might serve her well in the future. One of Roizen's colleagues remarked: "While lots of people are in networks and network fervently, there are very few people who become the nucleus of a network. Heidi is one of those people. As the nucleus of her own network, Heidi will forge a deep relationship with the nuclei of other networks within her vast constellation, which allows her to keep in touch with all the people in those other networks. I can only imagine how many networks Heidi touches."[12]

The strength of Heidi Roizen's network is a testament to her ability to build trusting relationships with others who are well connected in their own networks. According to one of her colleagues, Roizen functions as a central connector who forges deep relationships with central connectors in other networks. These central connectors are frequently powerful individuals and decision makers. Through the relationships she has developed with these individuals, Roizen is able to receive important information, learn about future opportunities, call in favors, and help people find new career opportunities.

1. How did Heidi Roizen invest in her network?
2. How did Roizen's network give her advantage at Apple?
3. Why do you think Roizen's network was important for her "mentor capitalist" role?
4. Why was trust a key contributor to the strength of Roizen's network?

In this chapter, we will discuss the value of social capital and explain how strategic networking enables individuals to create and leverage it. Because interpersonal networks are critical to disseminating information in a flat, flexible, and boundaryless organization, understanding the links between information is especially important. Individuals such as Roizen who build effective networks understand not only the value in linking similar groups but also the value in creating bridges between groups that may not otherwise be connected. Because effective networking is important to personal and professional success, the more equipped a person is to build a useful network, the greater the likelihood that his or her ideas will be put into action.

INTERPERSONAL NETWORKS

Interpersonal networks are not always depicted on a formal organizational chart, but they are intertwined with an organization's performance, with the way it develops and executes strategy, and with its ability to foster innovation.[13] **Interpersonal networks**, like Roizen's, are developed by forging relationships between people who work together, who have done business together, or who have engaged in some other joint activity.[14] The value individuals can extract from their interpersonal relationships is the basis of their social capital.

Interpersonal networks also play a large role in an individual's personal productivity, learning, and career success because the people he or she knows significantly impact what he or she comes to know.[15] By building relationships with influential mentors or other well-connected people, individuals create interpersonal networks that support their personal and professional development. Interpersonal networks include individuals both inside and outside the organization (e.g., developmental or career coaches, professional peers, senior executives, former professors, friends, and any other individuals that may provide helpful advice, important referrals, or assistance in a person's career). Individuals tend to leverage their personal networks when they are considering a significant career change or new developmental opportunity.[16] Although we have focused our attention on business ties, not personal ties, the two are not mutually exclusive. In many cases, business and personal relationships overlap. This is especially true when you consider that most people find their jobs through connecting with individuals outside of work. As such, it is important to apply the lessons of building interpersonal relationships to both business and personal connections.

Chapter 14 discussed task, career, and social networks and their relationship to power and influence. Another way of thinking about networks is in terms of the purpose they serve. From this vantage point, there are three distinct types of networks

Interpersonal networks
Relationships between people who work together, who have done business together, or who have engaged in some other joint activity.

that can be cultivated, and each of them serves a very distinct function. These include advice, communication, and trust networks. Despite the distinct objectives of each of these networks, the individuals in them sometimes overlap. Other times, they do not overlap, in which case we go to one person for advice, another for day-to-day communication, and yet another to build trust. Being a broker in any of these three distinct networks can be advantageous for those individuals.

In describing these networks, we consider them in the context of an organization but these networks can also be applied to personal matters. Both work-related and personal networks generally include individuals from our personal and professional lives.

Advice Networks

In organizations, more employees turn to colleagues for information than to databases, the Internet, or policy and procedure manuals.[17] When a computer problem arises, employees contact a technician in the technology support department. When they need an update on the status of a project, they contact the person who was last responsible for it or schedule a meeting with key people. As work flows through the organization, so does the information that is critical to solving problems and completing tasks.

An **advice network** includes the people in an organization to whom an individual typically goes for advice, either on solving problems or for technical information.[18] A particular person may seek advice from a broad array of individuals on various issues. At the same time, he or she may be providing advice to others who come to him or her for guidance on an array of issues. In this way, through the giving and receiving of advice, most individuals in an organization can become connected to each other. The resulting advice network can reveal the flow of information and the hubs of influence in the organization. For instance, if everyone in the organization goes to the same individuals for advice, they can become influential people in the day-to-day operations of a company. Essentially, people who are closer to the sources of information, regardless of their formal position in the organization, could have greater access to and control over the dissemination and use of that information. For example, employees in communication with senior managers who have decision-making authority may have access to valuable information and support.[19] They also may be responsible for mediating information to and from this group. Having this access provides them with control over important information, thus increasing others' dependence on them. If they leave the organization, connections between groups may collapse.

Communication Networks

Communication networks are used to exchange work-related information and can reveal the pattern of linkages between employees who talk about work-related matters on a regular basis. In organizations, communication networks can span across employees in all of the divisions and departments within a company. Examining communication networks can be helpful in identifying not only who communicates with whom but also in identifying gaps in information flow, inefficient use of resources, and connections that could enable the generation of new ideas.[20]

Employees who are connected to each other through a communication tie may perform tasks independently but may also be dependent on one another to achieve their goals. Seemingly, those who are connected through communication ties to a number of people in an organization have many alternative sources from which they draw the same information and, as a result, are likely to have more power. Those who are connected with people who have relationships with those with access to information and opportunities also tend to have more power.

Advice network
A network that includes people in an organization to whom an individual typically goes to for advice, either on solving problems or for technical information.

Communication networks
Networks that are used to exchange work-related information and can reveal the pattern of linkages between employees who talk about work-related matters on a regular basis.

Monkey Business Images/Shutterstock.com

Any good restaurant should have an effective communication network. At the front of the house, hosts greet customers and show them to their seats. Bussers set the tables with clean utensils and remove dirty ones, and servers take customers' orders, deliver the meals, present the check, and conduct financial transactions. In the kitchen, many people wash dishes, prepare food, and dress plates. For a restaurant's communication network to operate effectively, each employee must relay important information to another person in the restaurant in a timely manner. For instance, if a guest tells the host about food allergies, the host must ensure the information is relayed to the server who, in turn, needs to ensure that the information is communicated to the cooking staff.

Trust Networks

Trust is another important dimension in an interpersonal network. Most people in an organization have a core group of individuals that they trust. People who trust one another often share sensitive information and support one another in a crisis. These relationships also help people form alliances that give them greater access to information, opportunities, and rewards that can benefit them in the future.[21] These relationships together are called **trust networks**. An individual's trust network may or may not completely overlap with their communication or even advice networks. People may not trust everyone they communicate with or even go to for advice. Just as in the case of communication and advice networks, individuals who are trusted by many, and are therefore central in the trust network, are likely to be influential in an organization. Furthermore, gaps in trust networks in an organization often reveal problems.[22] Consider the following scenario.

Mary frequently spends time outside of work with her colleagues, attending social events and playing on the company softball team. Through these interactions, she has learned a lot about her colleagues' families, their career aspirations, and their experiences at the company. Mary is chosen to lead Team A. Even though she doesn't know most of the team members, Mary finds it relatively easy to guide the team to complete its task. It turns out that by virtue of the networks to which Mary belongs, she is connected to a number of people whom her team members consider trustworthy sources of information. So when the team members ask their confidants about Mary and her leadership skills, they are given information that suggests that Mary also is trustworthy and that she is the right person for the job.

Although John has a close group of colleagues who represent several departments in the company, he has limited interaction with his peers outside of work. When he does interact with colleagues, John's conversations are limited to work-related issues. John is chosen to lead Team B. John has never worked closely with any of the people assigned to his team, and he finds it difficult to motivate them and to keep them focused on their task. Although John seems to be well connected, he is not well connected to others in his team's trust networks. Therefore, when the team members ask their confidants about John and his leadership skills, they are not given much information. As a result, team members are not sure that John is acting in the team's best interest; therefore, team members may contribute less to the task.

While both Mary and John had successfully established relationships with colleagues, only Mary had actively pursued ways to develop trusting relationships throughout the organization that would benefit her in the future, especially when coming into contact with those who did not know her. To promote

Trust networks
The pattern of linkages among people in an organization who trust one another, share sensitive information, and support one another in a crisis.

Action to Promote Trust	Example
Act with discretion.	Keep sensitive information confidential.
Match words and deeds.	"Walk the talk"; that is, do as you say you are going to do.
Communicate often and well.	Interact face to face when possible.
Establish a shared vision and language.	Develop common goals and terminology.
Give away valuable information to promote reciprocity.	Advise someone on how to deal with a difficult peer or supervisor.
Help people refine unclear ideas.	Encourage inquiry in problem solving; help people define the question that will give them the answers they are seeking.
Make fair and transparent decisions.	Expose the process used to make a decision.
Hold people accountable for trustworthy behavior.	Recognize and reward trustworthy behavior.

Table 20.1 〉 Actions That Promote Trust

Source: Data adapted from R. Cross and A. Parker, *The Hidden Power of Social Networks* (Boston, MA: HBS Press, 2004).

interpersonal trust in networks, an individual can perform or adopt several key actions (see Table 20.1).

Advice and trust networks are often based on an individual's assessment of another person's competence and likability. One research study evaluated these two criteria and found that likability often outweighs competence when people are seeking advice or building trust and advice networks. The study found that if someone is strongly disliked, his or her advice will not be sought regardless of his or her level of expertise. Conversely, if someone is liked, others will seek out whatever level of competence that person has to provide (see Figure 20.1). Individuals are more inclined to seek advice and support from people who are competent and likable, the lovable stars. In contrast, individuals who are unlikable and incompetent are avoided and do not tend to last very long in an organization. Because lovable stars are rare in organizations, it is sometimes necessary to seek advice from individuals who are competent but unlikable (referred to as competent jerks), yet most individuals tend to limit this interaction as much as possible. Instead, they seek advice from people they like regardless of the individual's competence.[23] The implications of this behavior are profound and could hamper a firm's performance, especially if people with valuable information and knowledge are isolated. By seeking advice from the lovable fool instead of the competent jerk, managers may make suboptimal business decisions.

People gain social capital from belonging to networks, but many mistakenly believe that knowing a large number of people is enough to provide them with social capital. The actual source of social capital is the network, or the "conduit," while social capital is the product of those particular relationships. You have to work to build those ties, maintain them, and then know how to leverage them. For example, belonging to a network of colleagues throughout an organization is a source of social capital. Receiving information about new projects is the social capital created by belonging to that social network. As networks of relationships form, information flows and opportunities are generated. Being connected through advice, communication, and trust to different types of people who can create social capital is more important than the number of people someone can count in his or her network.[24]

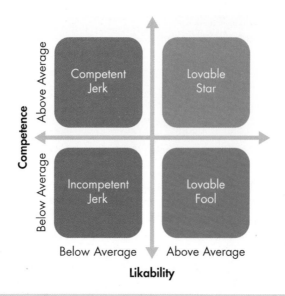

Figure 20.1 ⟩ Competence and Likability in Social Networks

NETWORK CHARACTERISTICS

As we consider how an individual's interpersonal network cumulates as social capital for them, there are a number of specific facets that we must review. Let us now dig a little deeper into the structure of the network itself and examine where the individual is placed within that network. To understand the strength of a person's network, it is important to consider its characteristics including: (1) how central a person is in his or her network; (2) the ability of the individual to act as a broker of important information; and (3) the types of contacts that the individual can access.

Centrality

Centrality
The extent to which an individual is centrally positioned in a network, giving them preferential access to information and influence.

Centrality is an indicator of how centrally located you are in a network (could be advice, communication, or trust). Another way to think of it is the ease with which you can access any other person in the network. It represents the breadth of information an individual can access through their interpersonal network by their participation in that network. It is not only an indicator of how much information one has access to, but also how much influence one has in an organization's social network. The individuals who are centrally located in an organization are likely to have greater access to information and thus greater influence in the organization than those who are peripheral to the network.

Let us try to illustrate the notion of centrality with an example. In an organization, the people who have the timeliest access to information are usually the office managers and the administrative assistants. Although they may or may not be central in the trust network of the organization (depending on their personal behavior), given their position within the organization, these individuals are likely to be central in the advice and communication networks. Typically, they are the go-to people for a higher-level manager or a group of influential people who need them to manage the day-to-day aspects

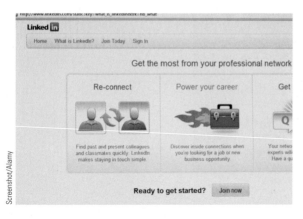

of a project or a department when they are indisposed. Although office managers and administrative assistants are often less central to the strategic aspects of a business, they play critical coordinating roles such as organizing meetings and managing information flows.[25] While they may not have immediate access to specific information, they know where and how to get it.[26] This is what makes officer managers and administrative assistants valuable resources in most organizations.

As should be clear by now, centrality refers to the extent to which someone is positioned centrally in a network with resultant preferential access to information and influence. There are three conceptions of centrality. Each captures a distinct way in which a central actor in a network is likely to be influential in the network. Underlying each measure is a set of assumptions about how and which specific types of central locations in a social network are likely to generate greater influence.

The three distinct conceptions of centrality are: degree, closeness, and betweenness.[27] **Degree of centrality** is the simplest measure and represents the number of contacts to whom a person is connected in a social network. This measure also represents the number of people a person can call when he or she needs information, a factor that may increase his or her opportunities and power. The assumption here is that information flow happens through direct contacts and, therefore, the more people you know, the better informed you will be.

Closeness centrality accounts for how easily a person can reach all other people in the network through his or her direct and indirect ties. Indirect ties refer to connections made to others through someone else (e.g., a friend of a friend of yours). This measure of centrality captures how easily (i.e., with the fewest number of direct or indirect contacts) you can reach everyone in your network. Connecting to others through long chains of indirect contacts (e.g., a friend of a friend of a friend of yours) makes it harder for you to access the information, knowledge, and advice offered by others. Hence, those individuals who can reach everyone in their network through either direct connections or the smallest number of intermediary contacts are more likely to have greater social capital than those who require a larger number of indirect connections to reach information. This form of centrality thus represents the extent to which one person can reach all the others in his or her network in the fewest steps.[28] We will further discuss closeness in the next section when we review the strength of ties.

Finally, **betweenness** accounts for the extent to which an individual falls between pairs of other people who may be trying to reach each other.[29] It is calculated as the extent to which an individual falls on the shortest path that may be used to connect any two individuals in a network. It captures the likelihood that others will have to go through him or her to reach any particular person in the network. This, in turn, makes those individuals central in the network. Betweenness therefore represents potential control over information and over connections that others may want to reach. The more you fall between others who may want to connect with each other, the more central you are in the network because others need to go through you to connect with each other.

The most central people on any of these three indicators of centrality are not always the formal leaders of a group, but instead are usually those who link many people in a group. As popular points of contact for the group, they know who to call on when information or expertise is needed. In Figure 20.2, AM is the central connector and has primary access to several people and secondary access to even more. For instance, AM can access LY through JL, and while AM does not have direct access to MN, AM can gain access through DJ, OC, DS, WR, and TP. In addition, AM can connect various individuals who know him but do not know each other. For instance, AM can connect JL to others in his network: NN, MW, and TC.

The first decade of the twenty-first century saw an influx of new businesses that enabled users to generate online content and then easily distribute it to fellow users. Examples include Flickr for photo sharing, Wikipedia for information sharing, and

Degree of centrality
Represents the number of contacts to whom a person is connected in a social network.

Closeness centrality
Represents how easily a person can reach all other people in his or her network through his or her direct and indirect ties.

Betweenness
Represents the extent to which an individual falls between pairs of other people in an interpersonal network who may be trying to reach each other.

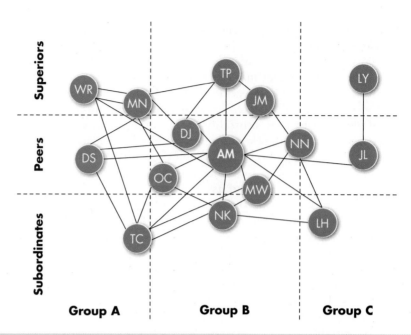

Superiors

Peers

Subordinates

Group A   Group B   Group C

Figure 20.2 ⟩ Sample Network Map

YouTube for video sharing. One of the most popular websites to come from this movement was LinkedIn, a social networking service that allows users to construct a profile, create a personal network, and communicate with fellow users in a fast and simple manner. LinkedIn is similar to other social networking sites (e.g., Facebook), but it focuses solely on professional networks. With LinkedIn, every professional can develop, visualize, and manage his or her own network and can then see connections between networks. By seeing their first-, second-, and third-degree connections, users have the ability to understand their own network centrality as well as their contacts' centrality.[30]

Brokerage

Brokerage
The act of leveraging network position to connect people who are not otherwise connected to one another to generate and control information.

As we have discussed above, social capital and its related benefits accrue to those who not only know a lot of people (i.e., those with a high degree of centrality) but also to those who can connect to many others through the fewest number of ties (closeness centrality). The role that one plays in connecting others (betweenness centrality) is also important. Individuals who play this connector role not only have greater access to information but also have the opportunity to control the flow of information. These individuals are known as brokers. Their high level of connectivity with people enables brokers to channel information from or to them, as well as to leverage relationships with those people. In fact, information and control are the two hallmark features of **brokerage**, and these features grant brokers tremendous access to social capital.[31] Having access to a valuable piece of information and receiving that information in a timely manner along with being able to influence outcomes are critical components of brokerage. Having control over how information gets disseminated is viewed by some to be even more powerful. When you have access to valuable information, you can decide whom to give it to. If you receive information early, you can even share it with your personal contacts before it is shared with others. If you have

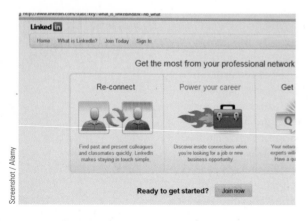

information about other people, you can mention their names at the right time in the right place so that opportunities are presented to them before anyone else.[32] This, in turn, could create an opportunity for a future favor. The same holds true for being able to influence outcomes. Being a connector affords individuals the opportunity to have the ability to shape outcomes and also enhance their own visibility within their organization.

Paul Revere is a classic example of an information broker. On the night of April 18, 1775, Paul Revere and William Dawes rode on horseback from Boston to sound the alarm that the British troops were landing in the harbor. This was a critical task because the Americans didn't have a standing army and so had to mobilize citizen volunteers as quickly as possible to fight the British.[33] At around midnight on what would become the eve of the American Revolution, Dawes rode west and Revere rode north to warn the local townspeople to get ready. The towns that Revere warned were prepared for the British invasion. Even towns that were over 40 miles away had heard Revere's warning, and they were able to successfully hold back the British troops. The towns along the western route that Dawes traveled were not ready for the British and struggled to form a resistance movement. Revere leveraged his network and connections to spread the news to a whole host of other networks. In contrast, Dawes, who was less connected, was not able to circulate the warning to a broader set of individuals.[34] Revere was able to bridge relatively disconnected groups of people to stimulate collaboration and get the message out quickly. As a result of Revere's warning to disparate yet well-connected groups that the British troops were on their way, his name went down in history as the man responsible for raising a militia to fight the British troops. William Dawes, who sounded the same alarm but to a smaller group of people with fewer connections, remains relatively unknown.[35]

Redundant contacts
Contacts in a network who know and communicate with each other and who therefore tend to provide similar information.

Nonredundant contacts
Contacts in a network who do not lead to the same people or provide the same information.

Structural holes
The existence of a gap between two individuals that provides access to nonredundant contacts.

Types of Contacts

So what relationships do people need to create to become a broker? While more contacts may mean more exposure to valuable information, having relationships with a large number of similar people who may be connected to each other tends to provide access to the same information. These contacts are connected to one another and tend to recirculate similar insights, knowledge, and information among themselves. These people are called **redundant contacts**.[36] In Figure 20.3, Network I and Network II are full of redundant contacts. Both A and E's contacts seem to know each other and so the same information keeps echoing back to them from different sources. The only difference is that E is connected to H in Network II. These types of networks are also called closed networks, where everyone knows everyone and there is little exposure or contact outside the network. These types of networks can be useful in efficiently working through routine or standardized operations, but they can be less helpful when engaging in novel or creative endeavors.[37]

What matters most, however, is the number of **nonredundant contacts** an individual has in his or her network, or the contacts that do not lead to the same people who provide the same information.[38] Ronald Burt proposes that an important benefit to individuals from his or her nonredundant contacts is to bridge what he calls **structural holes**.[39] A structural hole is the gap that exists between two individuals. Burt's research suggests that an individual whose networks are rich in structural

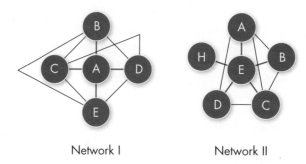

Figure 20.3 ⟩ Sample of Networks with Redundant Contacts

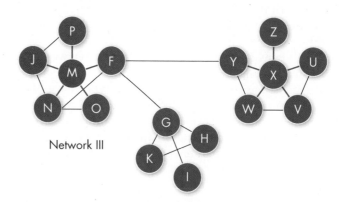

Figure 20.4 ⟩ Sample of Networks with Nonredundant Contacts and Structural Holes

holes, meaning they are connected to others who are not connected to each other, are the true brokers who typically have greater exposure to more rewarding opportunities.[40] He also proposed that networks with structural holes give those brokers an advantage in controlling how and to whom information is disseminated. In Figure 20.4, Network III with M at its center includes many nonredundant contacts that are connected through F. By virtue of M's relationship with F, she has contact with X's network and G's network.

Individuals who connect a network with other parts of the company or with other social networks in other organizations are a particular kind of broker. This is because they are linking their own work community to others that may exist inside or outside the organization. They are called **boundary spanners**.[41] In Figure 20.4, F, Y, and G function as boundary spanners between their respective networks. Boundary spanners regularly communicate, consult, advise, and nurture relationships with people outside the boundaries of their immediate task environment. Because of these activities, boundary spanners play an important role in establishing linkages within and across the organization.[42] Being a boundary spanner is very difficult because most people do not have the breadth of expertise, the wealth of social contacts, and the personality traits necessary to be accepted by different groups.[43]

STRENGTH OF RELATIONSHIPS

Thus far we have assumed that the strength of relationships between individuals in a social network doesn't vary. While they may differ in what flows through them (advice, communication, or trust), we have not accounted for the intensity of those ties that, in reality, may vary. We call this varying level of a tie's intensity the **strength of ties**.

Boundary spanners
Individuals who connect their immediate work group with other parts of the company or with groups in other organizations.

Strength of ties
The emotional intensity, intimacy, and frequency of interaction that characterize the relationship between two parties.

The strength of a tie refers to the emotional intensity, intimacy, and frequency of interaction that characterize it.[44] Some ties are stronger because they connect two people who have a lot in common and who have frequent contact.[45] Other ties are weaker because they connect people who are relative strangers. Some ties help improve knowledge transfer, whereas others make information flow more challenging.

Figure 20.4 depicts Network III connected to two other networks. We can graphically display the concept of strong and weak ties by the type of lines that connect two nodes. A solid line indicates a strong tie; a dotted line indicates a weak tie (see Figure 20.5). While M is directly connected to F (strong tie), his relationship with Y and W are based on his contact with F. In this case, Y and W are weak ties.

Strong Ties

Earlier we mentioned that Mary, the leader of Team A, frequently spent time outside work with her colleagues and that through these interactions, she had been able to establish more trusting relationships with her team members. In essence, Mary has been successful in cultivating strong ties. Strong ties, which are characterized by more frequent and close contact, can reduce resistance to an idea, provide comfort, and improve information sharing.[46] Trust, larger time commitments, and similar interests are also features of strong ties. Similarly, David Krackhardt proposed that *philos* relationships (that is, strong ties) have three characteristics that bring value to the network: interaction, affection, and time.[47] He suggested that each of these characteristics is necessary to create strong ties because without them, the basis for trust falls apart. Interaction creates opportunities for the exchange of information, some of which may be confidential. Affection creates motivation to treat the other person in positive ways.[48] And time creates the experiences necessary for each person to witness how the other person will use shared information.[49]

Weak Ties

While individuals with strong ties are effective in sharing information, they can provide redundant information because they are usually formed among similar individuals who are exposed to the same kind of data.[50] Mark Granovetter argued that in many instances individuals obtain their most valuable information like job leads through their weak ties. The underlying logic here is not simply that weak ties are inherently better, but rather that weak ties usually exist between people who are in different networks and so are bridges to novel information otherwise unavailable through redundant strong ties.[51]

Granovetter's evidence for "the strength of weak ties" arose from his research examining the relationship of network structure to job searches.[52] Of the

A DIFFERENT View

Nonprofit Networking

Some of the largest, most successful nonprofit organizations rely heavily on networking. Networks provide nonprofits with the ability to connect with each other and share ideas to facilitate initiatives, solutions, and innovation. Young Nonprofit Professionals Network, for example, supports leaders through professional development, networking, and social opportunities in the nonprofit community. These networks of organizations provide resources that would otherwise be unattainable for any single entity.

1. How do nonprofit leaders engage in networking? What aspects of networking are important to nonprofits?
2. What nonprofit organizations rely on networking? How has that improved their success?
3. What are the advantages that networking provides to the nonprofit sector that are different from the for profit sector?

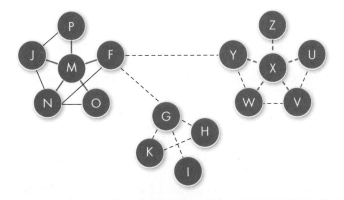

Figure 20.5 ⟩ Sample of Network with Strong and Weak Ties

individuals he interviewed about how they found their current jobs, he discovered that most of them rarely found work through close contacts or strong ties.[53] When they used a personal contact to obtain information about a job opportunity, the relationship was often distant, such as a high school acquaintance or someone they met at a recent social event.[54] In essence, although relationships between weak ties are not always founded on trust, frequent interactions, or similar interests, they do serve as bridges and are more likely to link members of dissimilar groups than are strong ones.[55]

Burt's structural holes theory and Granovetter's weak ties theory are similar in some ways and different in others. Both theories propose that new information and opportunities must come from those outside the immediate network. In contrast to Granovetter, however, Burt argues that the presence of a structural hole, not the strength of a relationship, actually leads to the spreading of new information and opportunities.[56] He goes further to suggest that the reason weak ties may be effective as sources of novel information is not that they are weak per se, but rather that they are usually connecting structural holes.

Effective networks include a proper balance between the breadth of contacts and the depth or strength of contacts. Networks characterized by breadth tend to have many nonredundant contacts that provide access to a wide range of potential opportunities and information. Sometimes having wide breadth means sacrificing the depth of contacts. Networks that include few but deep contacts tend to be better sources for dependable, high-quality information.[57] Managers must work to find the right balance between breadth and depth to ensure that they have proper access to the right people with the right information at the right time.

BUILDING USEFUL NETWORKS

We have spent much of this chapter discussing the importance and value of social networks. We also have explored the features of social networks that are more effective for information sharing and for providing access to opportunities that may not otherwise be known. In this section, we will focus on strategies and tips for building networks that are personally and professionally useful. First, though, we discuss six myths about building useful networks.[58]

- *Myth 1: To build better networks, we must communicate more.* Some people believe that the most effective way to network is to schedule regular meetings and to send frequent e-mail updates. However, these people mistakenly equate network building with communication and socializing. Although communication and socializing are important to network building, not all communication and social activities lead to outcomes that can enhance personal and professional development. Instead, you should define an effective social network by what it has done or is currently doing rather than how many times network members have met face to face.
- *Myth 2: We should build a large network.* Some people believe that if someone has a large number of ties, he or she is a great networker. As you have learned when assessing the quality of a network, the strength and diversity of ties are most important. Instead of focusing on maintaining relationships with a large number of people, an individual should invest in developing and maintaining relationships that have strategic value and focus on cross-boundary collaboration.
- *Myth 3: We can't do much to aid social networks.* Some people believe that social networks should be left to form naturally from personal relationships rather than be orchestrated by someone in a leadership role. Yet some

social networks can have strategic value to a business, especially when they encourage members to build collaborative practices, which is important to executing strategy. Therefore, managers and leaders should consider promoting less formal social networks in the workplace (for instance, employee affinity groups).

- *Myth 4: How people fit into networks is a matter of personality (which can't be changed).* Some people think of good networkers as being extroverted, social, and aggressive—traits associated with personality. Yet even highly introverted people can have strong and diverse social networks. Instead of thinking of social networking ability as innate, recognize that people can take specific steps to learn how to network effectively. In fact, introverts may be especially adept at creating relationships that are based on deep mutual trust.
- *Myth 5: Central people should make themselves more accessible.* Some people believe that just because they are central to an organization, they should make themselves available to others whenever needed. Unfortunately, central people can get bogged down in all of the tasks and requests they are juggling, which can slow down the whole group. Instead, central people should focus on delegating tasks and decision making and should learn to point people toward others in the network with the expertise to provide answers.
- *Myth 6: I already know what is going on in my network.* Some people believe that they do not have to regularly connect with people in their social networks because they would know if any new information or opportunity came about. The problem with this perspective is that social networking is an ongoing process that requires continued maintenance.

Building Internal Networks

A model for building a useful internal network includes three primary strategies: mapping your network, forging better connections, and cultivating brokers.[59]

Mapping Your Network

The first step in building a useful internal network is to map your network (see Table 20.2). The following instructions are useful for mapping your network:

1. Fill in the names of the most important contacts in your network, people you rely on for the exchange of private information, specialized expertise, advice, and creative inspiration. As you write each name, think of the resources you exchange with that person and the strength of the ties.
2. After you identify your key contacts, think about how you first met them. In the second column, write the name of the person who introduced you to your contact; if you met the person yourself, write "me." This column will reveal the brokers in your network and help you see the networking practices you used to connect with them.
3. In the third column, write the name of someone you introduced to your key contact. This column will show how you act as a broker for others.
4. In the next two columns, indicate whether the contact is someone from inside or outside your organization and what relationship they have to you (for example, your superior, peer, subordinate, or friend). This information will provide a snapshot about the breadth of your network.
5. Once your data is filled in, look at the number of times "me" appears in the second column. If you've introduced yourself to your key contacts more than 65% of the time, your network probably contains too many of the same types of people as well as people who are too close to you in proximity.

Name of Contact	Who Introduced You to the Contact?	To Whom Did You Introduce the Contact?	Inside/Outside Your Organization	Superior, Peer, Subordinate, or Friend

Table 20.2 〉 How to Map Your Network

Source: Adapted from B. Uzzi and S. Dunlap, "How to Build Your Network," *Harvard Business Review*, December 2005.

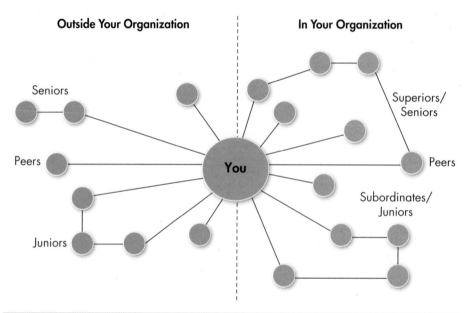

Figure 20.6 〉 Mapping Your Network

This initial analysis of a person's network can quickly outline the strengths and weaknesses of the network. Is the network too broad or too narrow? Does the network include a diverse array of individuals or are they very similar? A grid that pictures the nature of relationships (direct reports, peers, and superiors) also may be helpful in mapping a person's network (see Figure 20.6). Often a graphical representation of a person's network is useful in identifying gaps as well as opportunities.

Forging Better Connections

The next step in building a useful network is to focus on building better connections with a diverse group of people. Most individuals form ties around two key principles: spatial proximity and self-similarity. **Spatial proximity** refers to connections between people close to one another, due to having an office nearby or sharing work or private space. **Self-similarity** refers to the notion that we connect with those who are similar to us on a range of demographic or personal attributes and who may share similar interests. Both these principles lead us to form closed networks

Spatial proximity
Refers to connections between people close to one another, due to having an office nearby or sharing work or private space.

Self-similarity
Refers to the notion that we connect with those who are similar to us on a range of demographic or personal attributes and who may share similar interests.

with a lot of redundant ties. While such networks bring us a feeling of warmth and connectedness (which is why we should keep building such ties), they also preclude us from becoming a broker and bridge-builder in the organization.

A key to breaking out of the trap of having only closed networks is to embrace "shared activities" through which you are likely to meet people you would otherwise not meet. At the same time, you maintain an open mind to building bridges with people who are different from yourself and may be in a completely different part of the organization. For example, you can join a company softball team that represents employees from different levels, subunits, and groups in the organization. Participation in a shared activity allows you to enjoy close working relationships that may not have otherwise formed. Shared activities also strengthen ties between diverse individuals by changing their usual patterns of interaction and allowing them to break out of their day-to-day roles.[60]

To reinforce broader but also stronger ties, many companies host or support employee network groups. These allow current employees to openly interact with members of groups with which they identify. These groups are often formed by race, ethnicity or nationality, gender, sexual orientation, or ability. Other times, these groups are held together by common interests, backgrounds, and professions. Similar groups exist outside organizations as well. For example, the National Association of Black Accountants (NABA) is a professional social networking group that serves as a resource for African Americans and other minorities in the accounting profession.[61] Net Impact is another social networking group that serves as a resource for people interested in corporate social responsibility.[62]

Cultivating Brokers

The last step in building a useful network is to identify information brokers and the activities that can support the development of more frequent contact.[63] Look at the names of the people you listed in the first column of your map and think about how you met them. The people who introduced you to those individuals are the brokers in your network. To build a useful network, make sure you form relationships with such brokers, whether they have formal authority or not.[64] In addition, it is important to consider the following points:[65]

- Identify the people upon whom you depend for getting things done and focus your energies on cultivating relationships with them. Consider who you need to know now, then consider relationships that should be cultivated for the future.
- Develop awareness of key goals and resources valued by potential contacts and attempt to find areas of mutual benefit.
- Use different cultivation strategies with different people and be aware of personal preferences and interaction styles. Do you tend to gravitate to the same type of people? Is this limiting your access to key information or new opportunities?
- Provide information and services to others in exchange for the information and services you get from them. Remember the lessons of reciprocity discussed in Chapter 14.
- Avoid becoming overly dependent on one person. Make sure you use multiple network members when you need information because even the strongest relationships can sour.

Building External Networks

Networking clubs are community-based organizations that allow individuals to meet and develop professional relationships outside work.[66] Networking clubs are organized for making contacts and referrals with others who are committed

Networking clubs
A type of external network that provides members with opportunities to learn and develop professional relationships outside work.

to networking and are often vital to the development of an individual's personal network.

Networking clubs differ in four ways: focus of interest, size of membership, membership composition, and rules and procedures.[67]

- *Focus of interest.* Some networking clubs have very general missions. The National Association of Women Business Owners serves the career development and networking needs of women executives. Other networking clubs are dedicated to specific activities. For instance, the Boston-area 128 Venture Group brings together informal investors and high-tech innovators in need of financing.[68]
- *Size of membership.* Some networking clubs restrict their membership. NSACI Networkers, a networking club organized by the Northwest Suburban (Chicago) Association of Commerce and Industry, restricts its membership to a maximum of 45 people to allow members opportunities to develop stronger relationships. In contrast, the Chicagoland Association of Commerce and Industry organizes networking events in which more than 500 people attend.[69]
- *Membership composition.* Some networking clubs are comprised mainly of women entrepreneurs. Others are comprised of finance executives. Still others are comprised of MBA students interested in social responsibility.
- *Rules and procedures.* Some networking clubs operate with a great deal of structure: start and stop times are strict, each component of the event is purposeful, and members leave the event having achieved a concrete objective. Other networking clubs operate under a much looser schedule, with more socializing and fewer regulations.

As individuals seek to build external networks through clubs or associations, they should ask themselves some important questions (see Table 20.3). Networking clubs can have a significant impact on a person's career and potential success. For instance, in the first year a bank branch manager joined a networking club in his area, he secured seven new clients through his contacts, which represented one-third of his new sales.[70]

1.	What's the specific purpose of the club?
2.	Does the club serve the market or geographic region you're interested in?
3.	Is the composition of the membership suitable to meeting your needs? Can members help you learn and grow professionally?
4.	How often does the club meet? When does the club meet?
5.	Does the club have formal rules and regulations? (Clubs with established policies and procedures work best.)
6.	Is membership limited to a reasonable number so that members get to know each other well?
7.	Do members have regular opportunities to make presentations to the group?
8.	Are referrals required, recorded, and reported? Do current members have a say in who's allowed to join?
9.	What's the club's track record? (It's a good sign if the club keeps records of performance, such as number of referrals given and dollars invoiced.)
10.	Are competing businesses allowed to join the group?

Table 20.3 ⟩ Key Questions to Ask Before Joining a Networking Club

Source: Adapted from W. Baker, *Networking Smart: How to Build Relationships for Personal and Organizational Success* (Lincoln, NE: Iuniverse.com, 2000).

The Leadership Development Journey

Many leaders leverage their social capital to get things done. Social capital is the collective value of your networks and the inclination of network members to help you. Leaders build social capital through competence and by being trustworthy and reciprocating. Below are a few activities that you can experiment with to enhance your social capital.

- Spend time making high-quality connections with friends, classmates, professors, and family members.
- Nurture a relationship with a mentor or coach.
- Volunteer at a nonprofit organization.
- Write a thank-you note to someone that helped you accomplish a goal.
- Use your skills or talents to help another person.
- Make a connection by introducing two people that may have a common interest.
- Join a club that provides access to a new and different group of people.

Based on your experiment, how was your social capital enhanced? Do you have any other tips for your classmates to help them enhance their social capital?

Building social capital takes skill, time, and practice, but it also demands a high level of awareness of one's surroundings. Having social capital means having useful social networks, and highly effective networkers find ways to integrate relationship building into their busy lives. In this manner, networking becomes more of a natural occurrence rather than a forced activity that feels insincere.

SUMMARY

A boundaryless organization requires employees to develop interpersonal networks in which information can flow successfully throughout the company. It also mandates that people become more effective at building and managing relationships up, down, and across the company. While the impetus for creating boundaryless organizations is to promote an organizational structure that fosters a more flexible and cross-functional approach to decision making, individuals also can benefit personally and professionally from this new work method.

LO1 To benefit from interpersonal networking, individuals must develop effective relationships not only with those in their peer groups but also with dissimilar colleagues. Building bridges between groups that might not otherwise be connected is a powerful interpersonal networking skill that, if used effectively, can provide individuals with greater access to information and opportunities, and can help individuals reach their personal and professional goals. A key outcome of relationship building is the development of social capital. Individuals use social capital to influence important decisions or to gain access to vital information.

LO2 Individuals can rely on many different types of networks in their personal and professional lives, including advice, communication, and trust networks. Advice networks include individuals that a person seeks for help completing his or her work effectively. Communication networks generally correspond to the manner in which information flows throughout an organization. Trust networks include the individuals that a person seeks out for personal and professional development. They are characterized by the sharing of information and reciprocity. Trust is based on a person's competence as well as his or her likability.

LO3 To understand the strength of a person's network, it is important to consider its characteristics, including: (1) how central a person is in his or her network;

(2) the ability of the individual to act as a broker of important information; and (3) the types of contacts that the individual can access. Centrality can be defined by degree, closeness, and betweenness. Degree of centrality represents the number of contacts to whom a person is connected; closeness represents the proximity of a person to all other people in a network; and betweenness refers to the extent to which an individual falls between pairs of other people who are trying to reach each other. Individuals who are able to connect people who are otherwise not connected are referred to as brokers. Brokers generally have access to a large number of people and a vast array of information which they can leverage as a source of power.

Effective networks also include both redundant and nonredundant contacts—people that a person knows well and people that a person does not know as well. The advantage of nonredundant contacts is that they tend to provide access to new information and opportunities as well as access to even more people. If everyone knows everyone else in a network (characterized by redundant contacts), operations may be efficient but access to new ideas and opportunities may be impeded.

LO4 : Another way to assess a network is to evaluate the strength of the relationships in the network.

Individuals in a network that know one another well and share a mutual reciprocity are known as strong ties. These are based on more frequent and intimate contact. Weak ties are similar to nonredundant contacts in that they are based on less frequent contact and provide potential access to different information and individuals.

LO5 : To be successful, individuals need to build strong internal networks with people in their organization and external networks with people outside their organization. A first step in this process is to map one's network—identify what individuals compose the network and how the connections were made. With this map, a person can assess if and where there are potential vulnerabilities or constraints. For instance, is the network closed with too many people who have the same information and access to similar contacts, or is the network broad with many contacts characterized by weak ties? External networks can be extended through participation in networking clubs and other professional associations. These extended networks can be vital sources for future professional opportunities and/or business growth.

KEY TERMS

Advice networks
Betweenness
Boundary spanners
Brokerage
Centrality
Closeness centrality
Communication networks

Degree of centrality
Interpersonal networks
Networking
Networking clubs
Nonredundant contacts
Redundant contacts
Self-similarity

Social capital
Spatial proximity
Strength of ties
Structural holes
Trust networks

ASSIGNMENTS

Discussion Topics

1. Why is social capital so important? How does one build his or her social capital? How can social capital be used to influence others or to secure support for particular projects or objectives?

2. Organizations operate on a formal and informal level. The organizational chart often defines the formal structure and formal lines of authority. Sometimes the formal structure does not convey the true nature of power and influence within an

organization. How and in what ways does the informal organizational structure define the bases of power within a company? How would a new employee understand the role of the informal network?

3. Consider Figure 20.1. Why do people gravitate more to lovable fools than competent jerks? What strategies should one consider when he or she needs to interact with a competent jerk? In your own experience, what do you value

more—likability or competence? Why? What are the implications of your preference?

4. What are the advantages of being central in a network? What are the potential downsides?

5. In what situations is a closed network of relationships beneficial? How would you learn if your network consists of many redundant contacts? What strategies can one employ to build more nonredundant contacts?

6. In what ways is brokerage a source of power?

7. How has social media changed the landscape for networking?

8. In what situations or environments are weak ties more valuable than strong ties?

9. As one considers the development of his or her interpersonal network, what should he or she pay attention to? What criteria should one use to build his or her network?

10. Networking is sometimes viewed as a self-serving activity that is best pursued by extroverts. What are the fallacies in this viewpoint? How should one think about networking from a strategic perspective? How should one think about networking from a career development perspective?

Management Research

1. Write down the names of people in your various networks. Assess how strong these relationships are by rating them on a scale of 1 to 3 (for very strong, 2 for strong, or 3 for not strong). Put a star next to the relationship that you want to improve over the next 6 months.

2. Communities of practice are networks of people who share a concern or a passion for a cause and interact in order to work together to solve a problem or improve a situation. This type of network facilitates learning by the following actions:

- Collaborating to problem solve
- Sharing information, experiences, and resources
- Coordinating activities
- Documenting and mapping knowledge
- Discussing trends and best practices[71]

Research a community of practice, and then answer the following questions:

- What is the purpose of the community of practice?
- Who are the members in the community of practice?
- How does the community of practice facilitate learning?

In the Field

Identify a leader on your campus or in your community who is trying to solve a problem. Work with that leader to create a network map of the people who can help solve the problem. After the leader creates the network map, have the leader analyze how each person can contribute to solving the problem. Recommend that the leader contact people on the network map or convene them at a meeting to work on the problem. Report back to your class on the effectiveness of creating a network map to solve problems.

ENDNOTES

[1] John P. Kotter, *The General Managers* (New York: Free Press, 1982).

[2] Gretchen M. Spreitzer, "Leading to Grow and Growing to Lead: Leadership Development Lessons from Positive Organizational Studies," *Organizational Dynamics*, Vol. 35, No. 4, 2006, pp. 305–315.

[3] R. S. Burt, "The Contingent Value of Social Capital," *Administrative Science Quarterly*, Vol. 42, No. 2, June 1997, pp. 339–365.

[4] Herminia Ibarra, "Managerial Networks," Harvard Business School Note No. 9-495-039, rev. January 25, 1996 (Boston, MA: HBS Publishing, 1995).

[5] Don Cohen and Laurence Prusak, *In Good Company: How Social Capital Makes Organizations Work* (Boston, MA: HBS Press, 2001), p. 58.

[6] Rob Cross and Laurence Prusak, "The People Who Make Organizations Go—or Stop," *Harvard Business Review*, June 2002.

[7] Brian Uzzi and Shannon Dunlap, "How to Build Your Network," *Harvard Business Review*, December 2005.

[8] R. Burt, *Structural Holes* (Cambridge, MA: Harvard University Press, 1992).

[9] Ibid.

[10] Nicole Tempest and Kathleen McGinn, "Heidi Roizen," Harvard Business School Case No. 9-800-228, rev. April 28, 2010 (Boston, MA: HBS Publishing, 2000).

[11] Ibid.

[12] Ibid.

[13] W. Tsai and S. Ghoshal, "Social Capital and Value Creation: The Role of Intrafirm Networks," *Academy of Management Journal*, Vol. 41, No. 4. 1998; and R. Cross and A. Parker, *The Hidden Power of Social Networks* (Boston, MA: HBS Press, 2004).

[14] Don Cohen and Laurence Prusak, *In Good Company: How Social Capital*

Makes Organizations Work (Boston, MA: HBS Press, 2001), p. 69.

[15] H. Mintzberg, *The Nature of Managerial Work* (New York: Harper Row, 1973); and D. J. Brass and M. E. Burkhardt, "Centrality and Power in Organizations," *Networks in Organizations: Structure, Form, and Action*, N. Nohria and R. Eccles, eds. (Boston, MA: HBS Press, 1992).

[16] Herminia Ibarra and Mark Hunter, "How Leaders Create and Use Networks," *Harvard Business Review*, January 2007.

[17] A. Linden, R. Ball, A. Waldir, and K. Haley, Gartner's Survey on Managing Information, Note #COM-15-0871, Gartner, Inc.; and D. J. Brass and M. E. Burkhardt, "Centrality and Power in Organizations," *Networks in Organizations: Structure, Form, and Action*, N. Nohria and R. Eccles, eds. (Boston, MA: HBS Press, 1992).

[18] D. Krackhardt and J. R. Hanson, "Informal Networks: The Company Behind the Chart," *Harvard Business Review*, July–August 1993.

[19] D. J. Brass and M. E. Burkhardt, "Centrality and Power in Organizations," *Networks in Organizations: Structure, Form, and Action*, N. Nohria and R. Eccles, eds. (Boston, MA: HBS Press, 1992).

[20] D. Krackhardt and J. R. Hanson, "Informal Networks: The Company Behind the Chart," *Harvard Business Review*, July–August 1993.

[21] D. J. Brass and M. E. Burkhardt, "Centrality and Power in Organizations," *Networks in Organizations: Structure, Form, and Action*, N. Nohria and R. Eccles, eds. (Boston, MA: HBS Press, 1992).

[22] Ibid.

[23] Tiziana Casciaro and Miguel Sousa Lobo, "Competent Jerks, Lovable Fools, and the Formation of Social Networks," *Harvard Business Review*, June 2005.

[24] R. Burt, *Structural Holes* (Cambridge, MA: Harvard University Press, 1992).

[25] D. J. Brass and M. E. Burkhardt, "Centrality and Power in Organizations," *Networks in Organizations: Structure, Form, and Action*, N. Nohria and R. Eccles, eds. (Boston, MA: HBS Press, 1992).

[26] Rob Cross and Laurence Prusak, "The People Who Make Organizations Go—or Stop," *Harvard Business Review*, June 2002.

[27] Linton C. Freeman, "Centrality in Social Networks Conceptual Clarification," *Social Networks*, 1978, pp. 215–239; and D. J. Brass and M. E. Burkhardt, "Centrality and Power in Organizations," *Networks in Organizations: Structure, Form, and Action*, N. Nohria and R. Eccles, eds. (Boston, MA: HBS Press, 1992).

[28] D. J. Brass and M. E. Burkhardt, "Centrality and Power in Organizations," *Networks in Organizations: Structure, Form, and Action*, N. Nohria and R. Eccles, eds. (Boston, MA: HBS Press, 1992).

[29] Ibid.

[30] David B. Yoffie, Michael Slind, and Nitzan Achsaf, "LinkedIn Corp., 2008," Harvard Business School Case No. 9-709-426, rev. August 25, 2009 (Boston, MA: HBS Publishing, 2008), p. 2.

[31] R. Burt, *Structural Holes* (Cambridge, MA: Harvard University Press, 1992).

[32] Ibid.

[33] B. Uzzi and S. Dunlap, "How to Build Your Network," *Harvard Business Review*, December 2005; and M. Gladwell, *The Tipping Point* (Boston, MA: Little, Brown and Company, 2002).

[34] Ibid.

[35] Ibid.

[36] R. Burt, *Structural Holes* (Cambridge, MA: Harvard University Press, 1992).

[37] Ronald S. Burt, *Neighbor Networks: Competitive Advantage Local and Personal* (Oxford: Oxford University Press, 2010).

[38] R. Burt, *Structural Holes* (Cambridge, MA: Harvard University Press, 1992).

[39] Ibid.

[40] Ibid.

[41] D. J. Brass and M. E. Burkhardt, "Centrality and Power in Organizations," *Networks in Organizations: Structure, Form, and Action*, N. Nohria and R. Eccles, eds. (Boston, MA: HBS Press, 1992).

[42] Ibid.

[43] Ibid.

[44] D. Krackhardt, "The Strength of Strong Ties: The Importance of *Philos* in Organizations," *Networks and Organizations: Structures, Form, and Action*, N. Nohria and R. Eccles, eds. (Boston, MA: HBS Press, 1992).

[45] R. L. Moreland and R. B. Zajonc, "Exposure Effects in Person Perception: Familiarity, Similarity, and Attraction," *Journal of Experimental Social Psychology*, Vol. 24, 1982, pp. 283–292.

[46] D. Krackhardt, "The Strength of Strong Ties: The Importance of *Philos* in Organizations," *Networks and Organizations: Structures, Form, and Action*, N. Nohria and R. Eccles, eds. (Boston, MA: HBS Press, 1992).

[47] Ibid.

[48] Ibid.

[49] Ibid.

[50] R. S. Burt, "The Contingent Value of Social Capital," *Administrative Science Quarterly*, Vol. 42, No. 2, 1997, pp. 339–365.

[51] M. Granovetter, "The Strength of Weak Ties," *American Journal of Sociology*, Vol. 78, 1973.

[52] R. S. Burt, "The Contingent Value of Social Capital," *Administrative Science Quarterly*, Vol. 42, No. 2, 1997, pp. 339–365.

[53] M. Granovetter, "The Strength of Weak Ties," *American Journal of Sociology*, Vol. 78, No. 6, 1973, pp. 1360–1380.

[54] Ibid.

[55] Ibid.

[56] R. Burt, *Structural Holes* (Cambridge, MA: Harvard University Press, 1992).

[57] Kathleen L. McGinn and Elizabeth Long Lingo, "Power and Influence: Achieving Your Objectives in Organizations," Harvard Business School Note No. 9-801-425, rev. July 5, 2007 (Boston, MA: HBS Publishing, 2001).

[58] R. Cross, N. Nohria, and A. Parker, "Six Myths About Informal Networks—and How to Overcome Them," *Sloan Management Review*, Spring 2002.

[59] B. Uzzi and S. Dunlap, "How to Build Your Network," *Harvard Business Review*, December 2005.

[60] Ibid.

[61] National Association of Black Accountants, 2009, www.nabainc.org, accessed February 16, 2009.

[62] Net Impact, 2009, http://netimpact.org, accessed February 16, 2009.

[63] B. Uzzi and S. Dunlap, "How to Build Your Network," *Harvard Business Review*, December 2005.

[64] Ibid.

[65] Herminia Ibarra, "Managerial Networks," Harvard Business School Note No. 9-495-039, rev. January 25, 1996 (Boston, MA: HBS Publishing, 1995).

[66] W. Baker, *Networking Smart: How to Build Relationships for Personal and*

Organizational Success (Lincoln, NE: Iuniverse.com, 2000).

[67] Ibid.

[68] Ibid.

[69] Ibid.

[70] Susan G. Parker, "Are You Ready to Get Serious About Networking?" *Harvard Management Communication Letter*, February 2003.

[71] E. Wenger, R. McDermott, and W. M. Snyder, *Cultivating Communities of Practice* (Boston, MA: HBS Press, 2002).

Glossary

360-degree feedback A system in which employees conduct a self-assessment of key competencies and then compare their responses to others in the organization including managers, peers, direct reports, and clients. (Chapter 9)

Acquired needs theory The theory that individuals are driven or motivated by three needs: the need for affiliation, the need for power, and the need for achievement. (Chapter 18)

Activity-based costing (ABC) The accounting system used to assess the specific cost components of producing a product or service. (Chapter 10)

Adjourning stage The stage that occurs when a team has completed its task and the team is disbanded. (Chapter 17)

Adjustment heuristic The rule of thumb that contends that individuals make estimates or choices based on a certain starting point. (Chapter 15)

Administrative costs The costs of coordinating activities between a firm's business units. (Chapter 6)

Administrative model A model of decision making that acknowledges that managers may be unable to make economically rational decisions even if they want to because they lack sufficient information on which to base their decisions. (Chapter 15)

Advice network A network that includes people in an organization to whom an individual typically goes to for advice, either on solving problems or for technical information. (Chapter 20)

Affective conflict Conflict occurs when disagreements between individuals are attributed to personal characteristics instead of differences in how to approach a task or problem. (Chapter 16)

Alliances A structure where partners come together by contract to engage jointly in activities in a market. (Chapter 4)

Ambiguity Situations that are characterized by uncertainty and risk and where the optimal decision is not clear or obvious. (Chapter 15)

Appropriateness framework The process of making decisions based on societal norms or expectations. (Chapter 15)

Arbitrator An individual who listens to both sides of a disagreement and makes a final decision based on the arguments. (Chapter 16)

Artifacts Visible organizational structures, processes, and languages. (Chapter 8)

Assumption A behavior that stemmed from a belief held by a group that is no longer visible, but has become deeply embedded in the organization. (Chapter 8)

Availability heuristic The rule of thumb that contends that individuals assess the frequency, probability, or likely cause of an event by the degree to which instances or occurrences of that event are readily "available" in memory. (Chapter 15)

Backward integration Occurs when a firm owns or controls the inputs it uses. (Chapter 6)

Balance sheet Highlights the company's financial position by identifying the assets that the firm controls and the manner in which those assets are financed. (Chapter 10)

Balanced scorecard A method created to help businesses translate strategy into action by identifying the most critical measures to drive business success and linking long-term strategic goals with short-term operational actions; it uses four perspectives (financial, customer, business process, and learning and growth). (Chapter 10)

Bargaining power The pressure that a supplier or buyer can exert on a company. (Chapter 5)

Bargaining zone The range of settlements within which it is better for both parties to agree than not to agree. (Chapter 16)

Barriers to entry Obstacles a firm may face while trying to enter a market or an industry. (Chapter 5)

Behavior The actions and decisions of individual employees. (Chapter 10)

Behaviorists Those who support a more open organizational structure where roles and responsibilities are loosely defined. (Chapter 7)

Beliefs and values The meanings that members of an organization attach to artifacts. (Chapter 8)

Benchmarking The process of collecting data from the industry's best players and using their numbers as a goal or guideline for evaluating company performance. (Chapter 10)

Best alternative to a negotiated agreement (BATNA) The course of action that a person will take if a negotiation ends in an impasse. (Chapter 16)

Betweenness Represents the extent to which an individual falls between pairs of other people in an interpersonal network who may be trying to reach each other. (Chapter 20)

Blocking behaviors Behaviors that inhibit the team and its members from achieving their objectives. (Chapter 17)

Board of directors A group of individuals elected by shareholders and charged with overseeing the general direction of the firm. (Chapter 2)

Body language The use of posture, body movement, hand and arm gestures, facial expressions, and eye contact to convey meaning to messages. (Chapter 19)

Boundary manager A manager who determines how the team will work with clients, upper management, and others who have an interest in the team's product. They buffer the team from organizational infighting, persuade top management to support the team's work, and coordinate and negotiate with other groups on work deadlines. (Chapter 17)

Boundary spanners Individuals who connect their immediate work group with other parts of the company or with groups in other organizations. (Chapter 20)

Bounded rationality A set of boundaries or constraints that tend to complicate the rational decision-making process. (Chapter 15)

Brokerage The act of leveraging network position to connect people who are not otherwise connected to one another to generate and control information. (Chapter 20)

Budgeting process The process for allocating financial resources and measuring expected quantitative and qualitative outcomes of a firm. (Chapter 10)

Bureaucratic approach An extreme form of organizational control in which systems are highly formalized and are characterized by extensive rules, procedures, policies, and instructions. (Chapter 7)

Bureaucratic organization structure A clear differentiation of tasks and responsibilities among individuals; coordination through a strict hierarchy of authority and decision rights; standardized rules and procedures; and the vertical separation of planning and execution so that plans are made in the upper ranks of an organization and executed in the lower ranks. (Chapter 1)

Business environment The combination of all contextual forces and elements in the external and internal environments of a firm. (Chapter 1)

Business-level strategy The determination of how a company will compete in a given business and position itself among its competitors. (Chapter 4)

Business process perspective Focuses on the manner in which a company runs its operations. (Chapter 10)

Cafeteria plans An arrangement that allows employees to make their own choices about benefit options. (Chapter 9)

Cause–effect relationships A set of quantitative and qualitative measurements that are related and mutually reinforcing. (Chapter 10)

Centrality The extent to which an individual is centrally positioned in a network, giving them preferential access to information and influence. (Chapter 20)

Centralized organization An organizational structure characterized by formal structures that control employee behavior by concentrating decisions in a top-down, hierarchical fashion. (Chapter 7)

Character The core values and fundamental beliefs that drive behavior in variable situations. (Chapter 12)

Charismatic leaders Individuals who arouse strong followership through inspirational visions and/ or compelling personal attributes. (Chapter 12)

Claim value The process by which a negotiator attempts to gain benefits or concessions for his or her position. (Chapter 16)

Clan approach A type of organizational control that includes self-supervising teams that are responsible for a set of tasks. (Chapter 7)

Classical model A model of decision making that seeks to maximize economic or other outcomes using a rational choice process. (Chapter 15)

Closeness centrality Represents how easily a person can reach all other people in his or her network through his or her direct and indirect ties. (Chapter 20)

Coalitions Individuals and/or groups that have common interests and perspectives. (Chapter 14)

Coercive power A type of interpersonal power that gives someone the ability to punish another for his or her behavior. (Chapter 14)

Cognitive conflict Conflict that results from disagreements over work-related issues such as meeting schedules, work assignments, processes, or the task itself. (Chapter 16)

Cognitive skills A leader's ability to gather and process large amounts of information, create suitable strategies, solve problems, and make correct decisions. (Chapter 12)

Collective bargaining The process by which union representatives negotiate with the management of a firm to secure certain concessions on wages, benefits, job security, or seniority for union members. (Chapter 9)

Collocated teams Teams that use a significant amount of face-to-face communication to make operating decisions. They operate in close proximity, engage in a lot of social interaction, and provide quick feedback to the team's progress to one another. (Chapter 17)

Common information effect Teams that consider commonly held information to be more important and influential than uniquely-held information. (Chapter 17)

Communication The process of using sounds, words, pictures, symbols, gestures, and body language to exchange information. (Chapter 19)

Communication audit The process of reviewing the communication systems in an organization. (Chapter 19)

Communication channels The conduits used to deliver oral, written/print, and electronic media, including vertical channels and horizontal channels. (Chapter 19)

Communication media The formats used to convey messages, including oral, written, and electronic. (Chapter 19)

Communication networks Networks that are used to exchange work-related information and can reveal the pattern of linkages between employees who talk about work-related matters on a regular basis. (Chapter 20)

Communication style The ways in which someone interacts with and delivers information to others when communicating. (Chapter 19)

Communication systems The formal and informal structures that facilitate how communication is transmitted throughout an organization. (Chapter 19)

Comparative advantage An economic theory that proclaims countries should specialize in producing goods for which they have the lowest opportunity cost of production. (Chapter 2)

Competitive advantage A firm achieves a competitive advantage when it creates more economic value than competitors by engaging in a strategy that is difficult or impossible for others to duplicate. (Chapter 4)

Competitor Any organization that creates goods or services targeted at a similar group of customers. (Chapter 2)

Conditions of certainty Conditions in which individuals have all of the information they need to make the best possible decision. (Chapter 15)

Conditions of risk Conditions in which individuals have information about an organization's goals, objectives, priorities, and potential courses of action, but they do not have complete information about the possible outcomes for each course of action. (Chapter 15)

Conditions of uncertainty Conditions in which individuals have information related to an organization's objectives and priorities, but they do not have complete information about alternative courses of action or about the possible outcomes for each one. (Chapter 15)

Confirmation bias A bias in which people tend to seek information that confirms a decision before seeking information that disconfirms a decision, even if the disconfirming information is more powerful and important. (Chapter 15)

Conflict An emotional or cognitive response that occurs when interests, perspectives, and behaviors of one individual or group explicitly differ from those of another individual or group. (Chapter 16)

Conflict of interest Conflicts that occur when employees or managers engage in activities on behalf of the company and have a personal interest in the outcome of those activities. (Chapter 3)

Conformity The action of people behaving in line with a group's expectations and beliefs. (Chapter 17)

Conglomeration The act of growing through unrelated diversification, essentially by acquiring companies in different industries. (Chapter 4)

Content theories The study of the incentives and needs that motivate people to perform in a certain way. (Chapter 18)

Contextual intelligence The ability to understand the impact of environmental factors on a firm and the ability to understand how to influence those same factors. (Chapter 1)

Contingency planning The systematic assessment of the external environment to prepare for a possible range of alternative futures for the organization. (Chapter 1)

Contingent reward The exchange process between leaders and followers in which leaders offer rewards to subordinates in exchange for their services. (Chapter 12)

Contingent view A view of the firm where effective organizational structure is based on fit or alignment between the organization and various aspects in its environment. (Chapter 1)

Control cycle The four-stage process that provides the mechanisms and systems to monitor the transformation process, ensuring that outputs are produced to the desired quality, quantity, and specifications of an organization and its customers. (Chapter 10)

Core competencies A network of unique activities that strategically fit together and are difficult to replicate. (Chapter 4)

Corporate advantage Occurs when a firm maximizes its resources to build a competitive advantage across its various business units. (Chapter 6)

Corporate-level strategy The way a company seeks to create value through the configuration and coordination of multimarket activities. (Chapter 4)

Corporate social responsiveness The practice of businesses responding to pressure from society to engage in socially responsible ways. (Chapter 3)

Cost leadership A strategy that aims to provide a product or service at as low a price as possible to a broad audience. (Chapter 5)

Create value The process of expanding the opportunities or issues that can be evaluated in a negotiation. By expanding the issues, there is a greater likelihood that each party will achieve some level of satisfaction. (Chapter 16)

Creativity The ability to combine or link ideas in new ways to generate novel and useful alternatives. (Chapter 13)

CSR A business's obligation to pursue policies, decisions, and actions that align with the objectives and values of society. (Chapter 3)

Cultural intelligence The ability to understand and respond appropriately to different cultural contexts and situations. (Chapter 13)

Culture Culture provides employees with a road map and a set of rules for how work gets done and how people interact in a company. (Chapter 8)

Customer perspective Linking key customer-based metrics such as market share and retention to the financial performance of a firm. (Chapter 10)

Customers The people or organizations that buy a firm's products and services. (Chapter 2)

Decentralized organization An organizational structure where key decisions are made at all levels of the firm, not mandated from the top. (Chapter 7)

Decision making The process of identifying issues and making choices from alternative courses of action. (Chapter 15)

Decision rights Rights that include initiating, approving, implementing, and controlling various types of strategic or tactical decisions. (Chapter 7)

De-escalation The reduction or elimination of conflict. (Chapter 16)

Degree of centrality Represents the number of contacts to whom a person is connected in a social network. (Chapter 20)

Delegation The process by which managers transfer decision rights to individual employees. (Chapter 7)

Dependence asymmetry A phenomenon that exists when a firm is more dependent on a business partner than a business partner is on a firm. (Chapter 14)

Development A long-term process designed to build greater self-awareness, enhance managerial capabilities, and enable an individual to reach his or her potential. (Chapter 9)

Differentiation A strategy in which a firm seeks to be unique in its industry along a dimension or a group of dimensions that are valued by consumers. (Chapter 5)

Directness The amount of control an individual attempts to exercise in communication situations. (Chapter 19)

Disruptive technologies Innovative forces that include a different set of attributes than those valued by mainstream customers. (Chapter 11)

Dissatisfaction A component of the change process in which creating dissatisfaction with the status quo helps to free people and organizations from complacency or inertia. It often creates the spark needed to begin the change process. (Chapter 11)

Distributive justice A subset of justice that deals with the distribution of wealth among members of a society. (Chapter 3)

Distributive negotiations Single-issue negotiations that are assumed to be part of a "fixed pie" where one person's gain is the other person's loss. (Chapter 16)

Diversification A strategy in which a firm engages in several different businesses that may or may not be related in an attempt to create more value than if the businesses existed as stand-alone entities. (Chapter 6)

Division of labor The manner in which work in a firm is divided among employees. (Chapter 7)

Divisional structure A structure that groups diverse functions into separate divisions. (Chapter 7)

Downsizing A process of reducing the employee base of the company in an effort to be more competitive. (Chapter 9)

Economic dimension The general economic environment (e.g., GDP, inflation, and unemployment) in the markets where the firm performs activities. (Chapter 2)

Economic responsibilities A business's duty to make a profit and increase shareholder value. (Chapter 3)

Economies of scale Cost savings achieved when the volume of a product produced by a firm enables it to reduce per unit costs. (Chapter 5)

Economies of scope Exists when the costs of operating two or more businesses or producing two or more products with the same corporate structure is less than the costs of operating the businesses independently or producing each product separately. (Chapter 6)

Emotional intelligence The capacity for recognizing our own feelings and those of others, for motivating ourselves, and for managing our emotions and relationships in a productive manner. (Chapter 13)

Employees The people who make the products and provide the services that allow a firm to exist. (Chapter 2)

Empowerment The process of sharing power with subordinates and pushing decision making and implementation to the lowest possible level, increasing the influence and autonomy of all employees. (Chapter 14)

Environmental scanning A tool that managers use to scan the business horizon for key events and trends that will affect the business in the future. (Chapter 1)

Equity theory The theory that people will compare their circumstances with those of similar others and that this behavior motivates them to seek fairness in the way they are rewarded for performance. (Chapter 18)

ERG theory The theory that individuals are motivated by three primary needs: existence (basic physical needs), relatedness (connection with others), and growth (personal development). (Chapter 18)

Escalation An increase in conflict that occurs when one person's negative behaviors encourage or foster another person's negative behaviors. (Chapter 16)

Escalation of commitment Occurs when decision makers commit themselves to a particular course of action beyond the level suggested by rationality as a means of justifying previous commitments. (Chapter 15)

Ethical responsibilities A business's duty to meet the expectations of society beyond its economic and legal responsibilities. (Chapter 3)

Ethics The study of moral standards and their effect on behavior and conduct. (Chapter 3)

Expectancy theory The theory that employees expect that high effort should lead to good performance and that good performance, in turn, should lead to reward. (Chapter 18)

Expert power A type of interpersonal power based on an individual having specialized knowledge or skills. (Chapter 14)

Exporting Shipping a firm's products from its domestic home base to global markets. (Chapter 4)

External environment Represents all of the external forces that affect the firm's business. (Chapter 2)

Extinction The idea that a behavior stops because it has ceased to be rewarded or punished. (Chapter 18)

Extrinsic rewards Rewards used to facilitate or motivate task performance that include pay, promotions, fringe benefits, and job security. (Chapter 18)

Fiduciary A person who is entrusted with property, information, or power to act on behalf of a beneficiary. (Chapter 3)

Fiedler contingency model A contingency theory in which leaders are more effective depending on the favorability of a leadership situation, which is described by leader–member relations, task structure, and positional power of the leader. (Chapter 12)

Financial economies Cost savings that a firm achieves through the distribution of capital among business units. (Chapter 6)

Financial perspective Choosing the financial measurements that are most important for reaching strategic goals. (Chapter 10)

First-mover advantage A competitive advantage that occurs when a firm is first to offer desirable products or services that secure customer loyalty. (Chapter 5)

Focus A strategy in which a company "focuses" its sales efforts on a specific geographical region, a specific group of purchasers, or a specific product type. (Chapter 5)

Forming stage The stage that occurs when team members define the task that is to be done and how that task is to be accomplished, setting the ground rules for the team. (Chapter 17)

Forward integration Occurs when a firm owns or controls the customers or distribution channels for its main products. (Chapter 6)

Four-drive theory The theory that fulfilling four drives—the drive to acquire, the drive to bond, the drive to comprehend, and the drive to defend—underlies motivation and that the degree to which these are satisfied directly affects employees' emotions and behaviors. (Chapter 18)

Framing Alternative presentations of the same information that can significantly alter a decision. (Chapter 15)

Franchising Common arrangements in many retail businesses where a firm contracts with individual owners to operate its retail units. This arrangement typically involves a corporation sharing management and marketing techniques with the owner in exchange for a fee and some percentage of the unit's revenues. (Chapter 4)

Functional structure A structure that organizes a firm in terms of the main activities that need to be performed, such as production, marketing, sales, and accounting. (Chapter 7)

Gain-sharing A team-based compensation structure that rewards teams based on the achievement of certain metrics associated with productivity, efficiency, or quality. (Chapter 9)

Garbage can model A model of decision making whereby problems, solutions, participants, and choices flow throughout an organization. This decision process is not viewed as a sequence of steps that begins with a problem and ends with a solution. (Chapter 15)

General environment Includes the technological, economic, political/legal, and sociocultural dimensions that affect a firm's external environment. (Chapter 2)

Geographically distributed teams Teams that are made up of geographically or organizationally dispersed members who rely heavily on electronic tools such as e-mail, voice mail, telephone, and videoconferencing to interact with one another. (Chapter 17)

Global strategies Strategies that focus on developing overall scale economies and global efficiency instead of catering to local tastes. (Chapter 4)

Globalization The integration and interdependence of economic, technological, sociocultural, and political systems across diverse geographic regions. (Chapter 2)

Goal An organizationally desired result, product, or end state. (Chapter 4)

Goal-setting theory The theory that setting goals that are difficult, but achievable, is a significant motivator of performance. (Chapter 18)

"Great Man" theory A theory of leadership that explained leadership by examining the traits and characteristics of individuals considered to be historically great leaders. (Chapter 12)

Groupthink Extreme consensus during a decision-making process. (Chapter 16)

Heuristics Rules of thumb or short-cuts that individuals use to save time when making complex decisions. (Chapter 15)

Hierarchy of needs theory The theory that individuals have multiple needs that must be fulfilled in a specific hierarchical order to ensure the greatest level of satisfaction. (Chapter 18)

Horizontal teams Teams composed of employees from about the same hierarchical level but from several different departments in the organization. (Chapter 17)

Human relations movement The belief that organizations must be understood as systems of interdependent human beings who share a common interest in the survival and effective functioning of the firm. (Chapter 1)

Hygiene factors Job factors that are potential dissatisfiers that relate to physiological, safety, and belongingness needs. These factors are the primary components that comprise the work environment. (Chapter 18)

Income statement Summarizes the financial performance of the company over a specific period of time, usually monthly, quarterly, or yearly. (Chapter 10)

Incremental change A process in which small improvements or changes are made to processes and approaches on an ongoing basis. (Chapter 11)

Inertia The inability of organizations to change as rapidly as the environment. (Chapter 11)

Influence The means or vehicle by which power is exercised. (Chapter 14)

Insider trading Insider trading occurs when a manager uses inside information to bet for or against a company's stock before that information is publicly available. (Chapter 3)

Integrative negotiations Negotiations that focus on multiple issues to "expand the pie" and actively seek alternative solutions that satisfy both parties. (Chapter 16)

Intelligence A person's ability to profit from experience, acquire knowledge, think abstractly, and adapt to changes in the environment. (Chapter 13)

Intelligence quotient (IQ) A measure of the overall quality of an individual's mental abilities. (Chapter 13)

Interdependence A quality that exists whenever one individual requires another individual's assistance to achieve a goal. (Chapter 14)

Interests The underlying reasons or needs of each party involved in an issue. (Chapter 16)

Intergroup conflict Conflict that occurs between two or more groups. (Chapter 16)

Internal environment A group of parties or factors that directly impact a firm, including owners, the board of directors, employees, and culture. (Chapter 2)

International strategies Strategies that combine elements of multinational and global strategies by using foreign subsidiaries to produce and distribute products. (Chapter 4)

Interpersonal communication Communication that occurs in one-on-one or small group settings. (Chapter 19)

Interpersonal conflict Conflict that occurs between two or more individuals who are members of the same group. (Chapter 16)

Interpersonal effectiveness The ability to acknowledge and take responsibility for one's role in cultivating relationships and in communicating effectively with others. (Chapter 13)

Interpersonal networks Relationships between people who work together, who have done business together, or who have engaged in some other joint activity. (Chapter 20)

Interpersonal skills A leader's ability to interact with others. (Chapter 12)

Intrinsic rewards Rewards associated with "doing the job" that include interesting and challenging work, self-direction and responsibility, variety, opportunities to use one's skills and abilities, and sufficient feedback regarding one's efforts. (Chapter 18)

Intuitive decision making Insights that are tapped through intuition and are not always fully understood by the decision maker. (Chapter 15)

Issue The subject of a discussion. (Chapter 16)

Job analysis Analyzing information about specific job tasks in order to provide a more precise job description and define the characteristics of the ideal candidate for the position. (Chapter 9)

Job-based pay Pay that is determined by the nature of a particular job. (Chapter 9)

Joint dependence A phenomenon that exists when two firms are equally dependent on the other. (Chapter 14)

Joint venture A structure where two firms come together to form a new company in a market. (Chapter 4)

Justice An ethical philosophy that provides the framework for society to judge what is morally right or wrong, fair or unfair, and establishes ways to evaluate or punish those who behave in immoral ways. (Chapter 3)

Kantianism An ethical philosophy claiming that motives and universal rules are important aspects in judging what is right or wrong. (Chapter 3)

Ladder of inference A process by which an individual uses assumptions or biases formed from past experiences to make a judgment on the intentions of another individual. (Chapter 19)

Law of reciprocity The idea that people should repay in the future what another person has done for them in the present. (Chapter 14)

Leader–member exchange theory A method of leadership in which leaders treat each follower differently, and as a result, develop unique relationships with each member. (Chapter 12)

Leadership The ability to drive change and innovation through inspiration and motivation. (Chapter 1)

Leadership neutralizers Aspects of a situation that hinder a leader's ability to act a particular way. (Chapter 12)

Leadership style The pattern of behaviors that leaders use in situations. (Chapter 12)

Leadership substitutes Aspects of a situation that render leadership unnecessary. (Chapter 12)

Learning and growth perspective Identifies the infrastructure and skills needed to carry out business processes, interact with customers, and achieve long-term financial growth; it also helps to identify gaps in capabilities or resources. (Chapter 10)

Legal dimension The regulations and laws that a firm encounters in its markets. (Chapter 2)

Legal responsibilities A business's duty to pursue its economic responsibilities within the boundaries of the law. (Chapter 3)

Legitimate power A type of interpersonal power that is based on the formal position an individual holds in an organization. (Chapter 14)

Leverage ratios Ratios used to evaluate a company's debt levels. (Chapter 10)

Licensing A contractual arrangement whereby the licensor (selling firm) allows its technology, patents, trademarks, designs, processes, know-how, intellectual property, or other proprietary advantages to be used for a fee by the licensee (buying firm). (Chapter 4)

Liquidity ratios Ratios used to assess a firm's ability to meet its current or short-term financial obligations. (Chapter 10)

Listening The extent to which the receiver of the message hears what the speaker or the sender intended. (Chapter 19)

Locus of control The extent to which an individual believes that he or she can control or influence the outcome of events. (Chapter 13)

Management The act of working with and through a group of people to accomplish a desired goal or objective in an efficient and effective manner. (Chapter 1)

Management by objectives (MBO) The process of managing employees by outlining a series of specific objectives or milestones that they are expected to meet in a defined period of time. (Chapter 9)

Management-by-exception A method of leadership done passively or actively that prescribes when leaders should intervene to increase a subordinate's effort to meet standards. (Chapter 12)

Managerial grid A two-dimensional grid showing leaders' different levels of task-oriented and relations-oriented behavior, which results in particular styles of leadership. (Chapter 12)

Managerial view A business framework where the firm is seen as a mechanism for converting raw materials into products to sell to customers. (Chapter 1)

Manager-led teams Teams in which the manager acts as the team leader. (Chapter 17)

Market power Achieved when a firm attempts to increase the price at which it sells products to levels above the normal price seen in the market. (Chapter 6)

Matrix structure A structure where both divisional and functional managers have equal authority in the organization. (Chapter 7)

Measurement The process of evaluating behaviors and outputs to see whether standards have been met or objectives have been obtained. (Chapter 10)

Mediator An individual who does not make a final decision but works with each party to find some common ground on which both parties can agree. (Chapter 16)

Mission The activities a firm performs for its customers. (Chapter 4)

Mission statement A statement that defines a firm's reason for existence. (Chapter 4)

Model A vision for change. (Chapter 11)

Morality The standards that people use to judge what is right or wrong, good or evil. (Chapter 3)

Motivation The desire, stimulus, or incentive to pursue a particular course of action. (Chapter 18)

Motivators The direct consequences of doing the job and the primary cause of satisfaction on the job. (Chapter 18)

Multinational strategies Strategies in which the parent company organizes local subsidiaries and gives them autonomy to develop products tailored to local tastes. (Chapter 4)

Mutual adaptation The process by which firms impact the nature of their overarching industrial environment and adapt their organization in response to evolving contextual factors. (Chapter 7)

Need for achievement The need to set, meet, and exceed goals. (Chapter 18)

Need for affiliation The need to interact, socialize, and develop friendships. (Chapter 18)

Need for power The need to seek opportunities for personal aggrandizement (personalized power) or the need to make an impact on and influence others (socialized power). (Chapter 18)

Needs assessment A process by which an organization outlines what type of training needs to be done and who is best positioned to deliver it. (Chapter 9)

Negative bargaining zone The zone that exists when negotiators' acceptable positions do not overlap and no settlement will be acceptable to both parties. (Chapter 16)

Negative reinforcement The act of removing an aversive condition in response to a desired behavior. (Chapter 18)

Negotiation A process by which two parties attempt to reach agreement on an issue by offering and reviewing various positions or courses of action. (Chapter 16)

Network structure A structure where "knowledge workers" are organized to work as individual contributors or to be a part of a work cluster that provides a certain expertise for the organization. (Chapter 7)

Networking The activities associated with developing and managing relationships that are critical to a person's ability to accomplish tasks as well as develop personally and professionally. (Chapter 20)

Networking clubs A type of external network that provides members with opportunities to learn and develop professional relationships outside work. (Chapter 20)

Nonprogrammed decisions Decisions that are made in response to novel, poorly defined, or unstructured situations that require managers to use their best judgments. (Chapter 15)

Nonredundant contacts Contacts in a network who do not lead to the same people or provide the same information. (Chapter 20)

Nonverbal communication The use of body language, vocal qualities, and space and objects to convey meaning to messages. (Chapter 19)

Norming stage The stage that occurs when team members uncover ways to create new standards that encourage more collaborative behavior. (Chapter 17)

Objectives Series of quantifiable milestones or benchmarks by which a firm can assess its progress. (Chapter 4)

Offshoring Outsourcing a business activity to a contractor in a foreign country. (Chapter 9)

Openness The ease with which individuals show emotions and are emotionally accessible to other people when they communicate. (Chapter 19)

Organic change A process by which change emerges from individuals or teams as they innovate, solve problems, seek more effective ways to accomplish their work, react to large environmental shifts, or interact with others in cross-functional positions. (Chapter 11)

Organizational change The processes and activities that organizations go through to align themselves with internal and external changes in the business environment and to prepare for future potential opportunities. (Chapter 11)

Organizational commitment The desired end result of socialization whereby employees become committed to the organization and its goals. (Chapter 8)

Organizational design The formal systems, levers, and decisions an organization adopts or employs in pursuit of its strategy. (Chapter 7)

Organizational structure The pattern of organizational roles, relationships, and procedures that enable coordinated action among employees. (Chapter 7)

Organizers Those who believe that more control is warranted in organizational design to ensure that jobs are performed satisfactorily and efficiently. (Chapter 7)

Outputs The products and/or services that an organization produces. (Chapter 10)

Outsourcing Contracting with a firm outside the corporation to perform certain tasks or functions that the corporation used to do on its own. (Chapter 6)

Owners The people or institutions that maintain legal control of an organization. (Chapter 2)

Package reservation value The lowest value that a negotiator would be willing to accept for a package offer. (Chapter 16)

Participation The extent to which individuals engage in the process of generating solutions and articulating their opinions and perspectives. (Chapter 17)

Path–goal theory of leadership A theory that states that the most important aspect in leadership is the follower's expectation that a task can be accomplished and that it will lead to rewards. (Chapter 12)

Performance appraisal The identification, measurement, and management of individual performance in organizations. (Chapter 9)

Performing stage The stage that occurs when team members adopt and play roles that enhance the activities of the group. (Chapter 17)

Personal power Power that is obtained from having personal attributes that others desire. (Chapter 14)

Personality A system of enduring inner characteristics, tendencies, and temperaments that are both inherited and shaped by social, cultural, and environmental factors. (Chapter 13)

Persuasion A process by which an individual or a group captures an audience and influences, changes, or reinforces their perspectives, opinions, and behaviors. (Chapter 19)

Planned change A process where change efforts are predetermined and driven from corporate strategy departments or top-down directives. (Chapter 11)

Playfulness The deliberate, temporary relaxation of rules to explore many possible alternatives. (Chapter 15)

Political dimension Refers to the political events and activities in a market that affect a firm. (Chapter 2)

Political model A model of decision making that acknowledges that most organizational decisions involve many managers who have different goals and who have to share information to reach an agreement. (Chapter 15)

Position The perspective a person takes on an issue. (Chapter 16)

Positional power Power that comes from an individual's formal place within an organization's structure. (Chapter 14)

Positive bargaining zone The zone that exists when negotiators' acceptable positions overlap. (Chapter 16)

Positive reinforcement The act of rewarding a desired behavior. (Chapter 18)

Power The potential of one individual or group to influence the behavior, thinking, or attitudes of another individual or group. (Chapter 14)

Primary activities The activities involved in the physical creation of the product and its sale and transfer to the buyer. (Chapter 5)

Privacy A person's right to determine the type and extent of information that is disclosed about him or her. (Chapter 3)

Proactive change A process in which change is initiated based on some anticipatory event or opportunity on the horizon. (Chapter 11)

Procedural justice A subset of justice claiming that rules should be clearly stated, consistently obeyed, and impartially enforced. (Chapter 3)

Process A series of plans (communication, measurement, etc.) and approaches to implement a change effort. (Chapter 11)

Process theories Theories that explain how employees select behavioral actions to meet their needs and then assess whether these choices were successful. (Chapter 18)

Profitability ratios Ratios used to assess the firm's profits in relation to the source of those profits, including sales and assets. (Chapter 10)

Profit-sharing A team-based compensation structure that shares rewards based on improvements in profitability. (Chapter 9)

Programmed decisions Decisions that are made in response to recurring organizational problems that require individuals to follow established rules and procedures. (Chapter 15)

Psychologically safe An environment which encourages an open expression of ideas and feelings without a fear of being penalized. (Chapter 17)

Punishment The act of presenting an aversive stimulus in response to an undesired behavior. (Chapter 18)

Reactive change A process in which change is initiated in response to some known external threat or opportunity. (Chapter 11)

Realistic conflict theory A theory that proposes that limited resources will lead to conflict between groups. (Chapter 16)

Realistic job preview (RJP) When an organization provides information to job candidates that highlights the most important conditions of a job, including its positive and negative aspects. (Chapter 9)

Redundant contacts Contacts in a network who know and communicate with each other and who therefore tend to provide similar information. (Chapter 20)

Referent power A type of interpersonal power based on the personal liking an individual has for another. (Chapter 14)

Reinforcement theory The theory that positive and negative reinforcements can induce certain behavior. (Chapter 18)

Related diversification A firm that owns more than one business that uses a similar set of tangible and intangible resources. (Chapter 6)

Relational power Power gained from the types of networks to which an individual belongs, the types of people in those networks, and the strength of the relationships within the networks. (Chapter 14)

Relationship life cycle A concept marked by the stranger, acquaintance, and mature partnership phases in which a leader and follower undergo a process that dictates whether followers become part of the in-group or out-group. (Chapter 12)

Relations-oriented behavior Behaviors that prioritize interpersonal relationships, the value of workers as humans, and a strong commitment to the unit and its mission. (Chapter 12)

Representativeness heuristic The rule of thumb that contends that individuals tend to look for traits in another person or situation that correspond with previously formed stereotypes. (Chapter 15)

Reservation value The lowest offer a negotiator is willing to accept. It is the point at which a negotiator is indifferent between accepting a proposed offer and rejecting it in favor of pursuing his or her BATNA. (Chapter 16)

Resilience The belief that one can control or adapt to certain events and outcomes and be able to bounce back from difficulty. (Chapter 13)

Resource-based view of the firm A theory that a firm can develop a competitive advantage through the collection and harvesting of resources. (Chapter 5)

Resource scarcity The lack of sufficient resources, such as money and staff, that forces individuals in organizations to make critical decisions about how to best allocate the available resources throughout the company. (Chapter 14)

Reward power A type of interpersonal power that gives someone the ability to reward another for his or her behavior. (Chapter 14)

Satisficing The act of choosing a solution that is good enough. (Chapter 15)

Scenario building Forecasting the likely result that might occur when several events and stakeholders are linked together. (Chapter 1)

Scientific management A focus on how jobs, work, and incentive schemes could be designed to improve productivity using industrial engineering methods. (Chapter 1)

Self-awareness An understanding of one's thoughts, feelings, and behaviors. (Chapter 13)

Self-directed teams Teams that determine their own objectives and the methods by which to achieve them. (Chapter 17)

Self-efficacy The belief that one has the capabilities to accomplish organizational goals. (Chapter 18)

Self-monitoring The ability of individuals to read cues from their environment to assess their behavior. People can vary from being high self-monitors to being low self-monitors. (Chapter 13)

Self-similarity Refers to the notion that we connect with those who are similar to us on a range of demographic or personal attributes and who may share similar interests. (Chapter 20)

Shareholder view A business framework where the job of top managers is to produce the highest possible stock market valuation of the firm's assets. (Chapter 1)

Silos A functional or divisional unit that operates by its own rules and guidelines and does not openly share information with other units. (Chapter 7)

Single-product strategy A strategy in which a firm focuses on one specific product, typically in one market. (Chapter 6)

Situational leadership A leadership theory based on the interplay among (1) the amount of task-related behaviors a leader exhibits; (2) the amount of relationship-related behaviors a leader exhibits; and (3) the level at which followers are mature enough to perform a specific task, function, or objective. (Chapter 12)

Six Sigma A disciplined, quantitative approach to improve cycle time, reduce costs, and eliminate waste with a technical goal of 3.4 defects per million (six standard deviations from the mean). (Chapter 10)

Skill-based pay Pay that is determined by an individual's personal skills and knowledge. (Chapter 9)

Social capital The value that an individual can derive from his or her social relationships. (Chapter 20)

Social identity theory A theory that proposes that group members of an in-group will seek to find negative aspects of an out-group to enhance their self-image. (Chapter 16)

Social loafing Disengaging from the team process and failing to contribute to the team's recommendations or other deliverables. (Chapter 17)

Social values The deeply rooted system of principles that guide individuals in their everyday choices and interactions. (Chapter 2)

Socialization The process of understanding how work gets done and how individuals should interact in an organization. (Chapter 8)

Sociocultural dimension Demographic characteristics as well as the values and customs of a society. (Chapter 2)

Space and objects A nonverbal form of communication that conveys meaning through the way a meeting space is arranged, objects are used, or individuals are dressed. (Chapter 19)

Spatial proximity Refers to connections between people close to one another, due to having an office nearby or sharing work or private space. (Chapter 20)

Spot contracts Contracts that allow a buyer to purchase a commodity at a specific price. (Chapter 6)

Stakeholder view A business framework that identifies and analyzes multiple groups that interact with the firm and attempts to align organizational practices to satisfy the needs of these various groups. (Chapter 1)

Status quo bias The tendency to favor the "here and now" and to reject potential change. (Chapter 15)

Storming stage The stage that occurs when team members experience conflicts about interpersonal issues and differences in perspectives. (Chapter 17)

Strategic CSR Corporate social responsibility activities that are directly related to business activities so that they can combine social welfare with financial welfare. (Chapter 3)

Strategic flexibility The capability to identify and react to changes in the external environment and to mobilize internal resources to deal with those changes. (Chapter 5)

Strategic position A place in an industry that a firm occupies by way of the products or services it offers and the methods it uses to deliver them. (Chapter 4)

Strategic review process The process by which senior leaders of a corporation meet with business unit managers to review progress toward specific goals. (Chapter 1)

Strategy Pursuing a set of unique activities that provide value to customers; making tradeoffs about which businesses to pursue, what products to produce, and which customers to serve; and aligning resources to achieve organizational objectives. (Chapter 4)

Strategy formulation The process of identifying how a firm can best align its resources to carve out a defensible position in the marketplace. (Chapter 4)

Strength of ties The emotional intensity, intimacy, and frequency of interaction that characterize the relationship between two parties. (Chapter 20)

Structural holes The existence of a gap between two individuals that provides access to nonredundant contacts. (Chapter 20)

Subcultures Cultures that form around geographic or organizational units in a company. (Chapter 8)

Supplier A company that provides resources or services for a firm to help in its creation of products and services. (Chapter 2)

Support activities Activities that provide the support necessary for the primary activities to occur. (Chapter 5)

Supportive communication A process of offering advice and suggestions (advising), relating similar experiences (deflecting),

asking follow-up questions for clarification (probing), and reiterating the main points (reflecting). (Chapter 19)

Survivor syndrome A condition that can occur when certain employees who survive a downsizing become narrow-minded, self-absorbed, resentful, or risk-averse. (Chapter 9)

Sustainable technologies Innovative forces that improve the performance of established products, along the dimensions of performance that mainstream customers in major markets have historically valued. (Chapter 11)

SWOT analysis A tool that allows managers to take a snapshot of their firm's internal strengths and weaknesses as well as the opportunities and threats that are evident in the external environment. (Chapter 5)

Synergy Created when a firm generates sustainable cost savings by combining duplicate activities or deploying underutilized assets across multiple businesses. (Chapter 6)

Tactics The actions that a firm takes to enact its strategy. (Chapter 4)

Task complexity The amount of information that must be processed to understand the task, the degree of uncertainty about possible outcomes, the presence of many subtasks that require a range of skills and knowledge, or the absence of standardized procedures to conduct the task. (Chapter 17)

Task environment Includes entities that directly affect a firm on a constant basis and include competitors, suppliers, and customers. (Chapter 2)

Task interdependence The extent to which group members need to work with and rely on each other to produce the collective work of the group. (Chapter 17)

Task objectives Issues that orient team members toward their goals and priorities and help them understand how their work fits into the bigger picture. (Chapter 17)

Task-oriented behavior Behaviors that prioritize the accomplishment of a task in an efficient and reliable way. (Chapter 12)

Team A group of two or more people with complementary skills who are committed to working together to achieve a specific objective. (Chapter 17)

Team norms Expected team behaviors. (Chapter 17)

Technical skills A leader's knowledge about an organization and job-related activities. (Chapter 12)

Technological dimension The processes, technologies, or systems that a firm can use to produce outputs. (Chapter 2)

Theory of operant conditioning The theory that both positive and negative reinforcement increase behavior while punishment and extinction decrease behavior. (Chapter 18)

Theory of rational choice The theory that individuals make decisions based on a rational thought process that optimizes self-interest. (Chapter 15)

Theory X The belief that employees inherently dislike work and need to be constantly monitored and evaluated to ensure that they do what is expected. (Chapter 18)

Theory Y The belief that employees are motivated to do their best and to work to their potential. (Chapter 18)

Total cycle time The amount of time required to develop and deliver products and services to the customer. (Chapter 10)

Total quality management (TQM) A comprehensive and structured approach to identifying ways to improve the quality of a company's products and services. (Chapter 10)

Trade secret Any type of information used in conducting business that is not commonly known by others. It often provides a strategic advantage for a company over its competitors. (Chapter 3)

Traits-based leadership theory A theory of leadership that tries to reveal a set of universal traits and skills that are relevant in all leadership situations. (Chapter 12)

Transaction costs Costs to obtain products or services from a contractor or supplier as well as the costs associated with writing and administering the contracts for these products and services. (Chapter 6)

Transactional leadership The process by which a leader provides something to subordinates in return for something the subordinates want. (Chapter 12)

Transformational leadership A set of behaviors that leaders use to transform or change their organization and individuals for the better. (Chapter 12)

Transformative change A process in which change is radical or disruptive, typically in response to a major competitive threat and/or significant change in a firm's external or internal environment. (Chapter 11)

Transnational strategy Strategies that balance a firm's international activities among efficiency, local responsiveness, and organizational learning. (Chapter 4)

Trend analysis A tool where key variables are monitored and modeled to help predict a change that might occur in the environment. (Chapter 1)

Triarchic theory of intelligence The theory that individuals possess three components of intelligence: (1) computational (analytic), (2) experiential (creative), and (3) contextual (practical). (Chapter 13)

Trust networks The pattern of linkages among people in an organization who trust one another, share sensitive information, and support one another in a crisis. (Chapter 20)

Two-factor theory The theory that two conditions, hygiene factors and motivators, simultaneously act as drivers of satisfaction and dissatisfaction. Lower-order needs are hygiene factors and a potential source of dissatisfaction, while motivators are higher-order needs and a potential source of satisfaction. (Chapter 18)

Unrelated diversification A firm that manages several businesses with no reasonable connection. (Chapter 6)

Utilitarianism The ethical philosophy claiming that behaviors are considered moral if they produce the greatest good, or utility, for the greatest number of people. (Chapter 3)

Value The amount consumers are willing to pay for a product or service. It comes from offering a lower price than that of competitors or providing a unique product whose benefits outweigh a higher potential cost. (Chapter 5)

Value chain analysis A systematic way of examining all of the activities a firm performs and determining how they interact to form a source of competitive advantage. (Chapter 5)

Value propositions Quantitative and qualitative aspects of products or services that customers value most. (Chapter 10)

Verbal communication The use of sounds, letters, words, pictures, and symbols to convey a message. (Chapter 19)

Vertical integration Occurs when one corporation owns business units that make inputs for other business units in the same corporation. (Chapter 6)

Vertical teams Teams composed of a manager and his or her subordinates in the formal chain of command. (Chapter 17)

Virtue ethics An ethical philosophy claiming that morality's primary function is to develop virtuous character. (Chapter 3)

Vision A concept or picture of what a firm wants to achieve. (Chapter 4)

Vocal qualities Inflection patterns, rate of speech, fillers, and enunciation. (Chapter 19)

VUCA An acronym for volatile, uncertain, complex, and ambiguous that captures the context in which today's organizations compete. (Chapter 1)

Whistle-blowing The release of evidence by a member of an organization that proves illegal or immoral conduct to executives in a company or regulating agencies outside a company. (Chapter 3)

Wholly owned subsidiary A fully operational, independent entity that a firm sets up in a foreign country to conduct business in that market. (Chapter 4)

Zone of possible agreement (ZOPA) The set of all possible deals that would be acceptable to both parties. The ZOPA is the space between one party's reservation value and the other party's reservation value. (Chapter 16)

Name Index

Organization Index

Subject Index